ENCYCLOPEDIA OF
PREHISTORY

ENCYCLOPEDIA OF PREHISTORY

David Lambert
and
The Diagram Group

Facts On File, Inc.

Encyclopedia of Prehistory

Copyright © 2002 by The Diagram Group

Diagram Visual Information Ltd
195 Kentish Town Road, London, NW5 2JU
e-mail: diagramvis@aol.com

Senior artist:	Graham Rosewarne
Artists:	Darren Bennet, Ashley Best, Joe Bonello, Alastair Burnside, Ray Burrows, Richard Czapnik, Brian Hewson, Richard Hummerstone, Karen Johnson, Alison Jones, Robert Jones, Pavel Kostal, Lee Lawrence, Oscar Lobban, Arthur Lockwood, Chris Logan, Paul McCauley, Philip Patenall, Micky Pledge, Jane Robertson, Debbie Skinner, Jerry Watkiss,
Design:	bounford.com
Layout:	Denise Goodey/bounford.com
Production:	Richard Hummerstone
Editors:	Annabel Else, Randal Gray, Damien Grint, Peter Harrison, Denis Kennedy, Ruth Midgley, Sylvia Worth
Indexer:	Dr. Susan Boobis

Facts On File Inc.
132 West 31st Street
New York NY 10001

Library of Congress Cataloging-in-Publication Data
Lambert, David. 1932–
    Encyclopedia of prehistory / David Lambert and the Diagram Group.
        p. cm.
    Includes bibliographical references and index.
    ISBN 0-8160-4547-X
    1. Geology. 2. Paleontology. 3. Prehistoric peoples. I. Diagram Group. II. Title.

QE26.3 .L36 2001
550—dc2l

                                                                            2001033775

Facts On File books are available at special discounts when purchased in bulk quantities for businesses, associations, institutions, or sales promotions. Please call our Special Sales Department in New York at 212/967-8800 or 800/322-8755.

You can find Facts On File on the World Wide Web at http://www.factsonfile.com

Cover design by Cathy Rincon
Printed in the United States of America

EB DIAG 10 9 8 7 6 5 4 3 2 1

This book is printed on acid-free paper

Introduction

This thematic encyclopedia provides a concise, comprehensive, up-to-date key to the processes that forged our planet, and to the vast array of prehistoric animals, plants, and other organisms that appeared upon, and vanished from, its surface. The book is organized in four sections, subdivided into chapters containing one-page topics copiously illustrated by field guide–style artwork, explanatory diagrams, reconstructions of creatures from the past, and clearly labeled maps and charts. The book is in a broadly chronological, as opposed to an alphabetical, order so that explanations of the formation of the Earth and its features precede accounts of the major categories of life forms, and the chapters describing these in Section 2 largely reflect the sequence in which they evolved.

Section 1: The Evolving Earth surveys the world itself. Nine chapters cover its origins and the continuous processes forming and reforming the Earth's crust and oceans and raising mountains and wearing them away to fashion valleys and plains. The last chapter, tracing change through the ages, establishes the geological background for the sections that follow.

Section 2: Evolving Life is the core of the book: a guided tour in eight chapters through the great range of prehistoric life forms, here visually re-created as reconstructed skeletons and lifelike, whole-body restorations, with diagrams depicting their assumed relationships. After the first chapter's overview of fossils and evolution, the other seven chapters successively cover fossil plants, invertebrates, and (progressing up the evolutionary scale) fishes, early tetrapods and amphibians, reptiles, birds, and lastly synapsids: the mammals and their prehistoric kin.

Section 3: Dinosaurs focuses on this remarkable and long-lived vertebrate group, which included the largest land animals ever. After introducing these extraordinary reptiles, this section profiles 68 dinosaur genera in alphabetical order, showing when each genus lived on a time line marked off in millions of years ago. The section ends with a survey of dinosaur life: how dinosaurs' bodies were constructed, how they worked, and how these animals behaved.

Section 4: The First Humans presents humankind as the unique end-product of one evolving branch of the mammals known as primates. The first chapter reveals the evolutionary legacies concealed with our bodies. Three chapters then trace primate evolution from primitive "prosimians" to the advanced great apes, our closest living kin. The next chapters describe the australopithecines, prehistoric "ape men" descended from some prehistoric ape; their descendants, early forms of *Homo*; and their descendants, the Neandertals and *Homo sapiens*: ourselves.

Later chapters follow our species' Stone Age spread around the world and feature key cultural advances that led to our apparently unique control of our environment. The book ends with glimpses of the likely futures for humanity and our planet.

Encyclopedia of Prehistory is unique. The editorial team who worked on it specializes in the integration of visual forms of information with concise and clear text. This interrelationship of text and images is made even more effective by the care taken in presenting the elements on the page in an attractive, yet coherent, whole. Additionally, the use of two-color artwork, together with the painstaking concern for detail, brings creatures that no longer exist to life in a way that is both accurate and exciting.

A concise reference tool for students, researchers, and teachers, this user-friendly volume also gives the general reader an unparalleled overview of the remote past and its creatures–ancestors of the life forms that inhabit our planet today.

Consultants and advisers

Section 1 The Evolving Earth

Dr. D. Bell
University of Oxford, England

Professor G. S. Boulton
University of Edinburgh, Scotland

Dr. E. N. K. Clarkson
University of Edinburgh, Scotland

Dr. D. Drew
University of Dublin, Ireland

Dr. D. G. Fraser
University of Oxford, England

Professor H. G. Gade
University of Bergen, Norway

Dr. W. B. Harland
University of Cambridge, England

Dr. P. Homewood
University of Fribourg, Switzerland

Professor D. McKenzie
University of Cambridge, England

Dr. K. S. Richards
University of Cambridge, England

Dr. D. W. Strangway
University of Toronto, Canada

Section 2 Evolving Life

Dr. R. A. Fortey
British Museum (Natural History),
London, England

Dr. Angela Milner
British Museum (Natural History),
London, England

Dr. Ralph E. Molnar
Queensland Museum, Queensland,
Australia

Professor R. J. G. Savage
University of Bristol, England

Mr. C. A. Walker
British Museum (Natural History),
London, England

Section 3 Dinosaurs

General consultants

Dr. Angela Milner
British Museum (Natural History),
London, England

Dr. Ralph E. Molnar
Queensland Museum, Queensland,
Australia

Section 4 The First Humans

Contents

Section 1
The Evolving Earth

Section 2
Evolving Life

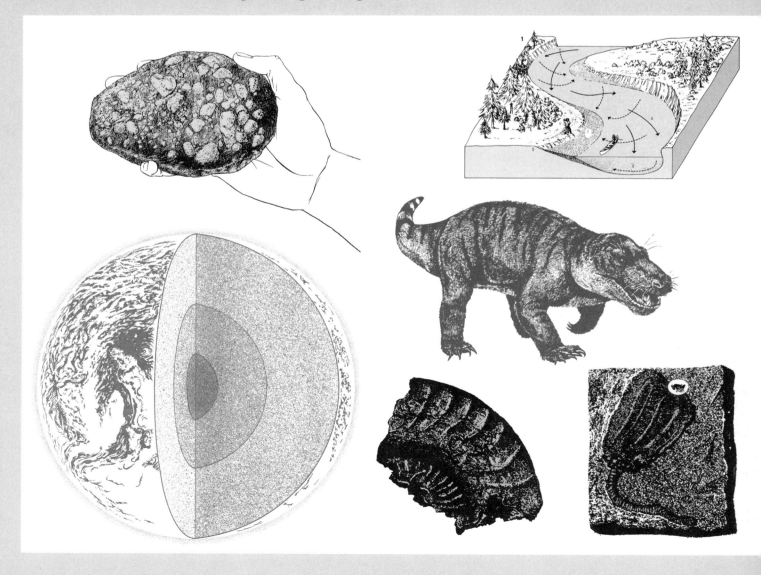

Section 3
Dinosaurs

Section 4
The First Humans

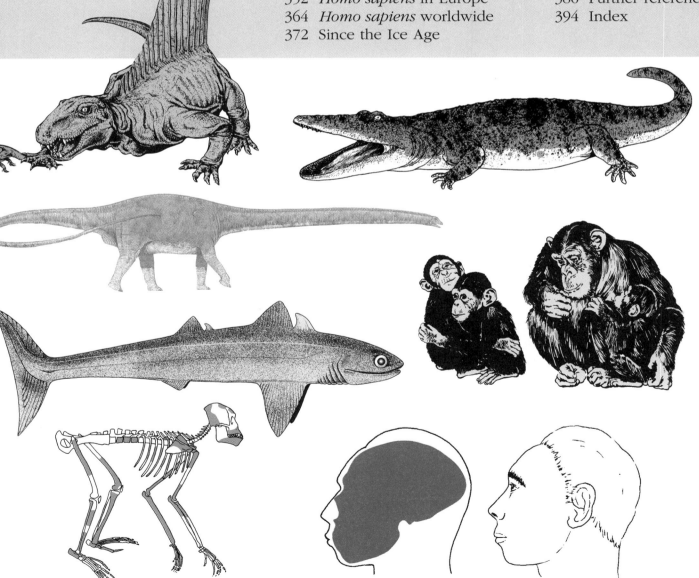

SECTION 1

THE EVOLVING EARTH

Sizing up the Earth

This book begins by putting our planet in its universal context. We see how matter, stars, and the solar system evolved and how the Earth acquired its layered structure and slightly bulging shape. There is a brief overview of elements, minerals, and rocks —Earth's building blocks. The chapter ends with a look at the forces that keep the sea and air in motion, disturb the crust, and turn the Earth into a mighty dynamo.

Sun and planets

Numbered items show (below) relative sizes of and (bottom) gaps between the Sun and planets. Asteroids (minor planets) lie between **5** and **6**.

1 Sun	**6** Jupiter
2 Mercury	**7** Saturn
3 Venus	**8** Uranus
4 Earth	**9** Neptune
5 Mars	**10** Pluto

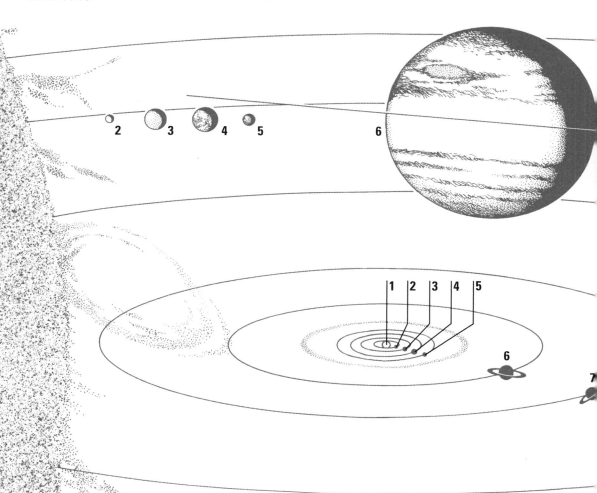

Earth in space

Earth is a rocky, spinning ball–one of nine planets and many lesser bodies (moons, asteroids, and comets) orbiting a star (the Sun). All of these together constitute our solar system.

The Earth is tiny compared to the four largest planets. But our solar system's largest and most influential body is the Sun, a glowing ball of gases a million times the volume of the Earth and far bigger than all the other objects orbiting the Sun. The Sun's immense gravitational force prevents the entities around it from flying outward into space. And its electromagnetic radiations produce the heat and light that help make life possible on Earth–the third nearest planet to the Sun. Most planets closer in or farther out appear too hot or cold for life.

Earth's behavior and that of its Moon determine time on Earth. Like all planets, Earth spins on a central axis with imaginary ends at the poles. Each rotation of about 24 hours produces day and night.

About once a month the Moon completes one revolution around the Earth. Earth itself completes one orbit of the Sun in about 365 days–an Earth year. Because Earth orbits in a tilted attitude, sunlight beams down directly upon its Northern and Southern Hemispheres at different times of year, creating seasons.

Immense distances separate the Earth from other bodies in space. From Earth to the Moon is about 1.25 light-seconds, the distance covered in that time by light, which travels at 186,000 mi per second (300,000 km per second). From Earth to the Sun is 8 light-minutes; the solar system is 11 light-hours across; from Earth to the nearest star beyond the Sun is 4 light-years. Our solar system plus dust, gas, and 100 billion stars (some certainly with solar systems of their own) comprise our galaxy–a flattened disk 80,000 light-years across. At least 10 billion galaxies are scattered throughout the universe.

The seasons

The Earth's tilt brings the midday sun overhead north or south of the equator at different times of year, creating seasons.

*21 March: **a** Sun over the equator*

*21 June: **b** Sun over the tropic of Cancer*

*23 September: **c** Sun over the equator*

*21 December: **d** Sun over the tropic of Capricorn*

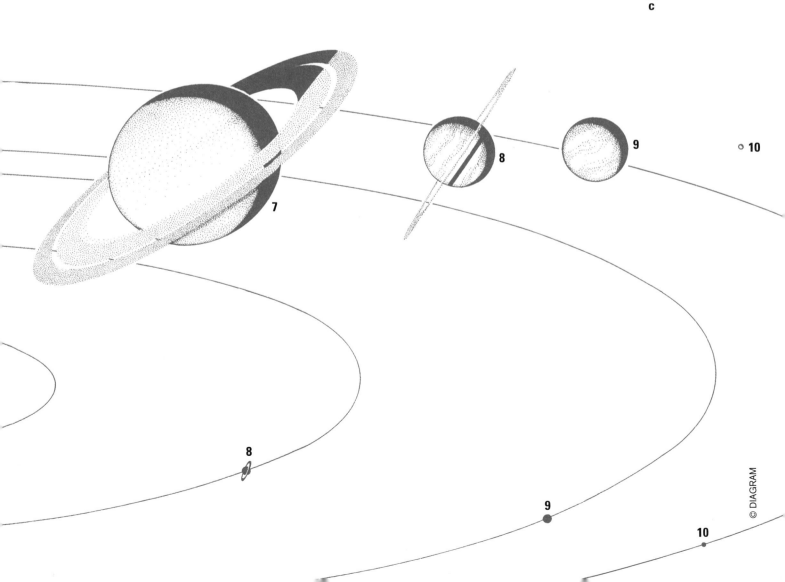

A

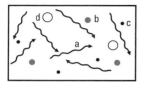

B

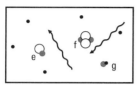

The first atoms (above)

A Post big-bang radiation (a) and subatomic particles: protons (b), neutrons (c), and electrons (d)

B Subatomic particles combined as nuclei of deuterium ("heavy hydrogen") (e), helium (f), and hydrogen (g)

1

2

3

4

5

6   **7**

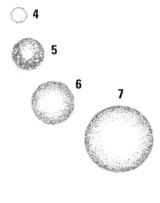

8

How everything began

Earth's origins lie in the creation of the universe. Just how this came about remains unclear, but many scientists accept some version of the big bang theory, which goes like this: At first all energy and matter (then only subatomic particles) were closely concentrated. About 15 billion years ago a vast explosion scattered everything throughout space. Star studies prove that the universe is still expanding, and background radiation hints at its initial heat.

The big bang sparked off processes that produced atoms that formed different elements–the chemically indivisible building blocks of stars and planets. More than 90 elements occur on Earth alone.

Hydrogen and helium, the lightest, most abundant elements, would have begun forming as subatomic particles within minutes of the big bang. Hundreds of millions of years later, condensing clouds of hydrogen formed galaxies. Here mighty blobs of gas contracted under gravitation. This process warmed the gas and triggered nuclear reactions. These converted hydrogen to helium and gave off energy, including light. Thus blobs of gas evolved into stars.

Stars that had used up all their hydrogen started "burning" helium and swelling into red giants. Inside their nuclear furnaces, atomic evolution sped up. First, helium nuclei combined to form carbon atoms.

Next, carbon gave rise to heavier elements, such as neon, nitrogen, and oxygen. Then came still heavier elements, including iron. From red giants such substances escaped into space.

Meanwhile massive "burned out" stars became supernovae, ending in immense explosions that forged such heavy elements as uranium and gold and hurled them into interstellar space.

New stars acquired these preformed elements. They make up only 1 percent of the Sun's mass. But much higher percentages occur in planets like the Earth. The next pages explain how the Sun and planets formed.

Life of a star (left)

Many stars go through the stages pictured on this page.

1 Gases make up a formless mass called a nebula.

2 Gravitation makes the nebula contract to a regular shape.

3 Contraction heats the center of the nebula until nuclear reactions turn hydrogen to helium and it becomes a star.

4 The star completes its main contraction and starts a long, stable phase of energy output as a so-called yellow dwarf.

5 The star's hydrogen exhausted, its core shrinks; its surface expands and cools.

6 The star grows brighter and expands into a red giant.

7 The star burns helium, heats up, and grows enormously.

8 The expanding star may reach 400 times its former size.

9 Its nuclear energy used up, the star collapses to a tiny, dense, dim white dwarf.

10 The star ends as a black dwarf, no longer yielding heat or light.

Building bigger atoms

"Star factories" forged heavier, more complex atoms, indicated by the number of electrons orbiting their nuclei.

A Hydrogen

B Carbon

C Phosphorus

D Calcium

A   **B**

C   **D**

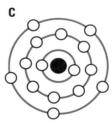

9 10

Rare and common elements

Elements made of large, complex atoms tend to be scarcer than those made of small, simple atoms.

a Logarithmic scale of universal abundance (relative to 1 million atoms of silicon)

b Atomic number (number of electrons per atom)

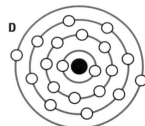

Selected elements:

1 Hydrogen

2 Carbon

3 Iron

4 Lead

5 Uranium

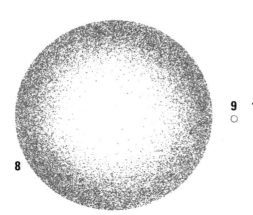

Birth of the solar system

Cosmologists believe that the universe was more than 10 billion years old when our solar system formed 4.6 billion years ago. Its raw material was a cloud of dust and gas in one spiral arm of our galaxy. Somehow that cloud became the Sun–a central star containing 99.8 percent of the solar system–and the planets, satellites lying roughly in one plane, most spinning in the same direction, that orbit the Sun.

Scientists have produced various theories to account for this arrangement. Here are four. (The fourth now seems most likely to be right.)

1 Nebular hypothesis A spinning, shrinking cloud of gas and dust produced the Sun and threw off rings, which condensed to form planets and their moons.

2 Tidal theory A passing star pulled a tongue of matter from the Sun. The tongue split into drops, then each drop became a planet.

3 Exploding supernova Our Sun supposedly had a companion star that exploded, leaving scattered debris that gave rise to planets.

4 Accretion theory Shock waves from supernovae made a cold cloud of gas and dust condense into smaller, denser clouds where complex molecules including methane formed. A collapsing portion of one cloud became a spinning disk of helium and hydrogen with 1–2 percent of heavier elements. Gravitational attraction produced the Sun and the giant gas-rich planets. Meanwhile, dust grains stuck together and created lumps attracting smaller debris and growing into so-called planetesimals 60–600 mi (100–1000 km) across. After 100 million years or so, coalescing swarms of planetesimals formed the Earth and Earth-like planets–largely stripped of hydrogen and helium gases by a stream of solar particles.

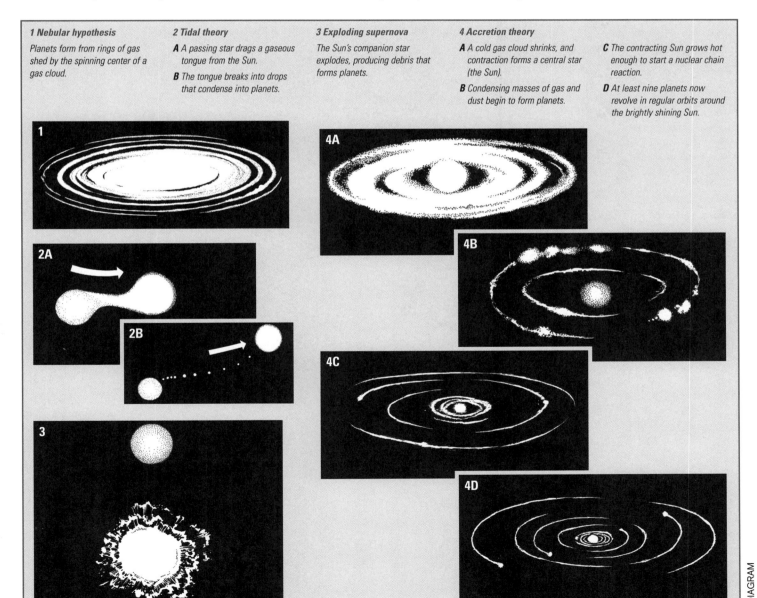

1 Nebular hypothesis

Planets form from rings of gas shed by the spinning center of a gas cloud.

2 Tidal theory

A A passing star drags a gaseous tongue from the Sun.

B The tongue breaks into drops that condense into planets.

3 Exploding supernova

The Sun's companion star explodes, producing debris that forms planets.

4 Accretion theory

A A cold gas cloud shrinks, and contraction forms a central star (the Sun).

B Condensing masses of gas and dust begin to form planets.

C The contracting Sun grows hot enough to start a nuclear chain reaction.

D At least nine planets now revolve in regular orbits around the brightly shining Sun.

© DIAGRAM

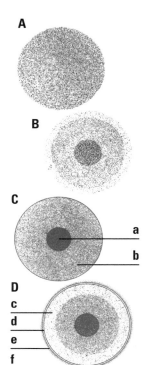

Our layered planet

Accumulating mini-planets, dust, and gases formed the Earth about 4.6 billion years ago. Compression caused by gravitation produced immense internal heat and pressure. Meanwhile gravity was sorting out the Earth's ingredients. Heavy elements tended to be drawn into the middle. Lighter elements and compounds collected near the surface. The lightest elements included an outer film of gases. This poisonous primeval atmosphere gave way to air in time, and Earth's molten surface cooled and hardened, but its interior remains intensely hot.

Such processes produced Earth's major layers:

1 Atmosphere An invisible film of gases (now mainly nitrogen and oxygen) that scientists have divided from the base up into the following areas: troposphere, stratosphere, mesosphere, ionosphere, thermosphere, exosphere, and magnetosphere.

2 Crust Earth's rocky outer surface is 4 mi (6 km) thick under oceans and up to 40 mi (64 km) thick under mountain ranges. The crust consists of relatively "light" rocks–largely granite below continents and basalt below oceans. Oceans cover about 71 percent of the crust.

3 Mantle A layer of rocks 1,800 mi (2,900 km) thick between the crust and outer core. Parts are semi-molten and evidently flow in sluggish currents. Mantle rock is more dense than crustal rock.

4 Outer core A layer of dense molten rocks 1,400 mi (2,240 km) thick between mantle and inner core. It may be mainly iron and nickel with some silicon.

5 Inner core A solid ball 1,540 mi (2,440 km) across. Intense pressure prevents it from liquefying despite a temperature of 3,700 °C. The inner core may be mainly iron and nickel.

Sorting out the Earth

Our planet might have formed in these four stages.

A Cloud of unsorted particles

B Particles sorted, the densest in the middle

C Primeval planet with:

a Dense iron and nickel core

b Material, as in carbonaceous chondrite meteorites

D Outer chondrite melted, yielding:

c Relatively dense mantle

d Primitive crust

e Ocean

f Early atmosphere

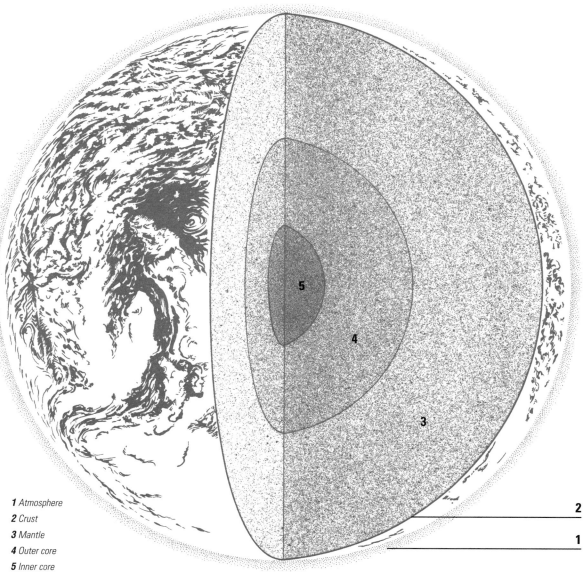

The Earth exposed

Cut open like a cake, today's Earth would show this "onion" structure. Scientists learn about its inner layers by studying how these interfere with waves set off by earthquakes. (See also p. 52.)

1 Atmosphere
2 Crust
3 Mantle
4 Outer core
5 Inner core

Earth's size and shape

Instruments, including artificial satellites, have helped scientists work out the Earth's size, shape, and other features. We now know ours is one of the smallest, lightest planets of the solar system–four others far exceed its mass and volume–but no planet has a greater density (5.5 times that of water).

Careful measurements prove that the ball-like Earth is not in fact a sphere. It measures 24,902 mi (40,075 km) around the equator, but only 24,860 mi (40,008 km) around the poles. So our planet bulges slightly at the equator and is slightly flattened at the poles. Centrifugal force created by Earth's spin produced this shape–an oblate spheroid. Even that description oversimplifies, for the Earth is very slightly pear-shaped.

Scientists accordingly use the term *geoid* ("earth shaped") to describe the Earth's hypothetical, mean sea-level surface–ignoring wrinkles formed by mountain chains and ocean floors. Geoid measurement involves taking sea-level gravity readings by gravimeter and studying "kinks" in the orbits of artificial satellites. Both reveal so-called gravity anomalies that reflect local differences in mass in the Earth's crust and mantle. Such differences account for vast but slight dips and bumps in the geoid's surface.

Gravity anomalies also reinforce the theory of isostasy–a state of balance in the Earth's crust where continents of light material float on a denser substance into which deep continental "roots" project like the underwater mass of floating icebergs.

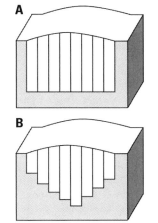

A

B

Ideas about isostasy (left)

A In 1856 John Pratt argued that high and low mountains were blocks of rocks of different density floating above the same base level.

B Sir George Airy thought that different heights showed blocks–of the same density but different thickness–floating at different depths. Airy's view prevailed.

The global geoid (below)

This world map shows the global geoid's surface areas (**a**) above and (**b**) below the surface of a true ellipsoid, as deduced from surface gravity and artificial satellites. The geoid's highest "bumps" are little more than 170 m (558 ft) above its lowest depressions.

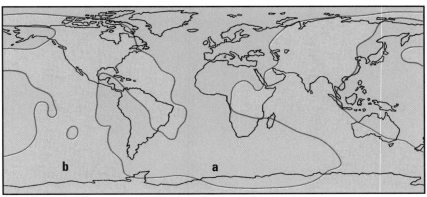

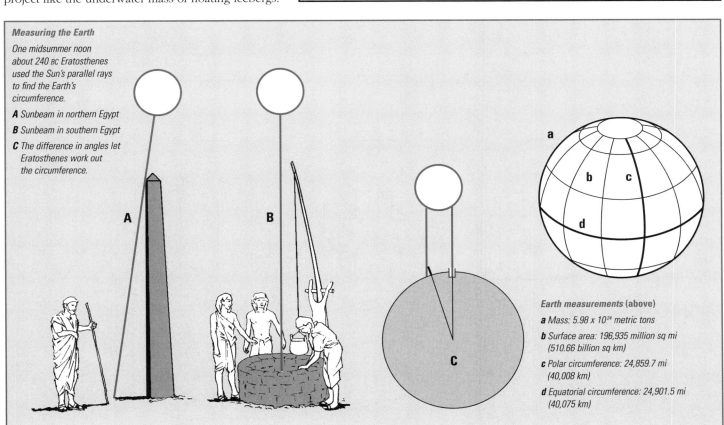

Measuring the Earth

One midsummer noon about 240 BC Eratosthenes used the Sun's parallel rays to find the Earth's circumference.

A Sunbeam in northern Egypt

B Sunbeam in southern Egypt

C The difference in angles let Eratosthenes work out the circumference.

Earth measurements (above)

a Mass: 5.98 x 10²⁴ metric tons

b Surface area: 196,935 million sq mi (510.66 billion sq km)

c Polar circumference: 24,859.7 mi (40,008 km)

d Equatorial circumference: 24,901.5 mi (40,075 km)

© DIAGRAM

Crustal elements

This pie chart shows the percentages of the most abundant elements in the Earth's crust.

a *Oxygen 46.6%*

b *Silicon 27.72%*

c *Aluminum 8.13%*

d *Iron 5.0%*

e *Calcium 3.63%*

f *Sodium 2.83%*

g *Potassium 2.59%*

h *Magnesium 2.09%*

i *Other elements 1.41%*

Earth's building blocks 1

Earth's building blocks are elements and minerals. Of our planet's 92 naturally occurring elements, eight account for 98 percent of the weight of the Earth's crust–the rocky layer scientists know best. Nearly three-quarters of its weight lies in two nonmetals, oxygen and silicon; most of the rest consists of the six metals, aluminum, iron, calcium, sodium, potassium, and magnesium.

Within the crust most elements occur as minerals– natural substances that differ chemically and have distinct atomic structures. The Earth's crust holds about 2,000 kinds of minerals. A few (including gold) occur as just one element; most comprise two or more elements chemically joined as compounds. Silicates (minerals containing silicon and oxygen) are the most abundant minerals in the crust and mantle, which make up four-fifths of our planet's volume. (See also pie chart, left.)

Most minerals formed from fluids that solidified–a process that arranged their atoms geometrically, producing crystals. Scientists identify six crystal systems based on axes–imaginary lines passing through the middle of a crystal. Each system yields crystals with distinctive symmetry. Within each system, each mineral crystal grows in a special shape or habit, though this can be modified by temperature, pressure, and impurities.

Traditional tests identify minerals by hardness, color, streak (color of the powdered mineral), luster, specific gravity, cleavage, fracture, form, tenacity (resistance to bending, breaking, and other forces), odor, taste, and feel. Sophisticated tests involve polarizing microscopes, X rays, and spectral analysis.

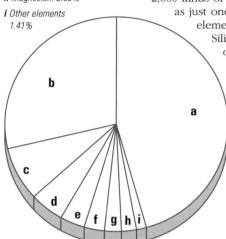

Crystal habits (right)

Three types of habit–crystal form determined by a crystal system but modified by factors such as temperature:

a *Cubic*

b *Columnar*

c *Tabular*

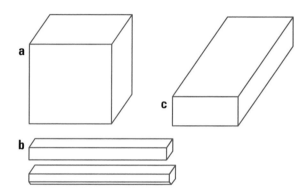

Crystal systems

Systems vary with the number, lengths, and angles of axes. Internal axes are shown by colored lines.

1 *Cubic*

1a *Example: halite*

2 *Tetragonal*

2a *Example: zircon*

3 *Orthorhombic*

3a *Example: staurolite*

4 *Hexagonal*

4a *Example: quartz*

5 *Monoclinic*

5a *Example: orthoclase*

6 *Triclinic*

6a *Example: albite*

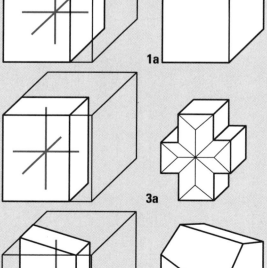
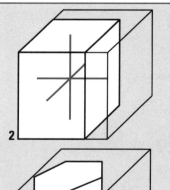

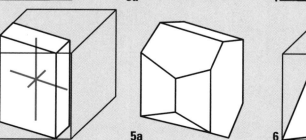
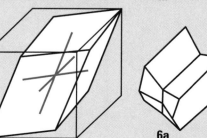

Earth's building blocks 2

Rocks are mixtures of minerals. Most rocks consist of interlocking grains or crystals stuck together by a natural cement. A few dozen minerals provide the main ingredients for the most common rocks. Here are some brief details about rock-forming minerals:

1 Silicates are the chief rock-forming minerals. Most feature a metal combined with silicon and oxygen. Examples: asbestos, mica, quartz, and feldspar

2 Carbonates are the second most abundant group of minerals and include carbon, oxygen, and one or more metals. Examples: calcite, dolomite, and aragonite

3 Sulfides are compounds of sulfur and one or more metals. Examples: galena and pyrite

4 Oxides are compounds of oxygen and one or more metals. Examples: hematite and magnetite

5 Halides are compounds of a halogen and a metal. Examples: Fluorite and halite (rock salt)

6 Hydroxides are compounds of hydrogen, oxygen and usually a metal. Examples: limonite and brucite

7 Sulfates are compounds of sulfur, oxygen, and a metal. Example: gypsum (the commonest sulfate)

8 Phosphates are chemical compounds related to phosphoric acid. Examples: apatite and monazite

9 Tungstates are salts of tungstic acid. Example: wolframite (a tungsten ore)

Rocks vary greatly in size, shape, and mineral proportions. But texture (influenced by origin) helps geologists identify three main groups: igneous, sedimentary, and metamorphic.

A Igneous rocks have interlocking crystals formed as molten rock cooled down. The smaller the crystals the faster the cooling.

B Sedimentary rocks mainly have rather rounded mineral grains joined by natural cements. Most derive from the deposited remains of older rocks.

C Metamorphic rocks have crystals with a tendency to banding or alignment. They are formed from older rocks recrystallized by heat and pressure.

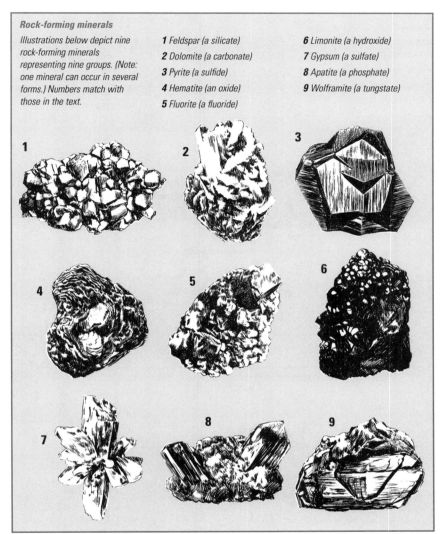

Rock-forming minerals

Illustrations below depict nine rock-forming minerals representing nine groups. (Note: one mineral can occur in several forms.) Numbers match with those in the text.

1 Feldspar (a silicate)
2 Dolomite (a carbonate)
3 Pyrite (a sulfide)
4 Hematite (an oxide)
5 Fluorite (a fluoride)
6 Limonite (a hydroxide)
7 Gypsum (a sulfate)
8 Apatite (a phosphate)
9 Wolframite (a tungstate)

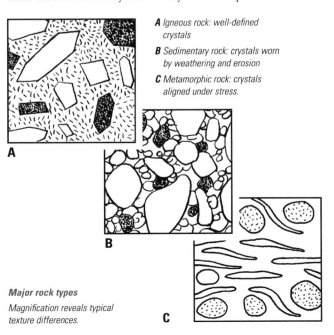

A Igneous rock: well-defined crystals
B Sedimentary rock: crystals worn by weathering and erosion
C Metamorphic rock: crystals aligned under stress.

Major rock types

Magnification reveals typical texture differences.

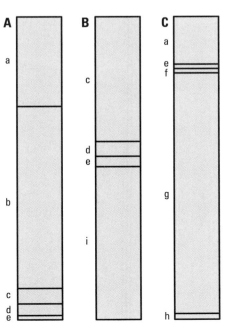

Mineral components

Bars show proportions of minerals in three rocks.

A Granite (igneous)
B Amphibolite (metamorphic)
C Shale (sedimentary)
a Quartz
b Alkali feldspar
c Plagioclase feldspar
d Biotite
e Magnetite
f Muscovite
g Clay minerals
h Calcite
i Amphibole

© DIAGRAM

Energy and the Earth

The flow of energy

This diagram shows Earth's energy input and output.

a Solar radiation

b Surface energy absorption

c Fossil fuel formation

d Surface heating

e Heat from Earth's interior

f Shortwave radiation

g Absorption by atmosphere

h Atmospheric warming

i Winds

j Waves

k Water cycle

l Longwave radiation

m Gravitational energy

n Oceanic tides

o Tides inside the Earth

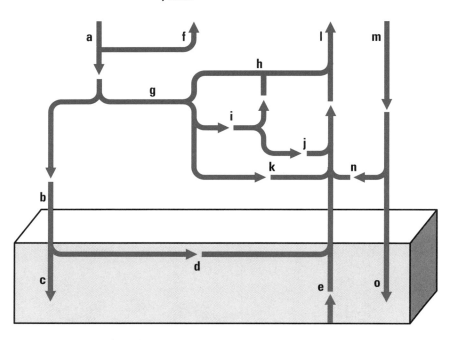

Temperature and depth (below)

This graph shows temperature increases from 59 °F (15 °C) near the surface to 100 °F (38 °C) at a depth of 1,000 m (3,280 ft). Rate of increase varies with the rock, as in our examples.

A Limestone

B Shale

C Granite

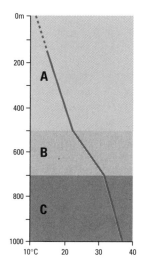

Heat-flow map (below)

The dark tone shows areas of highest heat flow (largely ocean ridges) from the Earth's interior. Coolest areas include the old parts of continents and ocean basins.

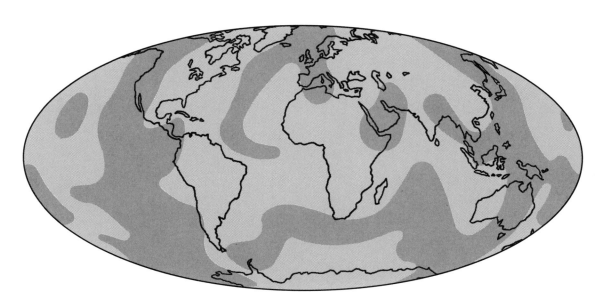

Huge quantities of energy are always acting on the surface of the Earth and its interior. Internal heat helps build and redeploy great sections of the Earth's crust. External energy from the Sun and Moon keeps sea and air in motion, and sculpts the crustal surface.

The immense amount of heat trapped below the Earth's crust has several origins, most dating from the Earth's formation. Thus there is impact energy from colliding planetesimals, energy released by core formation, heat produced by outer layers pressing on the core, and radioactive energy from isotopes incorporated in the early Earth.

From the Earth's core, convection currents convey heat through the mantle to the crust. More is added on the way by radioactive decay of crust and mantle minerals. Here some heat escapes in violent volcanic eruptions, hot springs, and earthquakes, but most simply leaks out quietly through continents and ocean floors–especially from the thin crust below some oceans.

The surface of the Earth's crust receives far more energy from above than below. Sunshine warms the atmosphere and crust. But sunshine warms the Tropics more than the polar regions. This uneven heating creates belts of differing atmospheric pressure. Winds blow from high- to low-pressure areas. In turn, winds drive ocean waves and surface currents. Between them, winds and currents help to spread heat more evenly around the world. The Sun's heat also drives the water cycle. The resulting rain, rivers, glaciers, and ocean waves sculpt the surface of the land in ways described in pp.56–89.

Besides gaining heat from above and below, the surface of the Earth's crust loses heat through radiation into space. Loss roughly matches gain, so surface temperature has long remained about the same.

Lastly, the gravitational energy provided by the Moon and Sun produces our ocean tides and the tidal energy inside the Earth itself.

Earth as a magnet

About 2,000 years ago the Chinese discovered that a freely turning lodestone spoon always ended pointing in the same direction. Such naturally magnetic lumps of iron oxide led later to the compass needle.

For centuries no one knew just why a magnetic compass worked. By AD 1600 experiments suggested that the Earth itself exerted a magnetic force on compass needles. Observations proved that the Earth indeed has a magnetic field whose force aligns compass needles with north and south magnetic poles fairly near the geographic poles. (The field in fact extends far into space: this extension into space is called the magnetosphere.)

Just why the Earth should be magnetic became clear only in the 1950s. Scientists now realize that the Earth is less a huge bar magnet than a self-excited dynamo. Inside the Earth, radioactive heat keeps streams of molten metal flowing through the outer core. This process generates electric currents that produce magnetic fields–much as an electric current flowing through a coil of copper wire creates a magnetic field around the wire. Earth's spin around its axis helps steer currents and create magnetic poles. Mighty eddies in the currents probably explain why magnetic poles slightly shift position from year to year. More puzzling are the hundreds of reversals of polarity occurring throughout Earth's history. Some rocks retain a record of the Earth's

polarity at the time those rocks were formed. Paleomagnetism–the study of the Earth's magnetic field in prehistoric times–helps geologists date certain rocks. It also helps them understand past and present movements of vast slabs of crust–the major subject of our second chapter.

Earth's magnetosphere (below)

a Solar "wind" streamlining Earth's magnetic field

b Shock front where solar wind meets magnetic field

c Magnetopause: edge of the magnetic field

d Van Allen radiation belts

e Earth

Magnetic fields compared

Below and right, two diagrams show the similarity between lines of force produced by an electric current flowing through a wire coil (**A**) and by the revolving Earth (**B**).

a Lines of magnetic force

b Mantle

c Core

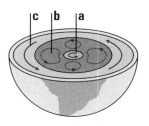

Inside the Earth (above)

The Earth cut open at the equator shows the internal differences of rotation producing the magnetic field.

a Inner core rotation

b Eddies in the outer core

c Rotation of mantle

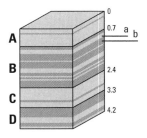

Polarity reversals (above)

This column shows epochs of predominantly normal (**a**) and reversed (**b**) polarity for the last 4.2 million years.

A Brunhes (normal)

B Matuyama (reversed)

C Gauss (normal)

D Gilbert (reversed)

© DIAGRAM

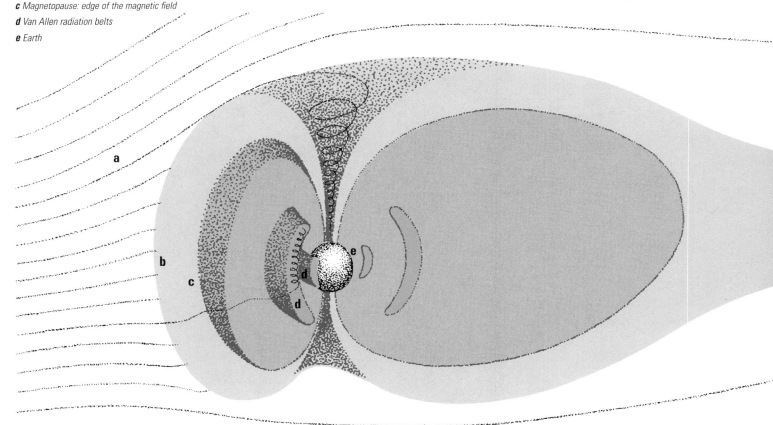

The restless crust

These pages explore the structure of the Earth's crust–the thin, hard outer layer that we live on. We look at rocks that form the continents and ocean floor. We glimpse the slow processes that make and then destroy the ocean floor; build, move, and split the continents; and thrust up mountain chains. Pushing up and wearing down creates a grand recycling of rocks whose processes and products shape the land in ways described in later chapters.

Tectonic plates

This map shows the major plates. Most plates are bounded by spreading ridges and collision zones or subduction zones (marked by oceanic trenches). Active boundaries give rise to earthquakes or volcanoes.

a Eurasian Plate

b African Plate

c Antarctic Plate

d Indo-Australian Plate

e Pacific Plate

f North American Plate

g Nazca Plate

h South American Plate

⊓⌐ Spreading ridges

— Collision zones

▲▲ Subduction zones

▭ Continental crust

⋮ Volcanoes

⋮ Earthquakes

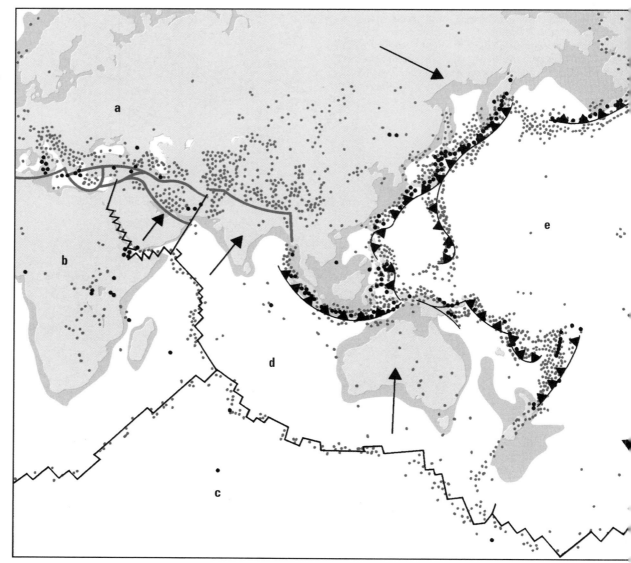

Earth's changing surface

Our planet's solid surface is a restless jigsaw of abutting, diverging, and colliding slabs called tectonic (or lithospheric) plates. How plates behave forms the subject known as plate tectonics.

Each plate involves a slab of oceanic crust, continental crust, or both, joined to a slab of rigid upper mantle. Collectively, these plates make up the lithosphere. This rides upon the asthenosphere, a dense, plastic layer of the mantle. Heat rising through this layer from the Earth's core and lower mantle seemingly produces convection currents that shift the plates above.

Plate activities produce three main kinds of plate margins. Constructive margins are suboceanic spreading ridges where new lithosphere is formed between two separating oceanic plates. Destructive margins are oceanic trenches where an oceanic plate dives down below a (less dense) continental plate. Conservative margins are where two plates slide past each other and lithosphere is neither made nor lost.

Geophysicists also talk about active margins (where colliding continental and oceanic plates spark off volcanic eruptions, earthquakes, and mountain building) and passive margins (tectonically quiet boundaries between continental and oceanic crust).

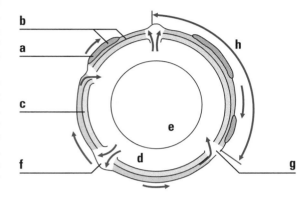

Plate tectonics in action

This cross section of the world suggests that lithosphere is made by currents rising in the mantle at constructive margins and lost at destructive margins where mantle currents sink.

a *Continental crust*

b *Lithosphere*

c *Asthenosphere*

d *Lower mantle*

e *Core*

f *Constructive margin*

g *Destructive margin*

h *Lithospheric plate*

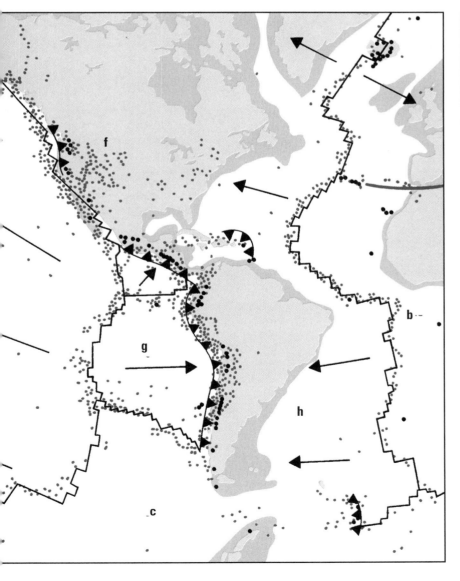

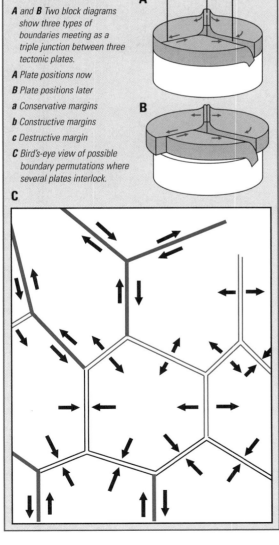

Plate boundaries

A and **B** *Two block diagrams show three types of boundaries meeting as a triple junction between three tectonic plates.*

A *Plate positions now*

B *Plate positions later*

a *Conservative margins*

b *Constructive margins*

c *Destructive margin*

C *Bird's-eye view of possible boundary permutations where several plates interlock.*

The ocean floor

This cross section of an imaginary ocean floor depicts the 10 major features explained in the text on the opposite page. (The vertical scale is exaggerated for effect.)

The ocean floor

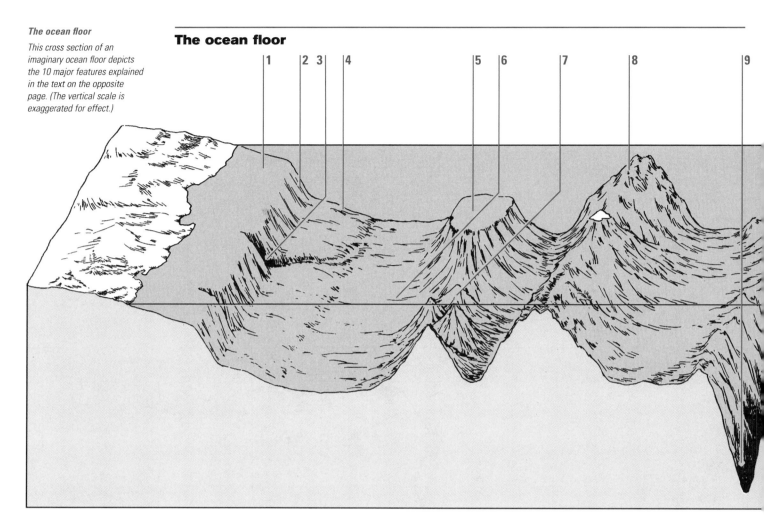

Oceanic crust

Dredging, boring, and seismic surveying suggest that oceanic crust is thinner, denser, and more simply made than continental crust. Oceanic crust is less than 6.2 mi (10 km) thick. Its rocks are richer than mantle rocks in aluminum and calcium, and their high silica and magnesium content earned oceanic crust the collective name of sima. Here are (simplified) details of oceanic crust's three layers and an associated fourth layer:

1 Layer 1 The top layer consists of sediments. Muds, sands, and other debris washed off continents lie up to 1/2 mi (l km) thick on continental shelves and nearby ocean floor.

The layered seabed

A block diagram shows one estimate of average depths of the four layers of oceanic lithosphere riding on the mantle. (Layer 1 thins away from continents.) Numbers match items in the text.

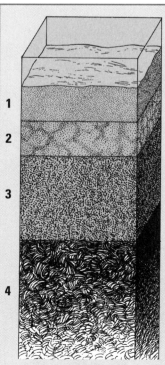

The open ocean's bed contains oozes (remains of dead microorganisms from the surface waters), clays, and (in places) nodules rich in substances including manganese. No sediment occurs on spreading ridges.

2 Layer 2 is chiefly igneous rock, especially basalt, derived from the mantle and released at spreading ridges as rounded lumps of pillow lava. Scientists think the lower part of Layer 2 is seamed by sheeted dikes (see p. 35). Much of Layer 2 is 0.9–1.2 mi (1.5–2 km) thick.

3 Layer 3 is about 3 mi (5 km) thick and largely made of gabbro–a coarse-grained rock equivalent to the fine-grained basalt found in Layer 2.

4 Layer 4 is a rigid upper mantle layer connected to the bottom of the ocean crust. It may be largely made of the dense igneous rock peridotite, consisting chiefly of the mineral olivine.

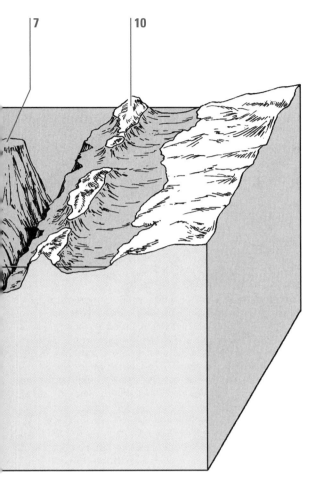

Oceans and their seas hold 97 percent of all surface water, and cover some 71 percent of the Earth to an average depth of 12,400 ft (3,800 m). Stripping off this watery sheath would reveal valleys, plateaus, peaks, and plains. Ten features of the ocean floor are explained below.

1 Continental shelf A continent's true but submerged and gently sloping rim; it descends to an average depth of 650 ft (200 m). Continental shelves occupy about 7.5 percent of the ocean floor.

2 Continental slope A relatively steep slope descending from the continental shelf. Such slopes occupy about 8.5 percent of the ocean floor.

3 Submarine canyon A deep cleft in the continental slope, cut by turbid river water flowing out to sea.

4 Continental rise A gentle slope below the continental slope.

5 Submarine plateau A high seafloor tableland.

6 Abyssal plain A sediment-covered deep-sea plain about 11,500–18,000 ft (3,500–5,500 m) below sea level.

7 Seamount A submarine volcano 3,300 ft (1,000 m) or more above its surroundings. Guyots are flat-topped seamounts that were once volcanic islands.

8 Spreading ridge A submarine mountain chain generally 10,000 ft (3,000 m) above the abyssal plain. A huge system of such ridges extends more than 37,000 mi (60,000 km) through the oceans.

9 Trench A deep, steep-sided trough in an abyssal plain. At 35,840 ft (10,924 m) below sea level (deep enough to submerge Mt. Everest), the Pacific Ocean's Marianas Trench is the deepest part of any ocean.

10 Island arc A curved row of volcanic islands, usually on the continental side of a trench.

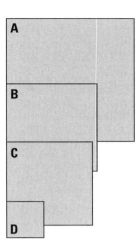

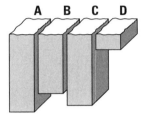

Ocean areas and depths

Diagrams contrast relative areas (above) and average depths (below) of the Earth's four oceans, omitting their marginal seas.

A Pacific Ocean

B Atlantic Ocean

C Indian Ocean

D Arctic Ocean

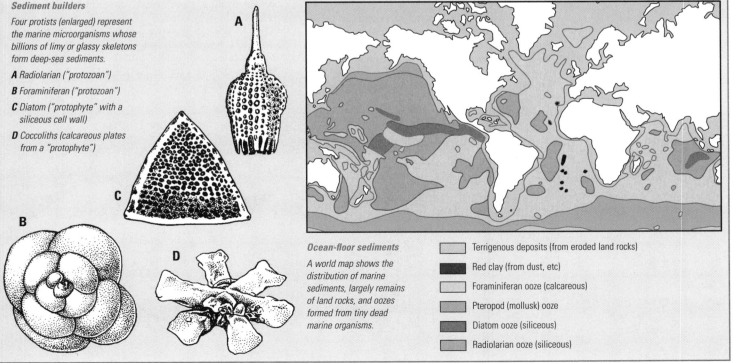

Sediment builders

Four protists (enlarged) represent the marine microorganisms whose billions of limy or glassy skeletons form deep-sea sediments.

A Radiolarian ("protozoan")

B Foraminiferan ("protozoan")

C Diatom ("protophyte" with a siliceous cell wall)

D Coccoliths (calcareous plates from a "protophyte")

Ocean-floor sediments

A world map shows the distribution of marine sediments, largely remains of land rocks, and oozes formed from tiny dead marine organisms.

Terrigenous deposits (from eroded land rocks)

Red clay (from dust, etc)

Foraminiferan ooze (calcareous)

Pteropod (mollusk) ooze

Diatom ooze (siliceous)

Radiolarian ooze (siliceous)

© DIAGRAM

Seafloor spreading

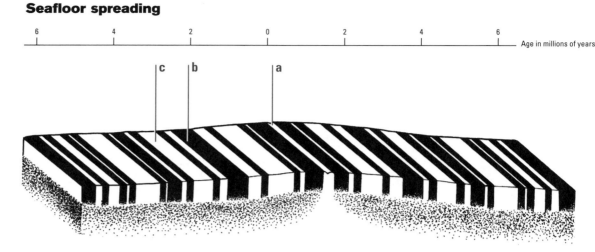

Age in millions of years

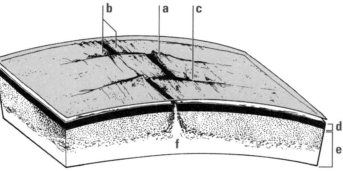

Scarcely any ocean floor is more than 200 million years old. Long ago a single mighty ocean incorporating the Pacific surrounded one landmass. The landmass developed splits that widened into basins. The Arctic, Atlantic, and Indian Oceans were created in this way.

Seafloor is always being made and destroyed by a process called seafloor spreading. Growth occurs at high heat-flow areas of oceanic crust where currents rising in the mantle hit the crust above. Seemingly this process helps tug apart vast chunks of crust, but the resulting gaps are continuously plugged by molten basalt and other rock originating in the mantle. Basalt sticking to the edges of such rifts formed the Mid-Atlantic Ridge and other vast underwater mountain chains called spreading ridges. Each widens by up to 10 in (25 cm) a year.

Scientists believe that the detailed process goes as follows. First, molten rock wells up from deep down in the upper mantle region called the asthenosphere. The upwelling molten mass partly melts the rocks around it to make the oceanic crust. Gravity pulls the ridge flanks down and sideways. The resulting tension opens two main cracks along the ridge. Between these cracks the ridge's middle sinks to form a central rift valley. Molten rock wells up through main and lesser cracks, then cools and hardens to become new ocean floor. Injections of fresh molten rock keep this spreading moving outwards from the central rift.

As upwelling continues, the rifting process is repeated. In time, rows of parallel ridges creep outward, cooling, growing denser, and sinking down to form the ocean's abyssal plains.

Meanwhile, great cracks called transform faults cut across the central ridge at right angles, offsetting the short, straight sections.

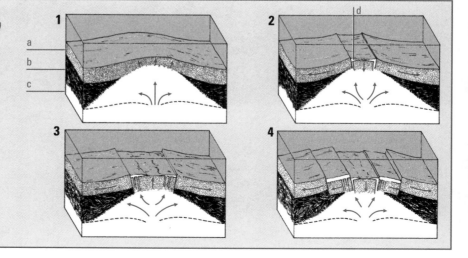

How seafloor disappears

While hot, light seafloor grows outward from the spreading ridges, old cooled and denser seafloor disappears elsewhere into the mantle. Oceanic trenches are the sites of these subduction zones, where leading edges of lithospheric plates plunge under less dense or less mobile plates and go below a continent or ocean floor. Most trenches lie around the rim of the Pacific Ocean; here the rocks originating from the spreading ridge that runs from Canada to south of New Zealand vanish.

Subducted oceanic crust injects a tongue of relatively cool material into the hot mantle rock beneath. The friction of its passage generates earthquakes.

As the subducted oceanic crust descends, its load of low-density sediments is largely scraped off and deformed. Meanwhile, 60 mi (100 km) down, the sinking lithosphere begins to melt; by 430 mi (700 km) down, it has completely broken up.

Less dense than the surrounding mantle, mantle melted by hot fluids from subducted lithosphere bobs up as it melts holes through the edge of the plate above the one subducted. Together with the scraped-off sediments, this process builds island arcs–rows of volcanic islands curved because they form upon the Earth's curved surface. (Pressing a ping-pong ball with your thumb forms a similarly arc-shaped fold.)

Examples of such arcs occur in the Aleutian, Japanese, Kurile, and Cycladic Islands.

Oceanic crust subducted below a continental rim throws up volcanoes on the mainland. Volcanoes formed this way crown the Andes mountain chain of western South America.

Spreading and subduction

This diagram shows the complete conveyor belt sequence of ocean-floor production, transportation, and destruction.

a Spreading ridge

b Transform fault

c Subduction zone

d Oceanic crust

e Continental crust

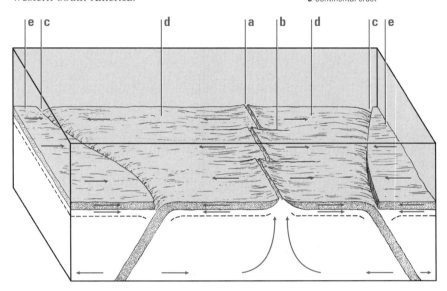

1 Oceanic subduction zone

a Oceanic trench

b Volcanic island arc

c Crust

d Mantle

e Area where oceanic crust is destroyed

2 Subduction zone beneath the South American continent

a Peru-Chile trench

b Seafloor (oceanic crust)

c Western cordillera (Andes)

d Eastern cordillera (Andes)

e Active volcano

f Continental crust

g Mantle

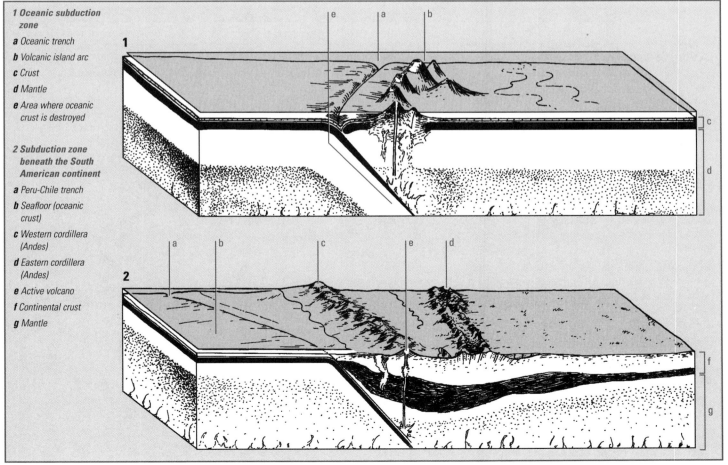

© DIAGRAM

The continental crust

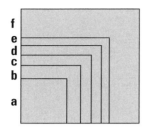

The continents

Relative areas of continental lands above sea level:

a *Australia*

b *Antarctica*

c *South America*

d *North America*

e *Africa*

f *Eurasia*

Continents are the great landmasses above the level of the ocean basins. The six major masses are North America, South America, Eurasia, Africa, Australia, and Antarctica. With their submerged offshore continental shelves, these form 29 percent of the Earth's surface and 0.3 percent of the Earth.

Continents are thicker, less dense, and contain more complex rocks than ocean crust. Continental crust averages 20 mi (33 km) in thickness, but can be twice that deep below high mountains. The top 9 mi (15 km) or so consists of sedimentary, igneous, and metamorphic rocks rich in silicon and aluminum, hence the collective name *sial* often used for

continental crust. The lower crust has denser igneous and metamorphic rocks. Continental lithospheric plates ride on the asthenosphere.

Continents average 2,950 ft (900 m) above sea level, but have wrinkles in the form of mountains, valleys, plains, and plateaus. According to geologists continents contain the following three main structural components:

1 Shields (or cratons) are stable slabs comprising outcrops of ancient masses of deformed crystalline rocks. Eroded shields plus overlying younger rocks are known as platforms. Shields and platforms form vast flat expanses, as in the plains of North America

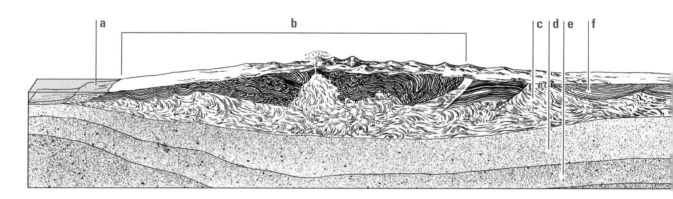

Clues to continental drift

Scientists suspected that continents had moved around before the discovery of seafloor spreading showed how this shifting might have occured. Here are five land-based clues to continental drift:

1 Geographical Some continents' coasts would almost interlock if they were rearranged like pieces of a jigsaw puzzle. For instance, South America fits into Africa.

2 Geological Old mountain zones of matching ages appear as belts crossing southern continents, if these are joined together in a certain way.

3 Climatic Glacial deposits and rocks scratched by stones in moving ice show that ice covered huge tracts of the southern continents 300 million years ago. This suggests that these landmasses once lay in polar regions.

4 Paleomagnetic Alignments of magnetized particles in old rock show that the southern continents all lay near the South Pole about 300 million years ago.

5 Biological Identical fossil land plants and land animals crop up in the southern continents now widely separated by the sea.

1 Geographical clues

*The Americas (**a**, **b**) fit into Europe (**c**) and Africa (**d**) if they are joined along their true rims, 6,600 ft (2,000 m) below the sea.*

2 Geological clues

Aligning shields and rocks of three mountain-building phases suggest how southern lands may have fitted together.

a *Shields*

b *Early Paleozoic rocks*

c *Early Mesozoic rocks*

d *Late Mesozoic–Early Cenozoic*

3 Climatic clues

About 320 million years ago South Polar ice sheets could have straddled southern lands in this way.

4 Paleomagnetic evidence

A *Apparent wander paths of South America and Africa in relation to magnetic poles 400–200 million years ago.*

B *Paths coincided, if both continents were joined.*

5 Biological clues

These three fossil land organisms crop up in several southern lands, as shown:

a *Glossopteris (plant)*

b *Lystrosaurus (synapsid "reptile")*

c *Mesosaurus (reptile)*

and Siberia, the Sahara Desert, the Congo Basin, and much of the Australian interior. Upraised parts of shields and platforms form high plateaus, especially in Africa and Asia.

2 Linear mobile belts include young fold mountains like the Alps, Himalayas, Andes, and North American Cordillera. (See p. 31.) Beveled, mobile belts probably comprise the long rock structures seen around the rims of ancient shields.

3 Sedimentary basins are broad, deep depressions filled with sedimentary rocks formed in shallow seas that sometimes covered parts of ancient shields or their flanking mobile belts.

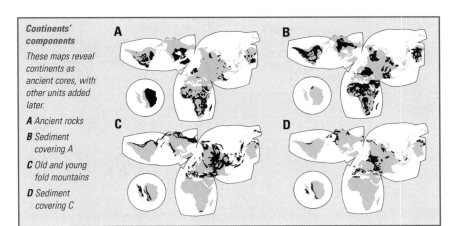

Continents' components

These maps reveal continents as ancient cores, with other units added later.

A Ancient rocks

B Sediment covering A

C Old and young fold mountains

D Sediment covering C

Inside a continent (left)

Section across an imaginary landmass:

a Continental shelf

b Young mobile belt (fold mountains with earthquakes and active volcanoes)

c Granitic/metamorphic rocks

d Granodioritic crust with intruded basic rocks

e Peridotite upper mantle

f Sedimentary basin

g Platform

h Shield

i Old mobile belt (old fold mountains without earthquakes or volcanoes).

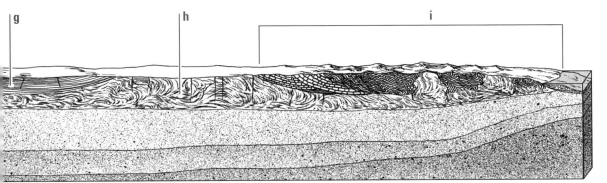

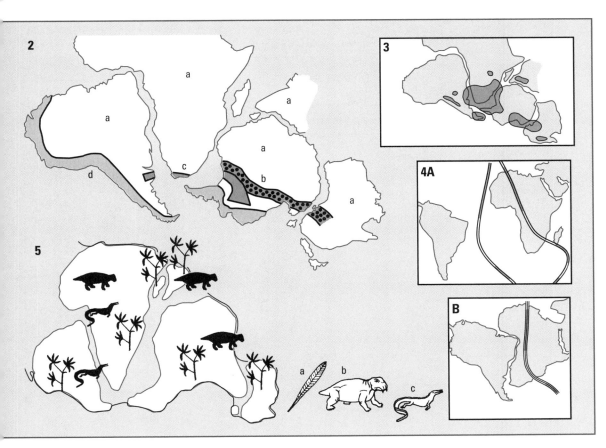

How continents evolve

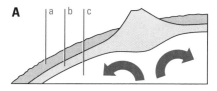

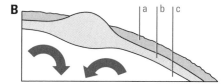

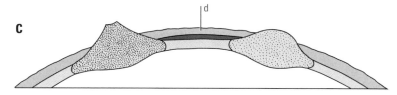

Emerging microcontinents (above)

Sections through the curved Earth's surface (above) suggest one way in which rock resorting of primal crust might have given rise to continental and oceanic crust.

A Greenstone island forms above rising mantle current.

B Granitic craton forms above sinking mantle current.

C Greenstone island belt, early oceanic crust, and embryonic craton.

a Ocean

b Primal crust

c Mantle

d Oceanic crust

Close study of the rocks of continents reveals ancient cores with progressively younger rocks tacked on to their rims. Each core, or craton, originated as a microcontinent, possibly like this. Two converging, cooling, horizontal currents in the mantle tugged on a tract of thin, early crustal rock, then sank. This squashed and thickened that patch of crust. Its base bulged down and melted, releasing light material that punched up through the crust above. Such rock resorting could have formed the first small slabs of continental crust. Later, sea-floor spreading swept island arcs and sediments against microcontinents as mobile belts – belts of deformed and buckled rock. Accretion of this kind formed full-blown continents.

About 5 per cent of today's continental crust had formed by 3.5 billion years ago, half by 2.5 billion years ago, most by 0.5 billion years ago. Once formed, continents are not immutable–they can be reworked, but not destroyed. Coalescing produced the supercontinent Pangea about 300 million years ago. Rifting later broke it up.

The Earth's crust splits open above "hot spots" fixed plumes of molten rock rising in the mantle. A plume formed the volcanic Hawaiian Islands by punching through the thin oceanic Pacific Plate passing over it. Plumes raise domes in the thick, rigid continental crust. A dome is liable to split in three as cracks grow outward from its top. Where three cracks widen, oceanic rock wells up into the spreading gaps. The continent is split apart, and a triple junction then separates three lithospheric plates. If spreading happens only in two cracks, two plates form. The third crack becomes an abandoned trough or rift. Nigeria's Benue Trough and Ethiopia's Afar Depression are two such so-called aulacogens.

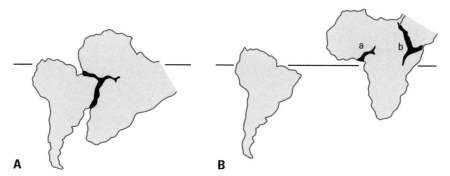

Triple junctions (above)

A A triple junction split South America from Africa.

B A triple junction splits Arabia from Africa. The Benue Trough (**a**) and Afar Depression (**b**) are both aulacogens.

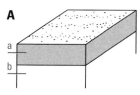

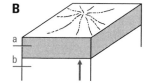

A rifting continent (right)

A Continental crust intact

B Crust bulges above a rising hot spot in the mantle

C Crust fractures

a Crust

b Mantle

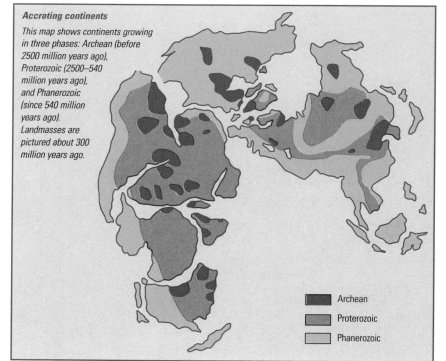

Accreting continents

This map shows continents growing in three phases: Archean (before 2500 million years ago), Proterozoic (2500–540 million years ago), and Phanerozoic (since 540 million years ago). Landmasses are pictured about 300 million years ago.

■ Archean

■ Proterozoic

■ Phanerozoic

Mountain building

Large regions of the Earth consist of mountains. Most occur in rows called ranges. Parallel ranges and intervening plateaus form chains such as the Andes and North American Cordillera. Related mountain chains and ranges make up mountain systems, notably the Tethyan (Alpine-Himalayan) and Circum-Pacific systems.

Orogenesis, or mountain building, occurs along mobile belts–places where colliding lithospheric plates disrupt the continental crust. Such mountain-building belts are known as orogens and orogenic belts are belts of fold mountains–mountains created by crustal deformation and uplift. Geologically recent orogenic belts mostly rim continents. But ancient orogenic belts (the Ural Mountains for example) can occur deep inside a continent where lithospheric plates were welded together long ago.

Mountain building is a complex process. Deep troughs of accumulated offshore sediment, volcanic rocks, bits of oceanic crust, and scraps of foreign continents can all be swept against one continent and welded on as mountain ranges. Most of mountainous western North America consists of more than 50 suspect terranes–mighty slabs of alien rock that independently rotated and migrated north along the western edge of North America.

Major mountain-building processes

We illustrate three major mountain-building processes. (For associated landforms see also pp. 32–41 and 48–55.)

1 Oceanic plate subduction below another oceanic plate. This process created the Aleutian Islands and other mountainous island arcs.

2 Oceanic plate subduction beneath a continent. Involving island-arc collision, this process helped produce the Andes.

3 Double continent collision. The way in which the Alps and Himalayas formed.

1 Island-arc orogeny

a Subducted oceanic crust

b Low outer island-arc of sediments squeezed by subducting oceanic crust.

c Inner island-arc of mountainous volcanoes, produced by the "bobbing up" of light, molten magma.

2 Cordilleran belt orogeny

A Island-arc (*c*) and continent (*d*) with offshore sediments (*b*) advance on two plates, one subducting below the other.

B Collision squeezes and rucks up sediments (*b*) between island-arc volcanoes (*c*) and continent (*d*), producing a cordilleran mountain chain such as the Andes.

C and D The old subduction zone is replaced by a new one.

3 Colliding continents

A Continents (*d*) advance on separate plates.

B Collision rucks up marginal sediments (*b*) and the ocean shrinks.

C The oceanic crust between is subducted and the two continents collide, forming mountain ranges like the Alps or the Himalayas

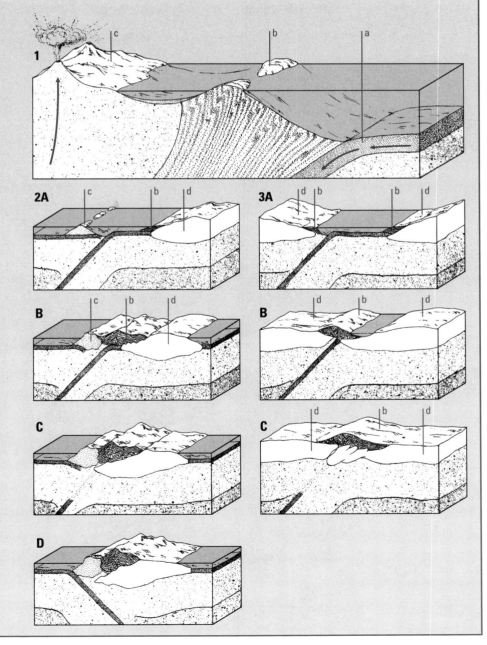

Fiery rocks

Molten rock welling up from deep down in the Earth's interior cools and hardens at or near the surface to create such rocks as lavas and granite. Igneous, or "fiery," rocks like these hold minerals that form the raw materials from which all crustal rocks derive. These pages describe major types and forms of igneous rocks, their ingredients, and the phenomena they yield—from mighty sheets and domes to tall volcanic cones, hot springs, and geysers. This chapter ends with a glimpse of fiery rocks from other planets.

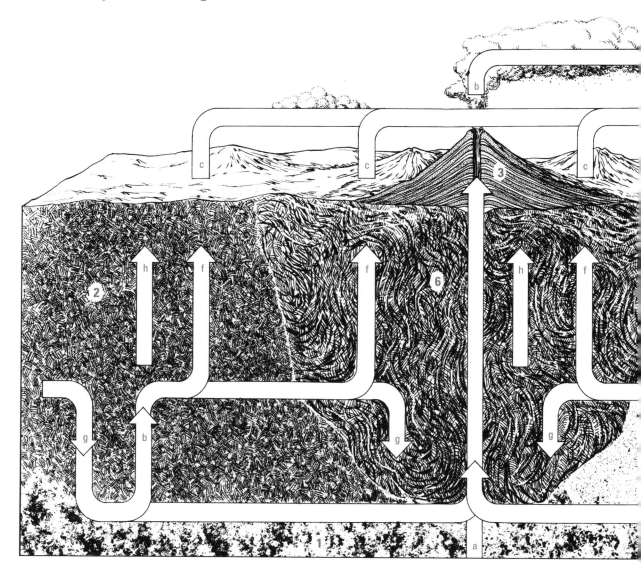

Materials

1 Molten rock in the mantle

2 Intrusive igneous rock

3 Extrusive (volcanic) igneous rock

4 Sediment

5 Sedimentary rock

6 Metamorphic rock

Rocks recycled

Internal and external forces produce a rock cycle that builds, destroys, and remakes much of the rock that forms our planet's crust. The internal forces are produced by currents of rock that rise and spread out in the mantle, thereby moving lithospheric plates around. The main external forces are the weather, determined and generated by the energy in sunshine.

Weather wears down the rocks exposed above sea level. Rainfall creates rivers that transport rock debris to the sea, where it collects as sediment. Some sediments consolidate into sedimentary rock.

Colliding lithospheric plates thrust much of the sedimentary rock above the sea. Subducting lithospheric plates bear igneous and sedimentary rock down into the mantle, where heat and pressure turn it into metamorphic rock. Molten igneous rock rises through the cooler, denser rocks above, creating island arcs, injecting new material into the continental crust, and baking preexisting rocks.

The rock cycle and its associated cycle of erosion involve the processes and products covered in pp. 32–89.

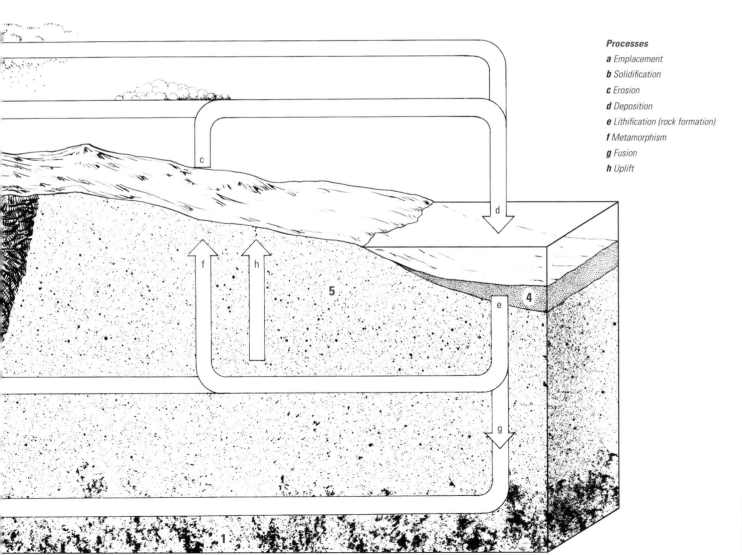

Processes

a Emplacement

b Solidification

c Erosion

d Deposition

e Lithification (rock formation)

f Metamorphism

g Fusion

h Uplift

Rocks from magma

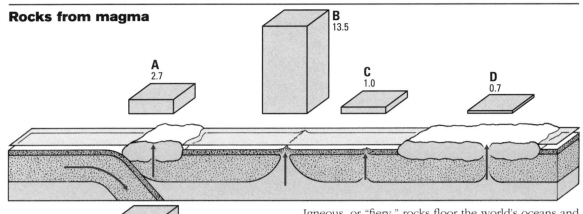

Magma production

Columns show annual magma output and loss in cubic kilometers from specific areas.

A Destructive plate boundaries (subduction zones)

B Constructive plate boundaries (spreading ridges)

C Within oceanic plates

D Within continental plates

E Plate material consumed at destructive plate boundaries

A 2.7

B 13.5

C 1.0

D 0.7

E 14.0

Igneous, or "fiery," rocks floor the world's oceans and form rock masses that rise from the roots of continents. Such rocks arise directly from the molten underground rock material–magma–that occurs where heat melts parts of the Earth's upper mantle and lower crust. Most magma that has cooled and solidified escapes up through the crust from oceanic spreading ridges. Smaller quantities come from destructive plate boundaries and colliding continents.

Igneous rocks hold many minerals, chiefly silicates (silicon and oxygen usually combined with a base or metal). The major silicates are feldspars– silicates of aluminum combined with certain other elements, notably potassium (in alkali feldspars) and sodium and/or calcium (in plagioclase feldspars). Other silicates include ferromagnesian minerals (rich in iron and magnesium); for instance, amphibole, biotite mica, olivine, and pyroxene are all ferromagnesian minerals. Quartz is the sole silicate comprising only silicon and oxygen.

Silica-rich igneous rocks are described as acid. In descending order of silica content, the other major groups are intermediate, basic (or mafic), and ultrabasic (or ultramafic).

Which type of rock evolves depends upon the type of parent magma and the processes it undergoes as it absorbs magma-melted rock, loses gas, and cools down. Different minerals "freeze out," or crystallize, and separate at different temperatures, so some magma yields rocks with layers of different minerals. But an igneous rock usually contains one set of minerals that solidified at roughly the same temperature. The rate of cooling influences crystal size; slow cooling gives large mineral crystals, and fast cooling yields fine-grained rocks.

The next pages describe igneous rocks formed in different conditions.

Igneous rocks' ingredients

Percentages of pale and dark minerals in coarse-grained and fine-grained rocks

Coarse-grained rocks:

1 Syenite

2 Granite

3 Granodiorite

4 Diorite

5 Gabbro

6 Peridotite

Pale and dark minerals:

a Orthoclase feldspar

b Quartz

c Plagioclase feldspar

d Biotite

e Amphibole

f Pyroxene

g Olivine

Fine-grained rocks:

7 Trachyte

8 Rhyolite

9 Rhyodacite

10 Andesite

11 Basalt

Crystals taking shape (right)

Minerals solidifying in sequence give igneous rocks an interlocking crystal texture

1 First mineral starts forming in molten magma

2 Second mineral forming

3 Last mineral to form fills any remaining space

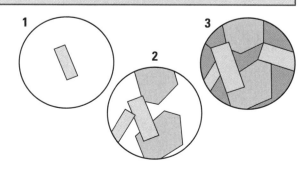

Solidifying minerals (right)

Temperatures in °C at which seven minerals crystallize:

a Amphibole

b Quartz

c Olivine

d Mica

e Pyroxene

f Orthoclase feldspar

g Plagioclase feldspar

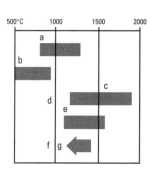

Fiery rocks formed underground

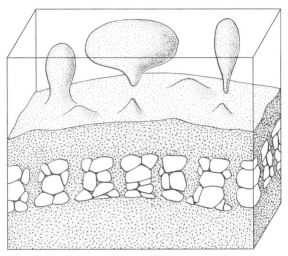

How granite forms

Light, molten blobs of granite rise from rocks melted deep down in the crust. Great blobs called plutons coalesce and cool as batholiths—immense rock masses in the cores of mountain ranges like the Sierra Nevada of California.

Intrusive igneous rocks are produced where magma cools and hardens underground. Geologists place intrusive rocks in two categories: plutonic and hypabyssal.

Plutonic rocks include great masses formed deep in mountain-building zones; some develop from partial fusion of lower continental crust, and others come from magma rising from the mantle. Slow cooling produces big mineral crystals, usually coarse-textured rocks, including (acid) granite and granodiorite; (intermediate) syenite and diorite; (basic) gabbro; and (ultrabasic) peridotite. Granite—mainly made of quartz, feldspar, and mica—is the chief igneous rock of all continental crust. Erosion of overlying rock exposes granite masses like the domes above California's Yosemite Valley and the tors of Dartmoor in southwest England.

Hypabyssal rocks are relatively smaller masses, often strips or sheets. Such rocks cooled at a lesser depth and faster than plutonic rock, so they hold smaller crystals. Hypabyssal rocks include (acid) microgranite and microgranodiorite; (intermediate) microsyenite and microdiorite; and (basic) diabase (dolerite).

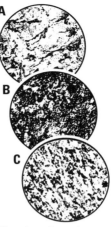

Three intrusive rocks

A *Granite, an acid rock rich in quartz and feldspar*

B *Diorite, an intermediate rock, mainly plagioclase feldspar with darker minerals such as biotite or hornblende*

C *Gabbro, a basic rock, mainly plagioclase feldspar and pyroxene*

Features of intrusive rocks

Intrusive rocks produce these features:

1 Batholith A huge deep-seated, dome-shaped intrusion, usually of acid igneous rock.

2 Stock Like a batholith but smaller, with an irregular surface area under 40 sq mi (about 100 sq km).

3 Boss A small circular-surfaced igneous intrusion less than 16 mi (26 km) across.

4 Dike A wall of usually basic igneous rock, such as diabase (dolerite), injected up through a vertical crack in preexisting rock.

5 Sill A sheet of usually basic igneous rock intruded horizontally between rock layers.

6 Laccolith A lens-shaped, usually acidic, igneous intrusion that domes overlying strata.

7 Lopolith A saucer-shaped intrusion between rock strata; can be up to hundreds of miles across.

Intrusive rocks
1 *Batholith*
2 *Stock*
3 *Boss*
4 *Dike*
5 *Sill*
6 *Laccolith*
7 *Lopolith*

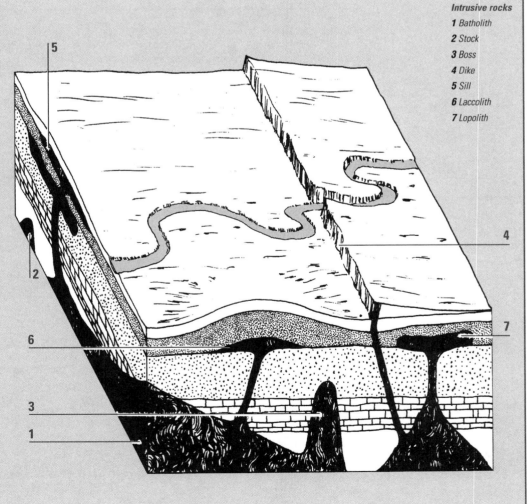

© DIAGRAM

Basalt columns (above)

As basalt lava cools, it shrinks and sometimes splits into vertical columns. Famous examples include Ireland's Giant's Causeway and Staffa in the Inner Hebrides.

Volcanic rocks

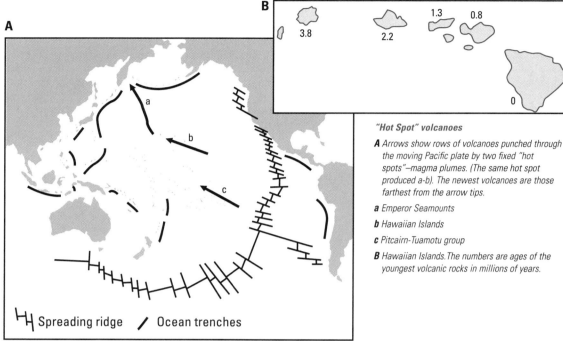

A

B 3.8 2.2 1.3 0.8 0

🔗🔗 Spreading ridge   ／ Ocean trenches

"Hot Spot" volcanoes

A *Arrows show rows of volcanoes punched through the moving Pacific plate by two fixed "hot spots"–magma plumes. (The same hot spot produced a-b). The newest volcanoes are those farthest from the arrow tips.*

a *Emperor Seamounts*

b *Hawaiian Islands*

c *Pitcairn-Tuamotu group*

B *Hawaiian Islands. The numbers are ages of the youngest volcanic rocks in millions of years.*

Where volcanoes erupt

a *Island arc*

b *Shield volcano*

c *Spreading ridge*

d *Cordilleran mountains*

e *Lava plateau*

f *Rift valley*

Extrusive, or volcanic, igneous rocks occur chiefly at volcanic vents along the active margins of lithospheric plates. Here magma erupts as lava, which cools and hardens quickly on the surface as fine-grained or glassy rock.

Basic lavas are rich in metallic elements but poor in silica. They flow easily and erupt relatively gently. The best-known product is basalt, which accounts for more than 90 percent of all volcanic rock. This dark, fine-grained rock contains the minerals plagioclase feldspar, pyroxene, olivine, and magnetite. Basalt is formed by a partial melting of peridotite, the chief rock of the upper mantle. Basalt wells up from oceanic spreading ridges and builds new ocean floor; it also appears in continental rift valleys and rows of volcanoes like the Hawaiian Islands–products of a fixed plume of magma punching through the Pacific plate moving over it.

Acid (silica-rich) lavas appear at destructive plate margins. They probably comprise selected substances

from basic lava of the upper mantle or reprocessed crust. Acid lavas are explosive and slow-flowing. They produce rocks such as dacite, rhyolite, and (black, glassy) obsidian.

Intermediate lavas contain plagioclase feldspar and amphibole, sometimes also alkali feldspar and quartz. They stem from partial melting of certain minerals in subducted oceanic crust. This process formed the lava andesite, named for the Andes Mountains. Found on the landward side of oceanic trenches, andesite builds island arc volcanoes and tacks new land onto the rims of continents.

More than 850 known volcanoes have erupted in the last 2,000 years. Those emitting continuously or from time to time are active; many form what is referred to as the "ring of fire" around the Pacific Ocean. Volcanoes not erupting in recent times are known as dormant. Long-inactive volcanoes are said to be extinct; some occur where colliding plates fused together many millions of years ago.

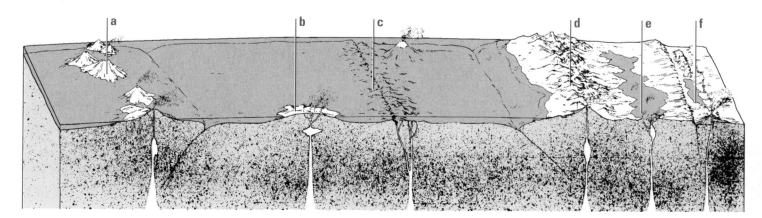

Anatomy of a volcano

Volcanoes take two main forms. Fissure, or linear, volcanoes chiefly emit basic lava from a crack in the Earth's crust. Central volcanoes yield lava, ash, and/or other products from a single hole. These products build a shield- or cone-shaped mound–the typical volcano shape. Central volcanoes can grow high and fast. In western Mexico in 1943, Parícutin grew 490 ft (150 m) high in a week and reached 1,500 ft (450 m) in a year. In western Argentina, extinct Aconcagua towers, 22,834 ft (6,960 m) above sea level; this is the highest mountain in the Western Hemisphere.

A cross section through an active central volcano would reveal these features: miles below the surface lies the magma chamber, a reservoir of gas-rich molten rock under pressure. This pressurized magma may "balloon" outward against the surrounding solid rock until it can relieve the pressure by escaping through a weakness in the crust above. From the chamber, magma then rises through a central conduit. As magma rises, the pressure on it is reduced, and its dissolved gases are freed as expanding bubbles. Finally the force of gases blasts open a circular vent on the Earth's surface. From this outlet ash, cinders, and flows of lava build the main volcano shield or cone. Vent explosions shape its top as an inverted cone or crater. Meanwhile, side vents on the flanks of the volcano release ash or lava that may build subsidiary cones.

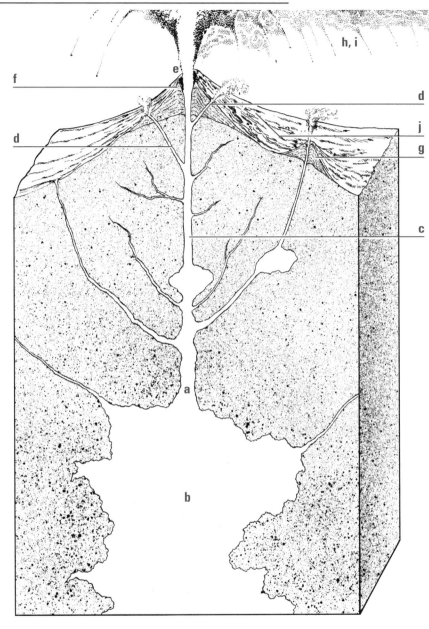

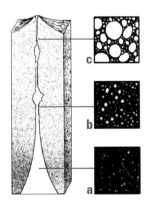

Gas and magma (left)

Inside a volcano as magma rises its pressure falls. Dissolved gases escape and form expanding bubbles (a, b, and c). These force magma out of the volcano.

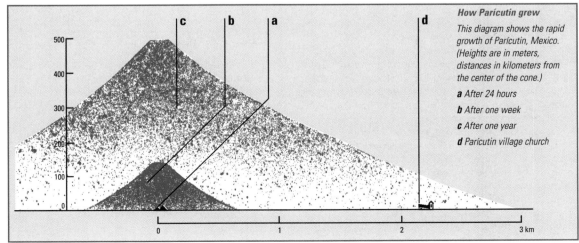

How Parícutin grew

This diagram shows the rapid growth of Parícutin, Mexico. (Heights are in meters, distances in kilometers from the center of the cone.)

a After 24 hours
b After one week
c After one year
d Parícutin village church

Volcanic features (above)

a Magma
b Magma chamber
c Pipe
d Side vents
e Vent
f Cone
g Subsidiary cone
h Gas
i Ash
j Lava

© DIAGRAM

Volcanic landforms

Volcanic basins (calderas)

These may be formed in several ways, one of which is shown.

a A lava plug bottles up explosive gases below.

b In time, pent-up gas pressure blasts off the top of the volcano.

c The explosion leaves a great shallow cavity–a caldera, or basal wreck.

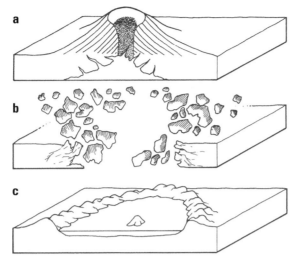

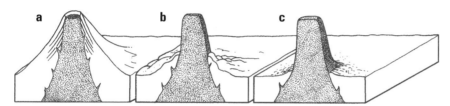

Volcanic plug (above)

a Upwelling lava fills the original volcano's central pipe.

b Erosion attacks the soft outer slopes.

c Only the resistant lava plug remains.

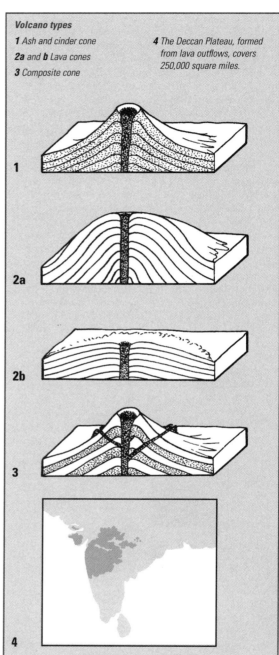

Volcano types

1 *Ash and cinder cone*

2a *and* **b** *Lava cones*

3 *Composite cone*

4 *The Deccan Plateau, formed from lava outflows, covers 250,000 square miles.*

Surface features of volcanic origin range from towering peaks and vast sheets of lava to craters small and low enough to jump across. Features vary depending on the type of eruption, material erupted, and effects of erosion. There are four major types of volcanic landform:

1 Ash and cinder cones, or explosion cones, occur where explosive eruption ejects solid fragments from a central crater and/or subsidiary craters. The resulting concave cone is seldom higher than 1,000 ft (300 m). Idaho's Craters of the Moon National Monument has many such examples.

2 Lava cones usually form from slowly upwelling lava. They come in two main types:

a Steep-sided volcanoes, like France's Puy de Dôme and Lassen Peak in California, grew from sticky acid lava that soon hardened. When squeezed out like toothpaste, very viscous lava builds spines like Wyoming's Devils Tower.

b Shield volcanoes (gently sloping domes) form from runny lava that flowed far before it hardened. From a seabed base 500 mi (800 km) across, Hawaii's Mauna Loa gradually rises 32,000 ft (9,750 m) to the broad crater at its summit.

3 Composite cones, or strato-volcanoes, have concave, cone-shaped sides that feature alternating ash and lava layers. Composite cones account for most of the highest volcanoes. Mount Fuji, Mount Rainier, and Vesuvius are three well-known examples. If solid lava plugs the main pipe to the crater, pent-up gases may blast the top off. If the magma chamber empties, the summit may collapse.

The product of either occurrence is a vast shallow cavity called a caldera. Calderas include Crater Lake in Oregon, Tanzania's Ngorongoro Crater, and Japan's Aso, whose 71 mi (112 km) circumference makes this the largest caldera in the world.

4 Plateau basalts, or lava plains, occur where fissures leaked successive flows of basic lava that have blanketed huge areas in basalt. Basalt up to 7,000 ft (2,100 m) thick covers 250,000 sq mi (650,000 sq km) in India's Deccan Plateau. Other outflows form the US Columbia River Plateau, South America's Paraná Plateau, the Abyssinian Plateau, and Northern Ireland's Antrim Plateau.

Volcanic products

Volcanoes produce gases, liquids, and solids.

Volcanic gases include steam, hydrogen, and sulfur as well as carbon dioxide. Steam condensing in air forms clouds that shed heavy rain. Interacting gases intensify the heat in erupting lavas, and explosive eruptions may yield nuées ardentes–burning clouds of gas with scraps of glowing lava.

Liquid lava is the main volcanic product. Acid, sticky lava cools and hardens before flowing far. It may block a vent, causing magmatic pressure build-up, relieved by an explosion. Basic, fluid lava flows far and quietly before hardening, especially if it is rich in gas.

Varying conditions produce the following lava forms: **Aa** features chunky blocks formed where gas spurted from sluggish molten rock capped by cooling crust. **Pahoehoe** has a wrinkly skin made by molten lava flowing fast below it. **Pillow lava** resembles pillows and piles up where fast-cooling lava erupts underwater.

Solid products of explosive outbursts are called **pyroclasts**. These can be fresh material or ejected scraps of old hard lava and other rock. **Volcanic bombs** include pancake-flat scoria shaped on impact with the ground, and spindle bombs twisted by whizzing through the air. Acid lava full of gas-formed cavities produces **pumice**, a volcanic rock light enough to float on water. **Ignimbrite** contains naturally welded glassy fragments. Hurled-out cinder fragments are called **lapilli**. Some volcanoes also spew vast clouds of **dust** or **volcanic ash**–tiny lava particles. Ash mixed with heavy rain produces mudflows like the one that buried the Roman town Herculaneum when Mt. Vesuvius erupted in AD 79. Immense explosions can smother land for miles in ash and hurl vast quantities of dust into the higher atmosphere, cooling climates on a global scale and adding layers to deep ocean sediments.

Violent eruptions destroy towns and farms, but volcanic ash also provides rich soil for crops.

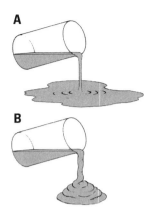

A

B

How lavas behave (above)

Lavas vary in viscosity–resistance to internal flow.

A Low-viscosity lava flows readily, like water.

B High-viscosity lava flows sluggishly, like molasses.

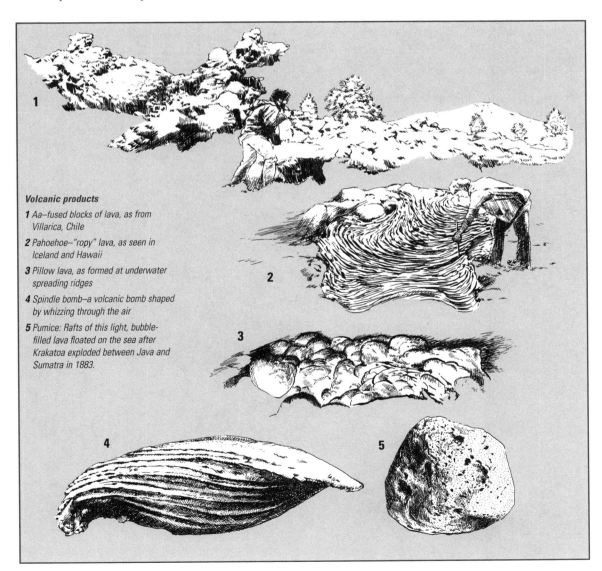

Volcanic products

1 *Aa–fused blocks of lava, as from Villarica, Chile*

2 *Pahoehoe–"ropy" lava, as seen in Iceland and Hawaii*

3 *Pillow lava, as formed at underwater spreading ridges*

4 *Spindle bomb–a volcanic bomb shaped by whizzing through the air*

5 *Pumice: Rafts of this light, bubble-filled lava floated on the sea after Krakatoa exploded between Java and Sumatra in 1883.*

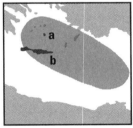

Volcanic fallout (above)

About 1628 BC, as redated in 1988, a huge volcano exploded on the Aegean island Thíra, also known as Santorin (a). The ash-fall (shown here tinted) covered much of Crete (b) and might have helped destroy Crete's great Minoan culture.

© DIAGRAM

Hot water, gas, and mud

Hot water, gas, and mud squirt or dribble from vents in the ground heated by volcanoes mostly near extinction. Such features are plentiful in parts of Italy, Iceland, New Zealand, and the United States. Here are brief definitions of these forms:

1 Hot spring Spring water heated by hot rocks underground. Hot springs shed dissolved minerals that produce sinters (crusts) of (calcium carbonate) travertine or (quartz) geyserite. Famous hot springs occur in Iceland, New Zealand's North Island, and Yellowstone National Park.

2 Smoker Submarine hot spring at an oceanic spreading ridge; the best known is the Galápagos Rise. Emitted sulfides build chimneys that belch black, smoky clouds.

3 Geyser Periodic fountain of steam and hot water forced up from a vent by water superheated in a pipe or cave deep down. Famous geysers occur in Iceland and Yellowstone National Park.

4 Mud volcano Low mud cone deposited by mud-rich water escaping from a vent. Iceland, New Zealand's North Island, and Sicily have mud volcanoes.

5 Fumarole Small vent emitting jets of steam, as at Mt. Etna, Sicily, and in Alaska's Valley of Ten Thousand Smokes.

6 Solfatara Volcanic vent emitting steam and sulfurous gas; named after one near Naples, Italy.

7 Mofette Small vent emitting gases including carbon dioxide. Examples occur in France (Auvergne), Italy, and Java.

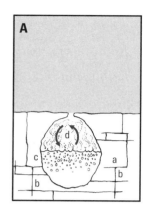

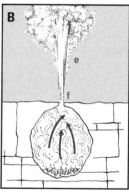

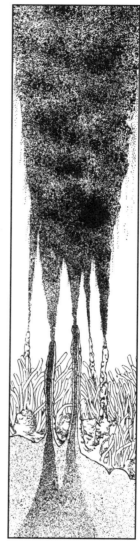

Geysers in action (above)

Two diagrams show how one type of geyser operates.

A *Hot rocks (**a**) heat water that flows through joints (**b**) and boils in a cave (**c**). Steam (**d**) collects under pressure.*

B *Pressure forces a jet of steam and water (**e**) from the cave's narrow mouth (**f**).*

Smokers (right)

Jets of sulfide-rich water heated to 650 °F (350 °C) escape from mineral chimneys in the ocean floor—a phenomenon of spreading ridges.

Sinter terraces (right)

These steps consist of minerals deposited by mineral-rich water escaping from the ground as hot springs.

Fiery rocks of other worlds

Face of the Moon

A *The Moon as seen from Earth reveals dark basalt plains (a), and pale highlands (b), largely of anorthosite.*

B *A block diagram reveals features of a basalt plain.*

a *Ancient crust (anorthosite)*

b *Breccia (rocks shattered by meteorite "bombs")*

c *Lava flows*

d *Volcanoes*

e *Impact craters*

f *Sinuous rille (perhaps a collapsed lava tunnel.)*

g *Linear rille (shallow rift valley)*

h *Wrinkle ridge*

i *Crater chain*

j *Regolith (surface debris)*

k *Fault scarp*

© DIAGRAM

Beyond the Earth space probes reveal an igneous rocky crust on the solid-surfaced planets Mercury, Venus, and Mars, and on some moons. Certain worlds possess volcanoes, though most of their craters were dug out by meteorites.

The landscape of much-cratered Mercury includes smooth plains, perhaps old basalt lava flows.

Basalt lava probably built the plains that largely cover Venus. Radar shows vast twin cones called Rhea Mons and Theia Mons. Perhaps the largest (shield) volcanoes in the solar system, they may contribute to the sulfuric-acid clouds that cloak this planet. Basalt lava plains sprawl over much of northern Mars. Mars also has four mighty, very old volcanoes. Olympus Mons, the highest, towers at least 14 mi (23 km) above the Martian plains. Only Venus's giant volcanoes may be larger.

The Moon's surface shows two major types of rock. Its pale highlands consist mainly of anorthosite (found on Earth only in old parts of continents) and related rocks rich in plagioclase feldspar. The Moon's dark "seas," or maria, are ancient basalt lava flows. These welled up, filling basins gouged out by the impact of asteroids or mini-moons. The Moon is now volcanically dead. But meteorite impacts melting surface rocks created breccias consisting of sharp stones in a glassy matrix.

The solar system's most volcanically active world is Io–a moon of Jupiter the same size as our Moon. Space probe images show hundreds of volcanic craters and some immense volcanoes. Hot rocks heat sulfur in pockets underground. The molten sulfur rises, melts sulfur dioxide in pipes above, then squirts it out like water from a geyser. Plumes of sulfur compounds reach 200 mi (300 km) above the surface. Then they splash back, coloring the surface yellow, orange, black, and white like some colossal pizza

The surface of Venus (above)

As seen from Russian space probe Venera 14, the Venusian surface revealed layered, weathered basaltic rocks similar to ones on Earth.

Mars' giant mountain (below)

This diagram contrasts the relative heights and sizes of three volcanoes:

a *Olympus Mons, Mars*

b *Everest (Earth's highest peak above sea level)*

c *Mauna Loa, Hawaii. (Lies mostly below the Pacific Ocean)*

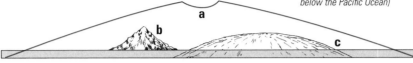

Sulfur fountains (right)

Molten sulfur compounds spurt high above the ever-active surface of a strange moon, Io.

Rocks from scraps

When weather breaks up igneous or other surface rocks, wind and rivers bear away their broken scraps. Most settle on the seabeds fringing continents. Heavy pebbles get washed just offshore; sand farther out; and light, fine particles of silt and clay farther still. Pressure and natural cements convert these layered sediments to conglomerate, sandstone, and shale rock types. Meanwhile compacted remains of swamp plants and shallow-water animals form coals and limestone. Elsewhere, accumulating chemical deposits create evaporites. Sedimentary rocks form only 5 percent of the Earth's crust, but they cover three-quarters of its land.

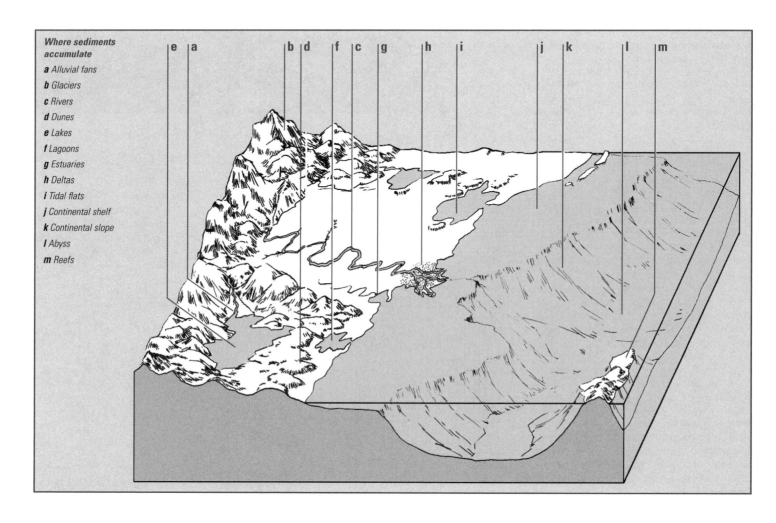

Where sediments accumulate

a Alluvial fans
b Glaciers
c Rivers
d Dunes
e Lakes
f Lagoons
g Estuaries
h Deltas
i Tidal flats
j Continental shelf
k Continental slope
l Abyss
m Reefs

Rocks from sediments

Sediment or sedimentary rock covers most of the ocean floor and three-quarters of the land. On land this skin is usually a few miles thick, but layers up to 19 mi (30 km) thick collect in offshore basins. Most sedimentary rock comes from scraps of older (igneous or other) rocks eroded from the land, carried into lakes or seas by rivers, deposited, and then consolidated into a solid mass. When parent rock breaks up its minerals behave in different ways. Some of the silicates (the main mineral ingredients of igneous rocks) dissolve; others–quartz, for one–endure; and weathering creates new minerals–especially the clays that bulk large in most sedimentary rock. Besides the clastic sedimentary rocks–rocks made from fragments–others come from chemical precipitates or from the durable remains of living things.

Processes converting sediment to rock are known as diagenesis. Two main processes occur. As sediments pile up, their pressure squeezes water from the sediments below and packs the particles together. Then, too, some minerals between the grains cement a mass of sediment together.

Changes converting sediment to rock leave traces in the finished product. Transportation of eroded sediments abrades and rounds their particles, sorts these by density or size, "rots" unstable minerals, and concentrates resistant minerals, including diamonds and gold.

Deposition lays down sediments in broadly horizontal sheets called beds or strata, each separated from the next in the pile by a division called a bedding plane. Beds with ripple marks reveal ancient currents. Graded bedding (beds with grain size graded vertically) may hint at turbidity currents–sediment rich water sliding soupily down a continental slope. Cross bedding (sands laid down at an angle between two bedding planes) shows features such as old dunes and sandbars.

A

B

Rock production (left)

A *Relative volumes of (**a**) sedimentary and changed sedimentary rocks and (**b**) igneous and changed igneous rocks in the Earth's crust contrast with:*

B *The same rocks' exposed areas*

A **B**

Two types of bedding (left)

A *Graded bedding–where large particles had time to settle before small particles*

B *Cross-bedding in sands laid down by migrating dunes or ripples*

Diagenetic processes (below)

1 *Before compaction*

2 *After compaction*

3 *Before cementation*

4 *After cementation*

 Clay particles

 Mineral particles

Natural cement

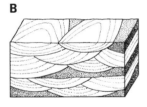

1

2

3 **4**

© DIAGRAM

Cross-bedding in Utah (below)

A human figure shows the scale of cross-bedded sandstone sediments in Zion National Park.

Rocks from fragments 1

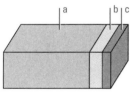

Sedimentary rocks (above)

Sedimentary rocks can be divided into the following:

a Shale: 81%

b Sandstone: 11%

c Limestone: 8%

Shale (below)

An outcrop reveals bedding planes in the fine-grained sedimentary rock, shale.

Sandstone (below)

Weathering accentuates the horizontal bedding planes and vertical joints in these sandstone masses.

Sandstones classified

Varying proportions of four components yield four types of sandstone, or arenite. Components:

a Matrix

b Quartz

c Rock fragments

d Feldspar

Sandstones:

1 Greywacke

2 Quartzite

3 Lithic arenite

4 Arkose

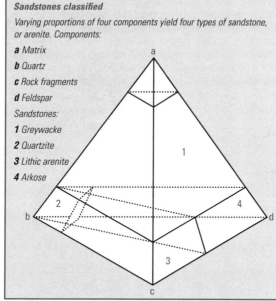

Four sandstones (right)

Variations in textural maturity hint at places of origin.

A Immature (river floodplain)

B Submature (river or tidal channel)

C Mature (beach)

D Supermature (desert dune)

○ ○ Mineral grains

☐ Clay matrix

▨ Natural cement

Most sedimentary rocks form from particles eroded from the rocks on land. Their main ingredients are clasts–rock fragments–of quartz, feldspar, and clay minerals. These fragments range in size from microscopic grains to boulders.

More than 90 percent of all sedimentary rock contains partides no bigger than a sand grain. Many geologists classify such partides by size into two main groups. The (fine-grained) lutites with grains less than 0.06 mm diameter produce mudstone, siltstone, and shale. The (medium-grained) arenites or sandstones with grains of 0.06–2 mm give arkose, graywacke, and orthoquartzite. Here are brief descriptions of six fine- and medium-grained rocks:

1 Mudstone Soft rock made of clay minerals of less than 0.004mm diameter.

2 Siltstone Rock formed of partides 0.004–0.06 mm in diameter.

3 Shale Mudstone, siltstone, or similar fine-grained rock of silt and clay split easily along their bedding planes. Shale accounts for more than 80 percent of all sedimentary rock.

4 Orthoquartzite A "clean," or pure, arenite mainly made of quartz after other substances have been removed. (Arenites account for more than 10 percent of all sedimentary rock.)

5 Arkose An arenite rich in feldspar derived from gneiss or granite.

6 Graywacke A muddy, often grayish sandstone with mixed-size particles including quartz, clay minerals, and others.

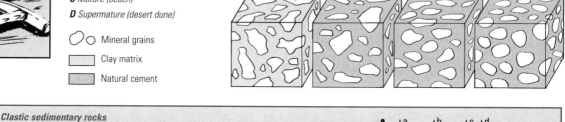

Clastic sedimentary rocks

A Right: Ingredients in a clastic sedimentary rock

a Clasts

b Matrix

c Cement

d Pore spaces

B Where rock-forming fragments settle

a River mouths (mud and sand)

b Inshore deposits (large sand particles form sandstones)

c Offshore deposits (fine mud particles form clay or shale)

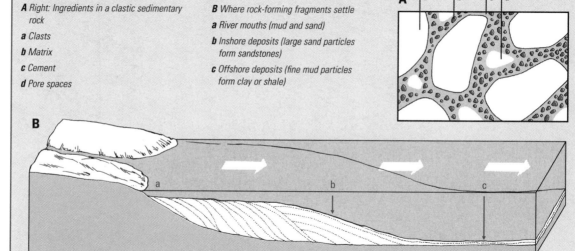

Rocks from fragments 2

Rudites (from the Latin *rudis*: "coarse") are clasts (rock fragments) coarser than a sand grain. Mixed with finer particles, rudites can be consolidated into natural concretes called conglomerates and breccias.

Conglomerates are named from the Latin for "lumped together." They contain rounded fragments –pebbles, cobbles, and/or boulders–and often represent waterborne and watersorted remnants of eroded mountain ranges or retreating rocky coasts. They accumulate along mountain fronts, in shallow coastal waters, and elsewhere, becoming mixed with sand, then bound by natural cement. How clasts in a conglomerate lie sorted, packed, and graded offers clues to how or where it was laid down. The thickest masses of conglomerate–as in the Siwalik Range, the southernmost part of the Himalayas' foothills– mark the aftermath of an orogeny.

Breccias (from the Italian for "rubble") are rocks containing sharp-edged, unworn, usually poorly sorted fragments, often embedded in a clay-rich matrix. Breccias usually form near their place of origin; their clasts have not been carried far enough to suffer rounding by abrasion. Many breccias originate in or from talus, deserts, mudslides, faulting, meteorite impact, or shrinkage of evaporite beds.

Authorities tend to separate conglomerates and breccias from tillites–poorly sorted, ice-eroded, ice-borne debris consolidated into solid rock. Many tillite clasts are faceted, with slightly rounded edges. Ancient tillites occur in South America, Africa, India, and Australia.

Types of conglomerate (below)

A Well sorted
B Poorly sorted
C Close-packed (clast supported)
D Loosely packed (matrix supported)
E Imbricated
F Graded bedding

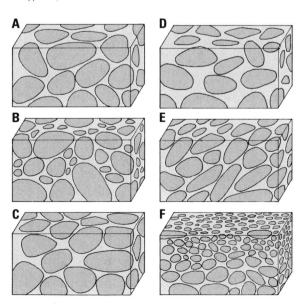

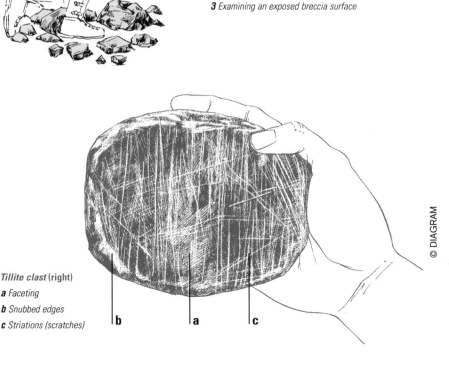

Natural concretes (above)

Main kinds of natural concrete.

1 Conglomerate (with rounded clasts)
2 Breccia (with sharp-edged clasts)
3 Examining an exposed breccia surface

Tillite clast (right)

a Faceting
b Snubbed edges
c Striations (scratches)

© DIAGRAM

Rocks from chemicals

Some sedimentary rocks and minerals consist of chemicals that had once been dissolved in water.

Certain limestones formed this way. Oolitic limestone consists of billions of oolites–tiny balls produced by calcium carbonate accumulating on particles rolled around by gentle currents in warm, shallow seas. Oolite forms like this today on the Bahama Banks. Dolomitic limestone (limestone mainly made of the mineral dolomite) occurs where certain brines chemically alter preexisting limestone or where dolomite deposits form in an evaporating sea.

Such so-called evaporites underlie one-quarter of the continents in beds up to 4,000 ft (1,220 m) thick. Evaporites now form where chemical deposits accumulate in evaporating desert lakes and coastal salt flats. But certain old evaporites could have been precipitated from chemically oversaturated deep

offshore waters of almost landlocked seas such as the Mediterranean.

Three main minerals tend to settle in a sequence. First comes calcium carbonate. Next is gypsum (a granular crystalline form of calcium sulfate combined with water). Then comes sodium chloride in the form of halite (rock salt). This is a soft, low-density rock that is liable to flow. Pressure from overlying rocks forces up huge plugs or domes of salt beneath the coast of Texas and Louisiana and in parts of Germany, Iran, and Russia.

Besides the rocks and minerals just named, there are other chemical deposits. A few have or had important economic uses–particularly borax, chert and flint, certain iron-rich compounds, nitrates, and phosphorites. But some of these are partly biological in origin, and scientists disagree about how certain forms of iron occurred.

Two evaporites (above)

1 Dolomite, derived from small shells, and named after the French geologist Dieudonné Dolomieu (1750–1801).

2 Gypsum, a sulfate mineral named from gypsos, the Greek word for chalk.

Oolites enlarged (left)

This much-magnified section of a Cambrian limestone shows spherical oolites (also called ooids) cemented by carbonate. Each oolite's growth around a sand grain or shell fragment produced a concentric, radial structure.

Flint knapping (right)

Stone-Age humans learned that controlled blows could split this fine-grained quartz into sharp-edged weapons and tools.

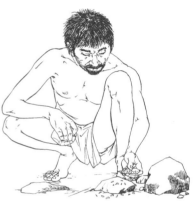

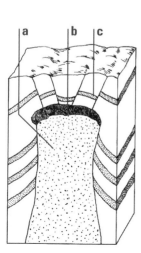

Salt dome (above)

a Salt core up to 6 mi (10 km) high

b Llimestone-anhydrite cap rock

c Strata uplifted by salt core

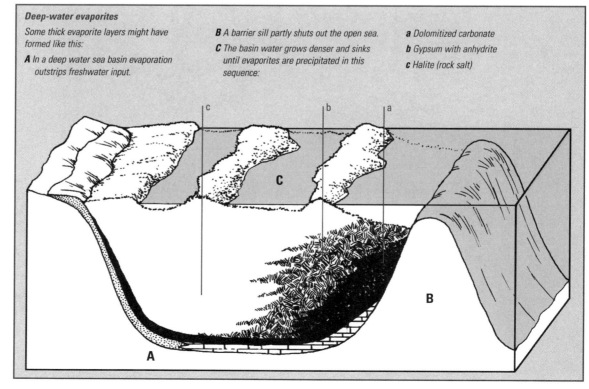

Deep-water evaporites

Some thick evaporite layers might have formed like this:

A In a deep water sea basin evaporation outstrips freshwater input.

B A barrier sill partly shuts out the open sea.

C The basin water grows denser and sinks until evaporites are precipitated in this sequence:

a Dolomitized carbonate
b Gypsum with anhydrite
c Halite (rock salt)

Rocks from living things

Organic sediments produce the rocks we know as coals and limestones.

Coals are rich in carbon derived from swampy vegetation. Coal type varies with the processes involved. Coal formation starts when plants die in wet acid conditions; instead of rotting completely, the plants turn into the soft, fibrous substance known as peat. Later, overlying sediments drive out moisture and squash the peat, converting it to lignite (soft brown coal). Even greater pressure gives bituminous coal–harder, blacker, and with a higher carbon content. The final stage is anthracite–a hard, black, shiny coal with the highest carbon content in the series. Most of the world's coal mines tap the remains of low-lying forests drowned by an invading sea and buried under sediments.

Limestones are rich in calcium and magnesium carbonates. They make up about 8 percent of all sedimentary rock; only shale and sandstone are more plentiful. Organic limestones contain calcium carbonate extracted from seawater by plants and animals that used this compound for protective shells. These rocks include reef limestones built up from the stony skeletons of billions of coral polyps and algae inhabiting the beds of shallow seas. Coquina is a cemented mass of shelly debris. Chalk is a white, powdery, porous limestone made up of tiny shells of fossil microorganisms, drifting in the surface waters before they died and fell to the sea bottom.

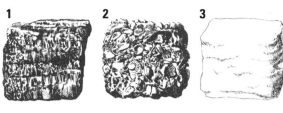

Three organic rocks

1 Bituminous coal (mainly carbon)

2 Coquina (shelly limestone)

3 Chalk (a powdery limestone)

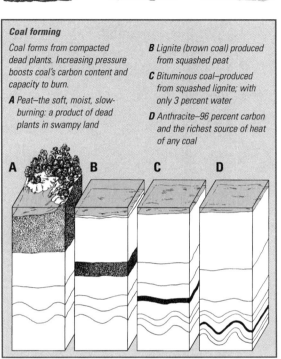

Coal forming

Coal forms from compacted dead plants. Increasing pressure boosts coal's carbon content and capacity to burn.

A Peat–the soft, moist, slow-burning: a product of dead plants in swampy land

B Lignite (brown coal) produced from squashed peat

C Bituminous coal–produced from squashed lignite; with only 3 percent water

D Anthracite–96 percent carbon and the richest source of heat of any coal

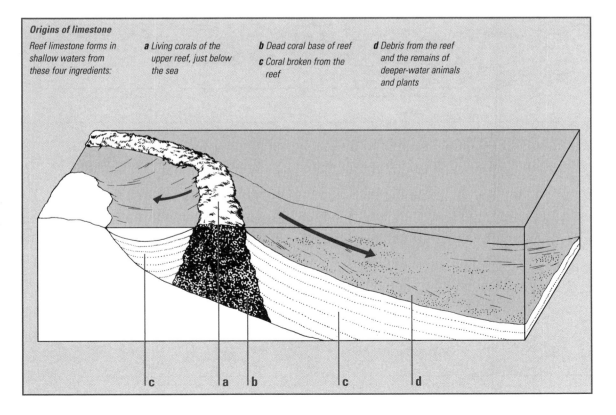

Origins of limestone

Reef limestone forms in shallow waters from these four ingredients:

a Living corals of the upper reef, just below the sea

b Dead coral base of reef

c Coral broken from the reef

d Debris from the reef and the remains of deeper-water animals and plants

© DIAGRAM

Deformed and altered rocks

Great loads of sediment or ice depress tracts of continental crust. Where a load has been removed, the land bobs up again. As lithospheric plates collide or split, tension or compression tilts, folds, squeezes, and breaks the rigid rocks, producing folds, faults, and earthquakes. Then, too, meteorites hurtling from space punch craters in the crust, while blobs of molten rock push up through the crust from below. Events like these produce heat and pressure that deform and alter solid rocks. This chapter ends with an account of rocks transformed that way.

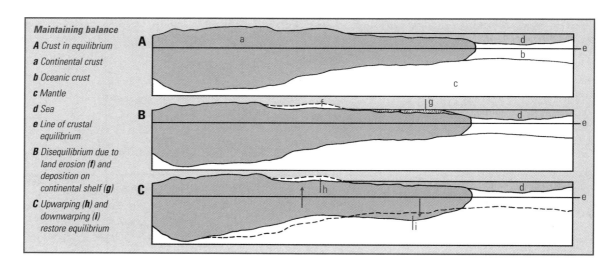

Maintaining balance

A Crust in equilibrium

a Continental crust

b Oceanic crust

c Mantle

d Sea

e Line of crustal equilibrium

B Disequilibrium due to land erosion (f) and deposition on continental shelf (g)

C Upwarping (h) and downwarping (i) restore equilibrium

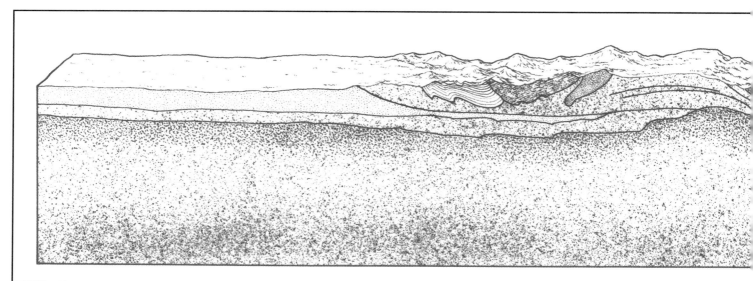

Rising and sinking rocks

Great tracts of the Earth's crust slowly rise or sink. Block mountains and the Black and Mediterranean Seas are products of such movement, called epeirogenesis. Its cause is a type of disturbance that affects isostasy–the state of balance of the Earth's crust floating on the denser underlying mantle. The crust is four-fifths as dense as mantle, so a mountain mass one mile high is "balanced" by four miles of crust below sea level.

Warping–the gentle rise or fall of crust–results from two pairs of processes: erosion and deposition, and freezing and melting.

Erosion that wears away a mountain mass reduces the weight pressing on the underlying crust, so the surface of the land bobs up. Such upwarping probably means that few large land surfaces get worn down to a level even with the sea. Indeed much of Africa is plateau, albeit perching on a superplume.

Deposition of eroded sediment depresses or downwarps deltas and tracts of the continental rim.

Sediments thousands of meters thick accumulate in eugeosynclines–depressions in a continent's deepwater margin. Shallow-water sediments including limestones form long lenses in continental-shelf depressions called miogeosynclines.

Growing ice sheets depress the crust beneath, squeezing out asthenospheric material, which pushes up the crust beyond the ice sheet's rim. When ice sheets melt, the land below bobs up again–a process that has lasted 10,000 years or more in Scandinavia and northeast Canada.

While isostatic change describes land moving up or down, eustatic change is a worldwide shift in the level of the sea. Eustatic change occurs if ocean basins grow or shrink, or if they gain or lose sea water. Sea level falls when much of the world's surface moisture becomes locked up in ice sheets on the land. But water freed by melting ice sheets lifts the level of the sea. Clues to eustatic and isostatic change include the drowned valleys and raised beaches of some coasts described in pp. 76 and 78.

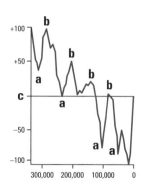

Changing sea level (above)

A graph depicts in meters the likely changes in the level of the Mediterranean in the last 300,000 years.

a Glacial periods

b Interglacials

c Present sea level

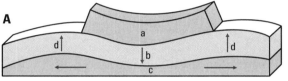

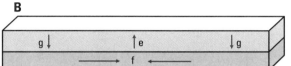

Downwarped crust (left)

*A section of crust between New York (**A**) and Maine (**B**) shows rocks up to 20,000 ft (6000 m) thick produced where offshore sediments downwarped crust 500 million years ago.*

1 Old miogeosyncline (shallow water limestones)

2 Old eugeosyncline (deeper water shales)

Effects of ice (left)

Simplified block diagrams show how an ice sheet makes land rise and sink.

A Ice sheet (**a**) depresses crust (**b**), displacing asthenosphere (viscous mantle) (**c**), which upwarps crust (**d**) around the ice sheet.

B After ice melts, depressed crust rises (**e**); displaced asthenosphere returns (**f**); and upwarped crust sinks (**g**).

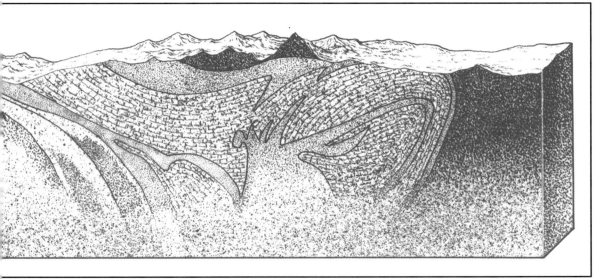

A cross section through the Alps

This block diagram shows rock layers contorted by the collision of the lithospheric plates.

© DIAGRAM

Tilting and folding rocks

Sediments and plateau basalts are laid down as horizontal beds or sheets. Old deposits lie almost undisturbed across great tracts of ancient, stable continental shields. But in unstable regions crustal tension and compression tilt, fold, squeeze, or break the level layers, and thrust them up as mountains. Which type of deformation happens depends on pressure, temperature, strain-rate (compression in a given time), and composition of affected rocks.

Folding occurs largely deep down along the edges of colliding continental plates. Here steady stress and high temperatures and pressures make normally brittle rocks bend instead of break. Thus in quartzite, quartz grains slide about and dissolve at stress points. Such processes produced repeated folding in the Alps and Himalayas.

Folded rocks exposed

This Cornish sea cliff reveals rock layers doubled over in a small recumbent fold. Rock folds of almost any kind can span just a few feet as here, or measure miles across, as in some regions of the Alps.

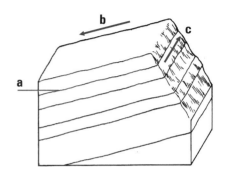

Tilted rocks (below)

Labels indicate key features of tilted rock beds.

a Bedding plane

b Dip

c Strike

Folds

Folds take various forms, especially these.

1 Monocline A steep step-like fold, bounded by upper and lower bends in a set of rock layers.

2 Anticline Rock beds upfolded into an arch from a few feet to many miles across. Anticlines form much of the Jura Mountains of France and Switzerland. An anticline containing many lesser folds is an anticlinorium. Huge anticlines are geanticlines.

3 Pericline An anticline in the form of an elongated dome. The Bighorn Mountains of Wyoming show a periclinal structure.

4 Syncline Downfolded sedimentary rock layers that form a basin such as the London Basin. A syncline with subsidiary synclines is a synclinorium. Immense synclines are called geosynclines.

5 Overfold A lopsided anticline with one limb (side) forced over the other. Extreme overfolds are called recumbent folds.

6 Nappe A recumbent fold sheared through so that the upper limb is forced forward, perhaps for many miles. Nappes feature prominently in the Alps. Nappes with rocks forced over each other in slices like a pack of cards are imbricate structures.

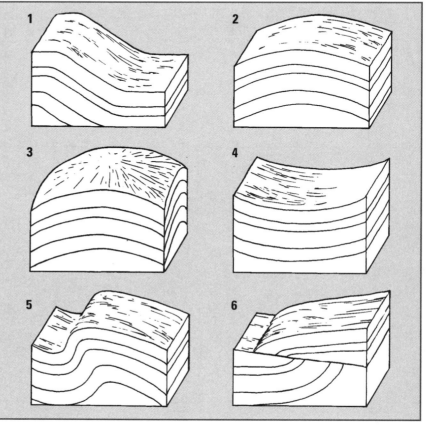

Breaking rocks: joints and faults

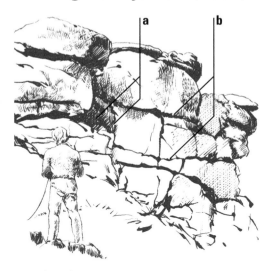

Joints (above)

In many sedimentary rocks, joints occur at right angles to bedding planes.

a *Joints*

b *Bedding planes*

Joints and faults are splits that form in stressed rock, particularly near the surface.

Joints are cracks with little movement of the rock on either side. They open up as cooling igneous rock contracts, and appear in other rock, subjected to tension or compression. Joints occur in parallel sets, sometimes at right angles to each other.

Faults are breaks in the Earth's crust, involving horizontal or vertical movement, or both, along a line of weakness called a fault plane. Block-faulting –breakup of a slab of crust into fault-bounded blocks– creates some of the world's great valleys and upland areas.

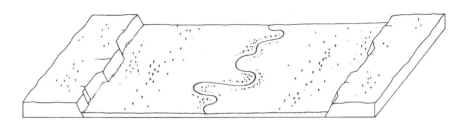

Rift Valley (above)

Such troughs lie between parallel faults with throws in opposite directions.

Major types of fault or fault block

Here are six major types of fault or fault block.

1 Normal fault Stretching breaks rocks along a steep fault plane, and one block drops or rises against the other.

2 Reverse fault Compression forces one block up and over another. A thrust fault is a reverse fault with a low-angled fault plane producing great horizontal movement.

3 Tear fault (alias strike-slip, transcurrent, or wrench fault) Horizontal shearing along a vertical fault plane, as in California's San Andreas Fault (see also p. 52). Transform faults are tear faults at right angles to oceanic ridges.

4 Graben A long, narrow block sunk between two parallel faults. Such blocks form the upper Rhine Valley, East African rift valleys, oceanic spreading ridges' central rifts, and other rift valleys.

5 Horst A horizontal block raised between two normal faults. Examples are the Black Forest, Vosges, Korea, and Sinai.

6 Tilt block An uplifted, tilted block. Tilt-blocks form the western US Basin and Range Province, Arabian and Brazilian plateaus, and the Deccan of India.

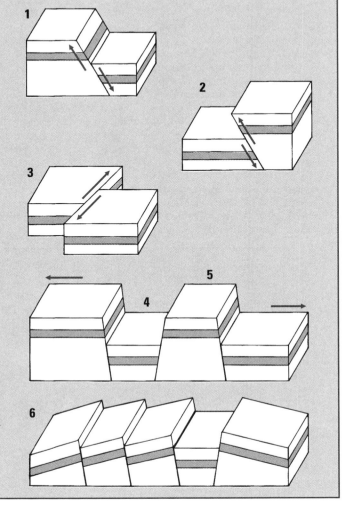

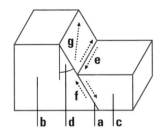

Anatomy of a fault (above)

a *Fault*

b *Upthrow*

c *Downthrow*

d *Hade (inclination to vertical)*

e *Heave (lateral shift)*

f *Throw (vertical shift)*

g *Net movement*

© DIAGRAM

Earthquakes

Evidence of earthquake (right)

Past 'quakes may leave such clues as these:

a *River bend*

b *Displaced railroad*

c *Disrupted orchard*

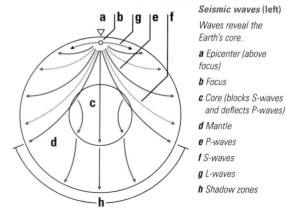

Seismic waves (left)

Waves reveal the Earth's core.

a *Epicenter (above focus)*

b *Focus*

c *Core (blocks S-waves and deflects P-waves)*

d *Mantle*

e *P-waves*

f *S-waves*

g *L-waves*

h *Shadow zones*

Earthquake shocks (right)

Isoseismal lines link places with equal intensity of shock.

a *Focus*

b *Epicenter*

c *Isoseismal lines*

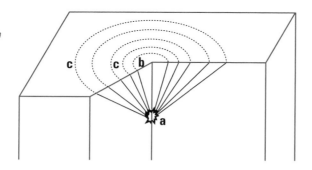

and lower, denser "gabbroic" crust; the Mohorovičić discontinuity between crust and upper mantle; and the Gutenberg discontinuity between the mantle and outer core (where S-waves cease because they cannot pass through the liquid outer core).

At the surface are long (L) waves subdivided into Love waves vibrating horizontally at right angles to their direction and Rayleigh waves that move through ground as waves move through the sea. By timing the arrival of these waves, three seismic stations can plot the epicenter (the surface point above the focus).

L-waves spark off landslides, avalanches, and other earthquake damage. Undersea earthquakes set off tsunami–mighty waves that devastate low coasts.

An earthquake's felt intensity is measured on the modified Mercalli scale, where 1 means "felt by few" and 12 means "damage total." The Richter scale measures magnitude, or energy released. Here each number stands for 10 times the energy of the number below; you would scarcely notice a 2, but an 8 would flatten a city. Many of the world's million earthquakes a year are fortunately slight.

Most occur at spreading ridges, oceanic trenches, and mountain-building zones. Strike-slip motion triggers earthquakes along California's notorious San Andreas Fault–a transform fault where western California moves northwest against the rest.

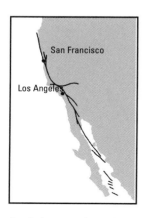

San Andreas Fault (above)

Lines show the San Andreas and associated faults. Land west of these is edging northwest.

An earthquake is a sudden shaking of the ground where stress-deformed rocks broke along a fault and now snap back into shape but in a new position.

An earthquake's point of fracture is its focus, which may be shallow, intermediate, or deep–down to about 430 mi (700 km). From the focus, two types of seismic wave pass through the rocks: Compressional waves (primary or P-waves) produce push-pull forces. Distortional waves (secondary, shear, or S-waves) are slower and make rock particles oscillate at right angles to wave direction.

Wave velocity increases with rock density and depth, and waves are reflected and bent on reaching the boundaries between two layers. But P- and S-waves differ in behavior. This helped scientists detect the Conrad discontinuity between upper "granitic"

Earthquake belts (right)

These often coincide with active boundaries between lithospheric plates. Shallow earthquake foci lie 0–62 mi (100 km) down. Deep foci lie 62–435 mi (100–700 km) down.

● Shallow

● Deep

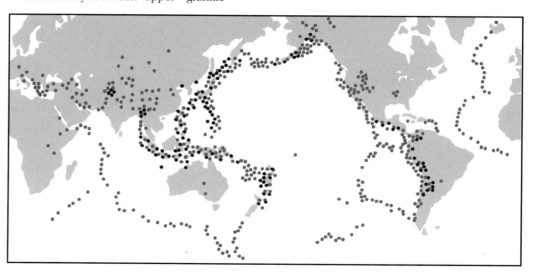

Bombs from space

Impact craters (left)

Dots mark 12 of the largest suspected craters—each more than 36 km (22 mi) across.

a Carswell, Canada

b Sudbury, Canada

c Charlevoix, Canada

d Manicouagan, Canada

e Araguainha Dome, Brazil

f Siljan, Sweden

g Vredefort, South Africa

h Puchezh-Katunki, Russia

i Kara, Russia

j Popigai, Siberia

k Chicxulub, Mexico

l Woodleigh, Australia

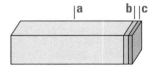

Meteorite percentages (above)

A bar diagram shows relative abundance of the three main types of meteorite.

a Stony: 93%

b Iron: 5%

c Stony iron: 2%

Whizzing specks, stones, and rocks bombard the surface of the Earth from space. About 10,000 short tons (9,000 metric tons) shower down each year. These missiles are meteorites–lumps weighing from a few ounces up to 100 tons or more. A few are bits of planets or the Moon struck off by other meteorites. Most are fragments of colliding asteroids–a belt of so-called minor planets between the orbits of the planets Mars and Jupiter. Some meteorites are 4,570 million years old, and their ingredients hold clues to the solar system's origin.

There are three main kinds of meteorite. Most are silicate-rich **stony meteorites**. The bulk of these are ordinary chondrites, containing solid silicate minerals. Carbonaceous chondrites include organic compounds, perhaps the building blocks that made life possible. Achondrites include basaltlike chunks, perhaps volcanic rock from big asteroids. **Iron meteorites**, the second major group, are iron with nickel. **Stony irons**, the third group, contain roughly equal amounts of nickel-iron and silicates.

Big stony meteorites break up and scatter before they hit the ground. Big iron meteorites vaporize upon punching impact craters in the ground. Circular depressions, shock structures in affected rocks, and tell-tale iridium and nickel deposits have helped scientists identify 90 sizable craters evidently gouged by meteorites. They include Canada's vast Manicouagan Crater, 43 mi (70 km) across; Arizona's famous Meteor Crater, 3/4 mi (1.2 km) across and 490ft (150 m) deep; and Mexico's immense Chicxulub crater, 112 mi (180 km) from side to side.

More evidence for ancient impact lies in small, black, glassy buttons, spheres, and teardrops collectively called **tektites**. Found mostly in the Southern Hemisphere, tektites are blobs of molten sedimentary rock that splashed high above the atmosphere, before cooling, hardening and falling–widely scattered–back to Earth.

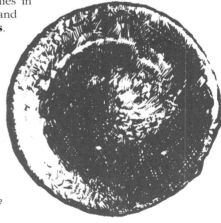

Two meteorite types (below)

A Stony meteorite. Its white bits, perhaps from an exploding star, may be among the oldest solid matter in our solar system.

B Iron meteorite, etched and polished. Bands form a triangular pattern of nickel-iron and other nickel alloys.

Tektite (right)

Such glassy "buttons" come from rocks melted and hurled high by meteorites punching craters like the one below.

© DIAGRAM

Rocks remade 1

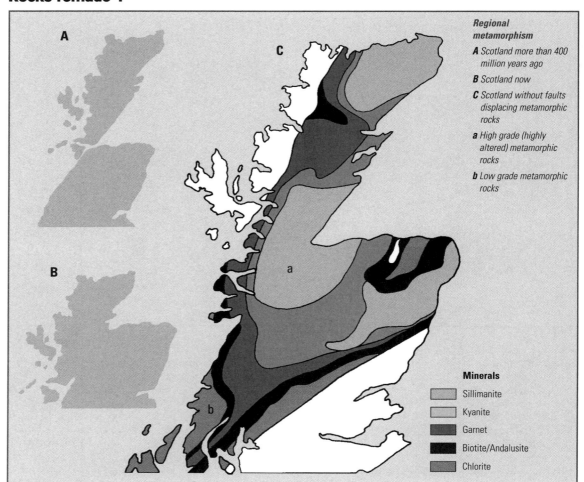

Regional metamorphism

A *Scotland more than 400 million years ago*

B *Scotland now*

C *Scotland without faults displacing metamorphic rocks*

a *High grade (highly altered) metamorphic rocks*

b *Low grade metamorphic rocks*

Minerals

- Sillimanite
- Kyanite
- Garnet
- Biotite/Andalusite
- Chlorite

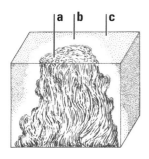

Contact aureole (above)

a *Injected igneous mass*

b *Contact or metamorphic aureole of altered country rock*

c *Unaltered country rock*

Heat and pressure

This diagram relates rock-forming processes to temperature and pressure (indirectly shown by depth). Metamorphic rocks form in conditions between those producing sedimentary and igneous rocks.

a *Diagenesis (sedimentary rock)*

b *Contact (thermal) metamorphism*

c *Burial metamorphism*

d *Regional metamorphism*

e *Anatexis or melting (igneous rock)*

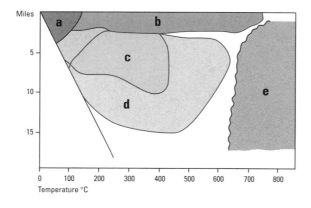

Great heat and pressure alter igneous and sedimentary rocks into metamorphic ("changed shape") rocks. These rocks' ingredients have undergone solid-state recrystallization to yield new textures or minerals. The greater the heat or pressure, the greater the change and the higher the grade of metamorphic rock produced. Here we summarize conditions that induce such changes. The next two pages describe the major types of metamorphic rock.

Metamorphism takes several forms. Burial metamorphism affects the base of immensely thick layers of sedimentary rock–the deeper the burial, the greater the pressure. Dynamic metamorphism transforms rocks crushed against each other in fault zones. Retrogressive (from high- to low-grade) metamorphism occurs at shear zones, for instance suboceanic transform faults where invading fluids introduce new elements that change the rocks' chemical composition–a process that is known as metasomatism. Impact metamorphism affects rocks struck by meteorites, but the best-known agents of change are contact and regional metamorphism.

Contact or thermal metamorphism occurs where a mass of magma invades and bakes country rocks (surrounding older rocks). Beyond a narrow baked zone extends a so-called contact aureole of altered rock. An injected granite batholith may change the rocks for several miles around.

Regional metamorphism covers much larger areas, downwarped where colliding continental plates built mountains. Intensely altered rocks produced this way show up in the exposed roots of old, eroded mountain ranges, as in the Canadian Shield and parts of Scotland and Sweden, in the newer Alps and Himalayas, and in old subduction zones detectable in California, New Caledonia, and Papua New Guinea.

Rocks remade 2

One type of sedimentary or igneous rock can produce a range of metamorphic rocks. Which type develops depends on such variables as the parent rock and the amounts of heat, pressure, and fluids passing through the rock. Contact (thermal) metamorphism tends to produce fine-grained textures. Heat plus pressure, as in regional metamorphism, favor coarse-grained rocks with foliated minerals–minerals flattened and aligned in parallel bands at right angles to the stress applied.

Index minerals, ones formed at different temperatures or pressures, indicate a rock's metamorphic grade. Most metamorphic rocks are harder than sedimentary rocks, and pelitic (clay-rich) rocks undergo more change than basaltic rocks.

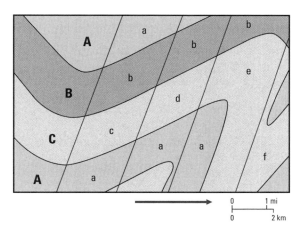

From shale to gneiss (left)

*Zones of intensifying heat and pressure (the parallel bands, read left-right) change surface belts of sedimentary rocks (**A–C**) to metamorphic rocks (**a–f**).*

A *Sandstone*

a *Quartzite*

B *Limestone*

b *Marble*

C *Shale*

c *Slate*

d *Phyllite*

e *Schist*

f *Gneiss*

Metamorphic rocks

We show eight common types of metamorphic rock: 1–4 formed largely by contact metamorphism; 2 and 5–8 by regional metamorphism. (Some types can be subdivided according to key minerals–for instance schist into talc schist and mica schist.)

1 Hornfels Fine-grained, dark, flinty rock with randomly arranged minerals; formed from mudstone and basalt.

2 Slate Fine-grained, often gray, foliated rock split easily along cleavage planes of mica flakes aligned by pressure; formed from shale.

3 Marble Granular or sugary-textured rock; formed from limestone.

4 Quartzite Very hard, granular quartz rock; formed from sandstone.

5 Phyllite Silky, foliated rock more coarsely grained than slate, its usual precursor.

6 Schist Foliated rock, more coarsely grained and of higher metamorphic grade than phyllite; formed from slate or basalt.

7 Amphibolite Foliated rock of higher metamorphic grade than schist; formed from basalt.

8 Gneiss Foliated, banded, rock; coarser grained than schist and of the highest metamorphic grade.

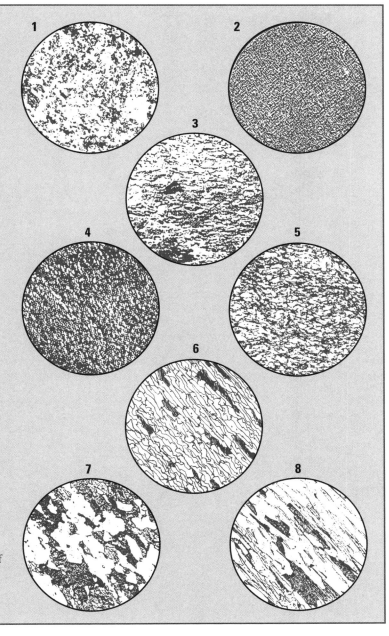

Foliation (above)

1 *Mica flakes haphazardly arranged in shale*

2 *The same flakes foliated–aligned by directed pressure–in slate, which splits along its foliation planes.*

© DIAGRAM

Crumbling rocks

As soon as rock is raised above sea level, weather starts to break it up. Water, ice, and chemicals split, dissolve, or rot the rocky surface until it crumbles. Crumbled rock mixed with water, air, and plant and animal remains form soil. Soil and broken rock fall, flow, or creep downhill. These movements help create the slopes that form the surface of the land.

Rocks attacked by weather 1

2 Block disintegration

3 Frost action

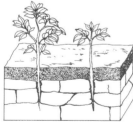

4 Tree root action

1 Exfoliation
Cutaway view of a boulder
subject to exfoliation

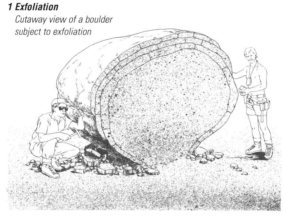

The wearing down of land begins as weather rots rocks at or near the surface. Different weather "weapons" probe different weaknesses; for instance, the joints in igneous rocks like basalt and granite, bedding planes in clays and shales, and natural cements in sandstones and conglomerates. Chemical weathering (opposite) attacks chemical ingredients in rocks. Physical (mechanical) weathering destroys rock but leaves its chemicals unchanged. Which kind of weathering predominates depends upon the type of rock and climate.

Physical weathering is active chiefly in cold or dry climates. Agents include sharp temperature changes (which reinforce the chemical effects), frost, drought, crystallizing salts, and growing plants.

1 Exfoliation, or spheroidal weathering, is the flaking of intensely heated surface rock as it expands more than the cooler rock below. This process produces rounded, isolated rock masses called exfoliation domes.

2 Block disintegration involves sharp temperature changes, which make desert rocks expand and contract. This helps enlarge the joints in rocks, thus splitting large masses into smaller blocks.

3 Frost action Water expanding as it freezes widens crevices in well-bedded or well-jointed rock and shatters it; this occurs in winter in mid-latitude regions and at night in high mountains everywhere. Products are piles of sharp-edged debris, including cone-shaped slopes of talus (scree) seen below steep peaks. Freezing also causes the granular disintegration of porous rocks like chalk.

4 Tree roots can widen cracks in rocks as they grow.

5 Pressure release, or unloading, follows the removal of overlying rock and its pressure on the rock below. Expansion of that rock then forms curved joints promoting sheeting (pulling off) of rock shells from the inner mass.

6 Slaking is the crumbling of clay-rich sedimentary rocks as they dry out during drought.

7 Crystallization of salts Dissolved salts expanding as they dry and crystallize in rock split the rock and honeycomb its surface.

5 Pressure release
Yosemite Valley domes

Rocks attacked by weather 2

Chemical weathering attacks rocks aggressively in humid climates. The chief destructive agents are rainwater and certain substances that it contains. These dissolve some kinds of rock or rot the natural cements that bind the particles in rocks together. But not all minerals are equally at risk; quartz proves much more resistant to attack than augite, biotite, hornblende, and orthoclase.

Granite tor (left)

Such massively jointed tors crown hills in Dartmoor, England. The tors formed from groundwater weathering or possibly from Ice Age freeze-thaw weathering.

Chemical weathering

The following items summarize important ways in which chemicals make rocks decay.

1 Carbonation is the dissolving of limy rocks by percolating rainwater armed with carbon dioxide from the atmosphere or soil. The resulting weak carbonic acid widens joints in carboniferous limestone surfaces, producing bare limestone pavements where clints (sharp ridges) alternate with grikes (solution grooves). With items such as caves, swallowholes, and gorges these features form karst landscapes, named for a limestone region in Yugoslavia (see also p. 69).

2 Hydration occurs when some minerals take up water and expand, thus breaking the shells from the rock containing them. Subsurface hydration probably produced southwest England's great, rounded granite moorland blocks called tors.

3 Hydrolysis is a water-rock reaction that can turn feldspar into clay, which then decomposes granite to produce white, powdery kaolin (china clay).

4 Solution occurs when water dissolves rock salt and (less readily) some other minerals.

5 Oxidation features the combining of atmospheric oxygen with the compounds in some rocks. Oxidized iron forms a brownish, crumbly, or (in dry lands) hard, protective crust of "rust."

6 Organic weathering is produced by the attack of organic acids from such organisms as bacteria, lichens, mosses, and decaying plants of many kinds on rock-forming minerals.

1 Carbonation

a Limestone pavement

b Clints

c Grikes

d Joints

e Bedding planes

2 Hydration: three likely stages in tor formation:

A Unweathered granite mass

a Ground surface

b Joints

B Weathering in process

c Joints widened

d Granite mass split into blocks between joints

C Tor bared by erosion of weathered material

e Massive blocks exposed

f Lowered ground surface

3 Hydrolysis

White mounds of waste quartz reveal a kaolin quarry, where rotting has changed and separated granite's mineral ingredients.

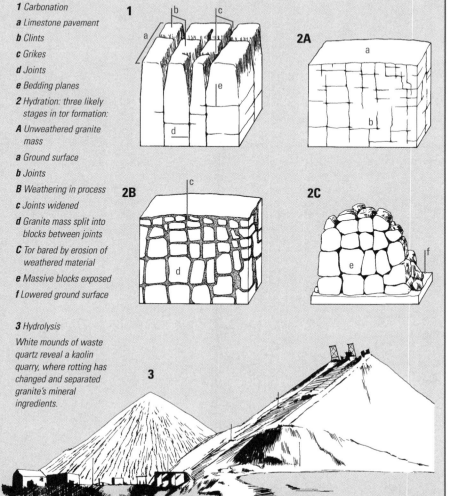

© DIAGRAM

Soil from rock

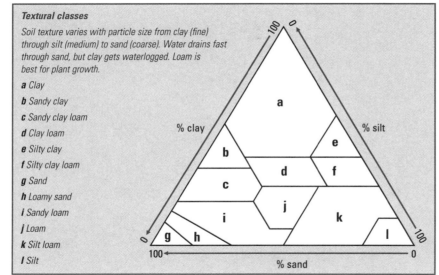

Life in the soil (right)

These organisms live in or help to form the soil.

A *Larger "aerators"*
a *Mole*
b *Earthworm*
B *Microorganisms*
c *Fungus*
d *Alga*
e *Virus*
f *Bacterium*
g *Protozoan*

C *Arthropods*
h *Wood louse*
i *Millipede*
j *Springtail*
k *Cockchafer larva*
l *Cricket*
m *Ant*
n *Mite*

Soil structure (above)

1 *Blocky*
2 *Prismatic*
3 *Platy*
4 *Crumb*

Soil profile (right)

Four simplified horizons:

A *Dark and humus rich*
B *Rich in minerals*
C *Infertile subsoil*
D *Unweathered bedrock*

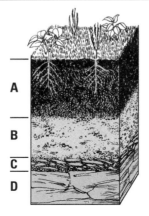

Textural classes

Soil texture varies with particle size from clay (fine) through silt (medium) to sand (coarse). Water drains fast through sand, but clay gets waterlogged. Loam is best for plant growth.

a *Clay*
b *Sandy clay*
c *Sandy clay loam*
d *Clay loam*
e *Silty clay*
f *Silty clay loam*
g *Sand*
h *Loamy sand*
i *Sandy loam*
j *Loam*
k *Silt loam*
l *Silt*

% clay   % silt

% sand

In time most weathered rock acquires a covering of soil–a substance most land life depends on.

Soil forms as weathering breaks rock into particles ranging in size from clay to silt, sand, and gravel. Air and water fill the gaps between the larger particles. Then chemical changes help bacteria, fungi, and plants to move in. Plant roots bind groups of particles together; leaves ward off destructive rain; and roots and stems raise minerals from deep down. Plants and their remains form food for burrowing insects, worms, and larger creatures. Bacteria and fungi decompose dead plants, animal droppings, and dead animals, converting it all into dark, fertile humus. So soil's main ingredients are (inorganic) minerals, (organic) humus, air, water, and living organisms.

A slice cut down through soil reveals a profile made up of layers called horizons, from top to bottom known as A, B, and C. A is dark and rich in humus. B is rich in minerals and substances washed down from A, but paler, more compact and less fertile. C, the subsoil, consists of infertile weathered rock, derived from the unweathered bedrock (sometimes known as the D horizon).

Few soils fit this description perfectly. Soil texture depends largely on the bedrock (parent rock), and soil type depends on topography, time, vegetation, and climate. Thus shales yield finer-textured soils than sandstones. Soils on limestones are rich in bases; others have an acid tendency. Soil depth can range from less than an inch (2.5 cm) on steep slopes to several yards on plains. Hillside soils are often better drained than those in valleys. Plants with different needs affect the proportions of some substances accumulating in the soil. But the chief influence on soils is climate (opposite).

Types of soil

Pedologists (soil scientists) have many ways of classifying soils. Thus the US Department of Agriculture labels soil types purely according to their properties, but the much-used zonal system stresses climatic origins.

Soils certainly owe more to climate and vegetation than to bedrock. Heavy rainfall causes much leaching (downward flow of dissolved substances), eluviation (downward movement of fine particles), and illuviation (redeposition of these substances at lower levels), and so it affects soil fertility. At the other extreme, hot deserts undergo salinization or alkalization as soil water brings salts and alkalis to the surface, then evaporates, leaving the chemicals to form a whitish crust.

Most of the following soil types come from the zonal system. The Arctic's tundra soils are often waterlogged or frozen, with a peaty upper layer and bluish mud below. The cool-climate podzol ("ash")

of northern coniferous forests is acid with a leached, ashy B horizon above a hard thin illuvial pan. Temperate forests of the world produced brown forest soil–humus-rich and slightly acid. Temperate grasslands (the steppe, prairie, pampas, and Australian downs) include chernozem, and/or prairie soil, and chestnut-brown soil. Chernozem's dark, humus-rich upper layer formed under light rainfall with little leaching. Prairie soil and chestnut-brown soil formed in drier climates. Alfisols ("degraded chernozems") have been identified in Spain, northwest Africa, India, and parts of Africa. Hot deserts have pale, coarse, soils, poor in humus and sometimes white with salty crust. Tropical grasslands indude dark, clayey grumusols. Deep, reddish, iron rich ferralsols underlie the humid tropics. Mountain soils include thin scree soils–little more than rock fragments.

A

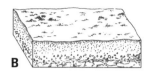

B

C

D

E

F

Six soil types (above)

Diagrams above show six soil types.

A *Tundra soil*

B *Desert soil*

C *Chernozem*

D *Ferralsol*

E *Brown forest soil*

F *A red-yellow podzol*

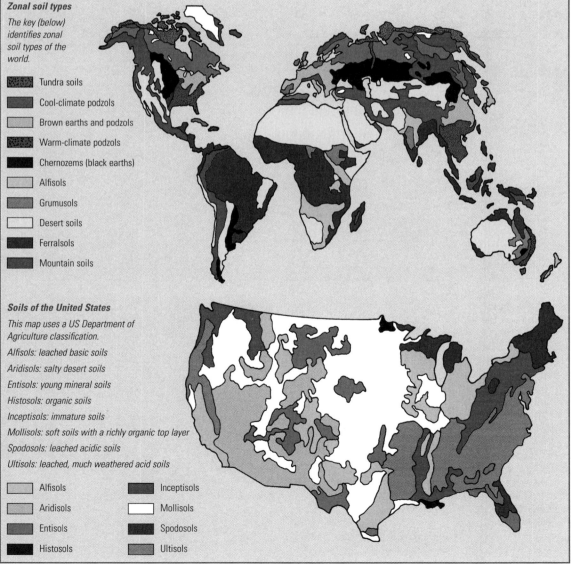

Zonal soil types

The key (below) identifies zonal soil types of the world.

- Tundra soils
- Cool-climate podzols
- Brown earths and podzols
- Warm-climate podzols
- Chernozems (black earths)
- Alfisols
- Grumusols
- Desert soils
- Ferralsols
- Mountain soils

Soils of the United States

This map uses a US Department of Agriculture classification.

Alfisols: leached basic soils

Aridisols: salty desert soils

Entisols: young mineral soils

Histosols: organic soils

Inceptisols: immature soils

Mollisols: soft soils with a richly organic top layer

Spodosols: leached acidic soils

Ultisols: leached, much weathered acid soils

- Alfisols
- Aridisols
- Entisols
- Histosols
- Inceptisols
- Mollisols
- Spodosols
- Ultisols

Mass movement

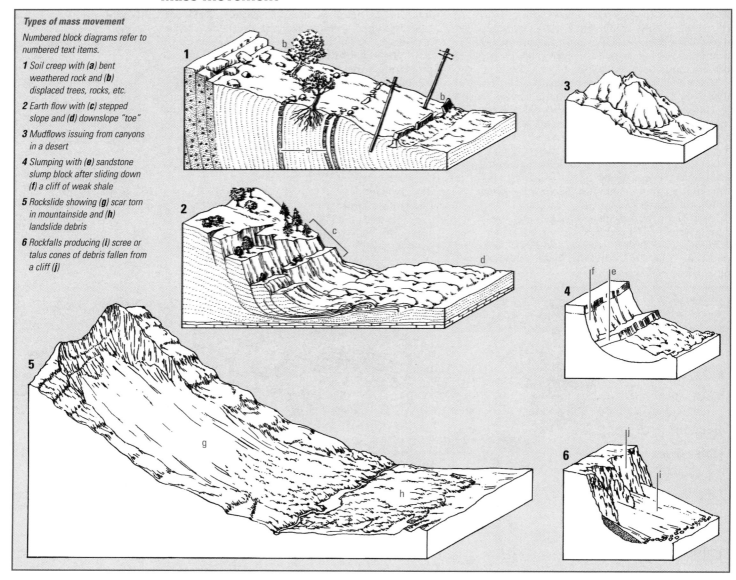

Mass movement (mass wasting) is the force of gravity shifting weathered rock and soil (the regolith) downhill. Water often lubricates and aids this process. Amounts and speeds involved vary with such things as slope steepness, underlying rocks, and quantity of moisture in the ground. Mass movement can affect a few square yards or a whole mountainside. Sodden regolith may flow; dry regolith will slide or fall. Slow movements include creeping and flowing. Swift movements include landslides and rockfalls triggered by such things as earthquakes, heavy rain, or quarrying.

1 Soil creep is the imperceptible downslope creep of soil, betrayed by items such as tilted and displaced trees and fences.

2 Earth flow This features a stepped slope where material has slumped downhill and a bulging downslope "toe" where it accumulates. Earth flow can occur in hours on saturated slopes.

3 Mudflows occur where mud holds so much water that it flows as slurry even down a gentle slope. A mudflow containing volcanic ash and dust from Mt. Vesuvius swallowed the Roman city of Herculaneum in AD 79.

4 Slumping is a landslide where rock masses tilt back as they slide from a cliff or escarpment – often where well-jointed sedimentary rocks overlie clay or shale. Resulting slump blocks can be 2 mi (3 km) long and 500 ft (150 m) thick.

5 Rockslides involve masses of bedrock slipping down a sloping fault or bedding plane. Rockslides have killed people and destroyed villages in the Canadian Rockies, Norway, and Switzerland.

6 Rockfalls are free falls of fragments of any size from a cliff. Frost-shattered fragments in time form cliff foot talus cones, with a talus (or scree) slope at an angle of about 35 degrees.

Slopes

Slopes steep or gentle make up almost all the surface of the land. Everywhere, mass movement, splashing raindrops, or rainwater flowing over land are forming slopes and wearing them away by shifting soil or broken bits of rock downhill.

Wherever the force of gravity is greater than the force of friction holding particles upon a slope, these tend to slide downhill. Most slopes have an average angle of less than 45 degrees. But a single slope usually has several (straight, concave, or convex) segments–parts with different angles. Slope angle varies with the amount of weathered debris entering and leaving a segment.

Slopes probably evolve in three main ways, all possible in one location:

A Slope decline Slope angle decreases through stages: (**a**) steep free face; (**b**) graded slope with convex curve above, concave curve below; (**c**) decreasing curvature; and (**d**) reduction in height. Slope decline predominates in moist temperate areas such as the northeastern US Appalachians.

B Slope retreat The retreating slope keeps a short convex top, long free face, debris slope, and (lengthening) pediment (thin sheet of debris). Such slopes abound in semiarid areas.

C Slope replacement Lower angle slopes extend upward to replace steep upper segments.

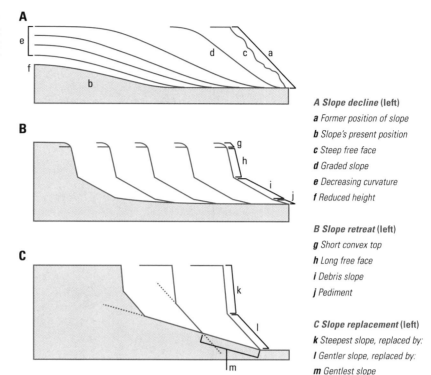

A Slope decline (left)
a Former position of slope
b Slope's present position
c Steep free face
d Graded slope
e Decreasing curvature
f Reduced height

B Slope retreat (left)
g Short convex top
h Long free face
i Debris slope
j Pediment

C Slope replacement (left)
k Steepest slope, replaced by:
l Gentler slope, replaced by:
m Gentlest slope

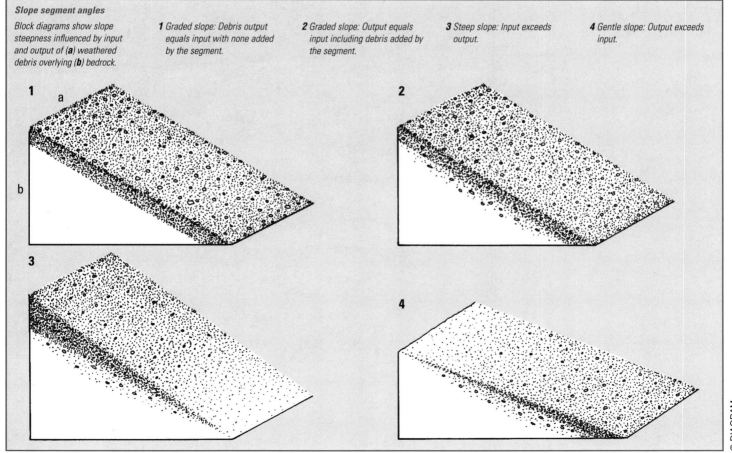

Slope segment angles

Block diagrams show slope steepness influenced by input and output of (**a**) weathered debris overlying (**b**) bedrock.

1 Graded slope: Debris output equals input with none added by the segment.

2 Graded slope: Output equals input including debris added by the segment.

3 Steep slope: Input exceeds output.

4 Gentle slope: Output exceeds input.

How rivers shape the land

Rain-fed rivers carve valleys in the hills and wash soil and weathered rock downhill, dumping them into the lakes and seas. Year by year the erosive work of rivers wears down the highest mountain ranges until some form flat plains that barely peek above the sea. Off some sheltered shores, though, sediments shed by rivers build deltas—muddy aprons of new land. This chapter describes the work of rivers and the landforms many help create.

Running water

Soon after land appears above the sea, rivers set about attacking it. Rivers rise in highlands and flow downhill to empty in a sea or inland drainage basin. The force of their moving water erodes and transports a load of soil and rock, so carving valleys that dissect mountains into peaks and ridges and reducing these to hills. But rivers also deposit the eroded debris to build lowland plains and offshore underwater platforms.

In theory, by degrading (eroding) some stretches of its bed and aggrading (building) others, a river tends to gain a graded concave profile, leaving it with just enough velocity to shift its load. In theory, too, rivers tend to bevel continents to peneplains–almost level plains just above sea level. In practice, earth movements and differences in rock formation and resistance to erosion interrupt both trends.

But calculations confirm running water's power to sculpt the continents. Rivers drain about 70 percent of all dry land. They contain only 0.03 percent of all fresh water, yet carry enough each year to drown all dry land 1 ft (30 cm) deep. Every year rivers dump about 20 billion tons of eroded material in the sea – enough to shave 1.2 in (3.13 cm) off the Earth's land surface every thousand years. The Mississippi River alone shifts an estimated 516 million tons a year; 340 million tons as fine suspended partides, 136 million tons in solution, and 40 million tons by saltation–the hopping of heavy particles along the river bed.

An individual river's power to erode and transport depends largely on its discharge–the product of its volume and velocity. The greatest mean discharge is the Amazon's 6,350,000 cu ft per second (180,000 cu m per second)–nearly ten times the Mississippi's. But for rivers such as China's Yangtze, wet and dry seasons affect the flow from month to month.

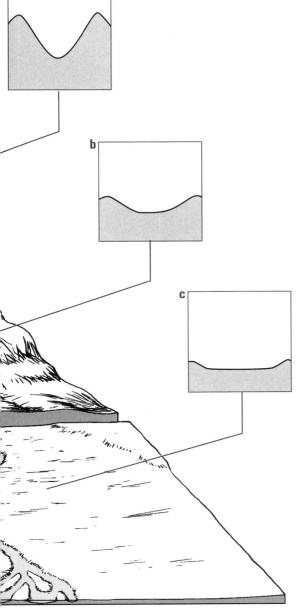

Water shapes land (left)

1 Streams erode mountains into ridges and intervening valleys. (**a**) "Youthful" river valley in cross section

2 River erosion reduces mountains to low hills. (**b**) "Mature" river valley in cross section

3 River action bevels hills to form a low flood-plain covered by river sediment. (**c**) "Old" river valley in cross section

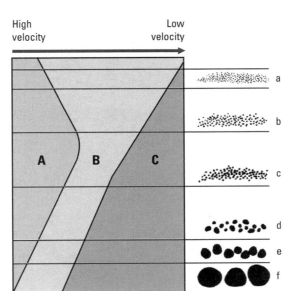

High velocity   Low velocity

A   B   C

a

b

c

d

e

f

Water transportation (left)

Stream velocity affects differently sized particles in different ways. Here we show how velocity decrease (from left to right) corresponds to erosion (**A**), transportation (**B**), and deposition (**C**) of the following.

a Clay

b Silt

c Sand

d Pebbles

e Cobbles

f Boulders

© DIAGRAM

Water comes and goes

The chief agent that wears down dry land is water flowing on the surface as part of the water cycle. Powered by the Sun and gravity, the cycle starts as the Sun's heat evaporates surface water, mostly from the oceans. Water vapor in the atmosphere cools and condenses into droplets that build clouds. Clouds shed this moisture as rain or snow. Much of this precipitation falls on the sea, but some falls on dry land. Vast quantities are locked in slowly moving sheets of ice (see pp. 80–81). But some water seeps underground, and smaller quantities run off the surface as rills, converging in rivers and lakes. Most water returns to the sea.

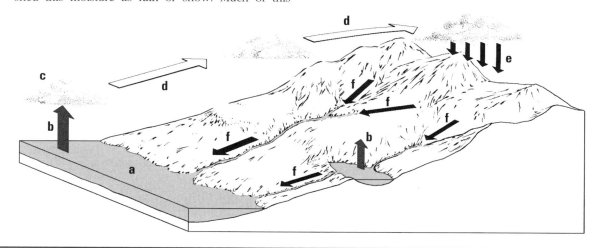

The water cycle (right)

Arrows indicate the circulation of moisture that keeps rivers running.

a Sea *d* Wind
b Evaporation *e* Precipitation
c Cloud formation *f* Rivers

Water underground

Rainfall is occasional, but many rivers are perennial, fed by underground water, which includes the following sources:

1 Ground water Below the soil, ground water saturates permeable rocks (rocks that let water through), filling the pores of porous rocks, such as sandstone, and cracks in pervious rocks, including limestone.

2 Aquifer This is a saturated layer of permeable rock lying on a layer of impermeable rock, such as slate or shale. The aquifer's surface is its water table. The table's level varies with rainfall, tends to follow slopes up and down, and is exposed in swamps, lakes, and springs.

3 Spring This is a flow of water escaping from the ground, such as where the water table outcrops on a hillside above impermeable rock. Springs are the sources of some major rivers.

4 Artesian basin This is a saucer-shaped aquifer sandwiched between layers of impermeable rock. Rain soaks down through its rim. Below rim level, water under pressure may gush from artesian wells and artesian springs. Artesian basins underlie London, Paris, much of the Sahara Desert, Australia, and North America.

1 Ground water
A Water percolates between the grains of sand in sandstone, a porous permeable rock.
B Water only percolates through joints in limestone, a non-porous permeable rock.

2 Aquifer
a Non-saturated rock
b Rock sometimes saturated
c Rock always saturated
d Impermeable rock
e (Variable) water table

3 Spring
a Porous rock
b Water table
c Impermeable rock
d Spring

4 Artesian basin
a Permeable rock (aquifer)
b Impermeable rock
c Rainfall
d Artesian well

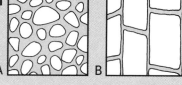

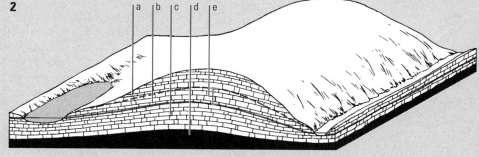

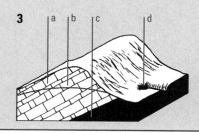

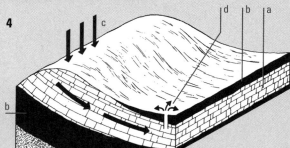

How river valleys form 1

River valleys grow where rivers cut down and sideways into rock, and weathering wears back the slopes on either side. Steep-sided valleys and broad, flat-bottomed valleys were once seen as erosion-cycle stages produced, respectively, by youthful and mature sections of a river. This takes no account of the effects of local rocks and climate. But upper, middle, and lower reaches of a river do often show distinctive differences.

Many valleys start to form high up on slopes, where springs erupt or rainwater successively produces splash, sheet, then rill erosion; deepened rills cut river channels. In its upper course a river may be a small, fast-flowing torrent cutting down into its bed and forming rapids and waterfalls (see also p. 66.) Floods accelerate this process, transporting rocks that gouge out rock pools. Mountain streams commonly reveal these features:

1 Headward erosion Undercutting, rain wash, and soil creep help a river valley to gnaw back into a hillside, thus lengthening the river.

2 Pot-holes Circular holes in a rocky stream bed show where waterborne scraps of rock were whirled around, deepening depressions. Stream-channel erosion also rubs bits off the rock fragments themselves, a process called attrition.

3 V-shaped valley Valleys develop deep, steep cross sections where streams erode downwards. Interlocking spurs are ridges projecting from both sides of the valley. The stream erodes most on the outsides of the bends, where the current flow is strongest, so the zigzags grow more pronounced.

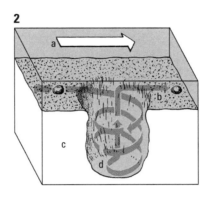

1 Headward erosion
a Rainwash
b Undercutting and soil creep
c Source of river
d Upper river valley

2 Pot-hole
a Stream flow
b Path of pebble
c Stream bed
d Pot-hole

3 V-shaped valley
a V-shaped cross section
b Interlocking spurs
c Stream

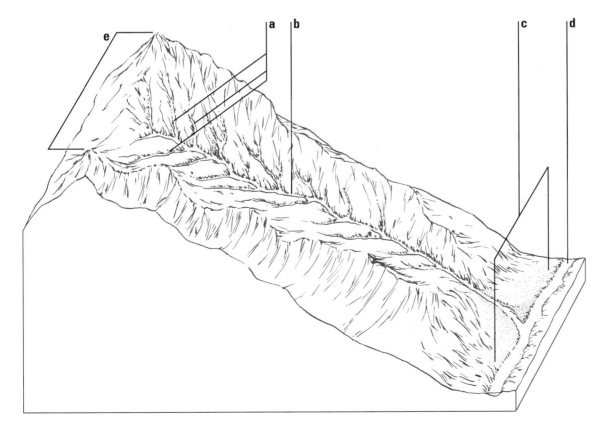

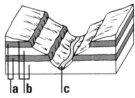

Resistant strata (above)

Alternating resistant and easily eroded horizontal strata help to produce river valleys with a stepped cross profile.

a Resistant strata
b Easily eroded strata
c River

A mountain valley (left)
a Gully
b Tributary stream
c Alluvial fan deposited by tributary
d River
e Divide

© DIAGRAM

How river valleys form 2

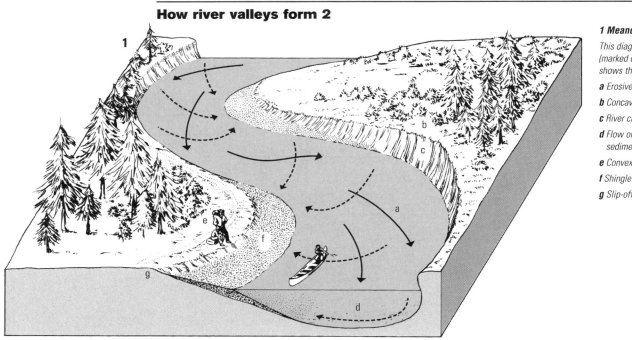

1 Meander

This diagram of a meander (marked curve in a river channel) shows these features.

a Erosive surface flow

b Concave bank

c River cliff

d Flow on river bed, shedding sediment

e Convex bank

f Shingle

g Slip-off slope

A river valley's middle section typically shows more mature features than its upper course. Weathering has broadened the valley sides. The river flows down a gentler gradient. Its current travels fast enough to shift the load of sediment acquired upstream. But the stream flows mostly over sediment it has deposited and no longer cuts down into the rock below its bed. Rather, it erodes from side to side, nibbling away its banks, thereby flattening and broadening the valley floor. Yet even in this middle section, land uplift or an outcrop of resistant rock may interrupt the valley's gently curving profile with a waterfall. The illustrations on the left show these processes at work.

1 Meander This is where a river current flows around a bend, hits its concave bank at speed, and gnaws that bank away to form a river cliff. Meanwhile, the river deposits sediment in slack water on the convex bend, where a sloping spur known as a slip-off slope grows out into the river. Thus the river migrates slowly sideways.

2 Valley broadening Meanders slowly migrate downstream, widening the river valley by lopping off the ends of interlocking spurs. This rims the valley floor with low cliffs called bluffs.

3 Waterfall This is a clifflike face down which a river plunges. Waterfalls form where resistant rock or land uplift interrupt the river's profile. Major falls include the Congo River's Boyoma (Stanley) Falls, the Paraná's Guaíra Falls, Niagara Falls, and the Zambezi's Victoria Falls. Vertical river erosion cuts back some waterfalls, so they migrate upstream above a long, deep gorge.

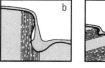

2 Valley broadening

A sequence of three diagrams shows migrating meanders widening a valley floor.

A Lateral erosion starts at concave banks.

B Lateral erosion lops off spurs.

C Large meanders migrating downstream broaden the valley floor, carving bluffs (a) and dumping gravel (b).

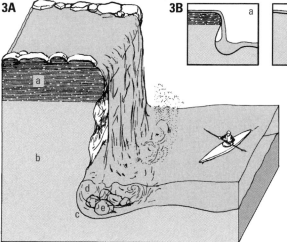

3 Waterfalls

A Waterfall features:

a Resistant rock

b Weaker rocks

c Undercutting

d Plunge pool

e Boulders

B Resistant rocks producing waterfalls:

a Horizontal cap rock

b Vertical rock

c Gently sloping rocks (creating rapids)

Where rivers shed their loads

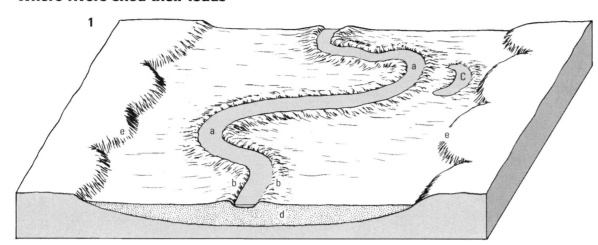

1

These features appear in a river's floodplain:

a Snaky meanders

b Levees

c Oxbow lakes

d Mud, silt, and sand

e Bluffs

In their lower courses, huge rivers like the Amazon and Mississippi flow down a gradient as slight as 3 in per mile (5 cm per km). Here, the rivers have beveled off all hills and cross a broad' low-lying plain thickly carpeted with sand and mud. Vast quantities of these river sediments built the floodplains of the Ganges, Mississippi, Niger, Nile, Rhine, and Rhône. Deposition blocks such rivers' mouths, producing deltas–swampy plains through which the river flows divided into several channels called distributaries. Deltas grow where a river sheds a large load of sediment faster than tides and currents can carry it away.

Illustrations show floodplain and delta features.

1 Floodplain This has a valley floor flattened and broadened by river erosion and floored with sediments deposited by migrating meanders and river floods. Cutoff meanders survive as oxbow lakes. The river flows above the level of the plain and between raised banks called levees.

2 Levees form because the river floods repeatedly. A flooding river sheds mud on its banks where current flow is slow, so banks grow higher. After flooding, the river deposits sediment on its bed, which raises it. After repeated flooding, both bed and banks are raised, and the river surface lies higher than the plain on either side.

3 Delta Deltas take the shape of a fan or bird's foot. They form in stages. Deposition splits a river into distributaries flanked by levees and separated by lagoons. Sediments turn lagoons into swamps and build bars and spits. Swamps become dry land (Louisiana, Mesopotamia, and the North China Plain were formed from deltas in this way).

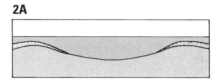

2A

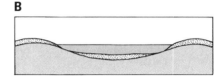

B

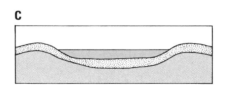

C

2 Levees (left)

Cross sections show how a river raises its banks.

A Sediment deposited by flooding

B Sediment deposited in normal flow

C Sediments and river after repeated flooding

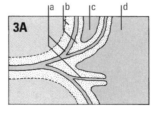

3A

B

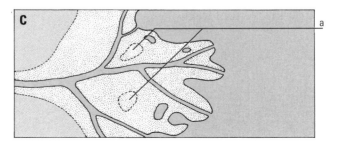

C

3 Deltas (right)

Plans and longitudinal sections show how a delta forms.

A The river splits

a Distributaries

b Levees

c Lagoon

d Sea

B The delta extends into the sea

a Spits and bars

b Swamps

C The delta expands.

a Infilled swamps become dry land.

Rivers revived

1 Knickpoint

Block diagrams and long profiles show a knickpoint receding upstream from a river mouth.

A *Before land uplift*

B *Soon after uplift*

C *Later*

a *Floodplain*

b *Sea*

c *Knickpoint*

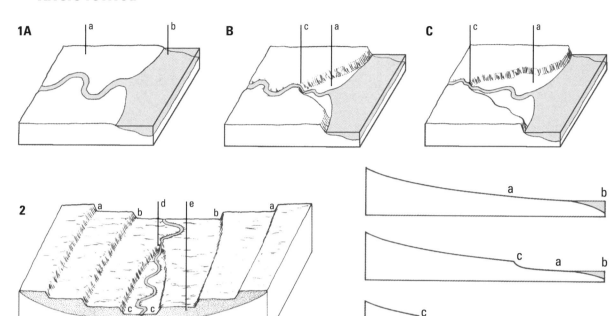

2 River terraces

a *Oldest terraces*

b *Younger terraces*

c *Present floodplain*

d *Present knickpoint*

e *Sediments*

3 Entrenched meanders

River erosion has kept pace with uplift of a floodplain by deeply incising old meanders in the rising land.

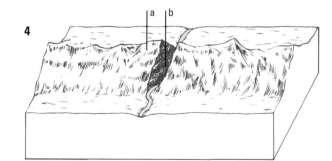

4 Gorges

River rejuvenation cut this long, steep, narrow gorge in land rising as earth movements built mountains.

a *Mountain*

b *Gorge*

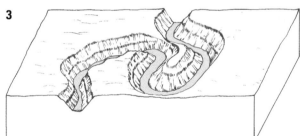

5 Natural bridge

Lateral river erosion whittled away cliffs flanked by an incised meander. Then the stream cut through the meander's narrow neck.

a *Old incised meander*

b *Present course of river*

c *Natural bridge*

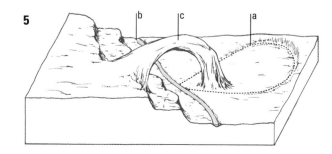

Mature, meandering rivers sometimes start vigorously cutting down into their beds like youthful mountain torrents. Called rejuvenation, this happens if a lasting rise in rainfall boosts a river's flow, or if land uplift or a fall in sea level leaves the river mouth above the sea. Either way the river will regrade its bed. Various landforms show where this has happened.

1 Knickpoint This is a sharp step in a river's long profile, often marked by rapids or a waterfall. In time a knickpoint starting at a river's mouth recedes upstream. Some rivers show several knickpoints resulting from successive uplifts of the land.

2 River terraces are remnants of old floodplain left when a river cuts down and sideways in the sediments through which it flowed before rejuvenation. Renewed rejuvenation cuts a second pair of terraces below the level of the first. Further episodes of uplift produce more terraces. Several pairs flank the Thames in London.

3 Entrenched (incised) meanders are floodplain meanders incised in bedrock by rejuvenation of a river. The Goose Necks of the San Juan River in Utah have been cut down through horizontal beds.

4 Gorges and canyons are deep, steep-sided, rocky valleys cut by rejuvenation in resistant rock or along a fault. Land uplift helped produce the 3 mi (4.8 km) deep Himalayan gorges of the Ganges and Brahmaputra, and Arizona's 1.5 mi (2.4 km) deep Grand Canyon–a desert gorge cut by the Colorado River, which is fed by distant melting snows.

5 Natural bridge This type of rock formation is formed by cutoff of an incised meander. Rainbow Bridge at Navajo Mountain, Utah, is a striking rock bridge rising 309 ft (94 m) from a gorge floor and spanning 278 ft (85 m).

Rivers underground

In most landscapes, rivers flow across the surface of the land. But rainwater sinks down through joints in permeable limestone rocks and invisibly attacks them underground. Carbon dioxide gas combines with falling rain to turn the water into weak carbonic acid, and this carbonic acid dissolves calcium carbonate– the main ingredient of limestone. In moist chalk countryside this process removes an estimated 35 tons of rock a year from every acre and forms depressions called solution hollows. In carboniferous limestone, water enlarges vertical and horizontal joints to gnaw complex channels underground. A slice cut through some limestone mountains would resemble a giant slice of Swiss cheese. Some limestone caverns and cave systems are immense. Several European cave systems descend 4,000 ft (1,219 m) or more. Mapped passages in Kentucky's Mammoth Cave National Park exceed 230 mi (370 km). Borneo's Sarawak Chamber could hold more than 7,000 buses, and five football fields would fit in the Big Room of New Mexico's Carlsbad Caverns.

Where dripping water evaporates and/or gives up carbon dioxide, the dissolved calcium bicarbonate becomes insoluble in the mineral form called calcite, building deposits such as these:

1 Stalactites "Icicles" of calcite hanging from a cave ceiling. Depending on conditions they take 4 to 4,000 years to grow 1 inch (2.54 cm).

2 Stalagmites Calcite spikes jutting upward from a cave floor.

3 Columns Calcite forms produced where stalactites and stalagmites meet.

4 Gours Calcite ridges formed where water rich in carbonate flows over an irregular surface.

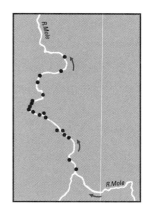

Swallowholes (above)

Dots show swallowholes in the chalk bed of England's River Mole. Water tends to vanish down these holes in dry weather.

How caves form (left)

Three illustrations trace the growth of caves in limestone.

A Rainwater trickles down through crevices produced by:

a Joints

b Bedding planes

B Rainwater acting as a weak carbonic acid dissolves the rocks it touches and removes the dissolved material. This widens vertical and horizontal crevices in limestone.

C Streams plunging underground widen crevices into vertical and horizontal caves. If the climate changes so that rainfall drops, many caves are left quite dry.

A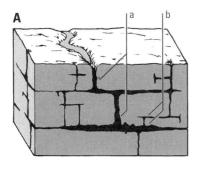

B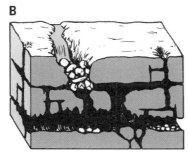

C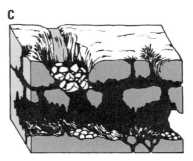

A limestone cave system

a Clints (blocks)

b Grikes (gullies)

c Sink-holes

d Galleries

e Stalagmites

f Stalactites

g Columns

h Gours

© DIAGRAM

Drainage patterns

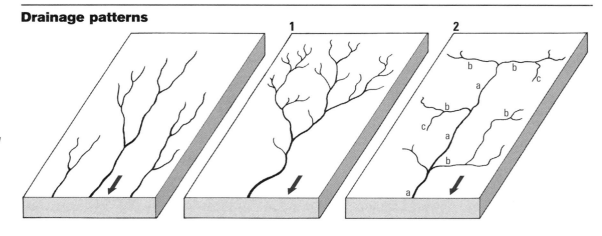

1

2

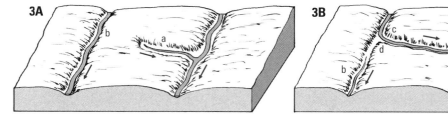

3A

3B

Land drained by a river and its tributaries comprises a watershed, also called a drainage basin, river basin, or catchment area. Some watersheds are immense. The Amazon's, the world's largest, embraces almost two-fifths of South America.

A drainage basin's river channels form a drainage pattern that depends on slope, rock types and formations, and crustal movements. Drainage patterns include the following types and features.

1 Dendritic pattern Named from the Greek *dendron*, or "tree," this is a tree-shaped pattern of small, branching tributaries feeding into a main "trunk" river. It forms on rocks of equal resistance.

2 Trellis pattern Here some tributaries flow parallel to the main river, others at right angles to it. This pattern appears where bands of hard and soft rock alternate.

3 River capture This involves a stream eroding headward until it captures another stream's headwaters at an elbow of capture. The "pirate" stream's flow increases, and the captured stream's flow dwindles. The victim stream may then rise below the elbow of capture, leaving a dry tract of valley called a wind gap.

4 Accordant drainage is where river channels relate to rock type and structure. On folded rocks, tributaries quickly attack tension cracks in (upcurved) anticlinal crests and often wear these down below intervening valleys formed in (downcurved) synclines. Synclinal crests occur in the Appalachian ridge-and-valley section. (Discordant drainage patterns show no relation to today's rock structure. They may be antecedent–formed before the land was raised or tilted–or superimposed on present rocks after developing on others that have worn away.)

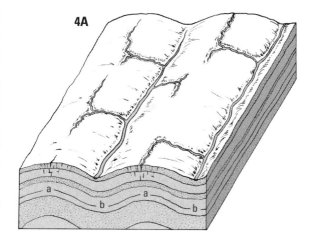

4A

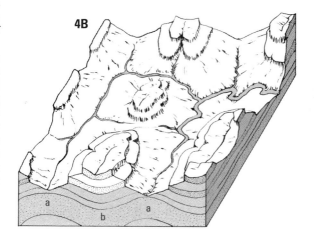

4B

Plateaus and ridges

As valleys eat into sedimentary rocks, they sculpt distinctive upland features determined largely by the types and angles of rock layer–especially where weak layers such as clay or shale alternate with more resistant layers like chalk, limestone, or sandstone.

A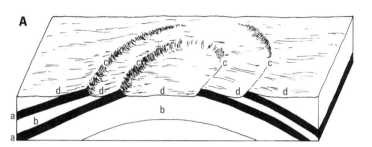

B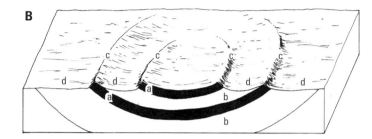

Upland features

Horizontal and tilted layers produce contrasting types of upland.

1 Plateaus develop where resistant rock caps other horizontal layers. River valleys may dissect a plateau into tablelands such as Brazil's *tableiros*, or the Colorado Plateau's steep-sided blocks called mesas, many now eroded into the smaller blocks called buttes (see also pp. 88–89). Plateaus may have "stepped" sides shaped by the different rates of erosion of alternating weak and resistant rock layers.

2 Cuestas are ridges formed by gently tilted strata. Each has a steep slope or escarpment and a gentle slope or dip slope. Beyond the cuesta lies lower land where erosion has eaten deeply into weaker rock. Cuestas abound in the US Southwest, and occur along the Gulf and Atlantic coasts. Cuestas overlooking clay vales dominate southeast England's landscape and rim part of the Paris Basin.

3 Hogbacks are steep, even-crested ridges formed by sharply dipping strata. They abound in the mid and southern Rockies and form most of the long parallel ridges of the Appalachian Mountains' ridge-and-valley system.

1A **B**

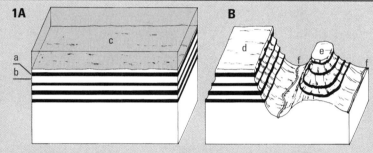

1 Plateaus

"Before and after" block diagrams show the origins of buttes and mesas.

A Horizontal rock layers laid down beneath the sea

a Resistant rock layers

b Easily eroded rock

c Sea

B The same rock layers after uplift and dissection by downcutting rivers

d Mesa

e Butte

f River valleys

2 Cuesta

a Scarp foot

b Escarpment

c Dip slope

d Backslope

e Resistant rock layer

f Easily eroded layer

3 Hoghack

a Steep slopes

b Steeply dipping bed of resistant rock

c Easily eroded rock bed

Cuestas and vales

Block diagrams (above) show the dissection of a dome and basin of sedimentary rock layers into cuestas with intervening vales.

A Dissected dome (dip slopes facing outwards)

B Dissected basin (dip slopes facing inward)

a Resistant rock layers

b Easily eroded rock layers

c Cuestas

d Vales

How lakes form

Lakes are bodies of water lying in depressions on land. They can be large or small, deep or shallow, fresh or salt. The largest lake is the Caspian Sea; the deepest, Lake Baikal in eastern Siberia.

Lakes are formed by earth movements, volcanoes, erosion, deposition, or erosion and deposition. Here are examples of lakes formed by each.

1 Earth movements Crustal uplift isolated the Caspian Sea from the Black Sea. Crustal warping (and later glacial action) formed Lake Superior. Fault blocks sinking between high valley walls produced the long, narrow trench containing Lake Malawi and other African Rift Valley lakes.

2 Volcanic action Water-filled volcanic craters include Oregon's Crater Lake. Lava flows damming river valleys held back the waters of lakes like the Sea of Galilee and Lac d'Aydat in south-central France.

3 Erosion Lakes fill ice-worn hollows, especially in Canada and Finland. Water dissolving limestone river banks broadened Ireland's Shannon River to create Lough Derg. Wind eroding rock to below the water table exposes lakes in deserts.

4 Deposition Rock slides damming rivers form lakes such as Montana's Earthquake Lake. Ice dams trap lakes against glaciers and ice sheets. Oxbow lakes form where a river cuts through the necks of meanders and leaves them isolated. River sediments help trap delta lakes. Bars and dunes pond back brackish coastal lakes.

5 Erosion and deposition Glacial erosion and glacial deposits called moraines form countless lakes. Moraine-dammed cirques (ice-eroded hollows) hold circular mountain lakes called tarns. End moraines at the mouths of glaciated valleys dam long narrow lakes such as New York's Finger Lakes, England's Lake District lakes, Sweden's Glint line lakes, and Italy's Lakes Como, Garda, and Maggiore.

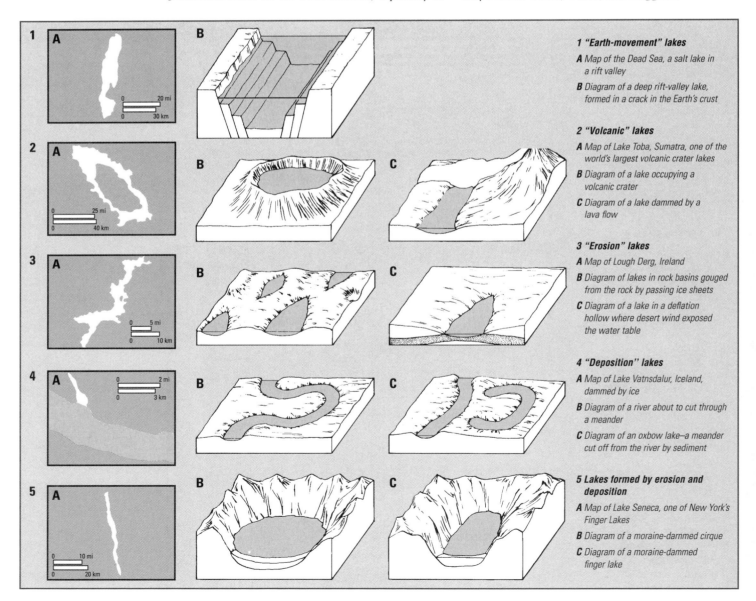

1 "Earth-movement" lakes

A Map of the Dead Sea, a salt lake in a rift valley

B Diagram of a deep rift-valley lake, formed in a crack in the Earth's crust

2 "Volcanic" lakes

A Map of Lake Toba, Sumatra, one of the world's largest volcanic crater lakes

B Diagram of a lake occupying a volcanic crater

C Diagram of a lake dammed by a lava flow

3 "Erosion" lakes

A Map of Lough Derg, Ireland

B Diagram of lakes in rock basins gouged from the rock by passing ice sheets

C Diagram of a lake in a deflation hollow where desert wind exposed the water table

4 "Deposition" lakes

A Map of Lake Vatnsdalur, Iceland, dammed by ice

B Diagram of a river about to cut through a meander

C Diagram of an oxbow lake—a meander cut off from the river by sediment

5 Lakes formed by erosion and deposition

A Map of Lake Seneca, one of New York's Finger Lakes

B Diagram of a moraine-dammed cirque

C Diagram of a moraine-dammed finger lake

Vanishing lakes

Most lakes are geologically short-lived; they dry up in only a few thousand years or so. A lake can disappear in several ways. Many lakes get clogged by mud and silt washed in by rivers. The Rhône River will fill Lake Geneva with mud in 40,000 years.

Huge prehistoric lakes drained away or shrank with the melting of ice sheets that had ponded back their waters. Once larger than all of today's Great Lakes combined, Canada's Lake Agassiz has been reduced to the remnant Lakes Winnipeg, Winnipegosis, and Manitoba. The Great Lakes themselves are shrunken relics of mighty prehistoric Lake Algonquin. And about 15,000 years ago, the bursting of an ice dam abruptly emptied Montana's mighty prehistoric Lake Missoula in a flood some 10 times greater than the flow of all the rivers in the world.

Some lakes dry up because the local rainfall dwindles and the lakes lose more water by evaporation than they gain from rivers. A drying climate helped shrink the Great Basin lakes of the United States.

Outlet rivers cutting down through bedrock are another factor. Utah's Great Salt Lake covers one-tenth the area of its precursor, Lake Bonneville, which lost one-third its volume in about six weeks through a breach at Red Rock Canyon.

Disappearing lakes and ponds produce many of the world's wetlands. Swamps are places that are always waterlogged; for instance, the Florida Everglades, Virginia's Dismal Swamp, and much of the Sudd in the Sudan. Marshes are low-lying lands that flood when rivers overflow. Bogs are soft, wet, spongy areas where moss fills shallow lakes and pools.

When even wetlands dry out, clues to vanished lakes remain in flat valley floors thickly carpeted with mud and silt, old overflow channels, and old beaches high on valley slopes.

A lake vanishes (below)

Diagrams show how a river fills in a lake.

A *River washes sediment into one end of the lake.*

B *River sediment builds a delta out into the lake.*

C *Sediment shrinks the lake into a small, shallow, reedy swamp.*

D *The lake floor is now filled in with sediment colonized by land plants.*

A

B

C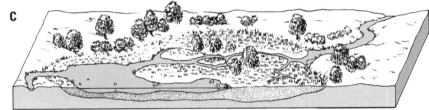

D

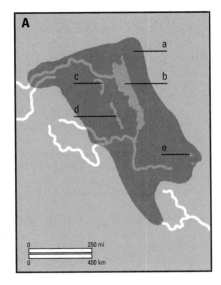

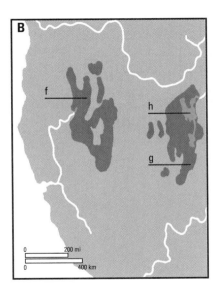

Lost lakes of North America (left)

Maps show lakes lost in relatively recent times, with their major modern relics.

A *North-central North America*

a *Former Lake Agassiz*

b *Lake Winnipeg*

c *Lake Winnipegosis*

d *Lake Manitoba*

e *Lake of the Woods*

B *Great Basin lakes*

f *Former Lake Lahontan*

g *Former Lake Bonneville*

h *Great Salt Lake*

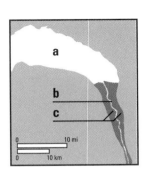

Lake Geneva (above)

A map shows how river sediment has filled in one end of this lake.

a *Lake Geneva*

b *Rhône River*

c *Former lake, now floored by river sediment*

The work of the sea

Seawater set in violent motion scours coasts around the world. On rocky shores, waves armed with stones batter the land away. Yet fragments torn from cliff-fringed coasts lodge on shores to raise new sand and shingle beaches. This chapter shows how the sea erodes and builds the land, and describes shores risen or submerged by the changing levels of the sea or land. It ends with a discussion of the growth of coral reefs and islands.

2 Underwater currents (below)

A Wave advances inshore against backwash from previous wave.

B Advancing wave peaks

C Advancing wave breaks

D Breaking wave thrusts water up the beach.

E Swash (water surging up the beach after a wave breaks)

F Backwash returns to sea, creating an undertow.

2
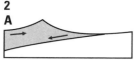
A

B

C

D

E

F

3 Tides (right)

A month's tides show how changes in tidal range follow changes in Earth, Moon, Sun alignment. Spring tides (high high tides and low low tides) and neap tides (low highs and high lows) each occur about every two weeks.

A Neap tide–Sun, Earth, Moon form a right angle

B Spring tide–Sun, Earth, Moon form a straight line

C Neap tide–Sun, Earth, Moon form a right angle again

D Spring tide–Sun, Moon, Earth form a straight line

The sea in action

1
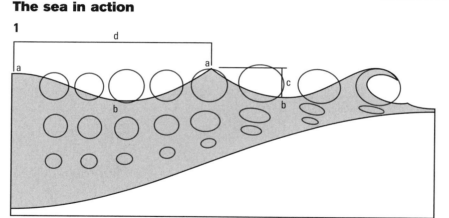

1 Waves (left)

Waves trigger the circling of water particles in a stack about half a wavelength deep. In shallower water the circles are flattened by their proximity to the bottom. The waves grow in height, and become unstable, and their crests topple and break.

a Wave crest

b Wave trough

c Wave height

d Wave length

Besides shaping inland surfaces, water sculpts the coast–the zone where land meets sea. Coasts include sea cliffs, shores (areas between low water and the highest storm waves), and beaches (shore deposits).

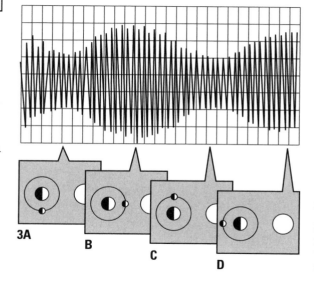

3A B C D

Seawater set in motion erodes cliffs, transports eroded debris along shores, and dumps it on beaches. Therefore, most coasts retreat or advance. The chief agents in this work are waves and currents, but tides contribute too.

1 Waves are undulations set in motion mainly by the wind. Wave height and power depend upon wind strength and fetch–the amount of unobstructed ocean over which the wind has blown. In the open sea, waves pass through the water without moving it forward. But in shallow water, wave crests crowd closer, pile up, and overbalance, causing forward movement of the water. The consequences are featured later in this chapter.

2 Underwater currents called undertows flow away from the shore, balancing the onshore pileup of water by waves. Rip currents are strong local currents of this kind.

3 Tides are two sets of huge progressive waves that sweep around the oceans each day. They are caused by the gravitational pull of the Moon and Sun. The Earth's spin, continents, coastlines, and underwater ridges affect local tidal height. Coinciding with storm waves, the highest tides affect the highest level of the shore.

Sea attacks the land

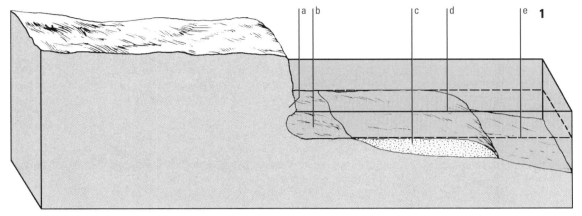

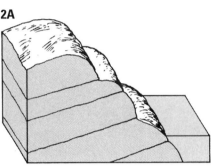

1 Cliff and wave-cut platform

a Sea cliff being forrned by undercutting wave erosion

b Wave-cut platform

c Beach deposits

d High tide level

e Low tide level

2 Cliff steepness

A Gentle cliff slope influenced by landward-tilted rock layers

B Steep cliff influenced by seaward-tilted rock layers

3 Headlands and bays

Diagrams show three stages in cliff erosion.

A Formation of headland (*a*) and bay (*b*)

B Erosion cuts sea caves (*c*) and a clifftop blowhole (*d*)

C Cave erosion creates arches (*e*) and, later, stacks (*f*)

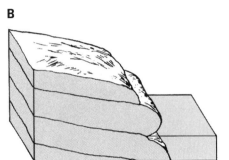

Where cliffs or rocks rim the land, the coast is probably retreating as waves erode the shore.

Wave erosion works chiefly by hydraulic action, corrasion, and attrition. As waves strike a sea cliff, hydraulic action crams air into rock crevices; as waves retreat, the explosively expanding air enlarges cracks and breaks off chunks of rock. Chunks hurled by waves against the cliff break off more pieces–a process called corrasion. Rubbing against each other and the cliff reduces broken rocks to pebbles and sand grains–a process called attrition.

Different combinations of wave action, rock type, and rock beds produce these features:

1 Cliff and wave-cut platform A sea cliff forms where waves undercut a slope until its unsupported top collapses. As waves eat farther back inland, they leave a wave-cut bench or platform jutting out beyond the cliff, below the sea.

2 Cliff steepness varies with rock hardness (usually the harder the rock, the steeper the cliff) and the angle of rock layers. Landward-tilted layers tend to produce a gentle cliff slope; seaward-tilted layers may give an overhanging cliff.

3 Headlands and bays Resistant rock juts out as a headland after erosion of nearby less resistant rock has eaten out a bay. Subsequent erosion produces caves, blowholes, arches, and stacks. At a sea cliff base, wave action may enlarge a horizontal crack to gnaw out a sea cave. Inside, erosion of a vertical joint may form a clifftop blowhole. A sea cave driven through a headland forms an arch. Roof collapse isolates the headland's tip as a steep-sided island called a stack.

3A

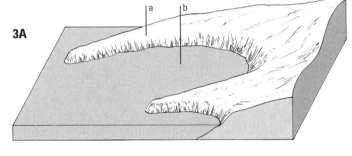

B

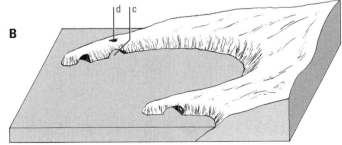

C

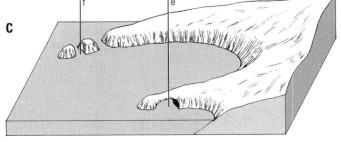

Drowned coastlines

If land subsides or sea level rises, the sea invades low-lying areas, drowning coastal plains, invading valleys, converting ridges to peninsulas, and isolating uplands as islands. Submerged upland coasts include the Dalmatian coastlines, fjords, and rias. Submerged lowland coasts may feature estuaries, fjords, and submerged glacial deposits.

1 Dalmation coastlines (also known as drowned concordant, longitudinal, or Pacific coastlines) feature mountain ridges that parallel the sea. Flooding formed valleys into sounds, and isolated ridges as long, narrow offshore islands. Croatia's Dalmatian coast and many British Columbian islands were shaped this way.

2 Fjords are submerged, glacially deepened inlets with sheer, high sides, a U-shaped cross profile, and a submerged seaward sill largely formed of end moraine. Fjords occur in south Alaska, British Columbia, south Chile, Greenland, New Zealand's South Island, and Norway

3 Rias are drowned river valleys forming long, funnel-shaped, branching inlets meeting the sea at right angles and with a V-shaped cross profile. Rias abound in southwest England, southwest Ireland, northwest France, and northwest Spain.

4 Estuaries are tidal river mouths, many of them drowned low-lying river valleys, flanked by mudflats and pierced by a maze of creeks submerged at high tide. Such estuaries include those of the Elbe, Gironde, Hudson, St. Lawrence, Chesapeake (Susquehanna), and Thames.

5 Fjards are ice-deepened lowland inlets often with small islands at the seaward end. They indent rocky, glaciated lowlands, as in southern Sweden, Nova Scotia, and the Shetland Islands.

6 Submergence of glacial deposits has left drumlins (see p. 83) as offshore islands in Boston Harbor and Northern Ireland's Strangford Lough.

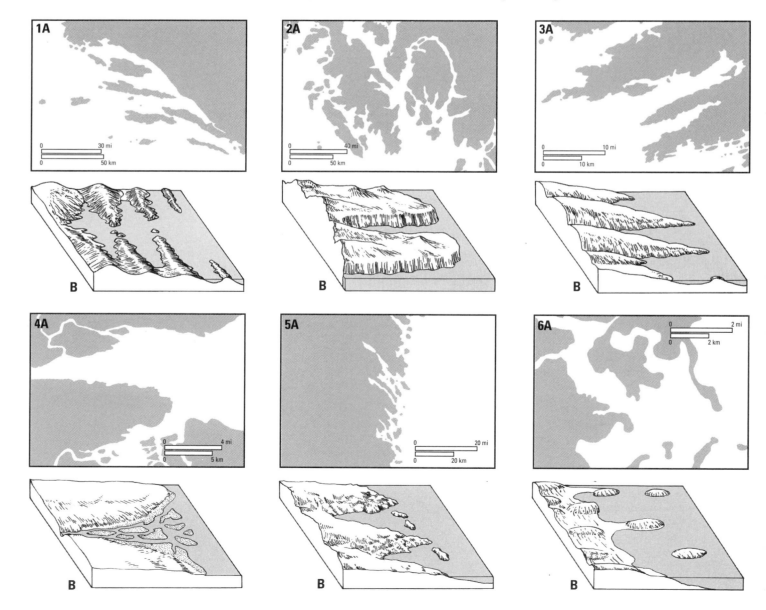

How sea builds land

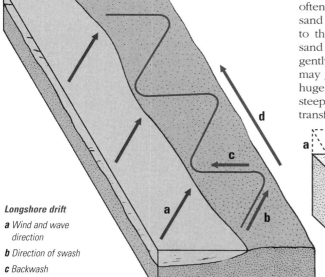

Longshore drift

a Wind and wave
  direction
b Direction of swash
c Backwash
d Direction of drift

Rock fragments torn from one stretch of coast are often added to another. Storm waves may hurl seabed sand and shingle inshore. Waves breaking at an angle to the land produce the longshore (littoral) drift of sand and shingle along the beach. Where land slopes gently to the waves, extensive beaches form, and land may grow into the sea. But storms shift or strip away huge quantities of loose material, especially on steeply sloping upper beaches. In the end, gravity transfers most beach material to the seabed.

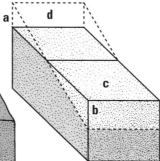

Shore deposition (left)

*On a gently sloping shore (**a-b**) sea erodes the lower part (**c**) and dumps it on the upper part (**d**). On a steeply sloping shore the opposite occurs. Most beaches are in near equilibrium.*

Depositional features (above)

a *Spit*
b *Double spits*
c *Bay-head beach*
d *Tombolo*
e *Barrier beach*
f *Hooked spit*
g *Cuspate foreland*

Coasts of deposition

Coasts of deposition include these items:

1 Boulder beaches are narrow belts of rocks and shingle at the base of sea cliffs.

2 Bay-head beaches are small sandy crescents. Each lies in a cove between two rocky headlands.

3 Lowland beaches are broad, gently sloping sandy beaches with a strip of shingle on the upper shore, often backed by dunes of sand blown inland by onshore winds. Such shores rim the southern Baltic and form the Landes of southwest France.

4 Bar A bar is an offshore strip of sand or shingle parallel to the coast. Bars border most of the US Southeast and Gulf coastline. They include the barrier islands that form Cape Hatteras.

5 Spit A spit resembles a bar, with one end tethered to the land. Special forms include bay-bars that link two headlands, tombolos linking islands to a mainland as in England's Chesil Beach, and (some) cuspate forelands–triangular shingle formations such as Cape Canaveral and Dungeness, England.

6 Mud-flats and **salt-marshes** form in estuaries and sheltered bays. Mud-flats are barren beds of silt and clay deposited by tides and drowned at high tide. Silt-trapping plants raise their level, and create salt marsh drained by tidal creeks. In the tropics, mud-flats colonized by mangrove trees form mangrove swamps.

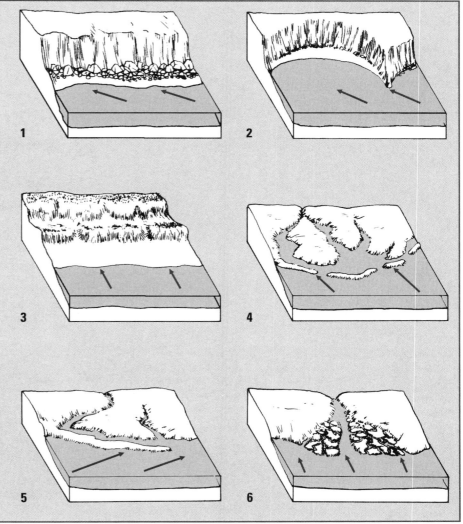

© DIAGRAM

Shores risen from the sea

While sinking land or rising sea level has drowned some coasts, rising land or falling sea level has stranded other coasts above the present level of the waves. Raised highland and lowland coasts have somewhat different characteristics.

1 Emergent highland coasts feature raised beaches. A raised beach, often covered with shells or shingle, stands perched high and dry above sea level. The raised beach is an old shoreline and adjoining wave-cut rock platform, up to 2,600 ft (about 800 m) across. Inland, above the raised beach, rises an old sea cliff, perhaps pierced by wave-cut caves. Below the raised beach, a new sea cliff and wave-cut platform form the seaward boundary. Successive earth movements can create a series of raised beaches, one above the other. Many formed where land depressed by ice bobbed up once the ice melted. Such beaches occur on North America's Arctic coasts, in western Scotland, and around the Baltic Sea. Others crop up as far apart as Malta and the South Pacific.

2 Emergent lowland coasts are coastal plains that slope gently to the sea and are rimmed by marshes, sandy beaches, bars, lagoons, and spits. The plains are uplifted continuations of the shallow offshore continental shelf, and thus may be floored by seashells, sand, and clay consolidated into limestone, sandstone, and shale. Inland, the plains may end abruptly below a line of hills marking the old coastline. This happens in the southeast United States–its coastal plain abuts the fall line where rejuvenated rivers flow steeply from the Appalachian Mountains to create a line of waterfalls. Other emergent lowland coasts include the northern Gulf of Mexico, the southern Rio de La Plata, and much of the east coast of India.

1 Emergent highland coast

a High tide level

b Low tide level

A Before emergence

c Sea cliff

d Sea caves

e Beach

f Wave-cut platform

B After emergence

g Old sea cliff

h Old sea caves

i Raised beach

j Exposed wave-cut platform

k New sea cliffs

l New beach

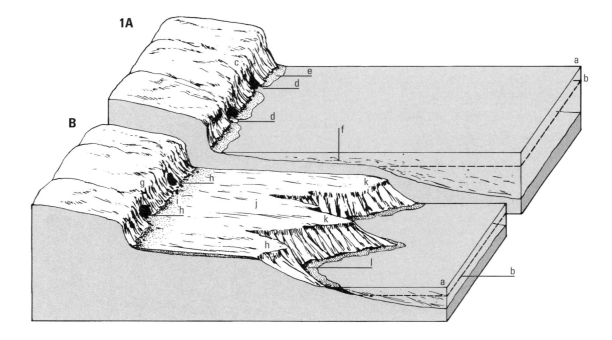

2 Emergent lowland coast

A Before emergence

a Gentle slopes

b River valleys

c Coastline

d Continental shelf

B After emergence

e Valleys deepened by rejuvenated rivers

f Old coastline

g New coastal plain

h New coastline

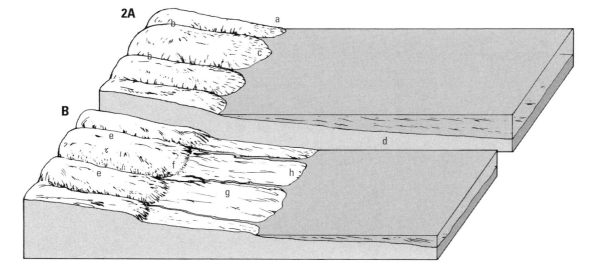

Where coral grows

Coral reefs rim shores and form low islands mainly in the world's warm seas and oceans. Coral is a limestone rock produced by tube-shaped skeletons of billions of coral polyps–animals resembling tiny sea anemones–and by limy algal plants called nullipores. Reefs grow up and out as new organisms build on the old skeletons. Waves pounding the seaward edge hurl broken chunks of coral on the reefs. Meanwhile sand accumulates upon the shoreward side, and reefs become low islands.

Coral polyps need clear, warm, shallow, salty water, found mostly in tropical seas and oceans to the east of continents. But many prehistoric reefs now lie inland in rocks outside the Tropics.

There are three main types of coral reef.

1 Fringing reefs are narrow offshore coral reefs, separated by a shallow lagoon from the nearby coast. Such reefs abound off the Bahamas and Caribbean islands.

2 Barrier reefs are broad coral platforms separated from the coast by a wide, deep channel. At least some formed upon subsiding coasts. The world's largest is northeast Australia's Great Barrier Reef, 1,260 mi (2,027 km) long.

3 Atolls comprise circular chains of coral reefs. Each atoll encloses a lagoon and probably started as a fringing reef around a volcanic island. As the island began to sink and/or sea level rose, coral growth kept pace. Thus the reef became a barrier reef and then an atoll. Borings show that Eniwetok Atoll in the Pacific Ocean grew upward from a volcanic base now more than 4,600 ft (1,400 m) below the surface. Atolls abound chiefly in parts of the Pacific and Indian Oceans. The Pacific's Marshall Islands include the world's largest atoll, Kwajalein–more than 170 mi (274 km) long.

1 Fringing reef

a Edge of land

b Narrow, shallow lagoon

c Living coral

d Mound of dead coral

e High water

f Low water

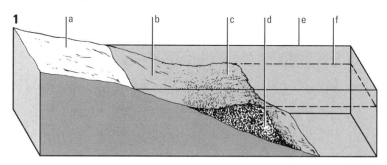

2 Barrier reef

a Edge of land

b Wide, deep lagoon

c Living coral

d Mound of dead coral

e High water

f Low water

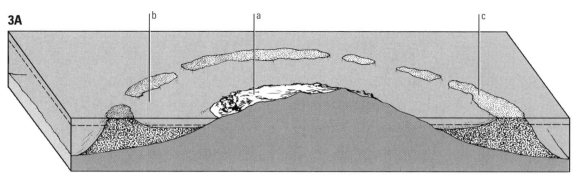

3A Atoll forming

a Slowly sinking volcanic island

b Lagoon

c Barrier reef

3B Atoll formed

a Submerged volcanic island

b Lagoon

c Coral reef

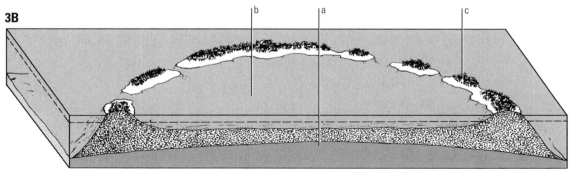

© DIAGRAM

The work of ice and air

Ice corrodes mountains into sharp-tipped peaks and saw-edged ridges. Moving rivers of ice deepen valleys and bevel hills. But melting ice sheds sheets and strips of debris on lowlands, and near an ice sheet, freezing and thawing rework the ground.

Where wind scours deserts, blown sand sculpts rocks and wears hollows in the land. But windblown particles accumulate as dunes and sheets. The work of wind and water creates distinctive landscapes.

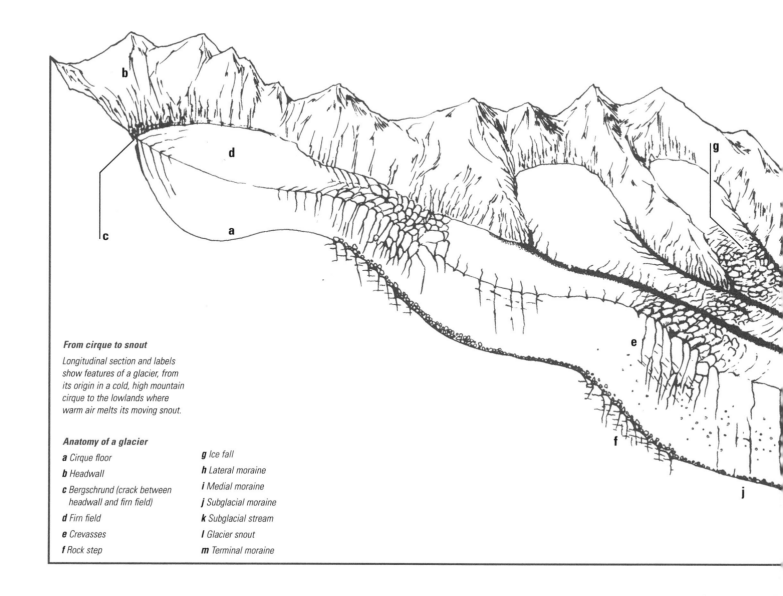

From cirque to snout

Longitudinal section and labels show features of a glacier, from its origin in a cold, high mountain cirque to the lowlands where warm air melts its moving snout.

Anatomy of a glacier

a Cirque floor
b Headwall
c Bergschrund (crack between headwall and firn field)
d Firn field
e Crevasses
f Rock step

g Ice fall
h Lateral moraine
i Medial moraine
j Subglacial moraine
k Subglacial stream
l Glacier snout
m Terminal moraine

Glaciers and ice sheets

Ice covers about 10 percent of all land and 12 percent of the oceans. Most lies in polar sea ice, polar ice sheets and ice caps, valley glaciers, and piedmont glaciers formed by valley glaciers merging on a plain.

Most of Antarctica lies beneath an ice sheet twice the size of Australia and up to 14,000 ft (4,300 m) thick. Another ice sheet covers Greenland. Such vast slabs of ice spread slowly, smothering all but a few projecting peaks, or nunataks. Smaller ice masses, called ice caps, crown parts of Iceland, Norway, and some Arctic islands.

Valley glaciers are tongues of ice in mountain ranges. They start in ice-worn rock basins called cirques. Here, old snow forms firn or névé–a mass of ice pellets compacted by the weight of snow above. Fed by fresh snowfalls, firn spawns a glacier that spills down a valley filling it with ice, perhaps for scores of miles.

Glaciers creep downhill at an inch (2.5 cm) to 100 ft (30 m) a day, depending on conditions. Pressure makes the lower ice plastic enough to flow, but the upper ice stays rigid. Varying gradients and differential rates of flow within the glacier split the surface with deep cracks called crevasses. Where a glacier plunges down a steep rock step, the surface forms an ice fall–a crisscross maze of crevasses and isolated pinnacles.

Frost-shattered rocks and stones falling on the glacier's flanks form lines of lateral moraines. Where a tributary glacier joins a major glacier, two lateral moraines merge as a medial moraine.

Most valley glaciers end in a moraine-rich snout where warm air melts ice as fast as the glacier flows. If ice melts any faster, the snout retreats.

In polar regions, glaciers and ice sheets extend down to the sea. Huge chunks of ice snap off and float away as icebergs. Antarctica's Ross Barrier is an example of a floating slab of ice as big as Spain that remains tethered to the land.

Castellated berg

These bergs plunge into the sea from Arctic glaciers. Vast flat-topped bergs break off the ice shelves that fringe Antarctica. Polar seas also bear vast tracts of sea ice.

Frozen landmasses

Maps locate two landmasses mostly under ice.

A *Antarctica*

B *Greenland*

Block diagrams compare their ice sheets with the areas of two other countries.

C *United States*

D *Mexico*

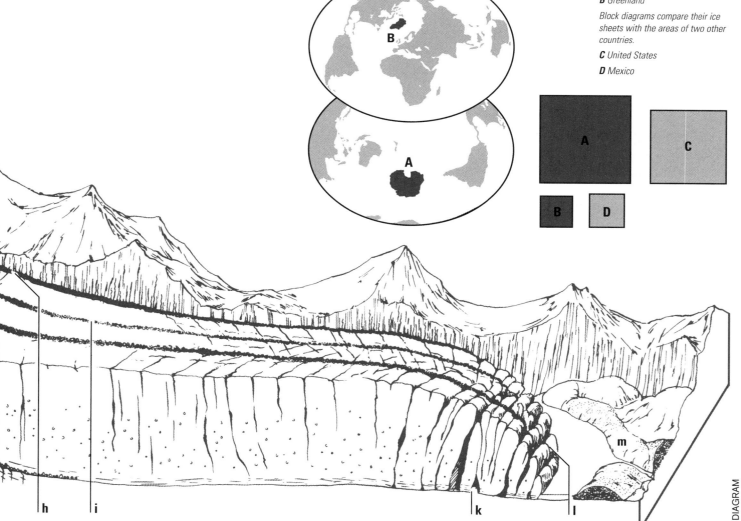

How ice attacks the land

A

B

Ice-worn hummocks (left)

A Roche moutonnée

a Gently sloping upstream side, grooved by stones in moving ice

b Steep, rough, ice-plucked downstream side

B Crag-and-tail

c Ice-rubbed resistant crag

d Protected tail of soft rock

narrow pass called a col. Where at least three cirques converge, arêtes meet in a pyramidal peak. The famous Matterhorn originated in this way.

A glacier that fills a mountain valley shoves loose material ahead and plucks rocks from the valley sides. Loosened stones embedded in the frozen river's flanks scrape more rock from the valley sides. Thus a glacier widens, deepens, and straightens; it changes a valley's V-shaped cross section into the U-shape of the glacial trough. (Glacial troughs invaded by the sea became the fjords of Alaska, Norway, and New Zealand.)

Glacial erosion truncates (lops off) the spurs that jut out into the main valley, and it leaves tributary streams to plunge from the lips of the hanging valleys that end high above the bottom of the trough. Yosemite's Bridalveil Fall is such a waterfall. Rock debris embedded in moving ice scratches and polishes the valley walls and floor, producing tell tale grooves. Similar striations betray the ice sheet that once covered New York's Central Park. Other telltale features include two distinctive types of ice-worn hummocks known as crag-and-tail and roche moutonnée.

When glaciers and icesheets melt, they leave a landscape scraped by moving ice. Ice sheets armed with broken rocks beveled huge tracts of northern Canada and Finland. Frost and moving ice have sharpened peaks and deepened mountain valleys in the Andes, Alps, Himalayas, and Rockies.

Valley-glacier erosion starts high up on hills or mountainsides. Here, freeze-thaw processes fracture rocks, as well as enlarge and deepen shallow snow-filled dips, to form the steep rock basins known as corries, cwms, or cirques. Two cirques eating back into a mountain may leave a knife-edged ridge called an arête, sometimes the cirques make a notched,

A

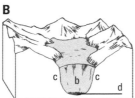

B

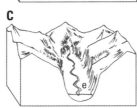

C

Gnawed by ice (above)

Three diagrams show the major changes wrought by glaciation in a mountain valley.

A Before glaciation

a V-shaped cross section

B During glaciation

b Glacier

c Ice-scoured valley sides

d Ice-deepened valley floor

C After glaciation

e Glacial trough with a U-shaped cross section

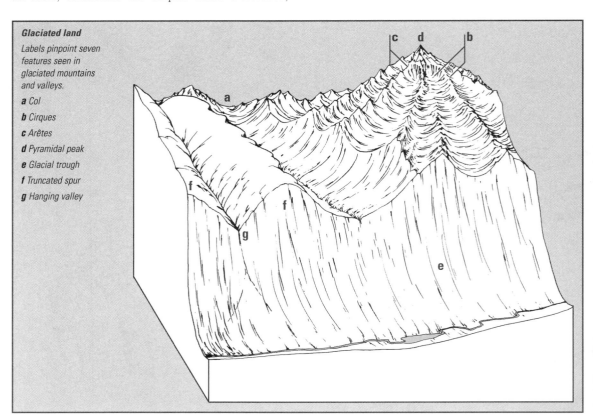

Glaciated land

Labels pinpoint seven features seen in glaciated mountains and valleys.

a Col

b Cirques

c Arêtes

d Pyramidal peak

e Glacial trough

f Truncated spur

g Hanging valley

Debris dumped by ice 1

Glaciers and ice sheets transport in, on, and beneath the ice from where they are formed, substances from finely powdered rock to mighty boulders. Streams emitted by the ice transport more ice-eroded debris. Where glaciers and ice sheets melt, this vast load of drift material remains and modifies the land. Experts calculate that more than one-third of Europe, nearly one-quarter of North America, and one-eighth of the world's land surface is cloaked in debris shed by ice or meltwater.

Debris dumped by glaciers themselves is an unsorted mass of stones and rock embedded in a sandy, clayey matrix known as till or boulder clay. Some till forms under active ice, and some accumulates where ice decays. How and where till forms determines the landscape features in huge tracts of lowland. Retreating ice left the undulating sheets called ground moraine that cover much of the North European plain. Drift added flat floors to many U-shaped glaciated valleys. And where an ice front paused, you will find the long, curved ridges of its terminal or end moraines.

Drumlins are elongated hummocks up to 300 ft (90 m) high and 1 mi (1.6 km) long. Many formed where valley glaciers shed and streamlined drift as they reached a plain and spread out.

Erratic blocks had other origins. Many of these ice-borne rocks lie far from where they started. Some Scottish rocks have ended up in southeast Ireland, and 600 mi (1,000 km) separate Kentucky's red jasper boulders from their nearest possible source north of Lake Huron. Erratic blocks can be enormous. One Albertan specimen reportedly exceeds 18,000 tons.

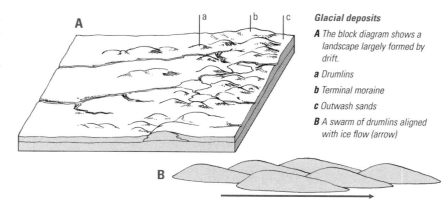

Glacial deposits

A The block diagram shows a landscape largely formed by drift.

a Drumlins

b Terminal moraine

c Outwash sands

B A swarm of drumlins aligned with ice flow (arrow)

Midwest drift deposits

This map marks the southern limits of the glacial deposits laid down by melting ice sheets in the Midwest. Each line marks the farthest advance of a different glacial stage, from Nebraskan (early) to Wisconsin (late).

Wisconsin ⸺ Illinoian ⸺ Kansan ⸺ Nebraskan

Erratic block

An immense granite boulder taller than a man lies on limestone. A melting ice sheet dumped the boulder more than 10,000 years ago.

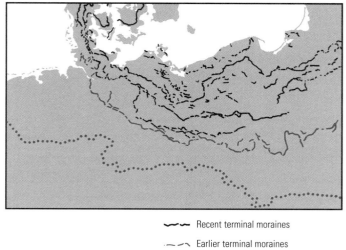

North European moraines

Here we show the southern limits of the glacial deposits laid down by successive, melting ice sheets based on the landscape of Scandinavia. Terminal moraines formed where a melting ice front paused.

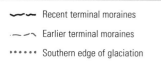

Recent terminal moraines

Earlier terminal moraines

•••••• Southern edge of glaciation

© DIAGRAM

Debris dumped by ice 2

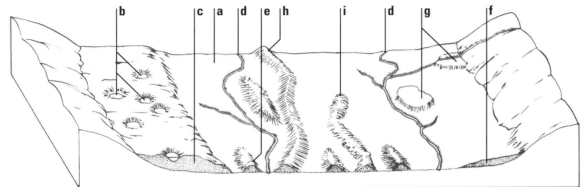

Glacial valley (right)

a Glacier

b Blocks of melting ice

c Lake filled by sediment

d Surface streams

e Crevasses containing sediment shed by streams

f Ice-margin lake

g Deltas

h Subglacial stream

i Englacial stream

Postglacial valley (right)

a Exposed valley floor

b Kettles (ex ice-filled hollows)

c Kame-terrace (old lake bed)

d Streams

e Kames (ex crevasse deposits)

f Kame-terrace (old lake bed)

g Kame-deltas

h Esker from subglacial stream

i Esker from englacial stream

Subglacial sediments (right)

Here we show two situations where a stream beneath a glacier may shed its load:

A The stream flows uphill and loses carrying power.

B The channel widens, so water flows at reduced pressure.

a Ice

b Stream

c Bedrock

d Sediment

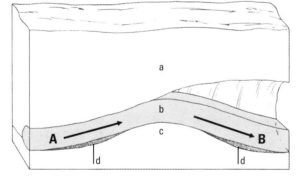

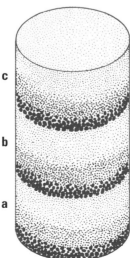

Varve clays (left)

This core sample shows three banded layers, representing sediments laid down in three successive years in a lake liable to winter freezing.

a First year

b Second year

c Third year

Meltwater streams that issue from a glacier or ice sheet produce layered sediments; these therefore differ from the unsorted drift directly dropped by ice. Geologists call them outwash or glaciofluvial deposits.

Outwash takes two main forms: outwash plains and valley trains. Outwash plains are layered sheets of clay, sands, and gravels that fan out over lowlands ahead of where an ice-sheet lay. The largest particles settle near the ice rim. Finer particles may travel many miles. Valley trains are thick outwash deposits covering the floors of deep, narrow, glaciated valleys.

Outwash deposits give rise to the following features:

1 Eskers These long, winding ridges are aligned with the flow of retreating glaciers or ice sheets. They are from a few feet to a few hundred feet wide, up to 100 ft (30 m) high and some extend for many miles. They grow where subglacial streams shed their loads in ice tunnels or at the tunnels' receding mouth. Eskers are plentiful in lowland areas around the Baltic Sea.

2 Kames are mounds that come in two main forms called kame-terraces and kame-moraines. A kame-terrace is a narrow, flat-topped, steep-sided ridge of sediments along a valley side. It formed below a stream or lake trapped between the valley side and a prehistoric glacier. Kame-moraines, or kame-deltas, are complex undulating mounds of sands and gravels dumped along a stagnant ice sheet's rim. Kame-moraines are plentiful in central Ireland and the United States between Long Island and Wisconsin.

3 Kettles are hollows in kame-terraces or kame-moraines, formed where ice blocks melted. Such ice blocks occur today in Iceland.

4 Varve clays are banded layers of fine and coarse material deposited in meltwater lakes fringing ice sheets. Coarse material washed in with the summer thaw. Fine material settled in winter when the lakes froze over. Counting the bands enables geologists to measure post-glacial time year by year in some areas of North America and Sweden.

Around an ice sheet's rim

Permafrost

Map and diagrams contrast the relative extent of permafrost in parts of Asia and North America.

a North Pole
b Arctic Circle
c Northeast Asia
d North America

A Cross section of Alaska showing the north-south extent and depth of permafrost (e) and active layer (f). (Length and depth are drawn to different scales.)

B Similar cross section of northeast Asia

Patterned ground (below)

a Stone polygons one yard (1 m) or more across, with sorted fine material inside

b Stone stripes: parallel lines of stones formed on steep slopes under the influence of soil creep

Ice
Water
Sediment

Pingo formation (above)

A Prepingo land surface
B Ice lens forms underground.
C Expanding ice lens pushes up a dome in the land surface.
D Tension cracks in the dome expose the ice lens.
E Melting ice creates a pond.
F Sediment collects on the pond floor.

Prolonged freezing and brief summer thawing around an ice sheet's rim produces the periglacial ("around the ice") or tundra landscapes of far northern Eurasia and North America. Some periglacial features dating from the last glaciation still show in lands much farther south.

A major feature is permafrost–permanently frozen ground beneath the surface. In places, Siberian permafrost extends 2,000 ft (610 m) deep. Above it lies the active layer, 6–20 ft (2–6 m) thick. In summer, meltwater fills and lubricates the active layer; sloping surfaces then creep downhill upon the frozen layer beneath. Known as solifluction, this process dumps head deposits of frost-shattered rocks, like the chalk-rubble coombe deposits still seen in parts of southern England.

Freeze-thaw affects both solid rock and loose materials. On north-facing slopes, freeze-thaw beneath snow patches loosens bits of bedrock, and meltwater and solifluction carry them away. Called nivation, this sequence wears big nivation hollows into the rock. Below loose surfaces, freezing water expands, so the ground heaves. Repeated heaving sorts out large and small soil particles. The result is patterned ground with stones arranged in circles, nets, polygons, and stripes.

Other hallmarks of the periglacial fringe include ice wedges, thermokarst, and pingos.

Ice wedges form where cracks appear in frozen ground. Meltwater fills the cracks and freezes as ice

wedges that taper downward for as much as 35 ft (l0 m). Gravel often fills old ice wedges.

Where ground ice melts it often leaves a surface pocked by hollows, superficially like a karst limestone surface, and thus called thermokarst.

The strangest periglacial features are pingos–cones or domes 20–300 ft (6–90 m) high. These earth or gravel humps occur where freezing water expands between an almost frozen surface and the permafrost, pushing up an earth or gravel blister.

Ice wedge (left)

Erosion of a subarctic river bank reveals a V-shaped ice wedge taller than a man.

© DIAGRAM

Wind the eroder

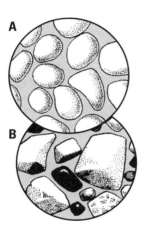

Wind the transporter (above)

Wind moves different particles at different levels.

a Dust particles

b Sand grains

c Tiny pebbles

Sands compared (above)

A *Polished, rounded, "frosted" desert grains*

B *More angular sand grains from a river bed*

In tropical and mid-latitude deserts, wind picks up specks of weathered rock and hurls them far across the barren land. Fine particles of silts and clays whirl high above the ground in dust storms. Sand grains hop and skip across the countryside. Tiny pebbles roll and slide. The process of sandblasting does the most to bevel desert rocks. Attacking pebbles, soft rocks, and rock crevices, windblown desert sand creates the erosion features shown below.

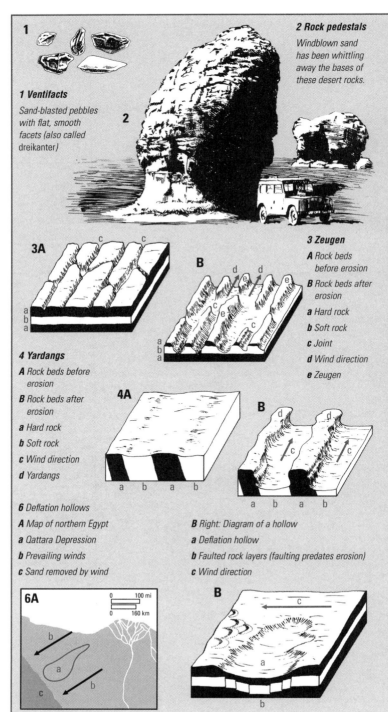

1 Ventifacts

Sand-blasted pebbles with flat, smooth facets (also called dreikanter)

2 Rock pedestals

Windblown sand has been whittling away the bases of these desert rocks.

3A

4 Yardangs

A *Rock beds before erosion*

B *Rock beds after erosion*

a *Hard rock*

b *Soft rock*

c *Wind direction*

d *Yardangs*

4A

3 Zeugen

A *Rock beds before erosion*

B *Rock beds after erosion*

a *Hard rock*

b *Soft rock*

c *Joint*

d *Wind direction*

e *Zeugen*

6 Deflation hollows

A *Map of northern Egypt*

a *Qattara Depression*

b *Prevailing winds*

c *Sand removed by wind*

B *Right: Diagram of a hollow*

a *Deflation hollow*

b *Faulted rock layers (faulting predates erosion)*

c *Wind direction*

6A

0 ___ 100 mi
0 ___ 160 km

Wind erosion

1 Ventifacts are stones with surfaces smoothed and flattened through prolonged attack by windblown sand.

2 Rock pedestals are mushroom-shaped rocks, often made of horizontal rock layers. Sand gnaws into their bases, but winds are seldom strong enough to lift sand grains above waist height. (Sand can similarly cut rock caves.)

3 Zeugen are parallel, flat-topped ridges of hard rock up to 100 ft (30 m) high. They are left standing when sand has widened joints in horizontal hard rock and gnawed into the softer rock beneath.

4 Yardangs are parallel ridges of hard rock up to 50 ft (15 m) high. They form where alternating hard and soft rock layers were upended. Wind gnaws the soft rock into furrows, but leaves the hard rock standing. Yardangs occur especially in Central Asia and Chile's Atacama Desert.

5 Rock pavement, or **hamada**, is a flat, wind-smoothed rocky desert surface (not shown).

6 Deflation hollows are worn or deepened in a desert surface by the wind. Egypt's Qattara Depression–the world's largest deflation hollow–is about as big as New Jersey, and as much as 400 ft (121 m) below the level of the sea. It is partly a tectonically formed feature, further eroded by the wind. Southwest Africa, western Australia, and Mongolia have smaller wind-worn "saucers." Some expose supplies of underground freshwater, which produces swamps or lakes, or supports fertile oases.

Windblown deposits

In barren lands wind freely moves huge quantities of tiny particles eroded from the rocks. In deserts and near prehistoric ice sheets, these windblown fragments cloak vast areas with shifting sands or layers of cemented dust.

In some deserts winds, slowed by passing over pebbles, shed sand in smooth or undulating sheets. But winds blowing steadily from one direction pile sand into the mobile hillocks known as dunes. Those described below are the best-known forms.

Windblown particles finer than sand settle far beyond their point of origin. Loosely cemented silt-sized grains from Mongolia's Gobi Desert form layers up to 1,000 ft (300 m) thick in northern China. Geologists call these deposits loess, from a German word for "loose." Known as adobe in the US and as *limon* in France, similar material covers parts of North America and Europe where winds blew dust from sands and clays deposited by ice sheets in the Pleistocene.

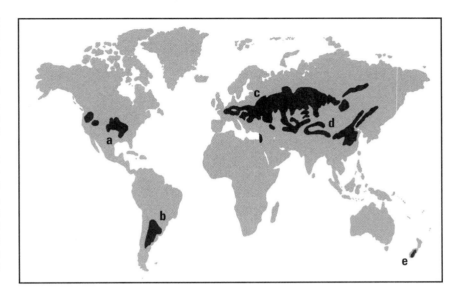

Loess deposits (above)

World map that locates loess and loess-like deposits in four continents and in New Zealand.
a *North America*
b *South America*
c *Europe*
d *Asia*
e *New Zealand*

Dunes

1 Head and tail dunes grow in dead air spaces near a rock or shrub. The long leeward tail can grow to almost half a mile (750 m) long.

2 Barkhans are dunes with low, curved flanks like horns, blown forward faster than the middle. Some barkhans grow 100 ft (30 m) high. Each migrates as wind pushes sand across its crest.

3 Seif ("sword") dunes form long, wavy ridges up to 700 ft (215 m) high; they are thrown up by vortices in a prevailing wind or where barkhans are elongated by a cross wind.

1 Head and tail dune

a *Obstacle impeding flow of windblown sand*

b *Head dune on windward side of obstacle*

c *Tail dune on leeward side*

d *Wind direction*

2 Barkhans

a *Gentle windward face*

b *Steep leeward face*

c *Horns*

d *Prevailing wind*

e *Eddy*

3 Seif dunes

A *Seif dune pattern*

a *Seif dunes: long, narrow, straight, and parallel*

b *Corridors*

c *Prevailing wind*

d *Eddies*

B *Barkhan into seif*

a *Barkhan and prevailing wind*

b *Wind shifts: one horn lengthens.*

c *Wind vacillates.*

d *Later: seif takes shape.*

© DIAGRAM

Lands shaped by wind and water

Eight desert features

Numbered items in this diagram correspond with items featured in the text.

1 Mesa
2 Butte
3 Inselberg
4 Pediment
5 Canyon
6 Wadi
7 Alluvial fan
8 Playa

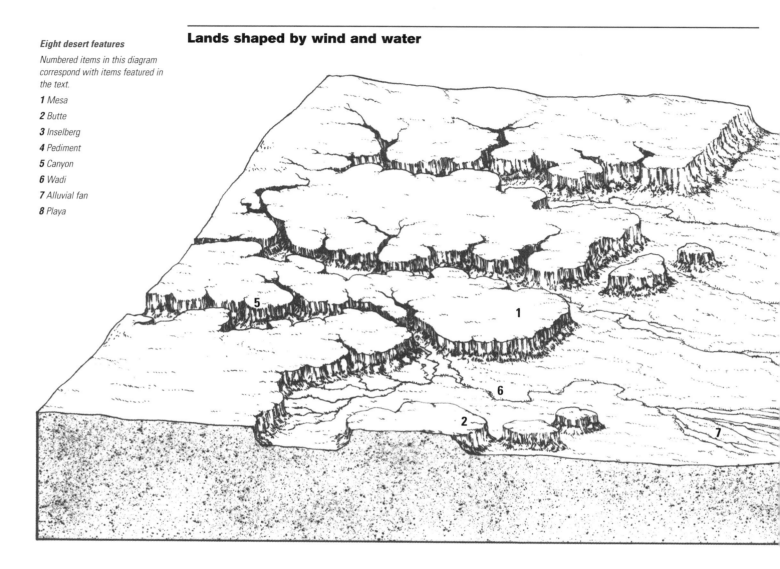

Desert weathering, flash floods, and/or windborne sand produce five main types of desert landscape: (**1**) jagged rock peaks, as in Sinai and the Sahara's Tibesti Mountains; (**2**) desert plateau with steep cliffs and deep, narrow river valleys; (**3**) stony, gravelly desert, also called *reg* or *serir*; (**4**) bare rock desert called a *hamada*; and (**5**) sand desert, also called *erg* or *koum*. Most have harsher features than you find in lands where vegetation softens the effects of sun, wind, frost, and rain. These five desert features figure mainly in such regions as the Colorado plateau:

1 Mesa Flat-topped, steep-sided plateau of horizontal strata capped by erosion-resistant rock.

2 Butte Isolated flat-topped hill, like a mesa but smaller.

3 Inselberg Steep, isolated hill with a narrow summit.

4 Pediment Gentle slope often covered with loose rock and lying below a mesa, butte, inselberg, or ridge. Pediments seem to be formed by weathering and floodwater.

5 Canyon Deep gorge of a river, often one flowing through a desert but fed by water from outside.

6 Wadi Usually dry desert watercourse, also called an *arroyo*, wash, or *nullah*.

7 Alluvial fan Fan-shaped mass of alluvial deposits shed by a fast-flowing mountain stream entering a plain or broad valley.

8 Playa (salt pan) Temporary brackish lake; many are found in Nevada and Utah.

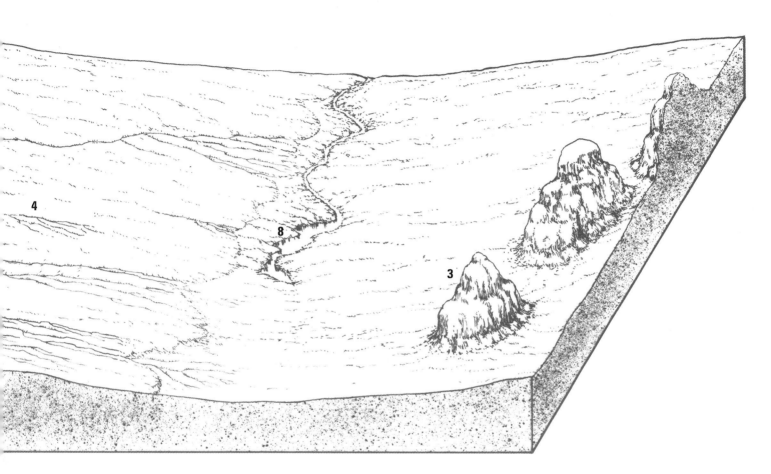

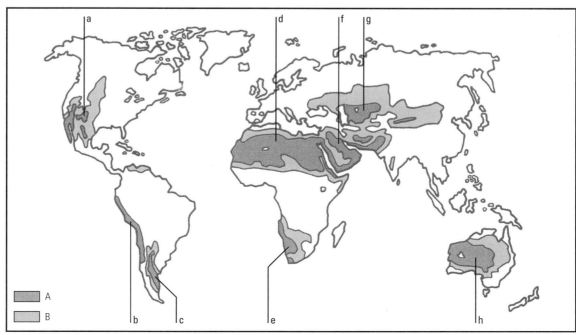

The world's deserts

*Arid (**A**) and semiarid (**B**) areas lie
mainly in the dry hearts of
continents.*

a North American desert

b Peruvian-Atacama desert

c Patagonian desert

d Sahara Desert

e Southwestern African deserts

f Middle Eastern deserts

g Central Asian deserts

h Australian desert

A

B

© DIAGRAM

Change through the ages

Processes producing and destroying land have shaped the crust ever since our planet developed its solid rocky skin. Geologist-detectives can now identify the broad sequence of events. Chronometric dating and relative dating based on layered rocks and fossils help scientists read the story in the rocks, but the first three of its four great volumes—time spans known as eons—are the least known and the longest.

Which formed when? (right)

*Volcanic ash (**a**) fell on limestone (**b**) laid down on glacial debris (**c**) dumped on slate (**d**) changed from preexisting shale by granite (**e**). A diabase (dolerite) dike (**f**) pierced **d** and **c** before **a** and **b** formed. Glacial erosion explains the unconformity at **g**.*

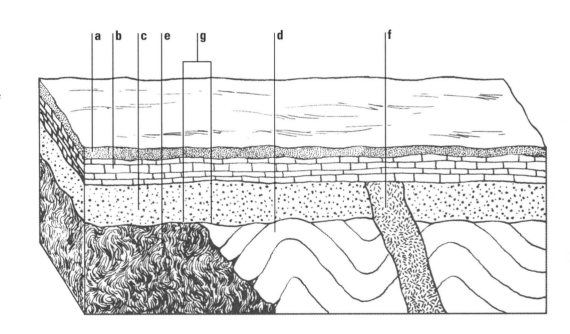

Migrating shoreline (below)

Facies change vertically where rising sea level moved a shoreline to the right.

A *Sea*

B *Beach*

C *Lagoon*

a *Limestone*

b *Fine sand*

c *Coarse sand*

d *Windblown sand*

e *Mud*

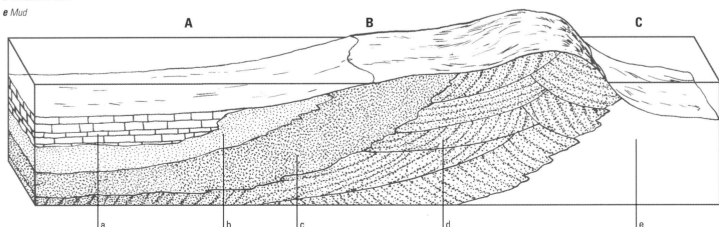

Relative dating: using rocks

Earth's history lies locked up in the rocks that form its crust. Sedimentary rock layers, or strata, were laid down on top of one another, like pages in a history book. Reading these pages is the study called stratigraphy. Much of this is based on studying the properties of rocks themselves.

Geologists identify individual strata largely by such properties as grain size, minerals, and color. These features and distinctive fossils (see p. 92) help experts to define rock units, or formations. Geologists may divide formations into members and beds or lump them together in subgroups, groups, or supergroups. (For time rock units see p. 94.)

Many pages in Earth's "book" are torn, turned upside down, displaced, or lost. Stratigraphy involves working out the true sequence in which rock strata formed in any given place, matching these with layers elsewhere, and noting local gaps where erosion has wiped strata from the record.

Various clues help rock detectives discover where earth movements or injected molten rock have tampered with the evidence. For instance, steeply sloping strata never formed that way. Faults, folds, and injections of molten rock are younger than the rocks they affect. Mud cracks, ripple marks, and pillow lava create distinctive patterns on a layer's upper surface, which becomes its base if the rock is overturned. A break between level rock layers above and crumpled layers below is an unconformity, suggesting a time gap when rock layers vanished by erosion.

Other clues help experts correlate the age of rocks formed at the same time in different places. Widely separated strata may share a unique set of characters, or facies. Migrating shorelines may mark a worldwide fall or rise in sea level. Widespread layers of volcanic ash could hint at an immense volcanic eruption. Lavas or sediments accumulating at the same time lock in particles aligned in the same direction by the Earth's magnetic field which has undergone a sequence of reversals. Matched alignments and matched fossils help geologists to correlate the relative ages of rock cores sampled from around the world.

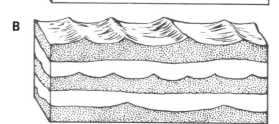

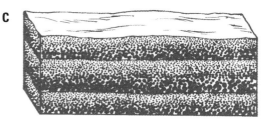

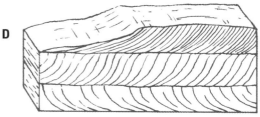

Clues to age sequences
Youngest rocks are at the top.
A *Mud cracks*
B *Ripple marks*
C *Graded bedding*
D *Cross bedding*
E *Pillow lava*

Sill or buried lava flow?
(below)

*The following clues help geologists tell a sill (**A**) from a buried lava flow (**B**).*
a *Chilled margin*
b *Baked contact*
c *Weathered lava surface*
d *Eroded bits of lava in an overlying bed*

Paleomagnetism (below)

As this volcano erupted, magnetic minerals in the lava aligned to match the lines of force in the Earth's magnetic field.
a *Magnetic north*
b *Lava*
c *Lines of force*
d *Aligned minerals, enlarged*

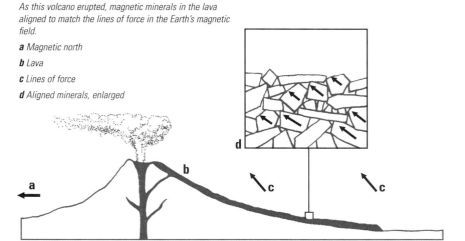

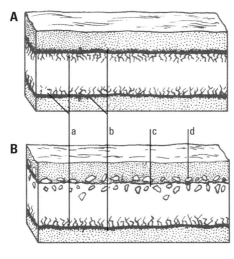

© DIAGRAM

Relative dating: fossils

Fossils offer valuable aids to relatively dating sedimentary rock strata and correlating these around the world. This process, biostratigraphy, involves identifying faunal zones–rock strata containing unique assemblages of fossils. Geologists name each faunal zone after a distinctive species called a zone fossil.

Besides providing guides to evolution and the ages of rocks, fossil individuals and groups reveal how prehistoric living things behaved and the kinds of place and climate they inhabited.

There are limits to our knowledge. Most soft-bodied organisms left no fossil record. Relatively few land plants and animals were fossilized. Billions of fossils vanished when erosion wore away the rocks containing them, or these were baked or crushed by metamorphic change. Billions more are inaccessible. But new kinds of fossil are discovered every year.

Faunal provinces (below)

*Two groups of fossil trilobite (**a**,**b**) and graptolite (**c**,**d**) mark two faunal provinces–shelf seas flanking a pre–Atlantic Ocean around 500 million years ago.*

A *Land (proto-Greenland)*

B *Land (proto-Europe)*

C *Iapetus (pre-Atlantic) Ocean*

D *Pacific province*

E *Atlantic province*

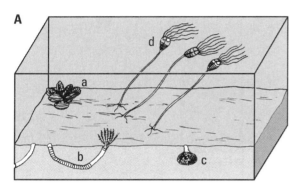

A

A Prehistoric community (left)

a *Shellfish*

b *Worm*

c *Sea urchin*

d *Crinoid (sea lily)*

B Fossils found (below)

Undisturbed fossils (below) aided reconstruction of the seabed community (left).

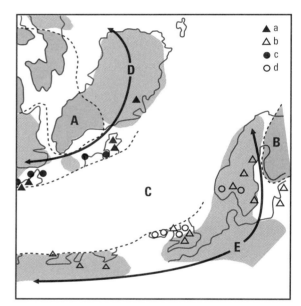

▲ a
△ b
● c
○ d

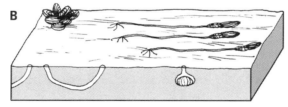

B

A

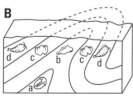

B

Fossils, faults, and folds (above)

*Key fossils help geologists date rock layers disturbed by (**A**) faults or (**B**) folding.*

a *Cambrian trilobite*

b *Ordovician crinoid (sea lily)*

c *Silurian brachiopod (lamp shell)*

d *Devonian eurypterid (sea scorpion)*

e *Carboniferous blastoid (kin to starfish and sea urchin)*

f *Permian ceratite ammonoid*

g *Triassic ammonite*

Zone fossils

A good zone fossil meets four requirements: Its species was extremely plentiful; spread far and fast (planktonic organisms are examples); left readily preserved remains; yet soon died out, thereby limiting its fossils to a few rock layers. Most such organisms lived in the sea. They ranged from sizable (macrofossil) animals and plants to tiny (microfossil) forms. Here are four examples:

1 Trilobites (three-lobed) were marine, segmented, distant relatives of wood lice; zone macrofossils for rocks 540–490 million years old.

2 Ammonoids were cephalopod mollusks with coiled, flat, wrinkled shells; zone macrofossils for rocks 370–65 million years old.

3 Bivalves are headless mollusks with hinged, two-part shells; zone macrofossils for rocks 370–65 million years old.

4 Foraminiferans are tiny one-celled protozoan organisms drifting in the seas and forming limy shells pierced by tiny holes; zone microfossils for rocks up to 65 million years old.

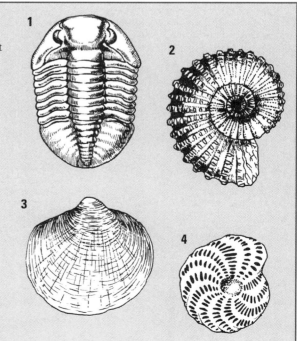

Clocks in rocks

Chronometric dating gives approximate ages in years for the rocks. Some rare sediments are datable from annually added layers. Some rocks are dated by the known rate of decay of a radioactive element into a more stable element. The more time that elapses, less of the parent element remains and more of the daughter element accumulates. So measuring the proportions of both elements within a rock reveals its age. For igneous rock this means how long ago its minerals crystallized; for sedimentary rock, it indicates when sedimentation produced certain minerals; for metamorphic rock, it shows when heat drove daughter elements from the rock and "reset" the geological clock.

Various elements and their isotopes (different forms of atom of a given element) give best results in different circumstances. Here are brief details of three radiometric techniques and one based on nuclear fission:

1 Potassium-argon dating uses the decay of the potassium-40 isotope into argon-40. Applications: mainly igneous and metamorphic rocks of any age greater than about 1 million years, and sedimentary rocks containing the mineral glauconite.

2 Rubidium-strontium dating uses the decay of rubidium-87 to strontium-87. Applications: igneous and metamorphic rocks (except basic types), and sedimentary rocks containing the mineral illite. This method is often best for rocks more than 30 million years old.

3 Uranium-thorium-lead methods employ radioactive isotopes in uranium. Uranium-235 decays to lead-207; thorium-232 decays to lead-208. Applications: igneous intrusions, metamorphic rocks, and sediments containing zircon. These methods are best for rocks more than 100 million years old.

4 Fission-track dating requires counting the fission tracks produced in rock by the splitting nuclei of uranium-238, whose nuclei split at a known and constant rate. The older the rock, the more fission tracks there are. Applications: many igneous and metamorphic rocks.

Fission-track dating

Fission tracks in a crystal are etched to make them show up, then counted under a microscope. The more tracks, the older the crystal.

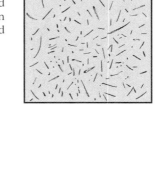

Dating diabase

Five illustrations depict six stages in dating a diabase (dolerite) dike injected into older rocks:

1 *This cross section shows a diabase dike (**a**) injected into preexisting granite (**b**) before overlying sandstone (**c**) formed.*

2 *A lump of diabase is dropped into a crusher that grinds the rock until it breaks up into component mineral grains.*

3 *Froth flotation separates micas from other minerals.*

4 *A mass spectrometer using a magnetic field separates and measures the amounts of isotopes of potassium and argon.*

a Gas inlet
b Electron beam
c Slits
d Ion accelerating voltage
e Ion beam
f Isotopes
g Detector slit
h Magnetic field

5 *A computer printout of the isotope data enables the calculation of the diabase's potassium argon age. (Potassium is the parent element, and argon is the daughter element.)*

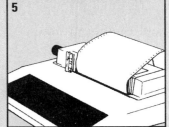
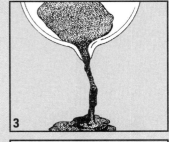
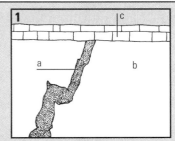

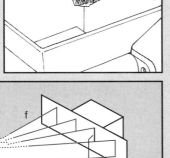

Radiometric dating (above)

By radiation potassium-40 loses half its mass every 1310 million years (one half life). Thus a sample's potassium-40 content can indicate its age.

A *Original sample*
B *After 1.3 billion years (one half life) half remains.*
C *After 2.6 billion years (two half lives) one quarter remains.*
D *After 3.9 billion years (three half lives) one-eighth remains.*
E *After 5.2 billion years (four half lives) one-sixteenth remains.*

© DIAGRAM

The geological column

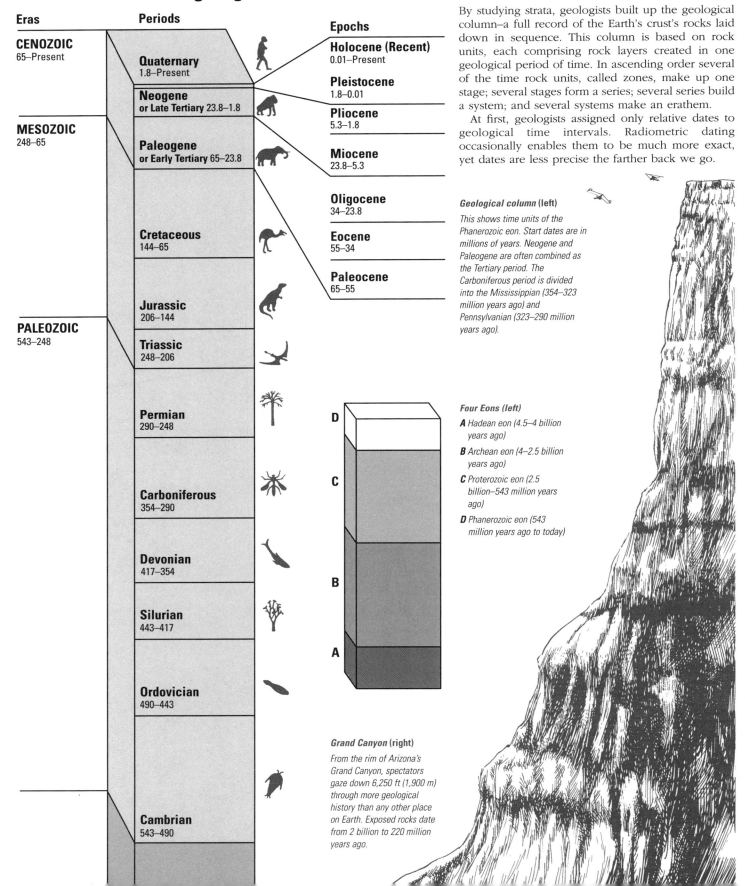

Eras

CENOZOIC
65–Present

MESOZOIC
248–65

PALEOZOIC
543–248

Periods

Quaternary
1.8–Present

Neogene
or Late Tertiary 23.8–1.8

Paleogene
or Early Tertiary 65–23.8

Cretaceous
144–65

Jurassic
206–144

Triassic
248–206

Permian
290–248

Carboniferous
354–290

Devonian
417–354

Silurian
443–417

Ordovician
490–443

Cambrian
543–490

Epochs

Holocene (Recent)
0.01–Present

Pleistocene
1.8–0.01

Pliocene
5.3–1.8

Miocene
23.8–5.3

Oligocene
34–23.8

Eocene
55–34

Paleocene
65–55

By studying strata, geologists built up the geological column—a full record of the Earth's crust's rocks laid down in sequence. This column is based on rock units, each comprising rock layers created in one geological period of time. In ascending order several of the time rock units, called zones, make up one stage; several stages form a series; several series build a system; and several systems make an erathem.

At first, geologists assigned only relative dates to geological time intervals. Radiometric dating occasionally enables them to be much more exact, yet dates are less precise the farther back we go.

Geological column (left)

This shows time units of the Phanerozoic eon. Start dates are in millions of years. Neogene and Paleogene are often combined as the Tertiary period. The Carboniferous period is divided into the Mississippian (354–323 million years ago) and Pennsylvanian (323–290 million years ago).

Four Eons (left)

A Hadean eon (4.5–4 billion years ago)

B Archean eon (4–2.5 billion years ago)

C Proterozoic eon (2.5 billion–543 million years ago)

D Phanerozoic eon (543 million years ago to today)

Grand Canyon (right)

From the rim of Arizona's Grand Canyon, spectators gaze down 6,250 ft (1,900 m) through more geological history than any other place on Earth. Exposed rocks date from 2 billion to 220 million years ago.

The ancient age

The first three eons of Earth history are the longest and least-known. The Hadean eon lasted from 4.5 to 4 billion years ago. Seemingly no rocks survive from the Hadean eon when the early Earth's crust was still molten. The Archean eon (Ancient Age) lasted from 4 to 2.5 billion years ago. The earliest-known surviving rocks on Earth are 3.9 billion years old. But they are older rocks reworked. The world probably already had some continental rock, an ocean, and an atmosphere–all produced by the resorting of the Earth's less dense ingredients. Geologists do not agree how that occurred–perhaps as follows:

The crust and mantle were probably more active at that time than today. Where two cooling mantle currents met and sank, they squashed, thickened, and melted the thin primeval crust above. Repeated melting could have resorted its ingredients until the lightest formed a scum of continental igneous rocks that with others metamorphosed into gneisses. There maybe appeared "granitoid" microcontinents in this way, with some still surviving as the ancient cores of continents.

Wrapped around these microcontinents were greenstone belts of lightly metamorphosed greenish dark volcanic rock, combined with shales and sandstones. The volcanic rock came perhaps from volcanoes spewing lava, ash, and gas from scores of hotspots in a weak, thin, early crust. Or they were island arc volcanoes, and the shales and sandstones formed from sediments washed off nearby microcontinents. Perhaps volcanic steam that cooled and turned to rain filled early ocean basins and the rivers that eroded rocks. Certainly volcanic gases formed an early atmosphere, rich in nitrogen and carbon dioxide.

Fossil organisms in the greenstone belts reveal that life appeared at least 3.5 billion years ago. Bacteria and blue-green algae were flourishing in shallow seas. Oxygen released each year by algae combined with iron, producing the banded iron formations now mined around the world. But iron and other chemical sponges left little oxygen for adding to the atmosphere.

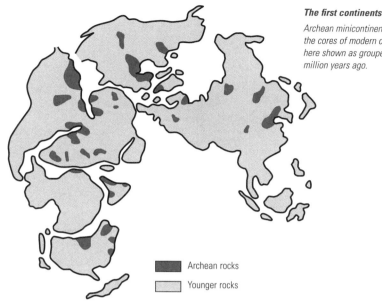

The first continents

Archean minicontinents became the cores of modern continents, here shown as grouped about 250 million years ago.

■ Archean rocks

▢ Younger rocks

Archean rocks (left)

A satellite view shows these features.

a Cratons (granitoid continental nuclei)

b Greenstone belts

© DIAGRAM

Continental growth (below)

Continental sediments (a) and volcanic rocks (b) increased in volume, while greenstone belt volcanic rocks (c) and sediments (d) decreased. The scale shows millions of years ago.

Stromatolites (left)

Blue-green algae formed intertidal pedestals like these, 3.5 billion years ago.

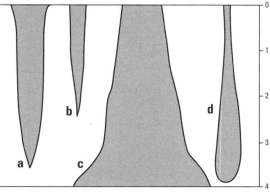

The age of former life

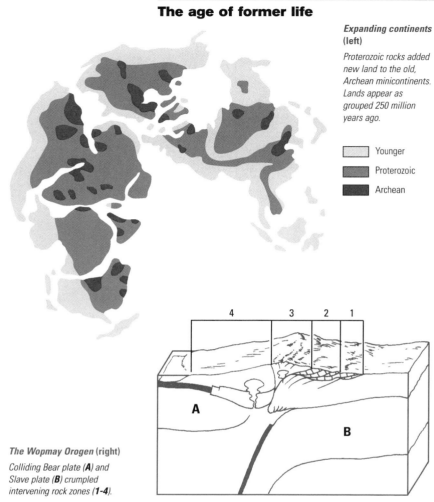

Expanding continents (left)

Proterozoic rocks added new land to the old, Archean minicontinents. Lands appear as grouped 250 million years ago.

	Younger
	Proterozoic
	Archean

About 2.5 billion years ago the first large continents appeared, and extensive, shallow, offshore seas gave new opportunities for living things to develop. These changes ushered in the third phase of Earth history. The Proterozoic eon (Age of Former Life) spanned 1.9 billion years, ending about 540 million years ago New "granitoid" and greenstone belts emerged, and vast masses of volcanic rocks and sediments were tacked on to Archean microcontinents.

Geologists detect three main construction phases, starting 1.9 billion, 1.2 billion, and 700 million years ago. The first produced the Wopmay Orogen–a long-since beveled mountain belt in northern Canada. Such ancient sites hold traces of old oceanic crust, island arcs, and colliding continents. This shows that plate tectonics was already molding continental and oceanic crust. Alignments of magnetic particles in rocks prove that continents were drifting and ocean floor was rifting and subducting by 1.5 billion years ago. Some evidence suggests that major continents were even stuck together at that time.

Meanwhile, the oceans and the atmosphere were undergoing change. Salts washed off land gave the sea its present saltiness. By about 2 billion years ago, cyanobacteria produced enough free oxygen for some to start accumulating in the sea and atmosphere. (Proof comes from compounds formed in certain rocks.)

Atmospheric oxygen began to build an ozone shield protecting living things from the Sun's lethal ultraviolet radiation. New, complex kinds of water life evolved, able to exploit the energy in oxygen. Soon after 700 million years ago, soft corals, jellyfish, worms, and other soft-bodied animals perhaps flourished in shallow seas off continental shores.

The Wopmay Orogen (right)

*Colliding Bear plate (**A**) and Slave plate (**B**) crumpled intervening rock zones (**1-4**).*

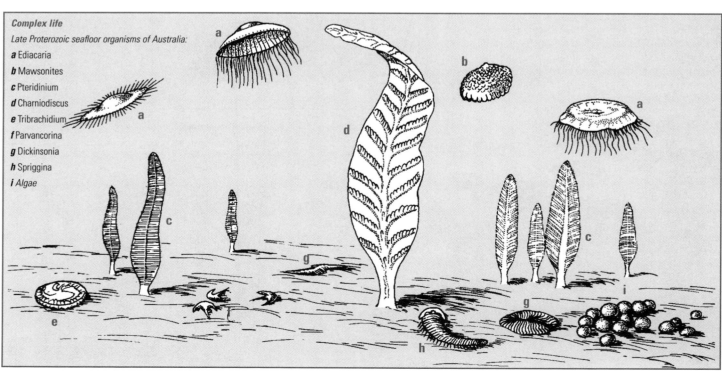

Complex life

Late Proterozoic seafloor organisms of Australia:

a Ediacaria
b Mawsonites
c Pteridinium
d Charniodiscus
e Tribrachidium
f Parvancorina
g Dickinsonia
h Spriggina
i Algae

The age of visible life

The last 540 million years or so form the Phanerozoic eon, or Age of Visible Life. The Phanerozoic saw complex modern life forms in the making.

Assemblages that lived at different times have led geologists to split the eon into three successive eras: the Paleozoic, or Age of Ancient Life (about 543–248 million years ago); Mesozoic, or Age of Middle Life (about 248–65 million years ago); and Cenozoic, or Age of Recent Life (about 65–0 million years ago). Fossil assemblages differing in time and place help experts reconstruct each era's climates, lands, seas, and oceans.

By coordinating fossil clues with those left by the rocks themselves, geologists have reconstructed how and why continents drifted, seas and oceans spread and shrank, mountain ranges rose and were worn down, and ice sheets waxed and waned.

Much remains unknown. For instance paleomagnetism reveals the past north-south positions of the continents, but their longitudes (east-west locations) lie open to dispute.

Even so, the following pages stress key events in each era's successive periods–the later chapters in the story of the Earth.

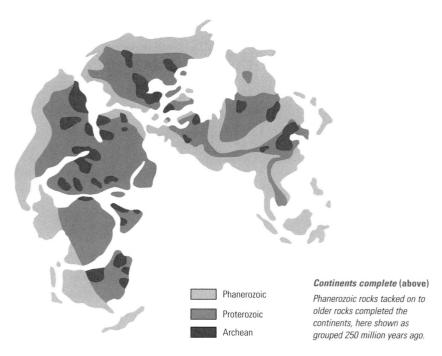

Phanerozoic

Proterozoic

Archean

Continents complete (above)

Phanerozoic rocks tacked on to older rocks completed the continents, here shown as grouped 250 million years ago.

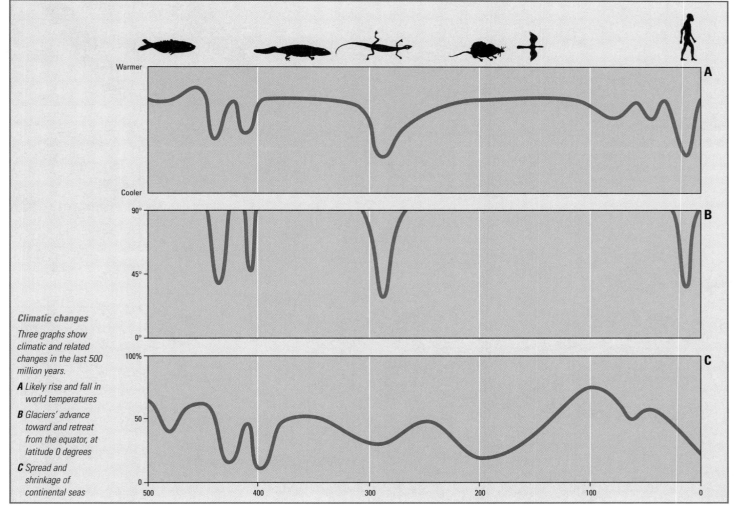

Climatic changes

Three graphs show climatic and related changes in the last 500 million years.

A *Likely rise and fall in world temperatures*

B *Glaciers' advance toward and retreat from the equator, at latitude 0 degrees*

C *Spread and shrinkage of continental seas*

Cambrian world (above)

Lands might have been arranged like this. Lines show the equator, Tropics, and Polar regions.

Cambrian period

The Cambrian period (about 543–490 million years ago) takes its name from the Latin word for Wales. Here geologists first studied Cambrian fossils—the first abundant animals with skeletons and shells. All life inhabited water. It teemed in shallow seas that invaded continents as ice sheets melted about 600 million years ago. Cambrian times were generally warmer than today.

Most continental lands probably lay on or close to the equator. South America, Africa, India, Antarctica, Australia, and bits of Asia were evidently welded into one southern supercontinent—Gondwanaland—with Africa "upside down." Among lesser chunks of continental crust were the cores of North America, Greenland, Europe, and northwest Africa. The Iapetus Ocean—a pre–Atlantic Ocean—had opened up between these once-fused lands. Within this ocean lay Avalonia, an archipelago whose rocks today lie scattered from the Carolinas, north through Newfoundland, to parts of Ireland and Wales.

By 570 million years ago mountains had sprouted in the Avalonian orogeny when a slab of land struck eastern North America to form New England. Elsewhere, the Andes mountains had begun to grow, and volcanoes spewed vast sheets of lava over parts of north and west Australia.

Sands that washed off land into shallow seas provided raw materials for sandstones. Animals with shells became a source of carbonates, and dolomite began to form. Other Cambrian sediments include blue clays that still survive in Russia.

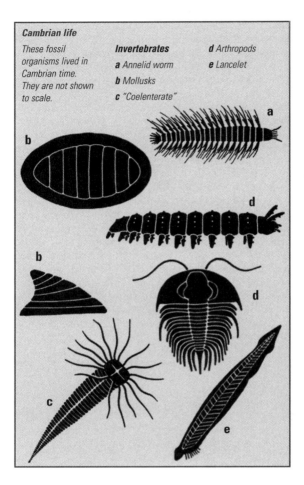

Cambrian life

These fossil organisms lived in Cambrian time. They are not shown to scale.

Invertebrates
a Annelid worm
b Mollusks
c "Coelenterate"

d Arthropods
e Lancelet

Cambrian rocks exposed (below)

Cambrian limestone overlying Cambrian quartzite form these high cliffs in Canada's Banff National Park. The cliffs' materials were laid down as immensely thick deposits in shallow water off what was then the northwest rim of proto-North America.

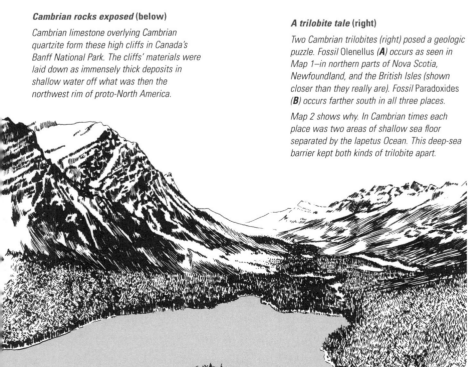

A trilobite tale (right)

*Two Cambrian trilobites (right) posed a geologic puzzle. Fossil Olenellus (**A**) occurs as seen in Map 1–in northern parts of Nova Scotia, Newfoundland, and the British Isles (shown closer than they really are). Fossil Paradoxides (**B**) occurs farther south in all three places.*

Map 2 shows why. In Cambrian times each place was two areas of shallow sea floor separated by the Iapetus Ocean. This deep-sea barrier kept both kinds of trilobite apart.

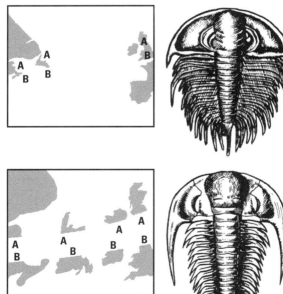

Ordovician period

Rocks from this time (about 490–443 million years ago) were first studied in Wales; an early Welsh tribe, the Ordovices, inspired the period's name.

Subduction brought slow shrinkage of the Iapetus Ocean and a closing up of its flanking continental cores: Laurentia (proto-North America and Greenland), Baltica (proto-Europe), and northwest Africa. Early on, subducting or colliding crustal blocks deformed rocks of the future Scottish Highlands. Later, the Taconic orogeny forced up the Green Mountains of Vermont. Volcanic rocks appeared in Scandinavia and Greenland.

Although large slabs of continental crust lay close to the equator, part of Gondwanaland moved deep into Antarctic latitudes. Indeed northwest Africa lay astride the South Pole. Late Ordovician ice-scoured rocks and ice-borne debris show that ice sheets covered northwest Africa and nearby parts of South America.

At their maximum extent the ice sheets locked up much of the world's water, and shallow continental seas withdrew. But from time to time, warm, shallow, salty water invaded lowlands including parts of proto-North America. Here lived trilobites, early corals, and many more invertebrates. The small colonial organisms called graptolites left fossils used for correlating the ages of Ordovician rocks from different areas. There were early jawless fishes, too.

Ordovician sediments up to 23,000 ft (7,000 m) thick formed in continental seas and offshore waters. North America, Europe, and north Australia all accumulated beds of limestone, dolomite, and coral.

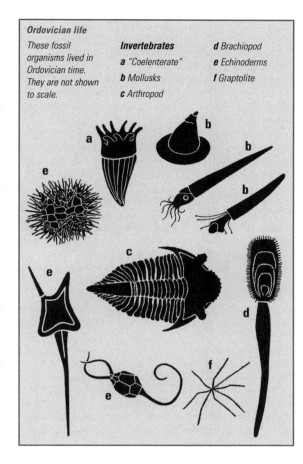

Ordovician life

These fossil organisms lived in Ordovician time. They are not shown to scale.

Invertebrates

a "Coelenterate"

b Mollusks

c Arthropod

d Brachiopod

e Echinoderms

f Graptolite

Ordovician world (above)

Lands might have been arranged like this. Lines show the equator, Tropics, and Polar regions.

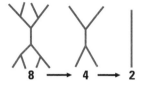

8 → 4 → 2

Evolving graptolites (above)

Ordovician times saw a reduction in the number of branches formed by colonies of tiny sea creatures, called graptolites.

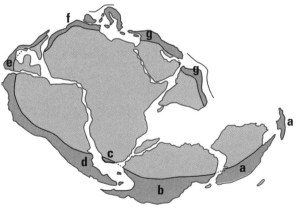

Future mountains (right)

Rocks eroded from Gondwanaland rimmed that land with belts of sediments in downwarped crustal troughs—a later source of mountain chains and ranges.

a Tasman Mio-/Eugeosyncline

b Transantarctic Geosyncline

c Cape Geosyncline

d Andean Mio-/Eugeosyncline

e Appalachian Geosyncline

f West African Geosyncline

g Southern Tethyan Geosyncline

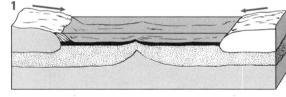

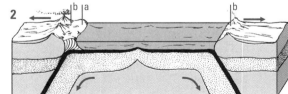

Ordovician rocks exposed (left)

The shales and sandstones above this road at South Africa's Cape of Good Hope contain late Ordovician fossils and pebbles scratched by Ordovician glaciers.

Taconic orogeny (above)

1 Cross section through the Iapetus Ocean in Cambrian times

2 Subduction of the Iapetus crust might have raised sediments (*a*) and spawned volcanoes (*b*), forming mountains on both shores.

Silurian life (above)

1 Cystiphyllum, *a solitary coral*

2 Baragwanathia, *a lycopsid–an early land plant*

3 Palaeophonus, *a scorpion–one of the first land animals*

Silurian period

The Lower Paleozoic ended with the Silurian period (443–417 million years ago). The Silures were an ancient British tribe of the Welsh border region where geologists first studied Silurian rocks. Rocks dating from this time occur on almost every continent. Some contain very early fossil land plants and animals.

As the pre-Atlantic Iapetus Ocean shrank, proto-North America and Greenland were beginning to collide with proto-Europe. The Caledonian orogeny crumpled up the edges of their plates, pushing up forerunners of the Scandinavian, Caledonian (Scottish), and Appalachian Mountains–a mighty chain of peaks that would extend in time from Scandinavia through the British Isles and Greenland to New York. Farther west, North America ended at eastern Nevada and Idaho. But as the continent began to override the oceanic plate beyond, new land would stick on to its western rim.

Some experts think Asia was mainly three ocean isolated blocks–Siberia, China, and part of South-East Asia. But the first two were closing by Silurian times. Indeed perhaps all northern continental slabs had almost fused to form a northern supercontinent, Laurasia.

In the southern supercontinent, Gondwanaland, Africa and South America were drifting north while Antarctica and Australia still headed south.

Melting southern ice sheets flooded continents with shallow seas. Off proto-North America the sea floor gained thick sheets of sands and gravels, the eroded ruins of high mountains raised in Ordovician times. Other sediments produced rich oil reserves in what is now the Sahara Desert. Widespread reefs marked the spread of (solitary) corals, and evaporites accumulated on the arid western coasts of continents.

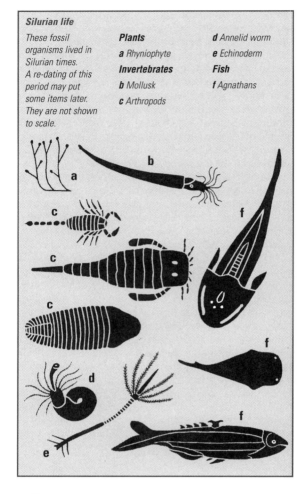

Silurian life

These fossil organisms lived in Silurian times. A re-dating of this period may put some items later. They are not shown to scale.

Plants
a Rhyniophyte

Invertebrates
b Mollusk
c Arthropods

d Annelid worm
e Echinoderm

Fish
f Agnathans

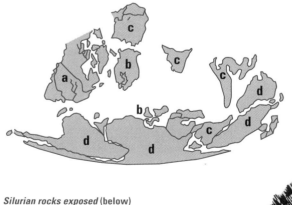

Alternative view (left)

Some experts think that today's northern continents remained largely unassembled.

a Bits of North America

b Bits of Europe

c Bits of Asia (perhaps even more than shown)

d Southern continents with bits of northern ones

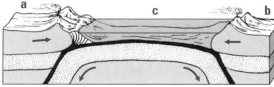

A closing ocean (above)

Proto-North America (**a**) and proto-Europe (**b**) advance on one another, closing the Iapetus Ocean (**c**) and starting the Caledonian orogeny.

Silurian rocks exposed (below)

These Silurian grits on the west Welsh coast formed horizontal layers until tilted by the Caledonian orogeny.

Devonian period

The Devonian period takes its name from Devon, England, where shales, slates, and Old Red Sandstone were laid down about 408–360 million years ago. But every continent has rocks dating from this first phase of the Upper Paleozoic. Devonian deposits include widespread coral reefs and rich oil reserves in Canada and Texas.

During the Devonian, subducting oceanic crust and colliding northern continents entirely closed the northern Iapetus Ocean. The Acadian orogeny uplifted much of northeast North America while the Caledonian orogeny was still affecting Europe. Eastern North America, Greenland, and western Europe fused to form an Old Red Continent. Its Old Red Sandstone rocks are formed from the eroded fragments of the huge mountain chain thrown up by the collision. Fossils in such rocks include freshwater fishes and the first "amphibians," whose Greenland home then straddled the equator. Devonian rocks also hold fossil remnants of the world's first forests.

At this time, Gondwanaland was moving north and pushing minicontinents ahead of it. Only a narrow, shrinking sea, the Tethys, separated South America and Africa from North America and Europe. Meanwhile the ocean separating Russia from Siberia was evidently closed. New collisions were inevitable. One theory holds that most of western Europe was created when the minicontinent Armorica slammed into Baltica, the proto-European continent. In Devonian times, this impact was foreshadowed by heavings that began pushing up the Hercynian mountain belt whose remnants include the Armorican Massif, Vosges, and Black Forest.

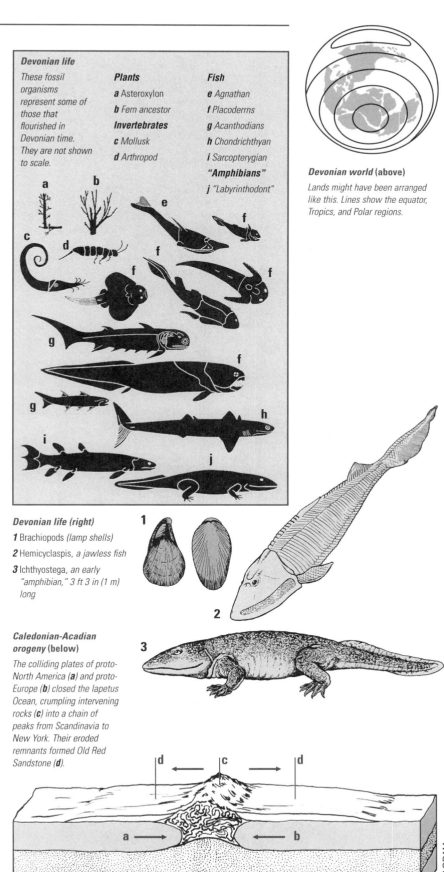

Devonian life

These fossil organisms represent some of those that flourished in Devonian time. They are not shown to scale.

Plants
a Asteroxylon
b Fern ancestor

Invertebrates
c Mollusk
d Arthropod

Fish
e Agnathan
f Placoderrns
g Acanthodians
h Chondrichthyan
i Sarcopterygian
"Amphibians"
j "Labyrinthodont"

***Devonian world* (above)**

Lands might have been arranged like this. Lines show the equator, Tropics, and Polar regions.

***Devonian life* (right)**

1 Brachiopods *(lamp shells)*

2 Hemicyclaspis, *a jawless fish*

3 Ichthyostega, *an early "amphibian," 3 ft 3 in (1 m) long*

***Caledonian-Acadian orogeny* (below)**

The colliding plates of proto-North America (*a*) and proto-Europe (*b*) closed the Iapetus Ocean, crumpling intervening rocks (*c*) into a chain of peaks from Scandinavia to New York. Their eroded remnants formed Old Red Sandstone (*d*).

***Devonian rocks exposed* (below)**

Gently dipping Upper Old Red Sandstone beds overlie more steeply dipping Lower Old Red Sandstone in eastern Scotland.

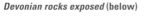

© DIAGRAM

Carboniferous period

The Carboniferous period (354–290 million years ago) takes its name from thick, coal-producing carbon layers. These are the remains of swampy tropical forests that were submerged when shallow seas invaded a vast, low-lying tract embracing much of North America and Europe. Smaller forests flourished in South America and Asia.

In North America this period is split in two. The Mississippian (354–323 million years ago) saw limestones laid down by a shallow sea that covered the Mississippi region. The Pennsylvanian (323–290 million years ago) is named for coal measures formed in Pennsylvania about 323–290 million years ago. Coal forests then flourishing in Nova Scotia contained the first known reptiles.

The Carboniferous saw North America and Europe colliding with the northern edges of Gondwanaland –the part containing South America and Africa. By about 350 million years ago, this process was fusing northern and southern continents into a single landmass, called Pangea.

The slow collisions forced up mountain ranges. About 300 million years ago South America seemingly struck Texas and Oklahoma, pushing up the Ouachita Mountains. Later, South America or Africa smashed into southeast North America. This resulted in the Alleghenian orogeny, crumpling up the southern Appalachians. Meanwhile the collision of South America or Africa with the south of Europe destroyed the intervening sea and continued raising the Hercynian mountains, whose eroded roots still run from southern Ireland to Bohemia. Such impacts also generated mountains in Gondwanaland.

As drifting carried parts of southern continents across the South Pole, ice sheets again smothered regions of the Southern Hemisphere. By late Carboniferous times, ice covered all of Antarctica, parts of Australia, and much of southern South America, Africa, and India.

Carboniferous world (above)

Lands might have reached these positions. Lines show the equator, Tropics, and Polar regions.

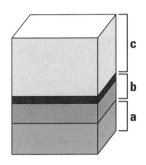

A sediment sequence (left)

*Non-marine sandstone (**a**), transitional sediments (**b**), including coal, and marine sediments (**c**) formed in recurring sequence in late Pennsylvanian times.*

Land and sea (below)

*A modern map shows (**A**) land under sea and (**B**) main lowlands often drowned by sea about 300 million years ago.*

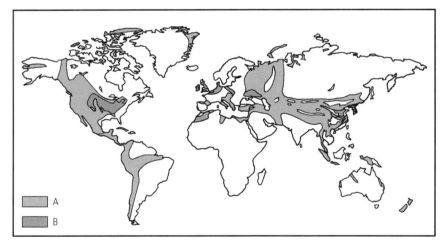

A

B

Carboniferous life (below)

1 *Conodont animal, a tiny sea creature, enlarged. Conodonts, or "cone-teeth," supported soft tissue in the gut area.*

2 *Meganeura, a giant proto-dragonfly*

3 *Hylonomus, an early reptile, was about 3 ft 3 in (1 m) long.*

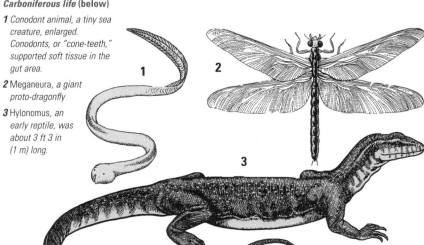

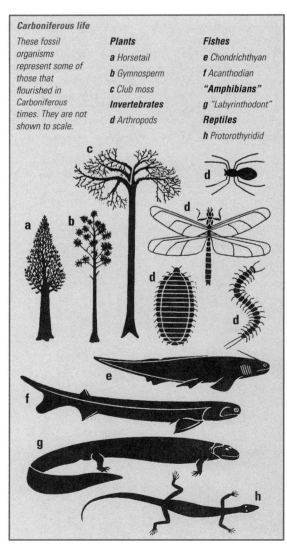

Carboniferous life

These fossil organisms represent some of those that flourished in Carboniferous times. They are not shown to scale.

Plants

a *Horsetail*

b *Gymnosperm*

c *Club moss*

Invertebrates

d *Arthropods*

Fishes

e *Chondrichthyan*

f *Acanthodian*

"Amphibians"

g *"Labyrinthodont"*

Reptiles

h *Protorothyridid*

Permian period

The Permian period (about 290–248 million years ago) is named after rocks from the old province of Perm in Russia's Ural Mountains.

This wall between northern Europe and Asia sprang up in Permian times when the Siberian plate collided with eastern Russia. Meanwhile other "pre-Asian" plates were quite likely docking and deforming the rocks of intervening mobile belts in forging most of the rest of Asia.

Elsewhere, Africa's (or South America's) collision with Europe's southern underbelly buckled up the mountains of Europe's Hercynian mobile belt. Farther west, Africa's (or South America's) collision with southeast North America went on crumpling up the southern Appalachians. On several continents collisions cracked open the crust, releasing basalt lavas.

Finally all continents lay jammed together as the supercontinent Pangea, surrounded by the single, mighty Panthalassa Ocean.

As Pangea drifted north, glaciers retreated south in South America, Africa, and India. They gripped Antarctica as that landmass crossed the South Pole, as well areas of Australia.

With much water locked up in ice and uplift of some continental masses, continental seas began to drain away. Large tracts of northern continents experienced a dry, continental climate with deserts that contained evaporites. Iron-rich minerals strongly oxidized in warm conditions produced the vivid rusty red beds typical of sedimentary rocks laid down in these conditions.

As the Permian period (and Paleozoic era) closed, the loss of many continental seas and vast volcanic eruptions helped produce the greatest mass extinctions in the fossil record.

Permian world (above)

Lands might have looked like this, omitting (much shrunken) continental seas. Lines show the equator, Tropics, and Polar regions.

Permian life (right)

1 Medlicottia, *an ammonoid*

2 Dimetrodon, *a flesh-eating reptile 11 ft 6 in (3.5 m) long*

3 Conifer, *a tree bearing seeds in cones*

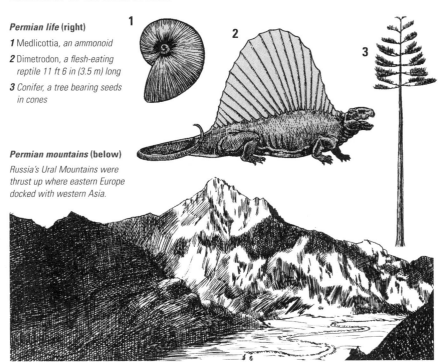

Permian mountains (below)

Russia's Ural Mountains were thrust up where eastern Europe docked with western Asia.

Permian ice sheets (above)

This map of early Permian Gondwanaland (fused southern continents) suggests that moving ice sheets covered much of South America, southern Africa, India, Antarctica, and southern Australia. Scoured rocks and glacial deposits hint at ice flow and its extent.

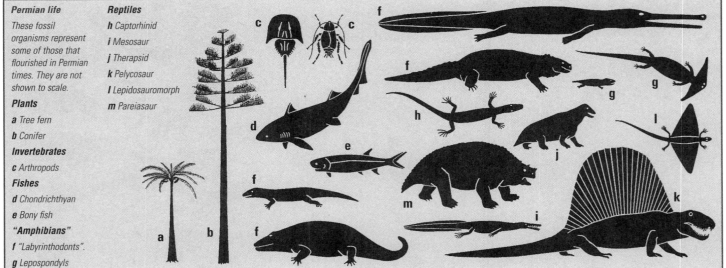

Permian life

These fossil organisms represent some of those that flourished in Permian times. They are not shown to scale.

Plants
a Tree fern
b Conifer

Invertebrates
c Arthropods

Fishes
d Chondrichthyan
e Bony fish

"Amphibians"
f "Labyrinthodonts".
g Lepospondyls

Reptiles
h Captorhinid
i Mesosaur
j Therapsid
k Pelycosaur
l Lepidosauromorph
m Pareiasaur

© DIAGRAM

Triassic world (above)

Lands might have looked like this, omitting continental seas. Lines show the equator, Tropics, and Polar regions.

Triasic life (below)

1 Tropites, a ceratite ammonoid

2 Gerrothorax, an "amphibian" 3 ft 3 in (1 m) long

3 Cynognathus, an advanced mammal-like therapsid 5 ft (1.5 m) long

Triassic period

The Mesozoic era, often called the Age of Dinosaurs, opened with the Triassic period, dating from about 248–206 million years ago. The name "Triassic" comes from the Latin *trias* ("three"), it is derived from three rock layers found in Germany.

Scarce marine sediments suggest a low sea level early in Triassic times, but red beds and evaporites accumulated on the land.

Betwen mid-Permian and mid-Triassic, the Pangean landmass drifted north about 30 degrees. North America, Europe, and northwest Africa seemingly lay locked together, but not, perhaps, immovably. Some experts think a 2,200 mi (3,500 km) east-west shearing of northern continents in relation to South America and Africa brought North America and Europe closer to the positions they occupy today. A gulf–the Tethys Sea–separated southern Eurasia from Afro-India.

Much of North America and Europe still lay inside the tropics. Gondwanaland no longer straddled the South Pole, and southern ice sheets had completely melted. World climates ranged from warm to mild, and deserts were extensive.

Pangea now showed signs of breaking up. Here and there, rising plumes of matter in the mantle domed the crust above until it split, creating block faults leaking lava. Indeed, such rifts dated back to Carboniferous times in Scotland's Midland Valley and a Permian rift opened up in Norway. Triassic rifts affected west and central Europe, eastern North America, and northwest Africa. But Pangea's true destruction lay ahead.

Cracked supercontinent (left)

The Palisades along New York's Hudson River are a Triassic or early Jurassic sill 400 ft (120 m) high. Its rnolten diabase (dolerite) rock rose through a crustal rift foreshadowing the break up of Pangea.

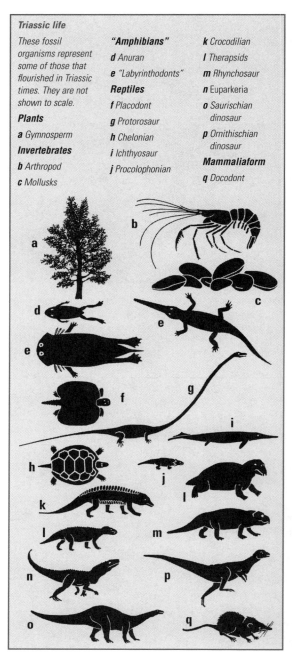

Triassic life

These fossil organisms represent some of those that flourished in Triassic times. They are not shown to scale.

Plants

a Gymnosperm

Invertebrates

b Arthropod

c Mollusks

"Amphibians"

d Anuran

e "Labyrinthodonts"

Reptiles

f Placodont

g Protorosaur

h Chelonian

i Ichthyosaur

j Procolophonian

k Crocodilian

l Therapsids

m Rhynchosaur

n Euparkeria

o Saurischian dinosaur

p Ornithischian dinosaur

Mammaliaform

q Docodont

Jurassic period

The Jurassic period (about 206–144 million years) takes its name from fossil-bearing limestone rocks formed in a sea but later raised as part of Europe's Jura Mountains. World climates were now mostly warm, and lands largely low, with old Paleozoic mountains worn down into stubs. Dinosaurs could have wandered overland across the world they shared with early birds and mammals. But the continental crust was growing restless.

Pangea had started breaking up into the continents we know today. Here and there crust domed, then split, creating triple-junction rifts. Later, linked rifts formed a spreading ridge that opened up the central part of the Atlantic Ocean, divorcing eastern North America from northwest Africa. Bits of the original continents became transposed; North America probably gained Florida from Africa. (Elsewhere, Asia would eventually gain Siberia's eastern tip from North America.)

Meanwhile, rifting was separating Africa/South America from Antarctica/Australia, although the Indian subcontinent was probably still stuck to eastern Africa. As cracks appeared vast flows of molten basalt welled up from southern Africa, through Antarctic mountains to Tasmania. More basalt flows show Australia preparing to cast off from Antarctica.

About 145 million years ago, Africa pushed east against southern Europe, shedding crustal chunks. These minicontinents eventually formed parts of Spain, Italy, Greece, Turkey, Iran, and Arabia. Meanwhile Eurasia had been fusing with Tibet.

Moving west to override the ocean floor, western North America produced three mountain-building episodes. Volcanoes sprouted as far south as the central Andes. Mighty blobs of molten granite bobbed up, melting solid rocks above. And slabs of crust—some possibly from Asia—were jammed against the western rim of North America.

Jurassic world (above)

Lands might have looked like this, omitting continental seas

A limestone house (above)

Jurassic limestone provided walls for this fine old English Cotswold manor house.

Rifting timetable

Tracts of the Atlantic opened in this order (figures are millions of years ago):

1 *Mid: 210–170*

2 *South: 145–125*

3 *Far north: 80–60*

4 *Mid-north: since 60*

a *North America*

b *Europe*

c *Africa*

d *South America*

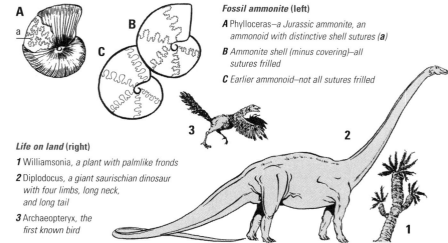

Fossil ammonite (left)

A *Phylloceras–a Jurassic ammonite, an ammonoid with distinctive shell sutures (**a**)*

B *Ammonite shell (minus covering)–all sutures frilled*

C *Earlier ammonoid–not all sutures frilled*

Life on land (right)

1 *Williamsonia, a plant with palmlike fronds*

2 *Diplodocus, a giant saurischian dinosaur with four limbs, long neck, and long tail*

3 *Archaeopteryx, the first known bird*

Jurassic life

These fossil organisms represent some of those that flourished in Jurassic times. They are not to scale.

Plants

a *Conifer*

b *Bennettitalean*

Invertebrates

c *Bryozoan*

d *Arthropod*

e *Mollusks*

Fishes

f *Bony fish*

g *Chondrichthyan*

Amphibians

h *Salamander*

Reptiles

i *Plesiosaur*

j *Ichthyosaur*

k *Crocodilian*

l *Pterosaur*

m *Ornithischian dinosaur*

n *Saurischian dinosaurs*

Birds

o *Archaeopteryx*

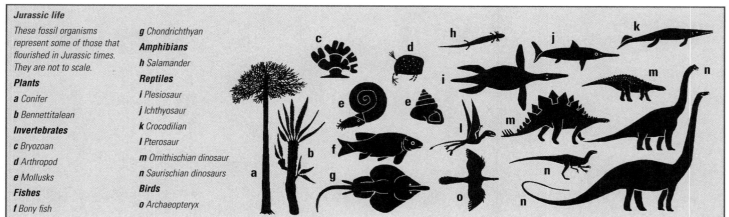

© DIAGRAM

***Cretaceous world* (above)**

Lands might have looked like this, omitting land bridges and continental seas.

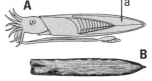

A

B

a

***Belemnite* (above)**

A *Reconstruction of a belemnite up to 31 in (80 cm) long. A calcite rod (**a**), the guard, provided internal support for this Mesozoic kin of the squid and octopus.*

B *Fossilized belemnite guard. Fossil guards abound in some marine Mesozoic rocks.*

Cretaceous period

The Mesozoic era closed with the Cretaceous period (144–65 million years ago). Its name comes from the Latin *creta*, meaning "chalk." Thick chalk deposits formed in shallow seas that invaded Europe, North America, and west Australia. Other deposits include 60 percent of today's known oil reserves.

Pangea was now fragmenting into (northern) Laurasia and (southern) Gondwanaland, and both of these supercontinents were also cracking up.

Early on, a spreading rift opened up the South Atlantic Ocean, driving South America and Africa apart. Much later, rifting separated Scandinavia from north Greenland, compressing and uplifting part of Siberia to raise the Verkhoyansk Mountains. But land still linked North America and Europe via south Greenland and the British Isles.

Farther south, the Bay of Biscay gaped open as north Spain pivoted away from west France. South of Europe, Africa moved east, forcing "Adriatica" against the Balkan plate, then moved west again. The Mediterranean was forming as a pinched-off portion of the Tethys Sea.

Dramatic changes added land and mountains to North America. Early on, one part projected far toward the North Pole. Then the north split open and the north-west pivoted west, reacting with the Pacific plate to ruck up rocks into the Brooks Range of north Alaska. The Arctic islands also probably rotated to where they lie today.

The overriding oceanic plates of western North America continued spawning a great island arc of batholiths and Andean-type volcanoes. Late in the Cretaceous, North America's westward drift accelerated, speeding up subduction of Pacific crust. This crumpled up the Rockies, exposing metals manufactured deep down in the crust and realigned the rivers of the continent.

Meanwhile, in the Southern Hemisphere, India had cast adrift from East Africa, and New Zealand had most likely torn free from Australia.

Cretaceous climates remained chiefly warm or mild. Flowering plants began to spread. But the Mesozoic ended with the mass death of the dinosaurs and many other creatures. The impact of a huge asteroid might have caused the climatic changes leading to this mass extinction.

***Cretaceous life* (below)**

1 Tyrannosaurus, *an immense flesh-eating dinosaur*

2 Magnolia, *a flowering plant*

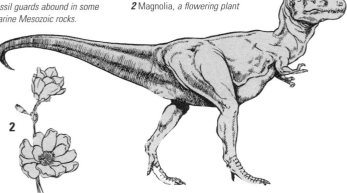

***Cretaceous cliffs* (below)**

Billions of shells of microorganisms helped build these chalk cliffs at Beer Cove in southwest England.

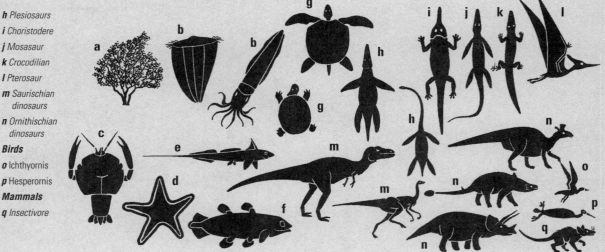

Cretaceous life

These fossil organisms represent some of those that flourished in Cretaceous time. They are not shown to scale.

Plants

a *Flowering plant*

Invertebrates

b *Mollusks*

c *Arthropod*

d *Echinoderm*

Fishes

e *Chondrichthyan*

f *Sarcopterygian*

Reptiles

g *Chelonians*

h *Plesiosaurs*

i *Choristodere*

j *Mosasaur*

k *Crocodilian*

l *Pterosaur*

m *Saurischian dinosaurs*

n *Ornithischian dinosaurs*

Birds

o *Ichthyornis*

p *Hesperornis*

Mammals

q *Insectivore*

Paleogene period

This term is often used for the combined Paleocene, Eocene, and Oligocene epochs–the first part of the Cenozoic era. The Paleogene (65–23.8 million years ago) saw continents taking on their present shapes and locations, and birds and mammals filled the roles once taken by the dinosaurs. Spreading ocean floors and colliding and subducting plates raised mountains and reconfigured the map.

Shallow continental seas withdrew at first. Later, for a time the sea invaded parts of Africa, Australia, and Siberia.

Western North America was thrusting west and overriding cool oceanic crust. This crust warmed up deep down and expanded, lifting all of western North America about 30 million years ago. Meanwhile the Rocky Mountains and Colorado plateau were evolving. Volcanoes spewed ash, and lowland sediments formed vast oil-shale deposits. In the northeast, by 45 million years ago the widening Atlantic Ocean had parted North America from Europe. To the south, immensely thick sediments pushed the Mississippi Delta out into the Gulf of Mexico, and North and South America separated.

About 45 million years ago, Africa thrust north, driving lithospheric platelets into Europe. Island Iberia struck France and crumpled up the Pyrenees. Farther east, the Adriatic plate overriding Europe's rim began pushing up the Alps. About 30 million years ago, part of France pivoted eastward, shoveling seabed sediments ashore on Italy to form the Apennines. Africa eventually added Sicily and the toe of Italy. Much of southeast Europe formed when two small Balkan plates struck southwest Russia.

In Africa itself great tracts warped up before splitting to release vast lava flows and open up the Red Sea rift.

By 40 million years ago, northward drifting India had struck Siberia and the small Kazakstan and Tarim plates to its south. The impact concertinaed the collision zones and began to raise the Himalayas.

By 30 million years ago, Antarctica formed an Antarctic island continent. Chilled by its location, it indirectly helped to lower temperatures worldwide.

Paleogene world (above)

The world looked roughly like this as India neared Asia in the Paleogene (alias early Tertiary) period.

Paleogene life (left)

1 Uintatherium, *a rhinoceros-sized hoofed herbivore from Eocene North America*

2 Gastornis, *a giant ground bird of Eocene North America and Europe*

Familiar fossil (left)

*Outer (**a**) and inner (**b**) views of one valve of a Venus shell. Dating from the Oligocene, this form of bivalve mollusk still flourishes.*

Paleogene peak

Mountaineers scale a peak in the Rockies–that was ice-sculpted as crustal heaving forced it high into the chilly upper air.

Palaeocene world

This world map shows landmasses in Paleocene time. Lines represent the equator, Tropics, and Polar regions.

Paleogene period: Paleocene epoch

The Paleocene ("old recent life") of 65–55 million years ago marks the first epoch of the Tertiary Period occupying most of the Cenozoic era ("age of recent life"). Retreating seas exposed dry land in much of inland North America, Africa, and Australia. But South America was cut adrift with its own unique evolving "ark" of mammals. Everywhere, new kinds of mammal were appearing. Primitive early species waned as more advanced placentals took their place; condylarths (the first hoofed herbivores), rodents, and squirrel-like primates shared the world with bulky pantodonts and primitive, early flesh-eating creodonts. Carnivorous mammals met some competition from big flightless birds of prey like *Gastornis*. Most fossil mammals come from North America, Europe, and Central Asia; in other places no extensive land-based sediments were laid down at this time.

At sea, gastropods and bivalves replaced ammonites as the leading mollusks. New kinds of sea urchin and foraminiferan replaced old ones. Among fish, sharks seem to have been particularly plentiful.

Eocene world

This world map shows landmasses in Eocene time. Lines represent the equator, Tropics, and Polar regions.

Paleogene period: Eocene epoch

Mountains rose and fissures leaked great lava flows in India and Scotland during the Eocene or "dawn of recent life" (55–34 million years ago). The rifting North Atlantic cut off North America from Europe, and South America lost its links to Antarctica. Seas invaded much of Africa, Australia, and Siberia. Climates were generally warm or mild. Tropical palms even flourished in the London basin.

Mammals continued to diversify. The first whales and sea cows swam in the seas. Rodents ousted multituberculates as the main small mammals. Insectivores gave rise to bats. Primates included forest-dwelling ancestors of today's lemurs and tarsiers. Ungainly uintatheres stomped around North America and Asia. But condylarths were giving way to more modern ungulates—early horses, tapirs, rhinoceroses, and piglike anthracotheres in Asia and Europe. Ancestors of elephants roamed Africa. Meanwhile, the isolated ungulates of South America produced a unique zoo of hoofed mammals, along with edentates and marsupials. Australia's mammal fauna at this time remains a mystery.

Oligocene world

This world map shows landmasses in Oligocene time. Lines represent the equator, Tropics, and Polar regions.

Paleogene period: Oligocene epoch

The Oligocene or "few recent" (kinds of life) lasted from 34–23.8 million years ago. Australia had hived off from Antarctica and left it isolated by ocean. This cooled world climates everywhere. Grasses and temperate trees ousted tropical vegetation from large areas. Grazing and browsing mammals multiplied–beasts like horses, camels, and rhinoceroses; while brontotheres ranged over Asia and North America. Dogs, stoats, cats, pigs, and ratlike rodents were on the increase. Africa was home to mastodonts, creodonts, hyraxes, anthracotheres, and the ape-ancestor *Aegyptopithecus*. Meanwhile isolated South America produced sloths, armadillos, rodents resembling guinea pigs, elephantlike pyrotheres, and others. While these creatures flourished, old fashioned hoofed and flesh-eating mammals–the ungulates and creodonts–were on the wane. Meanwhile at sea, early whales died out, largely replaced by toothed whales.

Paleocene life

These fossil animals represent some of those that flourished in Paleocene times. They are not shown to scale.

Invertebrates

a Phoronid

Amphibians

b Caecilian

Mammals

c Pantodont

d Dermopteran

e Primate

f Condylarth

g Multituberculate

h Perissodactyl

i Rodent

Eocene life

These fossil animals represent some of those that flourished in Eocene times. They are not shown to scale.

Invertebrates

a Coelenterate

b Nematode worm

Mammals

c Bat

d Tillodont

e Primate

f Creodont

g Carnivore

h Mesonychid

i Dinocerate

j Sea cow

k Proboscidean

l Perissodactyl

m Artiodactyls

n Edentate

o Whale

Birds

p Gastornithid

q Anseriform

Oligocene life

These fossil animals represent some of those that flourished in Oligocene times. They are not shown to scale.

Invertebrates

a Crustacean

Mammals

b Primates

c Creodont

d Embrithopod

e Pyrothere

f Perissodactyls

g Artiodactyls

Birds

h Coraciiform

i Apodiform

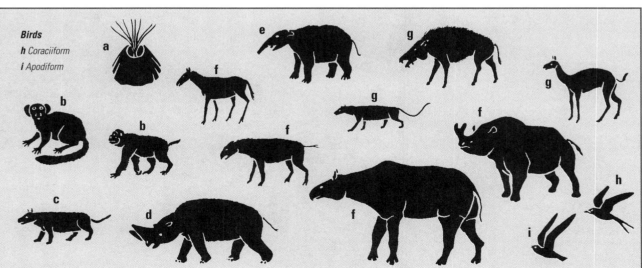

© DIAGRAM

Neogene world (above)

Lands reached present positions by the end of the Neogene (late Tertiary) period.

Neogene period

The Neogene period (23.8–1.8 million years ago) comprises the combined Miocene and Pliocene epochs. Continents had almost reached their present places, and crashing plates were pushing up great modern mountain ranges.

By mid-Cenozoic times, subducting seabed was forging island arcs around the west and north Pacific Ocean. Pacific area plate movements also cast adrift whole strips of continental crust. Japan probably split away from mainland Asia. The peninsula of Baja California was torn from mainland Mexico, and rode north-west along with California west of the San Andreas Fault.

Indeed faulting or volcanic eruptions racked western North America from Alaska to Mexico. The Coast and Cascade Ranges sprouted. Fissure flows built a vast basalt plateau in Oregon, Washington, and Idaho. Block faults from Nevada to Mexico formed the parallel ranges and valleys of the Basin and Range Province. But the rising of the Rockies and Appalachians suggests an upwarping of the whole continent. Rejuvenated mountain rivers eroded sharply downwards; the Colorado River was now carving out the Grand Canyon. Farther south a land bridge rejoined South and North America, and volcanic peaks were rising in the Andes.

Out in the Pacific Ocean, volcanoes were spawning the Hawaiian Islands chain. Australia moving north collided with the Pacific plate. This forced up mountains in New Guinea and island "stepping stones" between Australia and Asia.

Meanwhile Africa's impact with Europe was manufacturing the Alps and the Carpathian and Atlas Mountains. The Red Sea rift prised Africa away from Arabia, and volcanic peaks arose along the African rift system. Arabia and Iran crashed into Asia to create the Taurus and Zagros Mountains, and advancing India built the Himalayas and Tibetan plateau.

By 10 million years ago, Turkish and Arabian plates moving north had cut off the Mediterranean from the Indian Ocean, and Morocco had hit Spain. The isolated Mediterranean dried up and was refilled several times, leaving salt beds 20,000 ft (6,000 m) thick. Then, about 5 million years ago, a giant Atlantic waterfall burst in at Gibraltar and the sea refilled. Both polar regions now had ice caps.

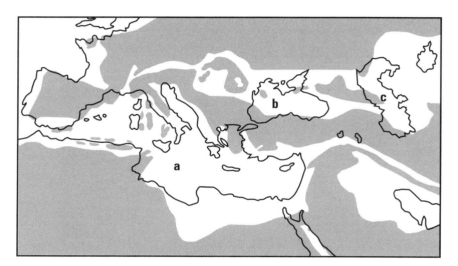

The shrinking Tethys (above)

A map shows Miocene remnants of the once mighty Tethys Sea and (*a–c*) outlines of their modern relics, cut off by shifting crustal plates. The Mediterranean (*a*) once linked the Atlantic and Indian Oceans, and the Black Sea (*b*) joined the Caspian (*c*).

Neogene fossil (left)

Cypraea, the cowrie, is a mollusk whose oldest fossils crop up in rocks formed on the floors of Miocene seas.

Rising land (right)

A section through one side of the Grand Canyon (*a*) shows multilayered and faulted ancient rocks laid bare as the Colorado River (*b*) gnawed down through a rising plateau (*c*).

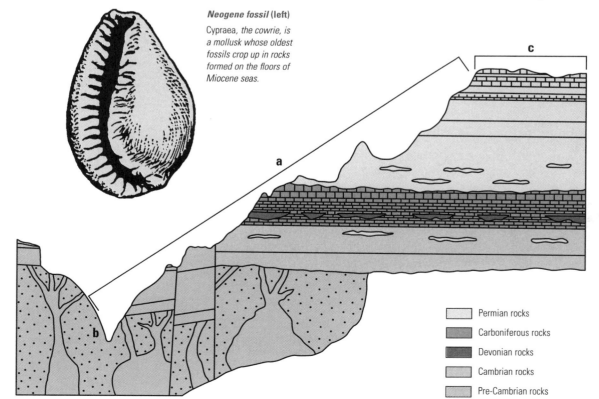

Permian rocks
Carboniferous rocks
Devonian rocks
Cambrian rocks
Pre-Cambrian rocks

Neogene period: Miocene epoch

The Miocene, or "less recent" (with fewer modern creatures than the next epoch), lasted from 23.8–5.3 million years ago, longer than any other epoch. The world changed greatly. Ice covered Antarctica; the Mediterranean Sea dried up; India crashed into Asia; the Himalayas, Rockies, and Andes rose. But sea still isolated South America and Australia. Grasslands spread extensively, and mammals reached their richest-ever variety. Many were hoofed grazers or browsers. Thus North America had horses, oreodonts, rhinoceroses, pronghorns, camels, protoceratids, and chalicotheres, with beardogs and saber-toothed cats among the predators. Eurasia's "zoo" included early deer and giraffes, while African mammals included mastodonts, apes, and Old World monkeys. Great migrations saw elephants spread out from Africa to Eurasia and North America. Cats, giraffes, pigs, and cattle went the other way–from Eurasia to Africa. Horses found their way from North America into Eurasia. Meanwhile glyptodonts, armadillos, anteaters, New World monkeys, and horselike litopterns evolved in isolated South America. Australia's Miocene marsupials and monotremes evolved in isolation too.

Miocene world (above)

This world map shows landmasses in Miocene times. Lines represent the equator, Tropics, and Polar regions.

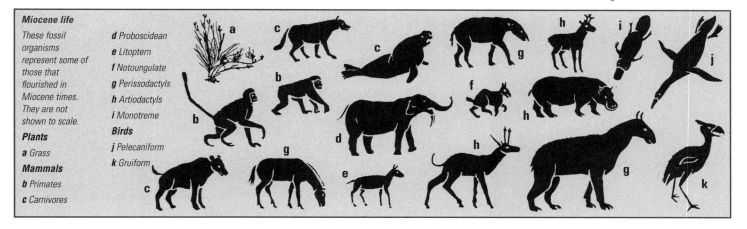

Miocene life

These fossil organisms represent some of those that flourished in Miocene times. They are not shown to scale.

Plants

a Grass

Mammals

b Primates

c Carnivores

d Proboscidean

e Litoptern

f Notoungulate

g Perissodactyls

h Artiodactyls

i Monotreme

Birds

j Pelecaniform

k Gruiform

Neogene period: Pliocene epoch

The Pliocene ("more recent") of 5.3–1.8 million years ago ended the second, Neogene period of the Cenozoic Era. Continents had taken up their present-day positions, and land linked North and South America. Antarctica's ice cap and new ones in the Northern Hemisphere cooled lands and oceans. Vegetation was like that of today. Grasslands replaced many forests, so grazing mammals spread at the expense of browsers. Cattle, sheep, antelopes, gazelles, and other bovids reached their peak in European lands. North American mammals included horses, camels, deer, pronghorns, peccaries, mastodonts, beavers, weasels, dogs, and saber-toothed cats. Rhinoceroses and protoceratids died out in North America. But ground sloths and other mammals moved in from South America. Meanwhile dogs, bears, horses, mastodonts, and others colonized South America from the north. Early elephants, antelopes, and the ancestors of man roamed Africa. But isolated Australia's only newcomers were rodents, rafting in on mats of vegetation drifting south from Indonesia.

Pliocene time (above)

This world map shows landmasses in Pliocene times. Lines represent the equator, Tropics, and Polar regions.

Pliocene life

These fossil animals represent some of those that flourished in Pliocene times. A redating of this period may put some items earlier. They are not shown to scale.

Mammals

a Marsupial

b Primates

c Desmostylan

d Proboscidean

e Notoungulate

f Litoptern

g Perissodactyl

h Artiodactyls

i Edentate

j Rodent

k Lagomorph

Birds

l Falconiform

© DIAGRAM

Quaternary world (above)

Continents have shifted little in the last two million years, though levels of the land and sea have changed.

Quaternary period

This followed the Tertiary period (also known as Paleogene and Neogene periods). The Quaternary began about 2 million years ago. It includes the Pleistocene or "Ice Age" epoch and the mild Holocene, or Recent, epoch in which we live today.

Pleistocene ice sheets smothered vast northern tracts, and glaciers filled mountain valleys worldwide. As the climate fluctuated ice repeatedly advanced and retreated–scouring valleys, damming lakes, rerouting rivers, and dumping debris over much of northern North America and Europe.

In intense glaciations sea level fell by as much as 330 ft (100 m). Meltwater torrents carved canyons in the rims of continental shelves. Land bridges joined Alaska and Siberia, mainland Asia and Indonesia, New Guinea and Australia, and the British Isles and mainland Europe.

Most of the northern ice sheets melted about 10,000 years ago. Sea levels rose, drowning the old canyons and land bridges. The Black Sea and Mediterranean were reunited. Along with the Caspian, both had once formed part of the prehistoric Tethys Sea until cut off by continental plates advancing from the south. As ice melted, crust once weighed down by ice bobbed up; it still rises in parts of Canada and Scandinavia. Meanwhile great subterranean forces were at work. Earthquakes, volcanic eruptions, oceanic trenches, and high peaks show where lithospheric plates still separate, collide, or grind against each other; shifting plates are still raising mountains and forcing oceanic crust into the mantle. Thus Cascades Range volcanoes sprout above the Farallon oceanic plate, which melts as it burrows under Oregon and Washington. And earthquakes shake the San Andreas Fault as the Pacific plate bears western California north.

Africa pushing under Europe forms a volcanic island arc in the Aegean and once raised Italy's volcanic Etna and Vesuvius. A rift broadens from the Dead Sea to the Gulf of Aden. Arabia thrusts against Iran. And farther east the Himalayas are still growing.

Humans evolved, but wildlife continues to wane as our inventive species competes with native plants and animals for food and living space.

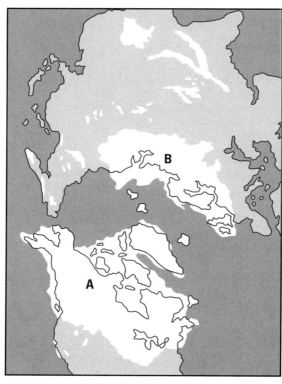

Lands under ice (above)

Pleistocene ice sheets sometimes covered these labeled parts of (**A**) North America and (**B**) Eurasia.

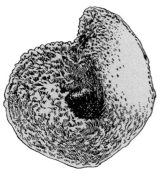

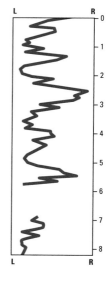

Volcanic power (left)

In 1980 Mt. St. Helens proved explosively that a Cascades Range volcano can still be dangerously active.

Clues to cold

Above: This (much enlarged) foraminiferan coils right in warm water, left in cold.

Right: proportions of left- and right-coilers from 8 m (26 ft) seabed cores hint at past climatic changes.

Quaternary period: Pleistocene epoch

The Pleistocene ("most recent") epoch of the short Quaternary period lasted from about 2 million to 10,000 years ago. Ice Age cold gripped northern lands as ice caps and glaciers waxed and waned. Advancing cold forced creatures south, though some returned in intervals of warmth. So much water lay locked up in ice that the level of the oceans fell. Horses, camels, deer, tapirs, mastodonts, mammoths, dogs, and saber-toothed cats lived in North America (though horses and camels died out there). Beasts migrating into South America helped wipe out many of its native creatures. Meanwhile, monkeys, hyenas, hippopotamuses, and straight tusked elephants thrived in Europe during a warm phase. Eurasia's cold-adapted beasts included woolly mammoth, woolly rhinoceros, cave bear, and cave lion—all now extinct. Australia was home to outsize marsupials including *Diprotodon*, a giant kangaroo, and a marsupial "lion." Spreading probably from Africa, humans developed efficient hunting skills. Maybe this explains the disappearance of most large mammals before the Pleistocene ended. About 10,000 years ago Ice Age cold gave way to the warm phase we call the Holocene, or Recent, epoch—the time we live in now.

Pleistocene life

These fossil animals represent some of those that flourished in Pleistocene times. They are not shown to scale.

Mammals

a Marsupials

b Primates

c Carnivores

d Proboscidean

e Perissodactyls

f Artiodactyls

g Edentate

h Rodent

Birds

i Ratite

Quaternary period: Holocene (Recent) epoch

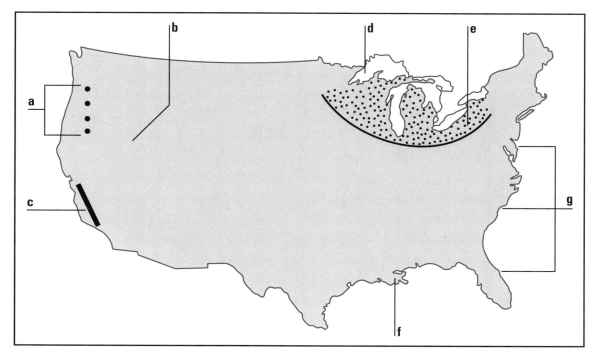

Some changes affecting the United States

a Cascades eruptions

b Growth and decline of Great Basin lakes

c San Andreas Fault earthquakes

d Great Lakes formed

e Glacial drift deposits left by melting ice

f Mississippi Delta growth

g Low coasts drowned

© DIAGRAM

SECTION 2

EVOLVING LIFE

Fossil clues to prehistoric life

This chapter explains fossils as keys that help us to unlock the puzzle of past life.

We show how parts of prehistoric organisms have survived as fossils in layered rocks, what paleontology (the study of fossil organisms) reveals about the evolution and extinction of past life-forms, and how and where prehistoric plants and creatures lived.

The chapter ends with a glimpse of paleontology in action: the kinds of work that made it possible to identify the plants and animals described on the later pages of this book.

A fossil's story

1 A fish that has just died lies on a seabed.

2 Flesh rots, revealing bones.

3 Mud or sand covers the bones, preventing decay.

4 Layers of mud and sand bury the bones, now reinforced and fossilized by minerals.

5 Weather exposes the fossil bones by eroding the layered sediments above, which have long since hardened into stone and been raised by uplift of the Earth's crust.

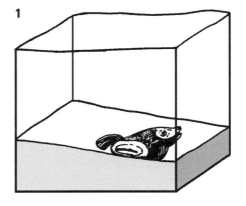
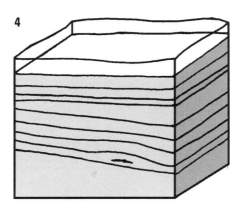
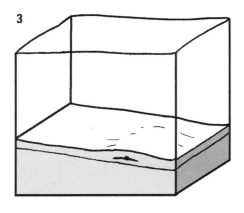
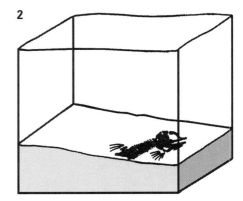
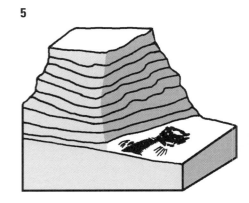

What fossils are

When plants or animals die, they usually decay. Sometimes, though, their hard parts get preserved in rock as fossils. Fossils are the clues that tell us what we know of long-dead living things.

Fossils form in several ways. The process usually happens under water. First, a newly dead plant or animal sinks to the bottom of a lake, sea, or river. Soft tissues soon rot, but before bone or wood decay, sand or mud may cover them, shutting out the oxygen needed by bacteria that cause decay. Later, water saturated with dissolved minerals seeps into tiny holes in the bone or wood. Inside these tiny pipes the water sheds some of its load of minerals. Layers of substances such as calcite, iron sulfide, opal, or quartz gradually fill the holes. This strengthens the bone or wood and helps it to survive the weight of sand or mud above. Sometimes bits of bone or wood dissolve, leaving hollows that preserve their shapes–fossils known as "molds." If minerals fill a mold they form a "cast."

Not only wood and bone become preserved. Skin, leaves, burrows, footprints, other tracks, and even droppings may form fossils. Soft-bodied creatures such as worms form fossils only in the finest fine-grained rock. Fossils also form under sands piled up by desert winds, while amber, frozen mud, and tar preserve some ancient organisms whole.

As a fossil hardens under water, layers of mud or sand grow above it. Their crushing weight and any natural cements that they contain may change thick layers of sand or soft mud into thin beds of hard rock. Millions of years later, great movements of the Earth's crust might heave up these beds to build mountains. Rain, frost, and running water slowly wear them down. In time, weather bares the mountains' inner layers and their fossils.

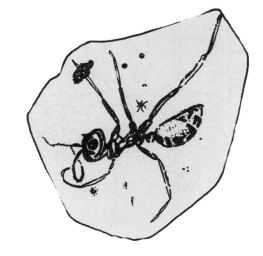

Ant in amber (left)

One hundred million years ago resin leaking from a tree trunk trapped this worker ant. The resin hardened into amber, preserving all but the ant's soft internal organs.

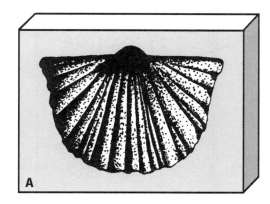

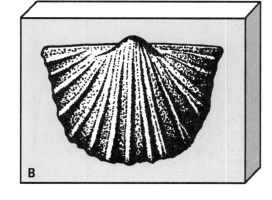

Mold and cast (left and below)

A A shell in rock dissolved to leave this shell-shaped hollow, called a mold.

B Minerals later filled the mold to form a cast.

a

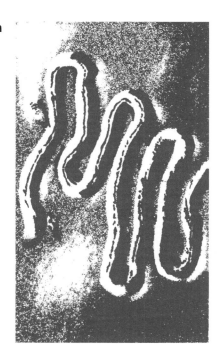

b

Fossil tracks (left)

Two examples show different types of fossil tracks (not drawn to scale).

a Trail probably made by a snail-like creature, and preserved in Pennsylvanian (late Carboniferous) rock.

b Footprints and beak marks left in mud by *Presbyornis*, an Eocene wading bird of North America. (Illustration after Erickson.)

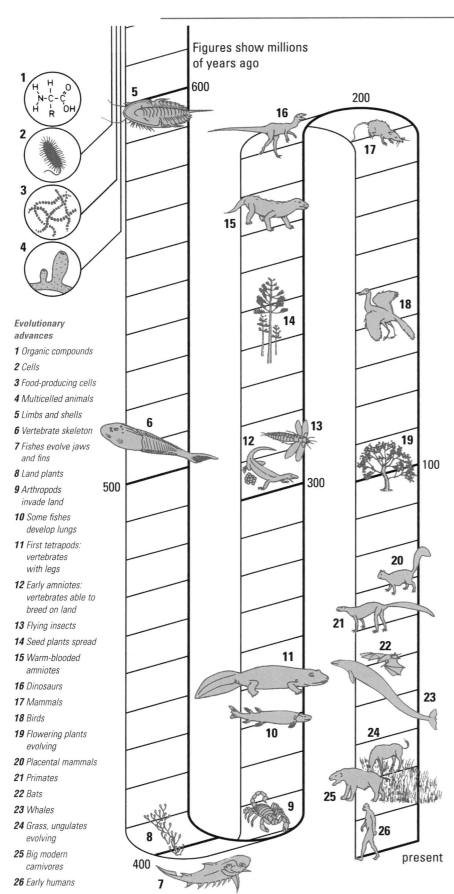

Figures show millions
of years ago

**Evolutionary
advances**

1 *Organic compounds*

2 *Cells*

3 *Food-producing cells*

4 *Multicelled animals*

5 *Limbs and shells*

6 *Vertebrate skeleton*

7 *Fishes evolve jaws
and fins*

8 *Land plants*

9 *Arthropods
invade land*

10 *Some fishes
develop lungs*

11 *First tetrapods:
vertebrates
with legs*

12 *Early amniotes:
vertebrates able to
breed on land*

13 *Flying insects*

14 *Seed plants spread*

15 *Warm-blooded
amniotes*

16 *Dinosaurs*

17 *Mammals*

18 *Birds*

19 *Flowering plants
evolving*

20 *Placental mammals*

21 *Primates*

22 *Bats*

23 *Whales*

24 *Grass, ungulates
evolving*

25 *Big modern
carnivores*

26 *Early humans*

Fossil clues to evolution

Fossils found in rocks of different ages show how living things evolved, or changed, through time. The first life-forms were microscopically tiny organisms. Later came soft-bodied sea creatures. Some gave rise to animals with shells or inner skeletons. One group of backboned animals, bony fishes, gave rise to tetrapods (four-legged vertebrates). Amphibious tetrapods produced ancestors of the mammals and the reptiles, which in turn gave rise to birds. Body changes producing each new type of organism arose from cumulative changes in inherited characteristics caused by the switching on or off of genes in the body's cells that control their complexity and shape.

Scientists can see such changes in the making by studying fossils in sequences of zones–biostratigraphic subdivisions of the rocks. "Key fossils" useful for this purpose include ammonites, brachiopods, and trilobites–fossil sea creatures widespread in rocks formed under ancient seas. (Most fossils were preserved in marine deposits.) Microfossils–fossil algae and other tiny fossils–are other valuable guides. So, too, are the minute fossil spores and pollen grains produced by plants. Indeed, palynology, the study of fossil spores and pollen, is a special branch of fossil studies. Gaps blur the fossil record: Some organisms left no trace; others have yet to be discovered. But enough remain for us to learn which organisms came from what; at least for many major groups. Wary paleontologists watch out for homeomorphs–unrelated "lookalike" species similarly adapted for the same lifestyle.

Most major groups are many millions of years old. Within these, though, each kind of organism endured only as long as it could fend off enemies and rivals. New kinds of lethal enemies or harsh climatic changes wiped out unresistant species by the dozen. Fossils show that major evolutionary changes came in fits and starts. After mass extinctions (see pp. 124) new life-forms sprang up and diversified explosively. New predators and herbivores soon populated habitats emptied of their former counterparts.

Evolving ammonites

These five fossils from successively younger rocks reveal one line of evolution among ammonites (mollusks with coiled shells).

a *Shell straight*

b *Shell curved*

c *Shell strongly
curved*

d *Shell loosely coiled*

e *Shell tightly coiled*

How living things are classified

Biologists classify or group all organisms, alive or extinct, according to how closely they resemble one another or how they are related. Either way, those that can breed among themselves but not with others form one "species." Different species resembling one another more than they resemble other species form a "genus." Similar genera make up a "family."

Similar families form an "order;" similar orders make a "class;" similar classes make a "phylum" or, if plants, a "division." Similar phyla or divisions form a "kingdom."

This so-called Linnaean classification system was once based on superficial similarities. Taxonomists, scientists who name organisms, now group them by evolved anatomical or molecular characters that separate them from the rest. Any group from species upward, with derived or advanced features not found in any other group, is called a 'clade.' Some clades match no Linnaean category, and many bear no category names. Clade-based "family trees" are cladograms, and the study of clades is cladistics.

Humans' fellow creatures

The diagram shows humans' relationships to other organisms living and extinct. You could construct a similar diagram to represent the relationships of any other species.

Each level shows a grouping made up of lesser groups with the status of the group above. Individual creatures stand for groups. For instance, each creature shown for the phylum Chordata stands for a different class of animal. Each creature shown for the kingdom Animalia stands for a different phylum, and so on. Animals shown as pale shapes stand for groups that are extinct. Some groups are not depicted.

1 Species Homo sapiens

2 Genus Homo, containing maybe five species

3 Family Hominidae, containing maybe 18 genera

4 Order Primates, containing maybe 18 families

5 Class Mammalia, containing more than 40 orders

6 Phylum Chordata, containing more than a dozen classes, 12 of which are vertebrates (backboned animals)

7 Kingdom Animalia, containing 36 phyla, all but one of which are invertebrates (animals without a backbone)

8 Domain Eucarya, containing more than 20 kingdoms (animals, plants, fungi, and some 18 groups of protists, slime molds, and seaweeds)

Humans' place in nature

Scientists classify humans in these progressively higher categories and (not illustrated) subgroups.

1 Species: Homo sapiens

2 Genus: Homo

3 Family: Hominidae Superfamily: Hominoidea

4 Order: Primates

5 Class: Mammalia in subphylum Vertebrata

6 Phylum: Chordata

7 Kingdom: Animalia

8 Domain: Eucarya

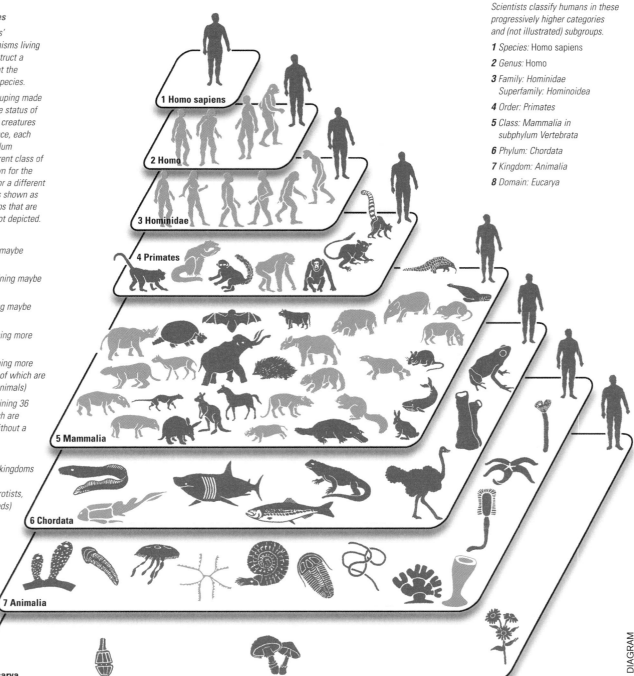

1 Homo sapiens
2 Homo
3 Hominidae
4 Primates
5 Mammalia
6 Chordata
7 Animalia
8 Eucarya

© DIAGRAM

The tree of life

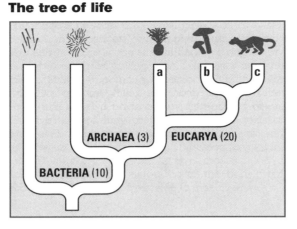

Major branches (right)

Here we show evolutionary relationships among life's three domains and number the kingdoms they contain.

Bacteria: 10 kingdoms

Archaea: 3 kingdoms

Eucarya: 20 kingdoms, the best known being:
a) Plantae (plants)
b) Fungi (mushrooms and other fungi)
c) Animalia (animals)

Scientists believe that all living things can be related to ancestors originating in minute one-celled organisms. Maybe lightning and ultraviolet radiation acting on a primeval atmosphere formed organic compounds from simple chemicals. Next, organic compounds organized in self-replicating committees formed into simple, one-celled organisms–Bacteria and Archaea collectively called prokaryotes. Committees of prokaryotes in time produced the large, complex cells of protists, fungi, plants, and animals, collectively called eucaryotes. Bacteria, Archaea, and Eucarya (eucaryotes), the three great types of life, are called domains. Their subdivisions form the branches and twigs of the evolutionary tree of life.

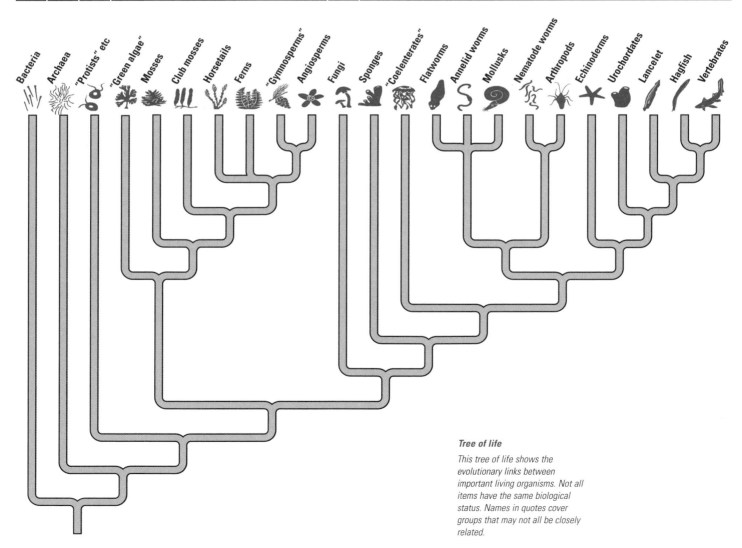

Tree of life

This tree of life shows the evolutionary links between important living organisms. Not all items have the same biological status. Names in quotes cover groups that may not all be closely related.

The oldest fossils

The earliest identifiable living things were bacteria, including cyanobacteria, among the best-known of the procaryotes, tiny one-celled organisms whose genetic blueprints did not lie in a single nucleus. Procaryotes probably evolved more than 3.8 billion years ago from combined amino acids created in the early ocean–a chemical-rich "test tube" shrouded by volcanic gases and intensively bombarded by solar radiation and electric storms.

Pioneer procaryotes consumed ready-made amino acids. Later came the cyanobacteria, containing the green pigment chlorophyll, which enabled them to use the energy in sunshine to build their own food compounds from carbon dioxide and water. This process, photosynthesis, yielded free oxygen as waste.

In time, free oxygen screened the Earth's surface from the Sun's harmful ultraviolet rays and formed a rich new source of energy. This was tapped by new, more complex life-forms with a cell nucleus: eucaryotes, including tiny one-celled protists ancestral to the many-celled and often much larger fungi, plants, and animals.

Early complex cells (below)

Fossils of cells multiplying by division hint at early complex life 1 billion years ago. Shown here much magnified are one-celled eucaryotic algae fossilized in chert at various stages of division. Genes within cell nuclei determine how each daughter cell develops. Most multicellular organisms undergo sexual reproduction, in which a fertile egg cell receives genes from both parents. This innovation increased the chance of genetic variation and evolution.

Early organisms

Our examples show two organisms (**1** and **2**) in the domain Bacteria and a third (**3**) in the domain Eucarya.

1 Kakabekia resembled a microscopic umbrella with a clubbed stalk. It might have been a bacterium dividing into two. Size: most bacteria are under 1 micron (0.001 mm) across. Time: Precambrian (2 billion years ago). Place: Canada. Kingdom: uncertain.

2 Nostoc, a "blue-green" alga, forms a necklace-like mass. It probably evolved from one-celled Precambrian ancestors. Kingdom: Cyanobacteria, mostly tiny, superficially plantlike organisms under 25 microns across.

3 Aspergillus is a mold, producing mildew on fruit, leather, or walls. Its growing, threadlike hyphae produce "side shoots" bearing spores from which new molds grow. Size: minute. Kingdom: Fungi (plantlike organisms that lack chlorophyll and feed on dead or living organisms). Fossil hyphae have been found in Precambrian rocks, but claims for a 3.8 billion-year-old fossil fungus found in Greenland proved mistaken.

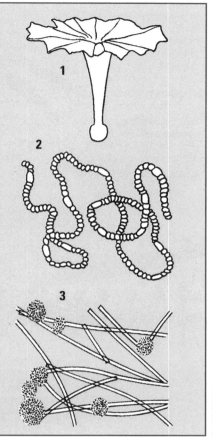

© DIAGRAM

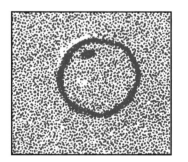 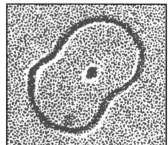 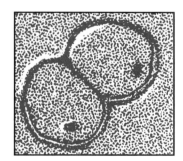 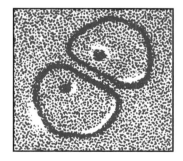

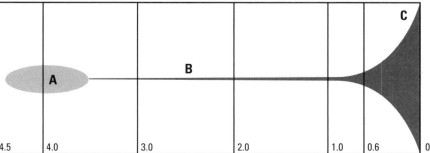

Accelerating evolution

Procaryotes played a crucial role in evolution, as we show here. The thicker the line, the more diversified the life-forms that it represents.

A Chemical evolution: amino acids, proteins, sugars, and other substances formed in water.

B Slow organic evolution: photosynthesizing procaryotes enriched the atmosphere with oxygen; some formed ozone.

C Rapid evolution, mainly of eucaryotes deriving energy from oxygen and screened from harmful solar rays by ozone in the atmosphere. Evolution accelerated 1 billion–700 million years ago as atmospheric oxygen reached more than 1% of its present level

| 4.5 | 4.0 | 3.0 | 2.0 | 1.0 | 0.6 | 0 |

billions of years ago

How ancient organisms lived

Fossils reveal much about how individual organisms lived. Sometimes we can even learn how prehistoric plants and creatures interacted, as prey or predators.

Just by looking at a fossil creature, experts may be able to work out how it ate, moved, sensed, or even grew. Clues often lie in jaws or other features similar to those of certain living animals with known habits. For instance, prehistoric sea reptiles called placodonts had broad, flat crushing teeth like those of skates–fishes that crunch up seabed shellfish. It seems that placodonts ate shellfish, too. Ichthyosaurs were reptiles with paddle-shaped flippers rather like a whale's. Ichthyosaurs, like whales, were accomplished swimmers, unable to walk on land. Trilobites were sea creatures resembling wood lice and with eyes rather like a fly's. Close study of one

fossil trilobite proves that it saw in all directions, detecting other creatures' sizes and movements, though not their shapes. Fossils also show that growing trilobites shed their outer "skin" from time to time to add an extra segment to the body. This gives a rough idea of individuals' ages. (Other clues to fossil organisms' ages include tooth wear in mammals and growth rings in tree trunks, fish scales, and mollusk shells.)

Where many different fossils crop up together in the same rock zone, paleontologists may be able to identify plants, plant-eating animals, and the predators that preyed upon these herbivores. In this way an expert can work out a prehistoric food chain whose links consist of eaters and eaten, and perhaps even a food web made up of interlinking chains.

Working out links is easy when fossils form a life assemblage–a group of organisms preserved as they once lived. Unfortunately many fossil groups are death assemblages. Such groups can include "outsiders" washed in by floods from other habitats. Then, too, predators, winds, currents, or chemicals destroy fragile bones and shells or carry them away, so certain species from a given habitat survive only as broken scraps or disappear completely.

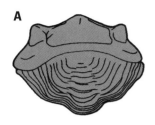

Trilobite abilities

A *This fossil trilobite was found curled up for protection.*

B *Study of the many lenses in its eyes shows that lenses at even higher levels detected the advance (from a to d) of objects of a certain height.*

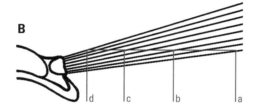

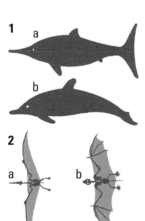

Convergent evolution (above)

Unrelated individuals evolved similar shapes suited for similar modes of life.

1 *Fishlike swimmers:*

a *Ichthyosaur (a reptile)*

b *Dolphin (a mammal)*

2 *Skin-winged fliers:*

a *Pterosaur (a reptile)*

b *Bat (a mammal)*

Death assemblage

This diagram shows how the remains of living creatures can get mixed and broken after death to form a fossil death assemblage.

1A *Prehistoric land and sea communities of organisms*

1B *Fossils from these sources and another source, mixed by erosion and undersea currents and incorporated in rock*

a *Fossil derived from an older rock layer*

b, c *Remains of land plants and a land animal*

d *Soft-bodied creature that has left no fossil trace*

e *Shellfish shell halves separated and realigned*

f *Fragile crinoids broken up*

Life assemblage

This shows how creatures' hard parts and tracks may be preserved intact in the positions where they lived.

2A *Prehistoric seabed community of organisms*

2B *Fossils of the community undisturbed by erosion or undersea currents before being incorporated in rock*

a *Shellfish shells intact and aligned as during life*

b *Tracks of a burrowing worm preserved in rock*

c *Burrowing bivalve and sea urchin with hollows that their soft parts made in sand*

d *Fragile crinoids unbroken*

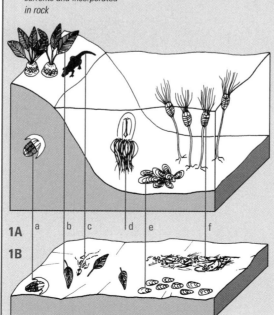

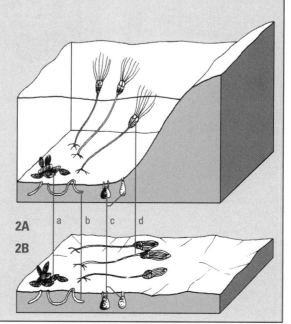

What lived where?

Fossils tell us much about the surface of the world in ancient times. Then, as now, different species were designed for life in different habitats–for instance forest, grassland, desert, swamp, or river. Fossils therefore tell us indirectly about the kind of place they lived in and about its climate. Widespread finds of fossil desert animals dating from a given time hint that desert climates were widespread too. Desert fossils crop up in Permian rocks as far apart as the United States, Russia, and South Africa.

Fossils of lush tropical vegetation show that much of North America and Europe had a warm, wet climate in later Carboniferous times, when northern lands lay close to the equator. Fossils have done much to prove that continents have drifted from their old positions. For instance, the Permian fossil plant *Glossopteris* occurs in all southern continents, now widely separated by oceans. Thus, when *Glossopteris* first grew, all southern continents lay locked together. Geologists believe that they were tugged apart by currents in the molten rock beneath the oceans, where Earth's crust of solid rock is thin and weak. But finds of certain fossil species only in specific regions suggest that natural barriers such as mountains, seas, or temperature boundaries also stopped those organisms from spreading.

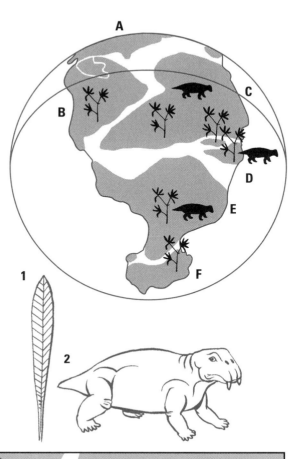

Supercontinent (above)

This global view shows the supercontinent Pangea in Permian times.

Worldwide life (right)

*Fossil finds of land organisms (**1–2**) and the matching rims of continents (**A–F**) are clues to the extent and shape of Pangea.*

1 Glossopteris, *a Permian tongue-shaped leaf, from a prehistoric tree*

2 Lystrosaurus, *an early Triassic synapsid*

A *North America*

B *South America*

C *Africa*

D *India*

E *Antarctica*

F *Australia*

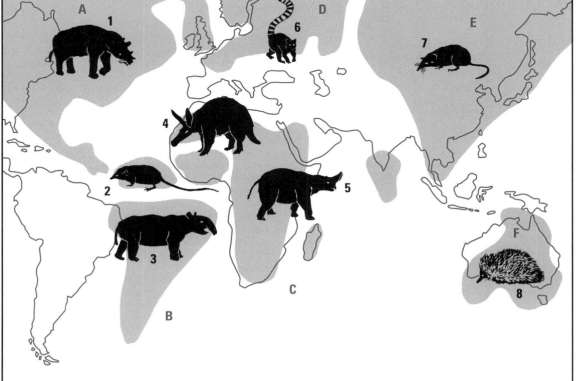

Isolated life

*Shown on this map (**1–8**) are mammals that evolved in isolation after Pangea broke up and continents (**A–F**) drifted apart, some split by seas.*

1 *Uintatheres*

2 *Opossum rats*

3 *Pyrotheres*

4 *Aardvarks*

5 *Embrithopods*

6 *Lemurs*

7 *Insectivores*

8 *Spiny anteaters*

A *North America*

B *South America*

C *Africa*

D *Europe*

E *Asia*

F *Australia*

© DIAGRAM

Mass extinctions

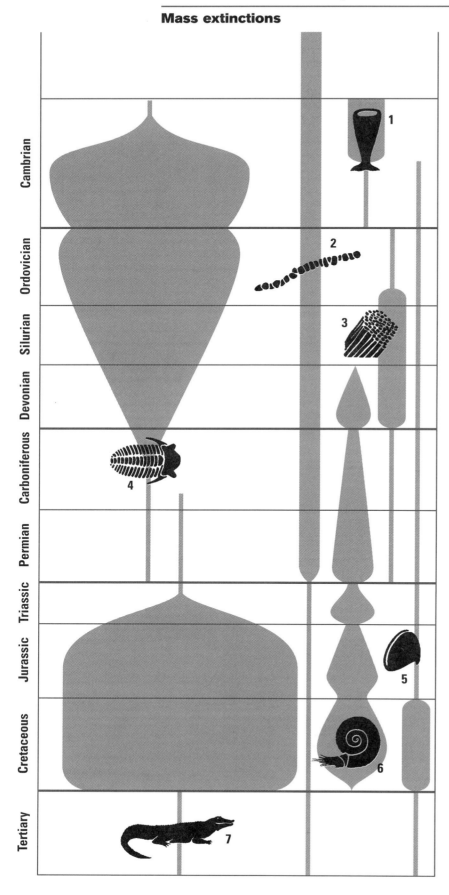

Plants and animals alive today account for most known species. Yet species that became extinct must have outnumbered these by far. One calculation suggests there are 4.5 million living species, but that 980 million species evolved in the last 600 million years. This estimate supposes each species lasted on average for only 2.7 million years.

In fact some forms were far more durable. The Australian lungfish may have survived for about 100 million years. Sea creatures like the king crab, coelacanth (a fish), and *Neopilina* (a mollusk) are close kin of beasts with even longer histories.

Somehow such living fossils resisted changes that wiped out many other organisms. Sometimes disasters struck down many groups together. The greatest mass deaths marked the ends of eras. Thus many sea creatures and a great group of reptilelike synapsids died out as the Paleozoic era ended. Major reptile groups, including dinosaurs and those once-abundant mollusks ammonites, all vanished as the Mesozoic era closed.

Experts disagree about what caused these mass extinctions. Perhaps cosmic rays from an exploding star deformed unborn young. Maybe deadly rays from space poured down when the Earth's magnetic field reversed. Or perhaps changes in the positions and levels of the continents caused killing periods of cold.

Some scientists blame huge lumps of rock that could have crashed on Earth from space like massive bombs. The impact of a rock 10 kilometres across could hurl enough dust and moisture into the air to darken skies around the world for months. Plants and plant-eating creatures would die in droves. The world would briefly freeze. But once dust settled, moisture still up in the sky would trap the Sun's incoming heat. Then overheating would destroy creatures unable to control their body temperature.

Yet no mass extinction theory convincingly explains why many groups of living things survived.

Lifelines

Thick and thin horizontal bands show the expansion and collapse of certain groups of organisms through prehistoric time. (Band thicknesses are not to scale.) Thick vertical lines show mass collapses that changed the makeup of marine communities. Widespread land and sea extinctions marked the end of the Cretaceous period.

1 *Archaeocyathids*

2 *Reef-forming stromatolites*

3 *Tabulate corals*

4 *Trilobites*

5 *Bivalves*

6 *Ammonites*

7 *Archosaurian reptiles (including dinosaurs)*

Finding fossils

Fossil hunters search where humans or weather have exposed sedimentary rocks–particularly limestones, shales, clays, and sometimes sandstone. Likely sites are sea cliffs, quarries, abandoned mines, road cuttings, building excavations, garbage dumps, streamsides with exposed bedrock, deserts, polar wastes, and mountainsides. Experienced collectors go armed with information obtained from local museums, guide books, and geological maps. They obtain landowners' consent; collect only in permitted areas (avoiding sites protected for their fossil rarities); and watch out for cliff falls, particularly after rain. Protective helmets may be needed, as well as old clothes and sturdy shoes, or rubber boots if working in soft mud. Fossil hunters pace slowly, scanning gullies, cliffs, or piles of weathered rock. Some rocks bristle with fossils; others seemingly hold none. But patient searching and a practiced eye reveal telltale shiny or discolored shapes in rock. Whole fossils are a rarity. Collectors mostly find just scattered teeth or broken bits of fossil leaf or bone. Yet even fragments can betray the organisms they belonged to. For example, short columns made of disklike plates could be the broken stems of crinoids, or "sea lilies." The broken plates of all echinoderms glint as they catch the light. Distinctive teeth help experts to identify fossil sharks and mammals. Deeply pitted bony plates come from crocodiles; less deeply pitted plates from turtles. Turtle plates are thicker than those from certain fossil fishes. Fossil fishes survive mostly just as scales and individual bones. The next two pages show how fossils small and large are extracted from the rocks.

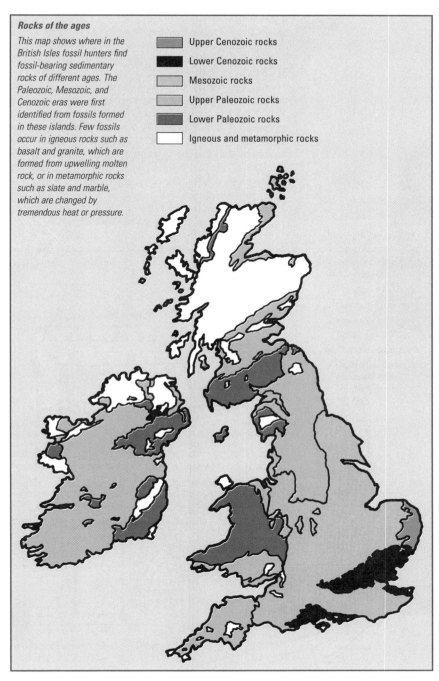

Rocks of the ages

This map shows where in the British Isles fossil hunters find fossil-bearing sedimentary rocks of different ages. The Paleozoic, Mesozoic, and Cenozoic eras were first identified from fossils formed in these islands. Few fossils occur in igneous rocks such as basalt and granite, which are formed from upwelling molten rock, or in metamorphic rocks such as slate and marble, which are changed by tremendous heat or pressure.

- Upper Cenozoic rocks
- Lower Cenozoic rocks
- Mesozoic rocks
- Upper Paleozoic rocks
- Lower Paleozoic rocks
- Igneous and metamorphic rocks

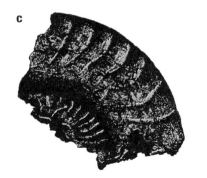

a

b

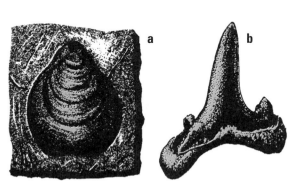

c

d

e

Fossil finds

Fossil hunters typically find specimens like those shown here. All but one are from marine invertebrates, the most widespread fossils, and most are broken, worn, or incomplete.

a Upper Cenozoic brachiopod

b Lower Cenozoic shark's tooth

c Mesozoic ammonite

d Upper Paleozoic crinoid

e Lower Paleozoic graptolite

Extracting fossils

Finding fossils is just the first stage of collecting. The fossil hunter must free fossils from their rocks, make a record of the finds, and transport these safely home.

You can go fossil collecting with just a geological hammer, hand lens, and old newspapers for wrapping finds, but collectors often take much more, inside a backpack with extra space for specimens. A broad-bladed chisel called a bolster will split rocks along their bedding planes, revealing hidden fossils. Cold chisels help to cut them free. A flat-bladed trowel is helpful in soft rock. Old kitchen knives, brushes, even picks and spades, can have their uses. Sieves help you separate small teeth and bones from even smaller particles of clay or sand. The hand lens helps you identify tiny but important features. A steel rule serves for making measurements.

To remove a fossil from a rock, trim away as much rock as possible. Leave the rest for careful work at home. If your fossil breaks, mark joins and number the pieces, using waterproof ink or a felt-tip pen. Wrap together fragments for later reassembly. Use a water- or solvent-based hardening solution to strengthen fragile fossils in soft clay or sand. When specimens have dried, wrap them in paper tissues, kitchen foil, moss, or sand and place them in tins or boxes. Stronger specimens can go in polythene or linen bags.

Gather samples of loose rock and sieve them back at home for tiny fossil teeth, bones, or seeds. Number each item, then use a notebook to record its number, name, locality, and details of its parent rock. A sketch or photograph of rock layers at the site gives useful future reference.

Collecting big fossils, such as bones of dinosaurs, calls for special skills and teams of workers. Report such finds to the paleontology department of a museum or university, or at least inform your nearest natural history museum.

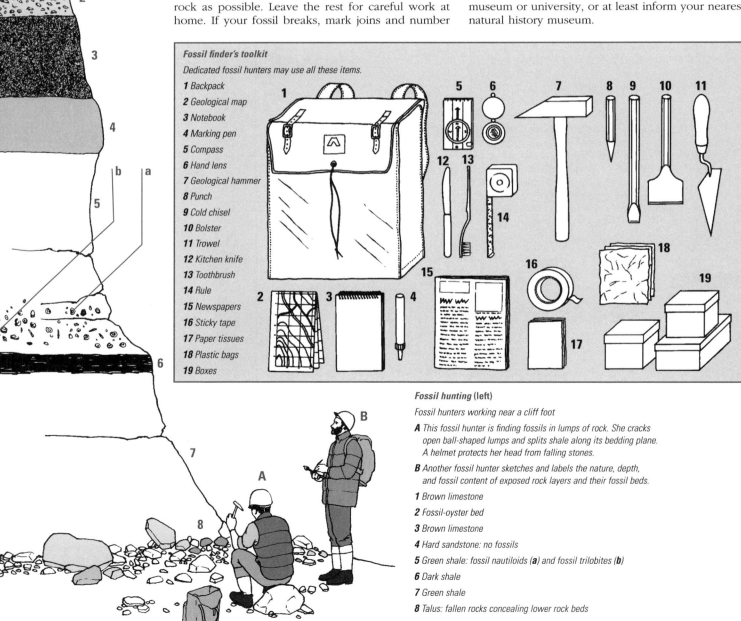

Fossil finder's toolkit

Dedicated fossil hunters may use all these items.

1 Backpack
2 Geological map
3 Notebook
4 Marking pen
5 Compass
6 Hand lens
7 Geological hammer
8 Punch
9 Cold chisel
10 Bolster
11 Trowel
12 Kitchen knife
13 Toothbrush
14 Rule
15 Newspapers
16 Sticky tape
17 Paper tissues
18 Plastic bags
19 Boxes

Fossil hunting (left)

Fossil hunters working near a cliff foot

A This fossil hunter is finding fossils in lumps of rock. She cracks open ball-shaped lumps and splits shale along its bedding plane. A helmet protects her head from falling stones.

B Another fossil hunter sketches and labels the nature, depth, and fossil content of exposed rock layers and their fossil beds.

1 Brown limestone

2 Fossil-oyster bed

3 Brown limestone

4 Hard sandstone: no fossils

5 Green shale: fossil nautiloids (**a**) and fossil trilobites (**b**)

6 Dark shale

7 Green shale

8 Talus: fallen rocks concealing lower rock beds

Digging up dinosaurs and primates

The slope above a single dinosaur bone may yield much of the skeleton still stuck in rock. A paleontologist tries to dig around the bones to judge the fossil's state and size, but freeing a large dinosaur from its rocky tomb may require the services of a team of experts and their workers. Power hammers, bulldozers, and explosives help them strip away hard overlying rock. Picks and shovels will remove soft and crumbly rock. (You can simply brush away the sand covering some Saharan Desert dinosaurs.) Careful scraping and chiseling begin as a team hones in on brittle bones.

Scientists number and photograph the bared bones and plot exactly where they lie. Then they spray resin or paint glue on fragile bones to harden them. Plastic foam, or sackcloth soaked in plaster, cushion big bones or bones in lumps of rock. Now the frail trophies are ready to withstand a bumpy truck ride across rough tracks to a museum.

Fossil bones or stone implements found scattered on the ground yield only isolated clues to early humans. But chance surface finds may lead to bones, tools, and pollen from a single time and place, still buried undisturbed in ancient sediments. Careful excavation of such sites can tease out information about our early ancestors, their ways of life, surroundings, and antiquity.

Excavation typically starts with mapping of the site to be explored. Paleoanthropologists or archaeologists mark it with a grid of meter squares, gather surface finds, then dig out the squares in blocks or trenches, working down through sediments a layer at a time. The team might use picks and shovels to clear overburden. Then work slows as diggers turn to finer tools like trowels. Dental probes and brushes remove rock matrix stuck to fossils, and sieves reveal small teeth and bits of bone.

Some excavations demand unusual methods. For instance, South African caves contain frail australopithecine bones set in a natural "concrete" called breccia that can only be drilled out in chunks, followed by weeks of treatment to remove the bones intact. Submerged sites involve work under water; relay teams of archaeologists trained as divers use special tools for shifting mud or silt, plotting finds, and raising them.

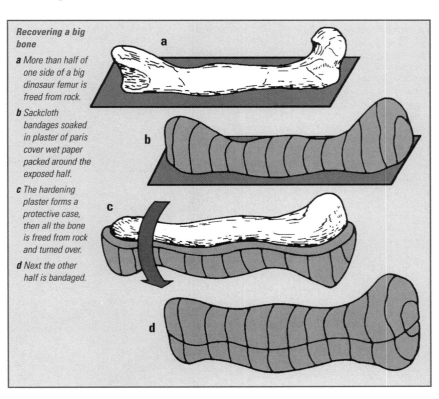

Recovering a big bone

a More than half of one side of a big dinosaur femur is freed from rock.

b Sackcloth bandages soaked in plaster of paris cover wet paper packed around the exposed half.

c The hardening plaster forms a protective case, then all the bone is freed from rock and turned over.

d Next the other half is bandaged.

Underwater excavation

An archaeologist trained in scuba diving uses a grid frame for plotting the positions of old wine jars lying on the seabed. The Roman ship conveying them foundered off southern Turkey more than 1,600 years ago.

Excavated burial (left)

This archaeologist is brushing soil from a double burial. He leaves enough to keep the skeletons intact. After a photographic record has been made the bones may be removed and studied.

Inside a fish's skull

This drawing of an ancient fish's brain is based on one made by the Swedish paleontologist Erik Stensio in the 1920s. Stensio used fine needles to remove the fossil skull, revealing rock formed in internal cavities that once contained brain, nerves, and blood vessels. Stensio's discovery proved cephalaspids had been early fishes, not salamanders as some people once supposed.

Cleaning and repairing fossils

Acid preparation (right)

Illustrations show four stages in using acid to reveal a fossil embedded in a rock.

1 *Rock encloses almost all the fossil.*

2 *The rock is soaked in acid for 2- to 6-hour periods.*

3 *Each time the soaked rock has been removed from the acid, it is washed in deionized water for a day, completely dried, and then the exposed fossil is painted with a plastic glue.*

4 *The prepared specimen is left to soak in water for up to two weeks.*

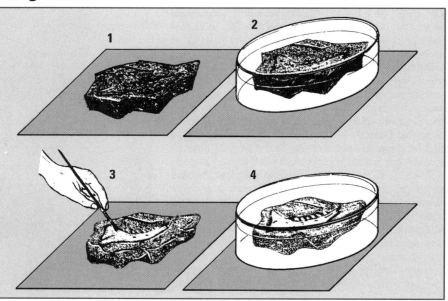

Museums receive many fossil skeletons resembling unsorted pieces of a jigsaw puzzle in rock. There are ways to free each bone or bit of shell and clean it for display.

The first task is soaking, sawing, slicing, or otherwise removing protective packing wrapped around a fossil still embedded in its rock. Next, technicians use special chemical solutions to harden exposed, fragile bones. Then they set to work with tools, chemicals, or both. People may chip away with hammer and chisel. Experts can work faster and more carefully with help from power tools, such as grinding burrs or dental drills with rapidly revolving diamond cutting wheels. Vibrating tungsten points of pneumatic power pens and gas jets firing an abrasive powder can cut through rock as if it were as soft as butter. Ultrasonic waves attack weaknesses in certain rocks. But sewing needles serve to clean tiny, fragile skulls.

Sometimes laboratory workers crush rock with a pestle and mortar, sieve the particles, and then inspect them with a microscope. All this separates and shows microfossils.

Chemicals have uses, too. Soaking limestone in dilute acetic or formic acid may remove the rock without dissolving fossils in it. Other acids attack rocks rich in iron and silica, while certain alkalis will break down shales and clays. Some chemicals are poisonous or burn the skin, so people handle these with special care.

Mending broken fossil bones and teeth is another job for the laboratory. Workers match two pieces at a time. They clean matching surfaces, then stick them together with a special adhesive. Rubber bands, metal clamps, or other aids hold the bits together until the adhesive dries.

Inside a brachiopod (right)

This much enlarged view shows the inside of one valve of a fossil brachiopod after acid treatment. Acid has etched away unwanted rock, revealing spiral riblike structures that once supported the creature's feeding system.

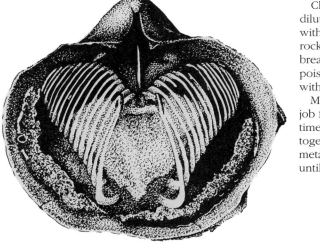

Cleaning tools (right)

Of the tools shown, the first two free fossils from hard rock; the others remove soft rock from fossils.

a *Speed engraver, with a fast-vibrating point*

b *Awl*

c *Fine-bristle brush*

d *Toothbrush*

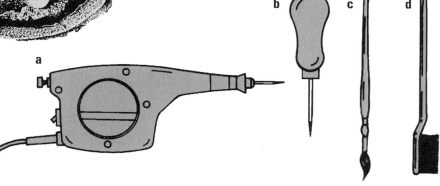

Preparing fossil dinosaurs

When fossil dinosaurs arrive at a museum, the work of studying their skeletons begins.

First a place must be found to house the bones–no easy task when a successful expedition brings back hundreds of colossal specimens.

Next, laboratory technicians known as preparators tackle the often tricky job of teasing out those fossil bones still stuck in chunks of rock. This process can take many months. Often it begins with soaking, sawing, and slicing off the hardened plaster jackets that saved specimens from damage on their journey from where they were found. Next, chemical solutions harden weak areas of exposed bone. Cushioning the rocky chunks against damage, preparators may then use an arsenal of power tools to free fossils from unwanted rock. They chip away with small pneumatic chisels, sandblast with abrasive powder fired by jets of gas, wield dental drills with diamond cutting wheels, or attack with vibropens whose fast-vibrating tips eat away hard rock. Sewing needles, though, are often best for cleaning out small, fragile skulls.

Certain kinds of rock are best removed by soaking in dilute acetic acid. Over several months, acid baths dissolve away the rock but leave the fossil bones intact.

Some fossil dinosaurs are difficult to tackle in these ways–for instance, embryos in stony, fossil eggs; skulls filled with solid stone; and skeletons buried deep in rocks almost too hard to excavate. Now, though, new techniques mean we can "see" these fossil objects without touching or cutting away their rocky cores or coverings. Devices used for taking human brainscans can scan a stone-filled dinosaur braincase and indicate how well that animal could see, hear, smell, and think. X rays and CAT (computerized axial tomography) scans can also show unhatched baby dinosaurs inside their eggs. A special "radar" scanner from New Mexico's Los Alamos National Laboratories probed the hard rock tomb of *Seismosaurus*, helping to detect its monstrous skeleton still hidden underground.

Back in the laboratory, preparators do more than clean up fossils. They may need to guard them from decay. Exposed to humid air, some fossil bones soon crack and crumble to dust. This problem once threatened Belgium's famous herd of *Iguanodon*. The fossil bones contained fool's gold (iron pyrites). Early hardening treatment trapped moisture, prolonging damage done as hard iron pyrites slowly turned to powdery iron sulfate. Modern preparators treat pyrite disease with ethanolamine thioglycolate, which neutralizes and removes the decay products.

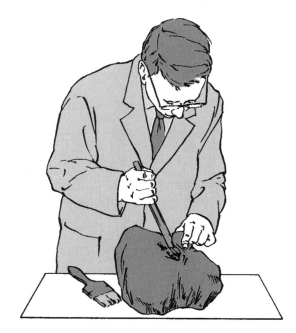

Removing packing (left)

A technician cuts away the plaster jacket that has protected a bone on its trip from excavation site to museum laboratory.

Acid bath (below)

Wearing protective mask and gloves, a preparator hauls a tray of bones from an acid bath. This has dissolved away the block of rock in which the bones had been embedded.

Removing rock

Powerful magnification helps this preparator wield a power tool with precision to free fragile bones from rock.

Understanding fossil dinosaurs

Cleaned, and maybe mended with a special glue, distinctive bones enable scientists to identify a dinosaur. Understanding how the bones once joined makes it possible to reconstruct the skeleton.

Study of a new kind of dinosaur means producing an illustrated article. First the scientist measures and describes the bones. Technical terms help the scientist name each bone and locate special features–ridges or hollows, for example. Photographs and detailed drawings show key bones from several aspects–dorsal (from above), ventral (from below), medial (from the inside), lateral (from the outside), proximal (closest to the point of attachment to the body), and distal (farthest from the point of attachment to the body). How the bones resemble or differ from bones of other dinosaurs suggests to which group of dinosaurs the animal belonged.

Fossils not only show how a dinosaur was built, they hint at how it lived. Braincase, eye sockets, teeth, backbone, limbs, muscle scars, and bony ridges that anchored muscles are clues to sight, hearing, and level of intelligence; how its jaws worked; what it ate; and how it walked or ran.

The paleontologist sums up such findings and gives the dinosaur a scientific name allotted to no other animal. Then he or she submits the written paper to a scientific journal. Independent experts approve the article before it is published.

Keeping up to date with new discoveries published in obscure journals and unfamiliar languages is difficult. Then, too, even writers of scientific articles make mistakes. Experts therefore do their best to visit museum collections worldwide, to study and compare specimens at first hand. This work has produced "new" kinds of dinosaurs from dusty storerooms where scores of bones had lodged for decades, misdescribed or nameless. Comparative dinosaur studies can also profit from computers. A paleontologist sitting at a desk can call up computer images of fossils in museums almost anywhere on Earth.

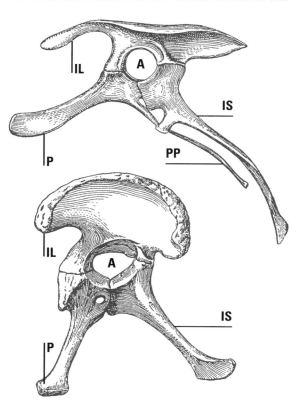

Hip design

Drawings from an article by the French-Belgian paleontologist Louis Dollo show differences in hip design between both main dinosaur groups.

Above:

Hip girdle of an ornithischian, Iguanodon

Below:

Hip girdle of a saurischian, Diplodocus

*Labeled bones are ilium (**IL**), ischium (**IS**), and pubis (**P** and **PP**). In Iguanodon **P** is an extension of the pubis. The acetabulum (**A**) is a socket for the hip bone.*

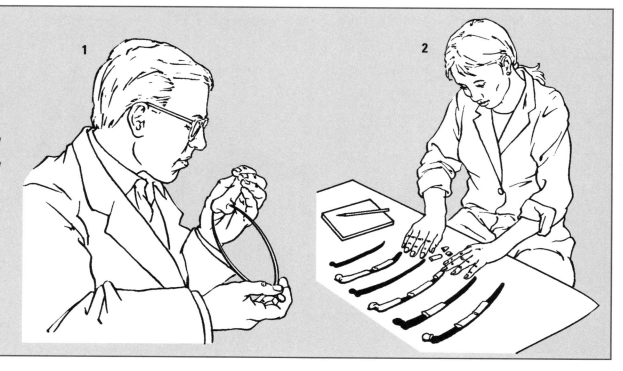

Studying a dinosaur

Careful study of even a few bones can help a scientist to work out the shape and size of the skeleton they came from.

1 *Using calipers to make key measurements of individual bones.*

2 *Extrapolating bones from fragments and plotting their relationships to one another. (Damaged bones can be repaired and missing bones may be replaced by casts.)*

Understanding fossil primates

To skilled interpreters, old bones and artifacts are encyclopedias of prehistoric primate life.

Comparing the measurements and structures of scores of bones and teeth has enabled scientists to identify individual bits of skull or limb bone as, say, Neandertal or dryopithecine ape.

Anatomy also offers clues to physical abilities and modes of life. Long bones indicate body build and height. Shoulder girdles betray which primates swung from trees. The position of the hole that lets the spinal cord in through the skull shows if a creature held its head erect or jutting forward. Thumb and finger bones and joints are guides to power grip, precision grip or, in very early primates, lack of any grip at all. Bones of hips, thighs, and toes distinguish quadrupedal climbers from bipedal walkers and upright walkers from those whose bodies tilt from side to side.

Skulls are guides to brain capacity and the ability to see and smell. Jaws and teeth–especially tooth structures, sizes, shapes, and wear–are powerful clues to what their owner ate.

Fossil bones can tell us more; from these an expert can deduce some kinds of injury or illness and if the victim had made a good recovery. Teeth and long bones may pinpoint the age at death.

Further information about prehistoric hominids comes from their enduring artifacts–at first mostly stone, bone, and charcoal, and later, pottery and post holes. These show how technology advanced and early humans found more efficient ways of securing food, warmth, and shelter.

New study methods also shed fresh light on early tools. Experimenters rediscover how our ancestors made and used stone implements. Lastly, tool and animal remains from camps of modern Stone Age hunters like the Inuit give glimpses into prehistoric social life. Comparing Inuit and ancient camp remains helps scientists work out the sizes of prehistoric hunting bands, activities their members shared, how long bands spent at individual sites, and at which times of year.

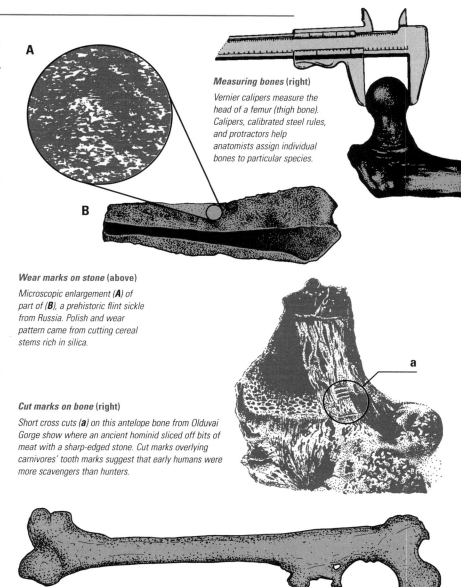

Measuring bones (right)

Vernier calipers measure the head of a femur (thigh bone). Calipers, calibrated steel rules, and protractors help anatomists assign individual bones to particular species.

Wear marks on stone (above)

*Microscopic enlargement (**A**) of part of (**B**), a prehistoric flint sickle from Russia. Polish and wear pattern came from cutting cereal stems rich in silica.*

Cut marks on bone (right)

*Short cross cuts (**a**) on this antelope bone from Olduvai Gorge show where an ancient hominid sliced off bits of meat with a sharp-edged stone. Cut marks overlying carnivores' tooth marks suggest that early humans were more scavengers than hunters.*

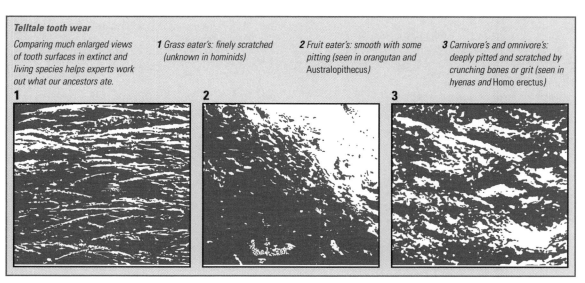

Telltale tooth wear

Comparing much enlarged views of tooth surfaces in extinct and living species helps experts work out what our ancestors ate.

1 *Grass eater's: finely scratched (unknown in hominids)*

2 *Fruit eater's: smooth with some pitting (seen in orangutan and* Australopithecus*)*

3 *Carnivore's and omnivore's: deeply pitted and scratched by crunching bones or grit (seen in hyenas and* Homo erectus*)*

Diseased bone (above)

*A bony growth (**a**) deforms this* Homo erectus *femur from Java– a possible result of food contaminated by fluoride compounds from a volcanic eruption.*

© DIAGRAM

Reconstructing dinosaur fossils

If most of a dinosaur has been recovered and described, preparators can rebuild the skeleton in standing pose, replacing missing bits with glass-fiber substitutes. Hip girdle, skull, ribs, limb bones, breastbone, and vertebrae (the bones of neck, back, and tail) may go up in a special sequence. If the skeleton is large, strong scaffolding is needed to hold heavy bones in place. Then metal rods or tubes are bent to fit and are clipped onto the jointed bones. After months of work, people can remove the heavy scaffolding, leaving almost all the skeleton on view.

A museum can make life-size replicas of its famous dinosaur skeletons. First, technicians produce silicone rubber molds of individual bones, then they fill the molds with glass-fiber casts. The museum can then sell its glass-fiber skeletons or swap these with other museums for casts of other beasts to add to its collection.

Reconstructed real or imitation skeletons enable artists and sculptors to produce lifelike restorations of the bodies of long-vanished creatures.

The dinosaurs of paintings, models, movies, books, and comic strips are all based on fossil evidence. Its study has transformed how scientists themselves see dinosaurs.

Even when a skeleton was largely known, scientists sometimes failed to realize how its owner stood or moved, or what it really looked like. They wrongly thought that most dinosaurs sprawled, with elbows stuck out at the sides. Many believed *Iguanodon* and *Tyrannosaurus* held their heads high like a kangeroo and walked with their tails dragging on the ground. *Hypsilophodon* was thought to be a tree-climber, while the great sauropods wallowed in water because their legs could not support their weight on land. Like theropods, ornithischians supposedly had mouths that ran from ear to ear. Patient probing of old bones disproved these notions and produced the images of dinosaurs depicted later in this book.

Build and stance

Illustrations spanning more than 120 years show changing ideas about what big predatory dinosaurs were like.

1 Megalosaurus *shown as a quadrupedal predator [From L. Figuier's* The World Before the Deluge *(1866)]*

2 Tarbosaurus *shown bipedally, but with legs stuck out sideways, heavy belly, kangaroo posture, and drooping tail [From Z. V. Spinar's* Life Before Man *(1972)]*

3 Tyrannosaurus, *with S-curved neck, legs directly below lean body, and horizontal back and tail–a beast combining strength and speed*

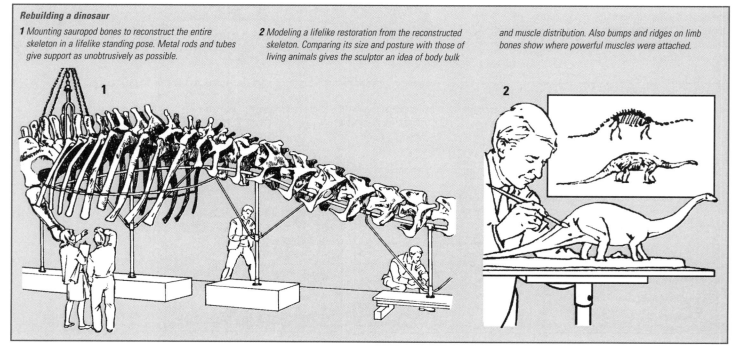

Rebuilding a dinosaur

1 *Mounting sauropod bones to reconstruct the entire skeleton in a lifelike standing pose. Metal rods and tubes give support as unobtrusively as possible.*

2 *Modeling a lifelike restoration from the reconstructed skeleton. Comparing its size and posture with those of living animals gives the sculptor an idea of body bulk* and muscle distribution. Also bumps and ridges on limb bones show where powerful muscles were attached.

Reconstructing fossil primates

Reconstructing fossil skulls and limbs and restoring lost, soft body parts helps us visualize the prehistoric ancestors of modern humans.

First, museum preparators clean the bones. Drills, vibrating tools, or sandblasting remove adhering sandy, gritty rock. Repeated washing and treatments with acetic acid free fossils stuck in breccia. Wet bones can be dried out by hanging them in n-Butyl alcohol. Laboratory experts will harden fragile porous bones with man-made plastics dissolved in solvents or emulsions in water.

Skilled anatomists then join bits of bone, like pieces of a jigsaw puzzle, to reconstruct a skull or skeleton, perhaps replacing missing bits with plastic imitations. The shapes and sizes of certain bones show how a fossil creature held its head and limbs. Making and mounting one reconstruction can take weeks or months of careful work.

From reconstructed skulls and skeletons, artists and sculptors expert in anatomy can restore whole heads and bodies. The strength and size of limb bones indicates the size of muscles used to operate them.

Bumps, grooves, and other features found on bones betray muscles' attachment points and shapes. Thus bony bumps and ridges on the skull show where large muscles held up a forward-jutting head or operated powerful jaws. All this helps artists to flesh out a skull or skeleton, first adding muscles and body fat, then skin and hair.

Yet restoring fossil bodies involves more uncertainty than joining a dismembered skeleton, for not all soft parts leave their marks on bones. Two sculptors working from one hominid skull may produce two very different heads—one more human looking than the other. Similarly, only informed guessing can reproduce skin, eye, hair color, and the amount of body hair.

Developing a fossil (below)

Dental picks, powered vibrating tools, scalpels, and magnifying lenses are among the tools and instruments that may be used to help a preparator free a fossil from its matrix.

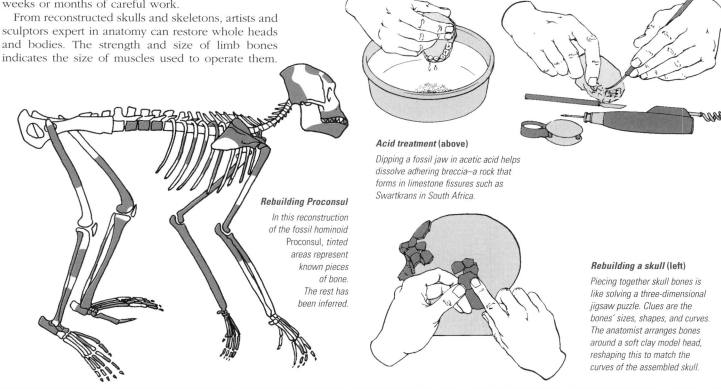

Acid treatment (above)

Dipping a fossil jaw in acetic acid helps dissolve adhering breccia—a rock that forms in limestone fissures such as Swartkrans in South Africa.

Rebuilding Proconsul

In this reconstruction of the fossil hominoid Proconsul, tinted areas represent known pieces of bone. The rest has been inferred.

Rebuilding a skull (left)

Piecing together skull bones is like solving a three-dimensional jigsaw puzzle. Clues are the bones' sizes, shapes, and curves. The anatomist arranges bones around a soft clay model head, reshaping this to match the curves of the assembled skull.

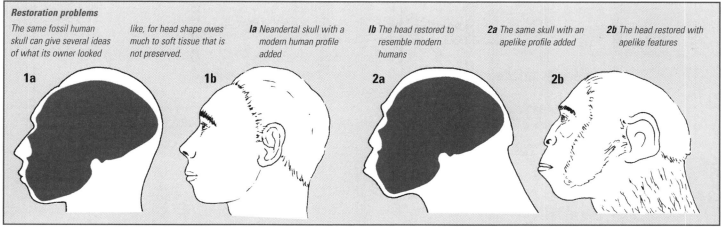

Restoration problems

The same fossil human skull can give several ideas of what its owner looked like, for head shape owes much to soft tissue that is not preserved.

Ia Neandertal skull with a modern human profile added

Ib The head restored to resemble modern humans

2a The same skull with an apelike profile added

2b The head restored with apelike features

1a

1b

2a

2b

© DIAGRAM

Plants and plantlike organisms

These pages include a brief evolutionary overview of the plant kingdom (Plantae), a vast group of organisms on which all animals depend directly or indirectly for their food. We describe major types with examples. Some groups' names and ranks are disputed; we call most clades.

The chapter includes primitive, plantlike seaweeds and one-celled "protists" in kingdoms of their own. Nine share the tree below with plants. The facing page shows some plantlike protists, once called "protophytes." Certain "protozoans" (protists with more similarities to animals) are described in the next chapter, along with invertebrates.

Plants and plantlike organisms

Of the selected kingdoms shown, *2–8* consist of one-celled protists.

1 *Rhodophyta (red seaweeds)*
2 *Foraminifera*
3 *Ciliata*
4 *Dinoflagellata*
5 *Radiolaria*
6 *Coccolithophorida*
7 *Bacillariophyta (diatoms)*
8 *Silicoflagellata*
9 *Phaeophyta (brown seaweeds)*
10 *Plantae (plants)*

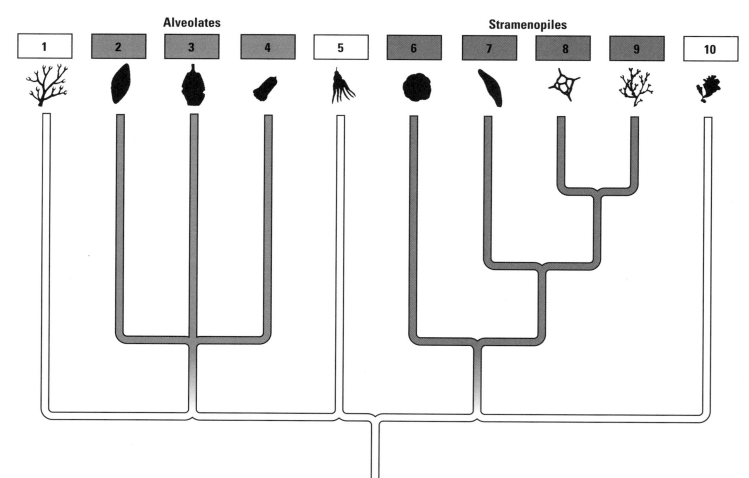

"Protophytes"

Four "protophytes"

1 Gonyaulacysta is known only from fossils of its resting form: a hard-walled cyst. Time: Silurian onward (guide fossils since Triassic times). Clade: Dinoflagellata (dinoflagellates), sea surface microorganisms 0.005-2 mm across. Each has a groove around the body and lashes itself along with two cilia ("whips").

2 A silicoflagellate has one or two "whips" and a tube or rodlike opal skeleton, often fossilized. Silicoflagellates are organisms 0.02–0.1 mm across, dating from Cretaceous times.

3 Cymbella has a two valved skeleton like a glass box with an overlapping lid. Length: 0.03 mm. Time: Pliocene onward. Clade: Bacillariophyta (diatoms)—oblong, round, and other microorganisms dating from Cretaceous times. Accumulations of their shells form diatomaceous earth.

4 Coccolithus is a ball-shaped sea microorganism covered in limy plates. Time: Pliocene onward. Clade: Coccolithophorida important rock formers since Jurassic times. Their plates 0.002–0.01 mm across sink on death, building layers of chalk or chalky mud.

Plants have cells surrounded by a cellulose wall, not just a membrane like that around animal cells. Plants use the green pigment chlorophyll to manufacture carbon dioxide and water.

Some protists that move about like animals have plantlike features. The main groups of these so-called "protophytes" are so distinct that they deserve to rank in kingdoms of their own.

Protists evolved by 1.2 billion years ago, from simple cells swallowing cyanobacteria ("blue-green algae") and other bacteria that then lived on inside them. The new "committee" microorganisms reproduced by dividing, like bacteria, but most of their ingredients also split, in complex ways.

Prehistoric protophytes mostly drifted in the sea. Their fossils help scientists date rocks formed in the last 200 million years.

Food factory (below)

This diagram shows (much magnified) structures in a tiny, living, one-celled "protophyte," Prymnesium. Even such microscopic scraps of life are highly organized.

a Haptonema

b Flagellum (a whiplike structure used in locomotion)

c Golgi body (rich in fat)

d Pyrenoid (a protein body)

e Chloroplast (food-producing unit containing chlorophyll)

f Fat (stored energy supply)

g Nucleus (control center essential for the cell's life and reproduction)

h Leucosin vesicle, containing food reserves

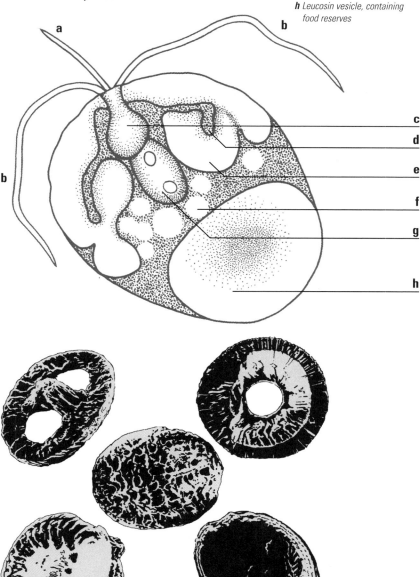

Coccoliths (right)

Shown here (much enlarged) are examples of coccoliths (literally "seed stones"). Many of these limy platelets, measuring less than one-hundredth of a millimeter across, cover each Coccolithus *and its relatives. Distinctive shapes and fast evolution make coccoliths good guides to the ages of such rocks as chalk.*

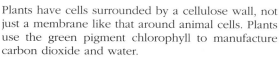

© DIAGRAM

Simple plants and seaweeds

Four examples

1 Stephanochara, an Oligocene stonewort, produced this female sex organ with a wall composed of helically arranged cells, shown magnified about 20 times. Clade: Charophyceae, an algal group that dates back to Devonian times.

2 Ulva, sea lettuce, is a green, shallow water seaweed. Size: 10–46 cm (4–18 in). Clade: Ulvophyceae (green algae), known since at least as early as Cambrian times.

3 Fucus is a brown shore seaweed. Height: 13–91 cm (5 in–3 ft). Clade: Phaeophyta (brown algae), perhaps dating from Ordovician times.

4 Ceramium is a red seaweed, banded and with forked, inturned tips. Height: 2.5–30.5 cm (1 in–1 ft). Clade: Rhodophyta (red algae), dating from Precambrian times.

5 Marchantia is a liverwort. Size: 5 cm (2 in). Clade: Marchantiopsida (liverworts), perhaps dating from Cambrian times.

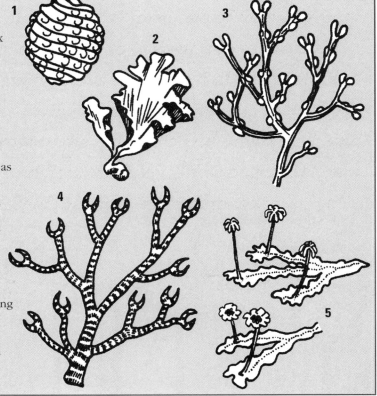

A brown seaweed (below)

Here we show features of the intertidal seaweed Fucus vesiculosus (bladder wrack).

a Receptacles (swollen branch tips containing mucilage filled conceptacles where sex cells develop)

b Air bladder, for buoyancy

c Blade

d Stipe

e Holdfast

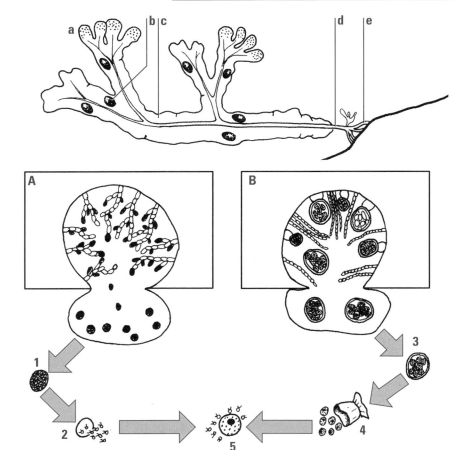

People once believed that the simplest, most primitive plants were the green, red, and brown "algae" known as seaweeds. Scientists now group the last two in kingdoms of their own. Only the "green algae," such as the Ulvophyceae, which include the sea lettuce pictured on this page, are still considered plants.

These fragile plants need water to support their flimsy bodies and stop them from drying up. Stoneworts form another primitive water-loving group. From some such moisture-loving organisms came all higher plants. The first land plants were probably ancestral to the liverworts and mosses, often collectively called bryophytes. Some have leaves but none has roots. All reproduce by spores. Ancient fossil spores described in the year 2000 show that land plants had appeared 0.5 billion years ago.

Sexual reproduction (left)

Fucus vesiculosus *has the life cycle shown in this diagram.*

A Male conceptacle

B Female conceptacle

1 Antheridium

2 Male sex cells being released

3 Oogonium

4 Female sex cells being released

5 Male sex cells surrounding a female sex cell; one male cell fertilizes the female

Vascular plants

Vascular plants–plants with internal channels for transporting liquids–include ferns, conifers, and flowering plants. Algal ancestors received support and nourishment in water, but vascular plants evolved for life on land. Roots give anchorage and obtain water from soil. Stems raise the food producing leaves up to the light. A waterproof cuticle prevents desiccation. Stomata–holes that can be closed–let gases in and out for food production and respiration. Above all, a "plumbing" system of tiny internal tubes transports water and salts up from the soil and dissolved food down from the leaves.

Vascular plants appeared about 400 million years ago. Pioneers had short, bare stems and neither roots nor leaves. Tall plants with woody stems became the first true trees. Among these were the giant club mosses and horsetails of swampy Carboniferous forests. Their compressed carbonaceous remains formed coal.

Here we describe prehistoric examples from three spore-producing groups: "rhyniophytes," lycopsids, and equisetopsids.

Early land plants

1 Cooksonia, the first known vascular plant, had simple forked, leafless stems, each ending in a spore-filled cap. Height: about 5 cm (2 in). Time: late Silurian. Place: Wales. Various species, known as "rhyniophytes."

2 Asteroxylon had a main stem with forked branches bearing tightly packed, tiny leaflets. Height: up to 1 m (3 ft 3 in). Time: early Devonian. Place: Scotland. Clade: Lycopsida (club mosses).

3 Lepidodendron was a giant club moss with a rootlike anchoring organ divided into four main branches: a broad, tall, bare trunk crowned by two sets of repeatedly forked branches bearing narrow leaves; and small and large spores, the latter borne in conelike structures. Height: 30 m (100 ft). Time: Carboniferous. Place: Europe and North America. Clade: Lycopsida.

4 Calamites had a tall, jointed stem and upswept branches bearing rings of narrow leaves. Height: up to 30 m (100 ft). Time: Carboniferous. Place: Europe and North America. Clade: Equisetopsida (horsetails).

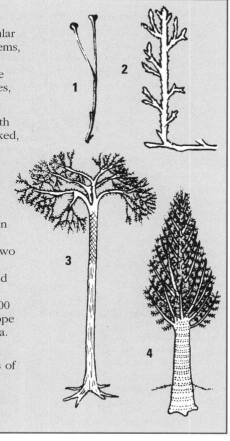

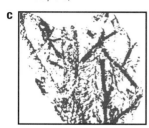

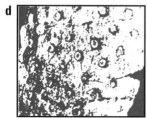

Lepidodendron restored

Fossil finds (below) enabled scientists to reconstruct the tree they came from (left).

a Piece of trunk scarred by shedding old leaves

b Piece of grooved, midlevel trunk

c Branches with leaves

d Surface of rootlike anchoring structure

e Whole tree, with a human to show its size. (Many other plant fossils left such fragmentary remains that we cannot even guess the shape and size of the whole plant.)

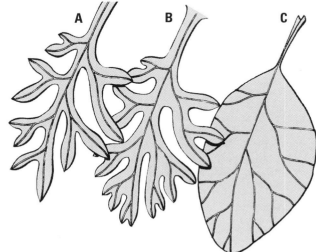

Leaves evolving (above)

These three illustrations retrace the likely evolution of compound leaves from stems.

A Branching stems of certain early plants probably had broad flat rims. These increased the surface area exposed to sunlight. Such stems trapped more light than others and so produced more food.

B Later plants produced more branches than their ancestors, which increased the surface area still further.

C Later still came plants whose many, wide-rimmed branches fused to form broad plates that faced the Sun. These plates were leaves.

© DIAGRAM

Ferns and gymnosperms

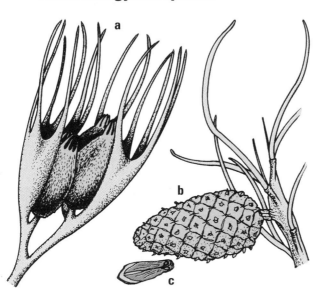

Seeds and cones (right)

These two examples contrast the seeds and seed containing structures of an early and a modern flowerless plant.

a Forked branches form the "bracts," which only loosely surround the seeds in a late Devonian plant called Archaeosperrna.

b A woody cone surrounds many individual seeds in a modern conifer. The cone opens when the seeds are ripe to let them fall.

c A conifer seed has a built-in winglike blade. Ripe seeds flutter down lightly, dispersing on the wind.

Ferns and "gymnosperms," an artificial group, probably arose from plants like *Cooksonia* more than 350 million years ago. Many ferns have feathery or straplike leaves called fronds. They lack flowers or seeds and disperse by spores shed from the fronds' undersides. A spore falling on damp soil grows into a minute "breeding" plant that produces male and female cells. Male cells fertilize female cells, which then develop into normal fern plants.

Gymnosperms ("naked seed" plants) include the ginkgo and conifers, flowerless plants reproducing by seeds not spores. Seeds develop when windblown pollen fertilizes egg cells still on the parent plant. The ripe seeds have food supplies and waterproof coats. Thus fallen seeds survive drought, sprouting when rain soaks the soil. Ferns and seed ferns flourished in warm, wet Carboniferous forests. Gymnosperms became diversified during Mesozoic times. This page shows spore-bearing fern and relatives (**1–3**); a seed-fern (**4**); seed-bearing gymnosperms (**6–9**); and a seed-bearing anthophyte (**5**).

Spore-bearers and seed-bearers

1 Cladoxylon was a primitive "fern ancestor" with a main stem, forked branches, forked leaves, and fanlike spore containing structures. Time: mid-late Devonian. Clade: Cladoxyliidae (extinct).

2 Stauropteris had forked stems tipped with spore-filled caps, much like ancestral *Cooksonia*. Time: Carboniferous. Clade: Stauropteridae (extinct).

3 Psaronius was a prehistoric tree fern. Height: about 7 m (23 ft). Time: Carboniferous/Permian. Clade: Marattiidae (still surviving in the Tropics).

4 Medullosa was a seed fern, producing seeds not spores. Height: 4.6 m (15 ft). Time: Carboniferous. Clade: Medullosaceae, seed ferns, (not true seed plants), abundant in Carboniferous forests.

5 Williamsonia sprouted stiff, palmlike fronds from a trunk. Height: 3 m (10 ft). Time: Jurassic. Clade: Bennettitales, also known as Cycadeoidophyta (extinct); in the Anthophyta, seed plants that include the flowering plants.

6 Zamia has leathery fronds rising from a short, fat, pithy stem. It is a survivor of the abundant Mesozoic cycads. Clade: Cycadatae (cycads).

7 Cordaites had a tall, slim, straight main trunk with a crown of branches bearing long, strap-shaped leaves. Seeds grew on stalks from conelike buds. Height: up to 30 m (100 ft). Time: Carboniferous. Clade: Cordaitidra (long extinct).

8 Ginkgo, a living fossil, has fan-shaped leaves. Height: up to 30 m (100 ft). Time: Permian onwards, widespread in the Jurassic. Clade: Ginkgoatae ("maidenhair trees").

9 Araucaria (monkey puzzle) is an evergreen, cone-bearing tree with stiff, flat, pointed leaves. Height: up to 45 m (150 ft). Time: similar species from the Jurassic onwards. Clade: Coniferidra (conifers).

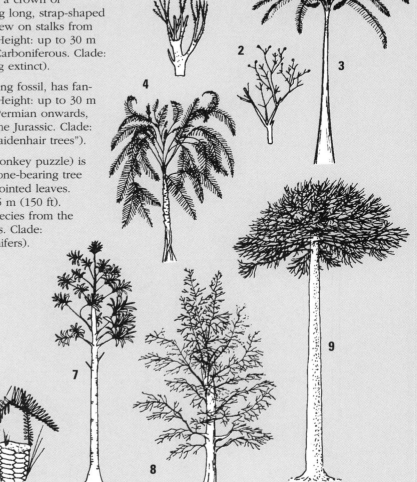

Flowering plants

Flowering plants are among the most successful land plants ever. They thrive from high latitudes to the equator, from seashore to mountaintop. They include most garden plants, farm crops, and broad-leaved trees, and range in size from 100-meter (330 ft) *Eucalyptus* trees to tiny duckweeds.

Reasons for success included a carpel–a protective covering that earns this major group of vascular plants its scientific name: Angiospermae ("enclosed seed plants"). Angiosperm seeds develop in greater safety than the "naked" seeds of gymnosperms, their likely ancestors. Finds of fossil leaves and pollen hint that flowering plants evolved about 120 million years ago. By 65 million years ago more than 90 percent of known fossil plants were angiosperms. Some resembled beeches, birches, maples, poplars, walnuts, and various other familiar kinds. Since Tertiary times the main change has been in distribution, as warmth-loving species tended to retreat from cooling polar regions.

Monocots and dicots

Our examples represent both main types of flowering plants: monocots, with one seed leaf, and dicots and eudicots with two seed-leaves. Dicots form the vast majority of angiosperms.

1 Buchloe, the living buffalo grass, represents the grasses–monocots that first became plentiful in the Miocene. Clade: Graminales (grasses and sedges).

2 Magnolia is a genus of dicot trees and shrubs with large leaves and showy flowers regarded as primitive in structure. Time: early Cretaceous onwards. Place: Asia and the Americas. Clade: Ranales, among the earliest of all known flowering plants.

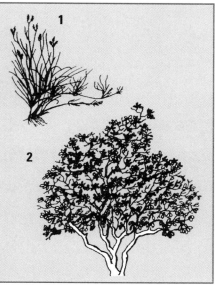

Fossil angiosperms

These Miocene plant fossil remains come from Switzerland. Fossil seeds and flowers are far rarer than fossil leaves, but most fossil angiosperms closely resemble living kinds.

1 Winged seeds of a Miocene maple, Acer trilobatum

2 The blossom of Porana oeningensis

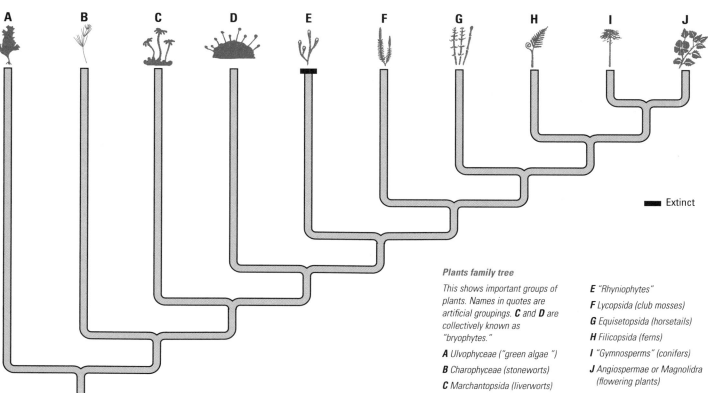

■ Extinct

Plants family tree

This shows important groups of plants. Names in quotes are artificial groupings. **C** *and* **D** *are collectively known as "bryophytes."*

A *Ulvophyceae ("green algae")*

B *Charophyceae (stoneworts)*

C *Marchantopsida (liverworts)*

D *Bryopsida (mosses)*

E *"Rhyniophytes"*

F *Lycopsida (club mosses)*

G *Equisetopsida (horsetails)*

H *Filicopsida (ferns)*

I *"Gymnosperms" (conifers)*

J *Angiospermae or Magnolidra (flowering plants)*

© DIAGRAM

Fossil invertebrates

Most phyla (the major groups of animals) are invertebrates–creatures with no backbone. According to some experts invertebrates account for 38 of 39 phyla comprising the kingdom Animalia. (Even the other phylum includes some groups without a backbone.) This chapter surveys the chief invertebrate groups significant as fossils, from simple sponges to complex echinoderms. It features, too, a page about the tiny protists with animal-like features, once lumped together as "protozoans" that can now arguably be divided into several kingdoms.

Early, soft-bodied invertebrates left few fossil traces. Most phyla may have appeared in the sea between 800 and 520 million years ago. This upsurge in evolution became possible as Earth's atmosphere became breathable and ozone shielded the surface of the sea from lethal ultraviolet radiation.

About invertebrates

"Invertebrates" is a name popularly used for the larger, lowlier section of the animal kingdom. This huge mixed group of animals without a backbone includes insects, worms, snails, and many more–living things with distinct body shapes and sizes, typically growing from an embryo or larva formed when male and female sex cells meet. Most invertebrates move about and, unlike plants, all feed upon organic matter, for no animals can manufacture food.

Invertebrates account for most creatures in the animal kingdom's three great groups: single-celled choanoflagellates; primitive, many-celled metazoans, such as sponges, containing cells very similar to choanoflagellates; and eumetazoans–animals made of many cells of different types, organized in tissues specialized to perform different tasks. The first two groups and, in the third group all but some of the Chordata (chordates), lack a backbone. All chordates have a notochord ("backstring"), a kind of body stiffener, but only one subgroup of chordates evolved a backbone made of vertebrae. From those first vertebrates came all the creatures featured in the chapters after this.

Borehole tracks from rocks in Zambia suggest that "protozoans" might have given rise to sponges and eumetazoans more than 1 billion years ago. Perhaps by 700 million years ago ancestral jellyfishes, worms, and other lowly eumetazoans lived beneath the sea. Step by step, evolution was forging creatures with three tissue layers, a digestive tube with mouth and anus at each end, symmetrical left and right sides of the body, and, eventually, a head. By 520 million years ago Cambrian seas probably teemed with all the major groups of animals alive today. Through time myriads of species died out, yet their fossils tell us what they looked like. Then, too, the living descendants of such prehistoric corals, mollusks, arthropods, echinoderms, and others help to show us how ancient organisms grew, fed, bred, and moved.

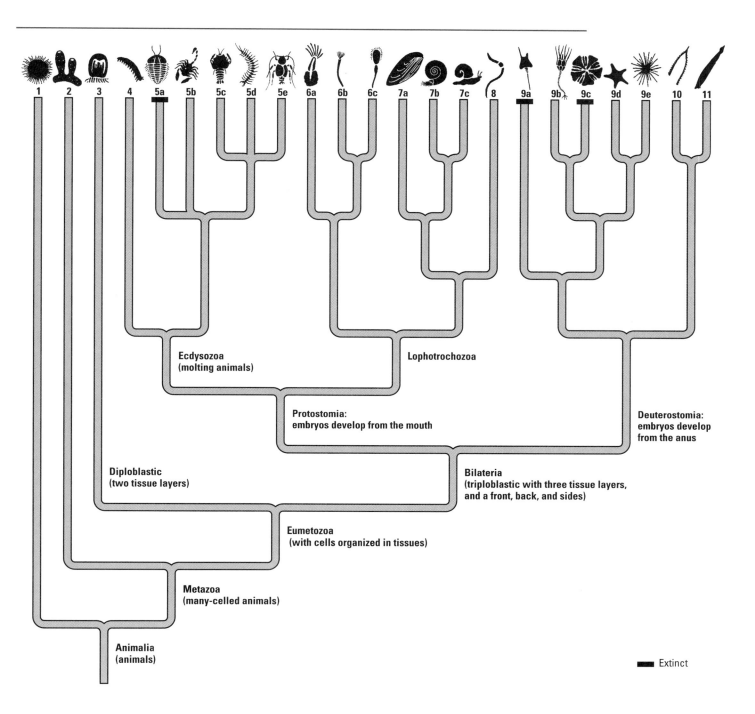

Ecdysozoa
(molting animals)

Lophotrochozoa

Protostomia:
embryos develop from the mouth

Deuterostomia:
embryos develop
from the anus

Diploblastic
(two tissue layers)

Bilateria
(triploblastic with three tissue layers,
and a front, back, and sides)

Eumetozoa
(with cells organized in tissues)

Metazoa
(many-celled animals)

Animalia
(animals)

■ Extinct

Many of these groups are significant as fossils.

1 Choanoflagellates

2 Porifera (sponges)

3 Cnidaria (jellyfishes and corals)

4 Onychophora (velvet worms)

5 Arthropoda (arthropods):

a Trilobita (trilobites)

b Chelicerata (scorpions)

c Crustacea (crustaceans)

d Myriapoda (millipedes, centipedes)

e Hexapoda or Insecta (insects)

6 "Lophophorates":

a "Bryozoans"

b Phoronida (phoronids)

c Brachiopoda (brachiopods)

7 Mollusca (mollusks):

a Bivalvia (bivalves)

b Cephalopoda (cephalopods)

c Gastropoda (gastropods)

8 Annelida (segmented worms)

9 Echinodermata (echinoderms):

a Homalozoa (carpoids)

b Crinoidea (crinoids)

c Blastozoa (blastoids and cystoids)

d Asteroidea (starfishes etc)

e Echinoidea (sea urchins)

10 "Hemichordates"

11 Chordata (chordates)

© DIAGRAM

Fusulinid features (below)

*Here the big foraminiferan
Fusulina is shown enlarged.*

a *Large test (skeleton)*

b *Spindle (sometimes
spherical) shape*

c *Composition: calcium carbonate*

d *Three- or four-layered
spirotheca (wall)*

e *Concentric chambers*

f *Fluted septa (divisions)*

g *Septal pores*

h *Foramen (opening)*

Protozoans

The name *protozoans* describes various groups of microscopic one-celled organisms with certain features seen in animals. Instead of making food as do many other protists, they tend to feed on other organisms or organic substances.

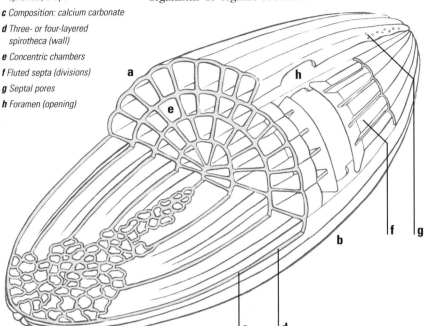

Protozoans include foraminiferans, radiolarians, and ciliates. Each is delicately shaped. Only prehistoric kinds with hard parts survived as fossils. The earliest date back more than 700 million years. Billions lived, and live, on seafloors or in surface waters. Their accumulating skeletons have formed thick rock layers in which some fossil types indirectly show the saltiness and warmth of ancient seas.

Four "protozoans"

Of our examples, numbers **1–3** belong to the phylum Rhizopoda, number **4** to the phylum Ciliata.

1 Fusulina had a large, chalky, spindle-shaped skeleton tapered at both ends. Size: 6 cm (2.4 in). Time: late Carboniferous. Kingdom: Foraminifera (foraminiferans: microorganisms usually known as fossils from their calcareous shells pierced by tiny holes. From these, in life, threadlike "false feet" projected for locomotion and seizing particles of food).

2 Nummulites belonged to a group of giant coin-shaped foraminiferans with limy, perforated shells comprising many chambers. Size: 1–6 cm (0.4–2.4 in). Time: Paleocene-Oligocene.

3 Cryptoprora resembles a lacy, pointed hat with ribbons hanging from the rim. Size: 0.1–1 mm (0.004–0.04 in). Time: Eocene onward. Kingdom: Radiolaria (protozoans with glassy, perforated skeletons shaped like hats, urns, or spheres).

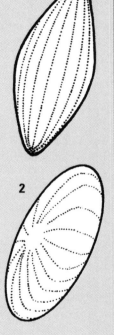

4 Tintinnopsis has a bell-shaped skeleton with a pointed "tail." Size: 0.1–0.2 mm (0.004–0.008 in). Time: Recent. Kingdom: Ciliata (ciliates), fringed by fine hairs (cilia) whose rhythmic beating helps them swim.

Problematic organisms (below)

Some fossil organisms fit no known group of protists, plants, or animals. They include the tiny aquatic acritarchs and chitinozoans, also the larger, many-celled Petalonamae, shown here.

A *Juvenile specimens*

B *Reconstructed group (smaller than life size) on a sandy seafloor, in late Precambrian times. Bodies comprised funnel-shaped colonies of branching tubes. The central cavity and scattered "needles" in the skeleton show that the Petalonamae had certain features found in sponges.*

Sponges

Sponges (Porifera) are among the simplest and most primitive of all metazoans. They are many-celled animals that lack true tissues or organs and can look misleadingly like plants. Sponges have simple baglike bodies open at one end and anchored to the seabed at the other. Mineral spicules (tiny rods) reinforce the body wall, which is pierced by tiny holes. The body cavity is lined with cells equipped with whips that draw in water through the holes. A sponge extracts food particles and oxygen from this water, and then whips drive the used water out through the osculum, the main body opening.

Some sponges live singly, others form colonies measuring from under 1 centimeter to more than 1 meter across (0.4 in–3.3 ft). Sponges grow as "vases," branches, or rock encrusting blobs. Fossil skeletal remains suggest that sponges evolved from protozoans 700 million years ago. Some prehistoric sponges built reeflike seabed rocks. Scientists divide the phylum Porifera (sponges) into four classes according to type of skeleton. Our examples show a fossil genus from each class.

Sponges and archaeocyathids

Here are five types of sponge, including an archaeocyathid. These were usually cup-shaped like a fossil coral, but with a sponge's perforated wall (in fact most had a double wall). They lived on seabeds in warm, clear seas worldwide, in early mid-Cambrian times. Some scientists put them in a phylum of their own, the Archaeocyatha.

1 Siphonia, about l cm (0.4 in) long, has lived since Cretaceous times. Class: Demospongea (horny sponges largely reinforced by networks of horny fibers).

2 Coeloptychium was a mushroom-shaped sponge common in late Cretaceous Europe. Diameter: 7.5 cm (3 in). Class: Hyalospongea (glass sponges with skeletons made up of six-rayed spicules).

3 Polytholosia resembled a string of pearls 5 cm (2 in) long. Time: Triassic. Class: Calcispongea (sponges with two- to four-rayed limy spicules).

4 Chaetetopsis, 4 cm (1.6 in) long, lived from Ordovician to Tertiary times. Class: Sclerospongea (coralline sponges with a skeleton of pin-shaped spicules).

5 Tabellaecyathus, was a cone shaped archaeocyathid, 4 cm (1.6 in) long. Time: Cambrian. Class: Irregulares (cup- and disc-shaped forms, often irregularly shaped).

Spicules and fibers

Scattered spicules are often the only clues to the fossil sponges in a rock layer. Here we show spicules from two classes of sponge and horny fibers from a third.

a *Calcareous spicules belonging to the Calcispongea*

b *Siliceous spicules belonging to the Hyalospongea*

c *Horny fibres belonging to the Demospongea; rare as fossils because they readily dissolve*

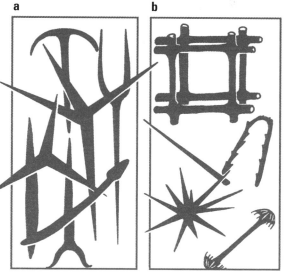

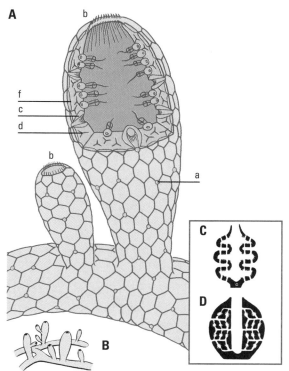

Sponge features

Shown here are different types of sponge, with features found in living specimens.

A *Simple sponge: cutaway view of part of a colony, shown much enlarged*

a *Incurrent pores let water enter*

b *Osculum lets water out*

c *Pore cell*

d *Spicule*

e *Collar cell*

f *Covering cell*

B *Simple sponge, actual size*

C *More advanced sponge, with a folded wall (shown in section)*

D *Complex sponge, with many canals and chambers (section)*

© DIAGRAM

Coelenterates

Coelenterates, or "hollow-gutted animals," are mostly jelly-like sea creatures. Each consists of many cells organized as tissues to produce a central body cavity with a mouth surrounded by tentacles and stinging cells for catching prey. Coelenterates are less primitive than sponges but have no central nervous system or systems for breathing, circulation, or excretion.

Cnidaria is the only phylum known from fossils. Cnidarians include jellyfishes, hydrozoans, sea anemones, and corals. Free swimming cnidarians (medusas) produce polyps "rooted" to the seafloor. Polyps produce medusas, and so on. Cnidarians evolved perhaps 700 million years ago. Limy cups enclosing colonial corals and hydrozoans in time built limestone reefs that formed rock layers.

Scarce survivors (left)

This fossil jellyfish came from Carboniferous rocks in Belgium. Fossils of soft bodied beasts like this are rare. They survive only in rocks such as shales or limestones formed from fine-grained particles of mud.

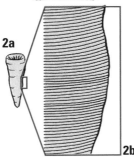

Growth of coral

Here we show how coral polyps form cups that have survived as fossils.

1 A living coral polyp in its coral cup. The creature builds its cup by adding a daily layer of calcium carbonate to its top.

2a Growth bands plainly show up on this Silurian coral cup, real height less than 2.5 cm (1 in).

2b This magnified view shows a few of the daily growth rings that produced the cup.

Cnidarians

Fossil cnidarians include these five examples. Numbers **3–5** are from the class Anthozoa (corals and sea anemones).

1 Conularia produced a polyp in a tall, hard, hollow "pyramid" inverted on the sea floor. Tentacles probably surrounded the broad mouth end. Length: 6-10 cm (2.4-4 in). Time: Cambrian-Triassic. Class: Scyphozoa (scyphozoans)–jellyfishes, or maybe in their own phylum.

2 Millepora comes in colonies of feeding polyps in central tubes, surrounded by protector polyps in other tubes. Size: 7 cm (2.8 in). Time: Recent. Class: Hydrozoa (hydrozoans).

3 Charnia, a sea pen, formed colonies of "feathers" growing from the seabed. Height: 14 cm (5l½ in). Time: Precambrian (about 570 million years ago). Subclass: Octocorallia (Alcyonaria), soft corals.

4 Streptelasma was a rugose ("wrinkled") coral, named for horizontal wrinkles on the skeleton's outer wall. Height: about 2.5 cm (1 in). Time: Ordovician-Silurian. Subclass: Zoantharia (stony corals). Order: Pterocorallia (rugose corals), mostly solitary, now extinct.

5 Halysites, a "chain coral," produced chains of tubes stuck together at the sides. Size: 5 cm (2 in) across. Time: Ordovician-Silurian. Subclass: Zoantharia. Order: Tabulata (tabulate corals, named from internal horizontal plates, or tabulae), extinct since Permian times.

6 Acropora produces a light, branching skeleton about 30.5 cm (1 ft) long. Time: Eocene–Recent. Subclass: Zoantharia. Order: Cyclocorallia (Scleractinia)–the major modern reef builders, probably evolved from naked sea anemones.

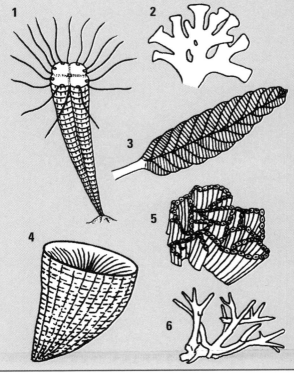

Mollusks 1

Mollusks ("soft" animals) include snails, clams, squids, and other creatures with a shell, muscular foot, or parts derived from these, and a digestive tract. Most live in the sea, grazing on algae, filtering food particles from mud or water, or hunting. Mollusks probably evolved in Precambrian times from animals like flatworms. By Carboniferous times, some mollusks invaded land and fresh water. No group of animals except the arthropods have diversified more. The phylum Mollusca produced many thousands of species, grouped into two subphyla with nine known fossil classes. Our examples all lived in the sea.

Four types of mollusk (below)

Shown here are sections through four of the main types of mollusk described on this page and the next.

A *Chiton (coat of mail shell)*

B *Clam (bivalve mollusk)*

C *Snail (gastropod)*

D *Squid (cephalopod). Despite differences, all share the same basic body plan, with the following common features:*

a *Shell (usually the only part preserved in fossils)*

b *Foot*

c *Digestive tract*

A

Unlikely bivalves

This restoration shows a seabed colony of rudists, 100 million years ago. In these bivalves, one valve was a lid that opened to let in food and water. Rudist shells built reefs before these mollusks died out at the end of the Cretaceous period.

B

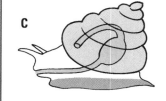
C

Six types of mollusk

1 Chiton (coat of mail shell) resembles a flattened wood louse guarded by a shell of seven or eight overlapping plates. It clings to rocks and grazes on algae. Chitons date from late Cambrian times. Only known fossil class: Polyplacophora.

2 Scenella was limpetlike, with a cap-shaped single shell. Size: 1 cm (0.5 in) across. Time: Cambrian. Class: Monoplacophora (maybe ancestral to the squids, octopuses, and other cephalopods).

3 Pleurotomaria was a primitive snail with a spiral, pointed shell about 5 cm (2 in) high. Time: Jurassic-Cretaceous. Class: Gastropoda (mollusks with head, foot, and a mantle that forms a bowl-shaped or spiral shell). They feed with a radula, a horny ribbon, armed with rows of rasping "teeth."

4 Dentalium lives in a slim, tusklike shell and burrows headfirst in soft sediment, extending threadlike tentacles to catch small organisms. Shell length: up to 12 cm (4.7 in). Class: Scaphopoda (tusk shells), known since Ordovician times.

5 Conocardium had a shell about 6cm (2.4in) across. Time: Ordovician-Permian. Class: Rostroconchia–extinct mollusks with a fused two-part shell that perhaps gave rise to bivalves.

6 Mytilus, the common mussel, is a bivalve, with a hinged, two part shell about 5 cm (2 in) long. Time: Triassic Recent. Class: Lamellibranchia (bivalves)– headless mollusks with a hinged, two valved shell.

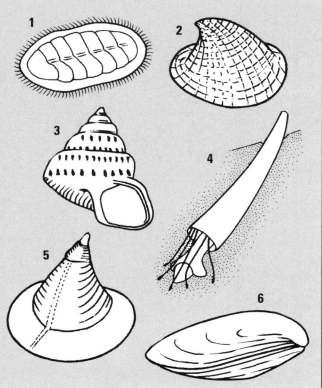

D
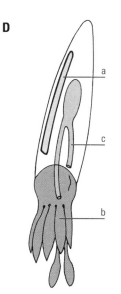

© DIAGRAM

Mollusks 2

A living nautiloid

Clues to fossil nautiloids come
from the surviving Nautilus.

A Head end, revealing the body in
the outer chamber

B Side view, with shell cut open to
reveal its structure

Squids, octopuses, and their kin form the
cephalopods ("head footed")–the most highly
developed class of mollusks. These big-brained,
keen-eyed sea beasts can swim backward fast by
squirting water forward. Tentacles at the head end
seize prey and feed it to the beaklike jaws. Some
cephalopods have an outside shell, some an inner
shell, others none at all. Cephalopods range from a
species only millimeters long to the giant squid–at up
to 22 meters (72 ft) long, the largest living
invertebrate. Cephalopods probably evolved in
Cambrian times, from gastropod-like mollusks. Our
examples come from the four cephalopod subclasses:
nautiloids, bactritoids, ammonoids, and coleoids.
Fossils show that extinct ammonoids and (coleoid)
belemnites were abundant in certain Mesozoic times.
Besides cephalopods, there were two more mollusk
classes: coniconchs and calyptoptomatids. These
were small beasts with straight, cone-shaped shells.
They died out in Permian times.

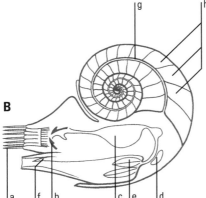

A

B

a Tentacles

b Jaws

c Gut

d Heart

e Gill

f Valve controlling water
used for jet propulsion

g Siphuncle–tube
connected to the inner
chambers

h Chambers, filled with
gas or air (Nautilus
pumps water in or out
to alter buoyancy, and
so sink or rise)

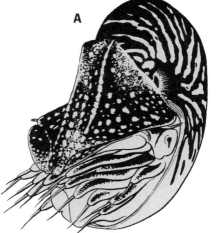

Shell sutures

Nautiloids, goniatites, ceratites,
and ammonites respectively
evolved ever more complex
sutures–lines formed where
internal partitions met the outside
shell. These four cut-open shells
show stages in this trend.

a Nautilus *(simple sutures)*

b Goniatites *(zigzag sutures)*

c Ceratites *(wavy sutures)*

d Phylloceras *(very complex
sutures)*

Complex sutures might have made
shells strong enough to endure
water pressure deep down.
Many ammonites were probably
bottom feeders.

Cephalopods

1 Orthoceras had a straight shell 15 cm
(6 in) long. Time: Ordovician-Triassic.
Subclass: Nautiloidea (nautiloids)–
cephalopods with a straight or curved
shell divided into chambers. Nautiloids
persisted from Cambrian times to today.

2 Cyrtobactrites had a tusk-shaped shell.
Length: 4.5 cm (1.8 in). Time: early
Devonian. Subclass: Bactritoidea
(ancestors of ammonoids).

3 Anetoceras had a loosely coiled shell
about 4 cm (1.6 in) across with zigzag
growth lines. Time: early Devonian. It
belonged to the goniatites, early members
of the subclass Ammonoidea. Ammonoids
resembled nautiloids but had shells with
wrinkled growth lines between chambers.

4 Stephanoceras had a coiled, ribbed,
disk-shaped shell 20 cm (8 in) across.
Time: mid Jurassic. It belonged to the
ammonoids called ammonites. Thousands
of species teemed in Mesozoic seas.

5 Gonioteuthis was a belemnite, with a
long, squidlike body known only from the
rear end's fossilized, bullet-shaped internal
guard. Guard length: 7 cm (2.8 in).
Time: late Cretaceous. Order: Belemnitida,
in the subclass Coleoidea (squids,
cuttlefish, octopuses, and belemnites).

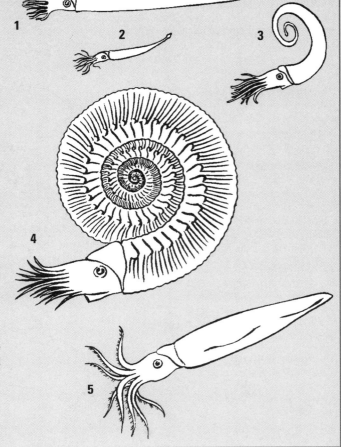

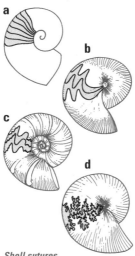

Worms

Annelids and others

1 Gordius, a "hair worm," resembles a living thread up to 15 cm (6 in) long. Adults wriggle in ponds and ditches worldwide. Young live inside aquatic insect larvae; adults invade land insects, then return to water to breed. Time: Eocene onwards. Phylum: Aschelminthes. Class: Nematomorpha.

2 Spriggina, one of the first known "worms," was probably a prearthropod. It was slim and flexible, with a long, strong, curved head shield, and up to 80 "limbs" with spiny ends. In late Precambrian times it swam offshore near what is now Australia. Length: up to 4.5 cm (1.8 in).

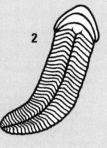

3 Dickinsonia had a broad, flat, oval body crossed by 20 to 550 ridges. Length: 0.25–60 cm (0.1 in–2 ft). It lived in a late Precambrian sea in what is now Australia. It resembled some flatworms but its identity remains uncertain.

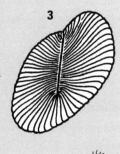

4 Canadia was a marine annelid with bristles and long "legs" projecting from its sides. Time: mid-Cambrian. Place: south-west Canada. Class: Polychaeta (segmented worms with "legs" and bristles). Order: Errantia (mainly active polychaetes, with a well-defined head and jaws).

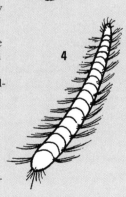

5 Serpula lives in a white, limy tube glued to an undersea shell or stone. Tentacles projecting from the head catch passing particles of food. Tube length: about 8 cm (3 in). Time: Silurian to present. Class: Polychaeta. Order: Sedentaria (jawless worms living in a tube or tunnel).

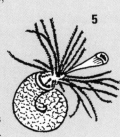

Soft-bodied beasts such as worms are seldom fossilized, but we know of prehistoric kinds from tracks, tunnels, tubes, jaw remains, and even impressions of their bodies left in fine-grained rocks. Such clues reveal that worms were crawling on and in, and swimming just above, the floors of shallow coastal waters some 580 million years ago, where South Australia's Ediacara Hills now stand. Southwest Canada's famous Burgess Shales reveal that many sea worms had evolved 520 million years ago. Of our examples, number **1** comes from the phylum Aschelminthes (roundworms, built on simple lines), **4–5** come from the Annelida (worms divided into many segments, often with complicated jaws, and tentacles projecting from the head). **2–3** have been thought annelids, arthropods, or in some completely extinct group.

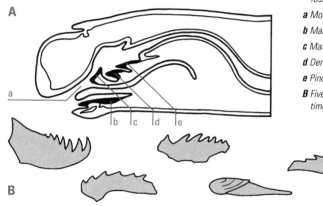

A

B

Durable mouth parts (below)

Prehistoric polychaete worms are known mostly from their mouth parts–the only hard parts of their bodies, and thus the only structures tending to be fossilized. Such fossils are called scolecodonts.

A *Enlarged section through a polychaete's head (items **b–e** are the hard parts likely to be fossilized)*

a *Mouth*

b *Mandible*

c *Maxilla*

d *Dental plate*

e *Pincer*

B *Five Permian scolecodonts 15 times larger than life*

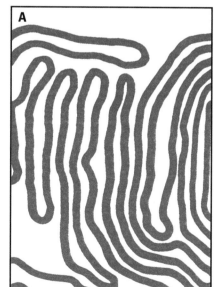

Worm trails (above and right)

Some rocks preserve worm tracks made in soft mud that later hardened into stone.

A *An unknown wormlike beast left this fossil track, seen from above. The creature plowed through underwater sediments. Most likely it was feeding on organic particles or tiny organisms.*

Worm trails (cont.)

B *This reconstruction shows how the track took shape.*

a *The width of churned up sediment fixed the distance of adjoining trails.*

b *The lengths of straight sections hint at the length of the worm that formed the U-turns seen in the track.*

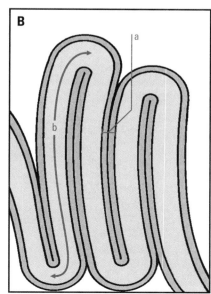

Arthropods 1

Insect features

This stonefly illustrates typical insect features, such as the three-part body. Early flying insects had two pairs of wings of equal size. They could flap each pair separately, but only up and down, and they could not fold their wings back at rest. In such later insects as butterflies, both pairs are coupled. In flies, hind wings are tiny and only serve as balancers.

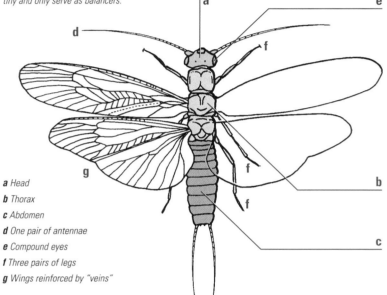

a Head

b Thorax

c Abdomen

d One pair of antennae

e Compound eyes

f Three pairs of legs

g Wings reinforced by "veins"

Arthropods 1

Most known kinds of animals belong to the phylum Arthropoda, or "jointed legged" animals. Arthropods include the extinct trilobites, as well as insects, spiders, crabs, centipedes, and relatives. All have jointed limbs and an exoskeleton shed from time to time as they grow. Maybe their ancestors looked like annelid seaworms. Early arthropods lived in the sea but some were colonizing land by 400 million years ago. These two pages give fossil examples of major groups based mostly on land. Onychophorans ("velvet worms") may be a primitive link with the arthropods' supposed worm ancestors. Many legged myriapods (centipedes and millipedes) were among the first land arthropods. From early, wingless insects came the bees and butterflies–winged pollinators evolving with, and feeding on, the flowering plants. Most fossil insects date from the last 60 million years. Some of the best fossil specimens occur in coal and amber.

Arthropleura

At 1.8 m (6 ft) Arthropleura was the largest ever land arthropod. This huge, flat millipede munched rotting vegetation of the floors of Carboniferous forests.

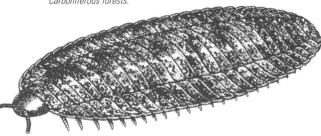

Arthropods 2

Living fossils

Trilobites died out more than 240 million years ago, but we show two kinds of living arthropods that have been regarded as close kin of these creatures.

1 Cephalocarids are tiny, primitive, shrimplike animals with segmented bodies much like trilobites'. First found in 1955, cephalocarids may be their nearest living relatives.

2 The horseshoe crab, actually a chelicerate, has a larval stage reminiscent of a young trilobite. This type of crab has lived for more than 400 million years.

Trilobites ("three lobed") were marine arthropods resembling wood lice. Their name comes from a central raised ridge along the back, flanked by flattish side lobes. There was a head shield and an armored thorax and tail, both divided into many segments. Each of these sprouted a pair of limbs designed for walking, swimming, breathing, and handling food. Trilobites crawled or swam, and many could curl up if threatened. Scientists know of several thousand genera and at least 15,000 species, from less than 4 mm (0.1 in) to 70 cm (28 in) long. Trilobites lived from about 540 to 250 million years ago. They dominated shallow seas in the Cambrian period. Ordovician genera included many specialized species with bizarre spines or knobs. These pages show a few contrasting kinds.

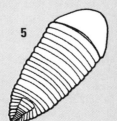

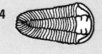

Trilobites

1 Ampyx was lightly built and filter fed. Length: 4 cm (1.6 in). Time: Ordovician.

2 Encrinurus had a relatively large, heavy head with eyes on stalks and was a bottom dweller. Length: 5 cm (2 in). Time: Ordovician-Silurian.

3 Lonchodomas had a long spike jutting forward from the head. Length: about 5 cm (2 in). Time: Ordovician.

4 Pliomera Toothlike ridges jutting from the front of the head interlocked with the tail tip when this animal rolled up. Length: about 4 cm (1.6 in). Time: Ordovician.

5 Trimerus was elongated and lived by burrowing in mud. Length: 8 cm (3 in). Time: Silurian-Devonian.

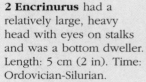

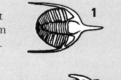

Insects and others

1 Aysheaia, an onychophoran "near arthropod," looked like a worm with a pair of stubby legs on each body segment and a pair of "feelers." It was arguably related to the living velvet worms but lived below the sea, in mid-Cambrian times.

2 Latzelia has been called an early centipede. It had poisoned fangs, a flat back, and a pair of walking legs on each of its many body segments. It roamed damp forest floors, hunting worms and soft insects. Time: Carboniferous. Subphylum: Myriapoda (centipedes and millipedes).

3 Rhyniella, a (wingless) insect, is a springtail, about 1 cm (0.5 in) long. Springtails live in soil, browse on decaying plants, and flip into the air if scared. Time: Devonian, about 370 million years ago. Subphylum: Hexapoda (insects) small invertebrates with six legs and a three-part body (head, thorax, abdomen). Many undergo great body changes (metamorphosis) as they grow.

4 Meganeura, the largest known winged insect, had a wing span of up to 70 cm (27.5 in). Time: late Carboniferous. Meganeura belonged to the Megasecoptera, primitive winged insects unable to fold back their wings held at rest.

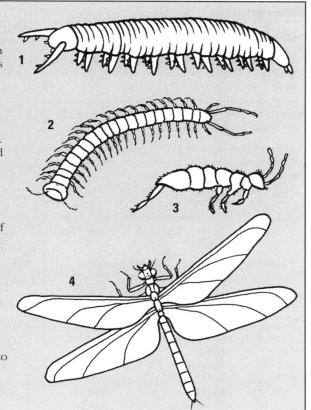

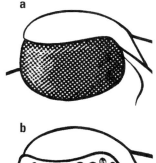

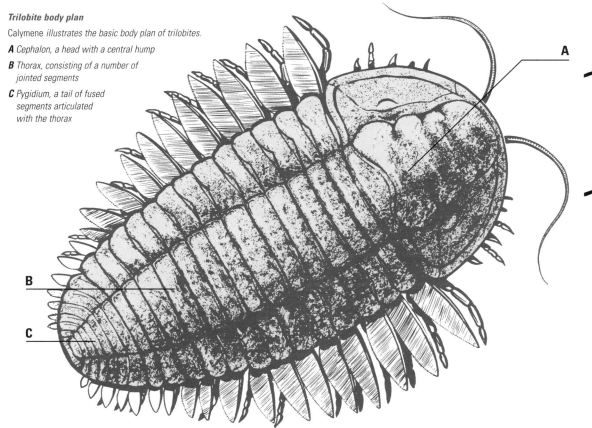

Trilobite body plan

Calymene *illustrates the basic body plan of trilobites.*

A *Cephalon, a head with a central hump*

B *Thorax, consisting of a number of jointed segments*

C *Pygidium, a tail of fused segments articulated with the thorax*

Amazing eyes (above)

Trilobites were among the first known animals with efficient eyes. These had many calcite-crystal lenses fixed at different angles to register movement and light from different directions.

a Compound or holochroal eyes consisted of 100 to 15,000 closely packed hexagonal lenses and resembled insects' eyes.

b Schizochroal eyes featured groups of lenses, relatively few in number.

Arthropods 3

Chelicerates

1 Palaeolimulus had a broad, horseshoe-shaped forepart with two large, many-faceted eyes. The narrow abdomen ended in a spiky "tail." Length: 6 cm (2.4 in). Time: Permian. Place: shallow seas. Class: Merostomata (perhaps a mixed group). Subclass: Xiphosura (horseshoe crabs).

2 Pterygotus, one of the largest arthropods ever, was a formidable predator. Its forepart had two long, strong pincers, eight legs, and two large, broad paddles for swimming. Twelve segments and a tail formed the long hind end. Length: up to 2.3 m (7ft 4 in). Time: Silurian. Place: seas. Class: Merostomata. Subclass: Eurypterida (eurypterids or sea scorpions).

3 Palaeophonus, a late Silurian scorpion, had big pincers and a large stinger on its tail. It might have been the first land animal. Class: Arachnida (spiders and scorpions). Order: Scorpionida (scorpions).

4 Arthrolycosa was a large, long-limbed early spider. It had eight legs and eight eyes and probably attacked insects with help from poisoned chelae ("fangs"). Time: Carboniferous. Class: Arachnida. Order: Araneae (spiders).

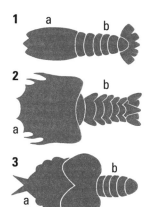

Spider in amber

Left: sticky sap trapped a spider 30 million years ago. Below: the sap hardened into amber, which still preserves the spider's lifelike body.

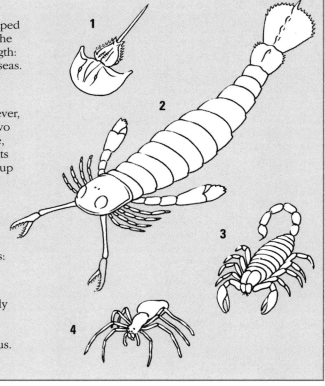

Arthropods 4

Crustaceans include crabs, barnacles, and relatives with flexible shells. Members of their subphylum, the Crustacea, have three main body parts (the first two often look like one), two pairs of antennae, and many more appendages. The limbs are forked. Crustaceans evolved by 540 million years ago. From early forms arose nine classes, all mostly found in water. Three produced a rich variety of fossils. These classes were the tiny ostracods, the cirripedes (barnacles and kin), and the malacostracans (including lobsters, crabs, and shrimps). Lobsterlike crustaceans date from Triassic times and gave rise to crabs in the Jurassic period.

Crabs in the making (below)

Shown here are the bodies of three prehistoric crustaceans (without their limbs).

1 Eryma
a Narrow cephalothorax (head and thorax)
b Abdomen as long as the cephalothorax

2 Eryon
a Broad, flat cephalothorax
b Long abdomen

3 Palaeinachus
a Big, broad cephalothorax
b Short, narrow abdomen

Ostracod body plan (right)

Experts identify fossil ostracods from the shapes and patterns of their shells. In life these small crustaceans (none larger than a bean) looked like the living specimen seen here enlarged. Such animals are found in seas and ponds.

a Hinged shell, shown in section; when shut it protected all parts of the body
b Short body
c Antennae (used as limbs)
d Mandibles (mouthparts)
e Maxillae (mouthparts)
f Trunk appendages
g Furca ("tail")

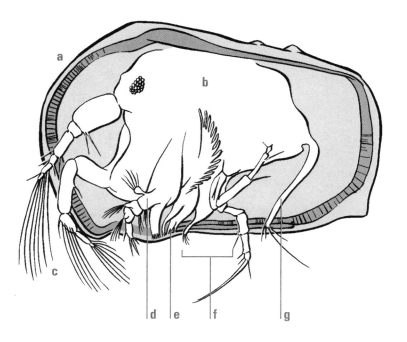

Spiders, scorpions, horseshoe crabs, and the extinct sea scorpions make up the subphylum Chelicerata. Prehistoric chelicerates included arthropods longer than a human: fish-eating terrors of ancient seas.

Chelicerates get their name from the two chelae ("biting claws") in front of the mouth. Behind these come a pair of pedipalps ("foot feelers"), used by horseshoe crabs as legs, by scorpions for seizing prey, and by male spiders to grip when mating. Then come four pairs of legs. The two-part body's limbless abdomen often ends in a flat or spiky tail. Horseshoe crabs and sea scorpions had gills and breathed under water. Modern spiders and scorpions breathe atmospheric air with help from "lung-books" or air holes called tracheae.

Chelicerates appeared in the seas more than 540 million years ago. They gave rise to sea scorpions soon after 500 million years ago. True scorpions evolved about 440 million years ago. The first known spiders were catching insects 385 million years ago. Most chelicerates grow a rather soft body covering, so few survive as fossils.

Eurypterid body plan

Shown here are two life-size views of the Silurian "sea scorpion" Eurypterus.

A *View of underside:*

a *Chelicerae (appendages with jointed pincers long and* formidable in beasts like Pterygotus, *which was capable of catching fishes)*

b *Four pairs of walking legs*

c *Large "paddles"*

d *Genital appendages*

B *View of upper side:*

a *Prosoma (forepart)*

b *Opisthosoma (hind part comprising 12 articulated segments) including:*

c *Telson ("tail")*

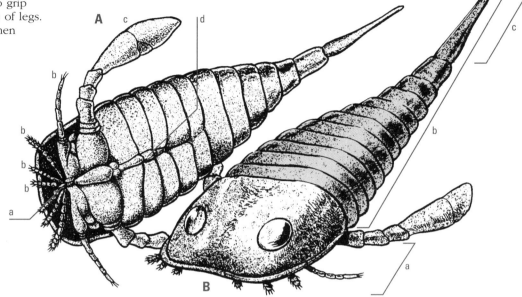

Crustaceans

1 Cypridea was a freshwater crustacean resembling a microscopic clam. Its body lay inside a two-valved shell with straight top and bottom edges and a knobbly surface. Time: mid-Jurassic–early Cretaceous. Class: Ostracoda–ostracods (mostly marine organisms, valuable as guide fossils from Cambrian times onward).

2 Balanus, an acorn barnacle, lives inside a domelike shell of six white limy plates, built on a tidal rock. At high tide curved, feathery appendages move in and out between shell plates to pull in scraps of food, and water. Size: about 1 cm (0.5 in) across. Time: Oligocene onward. Class: Cirripedia (barnacles)–crustaceans that fix their heads to rocks or other solid objects.

3 Aeger was a long-tailed ten-legged crustacean with a long bill-like rostrum and long antennae. Length: about 12 cm (4.7 in) excluding rostrum. Time: late Triassic–late Jurassic. Class: Malacostraca (advanced crustaceans with stalked eyes and a "shell" usually covering the head and thorax). Order: Decapoda (ten-legged crustaceans, including shrimps, crabs, and lobsters).

4 Eryon had a big, broad, flattened, crablike cephalothorax (fused head and thorax) but a longish abdomen. Crabs evolved from beasts like these that tucked the abdomen beneath the forepart of the body. Length: 10 cm (4 in). Time: mid-Jurassic–early Cretaceous. Order: Decapoda.

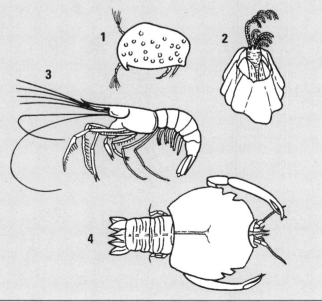

© DIAGRAM

Lophophorates

This name is used for three great groups of lowly sea beasts. Lophophorates have a lophophore, a "mouth" likened to a sugar scoop surrounded by a ring of tiny tentacles, used for pulling food and water into the mouth. Most live rooted to the seabed. Phoronids are wormlike creatures living in a hard protective tube. Bryozoans are two phyla of tiny, soft-bodied beasts that live in hard limy or horny cases. Colonies of bryozoans form mats or miniature "trees" on underwater rocks or shells. Brachiopods ("arm footed" animals) resemble bivalve mollusks on a fleshy stalk, but shell valves cover the body from above and below, not from side to side.

Brachiopods date from the early Cambrian, bryozoans from the Ordovician, and phoronids from the Cambrian period. The three groups were once mistakenly linked with conodonts, known only from tiny fossil teeth now recognized as belonging to an eel-like type of very early craniate (vertebrate).

Mistaken fossils (below)

Conodont tooth types, from a once unknown creature wrongly thought to be a lophophorate.

A Compound conodont

B Simple conodonts

C Platform conodont

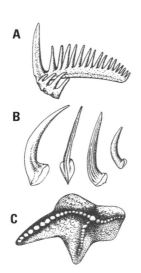

A

B

C

Brachiopods and bivalves (right)

At first glance you might mistake a fossil brachiopod for a bivalve mollusk, another creature with a two-valved shell. These illustrations show how to tell both apart.

A Brachiopod: both valves seen edgewise (1), and one valve seen from above (2)

a, b Shell valves differ in size and curvature

c Pointed beak at hinge end

d, e Each half of one valve is a mirror image of the other

B Bivalve: both valves seen edgewise (1) and one seen from above (2)

f, g Shell valves alike in size and curvature

h No beak at hinge

i, j Valves not symmetrical

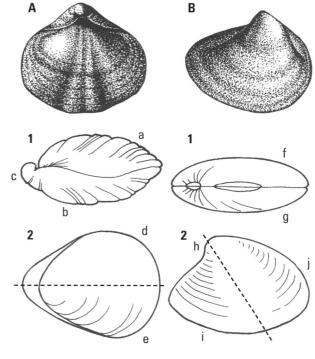

Three lophophorates

1 Phoronis is a wormlike tube dweller about 20 cm (8 in) long. It lives buried in sand offshore. Tiny whiplike cilia on its tentacles drive water and food into its mouth. Time: maybe Cretaceous onward. Phylum: Phoronida (phoronids).

2 Multisparsa was a bryozoan forming treelike colonies of tubes with touching sides. Colony size: 2 cm (0.8 in) across. Time: mid-Jurassic. Group: Bryozoans (sea mats).

3 Lingula lives inside a long, tongue-shaped shell growing from a strong stalk. It inhabits a burrow in soft undersea sediment. Diameter: 10 cm (4 in). Time: Ordovician onward (it is about the oldest living fossil). Phylum: Brachiopoda. Class: Inarticulata (brachiopods whose shell lacks a hinge).

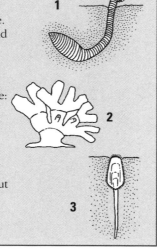

Evolved from worms (right)

Lingula's long wormlike body hints at the likely origin of brachiopods. Often called lampshells, they probably evolved from a tube-shaped worm that grew a pair of flat, protective shells.

Echinoderms and hemichordates

Echinoderms ("spiny skinned" animals) include starfishes, sea urchins, and their relatives. These tend to have a five-rayed body with a skeleton of chalky plates just below the skin. Some sprout protective spines. Water flows through tubes inside the body, and pumps up many tiny tube feet tipped with suckers and used for walking, gripping, or as breathing aids. Echinoderms lack a normal "head," but have a well-developed nervous system. They probably gave rise to backboned animals by way of a mixed group of phyla called hemichordates.

These small, soft-bodied, wormlike creatures with internal "gill baskets" include the pterobranchs and long extinct but once abundant graptolites. Such organisms produced the beginnings of a notochord or "backstring"–the precursor of a backbone. The Chordata (chordates), the phylum that includes all backboned animals, originated somewhere in this lowly group. Echinoderms and many hemichordates live on the sea bed. Hemichordates use tiny tentacles to catch passing scraps of food. Echinoderms include hunters, grazers, scavengers, and filter feeders. Both groups go back to Cambrian times. Examples **1–5** represent echinoderm subphyla. Examples **6–7** represent two phyla of hemichordates.

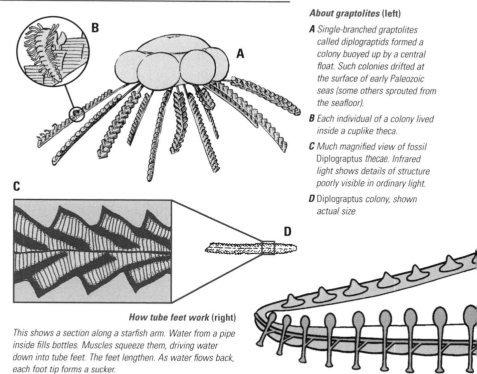

How tube feet work (right)

This shows a section along a starfish arm. Water from a pipe inside fills bottles. Muscles squeeze them, driving water down into tube feet. The feet lengthen. As water flows back, each foot tip forms a sucker.

About graptolites (left)

A Single-branched graptolites called diplograptids formed a colony buoyed up by a central float. Such colonies drifted at the surface of early Paleozoic seas (some others sprouted from the seafloor).

B Each individual of a colony lived inside a cuplike theca.

C Much magnified view of fossil Diplograptus thecae. Infrared light shows details of structure poorly visible in ordinary light.

D Diplograptus colony, shown actual size

Echinoderms and hemichordates

1 Dendrocystites looked like a double-ended thorn and probably laid flat on the sea bed, eating tiny organisms. Length: 9 cm (3.5 in). Time: Ordovician. Subphylum: Homalozoa (carpoids), extinct.

2 Pleurocystites sprouted two short, unbranched arms from a bud-shaped "cup" on a long stalk. Stalk height: 2 cm (0.8 in). Time: Ordovician. Subphylum: Blastozoa (blastoids and cystoids), extinct.

3 Botryocrinus was a flower-like seabed dweller with a stalk, crown, and feathery arms. Height: 15 cm (6 in). Time: Silurian. Subphylum: Crinoidea (sea lilies), Cambrian onward.

4 Crateraster had a broad central disk and five slim arms. Size: 10 cm (4 in) across. Time: Cretaceous. Subphylum: Asteroidea (starfishes), dating from Ordovician times.

5 Bothriocidaris resembled a small, prickly pincushion. Size: about 2 cm (0.8 in) across including spines. Time: Ordovician. Subphylum: Echinoidea (sea urchins), Ordovician on.

6 Rhabdopleura is a soft-bodied wormlike beast living in colonies in tubes on the seabed. Size: 2–3 mm (0.08–0.12 in). Phylum: Pterobranchia, dating from Ordovician times.

7 Dichograptus was an eight-branched graptolite a colony of tiny wormlike creatures, known from their flattened, "saw-edged" fossil tubes. Colony diameter: 6 cm (2.4 in). Time: Ordovician. Phylum: Graptolithina (graptolites), extinct, dating from Cambrian to Carboniferous.

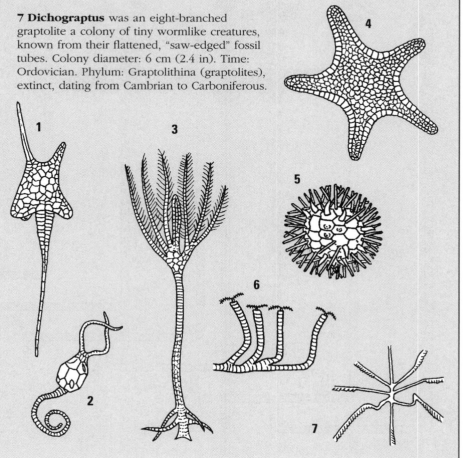

Fossil fishes

With fishes we reach the first of five chapters on fossil vertebrates, or animals with a backbone. Vertebrates are just one of several subphyla in the phylum Chordata (chordates), but their fossil record is by far the most impressive and varied. This chapter starts with the "agnathans," a mixed group of jawless fishes. We review the extinct placoderms and their nearest living relatives, chondrichthyans (sharks and kin). Lastly we look at the extinct acanthodians (spiny fishes) and their nearest living relatives, the osteichthyans (bony fishes), the group that gave rise to all vertebrates that live on land.

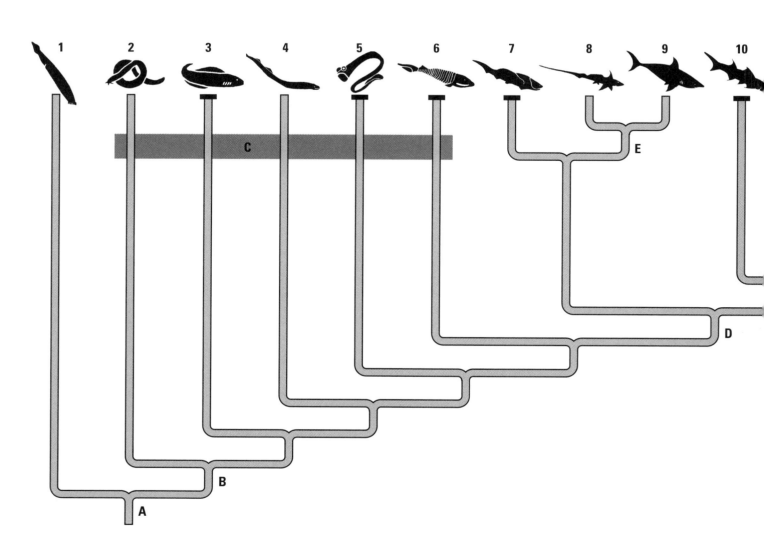

About fishes

Fishes are cold-blooded, backboned animals that live in water, breathing oxygen through gills. To swim forward most thrust water backward by waggling the tail and body.

As traditionally defined, fishes have jaws, paired fins, and also fins along the midline of the body, but this chapter includes creatures without jaws or true fins. Appearing more than 500 million years ago, they were the first known backboned animals or vertebrates: creatures with a brain housed in a skull, and gristly, and in time bony, vertebrae. Vertebrae provide bodily support and a protective channel for the spinal cord, which contains nerves connecting the brain with other parts of the body. From jawless fishes of types defunct there evolved four other major groups of fishes, two now extinct. Bony fishes, the most successful group, evolved a more flexible and mobile body than the fishes they replaced.

Fishes probably originated in the sea indirectly from echinoderms and hemichordates, but most early kinds inhabited fresh water. Prehistoric species ranged from creatures a few centimeters long to a 14-meter-long (46 ft) relative of the man-eating great white shark alive today.

Fossil fishes have been found in every continent. Appropriate rocks yield isolated bony plates, spines, scales, vertebrae, and teeth, but whole skeletons are rare, and many early fishes had gristly skeletons that seldom formed good fossils.

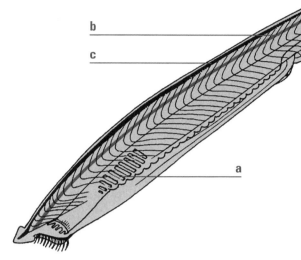

Fish ancestor?

Creatures like this tiny living lancelet were close to the ancestry of fishes. (A similar fossil 535 million years old is known from China.) Lancelets lack head, jaws, vertebrae, and paired fins, but have these fishlike features:

a *Gills*

b *Notochord (flexible rod foreshadowing the backbone)*

c *Nerve cord*

d *Tail fin (All animals with a notochord or backbone are chordates—members of the phylum Chordata. Lancelets belong to the subphylum Cephalochordata.)*

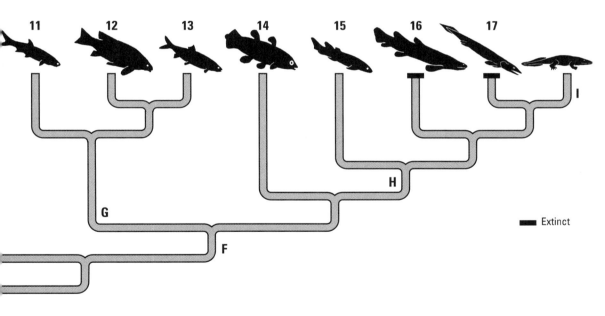

■ Extinct

Family tree of fishes

Capital letters indicate the presence or appearance of important groups and evolutionary innovations. Groups named in quotes contain kinds of organism now known to be not all close relatives.

A Chordata (chordates)

B Craniata; Vertebrata (craniates; vertebrates)

C "Agnathans"

D Gnathostomata (jawed vertebrates)

E Chondrichthyes (cartilaginous fishes)

F Osteichthyes (bony fishes)

G Actinopterygii (ray fins)

H Sarcopterygii (fleshy-finned fishes)

I Tetrapods (four-footed vertebrates)

1 Cephalochordata (cephalochordates: vertebrates' precursors)

2 Myxinoidea (hagfishes)

3 Myllokunmingia (Chinese fossil vertebrate more than 530 million years old)

4 Petromyzontiformes (lampreys)

5 Conodontia (conodonts: tiny eel-like fossil forms)

6 "Ostracoderms" (armored fishes)

7 Placodermi (placoderms)

8 Holocephali (chimeras)

9 Elasmobranchii (sharks etc)

10 Acanthodii (spiny fishes)

11 "Chondrosteans"

12 "Holosteans"

13 Teleostei (teleosts)

14 Actinistia (coelacanths)

15 Dipnoi (lungfishes)

16 "Rhipidistians"

17 Panderichthyidae (panderichthyids)

Jawless fishes

Agnathans ("jawless fishes") included the first backboned animals. Body armor earns most extinct agnathans the collective name *ostracoderms* ("shell skins"). Armor probably saved some from the fangs of eurypterids (sea scorpions). Ostracoderms flourished mainly in rivers and lakes about 500–350 million years ago. Most were small and lacked paired fins. Their armored heads had jawless slits or holes for mouths, through which they sucked in water containing particles of food. Some scavenged in mud, while others guzzled tiny organisms at the surface.

Ostracoderm fossils are plentiful in late Silurian and early Devonian rocks of Europe and North America.

Four ostracoderms

Here are examples from four orders in two (out of a total of four) classes of jawless fishes.

1 Hemicyclaspis was an armored fish with a solid bony head shield, usually backswept "horns," sensory fields in the head, eyes on top of the head, mouth below, body plated, triangular in cross section, tapering to the uptilted tail. Length: 13 cm (5 in). Time: late Silurian-Devonian. Place: northern continents. Order: Cephalaspida.

2 Birkenia was a small, deep-bodied ostracoderm, with small bony plates on the head, eyes at sides of the head, spines on the back, and tail angled downward. It had a fin along each side. Length: 10 cm (4 in). Time: mid-Silurian–early Devonian. Place: Europe. Order: Anaspida.

3 Pteraspis was a fish with a long, rounded head shield, no visible nostril, long sharp "beak," slit-shaped mouth below, one gill opening per side, long spine on the back, no paired fins, and a downward-angled tail. Length 5.7 cm (2.3 in). Time: early Devonian. Place: northern continents. Order: Pteraspidiformes.

4 Thelodus was a flat fish covered with small, toothlike denticles (not flat plates). It had a long upper tail lobe and eyes on the sides of the head. Length: 18 cm (7 in). Time: mid-Silurian–early Devonian. Place: Europe, North America. Order: Thelodontida.

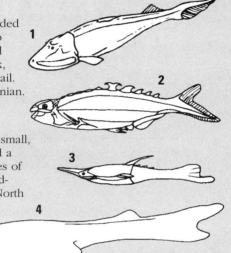

Spiny fishes

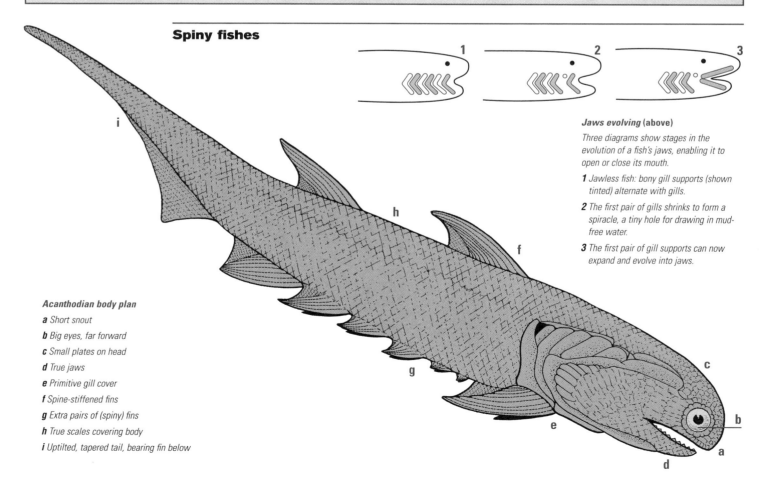

Jaws evolving (above)

Three diagrams show stages in the evolution of a fish's jaws, enabling it to open or close its mouth.

1 Jawless fish: bony gill supports (shown tinted) alternate with gills.

2 The first pair of gills shrinks to form a spiracle, a tiny hole for drawing in mud-free water.

3 The first pair of gill supports can now expand and evolve into jaws.

Acanthodian body plan

a Short snout

b Big eyes, far forward

c Small plates on head

d True jaws

e Primitive gill cover

f Spine-stiffened fins

g Extra pairs of (spiny) fins

h True scales covering body

i Uptilted, tapered tail, bearing fin below

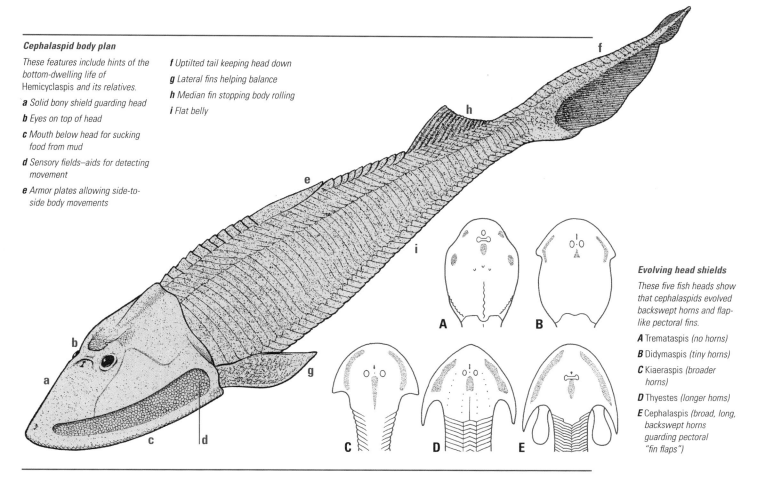

Cephalaspid body plan

These features include hints of the bottom-dwelling life of Hemicyclaspis *and its relatives.*

a *Solid bony shield guarding head*

b *Eyes on top of head*

c *Mouth below head for sucking food from mud*

d *Sensory fields–aids for detecting movement*

e *Armor plates allowing side-to-side body movements*

f *Uptilted tail keeping head down*

g *Lateral fins helping balance*

h *Median fin stopping body rolling*

i *Flat belly*

Evolving head shields

These five fish heads show that cephalaspids evolved backswept horns and flap-like pectoral fins.

A Tremataspis *(no horns)*

B Didymaspis *(tiny horns)*

C Kiaeraspis *(broader horns)*

D Thyestes *(longer horns)*

E Cephalaspis *(broad, long, backswept horns guarding pectoral "fin flaps")*

Nicknamed "spiny sharks" or "spiny fishes," the acanthodians had stout spines along the leading edges of their fins but were neither sharks nor bony fishes of a modern kind. These small freshwater species lived about 450–250 million years ago and were among the first vertebrates with jaws. They had a blunt head, small, studlike body scales, and a long, tapered upper tail lobe. Acanthodians swam at mid and surface levels. Some probably ate small, freshwater invertebrates. Others preyed on jawless fishes.

Fossils crop up in late Ordovician to Permian rocks and occur on almost every continent. Most are crushed flat in shale slabs. Early fossils are just spines and scales.

Three spiny fishes

Below are species from the three acanthodian orders: Climatiiformes (primitive types); Ischnacanthiformes (types with reduced spines); and Acanthodiformes (the last group, some degenerate).

1 Climatius had a short, deep body and five pairs of extra fins below its belly. Length: 7.6 cm (3 in). Time: late Silurian–early Devonian. Place: northern continents. Order: Climatiiformes.

2 Ischnacanthus was more advanced than *Climatius*, with fewer and slimmer but relatively longer and more deeply embedded spines. Time: early–mid-Devonian. Place: Europe. Order: Ischnacanthiformes.

3 Acanthodes looked more eel-like than earlier acanthodians; it was partly scaleless, with fewer fins and spines and no teeth. Length: 30.5 cm (1 ft). Time: late Devonian–early Permian. Place: northern continents and Australia. Order: Acanthodiformes.

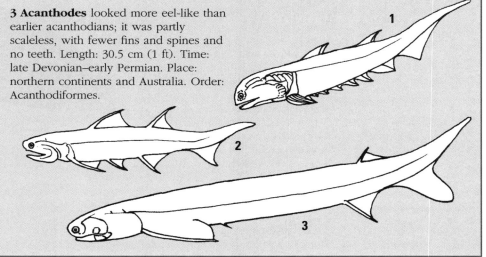

Placoderms

The placoderms, or "plated skins," were among the first fishes with jaws and paired fins. Bony armor covered the head and forepart of the body. In many, a movable joint between head and body armor let the head rock back to open the mouth wide. The primitive jaws had jagged bony edges that served as teeth. The tail end usually lacked protection and even scales. Placoderms mostly swam with eel-like movements. Many lived on the seabed. Some were the largest, most formidable creatures of their day. The group appeared in Silurian times, dominated Devonian seas (417–354 million years ago), and then died out under competition from sharks and bony fishes.

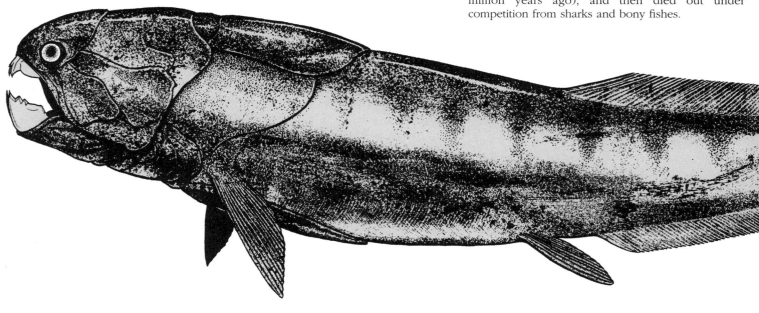

3

Sharks and their kin

Sharks and sharklike fishes make up the Chondrichthyes—one of two classes of so-called higher fishes. Chondrichthyans have skeletons of tough, gristly cartilage, not bone, and tiny toothlike scales. They have paired fins but lack gill covers and swim bladders to adjust buoyancy. Some are ferocious, streamlined killers with razor-sharp teeth. Skates, rays, and rat fishes include bottom dwellers with low, broad teeth for crunching shellfish. Most kinds live in the sea.

Sharks probably shared an ancestor with placoderms, appeared by 450 million years ago, and flourish still. Shark fossils occur worldwide. Many are just teeth, fin spines, or toothlike denticles from skin. The soft skeletons have mostly rotted, but fine-grained late Devonian Cleveland shales preserve fine specimens of early sharks along Lake Erie's southern shore.

These fishes represent five chondrichthyan orders.

1 Cladoselache had a torpedo-shaped body, short snout, big eyes, big pectoral fins, and long upper tail lobe. This early shark had unusual fin spines. Length: 50 cm–1.2 m (1 ft 8 in–4 ft). Time: late Devonian. Place: Europe and North America. Order: Cladodontiformes (extinct ancestral sharks).
2 Xenacanthus had a long dorsal fin, long tail ending in a point, and a spine jutting back from its head. Length: 76 cm (2 ft 6 in).

Time: late Devonian–mid Permian. Place: Americas, Europe, and Australia. Order: Xenacanthida (early freshwater sharks).
3 Hybodus had narrow based, maneuverable fins and a small anal fin. Length: more than 2 m (6 ft 6 in). Time: late Permian–early Cretaceous.

Tooth replacement (above)

This diagram shows how new teeth continuously grew forward in a shark's jaw to replace old teeth that fell out. Vast numbers survive as fossils.

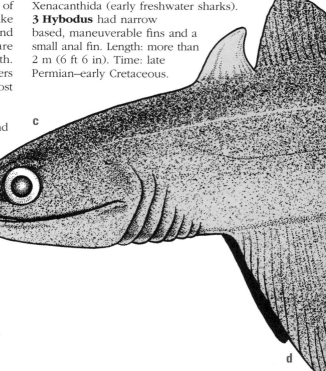

c

b

a

d

Placoderms are divided into eight orders. Here are examples of six of them, all Devonian.

1 Gemuendina was flat and broad. Length: 23 cm (9 in). Place: central Europe. Order: Rhenanida (placoderms resembling skates).

2 Lunaspis had armored skin all over and curved, bony shoulder spines. Length: 27 cm (10.5 in). Place: Europe. Order: Petalichthyida.

3 Dunkleosteus (Dinichthys), a huge predator, could kill large fishes. Length: up to 9 m (30 ft).

Place: North America and Europe. Order: Arthrodira (armored placoderms with jointed necks).

4 Rhamphodopsis had grinding jaw plates and a big shoulder spine. Length: 10 cm (4 in). Place: Europe. Order: Ptyctodontida (small, armored fishes).

5 Phyllolepis was flat, with little head armor. Length: 12.7 cm (5 in). Place: Australia, Europe, North America. Order: Phyllolepida (mostly flat and heavily plated placoderms).

6 Bothriolepis had a weak mouth, eyes on top of the head, and crablike arms encasing the front fins. Length: up to 30 cm (1 ft). Place: found on most continents. Order: Antiarchi (small fishes with jointed, movable, spiny front fins).

A late Devonian giant

Dunkleosteus (also called Dinichthys) appears here to the same scale as a human. Such fishes had a gristly backbone. They might have lurked on the seabed, with their large eyes seeking prey. This giant attacked by rocking back its head on ball-and-socket joints and dropping the lower jaw to expose the bony cutting edges that served as its teeth. Dunkleosteus perhaps grew more sharklike than our pictured monster and typically only half its length.

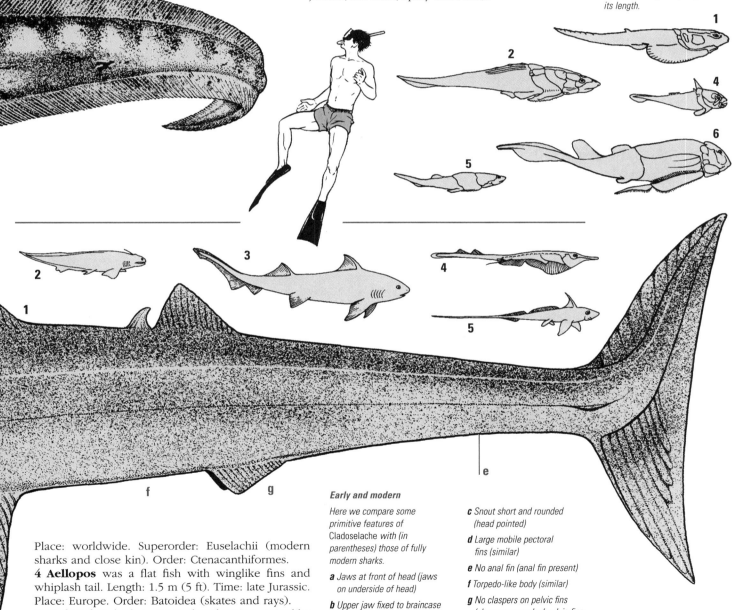

Place: worldwide. Superorder: Euselachii (modern sharks and close kin). Order: Ctenacanthiformes.

4 Aellopos was a flat fish with winglike fins and whiplash tail. Length: 1.5 m (5 ft). Time: late Jurassic. Place: Europe. Order: Batoidea (skates and rays).

5 Ischyodus had a stout dorsal spine, winglike pectoral fins, and whiplike tail. Length: 1.5 m (5 ft). Time: mid Jurassic-Paleocene. Place: worldwide. Order: Chimaeriformes ("rat fishes").

Early and modern

Here we compare some primitive features of Cladoselache with (in parentheses) those of fully modern sharks.

a Jaws at front of head (jaws on underside of head)

b Upper jaw fixed to braincase at back and front (upper jaw fixed to braincase at back only, allowing mouth to gape wide)

c Snout short and rounded (head pointed)

d Large mobile pectoral fins (similar)

e No anal fin (anal fin present)

f Torpedo-like body (similar)

g No claspers on pelvic fins (claspers on males' pelvic fins grip females during mating)

© DIAGRAM

Bony fishes 1

Bony fishes 1

Evolving tails and heads

*Here we show evolutionary trends in bony fishes, from chondrosteans (**a, d**) through holosteans (**b, e**) to teleosts (**c, f**).*

A *Heterocercal tail: the backbone's upturned end produces a long lower tail lobe that tends to drive the head down.*

b *Abbreviated heterocercal tail: upper lobe shortened; lift comes from swim bladder*

c *Homocercal tail: tail lobes seem equal, but most rays sprout from the backbone's still upturned end.*

d *Jaws work as a snap trap.*

e *Jaws are shortened but gape wide to suck in food.*

f *Jaws are shortened further but protrude when opened to create a suction tube.*

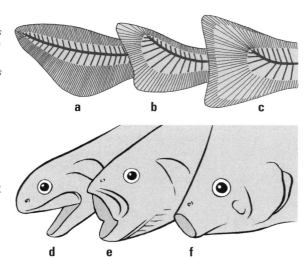

Ray-finned fishes–actinopterygians–account for almost all fishes now alive. Their ancestors grew far more plentiful and varied than the fleshy-finned fishes, the other subclass of Osteichthyes, or bony fishes (fishes with a bony skeleton). Instead of fleshy lobes, ray fins have straight bony rays jutting from the body to support their fins. Modern forms have an all-bony skeleton; short, widely gaping jaws; thin scales; mobile fins for precise body control; a symmetrical tail; and a lung evolved into a swim bladder to control buoyancy. These features evolved through species graded from the so-called chondrosteans and holosteans to teleosts.

Early ray fins were small species living more than 400 million years ago. Later came larger species, many living in the sea where they ousted placoderms. Fossil ray fins occur worldwide: chondrosteans mostly in Devonian-Triassic rocks; holosteans mostly in Triassic-Cretaceous rocks; and teleosts mostly in Jurassic and later rocks.

Ray-finned fishes

These three fishes represent evolutionary trends in the subclass Actinopterygii (ray fins).

1 Palaeoniscum had a long upper tail lobe, thick scales, bony head armor, long jaws hinged far back, and a kind of lung. Length: 30 cm (1 ft). Time: mainly Permian. Place: worldwide. Grade: Chondrostean.

2 Lepidotes differed from *Palaeoniscum* in its short upper tail lobe, thinner scales, swim bladder, deeper body, more maneuverable paired fins, and shorter jaws. Length: up to 1.2 m (4 ft). Time: mainly Jurassic. Place: worldwide. Grade: Holostean.

3 Leptolepis had a herring-like shape. It differed from *Palaeoniscum* amd *Lepidotes* in its symmetrical tail, thinner scales, shortened jaws with wide gape, and fewer skull bones. Length: 23 cm (9 in). Time: mainly Jurassic. Place: seas worldwide. Division: Teleostei.

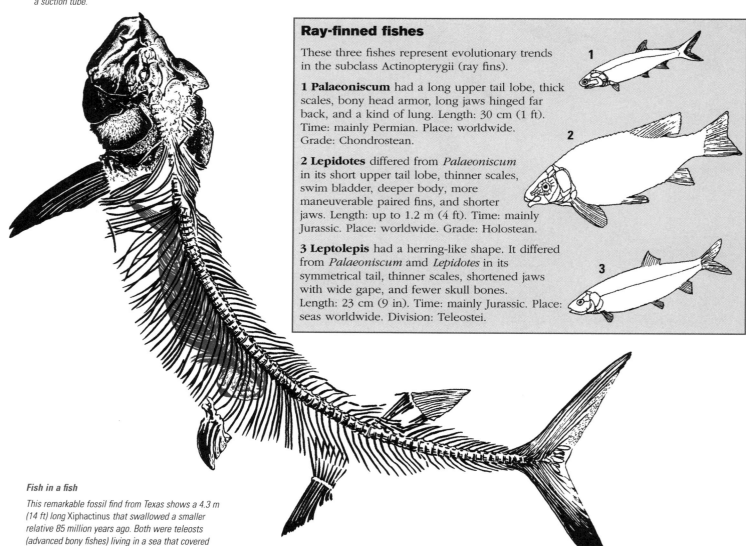

Fish in a fish

This remarkable fossil find from Texas shows a 4.3 m (14 ft) long Xiphactinus that swallowed a smaller relative 85 million years ago. Both were teleosts (advanced bony fishes) living in a sea that covered the southwest and southern areas of the United States.

Bony fishes 2

The Sarcopterygian subclass of bony fishes had paired fins borne on scaly lobes containing bones and muscles. Such fleshy fins gave rise to the limbs of backboned animals that live on land. Fleshy-finned fishes appeared about 400 million years ago. They included lung fishes, coelacanths, and the so-called rhipidistians, really several groups.

Rhipidistians were long-bodied flesh eaters that lurked in shallow waters–fresh and salt. Some could use fins as feeble legs and breathed air with lungs if hot weather made the water foul. All are extinct.

Coelacanths were mostly deep-bodied and lived in oceans. Their lungs became swim bladders that regulated buoyancy. All were thought extinct for more than 60 million years until an angler caught one off Southeast Africa in 1938.

Lungfishes had weaker limbs and a flimsier skeleton than other fleshy-finned fishes. Some could (and can) breathe atmospheric air if their ponds or rivers dry up.

Fishes

The animals here represent three main groups of fleshy-finned fishes. The first two were in the order Crossopterygii, the third in the order Dipnoi.

1 Eusthenopteron was a long-bodied, carnivorous freshwater fish with paired fins and a three-pronged tail fin. Skull, backbone, and limb bones resembled those of early tetrapods. Nostrils opened into the mouth. Length: 30–60 cm (1–2 ft). Time: late Devonian. Place: Europe and North America. Order: Osteolepiformes.

2 Macropoma was a deep-bodied coelacanth with a short, deep skull, three-pronged tail fin, and fan-shaped dorsal and anal fins. Nostrils did not open into the mouth. Length: 56 cm (22 in). Time: late Cretaceous. Place: oceans; fossils come from Europe. Order: Actinistia.

3 Dipterus had a long body tapered at both ends; paired, leaf-shaped fins; an uptilted tail; big, thick scales; and a braincase largely made of gristle. Length: 36 cm (14 in). Time: middle Devonian. Place: North America and Europe. Order: Dipnoi (lungfishes).

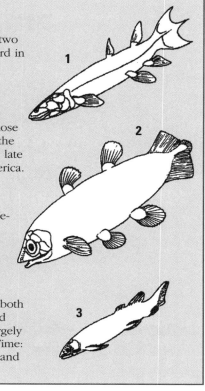

© DIAGRAM

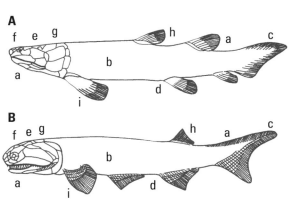

Fleshy-finned features (above)

Here we show similarities and differences between Osteolepis (**A**), an early fleshy-finned fish, and Cheirolepis (**B**), an early ray-finned fish.

Similarities:

a tapered at both ends

b covered with heavy scales

c primitive, uptilted tail

d paired fins similarly spaced

e bony plates covering skull

Differences:

f position and size of eyes

g proportions of skull bones

h number of dorsal fins

i fin design

Tetrapod ancestors? (right)

Agile young Eusthenopteron flipping ashore to escape hungry adults (**A**) was one notion of how fishes gave rise to tetrapods. Fishes like long-headed Panderichthys (**B**) now seem to be tetrapods' likeliest ancestors. Using four of only five fins as props they probably punted through weedy shallows.

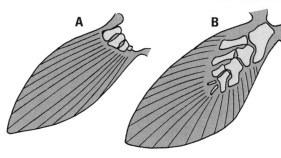

Two types of fin (left)

A Ray-finned fish's fin: rays spring from bones at the base.

B Fleshy-finned fish's fin: rays spring from bones along the center of the fin itself.

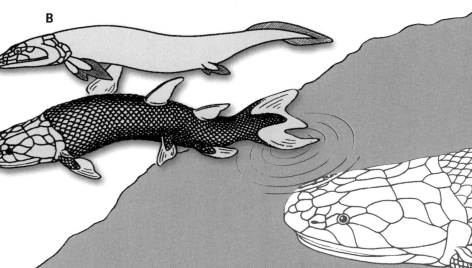

Fossil early tetrapods and amphibians

These pages look at early tetrapods (four-legged vertebrates) and their descendants, all of whom laid unprotected eggs in water. Once all were called amphibians (class Amphibia), divided into the extinct labyrinthodonts and lepospondyls and the living lissamphibians (frogs, salamanders, and caecilians). Many scientists now consider labyrinthodonts and lepospondyls artificial groupings and restrict Amphibia to lissamphibians and their closest prehistoric relatives.

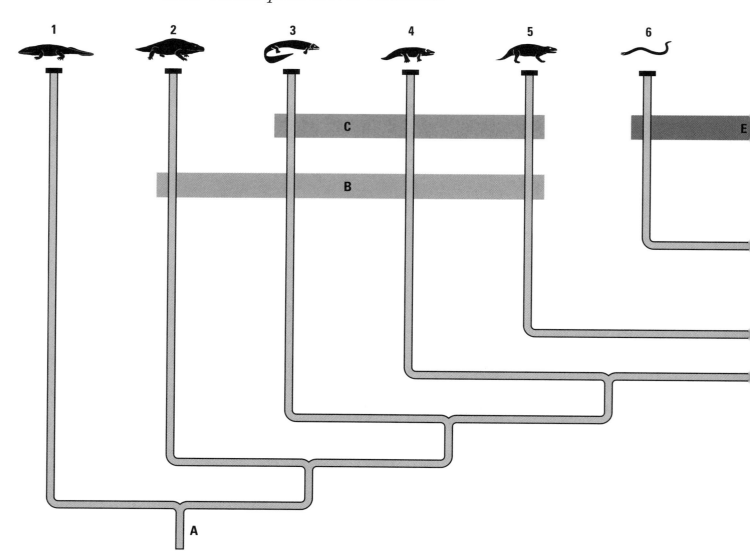

About early tetrapods

By 360 million years ago fleshy-finned fishes gave rise to the earliest four-limbed backboned animals. These first tetrapods punted through shallow water, but many later kinds could walk on land. Like frogs, though, early tetrpods laid their shell-less eggs in water to prevent them from drying up. The eggs hatched into tadpoles, which breathed through gills that later usually shrank. Some adults grew as big as a crocodile. Many had heavy skeletons, with powerful sprawling legs. They breathed through lungs and had a covering of fishlike scales or tough skin. (In contrast, modern amphibians are mostly small, with light skeletons and soft, moist skin; adults get more oxygen through skin than lungs.) Early tetrapods lived mainly in or near freshwater, hunting fishes, insects, or early reptiles. They dominated swamps that covered much of coastal North America and Europe in late Carboniferous (Pennsylvanian) and early Permian times. The fossils of many amphibious tetrapods come from rocks that formed during those periods.

Early goups of amphibious tetrapods died out by about 110 million years ago. Long before, one group gave rise to today's amphibians and another group gave rise to reptiles and the ancestors of mammals.

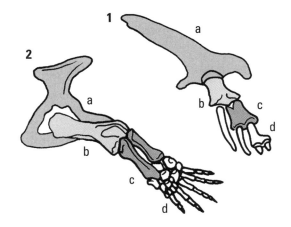

Limbs from fins

This comparison between the bones of a fish's fin and an early tetrapod's limb reveals that limb bones correspond to and evolved from the fin bones of fishes.

1 *Bones supporting a pelvic fin of a Devonian sarcopterygian fish, Eusthenopteron*

2 *Corresponding bones in a hind limb of the Permian temnospondyl Trematops*

a *Pelvis (hip region)*

b *Femur (thigh bone in land vertebrates)*

c *Tibia and fibula (leg bones in land vertebrates)*

d *Pes (foot): the small bones in the fish's fins evolved into the toes and fingers of early tetrapods and their descendants [Diagram after Colbert.]*

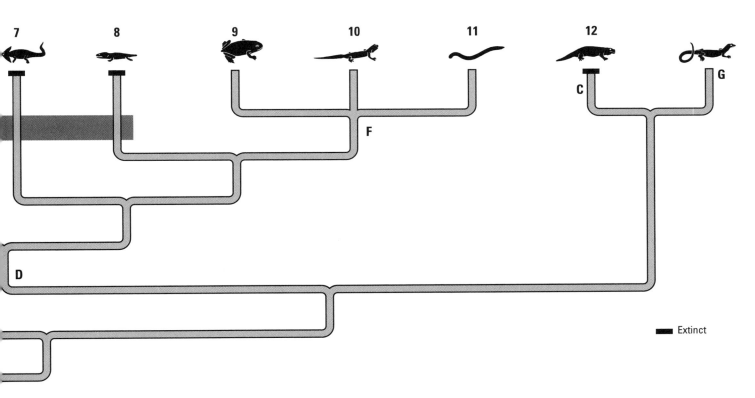

Early tetrapods and amphibians

Scientists do not agree how early tetrapods related to each other or which gave rise to living lissamphibians and amniotes (mammals, birds, and reptiles). This family tree is just one of several rival versions and shows only certain groups. Capital letters pinpoint the presence or

appearance of important groups or evolutionary innovations. Names of artificial or possibly artificial groups are in quotes.

A Tetrapoda (tetrapods)
B "Labyrinthodonts"
C "Anthracosaurs"

D Amphibia
E "Lepospondyls"
F Lissamphibia (modern amphibians)
G Amniota (amniotes)
1 Ichthyostega
2 Temnospondyli (temnospondyls)

3 Embolomeri (embolomeres)
4 Gephyrostegidae (gephyrostegids)
5 Seymouriamorpha (seymouriamorphs)
6 Aistopoda (aistopods)
7 Nectridea (nectrideans)

8 Microsauria (microsaurs)
9 Anura (frogs and toads)
10 Urodela (newts and salamanders)
11 Apoda (caecilians)
12 Diadectomorpha (diadectomorphs)

Extinct

© DIAGRAM

Early tetrapods 1

Labyrinthodont features

a This cross section through a labyrinthodont tooth shows the complex folds that earned labyrinthodonts their name.

b Seymouria's skull (actual size) had an otic notch (**1**) to hold an eardrum sensitive to airborne sounds. Its fish ancestors lacked eardrums.

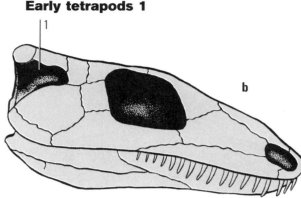

Early tetrapods had solid skulls and complex spinal bones. Some of them evolved strong backbones and strong, sprawling limbs. These became the first vertebrates to live on land. Others had weaker skeletons and eel-like bodies and lived in water. Between them these creatures ranged from a few centimeters (inches) long to 9 m (30 ft). They lived 360–110 million years ago and spread worldwide.

Scientists once identified a group of early tetrapods as labyrinthodonts from their labyrinthine tooth enamel, but this does not provide evidence of a uniquely shared relationship. Labyrinthodonts pictured on this page represent very different stocks. Very early forms including *Ichthyostega* were sprawing aquatic vertebrates with some fishlike features. These late Devonian tetrapods probably gave rise to all the rest. Late Paleozoic tetrapods here numbered **2–6** have been called anthracosaurs ("coal lizards"), probably another artificial lumping of very diverse groups. Of these, diadectomorphs seem near the ancestry of reptiles and synapsids, the group that includes mammals (but see p. 166).

1 Ichthyostega had well-developed limbs but traces of a fish's tail and scales. Length: 1 m (3 ft 3 in). Time: late Devonian. Place: Greenland.

2 Proterogyrinus, a very early anthracosaur, had a rather high skull and sturdy limbs. Length: 1–1.5 m (3 ft 3 in–4 ft 11 in). Time: late Carboniferous. Place: West Virginia. Group: Embolomeri ("typical" aquatic anthracosaurs).

3 Gephyrostegus had a small head and sturdy, sprawling limbs. Length: 45 cm (18 in). Time: late Carboniferous. Place: central Europe Group: Gephyrostegid (terrestrial anthracosaurs).

4 Eogyrinus had a long, eel-like body and tail, weak limbs, and a crocodile-like skull. It lived in water. Length: 4.6 m (15 ft). Time: late Carboniferous. Place: Europe. Group: Embolomeri.

5 Seymouria had longer, stronger limbs than the first amphibians and lived on land. Length: 60 cm (2 ft). Time: early Permian. Place: Texas and Germany Group: Seymouriamorpha (reptile-like anthracosaurs).

6 Diadectes, the earliest known plant-eating vertebrate, had heavy bones and shortened jaws with blunt teeth. Length: 3 m (10 ft). Time: early Permian. Place: Texas and Germany. Group: Diadectomorpha.

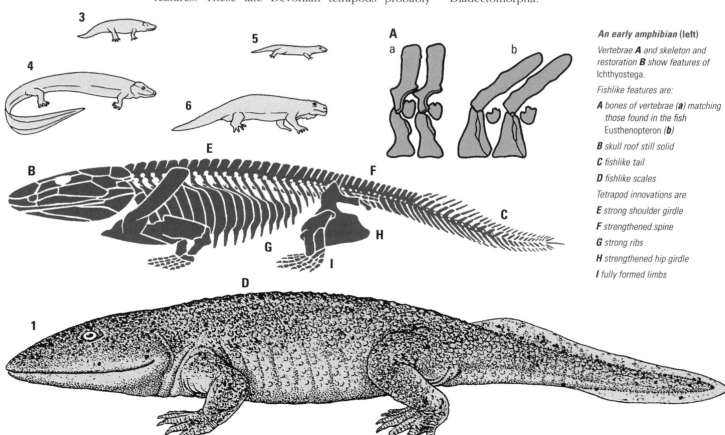

An early amphibian (left)

Vertebrae **A** and skeleton and restoration **B** show features of Ichthyostega.

Fishlike features are:

A bones of vertebrae (**a**) matching those found in the fish Eusthenopteron (**b**)

B skull roof still solid

C fishlike tail

D fishlike scales

Tetrapod innovations are

E strong shoulder girdle

F strengthened spine

G strong ribs

H strengthened hip girdle

I fully formed limbs

Early tetrapods 2: temnospondyls

Temnospondyls ("cut vetebrae") had distinctive ear, arm, and other bones that distinguish them from the anthracosaurs. Like them, some of these tetrapods lived on land, others in water. Temnospondyls persisted from Carboniferous to Cretaceous times and became extremely plentiful and varied.

The temnospondyls' many groups and subgroups included the stereospondyls, of mixed ancestry. These aquatic creatures with degenerate skeletons had no need of strong, bony, scaffolding to resist the tug of gravity. Some developed broad, flat bodies and huge heads. Such creatures included the largest of all early amphibious tetrapods. They dominated Triassic inland waters, but finally died out in the Cretaceous, outcompeted by crocodilians.

Plagiosaurs were even more grotesque aquatic temnospondyls of Permian to late Triassic times.

A landlubber (below)

The Permian temnospondyl Cacops *was one of the early tetrapods best designed for life on land. It had these features:*

a Length 40 cm (16 in)

b Sturdy limbs

c Large eardrum

d Armored skin on the back

e Large head with long jaws

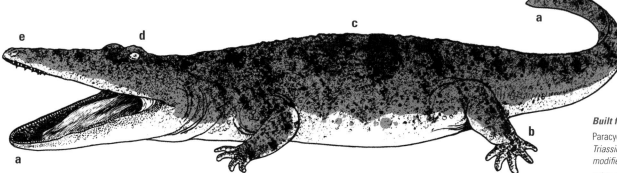

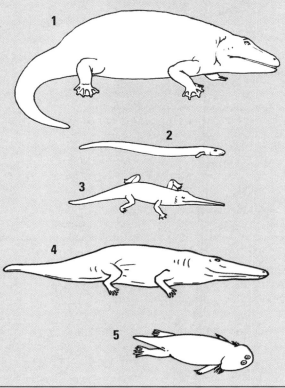

Built for water life (left)

Paracyclotosaurus, *an aquatic Triassic temnospondyl, was modified for life in water.*

a Length 2.25 m (7 ft 5 in)

b Short, rather weak limbs

c Somewhat flattened body

d Flattened skull

e Mouth opened by raising the skull instead of dropping the lower jaw

Temnospondyls

The creatures pictured on this page give some idea of the temnospondyls' range of shapes and sizes.

1 Eryops was heavy with a strong skeleton, short, strong limbs, and big, broad skull. It might have lived in water and on land, like crocodiles. Length: 1.5 m (5 ft). Time: early Permian. Place: Texas.

2 Trimerorhachis had a body protected by overlapping "fish scales." It probably swam in pools and streams. Length: 60 cm (2 ft). Time: early Permian. Place: Texas.

3 Aphaneramma had a head one-third its total length. It swam in seas and caught fishes with its long, slim, sharp-toothed jaws. Length: 60 cm (2 ft). Time: early Triassic. Place: worldwide. Fossils occur as far apart as Australia and Spitsbergen, Norway.

4 Cyclotosaurus, a stereospondyl capitosaur, was as large as a crocodile but had small, weak legs and needed the support of water. Length: 4.3 m (14 ft). Time: late Triassic. Place: Europe.

5 Gerrothorax was a plagiosaur with a short, wide head with gills; a flat, broad, armored body; short tail; and tiny limbs. Length: 1 m (3 ft 3 in). Time: late Triassic. Place: southern Germany.

Lepospondyls

Lepospondyls probably formed a mixed group of small tetrapods that thrived in Paleozoic swamps. They had simpler teeth and fewer skull bones than other early tetrapods and a type of vertebra with a bony cylinder firmly joined to an arch and pierced by a hole to fit a notochord. These insect-eating creatures tended to be smaller and more slightly built than many of those other early tetrapods, the temnospondyls and anthracosaurs.

Most lepospondyl fossils come from Carboniferous rocks. Their scarcity in later rocks hints that the group died out before modern amphibians evolved. However, a close comparison of fossils of different types of early tetrapods makes many paleontologists suspect that a late-surviving lepospondyl line gave rise to today's amphibians.

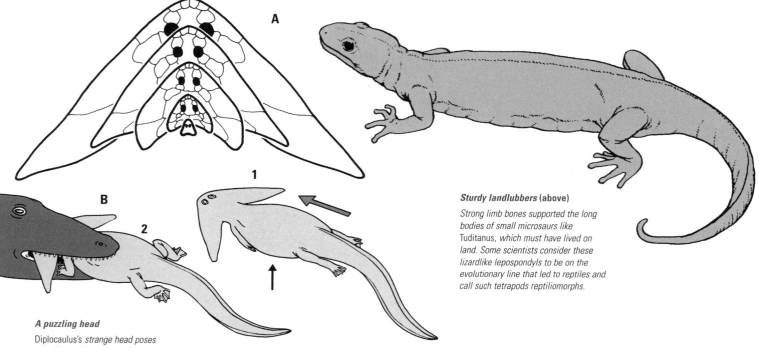

Sturdy landlubbers (above)

Strong limb bones supported the long bodies of small microsaurs like Tuditanus, *which must have lived on land. Some scientists consider these lizardlike lepospondyls to be on the evolutionary line that led to reptiles and call such tetrapods reptiliomorphs.*

A puzzling head

Diplocaulus's *strange head poses questions of design.*

A *Growth stages show that "horns" grew relatively longer as the head enlarged. This occurred because some skull bones outpaced others.*

B *Two illustrations suggest possible uses for a head with backswept "horns."*

1 *"Horns" might have acted as a hydrofoil, helping to lift and raise the animal through the water.*

2 *"Horns" might have made it difficult for predators to swallow Diplocaulus.*

Lepospondyls

Scientists recognize three main lepospondyl groups: the aistopods, nectrideans, and microsaurs. Aistopods were limbless burrowers that also very likely swam. Nectrideans were long-bodied, four-legged animals with deep tails flattened from side to side for swimming. Microsaurs had short legs and tails but ranged from lizardlike landlubbers to aquatic kinds that never lost their larval gills.

1 Ophiderpeton was a typical aistopod: aquatic, limbless, and snakelike, with forked ribs and 200 vertebrae. Length: 70 cm (27.5 in). Time: late Carboniferous. Place: Europe and North America.

2 Diplocaulus had a flat body, weak limbs, and a head like a cocked hat. Length: 1 m (3 ft 3 in). Time: early Permian. Place: Texas. Order: Nectridea (newt-like or snake-like).

3 Pantylus had a heavy body, small limbs, and a big, deep head. Length: 26 cm (10 in). Time: early Permian. Place: Texas. Order: Microsauria (mostly sturdy, land-based insect eaters).

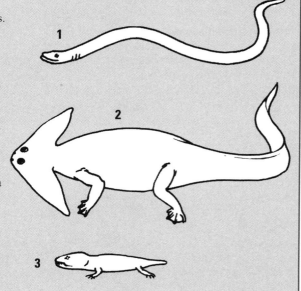

Modern amphibians

Frogs and toads, tailed amphibians, and caecilians (modern amphibians) have teeth on pedestals and form a group called Lissamphibia. Scientists had thought their ancestors were temnospondyls, but many now believe that their closest fossil relatives must lie among the lepospondyls known as microsaurs or another group quite close to these.

Of the three main forms of lissamphibians, the first known froglike fossil dates from early Triassic times, the earliest caecilian from early Jurassic, and the first salamander from the middle Jurassic.

A likely fourth lissamphibian group also appeared by mid-Jurassic times. Albanerpetontids resembled salamanders, but a Spanish fossil find described in 1995 revealed that these animals had scales. Their scales, distinctive teeth, and unusual joints between the jaws and head and neck seem to put these little creatures in a category of their own. Albanerpetontids ranged from North America through Europe into central Asia. Like other lissamphibians, this group had probably evolved more than 250 million years ago. Unlike the others, though, it became extinct at least 5 million years ago.

Lissamphibians

Here we give an example of each group of prehistoric lissamphibians.

1 Triadobatrachus, the first known fossil froglike lissamphibian, lived in early Triassic Madagascar. Length: 10 cm (4 in). Order: Anura.

2 Karaurus, an early salamander known from a complete skeleton, had a broad skull with sculptured bones. Length: 19 cm (7.5 in). Time: late Jurassic. Place: Kazakhstan. Order: Urodela (newts and salamanders).

3 Apodops, an early caecilian, is known from one vertebra. Time: Paleocene. Place: Brazil. Order: Apoda (caecilians: wormlike burrowers).

4 Celtedens, an albanerpetontid, resembled a little tough-skinned, scaly salamander, with strong bones and sturdy limbs designed for life on land. Length: 7.5 cm (3 in). Time: early Cretaceous. Place: Spain. Family: Albanerpetontidae.

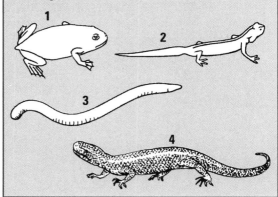

A frog ancestor

Here we show evolutionary changes that produced Triadobatrachus *from long-bodied amphibian ancestors.*

a Froglike skull

b Shortened back with reduced spinal bones (modern frogs have fewer still)

c Shortened tail (modern adult frogs have none)

d Shortened ribs (modern frogs have none)

e Leg design still primitive (modern frogs have very long hind limbs, for jumping)

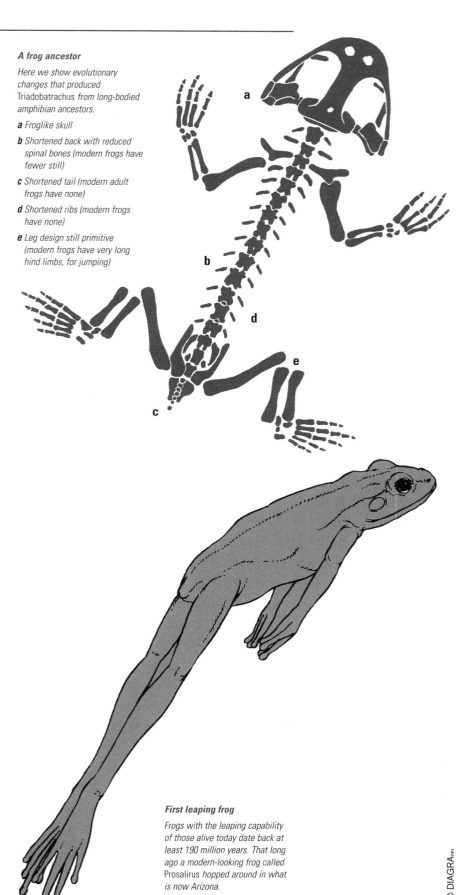

First leaping frog

Frogs with the leaping capability of those alive today date back at least 190 million years. That long ago a modern-looking frog called Prosalirus *hopped around in what is now Arizona.*

© DIAGRA...

Fossil reptiles

Reptiles (the Linnaean class Reptilia) form one of the two great groups of vertebrates able not only to live but also to breed on land. Both came from amphibious tetrapods that had evolved into amniotes–creatures laying waterproof eggs with their own food supply. Reptiles arose in the Paleozoic era, dominated land life in Mesozoic times, and flourish today. These pages explore fossil examples from most of the main reptile groups.

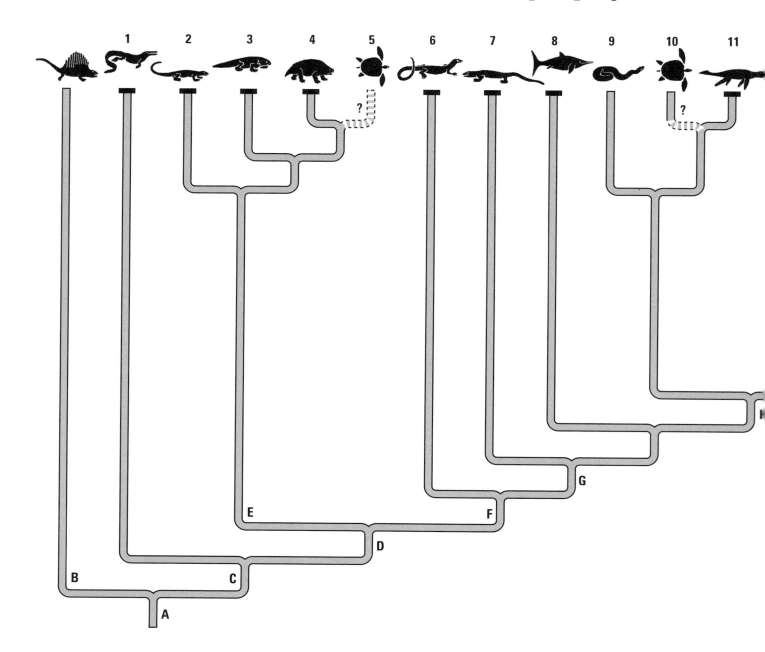

About reptiles

Reptiles were established by 300 million years ago. They probably evolved from tetrapods like *Casineria*, a 340-million-year-old early amniote described in 1999. Resembling a cross between a little lizard and a newt, this became the earliest known vertebrate with no more than five fingers on each hand. Its forelimbs were better built than those of early tetrapods for bearing weight on land.

Typical reptiles are cold-blooded animals with dry, scaly, waterproof skin, although we now know many dinosaurs were feathered and warm-blooded. Each reptile egg is fertilized inside a female. Most eggs develop only after being laid. Tough skin or a hard shell protects each fluid-cushioned embryo and its supply of nourishment and stops it from drying up. These devices freed reptiles from the waterside. They colonized dry lands and even deserts.

Reptiles gave rise to two main groups. They were identified by the number and type of holes, behind the eyes in the skull, with space for strong jaw muscles to contract. Many early reptiles lacked such holes. These so-called anapsids possibly include tortoises and turtles. Most reptiles are diapsids, with two openings behind each eye. Important diapsid subgroups are lepidosaurs, with snakes, lizards, and their ancestors, and archosaurs, with crocodiles, pterosaurs, dinosaurs, and others. Euryapsids, with one high cheek opening, were arguably diapsids that had lost a hole. Such reptiles included the large sea-going ichthyosaurs and plesiosaurs.

From late Paleozoic through Mesozoic times, big reptiles were the "lions" and "zebras" of their day. Land, air, and sea reptiles ruled the Mesozoic era, the Age of Dinosaurs.

Four types of skulls (below)

Reptiles were once put in four subclasses according to four types of skull design.

1 *Anapsida: no hole between postorbital (**A**) and squamosal (**B**) bones.*

2 *Synapsida: one hole between and below these bones. Synapsids ("mammal-like reptiles") branched off from the amniote stem before reptiles and are no longer considered reptiles. Their line includes mammals.*

3 *Euryapsida: one hole between and above these bones. Euryapsids have been reinterpreted as diapsids that lost a hole.*

4 *Diapsida: two holes between these bones. Most reptiles are diapsids.*

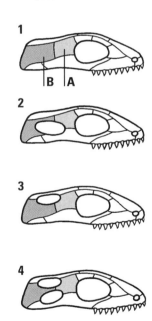

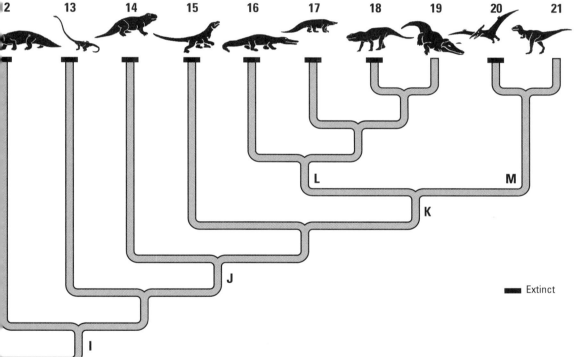

■ Extinct

Reptiles family tree

*This shows how reptile groups and some subgroups were perhaps related. (Turtles' origins are in dispute.) Capital letters pinpoint appearances of key evolutionary innovations. Reptiles as now formally defined only start at **D**. Most lines became extinct, but pelycosaurs led to mammals, and dinosaurs to birds.*

A *Amniota (amniotes)*

B *Synapsida (pelycosaurs, therapsids, and mammals)*

C *Sauropsida ("lizard faces")*
D *Reptilia (reptiles)*
E *Anapsida (anapsids)*
F *Eureptilia ("true reptiles")*
G *Diapsida (diapsids)*
H *Sauria (saurians)*
I *Archosauromorpha ("ruling reptile forms")*
J *Archosauriformes*
K *Archosauria ("ruling reptiles")*
L *Crurotarsi ("cross ankles")*

M *Ornithodira ("bird necks")*
1 *Mesosauria (mesosaurs)*
2 *Millerettidae (millerettids)*
3 *Procolophonoidea*
4 *Pareiasauria (pareiasaurs)*
5 *Chelonia (turtles)*
6 *Protorothyrididae*
7 *Younginiformes (representing basal diapsids)*
8 *Ichthyopterygia (ichthyosaurs)*

9 *Lepidosauria (lepidosaurs: lizards and snakes)*
10 *Chelonia (turtles)*
11 *Sauropterygia (placodonts, plesiosaurs)*
12 *Rhynchosauridae (rhynchosaurs)*
13 *Protorosauria (protorosaurs)*
14 *Erythrosuchidae*
15 *Euparkeria*

16 *Parasuchia or Phytosauria (parasuchians or phytosaurs)*
17 *Aetosauria (aetosaurs)*
18 *Rauisuchia (rauisuchians)*
19 *Crocodylomorpha (crocodilians)*
20 *Pterosauria (pterosaurs)*
21 *Dinosauria (dinosaurs)*

Reptile pioneers

Creatures shown on this page represent three grades of reptilian evolution. The five spanned nearly 100 million years, and they ranged from small and lizard-like animals to bulky beasts 3 m (10 ft) long, with solidly roofed skulls, sprawling limbs, and eardrums just above the jaw hinge. Most early, primitive reptiles lived in swamps, about 290–210 million years ago. Their fossils crop up worldwide, mostly in Permian and Triassic rocks.

Mesosaurs (**1**) were so-called sauropsids ("lizard faces"), the most primitive reptilian grade. They swam in shallow inshore waters of Africa and Brazil in early Permian times some 280 million years ago.

The four other animals shown here include three so-called parareptiles, with anapsid-type skulls: a procolophonian (**2**), a pareiasaur (**3**), and a millerettid (**4**). The protorothyridid (**5**), was an early eureptile ("true reptile") from 300 million years ago.

Reptilian features

Letters indicate features that help paleontologists to identify fossil bones as those of a reptile, not an amphibian, though certain tetrapods share some of these features.

a *Relatively deep skull*

b *Usually no otic (ear) notch*

c *Small size or distinctive position of some skull bones*

d *Any teeth on palate small not tusklike*

e *Two or more vertebrae join spine to hip girdle*

f *Pleurocentrum is the main part of each vertebra*

g *Enlarged ilium (a hip bone)*

h *Shoulder blade well developed but some bones in the shoulder girdle reduced*

i *Limb bones slimmer than in labyrinthodonts*

j *Fewer wrist and ankle bones than in amphibians*

k *Distinctive numbers of toe and "finger" bones*

Early reptiles

The five creatures drawn here represent three evolutionary grades: Sauropsida (**1**); "Anapsida" (parareptiles **2**–**4**), and Eureptilia (**5**).

1 Mesosaurus, a mesosaur, had a long, slim body, slender, sharp-toothed jaws, paddle-shaped limbs, and long, deep, swimmer's tail. Length: 71 cm (28 in). Time: early Permian. Place: Brazil and South Africa.

2 Hypsognathus was a lizard-like procolophonian, with broad cheek teeth, and spikes jutting back from its head. Length: 33 cm (13 in). Time: late Triassic. Place: New Jersey.

3 Scutosaurus belonged to the pareiasaurs: big, heavy, herbivorous animals, that stood more upright than many reptiles. The small, saw-edged teeth in its broad head probably sliced up vegetation. Length: 2.4 m (8 ft). Time: late Permian. Place: Russia.

4 Millerosaurus was a lizard-like reptile, with broad cheeks, short jaws, and in some individuals a skull hole behind each eye. Length: 1 m (3 ft 3 in). Time: late Permian. Place: South Africa.

5 Hylonomus, one of the first eureptiles, was a small, low protorothyridid, with sprawling limbs, long tail, short neck, short, pointed snout, and sharp teeth. Length: 1 m (3 ft 3 in). Time: late Carboniferous (lower Pennsylvanian). Place: Nova Scotia, Canada.

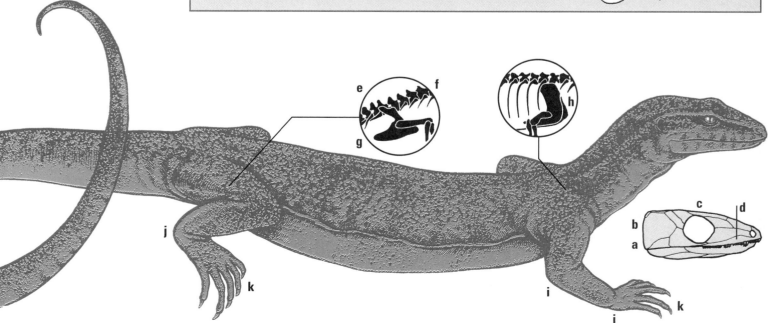

Turtles and tortoises

Chelonians (turtles and tortoises) form one of the oldest living reptile orders. They might be anapsids evolved from pareiasaurs, but molecular studies place them near crocodiles as reptiles that lost their diapsids' skull holes.

Most had a broad, short body protected by a bony shell covered with horny scutes. Many could (and still can) pull their heads, tails, and limbs inside the shells for protection. They evolved a toothless beak for slicing meat or vegetation. From the first chelonians came today's land tortoises and turtles designed to swim and hunt in rivers, pools, or seas. Of four (perhaps five) suborders, two survive.

The earliest fossils come from Triassic Germany and Thailand. Later fossils occur worldwide.

Chelonian body plan (right)

Archelon's skeleton (seen from above) and skull (seen from one side) show how chelonians evolved differently from other reptiles.

a *Skull roof often lacking certain bones*

b *Horny beak*

c *Short, broad body*

d *Heavy limbs projecting sideways*

e *Relatively few toe bones*

f *Relatively few vertebrae*

g *Two-part shell comprising bony carapace above and bony plastron beneath, covered with horny scutes; the shell is reduced in marine turtles, massive in slow-moving tortoises in need of protection*

h *Vertebrae and ribs fused to carapace*

i *Limb girdles and upper limb bones fitting inside ribs*

j *Short tail*

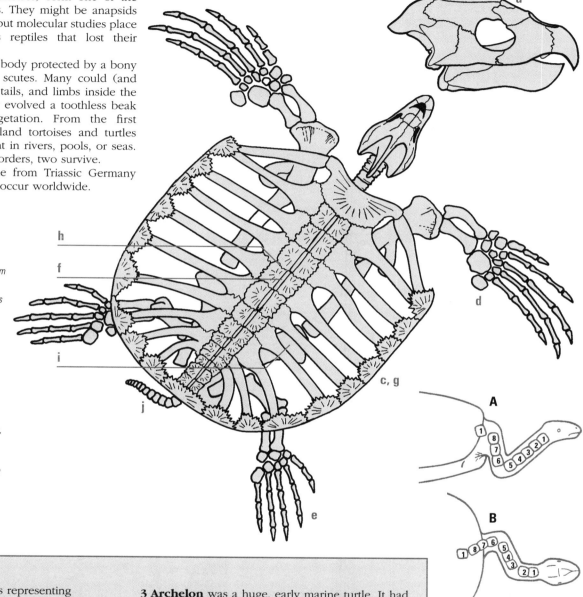

Neck benders (above)

These diagrams reveal how two types of chelonian pull the head inside the shell.

A *Cryptodires bend the neck down and back. Bending occurs mostly between cervical (neck) vertebrae 5 and 6, and between cervical vertebra 8 and dorsal (back) vertebra 1.*

B *Pleurodires bend the neck sideways. Bending occurs mostly between cervical vertebrae 2 and 3 and 5 and 6, and between cervical vertebra 8 and dorsal vertebra 1.*

Three chelonians

We show three chelonians representing evolutionary trends. Proganochelyids perhaps gave rise to amphichelyids (not shown) which led to cryptodires and pleurodires (both flourishing today).

1 Proganochelys had a well-developed shell but an "old-fashioned" skull with teeth as well as a beak. It probably could not pull its limbs, tail, or head inside its shell. Shell length: 61 cm (2 ft). Time: late Triassic. Place: Germany. Suborder: Proganochelydia (ancestral chelonians).

2 Podocnemis was and is a freshwater turtle (terrapin) that pulls its neck in sideways. Length: to 76 cm (30 in). Time: late Cretaceous onward. Place: once widespread, now South America and Madagascar. Suborder: Pleurodira (side-neck turtles).

3 Archelon was a huge, early marine turtle. It had a broad, light, flattened shell and long paddle-like limbs. Length: 3.7 m (12 ft). Time: late Cretaceous. Place: North America. Suborder: Cryptodira (vertical-neck turtles, including all living tortoises and most turtles).

© DIAGRAM

Early and primitive diapsids

The first diapsids (reptiles with two skull holes behind the eye) evolved from anapsid ancestors. Early diapsids were small, lizardlike creatures, but some of these gave rise to larger, crocodilelike forms. Early diapsid-type reptiles persisted about 290–50 million years, but their heyday was about 280-200 million years ago. Fossils of early diapsid-type reptiles crop up mostly in upper Permian rocks of South Africa, though finds occur elsewhere, especially in North America and Europe.

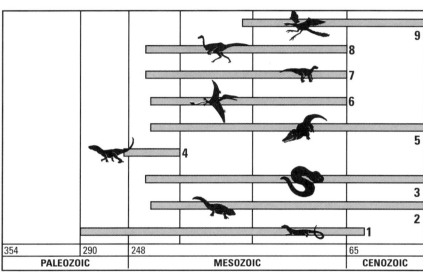

Diapsid time lines

This diagram shows likely time spans for selected groups of reptiles sharing a diapsid-type skull.

1 Primitive diapsids

2 Rhynchocephalians (sphenodonts: including the living tuatara)

3 Squamates (snakes, and lizards)

4 Archosauromorphs (early "ruling reptiles")

5 Crocodilians

6 Pterosaurs

7 Ornithischian dinosaurs

8 Saurischian dinosaurs

9 Birds (avian saurischian dinosaurs)

354	290	248		65
PALEOZOIC		MESOZOIC		CENOZOIC

Primitive diapsids

Primitive diapsids included the four diverse examples pictured below. Three were early forms, the fourth outlived the dinosaurs.

1 Araeoscelis was small, lightly built, and rather lizardlike, but with long, slim shins and "forearms." Length: 66 cm (26 in). Time: early Permian. Place: Texas. Clade: Araeoscelida.

2 Youngina had slim limbs; a long, slim tail and body; and a pointed skull of "old-fashioned" design, with teeth inside the mouth as well as set in sockets on the jaw rim. Length: 45 cm (18 in). Time: late Permian. Place: South Africa. Clade: Younginiformes (lizardlike).

3 Coelurosauravus glided from tree to tree on skin wings stretched between riblike bony struts. Length: 50 cm (20 in). Time: late Permian. Place: Europe. Family: Coelurosauravidae.

4 Champsosaurus resembled a slim-snouted crocodilian. Length: 1.5 m (5 ft). Time: late Cretaceous-Eocene. Place: North America and Europe. Clade: Choristodera (fish hunters).

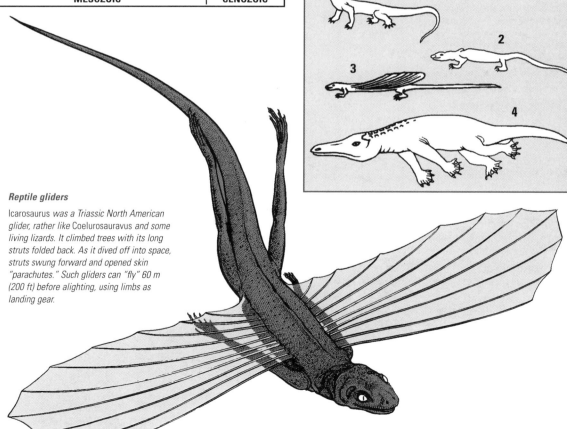

Reptile gliders

Icarosaurus *was a Triassic North American glider, rather like* Coelurosauravus *and some living lizards. It climbed trees with its long struts folded back. As it dived off into space, struts swung forward and opened skin "parachutes." Such gliders can "fly" 60 m (200 ft) before alighting, using limbs as landing gear.*

Early sauropterygians

Sauropterygians were mostly marine reptiles with a euryapsid-type hole high in the skull behind the eye; they may be diapsids that lost a skull hole. Placodonts and nothosaurs were two early groups, perhaps evolved from the semiaquatic claudiosaurids. Like those more highly accomplished swimmers thalattosaurs, claudiosaurids were diapsids of uncertain affinity. Placodonts had short, stout, armored bodies, paddle-like limbs, and blunt teeth. Nothosaurs were slimmer, with longer necks and bodies, and sharp teeth. Both groups hunted in the sea: placodonts for mollusks, nothosaurs for fishes. Placodonts and nothosaurs flourished in Triassic times until they were wiped out by competition from bony fishes and new aquatic reptiles. Fossils of both occur in Triassic rocks in parts of Europe, North Africa, and Asia that rimmed the ancient Tethys Sea.

Placodont body plan

The 2 m (6 ft 6 in) Placodus *from mid-Triassic Europe showed these typical placodont features:*

a Powerful jaws

b Peglike front teeth

c Flat, broad, crushing tooth plates at the back of the mouth

d Short, heavy, rounded body

e Short neck

f Extra set of (belly) ribs

g Small bones forming protective armor

h Limbs designed as paddles

i Skin joining toes and fingers

j Flattened tail (short in later placodonts)

Skulls compared

These diagrams contrast the jaws of two euryapsids that ate different foods.

A Nothosaurus *jaws were long and slim, with long, sharp teeth that interlocked to seize and grip slippery fishes.*

B Placodus *jaws were deep and strong and closed by muscles with great crushing force. Jutting front teeth were pincers to pluck molluscs from the seabed. Flat back teeth and bones in the skull roof and lower jaw crushed mollusc shells.*

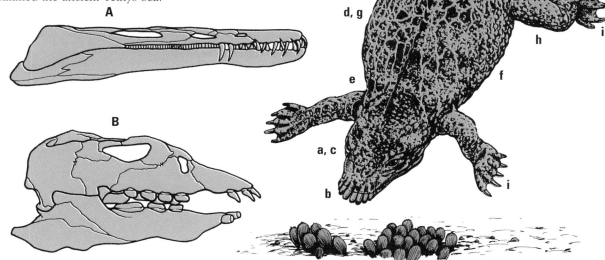

Sauropterygians

Here we show a thalattosaur, a claudiosaurid, and two early sauropterygians.

1 Claudiosaurus resembled a long-necked lizard. It swam by waggling its tail and foraged under inshore waters. Length: 2 ft (60 cm). Time: late Permian. Place: Madagascar. Family: Claudiosauridae.

2 Askeptosaurus had a long, slim body, long sharp-toothed skull, and small, paddle-like limb Length: 1.5 m (5 ft). Time: mid-Triassic. Place: Europe. Clade: Thalattosauria (aquatic hunters).

3 Henodus shows how later placodonts evolved like marine turtles, with flippers, a broad, flat body protected by a bony shell, and a horny, toothless beak. Length: 1 m (3 ft 3 in). Time: late Triassic. Place: Germany. Clade: Placodontia.

4 Nothosaurus had a long, slim neck and body, long forelimbs, and long, slim jaws bristling with sharp teeth shaped for catching fishes. Length: 3 m (10 ft). Time: mid-Triassic. Place: central Europe, North Africa, Southwest Asia, East Asia. Clade: Nothosauria.

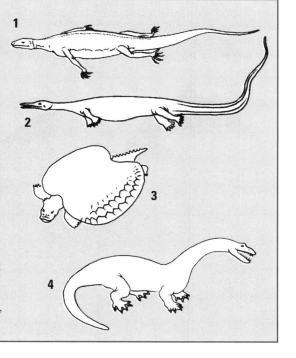

© DIAGRAM

Plesiosaurs

Plesiosaurs ("near lizards") were sauropterygians bigger than nothosaurs and better built for water life. They had a barrel-shaped body; broad ribs; "belly" ribs; four long, flat flippers; and a short tail. Along with ichthyosaurs they ruled Jurassic and Cretaceous seas and oceans, then died off.

Plesiosaurs comprised two main groups. Long-necked plesiosaurs were expert fishers at or near the surface. Short-necked plesiosaurs (pliosaurs) dived and preyed on ammonites. Both types swam with flippers, as marine turtles do. Perhaps flippers also helped move them ashore to lay eggs.

Fossil plesiosaurs occur in Triassic, Jurassic, and Cretaceous clays and limestones–especially Liassic (early Jurassic) rocks in England and Germany, late Cretaceous rocks in western North America, and early Cretaceous rocks in Australia.

Plesiosuars

These four plesiosaurs represent evolutionary trends in both main groups.

1 Peloneustes was a small short-necked plesiosaur. Length: 3 m (10 ft). Time: late Jurassic. Place: western Europe. Clade: Pliosauroidea.

2 Kronosaurus was a huge short-necked plesiosaur with massive teeth. Length: up to 17 m (56 ft), one-quarter of which was the head. Time: early Cretaceous. Place: Australia. Clade: Pliosauroidea.

3 Thaumatosaurus, an early long-necked plesiosaur, had a neck less than one-quarter of its total length. Length: 3.4 m (11 ft). Time: early–mid-Jurassic. Place: Europe. Clade: Plesiosauroidea.

4 Elasmosaurus was more than half neck, with more than 70 neck vertebrae. Length: 12 m (39 ft) or longer. Time: late Cretaceous. Place: North America. Clade: Plesiosauroidea.

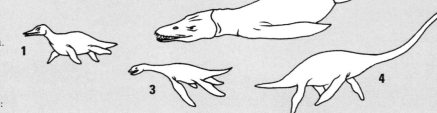
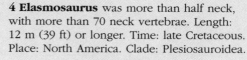

Ichthyosaurs

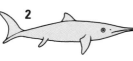

Ichthyosaurs ("fish lizards") were aquatic reptiles that flourished in shallow seas about 240 million to 90 million years ago. They had fins, flippers, long narrow jaws, and a superbly streamlined body. The largest individuals measured about 23 m (75 ft), but some species were no longer than a human. Ichthyosaurs ate cephalopods and fish and gave birth to their young in water.

These reptiles spread all around the world, but their fossils are most plentiful in lower Jurassic rocks about 180 million years old. Fossil ichthyosaur bones or feces occur in, for instance, Britain's Lias shales and limestones and in rocks in Germany, North and South America, Australia, and Indonesia.

These three ichthyosaurs represent evolutionary trends in the order Ichthyosauria.

1 Cymbospondylus, a Triassic ichthyosaur, had relatively long arm and thigh bones, a short skull, and a small tail, recalling the body build of the ichthyosaurs' land-based ancestors.

Dolphin's look-alike

Ichthyosaurs could have moved swiftly through the waves. Their bodies were designed for speed, much like those of dolphins—sea mammals evolved from ancestors that dwelt on land. But ichthyosaurs had vertical, not horizontal, tails; longer jaws; and simpler brains that made them less intelligent than dolphins.

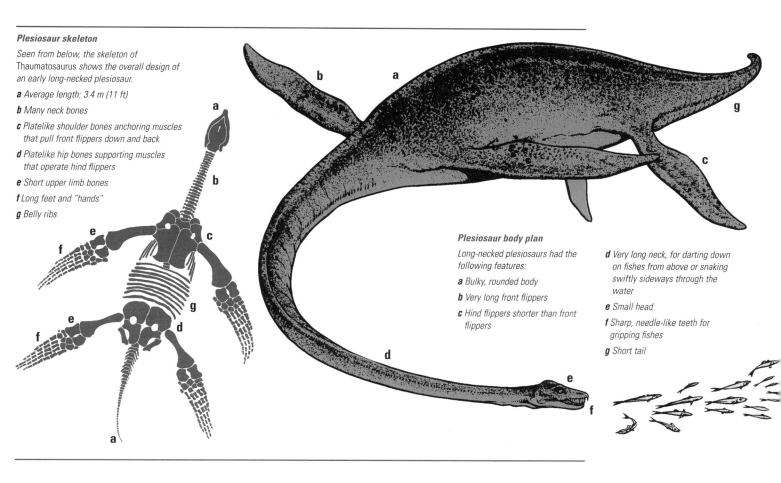

Plesiosaur skeleton

Seen from below, the skeleton of Thaumatosaurus shows the overall design of an early long-necked plesiosaur.

a *Average length: 3.4 m (11 ft)*

b *Many neck bones*

c *Platelike shoulder bones anchoring muscles that pull front flippers down and back*

d *Platelike hip bones supporting muscles that operate hind flippers*

e *Short upper limb bones*

f *Long feet and "hands"*

g *Belly ribs*

Plesiosaur body plan

Long-necked plesiosaurs had the following features:

a *Bulky, rounded body*

b *Very long front flippers*

c *Hind flippers shorter than front flippers*

d *Very long neck, for darting down on fishes from above or snaking swiftly sideways through the water*

e *Small head*

f *Sharp, needle-like teeth for gripping fishes*

g *Short tail*

2 Ichthyosaurus, from lower Jurassic rocks, was much more streamlined than *Cymbospondylus*. It had a large dorsal fin and tail; forelimbs broadened into paddles; and a long, tapered skull.

3 Ophthalmosaurus, from upper Jurassic rocks, reveals further evolutionary changes, including enlarged eyes and propulsive tail, tiny hind limbs, and teeth in a groove instead of separately socketed as in early ichthyosaurs.

Skin and bones

Fine-grained lower Jurassic rock preserved this fine Stenopterygius ichthyosaur fossil from Boll Holzmaden in southern Germany. Even skin remains survive. The fossil's biconcave vertebrae, bony eye ring, and slim, toothy jaws are typical of ichthyosaurs. Experts familiar with such features can often identify an ichthyosaur from just one bone.

© DIAGRAM

Lizards and snakes

Lizards, snakes, rhynchocephalians ("beak heads"), and extinct relatives make up a large group of diapsid reptiles called lepidosaurs ("scale lizards").

Lizards appeared about 230 million years ago. They gave rise to strange aquatic forms including aigalosaurs, dolichosaurs, and mosasaurs ("Meuse lizards"), a family of huge late Cretaceous sea lizards that seized fish and reptiles in sharp-toothed jaws. Mosasaur fossils are especially plentiful in Niobrara chalk from Kansas.

By about 130 million years ago, dolichosaurs or close relatives probably gave rise to snakes. Between them, snakes and lizards make up the Squamata, the most numerous, varied, and widespread reptile group in the world today.

Here are five examples of extinct lepidosaurs:

1 Paliguana was a small, early lizard, or maybe a lizard ancestor, from early Triassic South Africa.

2 Acteosaurus had a long, skinny body; slim tail; and short limbs. It was in the dolichosaurid family–semiaquatic Cretaceous European lizards. Length: about 40 cm (16 in).

3 Tylosaurus was a mosasaur up to 8 m (26 ft) long. Place: North America and New Zealand.

4 Dinilysia might have been an early relative of modern boas and pythons. Length: 1.8 m (6 ft). Time: late Cretaceous. Place: Patagonia, South America.

5 Homeosaurus was a lizardlike rhynchocephalian or sphenodont, related to the living tuatara found only in New Zealand. Length: 19 cm (7.5 in). Time: late Jurassic. Place: southwest Germany.

Mosasaur body plan

a Huge size

b Long head

c Nostrils high on skull

d Long jaws, with a joint in the lower jaw

e Sharp teeth set in sockets

f Short neck

g Long body

h Flattened, paddle-shaped limbs to steer and balance

i Long tail flattened from side to side for swimming

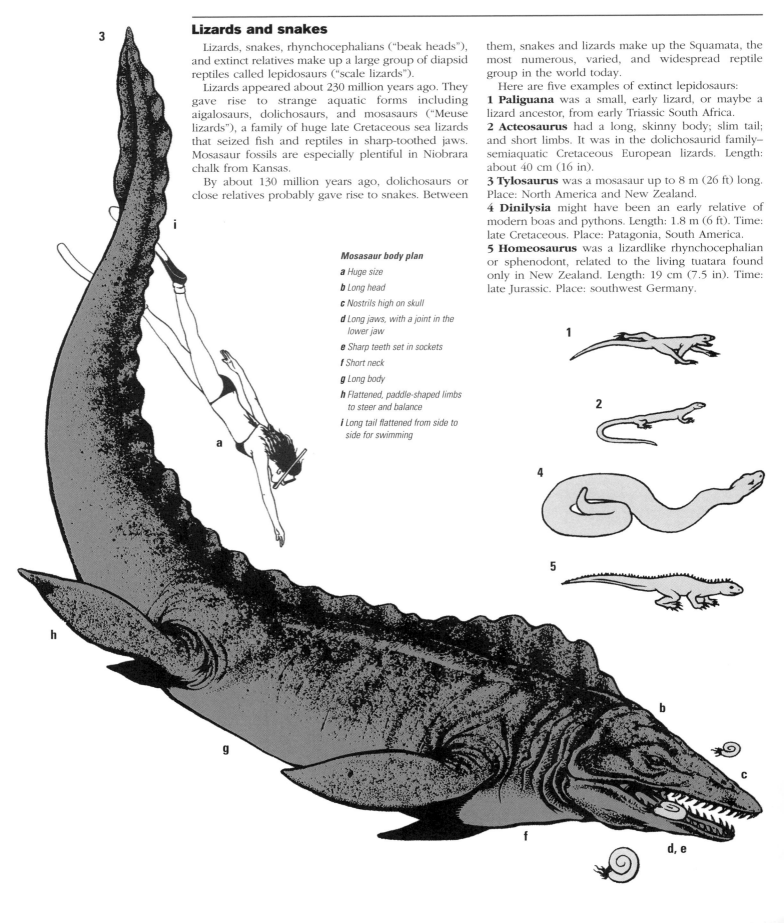

Early ruling reptiles

Archosauromorphs ("ruling reptile forms") were a very varied group of reptiles probably evolved from lizardlike diapsids. In Triassic times they spread worldwide and dominated life on land. Their shared features included distinctive neck ribs and teeth in sockets. Primitive forms represented on this page include piglike, plant-eating rhynchosaurs and lizardlike protorosaurs (or Prolacertiformes), as well as more advanced kinds known as Archosauriformes, with a skull hole in front of each eye. Among these were the lumbering quadrupedal erythrosuchids and small, slim, bipedal euparkerids that ran with their bodies held well off the ground and legs tucked in. From such lively, agile animals would evolve the Archosauria ("ruling reptiles"), featured on the next four pages. Archosaurs formed the world's largest, most diverse, and most successful group of vertebrates through most of Mesozoic times.

Euparkia *body plan* (below)

An advanced archosauriform had these features:

1 *Skull lightened on each side by two holes behind the eye (**a**), one in front of the eye (**b**) and one in the lower jaw (**c**).*

2 *Teeth set in sockets*

3 *About two dozen vertebrae between the head and hip region*

4 *Two sacral vertebrae (linked to the hips)*

5 *Hip socket shaped as a solid bony basin*

6 *Fairly straight thighbone, not sharply turned in at the top*

7 *Hind limbs (**a**) longer than front limbs (**b**)*

8 *Shin no longer than thigh*

9 *Five digits per hand and foot*

Clues to diet (left)

*Rhynchosaurs probably ate plants. Clues to their diet include features of skull and teeth, shown here from below (**A**) and side (**B**).*

a *rows of teeth on tooth plates*

b *groove to take the lower jaw as jaws shut like a penknife*

c *tonglike food-gathering beak, manipulated by a large tongue*

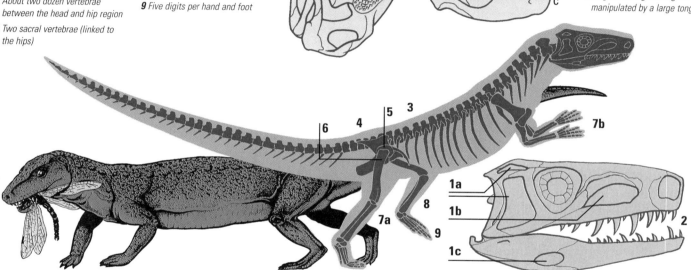

Early archosauromorphs

Early archosauromorphs included these four:

1 Scaphonyx was a rhynchosaur, a heavy-bodied herbivorous reptile with a deep skull, toothless, tonglike jaws; and rows of crushing toothplates in the mouth. It might have grubbed up roots and tubers or chopped and crushed up husked fruits. Length: 1.8 m (6 ft). Time: mid-Triassic. Place: South America.

2 Tanystropheus, a protorosaur, or prolacertiform, had a grotesquely long neck, probably used as a fishing rod. Adults maybe lived at sea, young on the shore. Length: up to 6 m (20 ft). Time: mid-Triassic. Place: central Europe and Israel.

3 Erythrosuchus, an erythrosuchid, had a stout, squat body, thick limbs, large head, and rather short tail. This creature, possibly amphibious, was the largest land vertebrate of its day. Length: up to 5 m (16 ft). Time: early Triassic. Place: South Africa.

4 Euparkeria was a small, lightly built hunter. It rose on long hind limbs to sprint, the tail balancing the head and neck. Rows of armor plates ran down the back. Length: 60 cm (2 ft). Time: early Triassic. Place: South Africa.

Two ways of standing (above)

A *Many archosauromorphs sprawled, with their knees and elbows stuck out and feet flat on the ground.*

B *Advanced archosauriforms tucked their knees and elbows down and in to lift the body and gain speed. Some ran on their toes.*

© DIAGRAM

"Cross ankles" 1

Advanced "ruling reptiles" (the Archosauria) included reptiles that walked on semierect and erect limbs. Distinctive ankle joints and other features have led scientists to split them into two main groups, Crurotarsi ("cross ankles") and Ornithodira ("bird necks"). Crurotarsi included the crocodilians and their close relatives, now extinct. Ornithodirans included the pterosaurs and dinosaurs.

This page features examples of four types of "cross ankles" (not all in fact had ankle bones designed in the same way). Ornithosuchids were large bipedal/quadrupedal carnivores. Parasuchians or phytosaurs were aquatic reptiles that looked like crocodiles. Aetosaurs were armored, quadrupedal plant eaters. Rauisuchians included large land-based, perhaps mainly quadrupedal, predators.

Rauisuchians appeared by 240 million years ago, the rest by 227 million years ago. All flourished in late Triassic times but died off as that period ended.

Crurotarsi

1 Ornithosuchus was an ornithosuchid predator with much longer legs than arms. It probably hurried on its hind limbs but ambled on all fours. Length: up to 4 m (13 ft). Time: late Triassic. Place: Europe.

2 Rutiodon resembled a crocodile but had nostrils in a bump almost between the eyes, not at the snout tip. It belonged to the parasuchians (phytosaurs). Such fish eaters dominated pools and rivers until they were replaced by crocodilians. Length: 3 m (10 ft). Time: late Triassic. Place: North America and Europe.

3 Stagonolepis was a heavy-bodied quadruped–an aetosaur with bony armor plates for built-in protection. It had a piglike snout with weak teeth.; perhaps it grubbed for roots. Length: 3 m (10 ft). Time: late Triassic. Place: Europe.

4 Postosuchus was a large-headed rauisuchian predator weighing about a ton. It had powerful jaws, sharp fangs, sharp-clawed hands, and an armored back. Despite long hind limbs it might have walked on all fours. Length: 6 m (20 ft). Time: late Triassic. Place: North America.

Ornithosuchus

With its upright stance, Ornithosuchus resembled theropod dinosaurs but, among other differences, had more toes and a "crocodile-reversed" type of ankle joint.

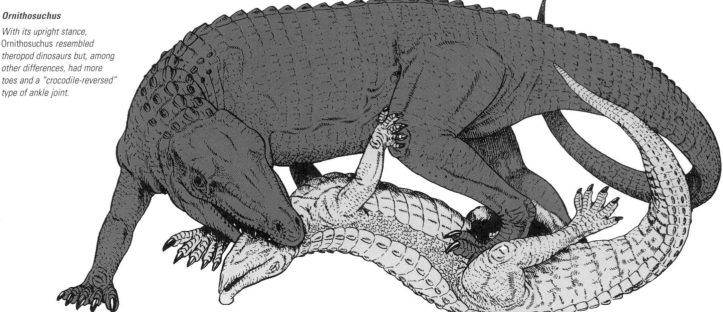

© DIAGRAM

"Cross ankles" 2: Crocodilians

Crocodilians are living fossils, and like birds, evolved from archosaurs. Their bulky, armored bodies; long, deep, flattened swimmers' tails; short, sturdy limbs; and long, strong, toothy, flesh eaters' jaws resemble those of crocodiles alive 100 million years ago.

Along with other archosaurs including dinosaurs, crocodilians had appeared before 200 million years ago. Fossils show that they dominated pools and rivers worldwide when climates almost everywhere were warm. Small, early kinds resembling *Protosuchus* gave rise to the thalattosuchians designed for life at sea and to the metasuchians, including the little-known sebecosuchids and the eusuchians the only group that survives today.

Here are four examples of crocodilian diversity.

1 Protosuchus from Arizona was an early form only 1 m (3 ft 3 in) long. It had a short, sharp-toothed skull and rather long hind limbs. Maybe it lived mainly on land. Time: early Jurassic.

2 Metriorhynchus was a thalattosuchian, with limbs evolved as flippers, a tail fin, very long jaws with sharp fish eater's teeth, and no bony armor. Length: 3 m (10 ft). Its mid-late Jurassic fossils occur in Europe and South America.

3 Baurusuchus was a sebecosuchid from Brazil. It had a short, deep, flattened skull, with few teeth (the front ones very large) and sideways-facing eyes. Probably it lived on land. Length: maybe 1.5 m (5 ft). Time: late Cretaceous.

4 Deinosuchus, an eusuchian with immense jaws, was the largest crocodilian ever. It lived in late Cretaceous Texas and must have eaten small- and medium-sized dinosaurs. Length: 10 m (33 ft).

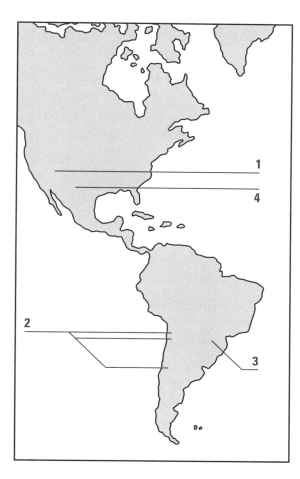

Where they lived (left)

This map shows finds of the four fossil crocodilians described on these pages.

1 Protosuchus

2 Metriorhynchus *(which lived in seas worldwide)*

3 Baurusuchus

4 Deinosuchus

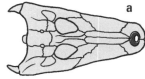

Nostrils fore or aft (above)

Nostril position helps us distinguish crocodilian fossils from those of phytosaurs.

a *Crocodilian nostrils (an enclosed nasal passage permits breathing while eating)*

b *Phytosaur nostrils*

Terror of the dinosaurs (below)

The huge crocodilian Deinosuchus lurked in rivers and ambushed dinosaurs that came to drink. Contrast this monster's size with that of a modern crocodile, shown to the same scale.

Pterosaurs

Pterosaurs ("winged lizards") included the first and largest flying backboned animals. Thought to be close kin of dinosaurs, they evolved from Triassic gliders, lasted 155 million years, and died out at the end of the Cretaceous period 65 million years ago. They had skin wings stretched between the limbs and body; light, but strong, skeletons; and well-developed powers of sight and wing control. On land they shuffled on all fours and roosted batlike. Most caught fish or other prey. Two main types evolved: first rhamphorhynchoids, with teeth and tails, then pterodactyloids, which lacked these and so shed needless weight. Large pterodactyloids were poor fliers and mostly soared or glided where air rose over heated land or winds blew up sea cliffs.

How pterosaurs began (above)

The gliding reptile Sharovipteryx might have given rise to pterosaurs (although these flew with their forelimbs). It lived in early Triassic times in what is now Kyrgystan, in West-central Asia.

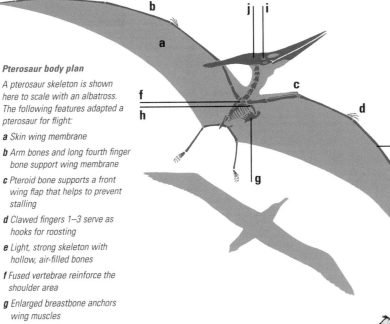

Pterosaur body plan

A pterosaur skeleton is shown here to scale with an albatross. The following features adapted a pterosaur for flight:

a Skin wing membrane

b Arm bones and long fourth finger bone support wing membrane

c Pteroid bone supports a front wing flap that helps to prevent stalling

d Clawed fingers 1–3 serve as hooks for roosting

e Light, strong skeleton with hollow, air-filled bones

f Fused vertebrae reinforce the shoulder area

g Enlarged breastbone anchors wing muscles

h Strong joint linking shoulder blade to spine and breastbone

i Large eyes with keen vision

j Brain well developed for sight and coordinated flight

"Winged lizards"

These examples show special features and trends.

1 Dimorphodon, an early Jurassic pterosaur from southern England, had a big head, biting teeth, and a long tail. Wingspan: 1.5 m (5 ft).

2 Sordes had fur to trap body heat (maybe all pterosaurs were warm-blooded). This small rhamphorhynchoid comes from late Jurassic rocks in West-central Asia (Kazakhstan).

3 Pteranodon was a huge, tailless, toothless pterodactyloid. Its "weather vane" head crest might have kept it heading into wind. It zoomed off sea cliffs, caught fish in its beak, and stored them in a throat pouch for its young. Wingspan: 8 m (26 ft). Time: late Cretaceous. Place: USA (Delaware, Kansas, and Texas) and Japan.

4 Quetzalcoatlus, or "feathered serpent, was the largest known pterosaur–a long-necked beast that soared on hot air and gobbled carrion. Wingspan: 11–12 m (36–39 ft). Weight: 86 kg (190 lb). Time: late Cretaceous. Place : Texas and Alberta.

Vultures and albatrosses

Weak fliers, giant pterosaurs relied on moving air to keep them borne aloft.

A Quetzalcoatlus soared on thermal currents rising from land heated by the Sun.

B Pteranodon launched into the winds that blew up sea cliffs.

Dinosaurs

Dinosaurs ("terrible lizards") were the most durable land vertebrates ever–reptiles with an erect stance, probably warm-blooded bodies, and ranging from no bigger than hens to as massive as whales. Evolving from small, bipedal/quadrupedal archosaurs about 230 million years ago, they spread around the world. One line, the saurischians, gave rise to bipedal carnivores large and small and to huge, four-legged plant eaters. Ornithischians, the other group produced two-legged and four-legged plant eaters, again with a huge range of sizes. All ornithischians and most saurischians died out 65 million years ago, but first carnivorous saurischians gave rise to birds.

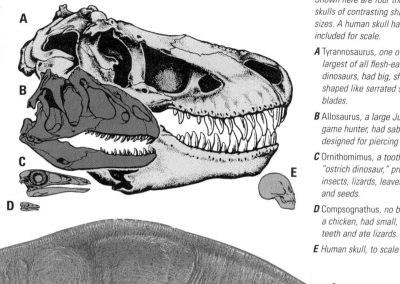

Theropod skulls (left)

Shown here are four theropod skulls of contrasting shapes and sizes. A human skull has also been included for scale.

A Tyrannosaurus, *one of the largest of all flesh-eating dinosaurs, had big, sharp teeth shaped like serrated steak knife blades.*

B Allosaurus, *a large Jurassic big-game hunter, had saberlike teeth designed for piercing flesh.*

C Ornithomimus, *a toothless "ostrich dinosaur," probably ate insects, lizards, leaves, fruit, and seeds.*

D Compsognathus, *no bigger than a chicken, had small, sharp teeth and ate lizards.*

E Human skull, to scale

Cetiosaurid body plan

Cetiosaurids were sauropods, which included the largest land animals ever.

a Small head, shape uncertain

b Teeth like flat spoons

c Long neck

d Bulky body

e Pillarlike limbs

f Long tail

Dinosaur groups

Here, five genera represent the main groups, and this book's next section is devoted to dinosaurs.

1 Tyrannosaurus was a huge theropod (carnivorous saurischian) with great fangs; massive jaws; very short arms with two-fingered hands; huge legs; three-toed, clawed feet; and a long tail balancing the front of the body. Length: up to 12 m (39 ft). Time: late Cretaceous. Place: North America.

2 Plateosaurus, a sauropodomorph saurischian, was a plant-eating prosauropod foreshadowing the vast sauropods. It had a bulky body, long neck, small head, long tail and hind limbs, but shorter forelimbs with great thumb claws. Length: 8 m (26 ft). Time: late Triassic. Place: western Europe.

3 Hypsilophodon, an ornithopod, was a speedy bipedal ornithischian "gazelle," with long shins and feet, short arms, a stiffened balancing tail, a beak, and self-sharpening cheek teeth. Length: 2.3 m (7 ft 6 in). Time: early Cretaceous. Place: western Europe and North America.

4 Triceratops, a marginocephalian ornithischian, was a great quadruped with a horned head, "parrot's" beak, scissorlike cheek teeth, and an immense bony neck frill. Length: 7.9 m (26 ft). Time: late Cretaceous. Place: North America.

5 Stegosaurus, a thyreophoran ornithischian, was a great quadruped with rows of tall, thin, bony plates on its neck and back, and a spiky tail. Length: 9 m (30 ft). Time: late Jurassic. Place: North America.

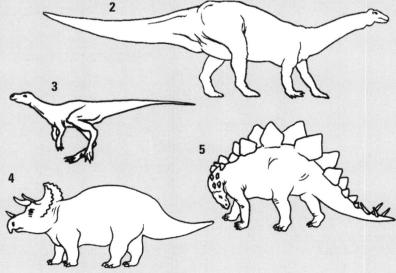

© DIAGRAM

Fossil birds

Birds are the most recently evolved of all the major groups of backboned animals. Since the 1980s, finds of fossil birds have shown the evolutionary shifts that transformed small, toothy, feathered dinosaurs into today's winged wonders. This chapter begins with a summary of those shifts (below and on the next page), followed by prehistoric examples from dozens of orders of birds identified by the Linnaean system, most of which survive.

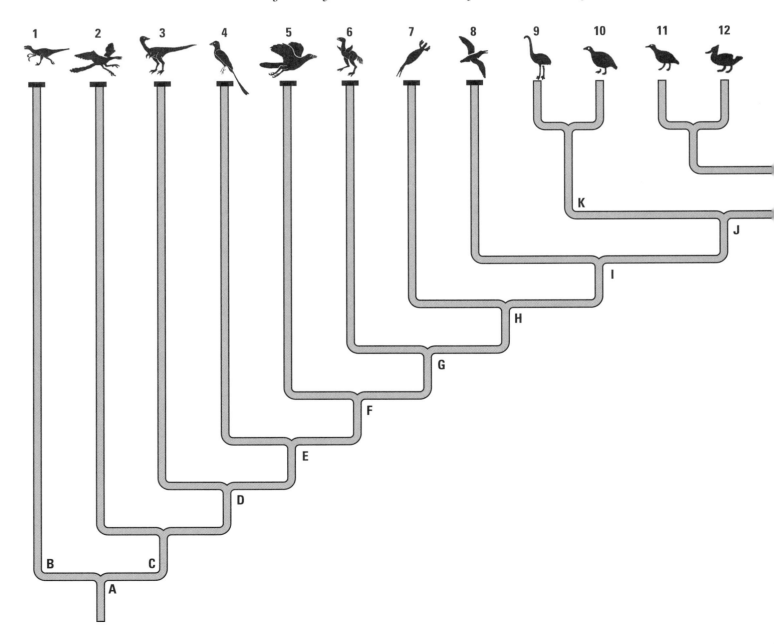

About birds

Birds are warm-blooded vertebrates with feathered wings and hollow, air-filled bones–features they almost certainly inherited from theropod dinosaurs. Like these, early birds that lived about 150 million years ago had teeth, clawed fingers, and a long bony tail core. Only small details such as their backturned hallux ("big toe") anatomically separate the first known birds from non-avian dinosaurs. However, later birds were redesigned on lighter lines for flight; they evolved a toothless beak and fused, shortened tail and hand bones. Most gained a deep breastbone for anchoring the big, strong muscles powering wings capable of flapping, soaring, or gliding flight.

At first, birds shared the air with pterosaurs, but birds have long outlived these creatures. This might be partly because birds' feathered wings survived injuries better than the pterosaurs' more fragile skin wings. Birds survived whatever caused the mass extinction that wiped out pterosaurs and non-avian dinosaurs 65 million years ago.

No one knows when all the more than 30 orders of Aves (birds) recognized by the Linnaean system began or how they are related. Molecular studies have not resolved this issue. Birds' fragile bones are seldom fossilized, and many bird fossils are just a footprint or a feather. Specimens of birds now long extinct have come from certain fine-grained rocks–limestones in southwest Germany and eastern Spain, shales of northeast China, the Niobrara chalk of Kansas, and mudstone rocks of Utah and Wyoming. Between them, fossil finds and molecular studies have now shown how early birds diversified and indicate that major living groups could date back to the Age of Dinosaurs.

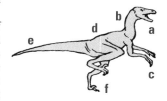

Theropods as ancestors

Dinosaurs similar to but smaller than dromaeosaurids, such as Velociraptor *probably gave rise to birds. The dromaeosaurids' many birdlike features apparently included these:*

a Kinetic jaw

b S-shaped neck

c Long, grasping hands

d Feathered body

e Stiff tail

f Erect legs with birdlike toes

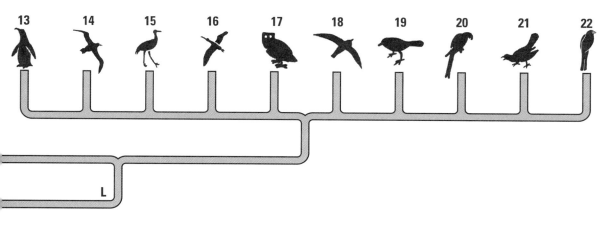

■ Extinct

Family tree of birds

This diagram shows evolutionary trends that turned descendants of one group of Theropoda (predatory dinosaurs) into modern birds (Neornithes). Capital letters signal the appearances of some key innovations. Relationships of various neornithine orders are still in doubt.

A *Maniraptora: feathered theropod dinosaurs with clawed hands that extended in a grasping "flight stroke"*

B *Dromaeosauridae: Maniraptorans with backswept pubic bones as in birds*

C *Avialae: with flight feathers and reversed hallux ("big toe")*

D *Metornithes: with fused wrist bones*

E *Pygostylia: with fused, shortened tail bones*

F *Ornithothoraces: with an alula or "bastard wing" for controlled slow flight, a feature shared by modern birds and Enantiornithes, a major evolutionary branch now long extinct*

G *Fused, long, foot bones*

H *Ornithurae: shortened back*

I *Carinatae: keeled breastbone and expanded braincase*

J *Aves or Neornithes: toothless and with distinctive neck and arm bones*

K *Palaeognathae: with an "old-fashioned" palate*

L *Neognathae: with a more mobile palate*

1 *Dromaeosauridae (dromaeosaurids)*

2 *Archaeopteryx*

3 *Alvarezsauridae*

4 *Confuciusornis*

5 *Iberomesornis*

6 *Patagopteryx*

7 *Hesperornis*

8 *Ichthyornis*

9 *Ratites (moa, emu, ostrich)*

10 *Tinamous*

11 *Galliformes (chickens)*

12 *Anseriformes (ducks)*

13 *Podicipediformes (grebes) Gaviiformes (divers) Sphenisciformes (penguins)*

14 *Pelecaniformes (pelicans) Procellariiformes (tube-noses)*

15 *Gruiformes (cranes, rails Charadriiformes (shorebirds) Columbiformes (pigeons) Ardeidae (herons)*

16 *Ciconiiformes (storks)*

17 *Falconiformes (eagles) Strigiformes (owls)*

18 *Caprimulgiformes (nightjars) Apodiformes (swifts)*

19 *Coraciiformes (kingfishers) Piciformes (woodpeckers) Passeriformes (perching birds)*

20 *Psittaciformes (parrots)*

21 *Cuculiformes (cuckoos)*

22 *Trogoniformes (trogons)*

Rival ancestors

Some scientists believe that birds came from an archosauriform such as Euparkeria *or another, undiscovered, reptile that predated dinosaurs. Most scientists, however, think that there is overwhelming evidence that dinosaurs gave rise to birds.*

© DIAGRAM

Early birds

Birds shown here represent three early groups with teeth. *Archaeopteryx*, the first known bird, resembled a small maniraptoran dinosaur but had flight feathers on its long "arms." Wings, wishbone, and the bones of its shoulder girdle adapted it for flight. Some experts think it climbed trees and fluttered down. Others believe it took off by sprinting into a headwind after insects. *Hesperornis* and its kin probably hunted fish just below the sea surface and nested on lonely coasts or offshore islands. *Ichthyornis* may have flown above the sea and plunged to seize small fish, as terns do now. It might have given rise to modern shore birds.

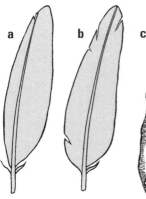

Feathers and flight (above)

Feathers help prove that Archaeopteryx *flew.*

a *Flying bird's wing feather: its asymmetrical design helps it act as an aerofoil.*

b *Flightless bird's wing feather: its symmetrical design is useless for flight.*

c Archaeopteryx *wing feather: its design is asymmetrical.*

The first known bird (above)

Archaeopteryx *might have used its clawed limbs for climbing trees, then flapped and fluttered down. The ability to climb and fly would have helped it escape enemies and capture agile prey.*

Three early birds

1 Archaeopteryx ("ancient wing") had feathered wings but also unbirdlike features: small teeth in the jaws, three-clawed fingers jutting from each wing, and a tail with a long, thin, bony core. Length: about 1 m (about 3 ft). Time: late Jurassic. Place: Bavaria, southwest Germany. Order: Archaeopterygiformes.

2 Hesperornis ("western bird") resembled a large diver. It had a long, slim, pointed beak rimmed with teeth and vestigial wings. It swam by thrusting water away with big lobed feet. Legs joined the body far back, so *Hesperornis* shuffled clumsily on land. Length: up to 1.5 m (5 ft). Time: late Cretaceous. Place: North America. Order: Hesperornithiformes (toothed divers).

3 Ichthyornis ("fish bird") was a small, stout, ternlike bird with long, pointed wings, small feet, and a long, slim beak armed with small curved teeth. *Ichthyornis* was one of the first birds with a keeled breastbone to help support flight muscles. Height: 20 cm (8 in). Time: late Cretaceous. Place: North America (Kansas, Texas and Alabama). Order: Ichthyornithiformes (toothed ternlike birds).

Flightless birds

Most extinct land birds make poor fossils–their fragile skeletons are soon eaten or just rot away–but big, flightless neornithine birds have left their remains in Cenozoic rocks. Many of these birds are collectively called "ratites" from the Latin *ratis* ("raft"), because the breastbone was flat and raftlike, not keeled to anchor powerful flight muscles like the breastbone of a flying bird. Most experts believe prehistoric ratites have living descendants in the emu, ostrich, and rhea. Molecular evidence of this shared ancestry appeared in 2001. Of the birds pictured below, **1** and **3** were ratites in the Palaeognathae, but **2** perhaps belonged with anseriforms (ducks) and **4** with gruiforms (cranes). Both were in the Neognathae.

The flightless birds shown here were huge. Some filled the roles of cattle, others behaved like big cats. Such monsters tended to appear in lands with no large mammal herbivores or carnivores. Early ratites left only fossils, but *Dinornis* and *Aepyornis* survive as actual bones, found preserved in swamps. Archaeologists have even identified some moas' stomach contents. There are also *Aepyornis maximus* eggs–the largest known eggs to have been laid by any bird.

1 Aepyornis maximus ("greatest of the high birds") was possibly the heaviest-ever bird at 440 kg (970 lb). A Madagascan elephant bird, it was the "roc" of the Sinbad legend, extinct by AD 1700.

2 Gastornis, a "terror crane," stood 2 m (6 ft 6 in) high and probably killed prey with its huge clawed feet and massive "parrot's" beak. It lived in North America and Europe 50 million years ago.

3 Dinornis giganteus ("giant terrible bird") was the tallest known bird, 3.5 m (11 ft 6 in) high. This New Zealand giant moa was a browser that may have died out only about 400 years ago.

4 Phorusrhacus longissimus stood 2 m (6 ft 6 in) tall and probably devoured goat-sized creatures with its huge "eagle's" beak. This savage hunter prowled Patagonia about 20 million years ago.

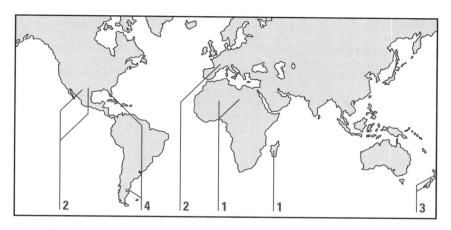

Where they lived (above)

This map depicts homes of the four groups of extinct flightless birds represented by those named on this page.

1 Elephant birds
2 Terror cranes
3 Moas
4 Phorusrhacids

Grounded giants

Four giant flightless birds appear here on the same scale as a chicken.

1 Aepyornis maximus
2 Gastornis
3 Dinornis giganteus
4 Phorusrhacus longissimus

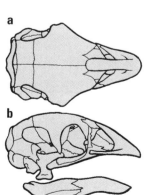

A moa's skull (above)

*These views show a moa skull seen from above (**a**) and from the right (**b**). The beak was shaped for cropping plants, not rending flesh.*

© DIAGRAM

Water birds

Birds shown here are fossil or living examples of the various groups of water birds and marsh birds. All except Ciconiiformes were probably derived from shorebirds.

1 Stictonetta, Australia's freckled duck is a primitive living member of the order Anseriformes (ducks, geese, swans), dating from Cretaceous times.

2 Presbyornis was a long-legged wader with a mainly ducklike skull. It might have given rise to ducks, geese, and swans. Vast flocks bred and fed on algae in salty, shallow lakes. Time: Cretaceous to Eocene. Place: North America, also maybe worldwide. Order: Anseriformes (some say Charadriiformes—shorebirds including gulls, terns, and waders).

3 Osteodontornis was among the largest-ever flying birds. Maybe it seized squid from the sea surface in its long bill rimmed with toothlike bony spikes. Wingspan: up to 5.2 m (17 ft). Time: Miocene. Place: California. Order: Pelecaniformes—web-footed, fish-eating seabirds including cormorants, gannets, and pelicans.

4 Puffinus, an early shearwater, lived in Eocene Europe and Miocene North America. Order: Procellariiformes (albatrosses, petrels, and shearwaters)—oceanic birds with long, slim, strong wings, webbed feet, and tube-shaped nostrils.

5 Pachydyptes, was a giant penguin about 1.6 m (5 ft 3in) high. Time: Eocene. Place: New Zealand. Order: Sphenisciformes (penguins)—flightless birds with wings evolved as swimming flippers. Penguins possibly evolved from petrels.

6 Colymboides was a diver (loon) no bigger than a small duck. Time: Eocene. Place: England. Order: Gaviiformes (divers)—swimming birds and strong fliers with webbed feet on legs set far back.

7 Podiceps was an early grebe. Time: Oligocene. Place: Oregon. Order: Podicipediformes (grebes)—swimming birds resembling divers but with lobed not webbed feet. They probably evolved from gruiforms (cranes, rails).

8 Proardea was an early heron. Time: Eocene. Place: England. Family: Ardeidae (herons, bitterns, and egrets)—long-legged, long-necked wading birds related to shorebirds.

Miocene seabirds

Strange birds in the order Pelecaniformes once fished the North Pacific Ocean.

a Osteodontornis seized prey at the surface.

b Plotopterids hunted underwater, swimming with their wings. They were the North's equivalent of penguins.

Land birds

This page gives early examples from 13 orders of land birds, including birds of prey.

1 Raphus, the dodo, was a flightless pigeon as big as a large turkey. It died out a mere three centuries ago. Order: Columbiformes (doves and pigeons)–birds derived from shorebirds as early as the Eocene epoch.

2 Archaeopsittacus was an early parrot. Time: late Oligocene. Place: France. Order: Psittaciformes (parrots)–tropical birds with a strong, hooked bill and two toes per foot turned back for perching. They might have evolved from pigeons.

3 Argentavis, a gigantic vulturelike bird of prey, was the largest-known bird able to fly. Wingspan: up to 7.6 m (25 ft). Weight: 120 kg (265 lb). Time: early Pliocene. Place: Argentina. Order: Falconiformes (birds of prey that mostly hunt by day) or maybe Ciconiiformes (storks).

4 Ogygoptynx, the first known owl, dates from Paleocene times. Order: Strigiformes (owls)–nocturnal birds of prey unrelated to falconiforms.

5 Gallinuloides was an early member of the Galliformes (chickens and their kin). These possibly derived from ducks and geese. Time: Eocene. Place: Wyoming.

6 Dynamopterus was an early cuckoo. Time: Oligocene. Place: France. Order: Cuculiformes (cuckoos, coucals, and touracos)–land birds, most with an outer toe turned back.

7 Colius has reversible hind and outer toes, and swings acrobatically from twigs. Time: Recent. Place: Africa. Order: Coliiformes (mousebirds), dating from Miocene times.

8 Caprimulgus has long, slim wings and a short, broad bill. It hunts at twilight. Time: Pleistocene on. Place: worldwide. Order: Caprimulgiformes (nightjars, oilbirds, frogmouth).

9 Aegialornis, an early swiftlike bird, had scimitar-shaped wings and flew fast to catch insects. Time: Oligocene. Place: France. Order: Apodiformes (swifts and maybe hummingbirds).

10 Geranopterus was an early roller from Oligocene France. Order: Coraciiformes (rollers, bee-eaters, kingfishers, hornbills, hoopoes)–colorful hole-nesters with the three front toes partly joined. These were the main land birds of the Oligocene epoch.

11 Archaeotrogon was an early trogon from Eocene France. Order: Trogoniformes–colorful hole-nesters resembling coraciiforms but whose affinities appear unclear.

12 Neanis, a primobucconid, lived in Eocene Wyoming. Order: Piciformes (barbets, toucans, woodpeckers)–perching birds with a reversed outer toe.

13 Lanius, the shrike genus, goes back to Miocene France. Order: Passeriformes ("true" perching birds)–birds with distinctively designed toes. They include the songbirds and account for three-fifths of all living bird species.

Teratornid tar trap

Teratornis, *a huge condor-like vulture, here plucks flesh from a mammoth stuck in a tar pool. Feasting teratornids also tumbled in, became stuck, and died. In fact the tar pools of Los Angeles are rich in late Pleistocene bird bones. Paleontologists have recovered those of condors, eagles, hawks, owls, ducks, geese, herons, storks, cranes, pigeons, ravens, turkeys, and many perching birds.*

© DIAGRAM

Fossil mammals and their kin

Mammals have dominated life on land for the last 65 million years, but mammal origins go back 320 million years, before even reptiles appeared. Mammals and reptiles share the same ancestors, however: vertebrates producing amniotic eggs.

This chapter covers prehistoric mammals and their ancestors, collectively a great group called synapsids. The first pages look at the ancient, reptilelike pelycosaurs and their descendants the therapsids that led directly to mammals. Later pages deal with major groups of mammals, from early prehistoric forms to advanced placental mammals of types familiar to us today.

Synapsid evolution

This diagram shows evolutionary relationships between some early synapsid groups and their mammal descendants. Capital letters signal the appearance of major groups or innovations on the line leading to mammals.

A Ancestral amniotes

B Synapsida (synapsids)

C Eupelycosauria ("true pelycosaurs")

D Therapsida (advanced early synapsids)

E Theriodontia (flesh eaters)

F Cynodontia (cynodonts)

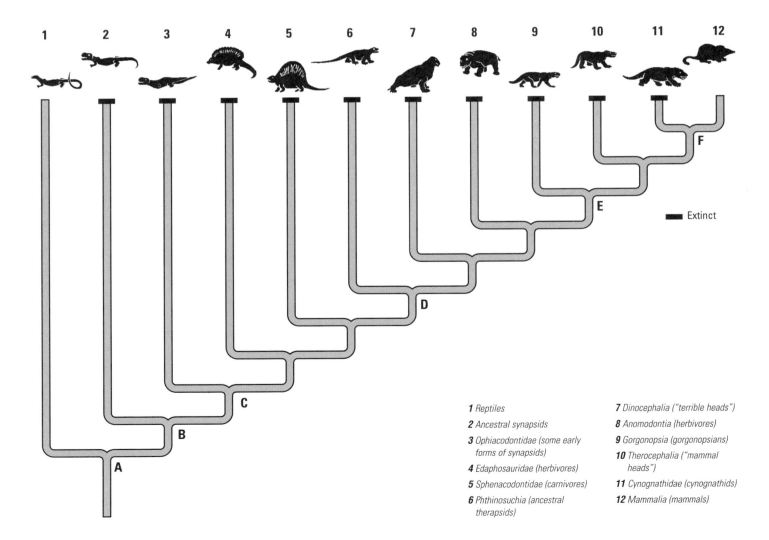

- Extinct

1 Reptiles
2 Ancestral synapsids
3 Ophiacodontidae (some early forms of synapsids)
4 Edaphosauridae (herbivores)
5 Sphenacodontidae (carnivores)
6 Phthinosuchia (ancestral therapsids)
7 Dinocephalia ("terrible heads")
8 Anomodontia (herbivores)
9 Gorgonopsia (gorgonopsians)
10 Therocephalia ("mammal heads")
11 Cynognathidae (cynognathids)
12 Mammalia (mammals)

Pelycosaurs

Three pelycosaurs

These examples show features of three major groups of pelycosaurs: ophiacodonts, sphenacodonts, and edaphosaurs.

1 Ophiacodon, an ophiacodontid, had a low-slung, lizardlike body; long hind legs; narrow deep, long head; and jaws equipped with many sharp teeth. Probably it hunted fish in rivers. Length: 3.7 m (12 ft). Time: early Permian. Place: Texas.

2 Dimetrodon was a sphenacodontid–a big flesh eater with long, sharp steak knife teeth and powerful jaws. It was one of the first backboned land animals able to kill beasts its own size. A huge skin sail rose from its back. Length: 3.5 m (11 ft 6 in). Time: early–mid-Permian. Place: Texas and Oklahoma and Europe.

3 Edaphosaurus, an edaphosaurid, was a large herbivore with blunt teeth, some in the mouth roof. A high skin sail ran down its back. Length: 3.3 m (11 ft). Time: late Pennsylvanian–early Permian. Place: USA and Europe.

Two types of jaws

Here we compare the skulls a flesh-eating Dimetrodon *and plant-eating* Edaphosaurus.

A Dimetrodon

a Long, deep, narrow skull

b Strong jaws with wide gape

c Small chewing teeth

d Two pairs of upper canine teeth: saw-edged blades

e "Step" in upper jaw

f Biting and grasping incisors

B Edaphosaurus

a Short, fairly shallow skull

b Straight-edged jaws (no step)

c Blunt teeth, all more or less alike

d Toothplates in mouth roof. Edaphosaurus *could have crushed tough seed-fern leaves and maybe even mollusk shells.*

The Synapsida ("fused arches") have a distinctive skull hole behind the eye. Misnamed "mammal-like reptiles," early, primitive forms included small-brained, carnivorous sprawlers: cold-blooded beasts with bony belly scales, maybe horny scales set in the skin, and several types of teeth as in mammals. Later kinds gave rise to warm-blooded species that stood more erect and grew body hair.

Pelycosaurs, or "basin-shaped pelvis lizards," were a major early synapsid group, with ophiacodontid pelycosaurs appearing by 320 million years ago. In early Permian times, big, sprawling pelycosaur flesh eaters and herbivores dominated life on land, at least in North America and Europe, where almost all their fossils have been found. They died out about 250 million years ago.

Sails as radiators

Long spines jutting from the backbone supported Dimetrodon's *skin sail. If the pelycosaur stood sideways to the Sun, it heated the sail's blood supply, which warmed the whole body. After chilly nights, it helped the cold-blooded creature become active.*

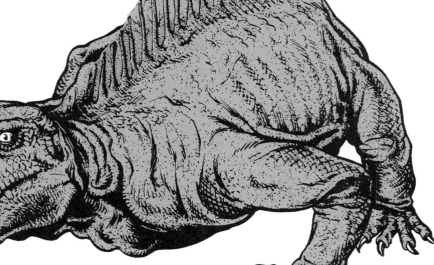

© DIAGRAM

Therapsids 1

Hunters and hunted

South Africa's Karroo rock beds hold fossil bones of big dinocephalians like Moschops *(**A**) and* Titanosuchus *(**B**).* Moschops *peaceably ate plants, but* Titanosuchus's *long, heavy jaws had sharp incisors and long, stabbing canine teeth, used to kill big game.*

A

B

In time, an advanced, varied order of mammal-like synapsids, the therapsids (literally "mammal arch"), took over from their ancestors the pelycosaurs. Therapsids flourished from mid-Permian to early Jurassic times. In the late Permian they were the chief flesh eaters and plant eaters living on dry land. Scientists have found Permian therapsid fossils worldwide, especially in South Africa and in Russia.

From such early therapsids as *Phthinosuchus* came dinocephalians ("terrible heads"), anomodonts, and theriodonts. All but the last are shown on this page. Dinocephalians included herbivores and carnivores. Anomodonts featured the plant-eating venjukoviids, galeopsids, and dicynodonts ("two doglike teeth"), the most numerous, diverse, and durable of all.

Five therapsids

1 Phthinosuchus belonged to the phthinosuchians–"old-fashioned" therapsids, but they had a large skull opening behind each eye, one pair of canine teeth per jaw, and a more upright stance than the pelycosaurs. Length: 1.5 m (5 ft). Time: mid-Permian. Place: Russia.

2 Galepus belonged to the galeopsids– little, lightweight plant eaters with jaws hinged well below the tooth row. Length: maybe 30 cm (1 ft). Time: mid-Permian. Place: South Africa.

3 Moschops was a plant-eating dinocephalian. It had a thick, short, dome-shaped skull; peglike cropping teeth; squat, heavy body; sloping back; and short tail. Stocky limbs held its body well off the ground. Big flesh-eating dinocephalians might have

attacked it. Length: 2.4 m (8 ft). Time: mid-Permian. Place: South Africa.

4 Venjukovia belonged to the venjukoviids–big, partly beaked herbivores with a deep lower jaw, mostly short teeth, and a few big, stubby front teeth. Time: mid-Permian. Place: Russia.

5 Lystrosaurus belonged to the dicynodonts–abundant, worldwide plant eaters. They had a short, broad body, short tail; strong legs; big holes in the skull behind the eyes; a horny beak; and a toothless mouth or just two upper tusks. *Lystrosaurus* was an early Triassic piglike animal at home by lakes and rivers. Length: 1 m (3 ft 3 in). Place: Antarctica, South Africa, India, and China.

Therapsids 2

The most mammal-like of all mammal-like synapsids was the therapsids' third main group: theriodonts ("mammal toothed"). These flesh eaters were mostly small- to medium-sized, with teeth and many bones designed astonishingly like those of a mammal. Some were warm-blooded and had a covering of body hair. A few perhaps even suckled young. Only the jaw and hearing mechanism marks these off from mammals, their direct descendants.

Theriodonts flourished about 260–170 million years ago. They spread worldwide, but South Africa's Permian rocks are the richest source of fossils. Here are examples from progressively advanced groups (some known well only from skulls). All but example **5** are from South Africa.

Cynognathus *skull* (right)

The skull reveals a tendency toward mammalian features.

A *Mouth and nasal passage separated, allowing breathing while eating*

B *Differentiated teeth: incisors, canines and ridged cheek teeth for fast chewing (speeding digestion to provide a high energy output)*

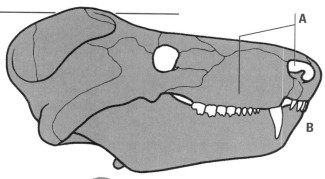

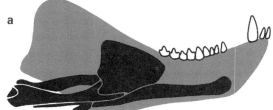

Mammal-like features (left)

This whole-body restoration of Cynognathus *is based on key features found in skeletal remains.*

1 *Body covering of hair inferred from whisker pits in the snout*

2 *Mammal-like posture (knees and elbows held beneath the body) inferred from bones of limbs, hips and shoulders*

Inner jaws (above)

The inner jaws of Cynognathus, *a "near mammal" and an early mammal (not to scale) illustrate a trend to fewer bones. The dentary is shown tinted.*

a Cynognathus *jaw: seven bones, the dentary relatively larger than in early synapsids*

b Morganucodon *jaw: four bones, the dentary by far the largest*

c Spalacotherium *jaw: one bone, the dentary*

Six theriodonts

1 Lycaenops belonged to the gorgonopsians–plentiful Permian flesh eaters derived from pelycosaur forebears. They had rather low-slung bodies, heavy skeletons, and saber teeth. Length: 1 m (3 ft 3 in). Time: late Permian.

2 Lycosuchus represents the therocephalians. These had as few toe and finger bones as mammals, a skull crest, and a large hole in the skull behind each eye. Some were powerfully built carnivores. Length: 1.8 m (6 ft). Time: late Permian.

3 Bauria was one of the therocephalians, with mammal-like teeth and skull but an old-fashioned lower jaw. *Bauria* seemingly had broad, grinding back teeth inset from the jaw rim, perhaps a space for cheeks to store half-chewed food. Length: maybe 1 m (3 ft 3 in). Time: early Triassic.

4 Cynognathus was a wolf-sized cynognathid cynodont predator or scavenger, with doglike skull and teeth and limbs held fairly well below the body, a help in running fast. Length: 1.5 m (5 ft). Time: early–mid-Triassic.

5 Oligokyphus belonged to the tritylodonts: small, rodentlike late survivors of the therapsid line. Length: 50 cm (20 in). Time: late Triassic–early Jurassic. Place: England and Portugal.

6 Diarthrognathus was a tritheledontid, in the group arguably ancestral to the mammals. Its jaw hinged almost like a mammal's. Length: maybe 40 cm (16 in). Time: early Jurassic.

About mammals

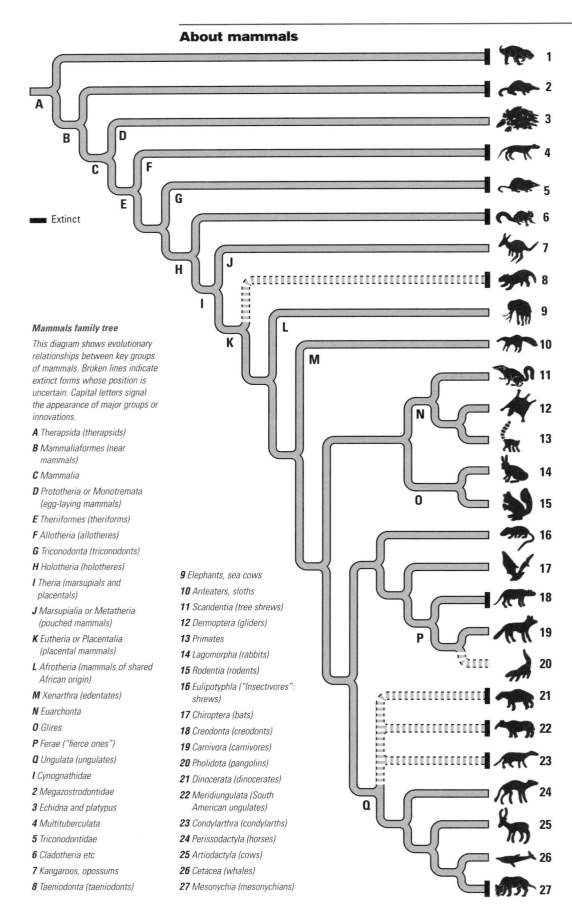

Mammals family tree

This diagram shows evolutionary relationships between key groups of mammals. Broken lines indicate extinct forms whose position is uncertain. Capital letters signal the appearance of major groups or innovations.

A Therapsida (therapsids)

B Mammaliaformes (near mammals)

C Mammalia

D Prototheria or Monotremata (egg-laying mammals)

E Theriiformes (theriforms)

F Allotheria (allotheres)

G Triconodonta (triconodonts)

H Holotheria (holotheres)

I Theria (marsupials and placentals)

J Marsupialia or Metatheria (pouched mammals)

K Eutheria or Placentalia (placental mammals)

L Afrotheria (mammals of shared African origin)

M Xenarthra (edentates)

N Euarchonta

O Glires

P Ferae ("fierce ones")

Q Ungulata (ungulates)

1 Cynognathidae

2 Megazostrodontidae

3 Echidna and platypus

4 Multituberculata

5 Triconodontidae

6 Cladotheria etc

7 Kangaroos, opossums

8 Taeniodonta (taeniodonts)

9 Elephants, sea cows

10 Anteaters, sloths

11 Scandentia (tree shrews)

12 Dermoptera (gliders)

13 Primates

14 Lagomorpha (rabbits)

15 Rodentia (rodents)

16 Eulipotyphla ("Insectivores": shrews)

17 Chiroptera (bats)

18 Creodonta (creodonts)

19 Carnivora (carnivores)

20 Pholidota (pangolins)

21 Dinocerata (dinocerates)

22 Meridiungulata (South American ungulates)

23 Condylarthra (condylarths)

24 Perissodactyla (horses)

25 Artiodactyla (cows)

26 Cetacea (whales)

27 Mesonychia (mesonychians)

■ Extinct

By 190 million years or so ago, cynodont therapsids had given rise to mammals–warm-blooded backboned animals with hair, an efficient four-chambered heart, and a muscular sheet (the diaphragm) that helps work the lungs. Most give birth instead of laying eggs, and all feed babies milk from special glands. Such soft parts do not survive as fossils, and experts distinguish fossil mammals from reptiles by differences between their bones, especially the jaws.

Smallish, early, and shrewlike Mammaliaformes are now not thought to be true mammals. The class Mammalia had two subclasses: the primitive egg-laying Prototheria, including the platypus, and Theriiformes, which includes the extinct allotheres, mostly small, with teeth much like a rodent's; the triconodonts, also with distinctive teeth; the holotheres, extinct form; and the Therians, marsupials (pouched mammals) and eutherians or placentals (mammals whose babies develop in the mother, nourished by food from a special structure, the placenta).

Only small, unobtrusive mammals coexisted with the dinosaurs. When these died out, therians more than took their place, evolving into shapes and sizes that suited them for life in almost every habitat. Small, early forms gave rise to bulky herbivores and carnivores. Others took to the air or water. Mammals have ruled most lands for the last 65 million years, throughout the Cenozoic era.

Early mammals

Of most known early mammals, little more than teeth or jaws survive. The first supposed mammals, small shrewlike late Triassic morganucodonts and early Jurassic docodonts, retained traces of the old therapsid type of jaw joint. No longer ranked as true mammals, they belong in the Mammaliaformes, along with others on the brink of mammal-hood.

About 100 million years separate late Triassic mammaliaforms from the earliest-known fossils of their possible descendants, the Prototheria (egg-laying mammals known only from the monotremes, including the echidna and platypus).

The Allotheria formed a long line of early mammals with multicuspid molars like rodents' (cusps are points on a tooth's grinding surface). Seemingly these were the first plant-eating mammals. Multituberculates, their only order, persisted 100 million years into the Oligocene, when rodents took their place.

The Holotheria included the extinct cladotheres with complex molars shaped to shear and crush and the symmetrodonts with simpler teeth. Both died out by mid-Cretaceous times (some 100 million years ago). Meanwhile, holotheres gave rise to the Theria–the marsupials and placentals profiled in the following pages.

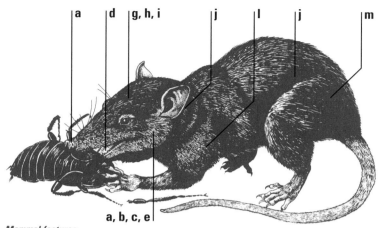

Mammal features

Unlike most reptiles, fossil mammals show these and other features:

a Distinctive jaw hinge

b Only one bone on each side of the lower jaw

c Three auditory bones in each ear, inside the skull

d Teeth only on jaw rims

e Complex cheek teeth, with two roots or more

f A single bony nasal opening

g Growing bones show epiphyses–ends separated by cartilage from the main parts of the bones

h Enlarged braincase

i No "third eye" in the skull

j No ribs in neck or lower back area

k Limbs hinged to move to-and-fro below the body

l Distinctive shoulder girdle

m Distinctive hip bones

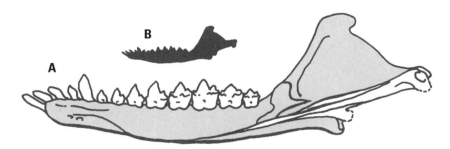

Distinctive jaw bones

Shown here much enlarged (A) and actual size (B) is the jaw of the early mammaliaform Morganucodon. Like reptile jaws, this jaw still comprises several bones, but the dentary (shaded) is by far the largest. In true mammals only this bone persists.

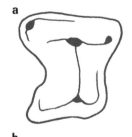

Early mammal and mammaliaform teeth (above)

Almost microscopically tiny teeth are the only known remains of many early fossil mammals. Shown here are crown views of three distinctive types of upper cheek teeth (mostly much enlarged).

a Docodont tooth shaped like a dumbbell

b Triconodont tooth, with three cusps in a row

c Multituberculate tooth, with many cusps

Early mammals and close kin

1 Megazostrodon, an early mammaliaform, was a tiny shrewlike docodont with a slim lower jaw. Length: 10 cm (4 in). Time: early Jurassic. Place: South Africa.

2 Echidna, a living spiny anteater, here stands for the monotremes of which the earliest fossils known are 110-million-year-old teeth from Australia. Some bones are primitive and reptilian. Like reptiles, monotremes expel all body wastes and give birth through one hole. They lack ears and have poor temperature control.

3 Taeniolabis, a beaver-sized multituberculate, had a heavy skull, strong jaw muscles, and big, chisel-like teeth. It probably ate nuts. Time: early Paleocene. Place: North America.

4 Crusafontia, an agile, squirrel-like climber that lived in late Jurassic Portugal. This dryolestid cladothere perhaps gave birth to tiny babies that suckled in a pouch.

© DIAGRAM

Pouched mammals

Australia's "hippo" (below)

Diprotodon *munched plants on salt flats at Lake Callabonna in southeast Australia. Fossil finds show that individuals fell through a dried salt crust and drowned in mud beneath.*

Marsupials (pouched mammals) give birth to tiny undeveloped young. Many grow up in a pouch located on the mother's belly and supported by so-called marsupial bones. Such bones and the teeth help experts identify fossil marsupials.

Marsupials evolved from the Tribosphenida, holotheres with distinctive molars, by mid-Cretaceous times (110 million years ago). They reached all continents except Africa, but only on the island continent Australia did they escape competition from advanced placental mammals. Both main marsupial groups, Ameridelphia and especially Australidelphia, produced many forms with placental counterparts—catlike and wolflike flesh eaters; insect-eating opossum rats and marsupial moles and mice; and rabbitlike, long-snouted bandicoots. Diprotodonts, the main group of marsupials that still flourishes, includes herbivorous kangaroos, koalas, and wombats. Their extinct marsupial kin, some of giant size (**2-4**), are shown below.

Marsupial features

The American opossum shows primitive marsupial features not found in placental mammals.

a *Relatively small braincase*

b *Holes in the bony palate (the roof of the mouth)*

c *Four molar teeth on each side of each jaw*

d *Shelf on the outer rim of the cheek teeth*

e *No full set of milk teeth*

f *Inturned lower jaw below the jaw hinge*

g *Marsupial (hip) bones*

h *Clawed second and third toes on the hind foot form a comb for grooming fur.*

Four extinct marsupials

1 Thylacosmilus, with long, curved, stabbing upper canines sheathed in the lower jaw, was a leopard-sized South American sparassodont equivalent of the placental saber-toothed cat. One of the last in its family (the borhyaenids), *Thylacosmilus* dates from Pliocene times.

2 Thylacoleo, an almost lion-sized marsupial "lion" from Pliocene and Pleistocene Australia, had unique tusklike incisors and huge premolar cheek teeth that sheared like scissors. It might have eaten flesh or fibrous fruits and tubers.

3 Sthenurus was a giant kangaroo with short jaws, a short tail, and a huge fourth toe. It stood about 3 m (10 ft) high and browsed on trees. Time: Pliocene and Pleistocene. Place: Australia.

4 Diprotodon, the largest-known marsupial, was hippolike, with big incisor tusks but cheek teeth like a kangaroo's. Length: 3.4 m (11 ft). Time: Pleistocene. Place: Australia.

Placental pioneers

Placental mammals (Placentalia or Eutheria) are named for the pregnant females' placenta–the organ that nourishes young in the womb. Placentals evolved from tribosphenids in mid-Cretaceous times. Advanced brains and babies already well developed at birth gave placentals major advantages. In the last 65 million years, they have produced 95 percent of all known mammal genera, past and present. Here we look briefly at five groups with early fossil records.

The first placentals were probably small nocturnal insect eaters, superficially similar to living insectivores, shrews and hedgehogs. Others with an early history include bats (chiropterans); gliding mammals (dermopterans); the large, ratlike taeniodonts; and the bearlike tillodonts. The last two died out in Eocene times. We give one prehistoric example from each group.

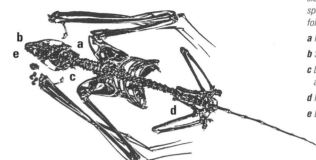

The first fossil bat (left)

Shown is a fossil of the first known bat, Icaronycteris. Fingers held up skin-membrane wings as in modern bats, and like them, it slept upside down. Even such specialized placentals shared the following common features:

a Relatively big brain case

b Solid bony palate

c Lower jaws lacking inturned angle

d No marsupial hip bones

e Distinctive teeth

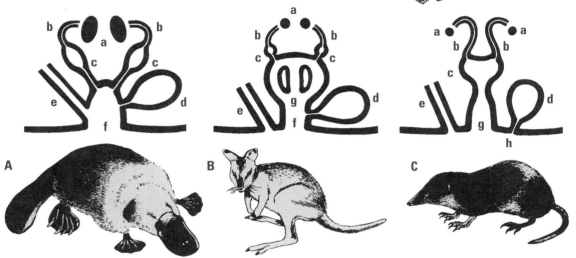

Three different designs (left)

*Here we show basic differences in body structure between three groups of living mammals: monotremes (**A**), marsupials (**B**), and placentals (**C**). All release body waste from the gut and bladder, and all produce egg cells in the ovaries, but the wastes and eggs or babies exit differently.*

a Ovaries

b Fallopian tubes

c Uterus(es)

d Bladder

e Anal canal

f Cloaca

g Vagina

h Urethra

One exit (A)

In monotremes such as the platypus, uteruses, bladder, and gut lead to a cloaca–a common exit by which eggs, liquid waste, and solid waste all leave the body. Hence the name monotreme, meaning "one opening."

Two exits (B)

In marsupials such as the wallaby, uteruses and bladder lead to a cloaca, but the gut's anal canal ends separately. Babies and liquid waste leave the body through the cloaca. Solid waste leaves from the gut's anal canal.

Three exits (C)

In placental mammals such as the shrew, uterus, bladder, and gut each have a separate body exit. Babies leave via a vagina, liquid waste via a urethra, solid waste via the anal canal.

Five early placentals

1 Zalambdalestes was an agile insectivore, with a long face; large eyes; small brain; long, sharp incisor teeth; "old-fashioned" molars; clawed feet; and a long tail. It belonged to the Anagelida, a group close to the ancestry of all main placental groups. Length: 20 cm (8 in). Time: late Cretaceous. Place: Mongolia.

2 Planetetherium, a squirrel-sized dermopteran, glided between trees on skin webs that joined legs and tail. Time: Paleocene. Place: Montana.

3 Icaronycteris, the first known bat, lived 50 million years ago in Eocene Wyoming. Order: Chiroptera (bats).

4 Stylinodon, a taeniodont leaf eater, resembled a huge rat with short, strong limbs, short toes, and powerful claws. Teeth were high-crowned, rootless pegs. Time: mid-Eocene. Place: North America.

5 Trogosus, a tillodont, resembled a big bear, with flat, clawed feet but chisel-shaped incisors like a rodent's and low-crowned molars. It was a herbivore. Time: mid-Eocene. Place: North America and Asia.

"Toothless" mammals

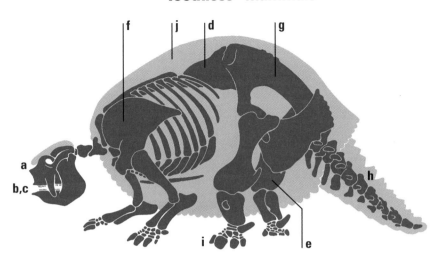

Glyptodon's *body plan*

a Deep, short skull with a small brain case

b Teeth only in sides of the jaw

c Each tooth was like three short pillars stuck together in a row and without enamel

d Many vertebrae fused to help support the shell

e Short, massive limb bones

f Broad shoulder girdle

g Massive hip bones

h Heavy, bony tail

i Five-toed feet with hooflike claws

j Solid armor (evolved from bony studs and plates set in the skin)

Edentates (Xenarthra) were mammals with few teeth. They evolved in the Americas while these were isolated. They include the living anteaters, sloths, and armadillos and their extinct relatives the huge, astonishingly armored glyptodonts and unwieldy ground sloths. Most edentates lack front teeth and have a few, simple, rootless cheek teeth. The brain is small. The limbs are short, strong, and tipped with long, curved claws. All edentates were and are slow-moving eaters of plants, carrion, or insects.

Perhaps the first known kinds were the so-called palaeanodonts from the North America of 60 million years ago, though possibly these led to the Old World's toothless pangolins, which molecular studies have surprisingly grouped with the Carnivora. Most fossil edentates arose in what was then the island continent of South America, though a land bridge later let some into North America. Finds of hairy hides hint that ground sloths survived in southern Argentina until four centuries ago, probably until they were killed off by people.

Megatherium's *life style*

Megatherium *is here shown to scale with a human. The monster walked on its knuckles and the sides of its feet. Females might have carried babies on their back. A strong tail propped up* Megatherium *as it reared to claw leaves into its mouth and chewed them with its peglike teeth.*

Three fossil edentates

These three examples show a palaeanodont and two enormous fossil edentates.

1 Metacheiromys was a palaeanodont with a long, low head, sharp canine teeth, and maybe horny pads instead of cheek teeth. It had short legs, sharp claws, and a long, heavy tail. Length: 45 cm (18 in). Time: middle Eocene (about 48 million years ago). Place: North America.

2 Glyptodon was a huge "mammal tortoise"–a glyptodont descended from early armadillos. Horny sheaths covered the many bony plates that formed a great dome-shaped shell around its body. A bony cap crowned its skull, and bony rings armored a thick, heavy tail, swung to fend off enemies. Length: about 3 m (10 ft). Time: Pliocene-Pleistocene. Place: South America.

3 Megatherium, the largest ground sloth, was an elephantine treetop browser. Length: 6 m (20 ft). Time: late Pliocene-Pleistocene. Place: South America to southeast USA.

Rodents and rabbits

In numbers, variety, and distribution, the most successful mammals have been members of the great group Rodentia: squirrels, rats, mole rats, cavies, beavers, porcupines, and many more. Rodents live in trees, on mountains, underground, in streams and swamps–everywhere from Polar wastes to steamy forests in the Tropics.

Small size, fast breeding, and the ability to gnaw and digest foods as hard as wood contributed to their success. This started when an insectivore-type ancestor gave rise to the first squirrel-like rodent more than 60 million years ago. From northern continents, that pioneer's descendants reached every continent except Antarctica.

Close relatives of rodents are the rodentlike lagomorphs: rabbits, hares, and pikas. Lagomorphs have eight long chisel-like incisor teeth (rodents have just four), and there are other differences. What we know of early lagomorphs and rodents owes much to finds of tiny fossil teeth.

Rodent relationships

Published in 2001, a molecular "family tree" showed how various rodent groups are related. It also confirmed that rodents and rabbits share the same ancestor, forming a group known as Glires. Rabbits, it seems, appeared before rodents.

A Glires
B Lagomorpha (lagomorphs)
C Rodentia (rodents)
1 Caviidae (guinea pigs)
2 Hystricidae (Old World porcupines)

3 Myomorpha (rats and mice)
4 Castoridae (beavers)
5 Sciuridae (squirrels)
6 Leporidae (hares and rabbits) and Ochotonidae (pikas)

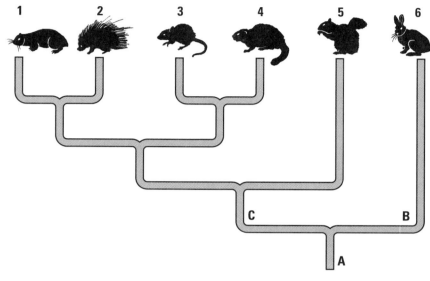

Rodent skeleton

This Paramys skeleton shows the following rodent features.

e Long, low skull
f Flexible forelimbs
g Strong hind limbs
h Five clawed toes per limb

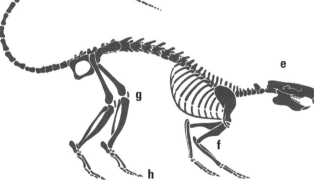

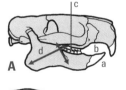

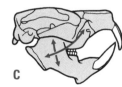

Rodent skulls

Shown here are the skulls of extinct creatures from three different rodent families:

A Paramys, an ischyromyid
B Cricetops, a murid
C Palaeocastor, a castorid
All have the following features:
a four chisel-like incisors
b gap behind the incisors
c tall, complex molars
d masseter muscles allowing lower jaw to move up and down, sideways, and to-and-fro

Six Glires (rodents and lagomorphs)

1 Paramys, a sciuromorph rodent, was a squirrel-like climber in the primitive family Ischyromyidae. Length 60 cm (2 ft). Time: late Paleocene–mid-Eocene. Place: North America and Europe.

2 Epigaulus, a two-horned gopher, was a burrowing sciuromorph rodent. Its horns served in defense or maybe as a pair of shovels. Length: 26 cm (10 in). Time: Miocene. Place: North America.

3 Sciurus, the squirrel genus found today in North America and Europe, is a "living fossil" in the rodent suborder Sciuromorpha; its history dates back 15 million years.

4 Castoroides was a land-based beaver almost as big as a black bear. Length: 2.3 m (7 ft 6 in). Time: Pleistocene. Place: North America.

5 Eocardia was a Miocene guinea pig-like member of the Hystricognatha, a South American rodent suborder. (*Eumegamys*, an almost hippo-sized Pliocene relative, was the largest rodent ever.)

6 Lepus, the modern hare, evolved 5 million years or so ago. Place: northern continents and Africa. Order: Lagomorpha.

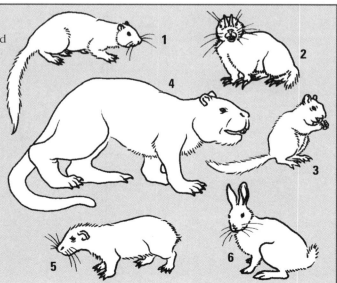

© DIAGRAM

Primates

Primates–humans, apes, monkeys, and their kin–include the most intelligent of all animals. Yet their early ancestors were insectivores–small, rather primitive placental mammals. Primates primitively kept five toes and fingers, but gained grasping hands, forward-facing eyes, and a big "thinking" region of the brain. Eyes and hands coordinated by the brain adapted early primates for an agile life among the trees. Meanwhile changes in the teeth adapted them for eating fruits or most other foods.

Primates resembling today's tree shrews probably appeared by 65 million years ago, giving rise to several groups. First came the relatively small and small-brained prosimians, including ancestors of today's lemurs and tarsiers. These were plentiful 60 to 40 million years ago in North America, Eurasia, and Africa. Prosimians led to the brainier and often bigger anthropoids (monkeys, apes, and humans) that largely replaced them. Below are examples of the five primate infraorders, as traditionally classified:

Primate features

These clues help experts recognize a primate fossil:

a Large brain case

b Often short jaws

c Low-crowned cheek teeth with low, blunt cusps (designed to eat almost any food)

d Usually no third molar or first premolar tooth

e Orbits (eye sockets) large and facing forward

f Bony bar behind the orbits

g Small nasal opening

h Long, flexible limbs

i Five toes and fingers, usually with nails–not claws

j Gap between thumb and big toe and other digits–an aid in grasping

Three flesh-eaters

1 Plesiadapis, a squirrel-sized, squirrel-like creature, had a long snout, side-facing eyes, big chisel-like teeth, long bushy tail, and claws, not nails. It could not grasp with its hands. It ate leaves, largely on the ground. Time: mid-Paleocene. Place: North America and Europe. Infraorder: Plesiadapiformes, perhaps not primates but close kin.

2 Adapis had a shorter snout than *Plesiadapis*, forward-facing eyes, relatively bigger brain, and grasping hands and feet with nails, not claws. It climbed forest trees, eating shoots, fruits, eggs, and insects. Length: 40 cm (16 in). Time: mid-late Eocene. Place: Europe. Infraorder: Lemuriformes (lemurs), probably ancestral to apes.

3 Necrolemur was small with huge eyes, big ears, a small "pinched" nose, long tail, and long tree climber's limbs with gripping toe pads. It was an Eocene European ancestor of modern tarsiers. Infraorder: Tarsiiformes.

4 Dolichocebus was small and squirrel-like with a bushy tail, and claws, not nails. It lived in Oligocene South America.

Infraorder: Platyrrhini ("flat noses"), New World monkeys. These have widely spaced, outward-facing nostrils and long tails, and lack good thumb-and-finger grip.

5 Mesopithecus was probably ancestral to the slim, long-legged, long-tailed monkeys known as langurs. It lived in late Miocene Greece and Asia Minor. Infraorder: Catarrhini ("down-facing noses"), Old World monkeys, apes, and humans. These have nostrils close together, good thumb-and-finger grip, and relatively big brains; tails become short in many later monkeys and are absent in apes and humans.

Creodonts

Creodonts were the first successful flesh-eating placental mammals. Many walked flat-footed on short, heavy limbs tipped with claws. The tail was long, the brain was small, and the teeth were less efficient than a cat's for stabbing flesh or shearing through it. Creodonts ranged from weasel size to beasts bigger than a bear. Small species might have eaten insects. Larger kinds probably included big-game hunters, carrion eaters, and omnivores. Creodonts roamed northern continents about 58–5 million years ago and were "top dogs" in the Eocene

(55–34 million years ago). Then there were still hoofed animals slow enough for them to catch, and they lacked competition from brainier, more lethal killers.

There were two creodont families: Oxyaenidae and the more durable Hyaenodontidae. Deltatheridians, once believed to be early creodonts, were not placental mammals but were related to marsupials.

A flesh-eating monster

Megistotherium *was one of the largest flesh-eating mammals ever. This huge creodont weighed about 900 kg (1,980 lb). The head was twice as large as any bear's and was armed with mighty canine teeth.* Megistotherium *quite likely killed elephant-like mastodonts. Miocene rocks in Libya contain this monster's fossils.*

Teeth to shear and chop

Early mammals had cheek teeth with triangular crowns. Those in flesh eaters worked to shear and chop, as shown here.

a *Skull with teeth, shown enlarged*

b *Crown view of upper cheek teeth, shown much enlarged*

c *Crown view of lower cheek teeth, shown much enlarged*

d *Upper and lower cheek teeth, here shown meshed together. The front edges of the lower teeth slid along the back edges of the upper teeth ahead of them. The low "heel" behind the main part of each lower tooth fitted into the surface of the upper tooth behind it, preventing further sliding. Partial meeting of cusps ("peaks") on the tooth crowns helped chop up food*

Three flesh-eaters

1 Deltatheridium, a deltatheridian, had creodont-like teeth (although it was related to marsupials). Length: maybe 15 cm (6 in). Time: late Cretaceous. Place: Mongolia.

2 Patriofelis was a bear-sized oxyaenid. Oxyaenids had a short, broad head; deep, strong jaws; and cheek teeth that crushed rather than sheared. Time: mid-Eocene. Place: North America.

3 Hyaenodon included wolf-sized species that tackled big, hoofed animals. It belonged to the hyaenodontids–a far bigger, longer-lasting group than oxyaenids, usually with a longer head, more slender jaws, a slimmer body, longer legs, and a tendency to walk on the toes. Teeth sheared rather than crushed. *Hyaenodon* lived in northern continents in Eocene and Oligocene times.

© DIAGRAM

Cats' claws (below)

Ability to unsheathe claws and spread toes provides most cats with formidable weapons.

a *Unsheathing: pulling a toe's lower tendon makes a claw curve down and out.*

b *Sheathing: pulling a toe's upper tendon makes a claw curve up and back.*

Modern carnivores 1

Modern carnivores form one order, Carnivora, with two suborders: Feliformia (with civets, cats, and hyenas) and Caniformia (including dogs, weasels, raccoons, pandas, bears, seals, and walruses). Carnivorans had bigger brains, keener ears, more deadly piercing canines and shearing cheek teeth, and longer limbs than creodonts. Cunning, agile carnivorans replaced creodonts as the top predators, for only they could catch and kill new kinds of speedy herbivores that replaced slower types.

Carnivora probably evolved from insect eaters by 60 million years ago. By 35 million years ago they dominated life on most continents. Six feliform families arose: the early Viverravidae, Nimravidae (false saber-tooths), Felidae (cats), Viverridae (civets), Herpestidae (mongooses), and Hyaenidae (hyenas). Below are five feliforms and a caniform.

Victor and victim (below)

Big stabbing cats like Smilodon *probably preyed on big, slow-moving herbivores like the large prehistoric ground sloth* Mylodon. *Remains of both occur in Los Angeles' famous tar pits. Tar trapped big herbivores that drank rainwater that concealed tar beneath. Creatures' struggles attracted predators.*

Stabbing and biting

Stabbing cats and biting cats evolved different techniques for using teeth as weapons.

A *Stabbing cats like* Smilodon *used strong neck muscles to strike downward with the head.*

B *Biting cats like the cheetah have strong jaw muscles and exert a formidable bite.*

Six carnivores

1 Miacis was a small, weasel-like, tree-climbing early caniform. Length: 60 cm (2 ft). Time: Eocene. Place: North America, Europe, and Asia.

2 Genetta, the genet, resembles Eocene members of its Old World civet family (Viverridae). It is a catlike forest dweller with short limbs, long tail, and retractile claws. Length: 96 cm (3 ft 2 in). Time: Pleistocene on. Place: Africa and Eurasia.

3 Percrocuta had a big head, strong jaws, bone-cracking teeth, and longish legs. Species of this early hyena were wolf size to lion size. Time: Miocene. Place: Africa and Asia.

4 Dinictis was a puma-sized member of the false saber-tooths (family Nimravidae). Time: early Oligocene–early Miocene. Place: North America.

5 Felis leo spelaea, the great "cave lion," was a biting cat one-third larger than the largest lion. It lived in mid-Pleistocene Europe.

6 Smilodon, the "saber-tooth tiger," was a heavy, lion-sized stabbing cat. Its daggerlike upper canines stabbed large prey or slashed blood vessels in their necks. Time: late Pliocene-Pleistocene. Place: North and South America.

Modern carnivores 2

The caniforms' varied families perhaps originated with weasel-like miacids. Caniforms mostly share a skull peculiarity involving the middle ear. They have less specialized teeth than cats and cannot sheathe their claws. Some eat almost any food. Land-based forms include the Canidae (dogs and wolves), Amphicyonidae (extinct bear-dogs), Ursidae (bears and giant panda), Mustelidae (weasels and badgers), and Procyonidae (raccoons and coatis).

By 25 million years ago, caniforms gave rise to sea mammals: the Otariidae (eared seals) and Phocidae (seals and walruses). This successful group of aquatic carnivores developed sleek, streamlined bodies, webbed limbs, and teeth designed for catching fish or for crushing clams (in walruses). Unlike whales or ichthyosaurs, seals kept a flexible neck and the tail is reduced to a stump.

Forrnidable jaws

*Here we compare skulls of a cave bear (**A**) and a fox (**B**), drawn to scale. Cave bears were omnivores, despite their massive jaws.*

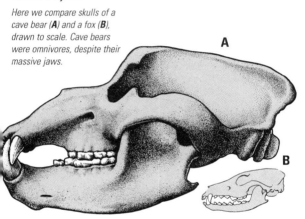

Carnivore relationships

Molecular studies of both groups of living Carnivora and their apparent nearest relative show these relationships:

A Feliformia
1 Domestic cat
2 Ocelot
3 Jaguar

B Caniformia
4 Dog
5 Bear

C Pholidota
6 Chinese pangolin (a scaly anteater)

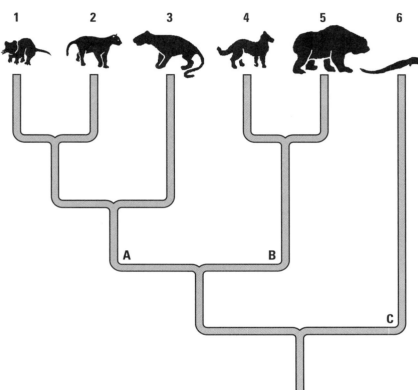

Caniforms

1 Cynodictis, a fox-sized amphicyonid, had a long, low body, long neck, long tail, sharp shearing cheek teeth, and longer legs and larger brain than miacids Time: late Eocene–early Oligocene. Place: Europe and East Asia.

2 Daphoenodon, a sizable predator, was a wolflike "bear-dog" from early Miocene North America. It had rather short limbs; spreading toes; a long, strong tail; and was perhaps omnivorous.

3 Osteoborus, a hyenalike canid scavenger, had a bulging forehead and strong jaws. It lived in Miocene North America.

4 Megalictis from early Miocene North America resembled a wolverine but was as big as a

black bear. It was the largest mustelid ever.

5 Ursus spelaeus, the great "cave bear" of Pleistocene Europe, was descended from the dog family. Bears walk flat-footed, not on toes like dogs, and most are omnivores. Length: 1.6 m (5 ft 3 in).

6 Phlaocyon was a small, raccoonlike procyonid (some say canid) from Miocene North America. It climbed trees, had grinding but not shearing cheek teeth, and was omnivorous.

7 Allodesmus, an early relative of sealions, probably resembled an elephant seal, the largest earless seal alive today. Time: early Miocene–mid-Miocene. Place: North Pacific Ocean.

© DIAGRAM

Early ungulates

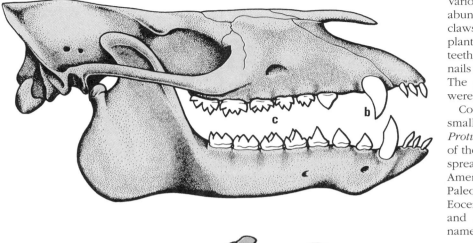

Various early ungulates (hoofed mammals) were abundant 65 to 40 million years ago. The first had claws, not hooves or nails, and some ate flesh, not plants. Later kinds developed chopping, grinding teeth for pulping leaves and long limbs tipped with nails or hooves for running away from carnivores. The pioneers were rabbit-sized; some later forms were longer than a large bear.

Condylarths like *Phenacodus* perhaps came from small early ungulates such as *Chriacus* and *Protungulatum* and maybe were near the ancestors of the more advanced hoofed mammals. Condylarths spread through northern continents and into South America and Africa. Most fossils come from Paleocene rocks in North America, as well as from Eocene rocks there and in South America, Europe, and Asia. This page profiles the three creatures named above.

A climbing ungulate (below)

Chriacus was an oxyclaenid, in a group of early ungulates called Procreodi. It grew about 1 m (3 ft) and had a long body, sturdy limbs, clawed digits, and a tail with grasping capability. It walked flat-footed but ran up trees, seizing fruits and insects between its crushing teeth. Chriacus *lived in Paleocene North America.*

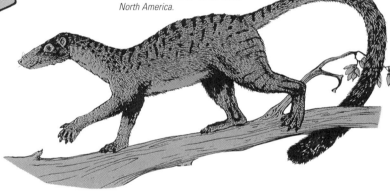

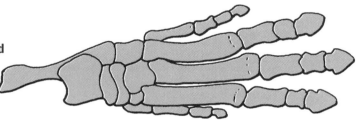

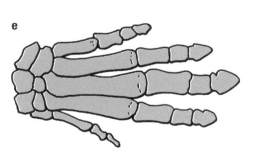

Early ungulate features (above)

Bones of Phenacodus *skull, manus (hand), and pes (foot):*

a *Long, low skull (shown half the actual length), resembling that of early carnivores*

b *Large canine teeth, as in early carnivores*

c *Ridged, square-crowned molars forming a battery of cheek teeth capable of crushing leaves*

d *Bones of hind foot, tipped with small, blunt hooves, not nails*

e *Bones of forefoot, also tipped with hooves*

Two early ungulates

1 Protungulatum, the first known ungulate, was rabbit-sized. It ate plants and maybe other foods. Time: late Cretaceous–early Paleocene. Place: North America. One of the most primitive of all known ungulates, it had a supple back; short limbs tipped with claws; a long tail; long, low head; and "old-fashioned" molars with triangular crowns.

2 Phenacodus, a phenacodontid condylarth, was a sheep-sized plant eater with big canine teeth and square-crowned molars. It was the earliest-known mammal with hooves, not nails or claws. Fossil skeletons show that it roamed woods and shrub lands in North America and Europe. Time: late Paleocene–early Eocene.

"Amblypods"

Amblypods ("slow-footed") was a name coined for a supposed related group of early ponderous, hoofed herbivores with broad, low, ridged cheek teeth. Many might have lived in swamps. Size, weapons, or habitat helped protect them from the creodonts. Such creatures flourished 60 to 30 million years ago, mostly in Paleocene and Eocene North America, but in Europe and East Asia also.

Scientists now think that amblypods held two quite separate groups: Dinocerata and Pantodonta. Dinocerates were early ungulates, many rhino-sized with strange bony horns, wicked-looking upper canines, and upper molars with a broad, V-shaped crest. Pantodonts, with short legs and long canine teeth arguably belonged inside the Ferae, a group including the flesh-eating Creodonta and Carnivora.

The Uinta beast (below)

Uintatherium's *low-crowned cheek teeth, massive postlike limbs, and stubby toes suggest it browsed on soft-leaved plants in grasslands and along the woodland edge. Fossil hunters found its bones where Colorado's Uinta Mountains jut north toward Wyoming.*

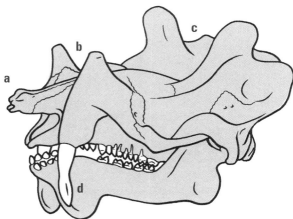

A "six-horned" head (left)

Uintatherium's *great grotesque skull 76 cm (30 in) long shows weapons used by jousting males or in defense.*

a Two small knobs on the nose

b Two larger knobs between the nose and eyes

c Two big broad knobs above and behind the eyes

d Huge upper canines, protected by a flange in the lower jaw

Four amblypods

Here we show three pantodonts from different families and the best-known dinocerate:

1 Pantolambda was one of the first hoofed mammals as big as a sheep. It had heavy legs, short feet, and a long, low head with large canine teeth. It might have wallowed, hippolike, and browsed on land. Time: mid-Paleocene. Place: North America and Asia.

2 Barylambda was pony-sized, with a heavy body, small head, and primitive teeth. It might have sat on its haunches to browse high up. It lived in late Paleocene–early Eocene North America.

3 Coryphodon had a long, heavy body, large head, wide muzzle, and knifelike upper canines. Length: 3 m (9 ft 10 in). Some think it lived largely in water. Time: late Paleocene–early Eocene. Place: northern continents.

4 Uintatherium was a massive dinocerate the size of a large rhinoceros. Thick limbs with spreading feet held up its heavy body. Three pairs of bony knobs sprouted from the head, and males had wickedly long, strong, upper canines. Time: Eocene. Place: North America.

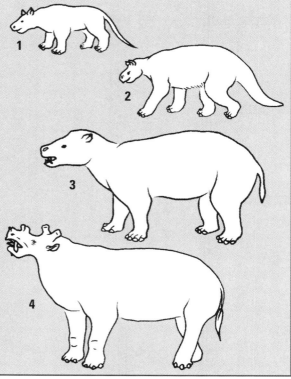

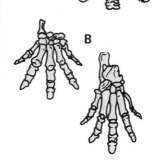

Two kinds of feet (above)

Big heavy herbivores tended to develop much more massive foot and toe bones than smaller, lighter forms.

A The short, thick, strong bones that bore the weight of mighty Uintatherium

B The relatively slim, thin bones of Pantolambda's fore and hind feet

© DIAGRAM

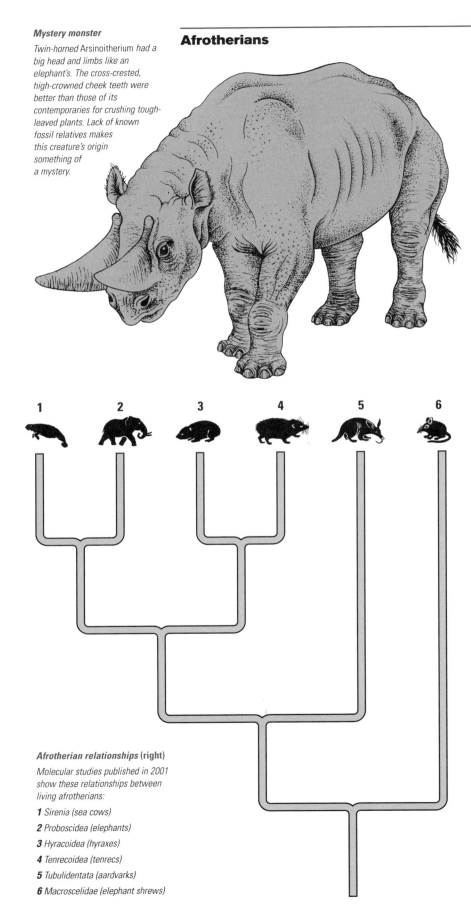

Mystery monster

Twin-horned Arsinoitherium *had a big head and limbs like an elephant's. The cross-crested, high-crowned cheek teeth were better than those of its contemporaries for crushing tough-leaved plants. Lack of known fossil relatives makes this creature's origin something of a mystery.*

Afrotherians

Molecular studies show that living sirenians (sea cows), proboscideans (elephants), hyraxes, and some others share an African ancestor and form a related group: the Afrotheria. Fossils reveal that afrotherians include the extinct embrithopods and desmostylans. Afrotherians tend to lack a collar bone but have five-toed feet with nails, not hooves. Many have few front teeth, one pair often tusklike, but enlarged premolars and grinding cheek teeth with crosswise ridges. Their common ancestor was possibly small, mouselike, and lived some 60 million years ago. This page is the first of three with examples of different prehistoric afrotherians.

Three afrotherians

1 Arsinoitherium, from early Oligocene Egypt, belonged to the embrithopods. This rhinoceros-sized mammal had a huge pair of horns side by side on its head. It probably munched coarse-leaved plants in swamps. Length: 3.4 m (11 ft).

2 Desmostylus, a heavy, walruslike desmostylan, swam or waded on North Pacific coasts from early Miocene to maybe early Pliocene times. Short tusks grew forward from both jaws. Rear teeth were closely-packed, heavily-enameled bundles, perhaps used for crunching shellfish or munching seaweed.

3 Protosiren was an early sea cow about 2.4 m (8 ft) long, from middle Eocene North Africa and Europe. Sea cows developed broad, beaklike snouts, flipperlike front limbs, and a broad, flat tail but lost their hind limbs. Living species browse on aquatic plants in tropical river mouths.

Afrotherian relationships (right)

Molecular studies published in 2001 show these relationships between living afrotherians:

1 *Sirenia (sea cows)*

2 *Proboscidea (elephants)*

3 *Hyracoidea (hyraxes)*

4 *Tenrecoidea (tenrecs)*

5 *Tubulidentata (aardvarks)*

6 *Macroscelidae (elephant shrews)*

Proboscideans 1

Elephants, their ancestors, and other kin make up the afrotherian order Proboscidea ("long snouted"). The first pig-sized, trunkless proboscideans lived in Africa 40 million years ago. From Africa, their evolving descendants invaded all continents except Australia and Antarctica. Meanwhile they grew in size. Many were immense slab-sided beasts with "tree trunk" limbs and a huge head armed with tusks and brandishing a flexible muscular trunk–a "hand" that could bring leaves and water to the mouth. In these two pages we show something of the astonishing variety of prehistoric proboscideans.

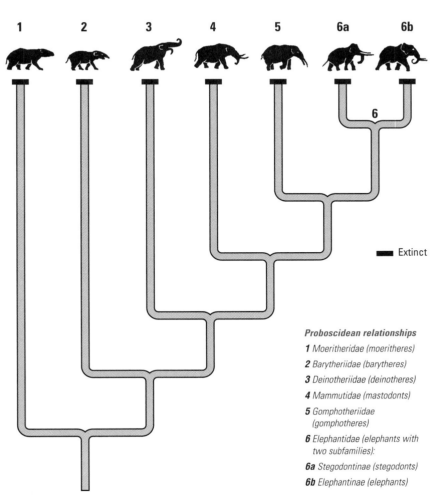

Extinct

Proboscidean relationships

1 *Moeritheridae (moeritheres)*

2 *Barytheriidae (barytheres)*

3 *Deinotheriidae (deinotheres)*

4 *Mammutidae (mastodonts)*

5 *Gomphotheriidae (gomphotheres)*

6 *Elephantidae (elephants with two subfamilies):*

6a *Stegodontinae (stegodonts)*

6b *Elephantinae (elephants)*

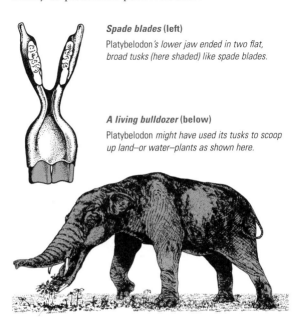

Spade blades (left)

Platybelodon's *lower jaw ended in two flat, broad tusks (here shaded) like spade blades.*

A living bulldozer (below)

Platybelodon *might have used its tusks to scoop up land–or water–plants as shown here.*

Six proboscideans

These come from six families, from **1** to **6**: Moeritheridae, Deinotheriidae, Phiomiidae, Gomphotheriidae, Mammutidae, and Elephantidae (the group that includes modern elephants).

1 Moeritherium, a pig-sized, heavy footed moeritherid, had a short, flexible snout and forward-jutting incisor teeth. It lived in swampy lands. Time: late Eocene–early Oligocene. Place: northern Africa (Egypt, Mali, and Senegal).

2 Deinotherium belonged to the deinotheriids: beasts up to 4 m (13 ft) high, with down-curved tusks in the lower jaw–forks for digging roots perhaps. Time: Miocene-Pleistocene. Place: Africa and Asia.

3 Phiomia, an early mastodont ("nipple-toothed") proboscidean,

had piglike cheek teeth, a long lower jaw, four short tusks, and a short trunk. Height: 2.4 m (8 ft). Time: early Oligocene. Place: Egypt.

4 Platybelodon, a so-called "shovel tusker," dug up plants with broad bladelike teeth jutting from its long lower jaw. Time: Miocene. Place: Asia and North America.

5 Mammut had long, curved upper tusks, strong crests across its cheek teeth, and a coat of reddish hair. It browsed in forests of North America, from Plicene times to 10,000 years ago.

6 Stegodon was a long-tusked possible ancestor of mammoths (see next page). Time: Pliocene-Pleistocene. Place: Asia and Africa.

Proboscideans 2

Prehistoric members of the elephants' subfamily included *Elephas* species related to the Asian elephant and mammoths ("giants") in the genus *Mammuthus*. More evolved than so-called mastodonts like *Mammut*, mammoths had higher skulls, shorter jaws, and more complex molars for grazing. Some were huge, some dwarfs, some hairy.

Mammoths appeared in Africa 5 million years ago, colonized the Northern Hemisphere, and died out only 3,700 years ago. Meanwhile, *Elephas* also spread and diversified into various species before declining. Our examples give an idea of the variety of both prehistoric groups.

Mammoth skull and teeth

A woolly mammoth skull appears here to scale with a human skull.

a Huge, curved tusks served in defense and maybe helped clear snow from a pasture.

b As it grew, each huge molar pushed out its predecessor(s).

c A crown view shows the many crosswise ridges that helped this molar grind like a mill.

Giant and dwarf

This illustration compares a woolly mammoth with a dwarf island species. The woolly mammoth's great bulk and shaggy coat helped to conserve body heat, enabling this elephant to survive in cold northrn climates. The dwarf elephant's head and feet differ from those of larger elephants in ways that reflect an overall design for more agility.

Five prehistoric elephants

1 Elephas falconeri from the island of Sicily was one of several dwarfed island elephants– an agile beast only one-quarter the size of its mainland ancestors.

2 Mammuthus trogontherii, one of the earliest mammoths, was the largest elephant ever, about 4.3 m (14 ft) at the shoulder.

3 Mammuthus imperator, the second-largest elephant, stood more than 4 m (13 ft) high and its tusks measured up to 4.3 m (14 ft). It flourished in North America in Pleistocene times.

4 Mammuthus primigenius, known as the wooly mammoth, had long, dark, brown hair and thick, wooly underfur. The vast tusks curved forward, up, and back. Height: 2.9 m (9 ft 6 in). This mammoth ranged north of the Arctic Circle.

5 "Palaeoloxodon" was a massive straight-tusked forest species of *Elephas* more than 4 m (13 ft) high. It lived in Europe, including England.

South American ungulates

A whole "zoo" of hoofed mammals evolved in South America while oceans cut it off from other lands. Many amazingly resembled rodents, horses, and other beasts that evolved elsewhere. The five orders of these so-called meridiungulates were the litopterns, notoungulates, astrapotheres, pyrotheres, and xenungulates. The litopterns probably evolved from condylarths, but the rest had other origins, and the meridiungulates may not be a related group.

Some orders of South American ungulate persisted many millions of years, but none survived for long once land linked North and South America about 2 million years ago and carnivores and ungulates invaded from the north.

Life by a pool

This restoration shows a likely scene in South America about 3 million years ago. A Macrauchenia *(**a**) drinks from a pool inhabited by two* Toxodon *(**b,c**). Alignment of the nose, eyes, and ears suggests that* Toxodon *could swim almost completely submerged. Perhaps this bulky mammal lived like a hippopotamus.*

Ten South American ungulates

1 Notostylops was a small primitive hoofed mammal from early Eocene Patagonia. It belonged to the Notioprogonia suborder of the notoungulates, the largest order of South American ungulates.

2 Toxodon was a rhinoceros-sized toxodont ("bow-toothed")–one of the largest and last notoungulates. It had short legs; broad, three-toed feet; big cropping incisor teeth; and tall cheek teeth. The molars curved in toward each other. Time: Pliocene-Pleistocene.

3 Protypotherium resembled a large rodent. It was a typothere notoungulate with claws not hooves. Length: 51 cm (20 in). Time: Miocene.

4 Pachyrukhos had long hind limbs and a stumpy tail. Probably it ran and even leaped like a hare. This Miocene creature belonged to the hegetotheres, the smallest notoungulates.

5 Thoatherium looked astonishingly like a small horse. It belonged to the proterotheriids, a family of litopterns. Time: Miocene.

6 Macrauchenia–camel-sized, and camel-like–might have had a trunk. It was a macraucheniid litoptern. Time: Pleistocene.

7 Astrapotherium belonged to the big astrapotheres. It had a "sawn-off" face, daggerlike canine teeth, and possibly a trunk. Hind limbs were weak. Perhaps it lived in water. Length 2.7 m (9 ft). Time: Miocene.

8 Trigonostylops was a small beast grouped with astrapotheres. It lived in South America and Antarctica. Time: Eocene.

9 Carodnia, one of two known xenungulates, might have resembled a uintathere. Time: late Paleocene.

10 Pyrotherium, a pyrothere, amazingly resembled a large early elephant in its trunk, chisel-like tusks, and type of teeth. Time: Oligocene.

© DIAGRAM

Horses

Horses, rhinoceroses, tapirs, and others make up the perissodactyls, or "odd-toed" ungulates—one of the two great surviving orders of hoofed mammals. Evolving more than 55 million years ago, perissodactyls became the most abundant ungulates, but then declined.

Few creatures left a richer fossil record than the horses—a large family in the hippomorph suborder. Dog-sized forest browsers living more than 50 million years ago gave rise to big, speedy grazers with teeth for chewing tough-leaved grasses that began replacing forests. From their home in North America, horses reached Eurasia, Africa, and South America. Only members of one genus still survive.

Evolving hooves

These illustrations show the hooves of Hyracotherium (**A**), Miohippus (**B**), Merychippus (**C**), *and* Equus (**D**). *Notice that side toes shrink and disappear, until each foot has only an enlarged middle toe ending in a big, broad hoof. Changes in foot design—like changes in skull design—adapted horses for life as grazers on open plains.*

A   B   C   D

Horse trends

These two early horses show important evolutionary trends.

a Orohippus, *a middle Eocene descendant of* Hyracotherium, *was only whippet-sized, but its teeth could cope with tough leaves. It lived in drier woodlands.*

b Merychippus, *a larger horse, could eat the hard, abrasive grasses of Miocene North America. A big gap separated cropping front teeth from grinding cheek teeth, and cement filled "pools" between the enameled ridges of each cheek tooth's crown. When* Merychippus *ran fast, its side toes did not reach the ground.*

Teeth for grazing

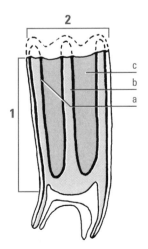

The cheek tooth of a modern horse is designed to chew hard, abrasive grass.

1 *High crown*

2 *Uneven grinding surface produced by wear on enamel (**a**), dentine (**b**), and cement (**c**)*

Evolving horses

1 Hyracotherium, the first known horse, was fox-sized. It had a short neck, curved back, long tail, slim limbs, and long four-toed forefeet and three-toed hind feet. Its low-crowned cheek teeth munched soft leaves in swampy North American and European forests. Time: early Eocene.

2 Mesohippus was bigger than *Hyracotherium*, with a straighter back, longer legs, three-toed forefeet, and enlarged premolar teeth. Height: 60 cm (2 ft) Time: mid-Eocene–early Oligocene.

3 Miohippus was a little larger still, with big middle toe, big molar-type premolars, and ridged cheek teeth. Time: late Eocene–early Miocene.

4 Merychippus was pony-sized, walked on each middle toe, and had a long neck and tall ridged cheek teeth for chewing grasses. Time: Miocene.

5 Pliohippus, 1.2 m (4 ft) tall, was the first one-toed horse. Time: Miocene.

6 Equus, the modern horse, 1.5 m (5 ft) tall, evolved 2 million years ago, and reached most continents. Surviving wild species are Przewalski's horse, the wild asses, and zebras.

7 Palaeotherium belonged to the palaeotheriids, a family evolved from early horses. It had three hooves per foot and seemed half horse, half tapir. Height: 75 cm (30 in). Time: late Eocene–early Oligocene. Place: Europe.

Brontotheres and chalicotheres

These were the strangest of all odd-toed ungulates. Both superfamilies belonged to the ceratomorph suborder that, like horses, perhaps evolved from condylarths. Brontotheres included massive beasts with elephantine limbs and a blunt, bony prong jutting from the nose. They ate only soft-leaved plants. The Brontotherioidea lived in northern continents about 50–30 million years ago.

Chalicotheres ranged from sheep size to horse size. They looked a bit like horses, yet their three-toed feet had big, curved claws that could be sheathed. Some think they walked on knuckles, using claws to dig up edible roots or pull down leafy branches. The Chalicotherioidea were never plentiful but persisted more than 50 million years until less than 2 million years ago. Fossils come from Europe, Asia, Africa, and North America.

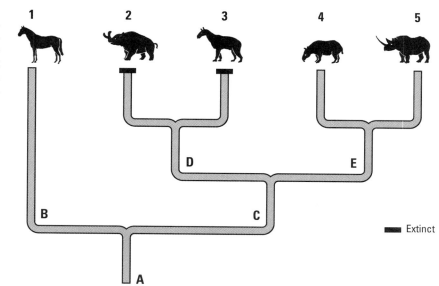

■ Extinct

Clash of titans

As shown here, two rival male brontotheres might have locked horns like stags or banged heads like bighorn rams. Winning stags and rams rule herds of females. Perhaps successful male brontotheres had harems, too.

Perissodactyls

This diagram shows relationships between the main groups of odd-toed ungulates, featured on these pages and the next page. Letters represent major groups; numbers, subsidiary groups.

A *Ancestral ungulates*

B *Hippomorpha*

C *Ceratomorpha*

D *Selenida*

E *Tapiromorpha*

1 *Horses*

2 *Brontotheres*

3 *Chalicotheres*

4 *Tapirs*

5 *Rhinoceroses*

Two ceratomorphs

1 Brontotherium was between a rhinoceros and elephant in size. Thick legs and short, broad feet with hoofed toes (four per forefoot, three per hind foot) supported its massive body. From its blunt snout jutted a thick Y-shaped horn, perhaps brandished at attacking creodonts. (Males might have used horns in jousting contests.) It lived in Eocene North America, probably on open plains, crushing soft leaves between the big, square, low-crowned but enamel-hardened molars. Shoulder height: 2.5 m (8 ft).

2 Moropus resembled a big horse, but like all chalicotheres, had claws, low-crowned teeth unsuited for eating grass, and longer front limbs than hind limbs so that its back sloped down from shoulders to hips. Length: 3 m (10 ft). Time: early–mid-Miocene. Place: North America and Europe.

Tapirs and rhinoceroses

Tapiromorphs (tapirs and rhinoceroses) appeared some 50 million years ago. Early kinds were small, agile beasts like early horses, but each of the two superfamilies had distinctive teeth for grazing. Rhinoceroses produced two families with scores of genera; some huge, many sprouting nasal horns. Tapirs remained small and primitive, with a heavy body; rounded back; short, stubby legs; and a flexible trunklike snout for grasping forest plants. Several families evolved.

Rhinoceroses and tapirs reached all northern lands and Africa, and tapirs entered South America. Now rhinos only live in Africa and Asia; tapirs in Asia and South America.

***Skulls compared* (below)**

*As these scale drawings show, Indricotherium's skull (**A**) dwarfed the skull of a large modern rhino (**B**).*

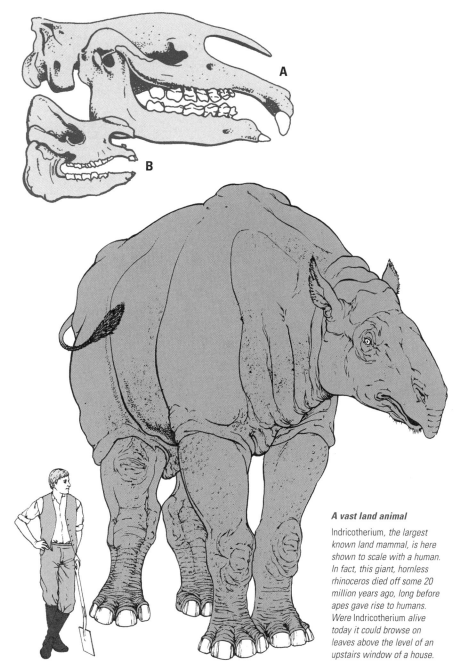

A vast land animal

Indricotherium, the largest known land mammal, is here shown to scale with a human. In fact, this giant, hornless rhinoceros died off some 20 million years ago, long before apes gave rise to humans. Were Indricotherium alive today it could browse on leaves above the level of an upstairs window of a house.

Seven tapiromorphs

1 Hyracodon was a small, agile member of the hyracodontids, early "running" rhinos with long, slim legs, long three-toed feet, and a grazer's molars. Length: 1.5 m (5 ft). Time: Eocene-Oligocene. Place: North America.

2 Metamynodon was a hippolike amynodontid rhino with short, thick limbs and short, broad feet. Time: Eocene-Oligocene. Place: Asia and North America.

3 Indricotherium, the largest land mammal ever, was a huge hyracodontid. Long legs and longish neck helped its small hornless head browse giraffelike among high branches. Shoulder height: 4.6 m (15 ft). Time: Eocene-Miocene. Place: Asia.

4 Elasmotherium, an elephant-sized rhinocerotid, had a huge horn measuring almost 2 m (6 ft 6 in). Time: Pleistocene. Place: Eurasia.

5 Coelodonta, the (rhinocerotid) woolly rhinoceros, survived Ice Age cold because of its shaggy coat. Time: Pleistocene. Place: Eurasia.

6 Helaletes was a small, early, agile helaletid tapir from Eocene North America and East Asia.

7 Miotapirus was a tapirid ancestor of modern tapirs from Early Miocene North America.

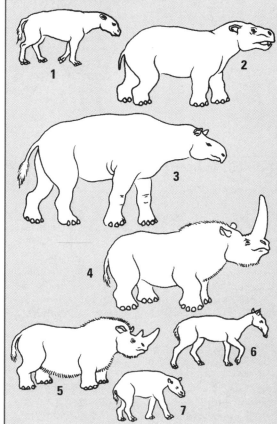

Early even-toed ungulates

Pigs, camels, giraffes, sheep, cattle, and their relatives and ancestors make up the artiodactyls or "even-toed" hoofed mammals. Appearing more than 50 million years ago, artiodactyls became today's major group of ungulates thanks largely to advances in digestion. We show below examples of more primitive types: (**1**) a dichobunoid, perhaps evolved from a Chriacus-like condylarth, and four bunodont Suiformes–piglike artiodactyls with rounded-cusped teeth. These four represent three superfamilies: (**2**) entelodonts ("giant pigs"); (**3**) piglike anthracotheres; and (**4** and **5**) suoids (pigs, peccaries, and hippopotamuses).

Artiodactyl relationships

This tree shows links between creatures on this page and the next four pages: 1–12 are superfamilies and a family, grouped in suborders BEF. Some relationships are uncertain. Letters ACDG mark the appearance of evolutionary innovations.

1 Dichobunoidea (dichobunoids)
2 Entelodontoidea (entelodonts)
3 Suoidea (pigs and close kin)
4 Anthracotherioidea (anthracotheres)
5 Oreodontoidea (oreodonts)
6 Anoplotherioidea (anoplotheres)
7 Cameloidea (camels and llamas)
8 Protoceratoidea (protoceratoids)
9 Tragulids etc
10 Giraffoidea (giraffes and kin)
11 Cervoidea (deer)
12 Bovoidea (sheep, goats, cattle, antelopes, pronghorns)

A Bunodonts, with rounded-cusped teeth
B Suiformes
C Selenodonts: with crescent-shaped cusps on teeth
D Neoselenodonts
E Tylopoda
F Ruminantia
G Pecorans: advanced ruminants

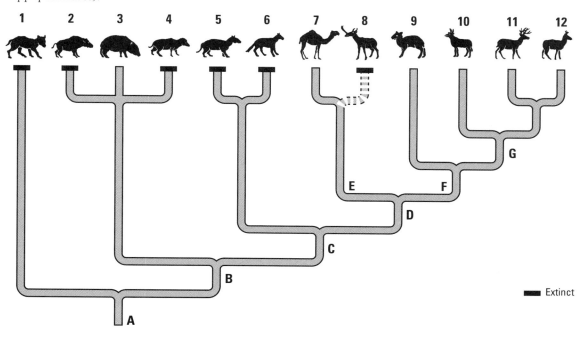

■ Extinct

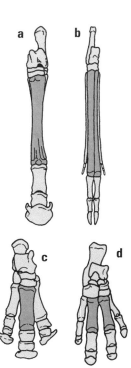

Sprinters and plodders

Bones from four living mammals show that odd-toed and even-toed ungulates of similar build have similar foot bones (shown shaded). These bones are longer in lightweight sprinters than in heavy plodders, and sprinters bear their weight on fewer toes.

a Foot bone of a horse, a speedy odd-toed ungulate that bears its weight on one toe

b Foot bones of a chevrotain, a speedy even-toed ungulate that bears its weight on two toes

c Foot bones of a rhinoceros, a plodding odd-toed ungulate that spreads its weight on three toes

d Foot bones of a hippopotamus, a plodding even-toed ungulate that spreads its weight on four toes

Piglike artiodactyls

1 Dichobune, a small dichobunoid, had short limbs, four-toed feet, and a low skull with long canine teeth and low-crowned molars. Time: mid-Eocene–early Oligocene. Place: Eurasia.

2 Archaeotherium was a huge warthoglike entelodont. It had humped shoulders, thin legs, and a long, heavy head with lumpy cheeks. Probably it grubbed up roots. Height: 1 m (3 ft 3 in). Time: late Eocene–early Miocene. Place: North America.

3 Bothriodon, an anthracothere, had a long body, short limbs with four-toed feet, and a long skull with 44 teeth including low-crowned molars. Length: 1.5 m (5 ft). Time: late Eocene–early Miocene. Place: northern continents.

4 Platygonus, a peccary, had a short deep skull, big, shearing canine teeth, and long legs with reduced side toes. Length: 1 m (3 ft 3 in). Time: Pliocene-Pleistocene. Place: North and South America.

5 Hippopotamus, one of two surviving genera in its family, is a huge, heavy, aquatic mammal with short, thick, four-toed legs, tiny ears and eyes, and a vast mouth armed with tusklike canine teeth. Length: up to 4.3 m (14 ft). Time: late Pliocene to today. Place: Africa (once Eurasia, too).

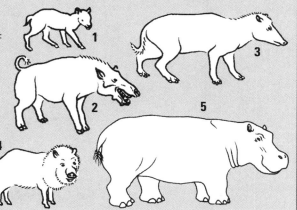

Evolving artiodactyls

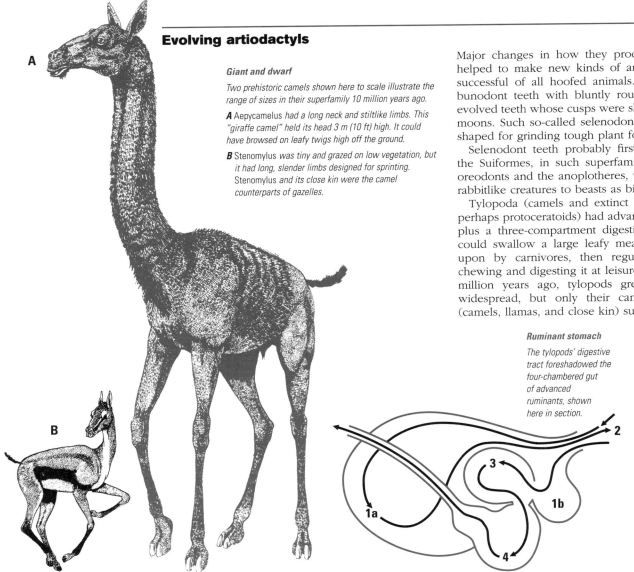

A

B

Giant and dwarf

Two prehistoric camels shown here to scale illustrate the range of sizes in their superfamily 10 million years ago.

A Aepycamelus *had a long neck and stiltlike limbs. This "giraffe camel" held its head 3 m (10 ft) high. It could have browsed on leafy twigs high off the ground.*

B Stenomylus *was tiny and grazed on low vegetation, but it had long, slender limbs designed for sprinting.* Stenomylus *and its close kin were the camel counterparts of gazelles.*

Major changes in how they processed plant foods helped to make new kinds of artiodactyl the most successful of all hoofed animals. First, in place of bunodont teeth with bluntly rounded cusps, some evolved teeth whose cusps were shaped like crescent moons. Such so-called selenodont teeth were better shaped for grinding tough plant foods.

Selenodont teeth probably first appeared among the Suiformes, in such superfamilies as the piglike oreodonts and the anoplotheres, which ranged from rabbitlike creatures to beasts as big as tapirs.

Tylopoda (camels and extinct relatives, including perhaps protoceratoids) had advanced chewing teeth plus a three-compartment digestive tract. Tylopods could swallow a large leafy meal, run away if set upon by carnivores, then regurgitate their food, chewing and digesting it at leisure. Appearing by 45 million years ago, tylopods grew numerous and widespread, but only their cameloid superfamily (camels, llamas, and close kin) survives.

Ruminant stomach

The tylopods' digestive tract foreshadowed the four-chambered gut of advanced ruminants, shown here in section.

1a Most swallowed food enters the rumen, the largest chamber; digestion starts here.

1b Tough plant fibers and stones go to the reticulum.

2 Pulped food returns to the mouth for extra crushing.

3 Reswallowed food has water squeezed out in the omasum.

4 Enzymes extract proteins from food in the abomasum.

Five selenodont-toothed artiodactyls

1 Cainotherium was a rabbit-sized cainotheriid anoplothere with big eyes, keen ears, and long hind limbs for bounding away at speed. Time: early Oligocene–mid-Miocene. Place: Europe.

2 Anoplotherium, an anoplotheriid anoplothere, was tapir-sized and heavily built with clawed toes and a long tail. Height: 1 m (3 ft 3 in). Time: late Eocene–early Oligocene. Place: Europe.

3 Merycoidodon was a sheep-sized, piglike oreodontid oreodont, with a large head, short neck, long body, and short limbs. Time: late Eocene–early Oligocene. Place: North America.

4 Agrichoerus was a sheep-sized agrichoerid anoplothere, with a rather long head, body, and tail and clawed feet, perhaps used for climbing trees or digging up edible roots. Time: mid-Eocene–early Miocene. Place: North America.

5 Poebrotherium was a sheep-sized early camel with short legs, two-toed feet, and a full set of teeth. It looked like a tiny llama. Time: late Eocene–early Oligocene. Place: North America.

Early ruminants

Cattle, sheep, deer, and close relatives make up the Ruminantia–artiodactyls whose multichambered gut thoroughly digests plant nutrients, which helps them survive food shortages. Many ruminants are graceful, with long, slim limbs. Their main defense is speed, though most have horns, antlers, or long, sharp canine teeth. They crop leaves by pressing them between the lower front teeth and an upper horny pad; the top front teeth are missing.

Ruminants first appeared more than 40 million years ago, perhaps in Asia, and spread to other continents. Three superfamilies evolved but this page shows three primitive, deerlike ruminants with simpler stomachs than true deer and two protoceratoids, supposed extinct tylopods but sharing certain features of the skull with ruminants.

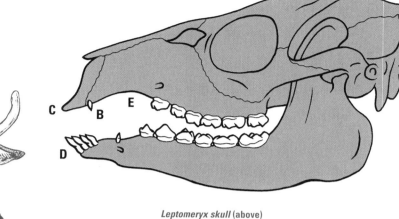

Leptomeryx skull (above)

This life-size skull of an early ruminant has these features:

A *No horns*

B *Sharp upper canine teeth*

C *Toothless cropping pad*

D *Cropping front teeth*

E *Gap developing between front and back teeth*

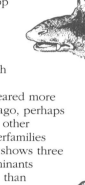

Pronghorned protoceratoid

Syndyoceras *from Miocene North America, a small deer-sized protoceratoid perhaps stockier than shown, had these features:*

a *Curved horns above the eyes*

b *Diverging horns above the nose*

c *Long, slim limbs*

d *Two-toed feet*

e *Metacarpal bones not fused as in advanced ruminants*

Primitive cud chewers

1 Archaeomeryx was a leptomerycid ruminant related to the little living chevrotains, or so-called mouse deer. No bigger than a large rabbit, it had a curved back, hind limbs longer than front limbs, and a long, caninelike premolar tooth in each lower jaw. Time: mid-Eocene. Place: Asia.

2 Synthetoceras was a protoceratid protoceratoid whose males had Y-shaped horns jutting up and forward from the nose and shorter horns curving back and up behind the eyes. Usually pictured like a deer, it might really have resembled a warthog. Time: late Miocene. Place: North America.

3 Tragulus, the Asian chevrotain, is one of only two survivors of the Tragulidae, a family of primitive ruminants. It looks very much like a rodent about 30 cm (1 ft) high. It lacks horns but has long, tusk-like upper canines and four toes per foot (the outer two toes are short and useless). Time: late Pliocene to today. Place: Southeast Asia.

© DIAGRAM

Deer and giraffes

Giraffoids, cervoids, and bovoids (giraffes, deer, cattle, and their relatives) are more "progressive" ruminants than tragulids and are known collectively as pecorans. In most, the upper canine teeth are short or lost, and their heads sprout horns or antlers. Certain bones inside their long, two-toed limbs have shrunk or almost vanished. Living members of these groups have a four-chambered stomach, better able to digest tough plant foods than the three-chambered stomach of the chevrotains.

Giraffes, deer, and their relatives live mostly in wooded countryside. Their low-crowned cheek teeth are designed to browse on trees or shrubs. Male deer grow and shed antlers each year; giraffes grow permanent skin-covered horns.

An early cervoid (below)

Little primitive Blastomeryx *had the following features:*

A *No antlers*

B *Canine tusks for defense*

C *Arched back*

D *Short tail*

E *Long legs and feet*

F *Two effective toes per foot*

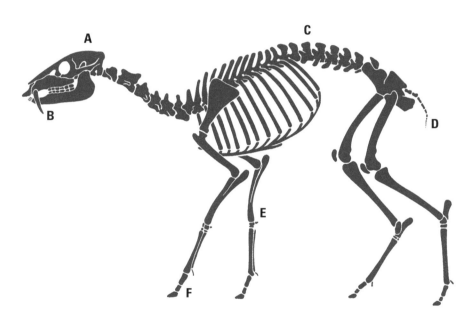

Cervoids and giraffoids

These cervoids (**1-3**) and giraffoids (**4-5**) represent groups with fossil records of more than 30 million and 20 million years, respectively.

1 Blastomeryx had "advanced" limbs but old-fashioned tusklike upper canines and no horns. It belonged to the primitive Moschidae (musk deer). Length: 76 cm (30 in). Time: Miocene–Pliocene. Place: North America.

2 Cranioceras, a North American palaeomerycid, had tall, pronged horns and a backswept third horn. Length: 1.5 m (5 ft). Time: Miocene.

3 Megaloceros, misnamed the "Irish elk," was a giant cervid, related to the fallow deer, with antlers 3 m (10 ft) across. It lived in Pleistocene Eurasia and died off about 2,500 years ago.

4 Palaeotragus, a giraffid ancestor of okapis and giraffes, resembled the okapi. Time: Miocene–Pliocene. Place: Eurasia and Africa.

5 Sivatherium was a large giraffid with a big head, but legs and neck shorter than a giraffe's. Males grew two pairs of horns, one long and branched. Shoulder height: 2.2 m (7 ft). Time: Pliocene–Pleistocene. Place: Eurasia and Africa.

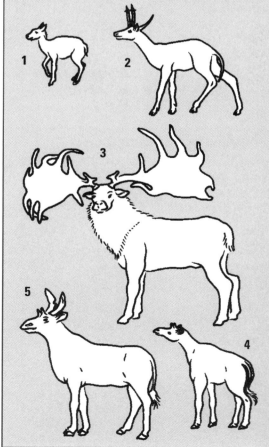

The antler cycle (below)

Like living deer, Megaloceros *would have grown and shed its antlers every year. The annual cycle went like this:*

A *New antlers sprout in summer, nourished and protected by a covering called velvet.*

B *Bony antlers reach their full extent in autumn, when rival stags perhaps locked them in combat.*

C *Antlers shed in spring reveal the pedicle or base from which next season's antlers grow.*

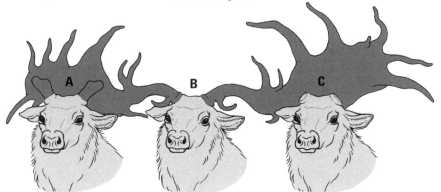

Cattle and their kin

The top grass eaters in the world today are bovoids–members of the cattle superfamily. Cattle, sheep, goats, antelopes, musk oxen, and relatives share almost all the grasslands of the world, with horses as their only large competitors. The bovoids' teeth, stomachs, legs, and feet superbly suit them for a life as grazers on the plains. Both sexes grow strong horns they never shed–living spears on which they can impale attacking carnivores.

Bovoids came from tragulidlike ruminants some 20 million years ago, later than giraffes or deer. Five million years ago great herds were spreading through the north. In time, they swarmed on grassy slopes and plains across Eurasia, Africa, and North America. This page shows five types of bovoid and also bovoidlike *Merycodus*, in fact a cervoid, related to the deer.

Bovoid features

Palaeoreas was a small Miocene ruminant of Eurasia. It was related to the musk ox, but had spiral horns, and is here shown somewhat like an antelope. Like other bovoids it owed success to features such as the following:

a *Both sexes permanently horned*

b *Wear-resistant teeth, with high crowns strengthened by folded ridges of enamel*

c *Lower incisors cropping against a hard toothless pad*

d *Sturdy body*

e *Four-chambered stomach for digesting tough leaves*

f *Long limbs for running*

g *Fused cannon bone reduced risk of sprains*

h *Two-toed cloven hooves*

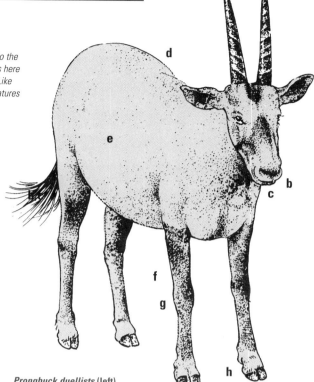

Prongbuck duellists (left)

Rival Merycodus *males could have locked their long forked horns in ritual combat, as shown here. As in most bovoid duels, such fights were probably trials of strength, not combats to the death. The weaker creature would have given up and run away.*

Bovoids and a prongbuck

1 Gazella, a small, delicately built antelope, is a desert and savanna sprinter. Shoulder height: 65–100 cm (26–40 in). Time: early Miocene onward. Place: Africa, Asia, and once also Europe.

2 Mesembriportax was a large, rather heavy-bodied antelope related to the living nilgai. It had long legs and uniquely forked horns. Time: early–late Pliocene. Place: South Africa.

3 Bison The long-horned species shown lived in late Pleistocene North America. Shoulder height: up to 1.8 m (6 ft).

4 Myotragus, the Balearic cave goat, lived on West Mediterranean islands from late Pliocene to Recent times. Its lower middle incisor teeth resembled rodents'. Shoulder height: 50 cm (20 in).

5 Merycodus was a small, early, deerlike prongbuck "antelope" with long forked horns. Prongbucks keep the bony horn cores but annually shed the horny sheaths. Time: early–late Miocene. Other prongbucks (some bizarrely horned) evolved, all in North America. Only one type survives.

Unusual horns (above)

Unlike deer, antilocaprids (prongbucks) never shed their horn cores. Unlike bovoids, they grow forked horns that annually shed their sheaths, seen here in section.

a *Permanent bony horn core*

b *Hair covering the core*

c *Horn formed by outgrowth of the hair growth takes four months from when the old horn has been shed.*

© DIAGRAM

Whales

Flippers and tail flukes adapt whales so well for water life that they cannot walk on land. Fossils hint that their suborder Cetacea shared ancestors with the carnivorous mesonychians (see opposite) and that artiodactyls were close kin of both. Molecular studies claim whales are artiodactyls close to the hippopotamuses. Both groups are hairless, neither sweats, and their young can suckle underwater.

By 50 million years ago, long-jawed meat eaters gave rise to *Pakicetus*, known from a skull found in Pakistan. About 1.8 m (6 ft) long and with features seen in whales and tapirs, *Pakicetus* lived near water but could not dive deep or hear well when submerged. By 25 million years ago, such archaeocetes had given rise to the ancestors of odontocetes and mysticetes (toothed and baleen whales). Buoyed by water, some mysticetes have become the largest animals ever.

A snaky whale

Here the big early archaeocete Basilosaurus, *also known as* Zeuglodon, *is shown chasing herring. At more than 20 m (66 ft), this monster matched many large modern whales for length, but it had a slender, rather snakelike body. The saw-edged teeth were suitable for seizing fishes.* Basilosaurus *fossils crop up in rocks of Eocene seabeds as far apart as Africa and North America.*

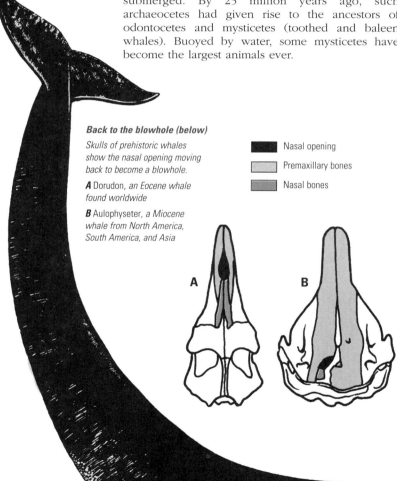

Back to the blowhole (below)

Skulls of prehistoric whales show the nasal opening moving back to become a blowhole.

A *Dorudon, an Eocene whale found worldwide*

B *Aulophyseter, a Miocene whale from North America, South America, and Asia*

■ Nasal opening
▨ Premaxillary bones
▨ Nasal bones

A   B

Prehistoric whales

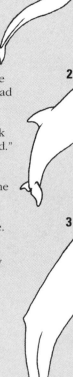

1 Dorudon, of mid–late Eocene seas worldwide, grew maybe 3 m (10 ft) long. It had a long snout, peglike front teeth, and three-ridged sawlike cheek teeth. It belonged to the Archaeocetes, a primitive Eocene Infraorder.

2 Prosqualodon, a more advanced small whale, had its blowhole above and behind the eyes, but its triangular sharklike cheek teeth were "old fashioned." This squalodontid whale resembled those small, living, toothed whales, the dolphins. Length: 2.3 m (7 ft 6 in). Time: Oligocene–early Miocene. Place: southern oceans.

3 Cetotherium probably resembled a small gray whale, or a mysticete (baleen whale). These toothless whales trap swarms of shrimplike creatures on the fringed baleen plates that hang from their upper jaws. Length: perhaps 4 m (13 ft). Time: Miocene. Place: Eurasia and North America.

Mesonychians

Mesonychians ("middle nails") were carnivorous, hoofed mammals considered close to the ancestry of whales. They ranged from wolflike carnivores to a ponderous beast bigger than the largest living bear. Many had sharp, piercing canine teeth and blunt-cusped cheek for crushing bones. Smaller agile kinds ran doglike on toes with flattened nails, not claws. Perhaps packs hunted herbivores.

Once grouped with condylarths, mesonychians have now been placed inside their own suborder, with the formal name Acreodi.

Mesonychians lived in northern continents for at least 30 million years. Appearing possibly as early as late Cretaceous times, before the dinosaurs died out, they vanished in the early Oligocene.

1 Andrewsarchus, a triisodontid mesonychian known only from a huge skull, might have been bearlike (**1a**) or resembled an immense hyena (**1b**). Either way it could have grown up to 6 m (22 ft) long, making it the largest carnivore ever. Besides meat, it probably ate wild fruits and insects, so it would have been as omnivorous as a grizzly bear. Time: late Eocene. Place: East Asia.

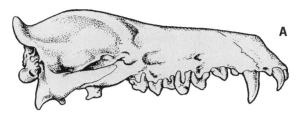

A

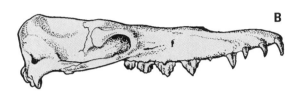

B

Skulls compared (left)

*Similarities between the skulls and teeth of mesonychians such as Andrewsarchus (**A**) and those of early whales like this example (**B**) convince most paleontologists that the whales and mesonychians share a common ancestor.*

1a

1b

© DIAGRAM

SECTION 3

DINOSAURS

Dinosaurs

This chapter takes a detailed look at dinosaurs, the most intensively studied and arguably successful of all prehistoric backboned animals. The first pages summarize some of the key features that help to identify this group, its two main subgroups– the saurischians and ornithischians–and their major branches. The next pages give A-to-Z profiles of scores of individual genera, along with time lines and fact files that put them into time, place, and other contexts.

What were dinosaurs?

Dinosaurs were reptiles that walked as erect as horses or humans, because their limbs transmitted body weight straight down, as seen here from the front (**A**) and side (**B**). Each femur, or thigh bone (**a**), turned in sharply at the top, where its ball-like head or top fitted into a deep hole–a perforate acetabulum (fully open socket) (**b**) in the hip bones (**c**). The supra-acetabular crest, a ridge on the hip bones, prevented the thigh bone from slipping out.

The main leg bone (tibia) (**d**) had a twist and a prominent cnemial (lower leg) crest (**e**). The ankle formed a simple hinge (**f**). Upper tarsal (ankle) bones, the astragalus (**g**) and calcaneum (**h**), closely joined the tibia, and part of the astragalus rose to fit into a notch in the tibia. Lower tarsal (ankle) bones (**i**) formed part of the foot, along with metatarsals (**j**) and phalanges (toe bones) (**k**). The middle toe was the longest. High ankles and long foot bones (**m**) show that dinosaurs walked on their toes.

Inturned femur head, fully open acetabulum, supra-acetabular crest, tall astragalus, plus reduced fourth and fifth fingers and–in all early dinosaurs–a grasping thumb were among the advanced features that set dinosaurs apart from their relatives, the crocodilians and other now extinct so-called archosaurs, or ruling reptiles.

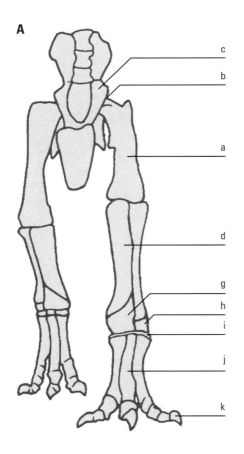

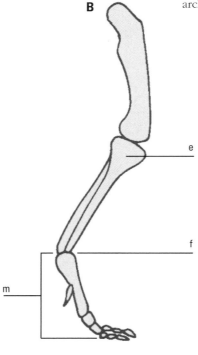

Hind limb features
a Femur
b Acetabulum
c Hip bones
d Tibia
e Cnemial crest
f Ankle joint
g Astragalus
h Calcaneum
i Lower tarsals
j Metatarsals
k Phalanges
m Foot bones

Two great groups

Paleontologists (scientists studying prehistoric life) divide dinosaurs into two great groups traditionally called orders, that are subdivided into successively lesser groups–suborders, infraorders, families, genera, and species.

The order Saurischia ("lizard-hipped") (**A**) included dinosaurs with long cervical vertebrae (neck bones), a long hand with the second digit longer than the others, and a big claw on the thumb. Like lizards, some but not all had a forward-pointing pubis, or front hip bone. There were two saurischian suborders: the two-legged, mainly flesh-eating Theropoda (**1**) (see below) and four-legged, plant-eating Sauropodomorpha (**2**) (see the next page).

The order Ornithischia ("bird-hipped") (**B**) included plant eating dinosaurs with a back-turned pubis, a horny beak covering an extra bone at the lower jaw tip, and blunt cheek teeth. Most had fleshy cheeks, or possibly a horny sheath outside the jaws. There were three ornithischian suborders: the plated and armored Thyreophora (**3**) (page 222), the largely two-legged Ornithopoda (**4**) (page 223), and horned dinosaurs and their kin, the Marginocephalia (**5**) (page 223).

Instead of grouping dinosaurs by rank, many scientists now put them in clades, each with features lacking in less highly evolved clades. Some clades hold just one species.

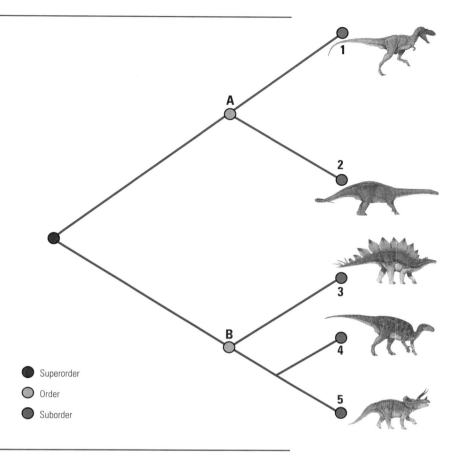

- ● Superorder
- ● Order
- ● Suborder

About theropods

Almost all predatory dinosaurs–except perhaps the earliest–belonged to the saurischian suborder Theropoda, or "beast feet" (**1**). Most of these bipeds had a broadly birdlike body plan but also had scales, sharp teeth, a long bony tail core, and arms with clawed fingers. Some forms evolved with reduced fingers, horny beaks instead of teeth, down as well as scales, and even feathered wings.

From early, lightly built, small-game chasers, some no bigger than a chicken, came big-game hunters or scavengers as heavy as an elephant.

There were two main theropod groups–the primitive Ceratosauria, or "horned lizards" (**2**), both large and small, and the more advanced Tetanurae, or "stiff tails" (**3**). Tetanurans included several subgroups. The Allosauroidea, or "strange lizards" (**4**), featured *Allosaurus* and its big relatives. Most other tetanurans belonged to the Coelurosauria, or "hollow-tail lizards" (**5**). Among these, the Arctometatarsalia, or "pinched metatarsal bones" (**6**), included the mainly toothless Ornithomimidae (**7**) and fearsome Tyrannosauridae (**8**). The Maniraptora, or "seizing hand" (**9**), coelurosaurs included birdlike *Velociraptor* (**10**) and birds themselves, from primitive Avialae, (**11**) such as *Archaeopteryx* (**12**), through more advanced forms to the modern birds, Neornithes (**13**).

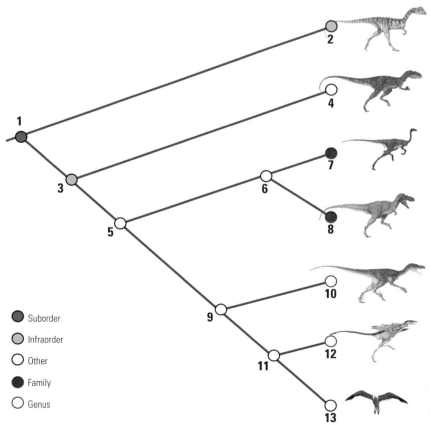

- ● Suborder
- ● Infraorder
- ○ Other
- ● Family
- ○ Genus

© DIAGRAM

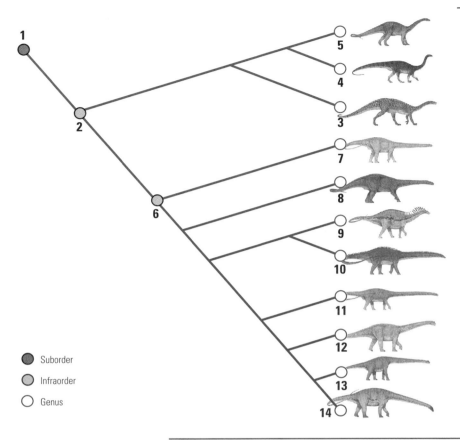

● Suborder

● Infraorder

○ Genus

About sauropodomorphs

Dinosaurs in the saurischian suborder Sauropodomorpha ("lizard feet forms") (**1**) featured a small head, long neck, bulky body, pillarlike limbs and long tail. They had plant eaters' teeth, shaped for cropping leaves but not chewing. Food was ground up by swallowed gizzard stones and broken down by bacteria living in the gut.

The Prosauropoda ("before sauropods") (**2**) probably began as small, bipedal beasts that gave rise to *Anchisaurus* (**3**) and bigger, bulkier quadrupeds like *Plateosaurus* (**4**) and *Melanorosaurus* (**5**).

Prosauropods gave way to the related Sauropoda ("lizard feet") (**6**), the biggest animals that ever lived on land. From early sauropods like *Barapasaurus* (**7**) and *Cetiosaurus* (**8**) evolved the lightly built giants *Amargasaurus* (**9**) and *Diplodocus* (**10**), the incredibly long-necked Chinese sauropod *Mamenchisaurus* (**11**), *Camarasaurus* (**12**), and immense heavyweights *Brachiosaurus* (**13**) and *Argentinosaurus* (**14**).

Some sauropods might have raised their heads to nibble treetops, but most had stiffened necks that they could not lift very high. Fossil tracks hint that sauropods went around in herds. Few theropods would have dared to attack a group of these gigantic animals.

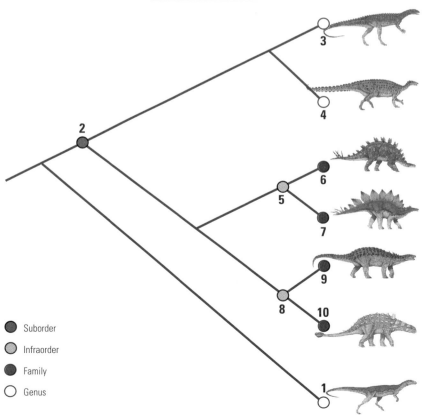

● Suborder

● Infraorder

● Family

○ Genus

About thyreophorans

Small bipedal plant eaters like *Lesothosaurus* (**1**) gave rise to all three main groups of ornithischian dinosaurs.

The group called Thyreophora ("shield bearers") (**2**) contained four-legged plant eaters protected by bony plates, spikes, or studs set in the skin. Most had rather low-slung heads and must have used their horny beaks and small cheek teeth to eat low-growing plants.

The earliest thyreophorans were relatively small, lightly armored beasts like *Scutellosaurus* (**3**) and *Scelidosaurus* (**4**).

Such creatures gave rise to the Stegosauria ("plated lizards") (**5**), dinosaurs with a small head and two rows of tall plates or spikes down the back. They included the primitive Huayangosauridae (**6**), which still had upper front teeth, and the more advanced Stegosauridae (**7**), which had a horny beak and no front teeth.

Early thyreophorans also gave rise to the Ankylosauria ("fused lizards") (**8**), dinosaurs covered with a mass of interlocking bony plates. Ankylosaurs included the Nodosauridae (**9**), with shoulder spines and a narrow beak, and the Ankylosauridae (**10**), with a bony tail club and a broad beak.

About ornithopods

The ornithischian suborder Ornithopoda ("bird feet") (**1**) ranged from small bipeds to very large dinosaurs that ambled on all fours but reared to hurry on powerful hind limbs much longer than their arms. All had long, stiff tails. Many looked a bit like the predatory theropods, but their horny beaks, teeth with leaf-shaped crowns, and powerful jaws were made for munching plants.

Small ornithopods such as the Heterodontosauridae ("different teeth lizards") (**2**), Hypsilophodontidae ("high ridge teeth") (**3**), and Dryosauridae ("tree lizards") (**5**) were agile sprinters.

From beasts like these came larger, more ponderous kinds: *Thescelosaurus* ("wonderful lizard") (**4**), the Camptosauridae ("flexible lizards") (**6**), Iguanodontidae ("iguana tooth lizards") (**7**), and Hadrosauridae ("bulky lizards"), or so-called duck-billed dinosaurs with two subfamilies–flat-headed or solid-crested Hadrosaurinae (**8**) and hollow-crested Lambeosaurinae (**9**).

As ornithopods evolved, claws became hooflike nails, fifth toes and fingers shrank or disappeared, and front teeth vanished, but the hadrosaurids had batteries of self-sharpening cheek teeth for pulping vegetation.

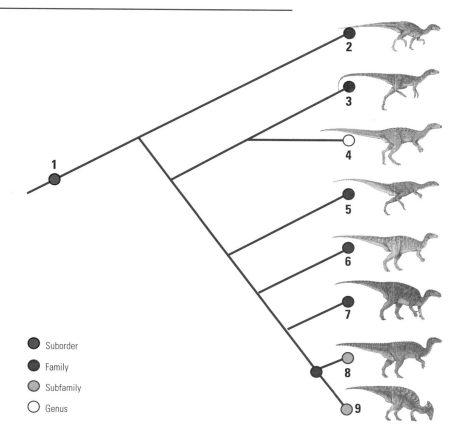

- ● Suborder
- ● Family
- ● Subfamily
- ○ Genus

About marginocephalians

Dinosaurs of the ornithischian suborder Marginocephalia ("margined heads") (**1**) were plant-eaters with a bony shelf, or frill, jutting from the back of the skull. The first known marginocephalians appeared in early Cretaceous times, later than any other major group of dinosaurs.

The infraorder Pachycephalosauria ("thick-headed lizards") (**2**) had two families of thick-skulled, bipedal plant eaters: the dome-headed Pachycephalosauridae (**3**) and flat-headed Homalocephalidae ("level heads") (**4**).

The infraorder Ceratopsia ("horned faces") (**5**) had flared cheekbones and a tall, narrow beak like a parrot's. There were three families. The Psittacosauridae ("parrot lizards") (**6**) were fairly small Asian bipeds. The Protoceratopsidae ("first horned faces") (**7**) were mostly small two-legged and four-legged dinosaurs with a bony skull frill. Some had bumps on the brows and nose. They lived in Asia and western North America and gave rise to the Ceratopsidae ("horned faces") (**8**) of western North America. These included large and very large four-legged, rhinoceroslike dinosaurs with big shelflike skull frills, horns jutting from the nose and brows, and batteries of self-sharpening teeth that sheared like scissors. There were two subfamilies: Centrosaurinae (**9**), with relatively short frills and faces, and Chasmosaurinae (**10**), with long frills and faces.

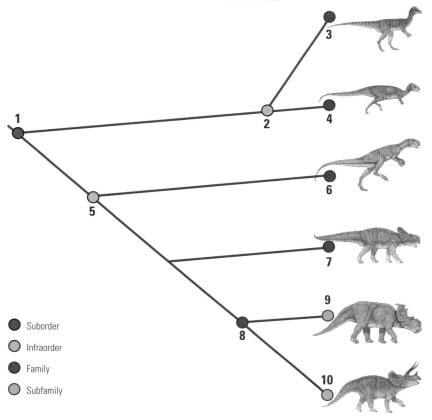

- ● Suborder
- ● Infraorder
- ● Family
- ○ Subfamily

© DIAGRAM

Allosaurus

This theropod was one of the most formidable big flesh eaters of late Jurassic North America. (A dwarfed relative reputedly lived on in Australia millions of years later.)

Allosaurus grew as long as a bus. Its great, lightly built skull had bony ridges and hornlets. Movable joints in the skull let the snout rise and the jaws move out sideways. *Allosaurus* could bolt down great mouthfuls of flesh bitten off by its curved, saw-edged fangs.

There was an S-shaped "bulldog" neck and a deep, narrow body. Each powerful arm had three clawed fingers. The great legs bore large three-toed feet. A long, stiffly held tail counterbalanced the body when *Allosaurus* walked or ran, with its head held low and back horizontal.

By hunting in packs, *Allosaurus* might have killed sauropods much larger than this kind of theropod.

Name *Allosaurus*
Pronunciation *al-loh-SORE-us*
Meaning *"Different lizard"*
Location *USA, Portugal, Tanzania and possibly Australia*
Length *Up to 12 m (40 ft)*
Food *Meat*
Period *Late Jurassic/possibly early Cretaceous*
Order *Saurischia*
Suborder *Theropoda*
Infraorder *Tetanurae*
Family *Allosauridae*

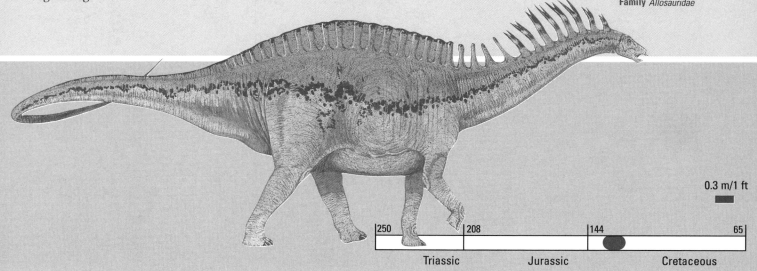

0.3 m/1 ft

250	208	144	65
Triassic	Jurassic		Cretaceous

Anchisaurus

Anchisaurus was a plant-eating dinosaur no heavier than an eight-year-old child. It walked on all fours but probably rose on its hind limbs to feed and run.

Dinosaurs like this had a small head, fairly long, flexible neck, long back, and long tail. Its hind limbs were much longer than its front limbs. *Anchisaurus*'s five-fingered hands and five-toed feet were much narrower than those of *Plateosaurus*, another prosauropod. Each thumb sprouted a great curved

claw. If a theropod attacked, *Anchisaurus* might have stabbed it with this weapon.

Anchisaurus walked on all fours because it was front-heavy, yet it was capable of rearing. It could snip leaves from twigs high on bushes with its saw-edged, leaf-shaped teeth. This prosauropod and others might have had cheek pouches for storing shredded leaves before they were swallowed and ground up by stones in the gizzard.

Name *Anchisaurus*
Pronunciation *AN-kee-SORE-us*
Meaning *"Near lizard"*
Location *Eastern North America and China*
Length *2.1 m (7 ft)*
Food *Plants*
Period *Early Jurassic*
Order *Saurischia*
Suborder *Sauropodomorpha*
Infraorder *Prosauropoda*
Family *Anchisauridae*

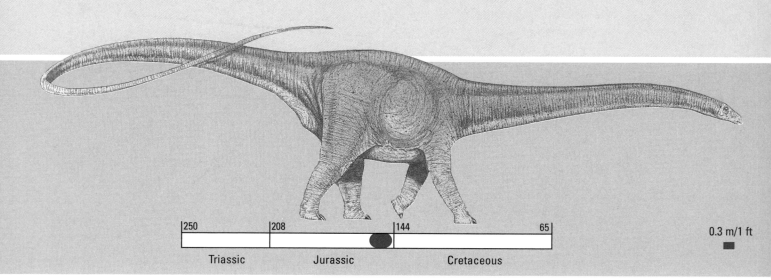

250	208	144	65
Triassic	Jurassic		Cretaceous

0.3 m/1 ft

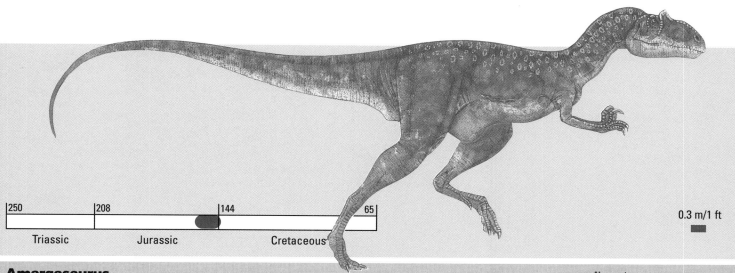

250	208	144	65
Triassic	Jurassic	Cretaceous	

0.3 m/1 ft

Amargasaurus

Amargasaurus was a weird sauropod with a skin "sail" or pair of "sails" rising from its neck and back.

Most of this dinosaur had the build of a typical sauropod: a heavy-bodied, four-legged plant eater with a small head and long neck and tail. *Amargasaurus* seems to have been shorter and more lightly built than most known sauropods, however.

The scientists who described this dinosaur thought it most closely resembled *Dicraeosaurus*, an African beast with a low skull like *Diplodocus's* but high spines on its vertebrae. *Amargasaurus's* vertebral spines were even taller–long pairs of bony spikes that stuck up from its neck and back. These might have carried skin "sails" or maybe a high, fleshy ridge. Either arrangement might have protected the neck and back from attack, scared off rivals, or helped to keep the body cool.

Name *Amargasaurus*
Pronunciation *ah-MAHR-gah-SORE-us*
Meaning *"[La] Amarga [Canyon] lizard"*
Location *West-central Argentina*
Length *10 m (33 ft)*
Food *Plants*
Period *Early Cretaceous*
Order *Saurischia*
Suborder *Sauropodomorpha*
Infraorder *Sauropoda*
Family *Dicraeosauridae*

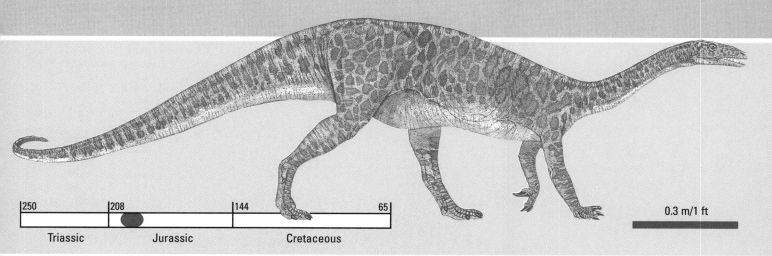

250	208	144	65
Triassic	Jurassic	Cretaceous	

0.3 m/1 ft

Apatosaurus

Apatosaurus is often misnamed "Brontosaurus" from the misidentification of bones that turned out to belong to an *Apatosaurus*, a beast already named.

This immense plant eater had a small, low head; long, thick neck; relatively short, deep body; heavy legs; and a long, whiplike tail. It was shorter than *Diplodocus* but maybe twice its weight, and its neck was relatively thicker than the necks of other diplodocid sauropods.

Like some of these, *Apatosaurus* might have had a saw-edged frill of skin along its back. Also parts of the neck and back had a double ridge created by forked spines rising from some vertebrae. Between these spines lay ligaments that helped to operate the neck and tail.

Studies published in 1999 show that *Apatosaurus* could swing its long neck 4 meters (13 ft) from side to side but raise its head only 6 meters (19 ft 8 in) off the ground. Often pictured browsing on leafy twigs high above the ground, perhaps this sauropod cropped low-growng ferns instead.

Name *Apatosaurus*
Pronunciation *ah-PAT-oh-SORE-us*
Meaning *"Deceitful lizard"*
Location *Western USA*
Length *21 m (70 ft)*
Food *Plants*
Period *Late Jurassic*
Order *Saurischia*
Suborder *Sauropodomorpha*
Infraorder *Sauropoda*
Family *Diplodocidae*

Argentinosaurus

Argentinosaurus is the largest known South American dinosaur. It might have been the heaviest of all land animals, weighing anywhere from 50 to 100 tons.

The few huge bones discovered include dorsal vertebrae as tall as a woman and the shin bone from a hind limb 4.5 meters (14 ft 9 in) long. Comparing these with bones of better-known sauropod relatives helps us guess at its appearance. Thus a sauropod skull found in 1997 hints at a head with a high-domed braincase, a long muzzle, and sturdy jaws rimmed with long, strong teeth. This skull made scientists suspect that South American sauropods such as *Argentinosaurus* were related to *Brachiosaurus*, a type of North American sauropod built like a massively constructed giraffe.

Quite likely, the vast, four-legged plant-eater's body had a back that sloped down from its shoulders to its hips. The neck and tail might have been rather short and thick.

It is possible that it could not raise its head higher than its shoulder, and so did not browse among the tree tops.

Name *Argentinosaurus*
Pronunciation *"AR-GEN-TINE-oh-SORE-us"*
Meaning *"Argentine lizard"*
Location *West-central Argentina*
Length *27.5 m (90 ft)*
Food *Plants*
Period *Early Late Cretaceous*
Order *Saurischia*
Suborder *Sauropodomorpha*
Infraorder *Sauropoda*
Family *Andesauridae*

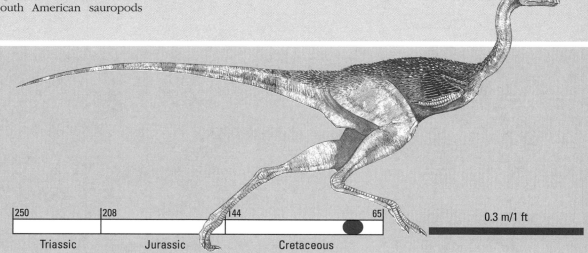

250	208	144	65	0.3 m/1 ft
Triassic	Jurassic	Cretaceous	

Barapasaurus

Barapasaurus was a great four-footed plant eater with saw-edged, spoon-shaped teeth; a long neck; a bulky body; slim limbs; and a long tail.

Most scientists consider this one of the earliest known sauropods. Its hip and spinal bones match those of other sauropods, yet some bones look like those of their more primitive relatives, prosauropods.

Scientists have found the remains of more than 300 individuals in India, yet none of them included a skull or foot bone. Without knowing just what *Barapasaurus*'s head looked like, scientists cannot be sure which were its closest relatives among the dinosaurs. Some experts put *Barapasaurus* in its own family, Barapasauridae. Others group it with the small early African sauropod *Vulcanodon* or with the primitive European sauropod *Cetiosaurus*.

Name *Barapasaurus*
Pronunciation *bah-RAP-a-SORE-us*
Meaning *"Big leg lizard"*
Location *India*
Length *18 m (59 ft)*
Food *Plants*
Period *Early Jurassic*
Order *Saurischia*
Suborder *Sauropodomorpha*
Infraorder *Sauropoda*
Family *Possibly Barapasauridae*

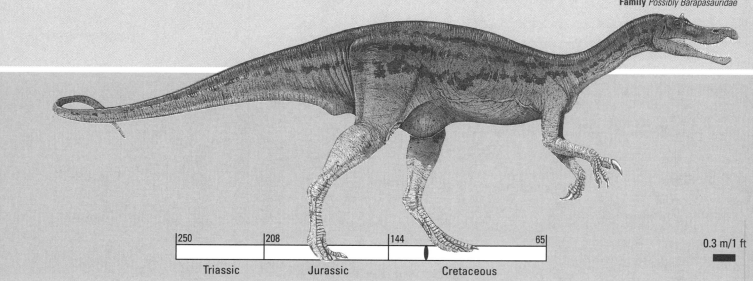

250	208	144	65	0.3 m/1 ft
Triassic	Jurassic	Cretaceous	

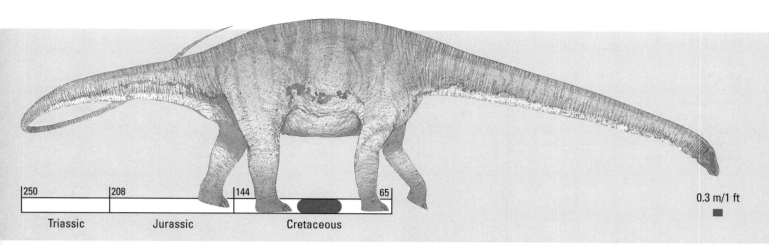

250	208	144	65		0.3 m/1 ft
Triassic	Jurassic	Cretaceous			

Avimimus

Avimimus has been called a birdlike running dinosaur with a toothless beak and maybe feathered arms (as illustrated on the left).

By 1999 discovered specimens included a fairly complete skeleton. This coelurosaurian theropod had a small, short, deep head; big eyes and fairly big brain; a long neck; short arms; and long, slim legs ending in three-toed feet with narrow, pointed claws. Some bones of the wrists and lower legs were fused as they are in birds, and the ridged forearms seem designed to take the shafts of feathers, although no fossil feathers have survived. *Avimimus* apparently could even fold its arms in the way birds fold their wings.

Avimimus roamed open plains. Most likely it ran down big insects, lizards and small mammals, then snapped them up in its beak. The beak's saw-edged upper half gripped wriggling victims until they could be swallowed.

Name *Avimimus*
Pronunciation *ay-vee-MEEM-us*
Meaning *"Bird mimic"*
Location *Mongolia*
Length *1 m (3 ft 3 in)*
Food *Probably small animals and plants*
Period *Late Cretaceous*
Order *Saurischia*
Suborder *Theropoda*
Infraorder *Tetanurae*
Family *Avimimidae*

250	208	144	65		0.3 m/1 ft
Triassic	Jurassic	Cretaceous			

Baryonyx

Baryonyx was a 2-ton fish-eating dinosaur more than 3 meters tall (9 ft 10 in) and as long as a bus.

This dinosaur had long, low, and narrow jaws like a crocodile's and crocodilelike teeth–twice as many teeth as most other theropods. *Baryonyx* also had a fairly long neck, straighter than the S-shaped necks of most other large theropods. Its long arms bore three clawed digits, with a great curved claw on the largest–the thumb.

Baryonyx might have fished like a brown bear, standing in shallow water and hooking big fish with its claws. Or maybe it seized fish in its mouth, as crocodiles do. Its jaws and teeth would have been just right for gripping these slippery creatures. We know that it ate fish, for the first *Baryonyx* skeleton to be found had the scales of a large freshwater fish in its ribcage, where its stomach would have been.

Name *Baryonyx*
Pronunciation *ba-ree-ON-iks*
Meaning *"Heavy claw"*
Location *western Europe and North Africa*
Length *10 m (33 ft)*
Food *Fish*
Period *Early Cretaceous*
Order *Saurischia*
Suborder *Theropoda*
Infraorder *Tetanurae*
Family *Baryonychidae*

Brachiosaurus

Brachiosaurus was one of the largest land animals that ever lived. Some people think a well-fed, full-grown specimen could have weighed as much as 10 elephants.

This sauropod was built rather like a monstrous giraffe, with forelimbs longer than hind limbs and a deep body that sloped down from the shoulders to a relatively short and thickset tail.

To lighten the huge load held up by its limbs there were deeply scooped out spinal bones and a skull partly made of bony struts. As in most sauropods, nostrils opened high up on the head, which allowed *Brachiosaurus* to breathe while it ate.

Worn, chisel-shaped teeth suggest that this sauropod cropped tough leaves. *Brachiosaurus* might have nibbled leafy twigs high above ground level.

Name *Brachiosaurus*
Pronunciation *BRAK-ee-oh-SORE-us*
Meaning *"Arm lizard"*
Location *western US, Portugal, and Tanzania*
Length *25 m (82 ft)*
Food *Plants*
Period *Late Jurassic*
Order *Saurischia*
Suborder *Sauropodomorpha*
Infraorder *Sauropoda*
Family *Brachiosauridae*

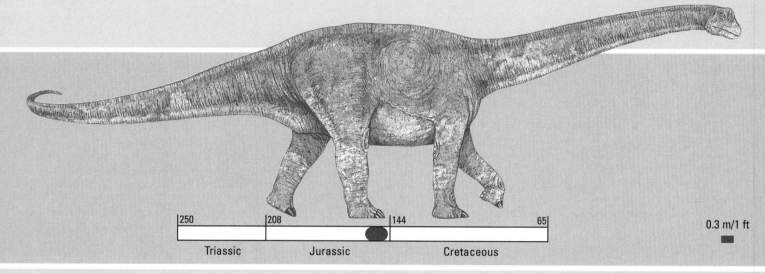

250	208	144	65
Triassic	Jurassic	Cretaceous	

0.3 m/1 ft

Camptosaurus

Bulky-bodied *Camptosaurus* was bigger and more advanced than its likely ancestors the hypsilophodontids. However, it was less advanced than those later ornithopods, the hadrosaurs, and smaller than most.

The head was long and low, with a sharp, horny, toothless beak and tightly packed, ridged cheek teeth.

The arms were short and sturdy. The strong wrists bore five-fingered hands with spiky thumb claws; these were shorter and blunter than *Iguanodon's*. Their long, strong thighs were longer than their shins, which hints that *Camptosaurus* could not run very fast. Its four-toed feet had fairly sharp, curved claws.

Camptosaurus walked on all fours to crop low-growing vegetation, but it would have hurried on its hind limbs, head and neck balanced by its long, stiffened tail.

Name *Camptosaurus*
Pronunciation *KAMP-toh-SORE-us*
Meaning *"Flexible lizard"*
Location *western US and Western Europe*
Length *6 m (20 ft)*
Food *Plants*
Period *Late Jurassic*
Order *Ornithischia*
Suborder *Ornithopoda*
Infraorder *Euornithopoda*
Family *Camptosauridae*

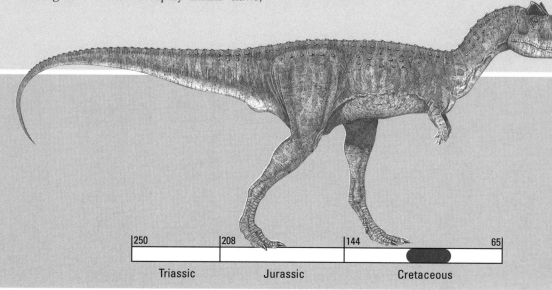

250	208	144	65
Triassic	Jurassic	Cretaceous	

0.3 m/1 ft

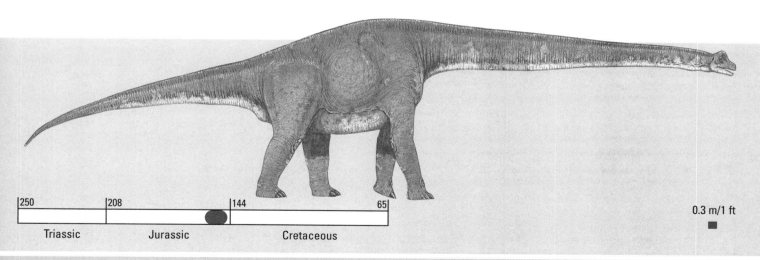

250	208	144	65
Triassic	Jurassic	Cretaceous	

0.3 m/1 ft

Camarasaurus

Camarasaurus was a very large four-legged plant eater, named for the hollow chambers in its spinal bones.

Its body was deep but fairly short, and most sauropods had a relatively longer neck and tail than this one. The front limbs were almost as long as the hind limbs, so its back was nearly level. Limbs like tree trunks and short, splayed, padded toes and fingers bore its weight. Like many sauropods it had large thumb claws.

The head was fairly big and deep, with nostril openings above and just in front of the eyes, and a muzzle rather like a bulldog's. Strong, chisel-shaped teeth rimmed its muscular jaws.

Camarasaurus could probably eat tough vegetation. Maybe it bit off and chopped up tough, fibrous fronds of cycadeoid trees, and even woody twigs, and branches.

Name *Camarasaurus*
Pronunciation *KAM-ah-rah-SORE-us*
Meaning *"Chambered lizard"*
Location *Western US and Portugal*
Length *18 m (59 ft)*
Food *Plants*
Period *Late Jurassic*
Order *Saurischia*
Suborder *Sauropodomorpha*
Infraorder *Sauropoda*
Family *Camarasauridae*

250	208	144	65
Triassic	Jurassic	Cretaceous	

0.3 m/1 ft

Carnotaurus

This big, bizarre theropod had a short, deep head with two horns sticking out sideways above the eyes, much like a cow's horns. Unlike cows' horns, though, these looked like short, stubby wings. Across the back of the braincase ran a crest that anchored jaw and neck muscles. Despite its powerful muscles, the lower jaw was slightly built, with slender teeth.

Other unusual features included forward-facing eyes, very short arms, vertebrae with wing-shaped projections, and rows of raised scales that ran along the back.

Scientists think that rival *Carnotaurus* males might have butted each other with their horned heads. More of a problem is how this dinosaur's weak-looking lower jaw and puny arms could have helped it to kill prey. Perhaps it hunted only young and sick sauropods and ate those that it found already dead.

Name *Carnotaurus*
Pronunciation *KAR-noh-TORE-us*
Meaning *"Meat [-eating] bull"*
Location *Patagonia, Argentina*
Length *7.5 m (25 ft)*
Food *Meat*
Period *Late Cretaceous*
Order *Saurischia*
Suborder *Theropoda*
Infraorder *Ceratosauria*
Family *Abelisauridae*

Caudipteryx

Twenty-five million years after dinosaurs seemingly gave rise to birds, long-legged "dinobirds" like this still lingered on in China. Turkey-sized *Caudipteryx* had birdlike, feathered wings and tail, yet the skull, hipbones, big toes, and other features were those of a theropod dinosaur.

Its unusual mixture of body parts also included a downy body covering; short arms with clawed fingers and long feathers; a fan of showy feathers sprouting from a brief bony tail; and a beak that was entirely toothless except for spiky buck teeth jutting from its upper tip.

Caudipteryx ran fast but could not fly. Its feathers had the wrong design and its wings were too short. Instead, the downy body feathers kept it warm, and males very likely fanned their tails and flapped their wings to show off to a rival or a mate. This dinobird ate plant foods, ground up by swallowed stones inside its gizzard.

Name *Caudipteryx*
Pronunciation *KOW-DIP-ter-iks*
Meaning *"Tail feather"*
Location *East Asia*
Height *70 cm (2 ft 4 in)*
Food *Plants*
Period *Early Cretaceous*
Order *Saurischia*
Family *Caudipteridae*
Suborder *Theropoda*
Infraorder *Tetanurae*

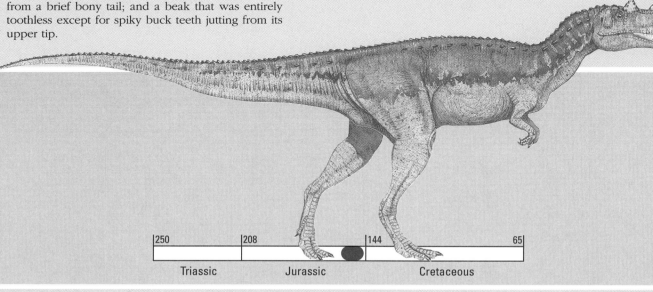

250		208		144		65
Triassic		Jurassic			Cretaceous	

0.3 m/1 ft

Cetiosaurus

Once considered very much like a whale, this was the first sauropod to be discovered and described.

Cetiosaurus was a very large, four-legged plant eater. No complete skeleton is known, but its head was very likely short and blunt. There was a fairly long neck, long back, bulky body, and rather short tail–all held up by limbs as thick as pillars.

This dinosaur's skeleton had some primitive features not seen in most other kinds of sauropod. For instance, its spinal bones had almost solid centers, instead of being hollowed out to cut down weight, nor were they forked at the top, like those of the more advanced sauropods.

Cetiosaurus could not raise its long neck high. Probably it cropped low-growing vegetation with its teeth, shaped like thick spoons with shallow bowls.

Name *Cetiosaurus*
Pronunciation *see-tie-oh-SORE-us*
Meaning *"Whalelike lizard"*
Location *Western Europe and possibly North Africa*
Length *18 m (59 ft)*
Food *Plants*
Period *Mid-Jurassic*
Order *Saurischia*

Suborder *Sauropodomorpha*
Infraorder *Sauropoda*
Family *Cetiosauridae*

250		208		144		65
Triassic		Jurassic			Cretaceous	

0.3 m/1 ft

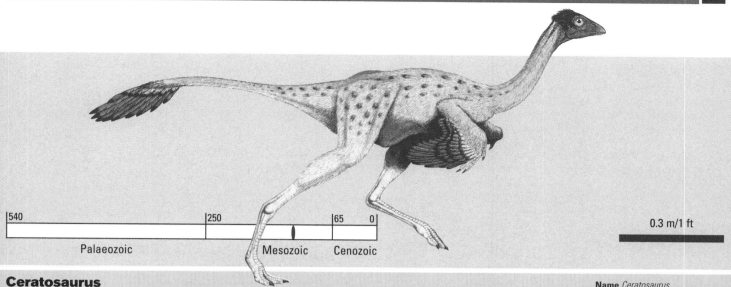

Ceratosaurus

A large bladelike nose horn and two low horns over its eyes inspired this dinosaur's name.

Ceratosaurus weighed about a ton; it was one of the largest of all the primitive theropod dinosaurs known as ceratosaurs.

This powerful killing machine had a big, deep head, with a lightly built skull, and huge, curved, bladelike teeth. Other weapons were the claws on its four-fingered hands and large three-toed feet. From its thick neck, small bony plates ran down a ridge on its back to a broad, deep tail.

Like the more advanced large theropod *Allosaurus*, *Ceratosaurus* chiefly roamed the fern meadows and riverside woodlands of what are now Colorado, Utah, and Wyoming. Its victims were most likely sick and young sauropods and the large ornithopod *Camptosaurus*.

Name *Ceratosaurus*
Pronunciation *Seh-rat-oh-SORE-us*
Meaning *"Horned lizard"*
Location *Western US and Tanzania*
Length *Up to 6 m (20 ft)*
Food *Meat*
Period *Late Jurassic*
Order *Saurischia*
Suborder *Theropoda*
Infraorder *Ceratosauria*
Family *Ceratosauridae*

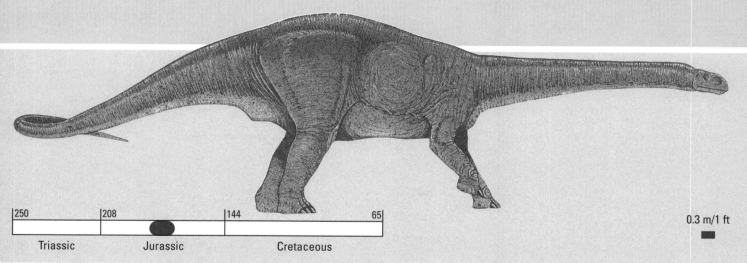

Chirostenotes

Slender hands earned this small birdlike theropod its name. Each hand had three long, thin fingers armed with long, slim claws. Each foot's three weight-bearing toes were also long and narrow. Females evidently had stronger feet and larger bodies than the males.

Upper foot bones tended to fuse together, as they do in birds. In fact the main three upper foot bones were squeezed so closely together that the middle bone was pinched in at the top. *Chirostenotes* shared this way of strengthening its feet with the far larger theropod *Tyrannosaurus*.

New finds made in the 1990s suggest that its nearest relatives included birdlike *Oviraptor*. Maybe this agile theropod chased lizards, or perhaps it used its narrow hands for prying insects out of holes in wood.

Chirostenotes lived late in the Age of Dinosaurs.

Name *Chirostenotes*
Pronunciation *kie-ROS-teh-NOH-teez*
Meaning *"Narrow hand"*
Location *Alberta, Canada*
Length *2 m (6 ft 6 in)*
Food *Small animals*
Period *Late Cretaceous*
Order *Saurischia*
Suborder *Theropoda*
Infraorder *Tetanurae*
Family *Caenagnathidae*

Coelophysis

Coelophysis was an early, lightweight, and bipedal hunting dinosaur that chased, seized, and ate big insects, lizards, and sometimes even its own young.

Coelophysis had a long, low head with a sharp narrow snout; a long flexible neck; long forelimbs; large, sharp-clawed hands; long sprinter's legs; a slim body; and a long tail held aloft to balance the front of the body.

Some individuals may have had head crests, and some had conical front teeth for seizing prey; other teeth were shaped like slashing blades. Strong and weaker individuals may represent males and females.

The discovery of hundreds of specimens killed by a flood suggests that *Coelophysis* roamed in packs.

Scientists studying this dinosaur reexamined one fossil and renamed it *Eucoelophysis*.

Name *Coelophysis*
Pronunciation *SEEL-oh-FIE-sis*
Meaning *"Hollow form"*
Location *Southwest US*
Length *Up to 3 m (10 ft)*
Food *Meat*
Period *Late Triassic*
Order *Saurischia*
Suborder *Theropoda*
Infraorder *Ceratosauria*
Family *Coelophysidae*

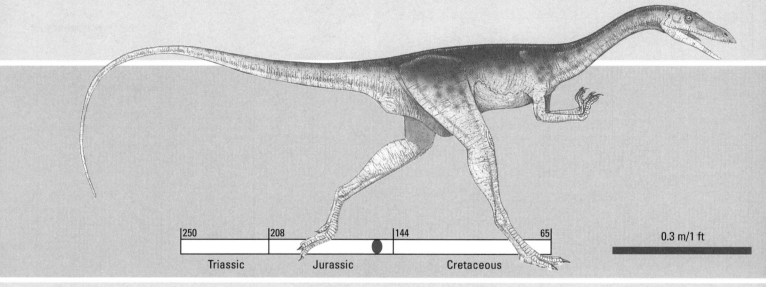

250	208	144	65	0.3 m/1 ft
Triassic	Jurassic	Cretaceous		

Deinocheirus

The bones of two gigantic, gangling forelimbs are our only clues to this theropod. *Deinocheirus* had longer arms than any known creature except *Therizinosaurus*.

Including its hand, each arm was longer than the tallest normal human. Bone for bone, the arms resemble those of *Ornithomimus* and other ostrich dinosaurs, but the hand was relatively wider than theirs, and its claws were stronger and more noticeably curved.

The owner of these amazing arms just might have been an ostrich dinosaur heavier than an elephant.

Some experts think *Deinocheirus* was a big-game hunter capable of ripping open a sauropod's belly with its claws; others think the claws were too blunt for that. An even more unlikely notion is that *Deinocheirus* used its claws as hooks for climbing trees, as sloths do now.

Name *Deinocheirus*
Pronunciation *DIE-noh-KIE-rus*
Meaning *"Terrible hand"*
Location *Mongolia*
Length *Uncertain*
Food *Probably plants and animals*
Period *Late Cretaceous*
Order *Saurischia*

Suborder *Theropoda*
Infraorder *Tetanurae*
Family *Deinocheiridae*

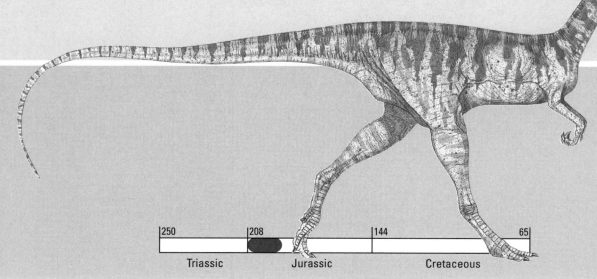

250	208	144	65	0.3 m/1 ft
Triassic	Jurassic	Cretaceous		

250   208   144   65

Triassic   Jurassic   Cretaceous

0.3 m/1 ft

Compsognathus

This little hunter was one of the smallest of all dinosaurs. A fully grown specimen was no bigger than a turkey.

Compsognathus had a long, narrow head with small, sharp teeth; a long, curved neck; a slim body; short arms with two-fingered or three-fingered hands; long legs with shins longer than thighs; and clawed, three-toed feet. The tail was also very long.

Some scientists think that this was merely a primitive tetanuran theropod. Yet some of its bones seem advanced in design and rather like a bird's.

Compsognathus lived on desert islands that are now parts of France and Germany. Because scientists found the skeleton of one individual that had swallowed a lizard, we know that it crept and darted about in the undergrowth, seizing and eating creatures small enough to cram into its mouth.

Name *Compsognathus*
Pronunciation *komp-SOG-na-thus*
Meaning *"Elegant jaw"*
Location *Southwest Germany and southeast France*
Length *Up to 1.4 m (4 ft 6 in)*
Food *Small animals*
Period *Late Jurassic*
Order *Saurischia*
Suborder *Theropoda*
Infraorder *Tetanurae*
Family *Compsognathidae*

250   208   144   65

Triassic   Jurassic   Cretaceous

length uncertain

Dilophosaurus

"Two-ridge lizard" had a pair of head crests, which looked a bit like halved plates. Males might have displayed these to rival males, the one with the biggest crests probably scared off his rivals. The winner would then mate with the females who lived on his land.

This was one of the lengthiest yet most lightly built of all the early meat-eating dinosaurs. Long legs and a very long, balancing tail made it speedy and agile. Perhaps it outran and killed early plant-eating dinosaurs.

Dilophosaurus could have struck out with its clawed toes and fingers as it bit into their flesh. But grappling with a big animal risked snapping off its frail head crests. Some scientists suppose it ate carrion instead of fighting.

The kink in its upper jaw and some other features show that *Dilophosaurus* belonged to the primitive theropods known as ceratosaurs.

Name *Dilophosaurus*
Pronunciation *die-loh-foh-SORE-us*
Meaning *"Two-ridge lizard"*
Location *Southwest US and maybe China*
Length *6 m (20 ft) or more*
Food *Meat*
Period *Early Jurassic*
Order *Saurischia*
Suborder *Theropoda*
Infraorder *Ceratosauria*
Family *Coelophysidae*

Diplodocus

Diplodocus is the longest dinosaur known from a whole skeleton. This sauropod grew longer than a tennis court, thanks to a snaky neck and an even lengthier tail. It might have whipped enemies with the tail's tapered tip.

For such a huge animal the low, sloping head seems tiny. Other odd features included weak, peg-shaped teeth only at the front of the jaws, and perhaps a spiny frill that ran down its back.

Despite its enormous length *Diplodocus* was gracefully designed and probably no heavier than two large elephants. Deep hollows in its backbone helped to reduce the weight supported by its limbs. These were less massive than those of heavyweights like *Brachiosaurus*.

Although it had a long neck, *Diplodocus* could only lift its head 4 meters (13 ft). Instead of nibbling treetops, it probably cropped low-growing ferns and shrubby trees.

Name *Diplodocus*
Pronunciation *di-PLOH-de-kus*
Meaning *"Double beam"*
Location *western US*
Length *27 m (88 ft)*
Food *Plants*
Period *Late Jurassic*
Order *Saurischia*
Suborder *Sauropodomorpha*
Infraorder *Sauropoda*
Family *Diplodocidae*

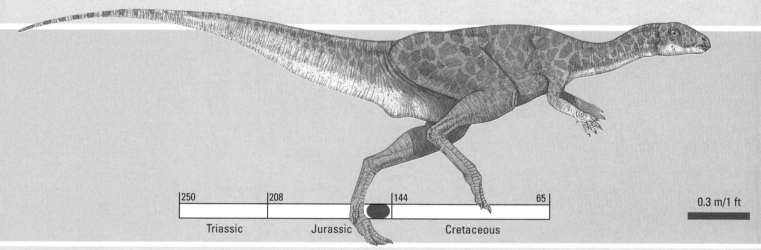

250	208	144	65
Triassic	Jurassic	Cretaceous	

0.3 m/1 ft

Dryptosaurus

Dryptosaurus is one of the few big flesh-eating dinosaurs found in eastern North America.

This large but lightly built theropod had a confusing mixture of features. Its curved teeth and claws resembled those of *Megalosaurus*, yet its thigh bones looked a bit like those of *Iguanodon*, a plant-eating dinosaur.

Its powerful arms bore very large, grasping claws, and the big, muscular legs had an "advanced" type of ankle unlike any other theropod's.

Dryptosaurus's discoverer thought this monster leapt upon its enemies. He called it *Laelaps*, after a mythological Greek dog that was turned to stone while leaping.

Dryptosaurus probably attacked and killed large plant-eating hadrosaurs (duck-billed dinosaurs).

Name *Dryptosaurus*
Pronunciation *drip-toh-SORE-us*
Meaning *"Tearing lizard"*
Location *Eastern North America*
Length *6 m (19 ft 6 in)*
Food *Meat*
Period *Late Cretaceous*
Order *Saurischia*
Suborder *Theropoda*
Infraorder *Tetanurae*
Family *Dryptosauridae*

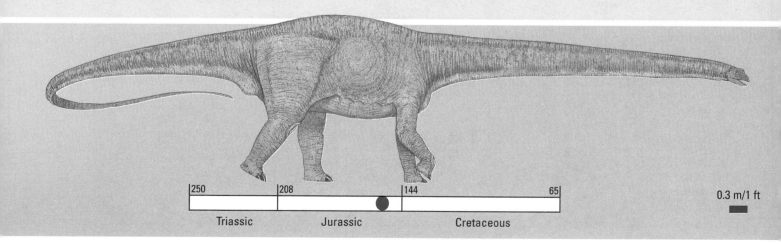

250	208	144	65
Triassic	Jurassic	Cretaceous	

0.3 m/1 ft

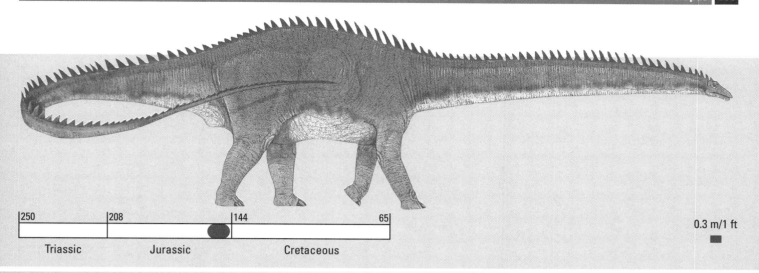

250	208	144	65

Triassic   Jurassic   Cretaceous

0.3 m/1 ft

Dryosaurus

Dryosaurus was a two-legged plant eater like little *Hypsilophodon* but was as long as a small car. Half its length or more was in its long, stiffened tail.

This dinosaur had a small, narrow head with large eyes and cheek pouches. Its tall, ridged, self-sharpening cheek teeth could cut and chew the leaves cropped by its beak.

Like *Hypsilophodon*, *Dryosaurus* had short arms but long legs. Their elongated shins and toes show

that this dinosaur could sprint. Running away would have been its only defense against hungry meat-eating dinosaurs.

Apart from being larger, *Dryosaurus* differed from *Hypsilophodon* in several ways. For instance, its head was smaller for its body size and the front upper jaw was toothless. Some bones of its skull, arms, thighs, and legs also showed distinctive features.

Name *Dryosaurus*
Pronunciation *DRY-oh-SORE-us*
Meaning *"Tree lizard"*
Location *Western US and East Africa*
Length *3.5 m (10 ft)*
Food *Plants*
Period *Late Jurassic*
Order *Ornithischia*
Suborder *Ornithopoda*
Infraorder *Euornithopoda*
Family *Dryosauridae*

250	208	144	65

Triassic   Jurassic   Cretaceous

0.3 m/1 ft

Euhelopus

Euhelopus was a plant eater with a small head, very long neck, long tail, four feet, and massive body.

Parts of it resemble sauropods from three different families. Like *Camarasaurus* it had a short, steep-snouted skull and strong teeth. Like *Diplodocus* it had spinal bones with split projections and "skids" below its tail bones, as if to shield blood vessels if its tail dragged on the ground. Like *Brachiosaurus* it had long forelimbs compared to the hind limbs.

Euhelopus's most distinctive features were its delicately designed skull bones and remarkable neck, which measured an astonishing 5 meters (16 ft).

Arguably such features put *Euhelopus* and several other dinosaurs in their own family of sauropods, called euhelopodids. These sauropods lived only in East Asia.

Name *Euhelopus*
Pronunciation *YOU-hel-OH-pus*
Meaning *"Good marsh foot"*
Location *China*
Length *15 m (49 ft)*
Food *Plants*
Period *Late Jurassic*
Order *Saurischia*
Suborder *Sauropodomorpha*
Infraorder *Sauropoda*
Family *Euhelopodidae*

Euoplocephalus

This large, four-legged, plant-eating ornithischian was one of the most heavily armored of all dinosaurs.

Euoplocephalus had a broad, heavy body; short neck; sturdy limbs; and a long tail held off the ground. Its reinforced skull was at least as wide as long, with a broad, toothless beak and convoluted nasal passages.

Everything except its underside was armored. The head had bony horns, and thick bone patterned like crazy paving formed the skull roof. There were even bony eyelids that flipped down like shutters to protect its eyes. Short, pointed, horn-sheathed, and bony plates jutted from the shoulders and back. Bands of hollow-based plates set in the skin ran across the back and tail to protect them yet also allowed some flexibility. The swollen tail tip formed a heavy bony club. Swung from side to side, it might have knocked even an attacking tyrannosaurid off its feet.

Name *Euoplocephalus*
Pronunciation *YEW-oh-ploh-SEF-a-lus*
Meaning *"Well-protected head"*
Location *Alberta, Canada*
Length *6 m (20 ft)*
Food *Plants*
Period *Late Cretaceous*
Order *Ornithischia*
Suborder *Thyreophora*
Infraorder *Ankylosauria*
Family *Ankylosauridae*

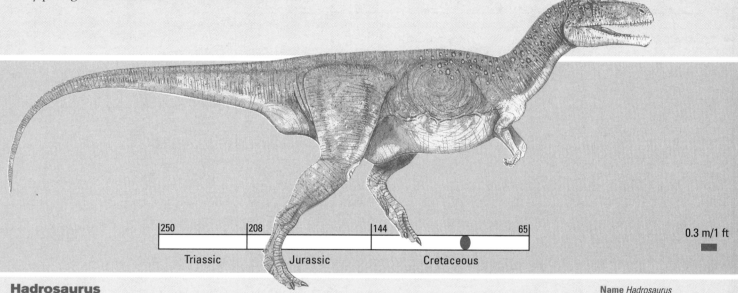

250	208	144	65
Triassic	Jurassic	Cretaceous	

0.3 m/1 ft

Hadrosaurus

Hadrosaurus was a large bipedal or quadrupedal plant eater with a toothless beak and batteries of cheek teeth. It belonged to the hadrosaurine hadrosaurs—duck-billed dinosaurs, with either a flat head or a solid bony head crest.

This ornithopod's skull might have had a bony arch between its nostrils. Such a ridge possibly supported skin flaps that blew up like balloons to amplify its calls.

Hadrosaurus had a wide, flat, toothless beak for cropping vegetation. Inside its powerful jaws, hundreds of self-sharpening cheek teeth formed ridged pavements that pulped the leaves and twigs cropped by its beak.

Hadrosaurids had relatively longer limbs and deeper tails than their likely forebears, such as *Iguanodon*. Unlike that dinosaur, *Hadrosaurus* had only four fingers on each hand, all cushioned in a padded paw.

Name *Hadrosaurus*
Pronunciation *HAD-roh-SORE-us*
Meaning *"Big lizard"*
Location *New Jersey*
Length *7 m (33 ft)*
Food *Plants*
Period *Late Cretaceous*
Order *Ornithischia*
Suborder *Ornithopoda*
Infraorder *Euornithopoda*
Family *Hadrosauridae*

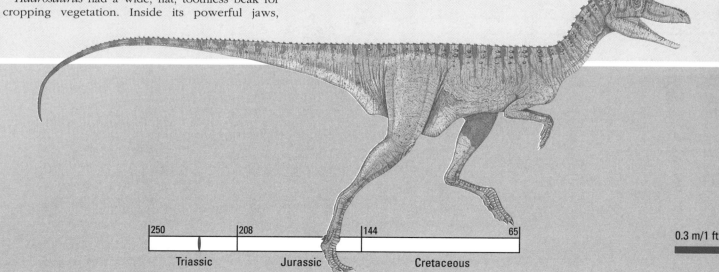

250	208	144	65
Triassic	Jurassic	Cretaceous	

0.3 m/1 ft

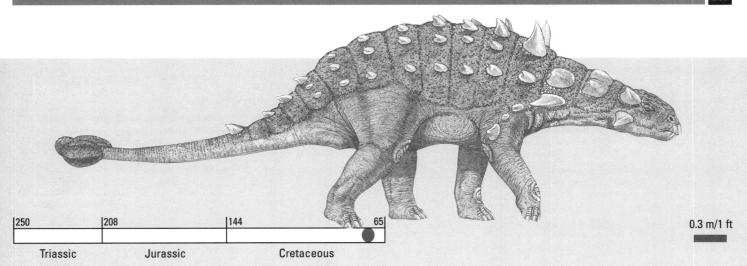

250	208	144	65
Triassic	Jurassic	Cretaceous	

0.3 m/1 ft

Giganotosaurus

In 1994 Argentinian paleontologists stunned the world with news of the discovery of a flesh-eating dinosaur more massive, yet far older, than *Tyrannosaurus*.

Giganotosaurus was heavier and more powerfully built than that terrifying predator. It could have weighed 8 tons. The theropod's huge head alone measured more than 1.5 meters (about 5 ft), and the vast jaws bore fangs longer than a man's hand.

Hurrying along on its great hind limbs, *Giganotosaurus* could have caught and killed herbivores even bigger than itself, living on the floodplain where it roamed. Maybe it stretched out its short, sturdy arms to grapple with medium-sized sauropods, such as *Andesaurus*. *Giganotosaurus*'s teeth would have stabbed through the tough hide of its victims and chopped out mighty mouthfuls of meaty muscle, to be swallowed whole.

Name *Giganotosaurus*
Pronunciation *JIE-GA-noh-toh-SORE-us*
Meaning *"Giant southern lizard"*
Location *western Argentina*
Length *12.5 m (41 ft)*
Food *Meat*
Period *Early Late Cretaceous*
Order *Saurischia*
Suborder *Theropoda*
Infraorder *Tetanurae*
Family *Carcharodontosauridae*

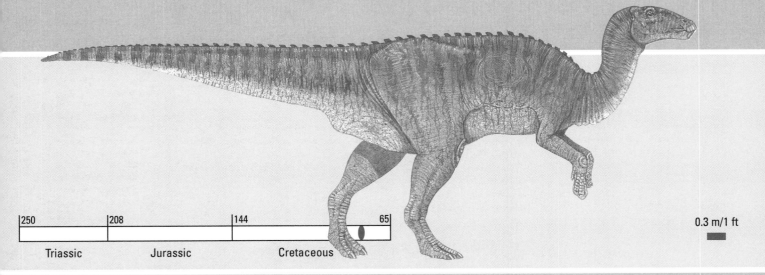

250	208	144	65
Triassic	Jurassic	Cretaceous	

0.3 m/1 ft

Herrerasaurus

Herrerasaurus was one of the earliest known hunting dinosaurs–a formidable beast as big as a small car.

Like *Staurikosaurus* it had curved, pointed teeth and long claws, but it also had a shorter neck, distinctive hip and leg bones, and thighs longer than shins. Each hand had a sharp-clawed thumb that swung in to help two clawed fingers seize prey. The other two fingers were stubs.

In some ways *Herrerasaurus* was surprisingly advanced. Double-hinged jaws helped the theropod

grip victims tightly in order to bite and bolt down big mouthfuls of flesh. Also some of this dinosaur's bones were surprisingly birdlike, especially its straplike shoulder blade, hip joint, and the backward-angled pubic bones.

Herrerasaurus hunted plant-eating reptiles that lived in the woody countryside beside South American rivers.

Name *Herrerasaurus*
Pronunciation *Eh-ray-ra-SORE-us*
Meaning *"Herrera's lizard"*
Location *Northwest Argentina*
Length *4.2 m (14 ft 9 in)*
Food *Meat*
Period *Late Triassic*
Order *Saurischia*
Suborder *Possibly Theropoda*
Infraorder *Unclassified*
Family *Herrerasauridae*

Heterodontosaurus

Heterodontosaurus was a lightly built plant eater with a skull no bigger than a rabbit's.

This early ornithischian had a remarkable variety of teeth. There were small, sharp teeth in the front upper jaw; tall cheek teeth with crowns like chisel blades; and, in between, four pointed canine teeth. In males, at least, both lower canines formed wicked-looking tusks that slotted into sockets in the upper jaw. As in other ornithischians, the lower jaw ended in a toothless beak.

Arms were sturdy, wrists flexible, and there were five long fingers on each hand. Legs had long sprinters' shins, and each foot had three long, forward-facing toes. Bony rods stiffened the back, hips, and tapered tail.

Heterodontosaurus probably walked and browsed on all fours but could run fast on its hind limbs.

Name *Heterodontosaurus*
Pronunciation *HET-er-oh-DON-toh-SORE-us*
Meaning *"Different teeth lizard"*
Location *Southern Africa*
Length *1.2 m (4 ft)*
Food *Plants and maybe insects*
Period *Early Jurassic*
Order *Ornithischia*
Suborder *Ornithopoda*
Infraorder *Unclassified*
Family *Heterodontosauridae*

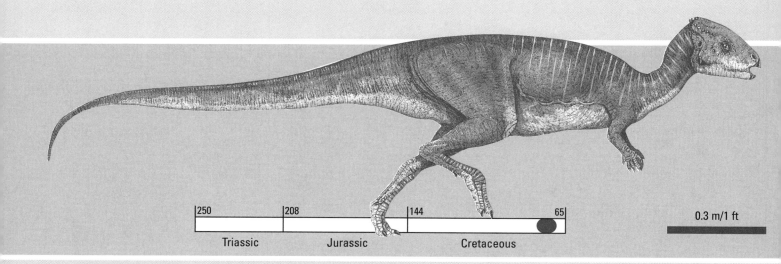

250	208	144	65
Triassic	Jurassic	Cretaceous	

0.3 m/1 ft

Huayangosaurus

Spiky-backed *Huayangosaurus* belonged to a group of early plated dinosaurs that lived in China, where that type of dinosaur perhaps arose.

Like all plated dinosaurs, *Huayangosaurus* was a four-legged plant eater with a bulky body; small, low-slung head; and two rows of bony armor on its back.

Huayangosaurus seems to have been more primitive than such later relatives as *Stegosaurus*. It was much smaller than that dinosaur. Also, *Huayangosaurus* had front teeth instead of a

toothless beak, for cropping leaves. Then, too, its front limbs were relatively longer than those of *Stegosaurus*. And, instead of bony plates, rows of bony spikes stuck up to shield its neck and back and halfway down its tail. Like *Stegosaurus*, though, this early plated dinosaur seemingly had two long shoulder spikes and four long spikes guarding the tip of its tail.

Name *Huayangosaurus*
Pronunciation *hoy-ANG-oh-SORE-us*
Meaning *"Huayang [Sichuan] lizard"*
Location *Sichuan, China*
Length *4.6 m (15 ft)*
Food *Plants*
Period *Mid-Jurassic*
Order *Ornithischia*
Suborder *Thyreophora*
Infraorder *Stegosauria*
Family *Huayangosauridae*

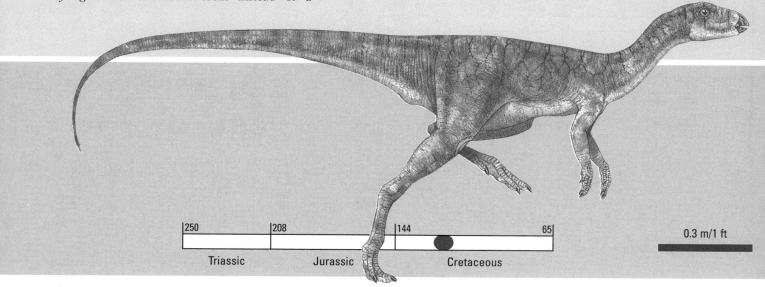

250	208	144	65
Triassic	Jurassic	Cretaceous	

0.3 m/1 ft

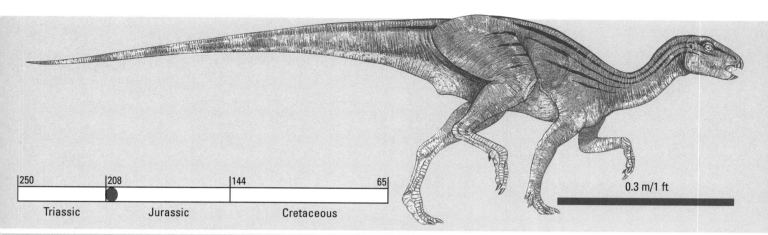

250	208	144	65
Triassic	Jurassic	Cretaceous	

0.3 m/1 ft

Homalocephale

Homalocephale was a flat-headed relative of dome-headed ornithischians, such as *Pachycephalosaurus*.

Like those dinosaurs, *Homalocephale* had a thick skull with rows of knobs and a shelf at the back. It was also a two-legged plant eater with arms much shorter than its legs, and it would have walked with its head held forward, its back level, and its stiffened tail held well above the ground.

However, *Homalocephale* was much smaller than *Pachycephalosaurus*. Then, too, instead of being domed, its skull was flattened on top. This makes scientists suppose that rival males fought in a different way from the dome-headed dinosaurs. Instead of butting one another's flanks, like bison, *Homalocephale* males quite likely pushed against each other, standing head-to-head, like marine iguanas.

Name *Homalocephale*
Pronunciation *HOME-a-loh-SEF-a-lee*
Meaning *"Level head"*
Location *Mongolia*
Length *2 m (6 ft 6 in)*
Food *Plants*
Period *Late Cretaceous*
Order *Ornithischia*
Suborder *Marginocephalia*
Infraorder *Pachycephalosauria*
Family *Homalocephalidae*

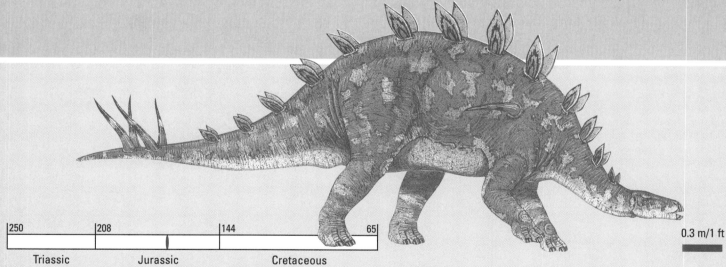

250	208	144	65
Triassic	Jurassic	Cretaceous	

0.3 m/1 ft

Hypsilophodon

This small, speedy plant eater was the dinosaur equivalent of those agile mammals, the gazelles.

Hypsilophodon had a small head, large eyes, strong jaws, and a horny beak with upper teeth. This beak cropped leaves, perhaps then stored in cheek pouches before being mashed up by self-sharpening cheek teeth. As its flexible jaws closed, top and bottom teeth slid sideways against each other with an effective shearing motion.

Powerful hind limbs with long shins and feet show that *Hypsilophodon* could run extremely fast. Its stiffened tail acted as a balancer if it had to dodge from side to side to escape a chasing theropod.

This ornithopod had five-fingered hands and four forward-facing toes. More advanced kinds of ornithopod had only four fingers and three toes.

Name *Hypsilophodon*
Pronunciation *HIP-si-LOH-foh-don*
Meaning *"High ridge tooth"*
Location *UK, Spain, and South Dakota*
Length *2.3 m (7 ft 6 in)*
Food *Plants*
Period *Early Cretaceous*
Order *Ornithischia*
Suborder *Ornithopoda*
Infraorder *Euornithopoda*
Family *Hypsilophodontidae*

Iguanodon

Iguanodon was built much like *Camptosaurus*, but it had more teeth, relatively bigger arms, straighter thigh bones, and other differences. Also, at least one of the several species grew much larger than *Camptosaurus*.

Iguanodon had a fairly large head, long snout, and tightly packed, ridged cheek teeth. Possibly there was a long, prehensile tongue for pulling leafy twigs into its mouth to be snipped off by its toothless beak.

The large, muscular hind limbs with three-toed feet were capable of supporting its heavy body. However, it seems likely that *Iguanodon* often walked on all fours because the shoulders, arms, and sturdy fingers tipped with hooflike claws could bear considerable weight.

This ornithopod had big, sharp thumb spikes capable of stabbing a rival *Iguanodon* or an aggressive theropod.

Name *Iguanodon*
Pronunciation *ig-WAH-noh-don*
Meaning *"Iguana tooth"*
Location *Western Europe and western US*
Length *10 m (33 ft)*
Food *Plants*
Period *Early Cretaceous*
Order *Ornithischia*
Suborder *Ornithopoda*
Infraorder *Euornithopoda*
Family *Iguanodontidae*

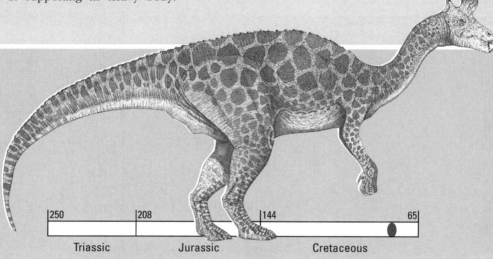

250	208	144	65
Triassic	Jurassic	Cretaceous	

0.3 m/1 ft

Lesothosaurus

This lightly built, bipedal plant eater was one of the smallest and most primitive of all the ornithischians.

Lesothosaurus's fairly long neck supported a small head with big eyes and a long snout. The lower jaw ended in a toothless beak, but the upper jaw had small front teeth. Most ornithischians lacked these. Also, its leaf-shaped cheek teeth were not set in from the edges of its jaws like theirs, so perhaps it had no roomy cheeks to store food as it ate. Then, too, its jaws' simple up-and-down motion meant teeth could only crush, not chew.

The arms were short, with five-fingered hands. The legs were long, with four-toed feet. Bony tendons stiffened the long tail, which balanced the head and body as it ran.

Lesothosaurus nibbled low-growing shrubs, but it was always ready to dash away from danger.

Name *Lesothosaurus*
Pronunciation *le-SOH-thoh-SORE-us*
Meaning *"Lesotho lizard"*
Location *Southern Africa and Venezuela*
Length *1 m (3 ft 3 in)*
Food *Plants and maybe insects*
Period *Early Jurassic*
Order *Ornithischia*
Suborder *Unclassified*
Infraorder *Unclassified*
Family *Lesothosauridae*

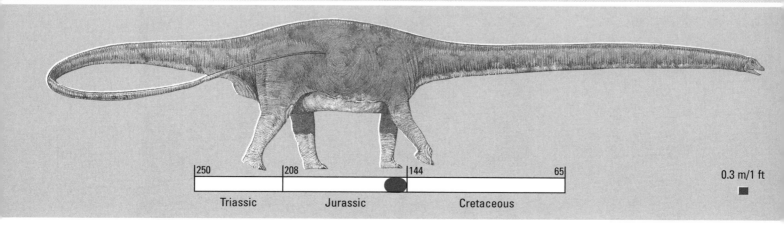

250	208	144	65
Triassic	Jurassic	Cretaceous	

0.3 m/1 ft

250	208	144	65		0.3 m/1 ft
Triassic	Jurassic	Cretaceous			

Lambeosaurus

Lambeosaurus was one of the largest hadrosaurids, or duck-billed dinosaurs. It belonged to the lambeosaurines, a subgroup with hollow head crests and relatively short lower jaws.

This huge bipedal/quadrupedal plant eater had pebbly skin, a toothless beak, hundreds of cheek teeth, and a hatchet-shaped skull crest. The crest's backward-pointing bony spike might have anchored a neck frill.

Inside the crest were two airways connected to the nostrils. Possibly they helped to give this dinosaur a distinctive voice or intensified its sense of smell.

The several species of *Lambeosaurus* had somewhat differently shaped crests. However, some large-crested and small-crested individuals turn out to have been males, females and young of a single species.

Name *Lambeosaurus*
Pronunciation *LAM-be-oh-SORE-us*
Meaning *"Lambe's lizard"*
Location *Western North America*
Length *Up to 15 m (49 ft)*
Food *Plants*
Period *Late Cretaceous*
Order *Ornithischia*
Suborder *Ornithopoda*
Infraorder *Euornithopoda*
Family *Hadrosauridae*

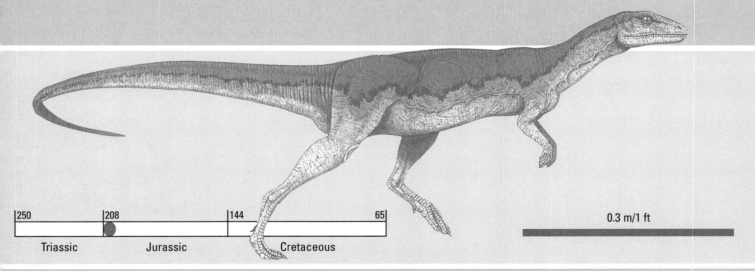

250	208	144	65		0.3 m/1 ft
Triassic	Jurassic	Cretaceous			

Mamenchisaurus

The Chinese sauropod *Mamenchisaurus* had the longest neck of any animal that ever lived. One species' neck might have measured an unbelievable 15 meters (49 ft). This is the biggest dinosaur yet found in Asia.

Supporting *Mamenchisaurus*'s long neck were 19 cervical vertebrae–more neck bones than in any other sauropod. Below these vertebrae, long, overlapping, rodlike ribs helped make the neck both straight and stiff.

Some people have supposed that *Mamenchisaurus* could lift its long, light neck to browse on treetops. Others think it ate low-growing plants, swinging the neck from side to side to gather up fern fronds and other vegetation.

Mamenchisaurus shared some of *Diplodocus*'s features but probably belonged to a different family, along with other very long-necked Chinese sauropods.

Name *Mamenchisaurus*
Pronunciation *mah-MEN-chi-SORE-us*
Meaning *"Mamen Brook lizard"*
Location *China*
Length *25 m (82 ft)*
Food *Plants*
Period *Late Jurassic*
Order *Saurischia*
Suborder *Sauropodomorpha*
Infraorder *Sauropoda*
Family *Possibly Euhelopodidae*

Megalosaurus

Megalosaurus was a large, heavily built, two-legged predator that weighed a ton or more.

The monster had a massive head and jaws armed with large, curved, flattened, saw-edged teeth. Its neck was strong and thick. The arms and legs were muscular, with formidable talons on the three-toed feet and three-fingered hands.

Megalosaurus could have seized prey in its clawed hands and feet while taking great bites. Slow-moving thyreophorans might have been its chief victims.

Megalosaurus was one of the first dinosaurs to be named and described, in 1824. Only bits of its skeleton were known, so at first people had little idea what it looked like. One lifesize model showed this two-legged beast on all fours, as if it were a giant, stockily built lizard.

Name *Megalosaurus*
Pronunciation *MEGA-loh-SORE-us*
Meaning *"Great lizard"*
Location *Western Europe*
Length *8 m (26 ft)*
Food *Meat*
Period *Mid-Jurassic*
Order *Saurischia*
Suborder *Theropoda*
Infraorder *Tetanurae*
Family *Megalosauridae*

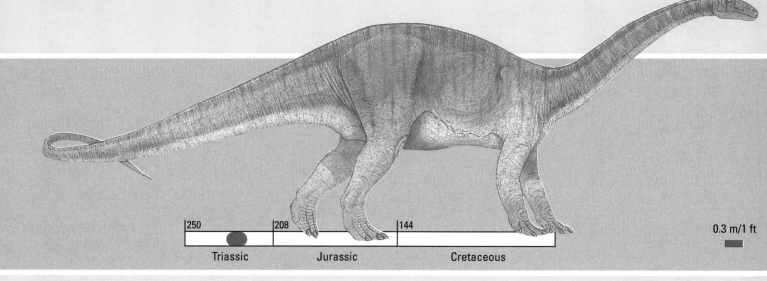

250 | 208 | 144

Triassic | Jurassic | Cretaceous

0.3 m/1 ft

Microceratops

No bigger than a one-year-old child, little *Microceratops* was one of the smallest of all dinosaurs. It was one of the last ceratopsians, yet one of the most primitive.

This horned dinosaur had a skull with a sharp parrotlike beak and a long, bony shelf at the back, but probably no nose horn or horns on its brows. Instead of cheeks, horny sheaths might have covered the jaws, as some scientists believe they did in all the ornithischian dinosaurs.

Microceratops was more delicately built than its mostly much larger relatives. Its head was smaller than theirs compared to the rest of the body, and its limb bones were relatively slimmer. The front limbs were long but the hind limbs were much longer.

Microceratops probably walked on all fours, but to escape predators it reared on its hind limbs and ran.

Name *Microceratops*
Pronunciation *MY-kroh-SERRA-tops*
Meaning *"Tiny horned face"*
Location *China and Mongolia*
Length *76 cm (2 ft 6 in)*
Food *Plants*
Period *Late Cretaceous*
Order *Ornithischia*
Suborder *Marginocephalia*
Infraorder *Ceratopsia*
Family *Protoceratopsidae*

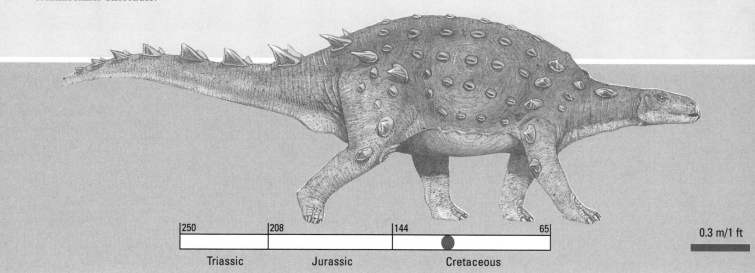

250 | 208 | 144 | 65

Triassic | Jurassic | Cretaceous

0.3 m/1 ft

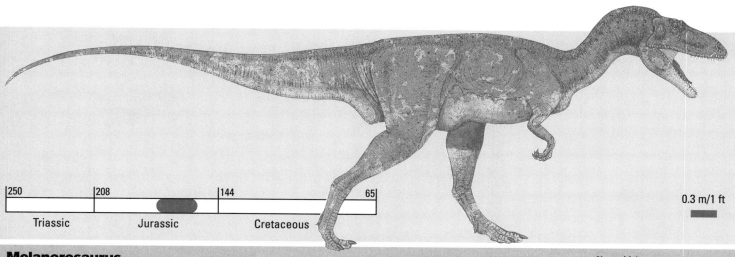

| 250 | 208 | 144 | 65 |
| Triassic | Jurassic | Cretaceous | |

0.3 m/1 ft

Melanorosaurus

The very early prosauropod *Melanorosaurus* grew as big as some of the gigantic sauropods.

Like other prosauropods it had a small head with serrated, leaf-shaped teeth, and a fairly long neck and tail. But its great body and sturdy limbs made it even more bulky and ponderous than sizable *Plateosaurus,* a beast better known from more complete remains. It must have walked and run on all fours, never rearing to hurry.

Limb bones were massive and weighty, like sauropod limb bones. But, like most sauropods' vertebrae, its spinal bones had hollows that helped to reduce weight.

Melanorosaurus lived well before the first known sauropod. You might think sauropods came from big prosauropods like this. Yet differences in the design of their ankle bones make some suppose that prosauropods and sauropods merely shared the same ancestor.

Name *Melanorosaurus*
Pronunciation *meh-LAN-oh-roh-SORE-us*
Meaning *"Black mountain lizard"*
Location *South Africa*
Length *12 m (40 ft)*
Food *Plants*
Period *Late Triassic*
Order *Saurischia*
Suborder *Sauropodomorpha*
Infraorder *Prosauropoda*
Family *Melanorosauridae*

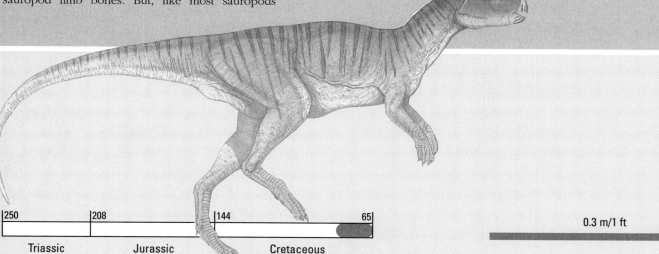

| 250 | 208 | 144 | 65 |
| Triassic | Jurassic | Cretaceous | |

0.3 m/1 ft

Minmi

This four-legged, armored plant eater was not only the first ankylosaur ever found in the southern half of the world but was also unique in several ways.

Horn-covered bony plates protected most of its body from the sharp teeth and claws of flesh-eating dinosaurs. Armor plating covered its skull, neck and shoulders. Rows of scutes (bony plates) ran down its back and flanks. Low, sharp plates stuck out from its hips, and thorn-shaped plates protected the tail. Bony plates also protected the shins.

One remarkable find was the mass of small scutes protecting its belly. Another was its unique system of bony rods reinforcing its spine.

Minmi had a low head, like a turtle's. Its narrow beak snipped off low-growing plants to be chewed up by its little, leaf-shaped cheek teeth.

Name *Minmi*
Pronunciation *min-MY*
Meaning *"Minmi [Crossing]"*
Location *Queensland, Australia*
Length *3 m (10 ft)*
Food *Plants*
Period *Early Cretaceous*
Order *Ornithischia*
Suborder *Thyreophora*
Infraorder *Ankylosauria*
Family *Unclassified*

Noasaurus

This small South American predator in one way resembled those advanced killing machines the dromaeosaurids of northern continents. The second toe of each foot had a large, sharp, curved claw that it could flick forward for slashing an enemy, or pull back and up out of the way for walking. Yet the tendon that pulled the claw back was not arranged like a dromaeosaurid's tendon. This shows that *Noasaurus* must have evolved its switchblade claw independently.

The neck bones, fairly deep head, and lightly built jaws recall those of an abelisaurid–a much less advanced kind of theropod than the dromaeosaurids. Perhaps *Noasaurus* was a late survival of a group of theropods designed on old-fashioned lines.

This agile hunter might have hunted in packs, killing creatures up to the size of young sauropods.

Location *Northwest Argentina*
Length *1.8 m (6 ft)*
Food *Meat*
Period *Late Cretaceous*
Order *Saurischia*
Suborder *Theropoda*
Infraorder *Ceratosauria*
Family *Noasauridae*

Name *Noasaurus*
Pronunciation *NOH-a-SORE-us*
Meaning *"Noa [Northwest Argentina] lizard"*

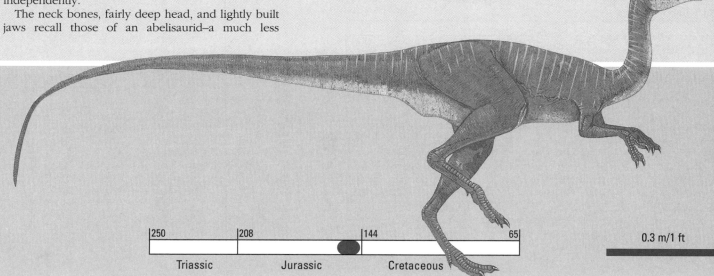

250	208	144	65
Triassic	Jurassic	Cretaceous	

0.3 m/1 ft

Ornithomimus

Ornithomimus was very ostrichlike. It had a small light head, a rather big brain, large eyes, and a narrow, toothless beak. The neck was long, slim, curved, and mobile. There was a compact body, and its sprinter's legs had muscular thighs shorter than the shins.

In other ways, *Ornithomimus* was unmistakably a dinosaur. Instead of wings it had long, thin arms with clawed, three-fingered hands that might have served as a hook. Its tail was long, stiff, and fleshy and had a bony core. Held level with its back, the tail balanced *Ornithomimus's* head, neck, arms, and body when it ran.

Ostrich dinosaurs probably ate plants and maybe insects and small reptiles. If attacked by a big meat-eating dinosaur, they might have lashed out with their long clawed toes. But a fast getaway was their best defense–*Ornithomimus* could run as quickly as a horse.

Name *Ornithomimus*
Pronunciation *OR-nee-thoh-MEEM-us*
Meaning *"Bird mimic"*
Location *Western US and Canada*
Length *3.5 m (12 ft)*
Food *Plants and small animals*
Period *Late Cretaceous*
Order *Saurischia*
Suborder *Theropoda*
Infraorder *Tetanurae*
Family *Ornithomimidae*

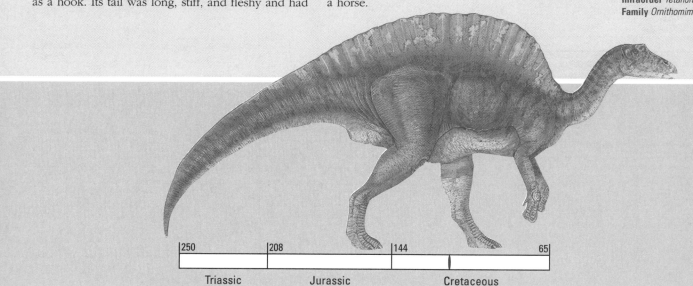

250	208	144	65
Triassic	Jurassic	Cretaceous	

0.3 m/1 ft

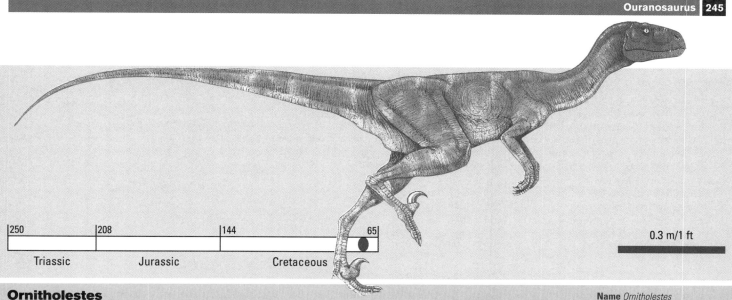

| Triassic | Jurassic | Cretaceous |

0.3 m/1 ft

Ornitholestes

This slender, bipedal predator belonged to the group of theropods that included the ancestors of birds.

Ornitholestes had a low, narrow head with sharp-toothed jaws, large nostrils, and probably a crest or horn on its snout. Neck, arms, and legs were long. Each foot had three main, clawed toes and each hand had three fingers with strongly curved claws. *Ornitholestes*' paired pubic hip bones ended in "boots"; this was a more advanced design than you find in *Compsognathus*, another small theropod that lived about the same time.

Ornitholestes would have been a speedy hunter, capable of chasing and seizing small birds, lizards, pterosaur, and mammals.

Perhaps this dinosaur also scavenged meat from the kills of larger predators, as jackals and hyenas do today.

Name *Ornitholestes*
Pronunciation *OR-ni-thoh-LES-teez*
Meaning *"Bird robber"*
Location *Western US*
Length *Up to 2 m (6 ft 6 in)*
Food *Meat*
Period *Late Jurassic*
Order *Saurischia*
Suborder *Theropoda*
Infraorder *Tetanurae*
Family *Coeluridae*

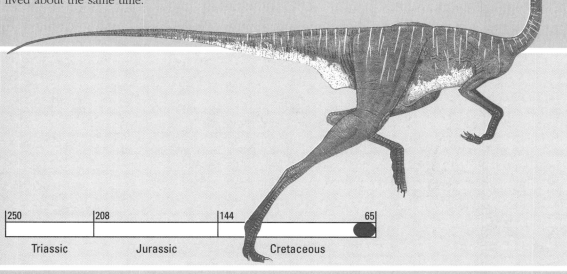

| 250 | 208 | 144 | 65 |

| Triassic | Jurassic | Cretaceous |

0.3 m/1 ft

Ouranosaurus

Ouranosaurus broadly resembled *Iguanodon*. Both of these plant eaters had high-crowned cheek teeth; long, strong hind limbs; hoof-shaped nails on toes and fingers; and spiky thumbs. But there were also remarkable differences.

Ouranosaurus had a tall ridge on its back, held up by bladelike spines that rose from its vertebrae. If these spines formed a skin sail, this might have helped its body to warm up when *Ouranosaurus* turned broadside to the Sun. If the ridge was a fat-filled hump, its purpose was to store food and help keep the body cool. Or perhaps males used their tall backs for showing off.

Other differences included aspects of the head. *Ouranosaurus's* flat-topped skull had bumps over the eyes and sloped evenly down to a low, narrow, flared beak like a duck's.

This dinosaur lived at the same time and in the same part of Africa as ridge-backed relatives of the theropod *Spinosaurus*.

Name *Ouranosaurus*
Pronunciation *oo-RAN-oh-SORE-us*
Meaning *"Brave [monitor] lizard"*
Location *Niger*
Length *7 m (23 ft)*
Food *Plants*
Period *Early Cretaceous*
Order *Ornithischia*
Suborder *Ornithopoda*
Infraorder *Euornithopoda*
Family *Maybe Iguanodontidae*

Oviraptor

Oviraptor's body was much like that of other birdlike, running theropods. Its head, though, was bizarre.

The short, deep skull was crested like a cassowary's, maybe for display. The toothless beak rather resembled a parrot's, but two small, sharp, bony points jutted down from the mouth's roof, perhaps for crushing shells.

Oviraptor's tail was short, but its legs were long and powerful with effectively three-toed feet. It had a wrist and wishbone rather like a bird's, and birdlike features in its hips. Each finger had a huge, sharp, hooked claw.

Paleontologists once thought *Oviraptor* stole and ate *Protoceratops* eggs. Then they found a nestful of such eggs beneath an *Oviraptor* that had died trying to protect them from a storm. So it seems that *Oviraptor* laid and incubated eggs, much as ostriches and emus do.

Name *Oviraptor*
Pronunciation *OHVE-i-RAP-tor*
Meaning *"Egg robber"*
Location *Mongolia*
Length *1.8 m (6 ft)*
Food *Fruits, eggs, or small animals*
Period *Late Cretaceous*
Order *Saurischia*

Suborder *Theropoda*
Infraorder *Tetanurae*
Family *Oviraptoridae*

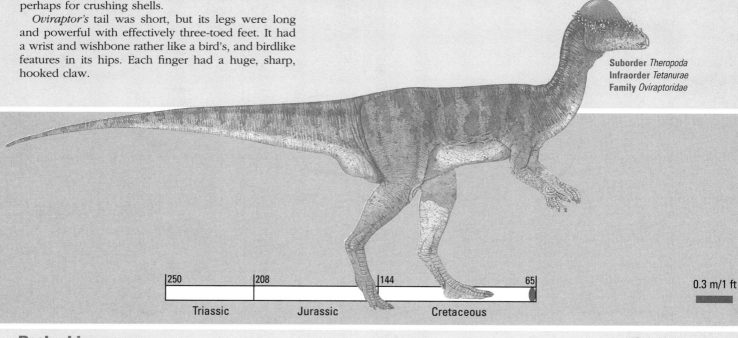

250	208	144	65
Triassic	Jurassic	Cretaceous	

0.3 m/1 ft

Pachyrhinosaurus

Pachyrhinosaurus was a horned dinosaur but had thick lumps of spongy bone instead of horns on its face. Up to 2 meters (6 ft 6 in) high at the hips, it was the biggest of the short-frilled horned dinosaurs, or centrosaurines.

This heavily built, four-legged plant eater had a large, low head with jaws ending in a deep, narrow, toothless beak. There was a big flattish bony lump above its nostrils, and a smaller lump above each eye. Two short horns curved forward from the back

of its bony neck frill, and a short spike stuck up from its center.

Scientists suppose that rival males met head to head to use the bony lump above the nose in pushing contests.

Fossil finds suggest that herds made regular migrations to Arctic feeding grounds. In Alberta, a flood apparently once drowned a migrating herd of up to 1,000 *Pachyrhinosaurus*.

Name *Pachyrhinosaurus*
Pronunciation *PAK-ee-RYE-noh-SORE-us*
Meaning *"Thick nose lizard"*
Location *Alberta, Canada and Alaska, US*
Length *6.5 m (21 ft 4 in)*
Food *Plants*
Period *Late Cretaceous*
Order *Ornithischia*
Suborder *Marginocephalia*
Infraorder *Ceratopsia*
Family *Ceratopsidae*

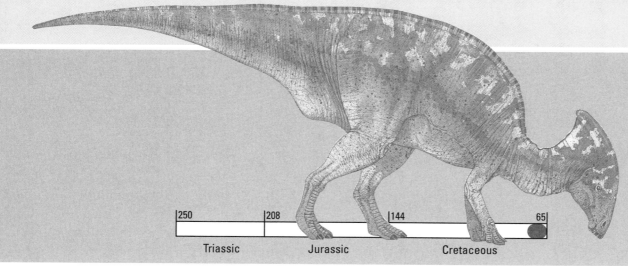

250	208	144	65
Triassic	Jurassic	Cretaceous	

0.3 m/1 ft

250	208	144	65
Triassic	Jurassic	Cretaceous	

0.3 m/1 ft

Pachycephalosaurus

A two-legged plant eater the length of a large car, this was the biggest of all known thick-headed dinosaurs.

Pachycephalosaurus's extraordinary skull had a knobbly shelf at the back; a high, thick dome shielding its brain; and bony spikes on a short, narrow snout. Like bison, rival *Pachycephalosaurus* males might have used their heads for butting one another's sides.

Only the skull is well known, but *Pachycephalosaurus* probably had a rather short neck, solid body, short arms, strong hips and legs, and tendons that stiffened its tail.

This kind of dinosaur would have walked around using its small, ridged teeth for eating seeds, fruits, leaves, and maybe insects. Sharp eyes and a keen sense of smell helped it to keep away from dangerous theropods. It was unlikely to be able to outrun them.

Name *Pachycephalosaurus*
Pronunciation *PAK-ee-SEF-a-loh-SORE-us*
Meaning *"Thick head lizard"*
Location *Western North America*
Length *4.5 m (15 ft)*
Food *Plants*
Period *Late Cretaceous*
Order *Ornithischia*
Suborder *Marginocephalia*
Infraorder *Pachycephalosauria*
Family *Pachycephalosauridae*

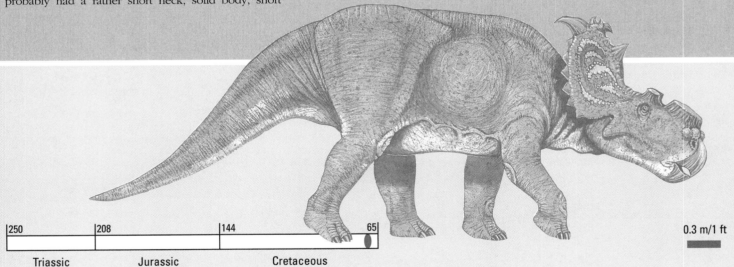

250	208	144	65
Triassic	Jurassic	Cretaceous	

0.3 m/1 ft

Parasaurolophus

Parasaurolophus was the most highly evolved of all lambeosaurine hadrosaurs–duck-billed dinosaurs with a hollow, bony head crest, which was larger in males than in females.

From *Parasaurolophus's* head, a bony, curved tube 1.5 meters (5 ft) long projected back over the neck, perhaps connected to it by a skin frill. The tube ran from the back of the throat to the nostrils, doubling back on itself like the tube of a trombone. Also like a trombone, it amplified sound. *Parasaurolophus's* honking cry might have carried for miles. Like the showy head crest, this call could have attracted mates or warned off rival males.

Apart from its built-in "trombone," this big, bulky plant eater's head looked rather like a horse's, but with a blunt toothless beak and many self-sharpening cheek teeth for grinding up the leaves stored in cheek pouches. It walked on all fours but ran on the hind limbs.

Name *Parasaurolophus*
Pronunciation *PAR-a-SORE-oh-LOAF-us*
Meaning *"Beside Saurolophus"*
Location *Western North America*
Length *9 m (30 ft)*
Food *Plants*
Period *Late Cretaceous*
Order *Ornithischia*
Suborder *Ornithopoda*
Infraorder *Euornithopoda*
Family *Hadrosauridae*

Pelecanimimus

Pelecanimimus was an early ostrich dinosaur. Discovered in 1993, this was the first known ornithomimosaur to be found in Europe.

Like all ostrich dinosaurs, *Pelecanimimus* resembled a big flightless bird except for its long bony tail and long, gangling arms with clawed, three-fingered hands. Instead of a toothless beak, *Pelecanimimus* had long, narrow jaws crammed with more than 200 sharp little teeth, so closely packed that they formed a long cutting edge. Scientists suspect that the later toothless ostrich dinosaurs evolved from ancestors like this, whose teeth had multiplied but become extremely small.

Fossil impressions left by the skin seem to show another curiosity–a flap like the pouch where a pelican stores captured fish. *Pelecanimimus* lived near lakes inhabited by fish and crustaceans; perhaps it fished by standing patiently at the water's edge like a heron.

Name *Pelecanimimus*
Pronunciation *pel-e-kan-i-MEEM-us*
Meaning *"Pelican mimic"*
Location *Spain*
Length *2.5 m (8 ft)*
Food *Perhaps fish*
Period *Early Cretaceous*
Order *Saurischia*
Suborder *Theropoda*
Infraorder *Tetanurae*
Family *Possibly Ornithomimidae*

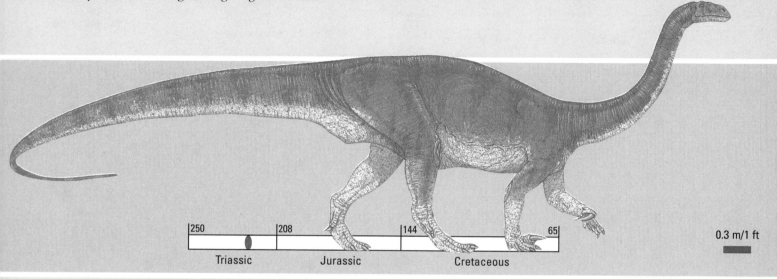

250	208	144	65	0.3 m/1 ft
Triassic	Jurassic	Cretaceous		

Probactrosaurus

This large, bipedal/quadrupedal plant eater had a toothless beak and hooflike claws. It looked much like *Iguanodon*. However, it shared certain features with those more advanced ornithopods, the hadrosaurids, also known as duck-billed dinosaurs.

Like *Iguanodon*, *Probactrosaurus* had a long, narrow snout; a long, lower jaw; and two-layered rows of teeth.

Like hadrosaurids, *Probactrosaurus* grew more than one replacement tooth at each position in its jaw. Then, too, some details of its teeth, hip bones, and foot bones were more like those of duck-billed dinosaurs than *Iguanodon*.

Probactrosaurus seems something of a missing link between the iguanodontids and the hadrosaurids. Instead of grouping it with either, scientists put it in a family of its own, a family so far without a name.

Name *Probactrosaurus*
Pronunciation *proh-BAK-troh-SORE-us*
Meaning *"Before Bactrosaurus"*
Location *China*
Length *6 m (19 ft 6 in)*
Food *Plants*
Period *Late Cretaceous*
Order *Ornithischia*
Suborder *Ornithopoda*
Infraorder *Euornithopoda*
Family *Unclassified*

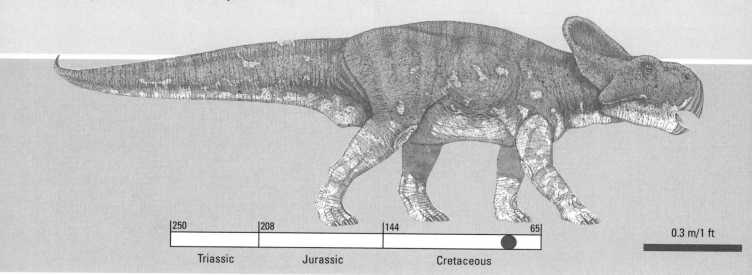

250	208	144	65	0.3 m/1 ft
Triassic	Jurassic	Cretaceous		

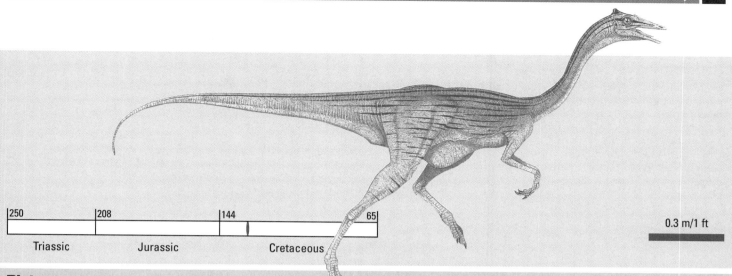

| 250 | | 208 | | 144 | | 65 | |
| Triassic | | Jurassic | | Cretaceous | | | |

0.3 m/1 ft

Plateosaurus

Bus-length *Plateosaurus* was one of the largest of the early dinosaurs. It was also one of the most plentiful of all known kinds of dinosaurs that ever lived in what is now Europe. Some people think it roamed around in herds.

Like most prosauropods, *Plateosaurus* had a small head, long neck, long and bulky body, and long tail. But it was much bigger than its relative *Anchisaurus*. It also had much broader feet and hands and a larger, stronger skull.

The jaw hinge was set below the level of the teeth to give a powerful bite. *Plateosaurus* probably used its pointed, ridged teeth to chop up tree fern fronds and other leaves.

This heavy herbivore walked on all fours, maybe with its great clawed thumbs held off the ground. But it could also rear to hurry or to use its claws to stab enemies or rake leafy twigs toward its mouth.

Name *Plateosaurus*
Pronunciation *PLAT-ee-oh-SORE-us*
Meaning *"Flat lizard"*
Location *Western Europe*
Length *8 m (26 ft)*
Food *Plants*
Period *Late Triassic*
Order *Saurischia*
Suborder *Sauropodomorpha*
Infraorder *Prosauropoda*
Family *Plateosauridae*

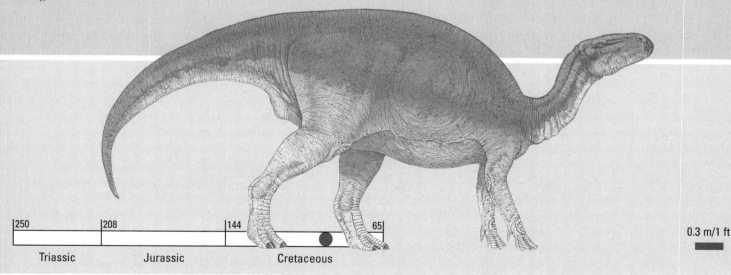

| 250 | | 208 | | 144 | | 65 | |
| Triassic | | Jurassic | | Cretaceous | | | |

0.3 m/1 ft

Protoceratops

Protoceratops was a small, early, horned dinosaur.

This four-legged plant eater was as long as a very tall man but much heavier. It had a big head with a broad, bony frill at the back; thickened bone above the eyes and snout; flared cheek bones; sharp, shearing cheek teeth; and a deep, narrow beak like a parrot's.

Skulls with the largest frills and a prominent bump on the snout probably belonged to males. Rival males could have displayed their frills by nodding heads. Perhaps they used their ridged noses for butting each other.

Long, strong forelimbs with blunt-clawed, three-toed digits supported its heavy head when *Protoceratops* walked. Its hind limbs were even longer and stronger, with elongated, four-toed, blunt-clawed feet. This dinosaur had a rather thick, heavy tail.

Name *Protoceratops*
Pronunciation *PROH-toh-SERA-tops*
Meaning *"First horned face"*
Location *Mongolia*
Length *2 m (6 ft 6 in)*
Food *Plants*
Period *Late Cretaceous*
Order *Ornithischia*
Suborder *Marginocephalia*
Infraorder *Ceratopsia*
Family *Protoceratopsidae*

Psittacosaurus

Psittacosaurus is the earliest known and most primitive of the ceratopsians, or horned dinosaurs. A bipedal plant eater, it grew the length of a tall man. A number of species have been found, all of them in Asia and most of them in China.

Like all ceratopsians, *Psittacosaurus* had a deep, cutting beak like a parrot's. Perhaps this sharp beak helped it to crop tough, fibrous, and new kinds of plants.

Unlike later ceratopsians, *Psittacosaurus* lacked horns on the front of its face, which was narrow. However, its pointed cheek bones formed little horns at the sides. The eyes and nostrils were set high in its short, deep head.

Psittacosaurus had long hind limbs, and strong, short forelimbs with blunt claws, suitable for walking on or grasping leaves. A long tail counterbalanced the front of its body when it walked or ran.

Name *Psittacosaurus*
Pronunciation *sit-AK-oh-SORE-us*
Meaning *"Parrot lizard"*
Location *China, Mongolia, Russia, and Thailand*
Length *2 m (6 ft 6 in)*
Food *Plants*
Period *Early Cretaceous*
Suborder *Marginocephalia*
Infraorder *Ceratopsia*
Family *Psittacosauridae*

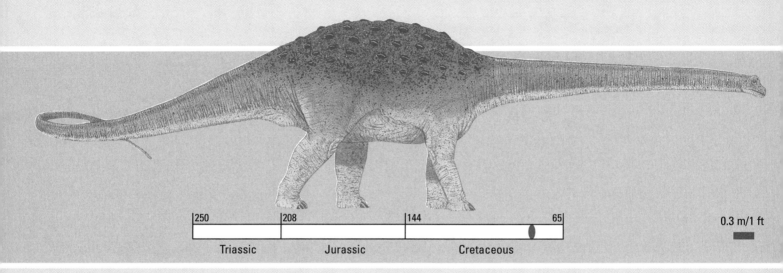

250	208	144	65
Triassic	Jurassic	Cretaceous	

0.3 m/1 ft

Sauropelta

Sauropelta, an early North American nodosaurid dinosaur, was a large, four-legged, armored plant eater.

The heavy-bodied creature had a rather narrow head with massive jaws but only small, leaf-shaped teeth and a horny, toothless beak. Its neck was short, its tail long and stiffened. Sturdy limbs with short, broad toes and fingers bore its weight.

Bands of bony plates, spines, and nodules

"floating" in the skin protected *Sauropelta's* head, neck, back, and hips. Sharp-edged spines, longest at the neck, and shoulders, stuck out to the sides. Unlike *Euoplocephalus*, though, it did not have a tail armed with a club.

Sauropelta ate low-growing plants. This nodosaurid walked with its body high above the ground, but if attacked it might have crouched to shield its belly.

Name *Sauropelta*
Pronunciation *SORE-oh-PEL-ta*
Meaning *"Small shield lizard"*
Location *Kansas and Wyoming*
Length *7 m (23 ft)*
Food *Plants*
Period *Early Cretaceous*
Order *Ornithischia*
Suborder *Thyreophora*
Infraorder *Ankylosauria*
Family *Nodosauridae*

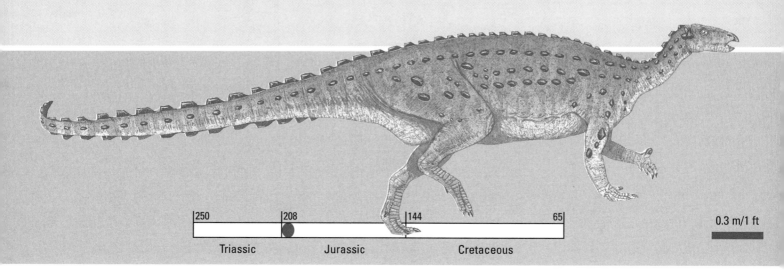

250	208	144	65
Triassic	Jurassic	Cretaceous	

0.3 m/1 ft

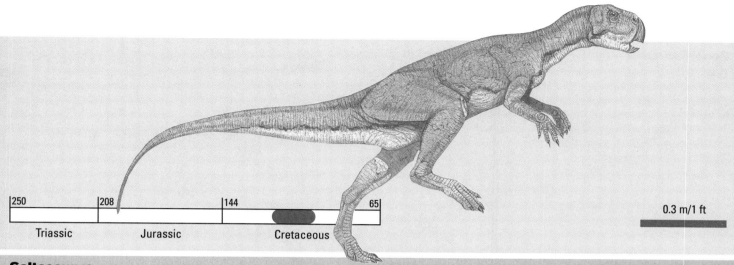

250	208	144	65
Triassic	Jurassic	Cretaceous	

0.3 m/1 ft

Saltasaurus

The discovery of this medium-sized sauropod proved that some of these four-legged giants had body armor.

Along with its skeleton, scientists unearthed hundreds of pea-sized bony lumps and a few ridged bony plates as big as the palm of a human hand; both had been embedded in this creature's skin. Any theropod that tried attacking *Saltasaurus*'s back or sides risked badly damaging its teeth or claws.

Large sternal plates (breast bones) and distinctive spinal bones show that *Saltasaurus* belonged to the titanosaurid family of sauropods.

Before *Saltasaurus*'s discovery, people supposed that armor found with scrappy titanosaurid remains had come from ankylosaurs. Now it seems that many, maybe all, titanosaurids' hides were reinforced against attack.

Name *Saltasaurus*
Pronunciation *SAL-ta-SORE-us*
Meaning *"Salta [province] lizard"*
Location *Argentina and Uruguay*
Length *12 m (39 ft)*
Food *Plants*
Period *Late Cretaceous*
Order *Saurischia*
Suborder *Sauropodomorpha*
Infraorder *Sauropoda*
Family *Titanosauridae*

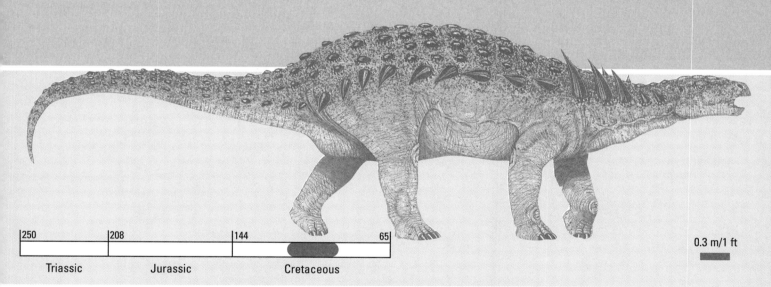

250	208	144	65
Triassic	Jurassic	Cretaceous	

0.3 m/1 ft

Scelidosaurus

Bony studs embedded in the skin protected this primitive four-legged ornithischian plant eater.

Scelidosaurus had a small head, held low on a relatively longer neck than that of its later and much larger relatives, the armored dinosaurs called ankylosaurs. The jaws were narrow, with small leaf-shaped teeth and a horn-sheathed bony beak.

Four sturdy limbs with four-toed feet supported a long, heavy body, which was highest at the hips.

Scelidosaurus was not a fast mover. It probably plodded around, cropping soft-leaved, low-growing plants. If threatened by a theropod, it might have crouched, relying on its armor for defense, instead of running away. Thorny plates guarded the back of the head and rows of sharp bones sheathed in horn guarded the neck, back, and flanks. The skin between the rows was covered in tough scales.

Name *Scelidosaurus*
Pronunciation *SKEL-eye-doh-SORE-us*
Meaning *"Hind leg lizard"*
Location *England, possibly Arizona US, and possibly Tibet*
Length *4 m (13 ft)*
Food *Plants*
Period *Early Jurassic*
Order *Ornithischia*
Suborder *Thyreophora*
Infraorder *Unclassified*
Family *Scelidosauridae*

Scutellosaurus

This unusual early dinosaur was a two-legged armored ornithischian no bigger than a collie dog. The big four-legged plated and armored dinosaurs all probably evolved from a common ancestor like this.

Scutellosaurus bore body armor comprising rows of hundreds of little bony plates. There were six types of these–some flat, some ridged like tiny roofs. All maybe had a covering of leathery or horny scales.

A very long tail helped to counterbalance this armor's weight. Scutellosaurus could walk and run on its long hind limbs, but fairly long arms suggest that it often went down on all fours to help support its relatively heavy body. The toes and fingers bore small, pointed claws.

Scutellosaurus probably cropped low-growing leaves, then chopped them up with its ridged cheek teeth.

Name Scutellosaurus
Pronunciation SKOOT-el-oh-SORE-us
Meaning "Small shield lizard"
Location Arizona, US
Length 1.2 m (4 ft)
Food Plants
Period Early Jurassic
Order Ornithischia
Suborder Thyreophora
Infraorder Unclassified
Family Possibly Scelidosauridae

0.3 m/1 ft

250	208	144	65
Triassic	Jurassic	Cretaceous	

Spinosaurus

Spinosaurus was one of the longest, though not the heaviest, of all theropods. It was also one of the strangest looking of all dinosaurs.

Long "swords" sticking up from its backbone supported a tall skin sail or maybe a tall hump on its back. Other remarkable features included a lower jaw like a crocodile's, and straight, pointed teeth with smooth, rounded sides–more like a crocodile's teeth than the saw-edged, rather knifelike, blades of a typical theropod dinosaur.

Scientists think rival males might have displayed their tall backs to threaten each other. But a skin sail could have served as a solar panel. If Spinosaurus was cold blooded, turning its sail to the Sun on chilly mornings might have warmed it up enough to make it active. If it had a hump, though, this could have stored food as fat and insulated the body against fierce sunshine.

Name Spinosaurus
Pronunciation SPY-noh-SORE-us
Meaning "Spine lizard"
Location North Africa
Length Up to 15 m (49 ft)
Food Meat and fish
Period Late Cretaceous
Order Saurischia
Infraorder Tetanurae
Family Spinosauridae

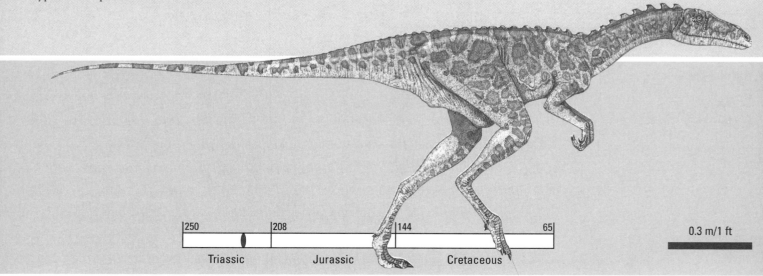

250	208	144	65
Triassic	Jurassic	Cretaceous	

0.3 m/1 ft

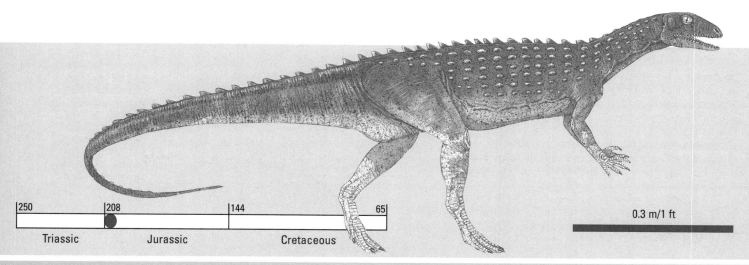

250	208	144	65
Triassic	Jurassic	Cretaceous	

0.3 m/1 ft

Sinosauropteryx

Scientists have long puzzled about how scaly dinosaurs could have given rise to feathered birds. By the middle 1990s the discovery of *Sinosauropteryx* hinted at an answer. Fuzzy down like a newly hatched chicken's seems to have covered this small theropod's body. Perhaps feathers evolved from scales that went wrong and split.

Sinosauropteryx was no larger than a big chicken. Apart from its downy covering, this Chinese dinosaur looked rather like its European cousin, *Compsognathus*. The body was deep and slender, the arms were short, but the tail was very long indeed.

An odd feature of its three-fingered hand was a huge thumb with a big, vicious-looking claw, perhaps for killing prey. One discovered individual had caught and eaten a tiny mammal. Another had swallowed a lizard. The lizard-eater was also about to lay two little eggs when it died.

Name *Sinosauropteryx*
Pronunciation *SINE-oh-sore-OP-teriks*
Meaning *"Chinese lizard wing"*
Location *Northeast China*
Length *90 cm (2 ft 4 in)*
Food *Small animals*
Period *Early Cretaceous*
Order *Saurischia*
Suborder *Theropoda*
Infraorder *Tetanurae*
Family *Compsognathidae*

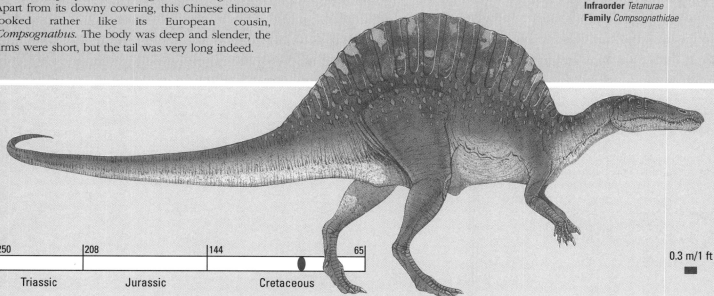

250	208	144	65
Triassic	Jurassic	Cretaceous	

0.3 m/1 ft

Staurikosaurus

This two-legged dinosaur was longer than a man yet weighed less than a big dog. It had a large head, with big, sharp teeth. There were short arms and maybe four-fingered hands. Its agile legs had shins longer than thighs, and each foot probably had five sharp-clawed toes. The tail was long and slender.

Staurikosaurus had more fingers and toes than most later flesh-eating dinosaurs, but only two

vertebrae joined the backbone to the hips–fewer than almost any other dinosaur.

Such creatures were among the earliest and most primitive dinosaurs. They might have been too primitive to be theropods or even saurischians.

Despite its modest size, *Staurikosaurus* might have been one of the first dinosaurs to run down and kill big game.

Name *Staurikosaurus*
Pronunciation *STOR-ik-oh-SORE-us*
Meaning *"[Southern] Cross lizard"*
Location *Southern Brazil*
Length *2 m (7 ft)*
Food *Meat*
Period *Late Triassic*
Order *Saurischia*
Suborder *Possibly Theropoda*
Infraorder *Unclassified*
Family *Herrerasauridae*

Stegosaurus

Stegosaurus was the largest known plated dinosaur. It walked on all fours, with its deep, narrow body highest at the hips. The small, low-slung head was long and narrow, with a brain perhaps smaller than a dog's, tiny cheek teeth, and a toothless beak.

Stegosaurus might have been a choosy feeder, foraging for the flowers and fruits of cycadeoids and seed ferns. Perhaps it reared to nibble tidbits above head level.

This slow-moving herbivore had armor for defense; bony studs guarded its throat, and maybe other areas, and its long tail spikes could have swiped an enemy. Two staggered rows of tall bony plates rose from the

neck, back, and upper tail. Too weak for armor, these might have scared rivals or attracted mates. Maybe they also cooled or warmed *Stegosaurus,* depending on whether it turned away from or broadside to the Sun.

Name *Stegosaurus*
Pronunciation *STEG-oh-SORE-us*
Meaning *"Roof lizard"*
Location *Western US*
Length *9 m (30 ft)*
Food *Plants*
Period *Late Jurassic*
Order *Ornithischia*
Suborder *Thyreophora*
Infraorder *Stegosauria*
Family *Stegosauridae*

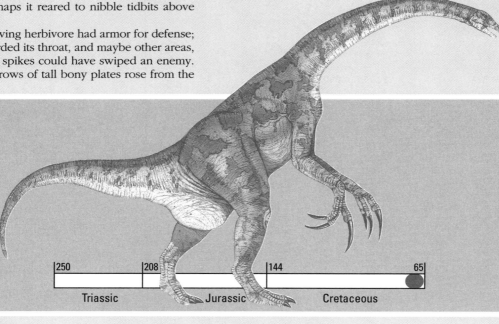

250	208	144	65
Triassic	Jurassic	Cretaceous	

0.3 m/1 ft

Thescelosaurus

Thescelosaurus was a late ornithopod of primitive design. It had a small head; thickly enameled, strongly ridged cheek teeth; a moderately long neck; a bulky body; and a long tail. From snout to tail tip *Thescelosaurus* was the length of a small car.

Finds of incomplete skeletons hint at five-fingered hands, four-toed feet with hooflike claws, and even rows of bony studs on its back.

Thescelosaurus was longer, bulkier, and sturdier than *Hypsilophodon*, and it had a relatively broader

head. Also its thighs were longer than its shins, so it could not run so fast. It might even have foraged on all fours.

Some experts have thought *Thescelosaurus* was an iguanodontid. Many consider it just a bulky hypsilophodontid. Others put it in a family of its own.

Name *Thescelosaurus*
Pronunciation *THES-kel-oh-SORE-us*
Meaning *"Wonderful lizard"*
Location *Western US and Canada*
Length *3.5 m (12 ft)*
Food *Plants*
Period *Late Cretaceous*
Order *Ornithischia*
Suborder *Ornithopoda*
Infraorder *Euornithopoda*
Family *Possibly Thescelosauridae*

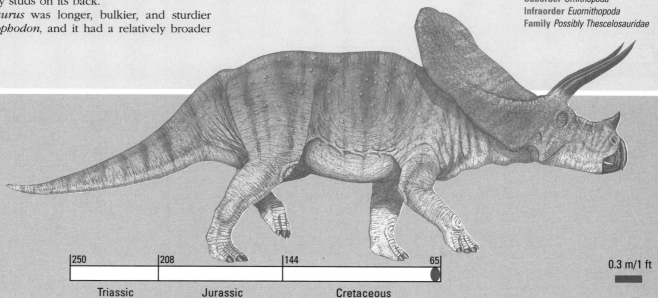

250	208	144	65
Triassic	Jurassic	Cretaceous	

0.3 m/1 ft

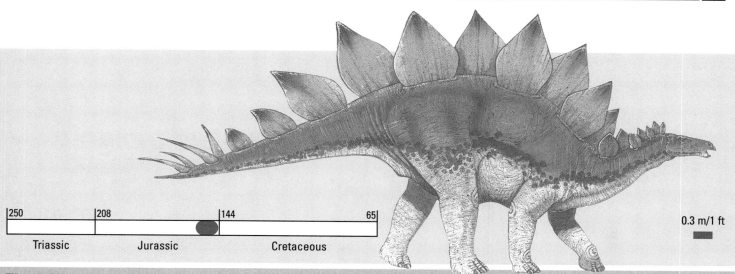

| 250 | | 208 | | 144 | | 65 |
| Triassic | | Jurassic | | Cretaceous | | |

0.3 m/1 ft

Therizinosaurus

Therizinosaurus's only certain remains are arms longer than a man and three-fingered hands tipped with long curved claws. Foot bones found nearby probably came from the same animal. By matching these finds with the bones of similar dinosaurs, scientists have built up a picture of what *Therizinosaurus* might have looked like.

The result is the weirdest-looking dinosaur of all–a two-legged beast as heavy as an elephant, with a small skull and beaked, toothless jaws. The long neck

and the back slope steeply upwards, like a giraffe's. The tail is short. The arms are strong, and the hands' great claws can rest upon the ground, propping up the chest. Each long, muscular leg ends in a flat foot with four toes.

If *Therizinosaurus* really looked like this it probably ate plants. Sitting on the ground, it could have used its hands to push the leafy twigs of shrubs and trees into its mouth.

Name *Therizinosaurus*
Pronunciation *THER-ee-ZINE-oh-SORE-us*
Meaning *"Scythe lizard"*
Location *Mongolia*
Length *12 m (39 ft)*
Food *Probably plants*
Period *Late Cretaceous*
Order *Saurischia*
Suborder *Theropoda*
Infraorder *Tetanurae*
Family *Therizinosauridae*

| 250 | | 208 | | 144 | | 65 |
| Triassic | | Jurassic | | Cretaceous | | |

0.3 m/1 ft

Torosaurus

This long-frilled, horned dinosaur might have had the longest skull of any land animal that ever lived.

Torosaurus was a big, four-legged plant eater with a parrot's beak and shearing cheek teeth in its powerful narrow jaws. Its huge head had two long brow horns, a short nose horn, and a great, skin-covered, bony frill. Up to 2 meters (6 ft 6 in) long, this frill jutted backward from the skull, above the neck and shoulders.

Some people think the skull frill anchored jaw muscles. More likely it frightened rivals when a male displayed his frill by nodding his head. Another notion is that the frill helped to control body temperature by acting as a solar panel or a radiator, depending on the time of day.

If a *Tyrannosaurus* attacked, a *Torosaurus* might have countered with its horns.

Name *Torosaurus*
Pronunciation *TOR-o-SORE-us*
Meaning *"Perforated [skull frill] lizard"*
Location *Western North America*
Length *7 m (23 ft)*
Food *Plants*
Period *Late Cretaceous*
Order *Ornithischia*
Suborder *Marginocephalia*
Infraorder *Ceratopsia*
Family *Ceratopsidae*

Triceratops

Triceratops was one of the last and largest of the horned dinosaurs. Despite its short, bony frill, other features of the skull persuade scientists that it belonged with the chasmosaurines, or long-frilled horned dinosaurs.

This great four-legged plant eater weighed as much as an elephant and rather resembled a huge rhinoceros with an immense three-horned head. With its broad, bony frill at the back, it was up to 2.4 meters (7 ft 10 in) long–one-third of this dinosaur's length. The nose horn was short, but two very long brow horns jutted out over the eyes.

Old, healed injuries to *Triceratops* skulls might have been caused by these dinosaurs trying to fend off attacks by *Tyrannosaurus*. More likely they happened when rival males locked horns in battle. Usually, though, they probably just threatened each other by nodding their heads. The male with the largest head would have won.

Name *Triceratops*
Pronunciation *try-SERA-tops*
Meaning *"Three-horn face"*
Location *Western North America*
Length *7.9 m (26 ft)*
Food *Plants*
Period *Late Cretaceous*
Order *Ornithischia*
Suborder *Marginocephalia*
Infraorder *Ceratopsia*
Family *Ceratopsidae*

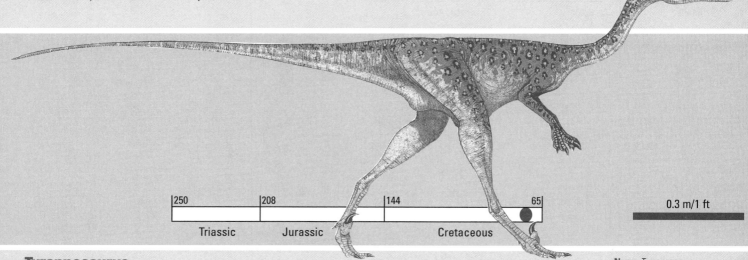

250	208	144	65
Triassic	Jurassic	Cretaceous	

0.3 m/1 ft

Tyrannosaurus

Tyrannosaurus was one of the last and largest theropods. The biggest specimens weighed more than 6 tons. (Females perhaps became even larger than males.)

The body was short and deep, and the legs were immense; yet the arms were tiny, with just two fingers on each hand.

A strong, thick neck supported a colossal head more than a meter (about 3 ft) long, with saw-edged fangs in jaws big enough to swallow humans whole, had any been around. Yet the skull was lighter than

might be expected, because for its size many of its bones were only hollow struts.

Both forward-facing eyes could focus on a single object. This might have helped *Tyrannosaurus* to judge if a horned dinosaur or hadrosaur was near enough to catch. It could not run fast enough to grab fast moving prey. Some scientists think it ate only already dead dinosaurs.

Name *Tyrannosaurus*
Pronunciation *Tie-ran-oh-SORE-us*
Meaning *"Tyrant lizard"*
Location *Western North America*
Length *Up to 12 m (39 ft)*
Food *Meat*
Period *Late Cretaceous*
Order *Saurischia*
Suborder *Theropoda*
Infraorder *Tetanurae*
Family *Tyrannosauridae*

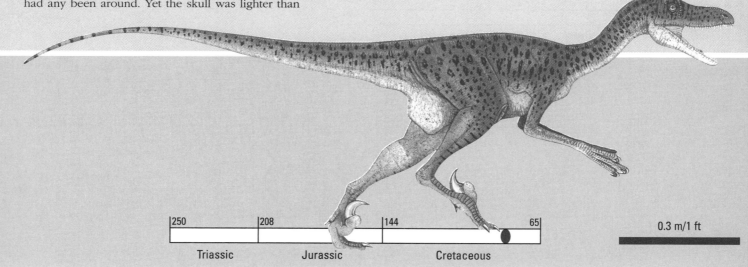

250	208	144	65
Triassic	Jurassic	Cretaceous	

0.3 m/1 ft

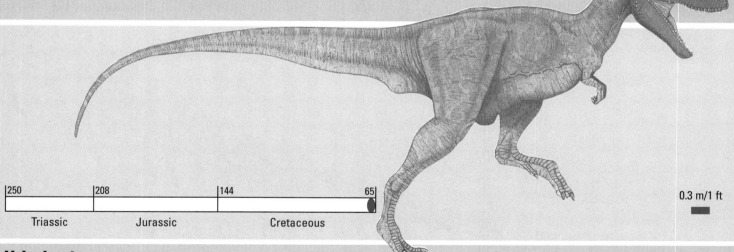

0.3 m/1 ft

250 | 208 | 144 | 65

Triassic | Jurassic | Cretaceous

0.3 m/1 ft

Troodon

Small, lightweight *Troodon* was a lithe and speedy hunter, perhaps the two-legged dinosaur equivalent of a lynx or caracal. Quick and agile, it probably grabbed small mammals, birds, and reptiles with its hands.

Troodon's long, narrow skull contained a relatively bigger brain than any other dinosaur. Its wide-set eyes were large and keen, maybe capable of spotting prey in twilight. A capsule in the skull was similar to that in the toothless ostrich dinosaurs, but *Troodon's* slim jaws contained sharp, bladelike teeth.

Like *Velociraptor*, this theropod had long arms with grasping hands and probably tail-stiffeners formed by bony rods. It also had a retractable second toe, but this was weaker than *Velociraptor's* and had a smaller claw. A pinched upper foot bone hints that *Troodon's* near relatives included *Chirostenotes* and *Ornithomimus*.

Name *Troodon*
Pronunciation *TROH-oh-don*
Meaning *"Wounding tooth"*
Location *Western North America*
Length *1.75 m (6 ft)*
Food *Meat*
Period *Late Cretaceous*
Order *Saurischia*
Suborder *Theropoda*
Infraorder *Tetanurae*
Family *Troodontidae*

250 | 208 | 144 | 65

Triassic | Jurassic | Cretaceous

0.3 m/1 ft

Velociraptor

As long as a man, yet only the weight of a wolf, *Velociraptor* might have been one of the fiercest, most frightening of all flesh-eating dinosaurs for its size.

This dromaeosaurid had a long head with a rather big brain, keen eyes, and sharp fangs. Each long arm bore a hand with three grasping fingers tipped with curved claws. When *Velociraptor* ran and leapt, only the third and fourth toes bore its weight. The

retracted second toe had a great switchblade claw that could be flicked forward for a sudden attack.

Thin bony rods stiffened its tail, helping *Velociraptor* to balance as it ran or stood on one leg to deliver slashing kicks that cut through victims' hides and pierced their entrails.

Birds and dromaeosaurids share so many anatomical features that most scientists now think that birds evolved from close kin of these theropods.

Name *Velociraptor*
Pronunciation *vel-o-see-RAP-tor*
Meaning *"Quick robber"*
Location *Mongolia and China*
Length *1.8 m (6 ft)*
Food *Meat*
Period *Late Cretaceous*
Order *Saurischia*
Suborder *Theropoda*
Infraorder *Tetanurae*
Family *Dromaeosauridae*

Dinosaur life

How dinosaurs were built, how their bodies worked, and how they lived are the themes of this chapter. We explore the dinosaurs' bone structures; muscles and limbs; heart-lung systems; brains and senses; digestive systems; and heads, necks, limbs, tails, skin, and scales. After a look at how dinosaurs kept their bodies warm, we explain how they moved, fed, fought, and bred. The chapter ends with an analysis of life expectancy and death. Much of what we say and show is not proven fact, just plausibly inferred from careful scientific study and research.

Spinal bone

A *Cross section through a Brachiosaurus spinal bone, showing its thin bony core and deeply hollowed sides.*

B *An I-section steel girder designed on similar lines. Both structures provide great strength yet economize on weight.*

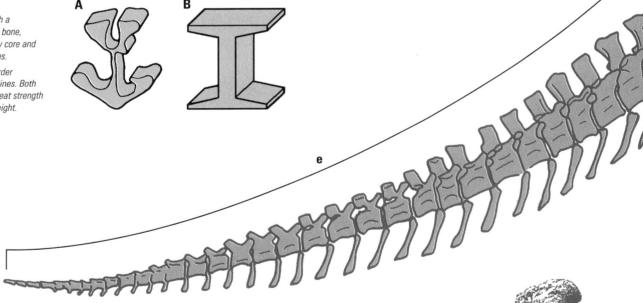

Tyrannosaur skeleton

Labels indicate main bones or groups of bones in a big predatory dinosaur.

a *Skull*

b *Cervical vertebrae*

c *Dorsal vertebrae*

d *Sacral vertebrae*

e *Caudal vertebrae*

f *Ribs*

g *Gastralia (belly ribs)*

h *Scapula (shoulder blade)*

i *Humerus (upper arm bone)*

j *Radius/ulna (forearm)*

k *Carpus (wrist)*

l *Phalanges (digit bones)*

m *Pelvis (hip region)*

n *Femur (thigh bone)*

o *Tibia (main shin bone)*

p *Fibula*

q *Tarsus (ankle)*

r *Metatarsal bones*

Giant femur

A man beside a sauropod femur shows its colossal size. Such pillarlike thigh bones transmitted body weight from hips to lower legs. Experts once wrongly thought that even this massive bone could only hold up the largest dinosaurs if they were buoyed in water.

Bony scaffolding

A dinosaur's skeleton supported the body, formed levers that enabled it to move, guarded vital organs, and stored blood-forming bone marrow. Thick, solid limb bones propped up heavy dinosaurs; lighter kinds had thin-walled hollow bones; and in large theropods and sauropods, holes and hollows lightened the skull or vertebrae. The spine ran the length of the body, reinforcing the neck, back, and tail, and supporting the skull and ribs–shields for the brain, heart, and lungs. Vertebrae fused to the pelvic (hip) bones linked the spine to bones in the thighs, legs, and feet. Shoulder blades supported arm and hand bones. All bones met at joints, which were either immovable, as in many skulls, or movable, as those in the limbs, where fibrous cartilage buffered hinge, or ball-and-socket, joints, held in place by strong flexible bands called ligaments.

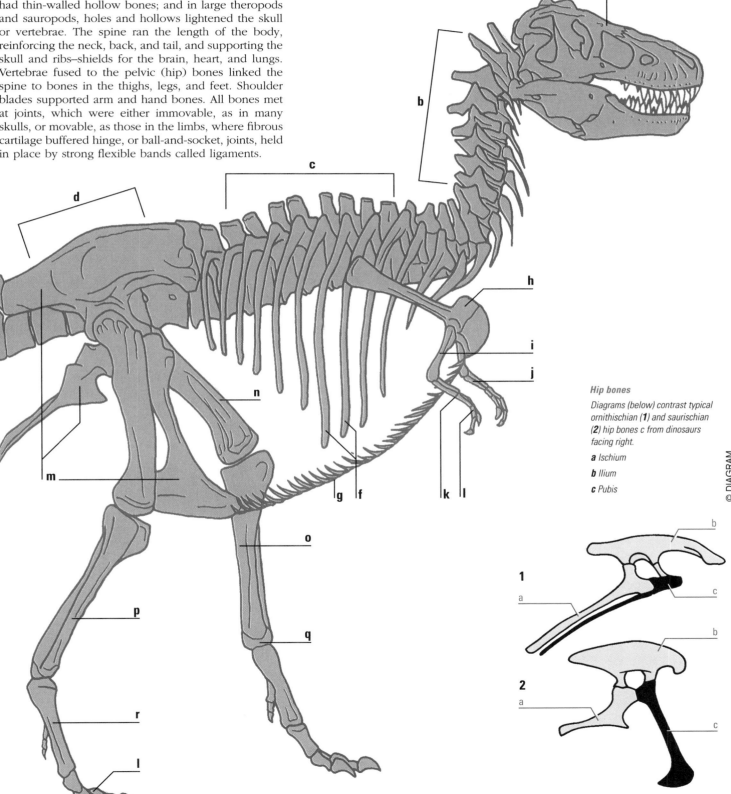

Hip bones

Diagrams (below) contrast typical ornithischian (**1**) and saurischian (**2**) hip bones c from dinosaurs facing right.

a Ischium

b Ilium

c Pubis

© DIAGRAM

Muscles

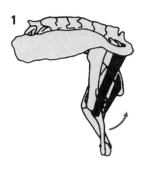

The muscles of a dinosaur held its bones together, gave its body shape, and made it move. Muscles are elastic fibers grouped in sheets and bundles that contract and relax under orders from the nervous system. Nerve signals shortened muscles and operated a dinosaur's jaws, head, neck, limbs, and tail; pumped blood through its heart; and pushed food through its gut. Each end of every long skeletal muscle joined a separate bone (at some ends via a tough flexible tendon). When the muscle contracted, usually one bone moved. By alternating paired flexor and extensor muscles, a dinosaur could bend and straighten joints to operate its limbs.

Hips (right)

These two diagrams illustrate muscles joining the legs to hips in the same armored dinosaur whose shoulder muscles figure on this page.

1 *Flexor tibialis anterior and ilio-fibularis were the muscles between the ilium (top hip bone) and lower leg bones which contracted to bend the leg along with the caudo-femoralis (tail-thigh) muscle, not shown.*

2 *Ilio-tibialis muscles joined the ilium to the main shin bone and contracted to straighten the leg.*

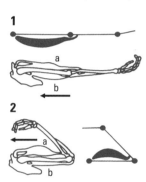

Jaw muscles (right)

These diagrams show three muscles operating the jaws of the predatory dinosaur Deinonychus. Each muscle had one end fixed to the mandible (the lower jaw).

1 *Adductor mandibularis: the big strong muscle that powerfully shut jaws when these were almost closed*

2 *Pterygoideus: the muscle that smartly snapped shut wide-open jaws*

3 *Depressor mandibulae: a small muscle at the back of the skull, used to open the jaws*

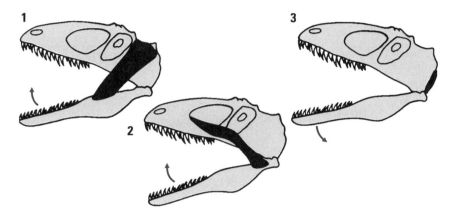

To and fro (above)

Alternate action of paired muscles in the human arm indicates how dinosaurs bent and straightened limbs. Muscles causing active movement are prime movers; those opposing them are antagonists.

1 *Extending the elbow the biceps muscle (a) relaxes and the triceps muscle (b) contracts.*

2 *Bending the elbow the biceps muscle (a) contracts and the triceps muscle (b) relaxes.*

Shoulders (right)

These four diagrams show the shoulder muscles of armored Euoplocephalus or Dyoplosaurus. The arms served as weight-bearing forelimbs, not for grasping as in theropods.

1 *Supracoracoideus and scapulo-humeralis anterior raised the arm.*

2 *Teres pulled the arm back.*

3 *Coraco-brachialis and pectoralis pulled the arm forward.*

4 *Triceps straightened the arm.*

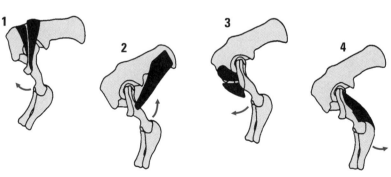

Levers

Body movements used joints that worked as three main types of levers. In each, muscular effort (E) moved a load (L) about a fulcrum (F).

1 *A first-class lever (LFE): nodding the head.*

2 *A second-class lever (FLE): walking foot action.*

3 *A third-class lever (LEF): bending the elbow.*

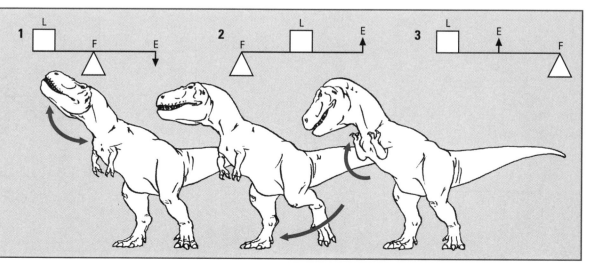

Heart-lung system

Dinosaurs' hearts pumped nutrient-rich blood around their bodies, building and repairing cells and washing wastes away. Meanwhile lungs breathed in air containing oxygen that "burned" carbon in the muscles, releasing energy for growth and movement. The chemical reaction gave off carbon dioxide gas as breathed-out waste. Because dinosaurs stood and walked erect like elephants and ostriches, some scientists believe they had big, efficient hearts and lungs as birds and mammals do. Certainly some dinosaurs had rib cages roomy enough for large hearts and lungs, and hollow bones perhaps for air sacs like those found in living birds.

Air sacs (right)

1 *Inside a bird, air sacs (**a**) assure a steady one-way flow of fresh air through the lungs (**b**).*

2 *Inside a birdlike theropod dinosaur, belly ribs (**c**) might have squeezed similar air sacs so that they filled and emptied like bellows.*

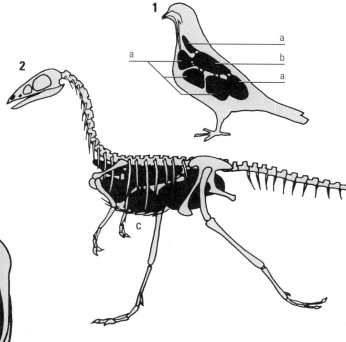

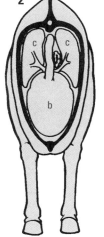
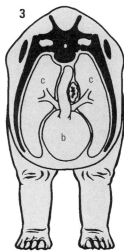

Lungs and hearts (left)

Cross sections (not to scale) through two living animals hint at the likely size of lungs and heart in a sauropod dinosaur.

1 *Crocodile. Ribs (**a**) enclose a shallow chest cavity with small heart (**b**) and lungs (**c**).*

2 *Horse. Its deep chest cavity holds large powerful heart and lungs.*

3 *Apatosaurus. Its deep chest cavity suggests heart and lungs more like a horse's than a crocodile's.*

Four types of hearts

1 *A lizard's heart lacks a wall to separate fresh blood from the lungs and used blood from the body.*

2 *A crocodile's heart, with a valve in a dividing wall, sometimes separates fresh blood from used.*

3 *A bird's heart always separates fresh blood from used, which provides body tissues with a rich supply of oxygen for active movement.*

4 *Some people think dinosaurs had efficient, birdlike hearts. Maybe some had birdlike hearts, while others had hearts similar to those of crocodiles.*

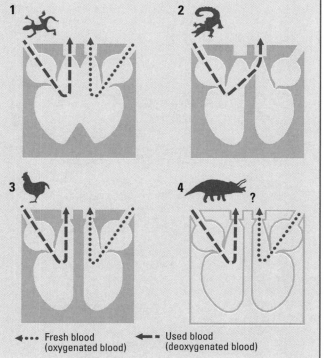

◄••• Fresh blood (oxygenated blood)

◄– – Used blood (deoxygenated blood)

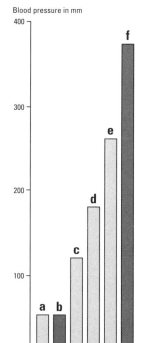

Blood pressure in mm

Blood pressures

Bars show likely heart-level blood pressure for two dinosaurs and known blood pressure for four living animals. High pressure produced by efficient hearts is needed to pump blood to the brain in beasts with heads high above their hearts, so arguably Apatosaurus had a heart designed like those of birds and mammals. (However scientists now suspect that its neck could rise not much higher than its shoulders.)

a *Alligator*

b Triceratops

c *Human*

d Duck

e *Giraffe*

f Apatosaurus

© DIAGRAM

Heads

Horned dinosaurs and big flesh eaters had huge heads with powerful jaws. Yet sauropods the size of several elephants had heads no larger than a horse's. Small theropods and most ornithischians had moderately sized heads and jaws. Beneath the skin, the skulls' sides were pierced by windows, or holes, as in other archosaurs. In certain sauropods and theropods, gigantic holes meant skulls were little more than jaws and braincase linked by bony struts. Besides lightening the skull, certain holes left extra room for muscles to close jaws. In ankylosaurs, however, solid bony armor overgrew the windows in the skull.

Head sizes (above)

1 Brachiosaurus, one of the largest of all dinosaurs, had a relatively tiny head. All sauropod heads were small compared to their body size.

2 Torosaurus, a horned dinosaur, had the longest head of any animal that ever lived on land.

Hint of a trunk (below)

Top (**A**), and side (**B**) views of a Diplodocus skull show nostril openings (**a**) above the eyes. High nostril openings in mammals, such as elephants, usually indicate the presence of a trunk. Perhaps some sauropods had trunks as well. If so, Diplodocus might have had a head like this (**C**). Most scientists doubt this theory, however.

Hollow and solid

Windows in the skull, as in the theropod Compsognathus (**1**), became closed in the armored skulls of such dinosaurs as Panoplosaurus (**2**).

a Nasal opening

b Antorbital opening

c Orbit (for eye)

d Upper temporal opening

e Lower temporal opening

f Mandibular opening

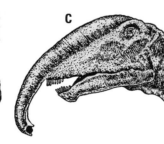

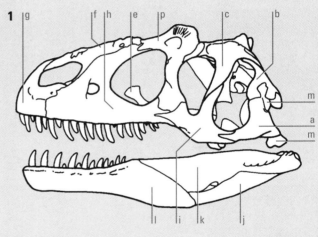

Skull bones

Dinosaur skulls, like other vertebrates' skulls, formed a mosaic of bones. Bone shapes and proportions and joint rigidity varied within both major groups of dinosaurs. Some had certain skull bones fused together. The main difference between both groups is the predentary bone of ornithischians.

1 Skull of Allosaurus, a saurischian dinosaur

2 Skull of Camptosaurus, an ornithischian dinosaur

a Quadratojugal	**f** Nasal	**k** Surangular	**p** Lacrimal
b Squamosal	**g** Premaxilla	**l** Dentary	**q** Predentary
c Postorbital	**h** Maxilla	**m** Quadrate	
d Prefrontal	**i** Jugal	**n** Parietal	
e Parasphenoid	**j** Angular	**o** Frontal	

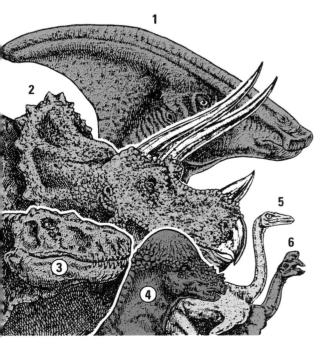

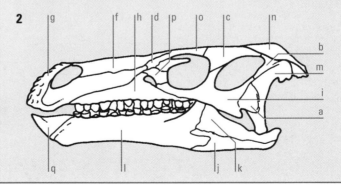

Head shapes (left)

Dinosaurs' head shapes came in a remarkable variety that reflected different modes of feeding, fighting, or communication.

1 A duck-bill's head had a hollow resonating tube that amplified its calls.

2 A horned dinosaur's head had a parrotlike beak, brow horns, and bony frill.

3 A big theropod's head had huge powerful jaws.

4 The domed head of a bone-headed dinosaur that might have used its skull in combat.

5 A lightweight theropod had a long, narrow head and jaws.

6 The strange, short head of birdlike Oviraptor, possibly an egg eater, had a crest that may have helped individuals to identify their own kind.

Brains and intelligence

People think of dinosaurs as small-brained, stupid creatures. Was this really true? No dinosaur brains survive, but we can judge their size and weight from fossil skulls. A skull includes the bony, hollow braincase; over time, some skulls filled with sediment that formed a mold of brain-shaped rock.

Such molds reveal that some dinosaurs had very tiny brains. *Stegosaurus* had a brain no bigger than a dog's. Sauropods, with a head as big as a horse's, had a brain no larger than a cat's.

Small brains do not necessarily imply stupidity. Brain size in relation to body size is a better indicator of mental ability. Weight for weight, most dinosaurs had smaller, lighter brains than birds or mammals. But a huge python with a relatively smaller brain than that of a small snake may be no less intelligent. Relative brain size plus brain complexity give a truer guide to a creature's levels of behavior and activity.

Dinosaurs' relative brain weights and sizes matched their lifestyles. The great plant-eating, plodding sauropods had relatively smaller, lighter brains than any other backboned animal. A sauropod brain weighed a mere one-hundred thousandth as much as its colossal body. (Your own brain is one-fortieth your body's weight.) Slow-moving armored and plated dinosaurs had the next smallest brains. Then came the seemingly more active, agile horned dinosaurs. Big ornithopods had relatively larger, better-developed brains, which were linked with their high ability to interact, sense enemies, and run from danger on two legs. Yet a duck-billed dinosaur's brain was a mere one-twenty thousandth of its body weight.

The brainiest dinosaurs were theropods–bipedal hunters with forelimbs freed for grasping. Yet *Tyrannosaurus's* brain mainly handled sight, smell, and limb coordination–the cerebrum containing the brain's "thinking part" was far tinier than ours. Easily the best developed brains belonged to speedy, agile, keen-eyed coelurosaurs such as *Troodon*. This creature's brain was at least one-thousandth as heavy as its body, and its well developed forebrain allowed for fine hand-eye coordination.

Only small hunting dinosaurs like this had brains relatively as big and complex as those of some birds and certain mammals. All other dinosaurs were probably no more intelligent than modern reptiles.

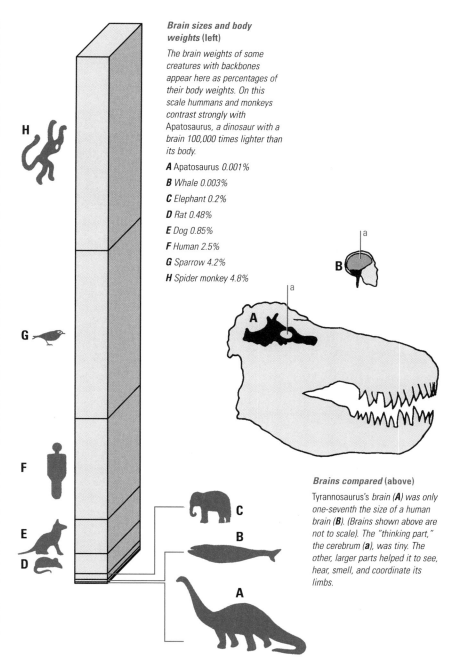

Brain sizes and body weights (left)

The brain weights of some creatures with backbones appear here as percentages of their body weights. On this scale hummans and monkeys contrast strongly with Apatosaurus, a dinosaur with a brain 100,000 times lighter than its body.

A Apatosaurus *0.001%*

B Whale *0.003%*

C Elephant *0.2%*

D Rat *0.48%*

E Dog *0.85%*

F Human *2.5%*

G Sparrow *4.2%*

H Spider monkey *4.8%*

Brains compared (above)

Tyrannosaurus's *brain (**A**) was only one-seventh the size of a human brain (**B**). (Brains shown above are not to scale). The "thinking part," the cerebrum (**a**), was tiny. The other, larger parts helped it to see, hear, smell, and coordinate its limbs.*

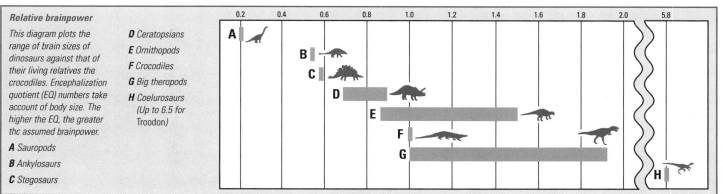

Relative brainpower

This diagram plots the range of brain sizes of dinosaurs against that of their living relatives the crocodiles. Encephalization quotient (EQ) numbers take account of body size. The higher the EQ, the greater thc assumed brainpower.

A Sauropods

B Ankylosaurs

C Stegosaurs

D Ceratopsians

E Ornithopods

F Crocodiles

G Big theropods

H Coelurosaurs (Up to 6.5 for Troodon)

© DIAGRAM

Sight, smell, and hearing

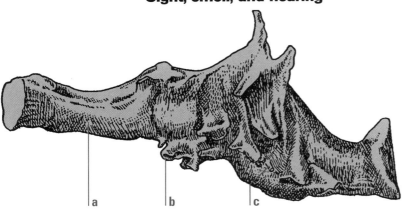

Coordination center (above)

Tyrannosaurus *brain based on a skull endocast.*

Labels show areas of brain receiving signals from the nose, eyes, and ears.

a Olfactory bulb, the brain's smell center

b Optic nerve: handles visual signals

c Auditory nerve: processes sound signals

Hearing and voice (right)

*Supposed vocal structures hint at keen hearing in the duck-billed dinosaurs. Saurolophus (**1A**) had a solid bony crest jutting from the back of the head. This probably supported a skin balloon, which inflated (**1B**) when the creature called, amplifying its voice and so giving distinctive resonance.*

Because most dinosaurs were active during the day, they relied especially on sight for sensing food, friends, and enemies. Ostrich dinosaurs and troodontids had big, keen eyes; predators with forward-facing eyes judged distance with precision. Large-snouted dinosaurs had a well-developed sense of smell, and diplodocids' high nasal openings hint at a sensitive trunk. Dinosaurs lacked external ears, yet skulls and brain casts suggest an acute sense of hearing in hadrosaurs and their tyrannosaurid enemies. Doubtless dinosaurs had voices too, and bellowings arose from hadrosaurs with ballooning facial flaps or hollow head crests.

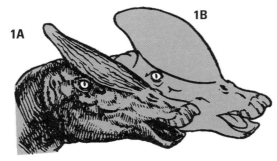

Sight

*As with mammals, what dinosaurs saw depended largely on the positions of the eyes within the skull. (Like living reptiles, but unlike most mammals, dinosaurs probably saw their world in color.) Predatory Troodon (**1**) had large forward-facing eye, somewhat like a cat's (**2**), so like a cat it* *would have judged distance well, an important aid in stalking and seizing prey. An ostrich dinosaur (**3**) had eyes on the sides of its head, somewhat like a horse (**4**). Creatures with eyes in this position can see danger approaching from behind, so enemies seldom catch them unaware.*

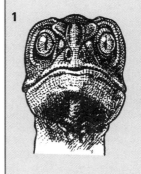

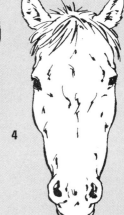

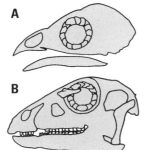

Bony eye rings (above)

*Skulls of a chicken (**A**) and the dinosaur Hypsilophodon (**B**) each show a bony ring inside a large eye socket. Bony eye rings occur in many fossil dinosaurs and living birds and reptiles. Such rings help to support the eyes and maybe help them focus. Like living birds and reptiles, many dinosaurs were sharp-sighted.*

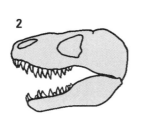

Sense of smell (above)

*The large snout of a big predatory dinosaur (**2**) and the large nasal openings (**a**) in dinosaurs such as Brachiosaurus (**3**) suggest that these dinosaurs had a keen sense of smell. Yet ostrich dinosaurs lacked a sharp sense of smell, and even large-snouted dinosaurs may not have been able to detect faint scents as well as dogs do.*

Pupil shapes and sizes (below)

1 Diurnal gecko with rounded pupils

2 Nocturnal gecko with slit-shaped pupils. Because these pupils open up at night they give good nocturnal vision.

3 Troodon appears to have had large eyes, perhaps with good light-gathering ability. If it hunted at dusk, it might have had slit-shaped pupils like a nocturnal gecko's.

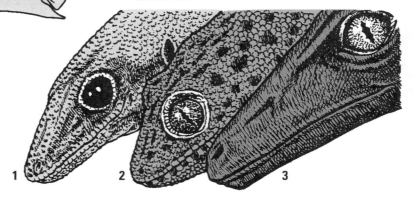

Necks

Dinosaurs' necks joined their heads to their bodies in ways that matched their skeletal structure and lifestyles. Short necks were long enough for the low-grazing horned and armored dinosaurs, and horned dinosaurs' necks were protected by a backswept bony skull frill. Necks that curved like those of bisons probably suited the hadrosaurs' habit of feeding near the ground. A sauropod's long, lightweight neck operated like a crane's boom, raising the head to browse at shoulder height or dropping it to graze on ferns and drink from pools and streams. A theropod's birdlike neck formed an S-shaped curve like a spring as, jaws agape, the head struck out at prey.

Two necks compared

*Similarity between spinal curves in an American bison (**1**) and a hadrosaur (**2**) sheds light on the duck-billed dinosaur's likely feeding habits. Scientists note that in both the backbone bends down sharply at the shoulders. This bend keeps a bison's head down low for grazing. Hadrosaurs were also evidently built for feeding on low-growing vegetation. Even when a hadrosaur raised its head as high as possible (**3**), its mouth was still below the level of its back unless the creature reared.*

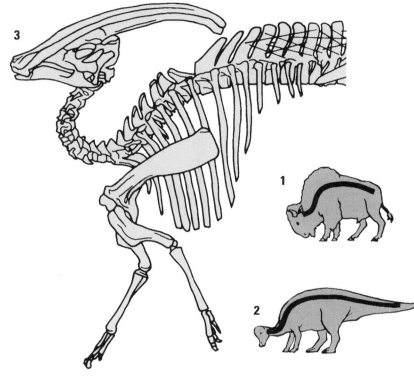

Neck bones

*Units are numbers of neck bones in two mammals (**A, B**) and three dinosaurs (**C, D, E**).*

A *Human*

B *Giraffe*

C *Psittacosaurus*

D *Most theropods*

E *Mamenchisaurus*

Most mammals have the same number of cervical vertebrae—long-necked mammals simply have longer neck bones—but long-necked dinosaurs had more bones than short-necked dinosaurs.

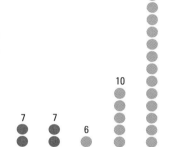

19

10

7 7

6

A B C D E

Longest neck

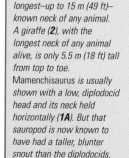

Mamenchisaurus (**1**) had the longest—up to 15 m (49 ft)—known neck of any animal. A giraffe (**2**), with the longest neck of any animal alive, is only 5.5 m (18 ft) tall from top to toe. Mamenchisaurus *is usually shown with a low, diplodocid head and its neck held horizontally (**1A**). But that sauropod is now known to have had a taller, blunter snout than the diplodocids, and an upward bend in joints below the neck led to a suggestion that this was held aloft (**1B**).*

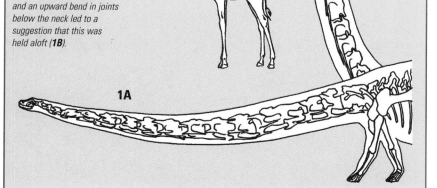

Neck curvatures

Diagrams contrast neck bones of an early archosaur, predatory dinosaur, and diving bird.

1 *The archosaur Euparkeria had a fairly straight neck like most reptiles and mammals.*

2 *Velociraptor and other theropods had neck bones that formed an S-shaped curve.*

3 *Loons have necks that are even more strongly curved. In all three, ribs made the neck strong and supple.*

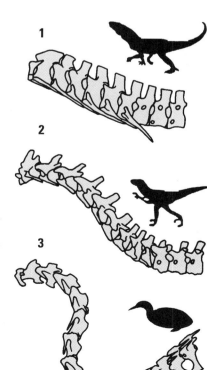

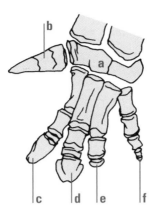

An ornithischian hand (above)

The wrist bones and specialized phalanges (digit bones) in Iguanodon's *hand*

a Fused wrist bones

b Digit 1: a thumb spike

c, d, e Digits 2–4 had hooflike nails, designed for bearing weight when Iguanodon *walked or rested on all fours*

f Digit 5: a flexible little finger, perhaps used for hooking leafy twigs into Iguanodon's *mouth*

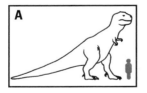

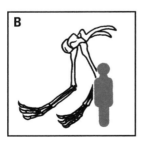

Arms small and large (above)

A For its size, Tarbosaurus *had the smallest arms and hands of almost any predatory dinosaur.*

B For its size, the unknown theropod Deinocheirus *might have had the longest arms and hands of all dinosaurs.*

Arms and hands

Theropods and ornithopods mainly had far shorter arms than legs, and some had grasping hands that seized the animals or plants they ate. Theropods' hands bore from two to five fingers tipped with sharp curved claws. Ornithopods' four- to five-fingered hands ended in hooflike nails. Sauropods, most prosauropods, and plated, horned, and armored dinosaurs stood and walked with the front part of the body borne on long forelimbs and with the elbows held tucked in. The hands of these creatures were broad, fleshy pads, with stubby, hooflike nails. In contrast, however, sauropods, prosauropods, and iguanodontids had spiky thumb claws designed as weapons of defense.

Saurischian hands

Saurischian hands varied in the number of digits and design. Here four sets of digits contrast the hand bones of two predators (A,B) and two plant-eating sauropodomorphs (C,D)

A Bones of Albertosaurus's *two-fingered hand*

B Bones and sharply curved claws of Deinonychus's *three-fingered hand*

C Bones and thumb claw of the five-fingered weight-bearing hand of the sauropod Diplodocus

D Bones and thumb claw of the five-fingered hand of a prosauropod, Plateosaurus

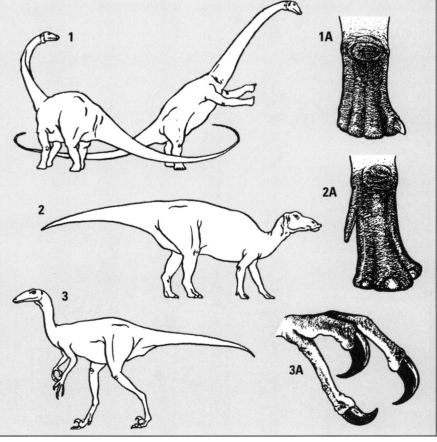

1 Elephantine pads
Sauropods could rear to feed or fight but walked on all fours. A sauropod hand (1A) resembled an elephant's front foot, but had a sharp thumb claw and hooflike nails or (in some) blocklike bones encased within a fleshy pad.

2 Duckbills' hands
Hadrosaurs walked on all fours. Each forepaw (2A) left a smooth curved print. Fleshy pads probably cushioned the digits and spread when pressed on the ground. Flattened pads in mummified hadrosaurs once made people think the creatures had webbed fingers.

3 Grasping hands
Troodon has been pictured with sharp-clawed digits opposable (3A) for grasping prey. Yet in many predatory dinosaurs, extending the fingers made the thumb claw turn away from these to form a vicious weapon. Some such birdlike theropods had a wrist-elbow system for folding arms much as birds fold their wings.

Digestive system

Sauropods' spoon-shaped or peg-shaped teeth cropped leaves; these were then ground to pulp by gizzard stones. Ornithischians and certain prosauropods had horny beaks for cropping leaves; they stored the leaves in cheek pouches until they chopped up or sliced them with cheek teeth (some self-sharpening). Many theropods had bladelike teeth for biting flesh from prey, and *Tyrannosaurus* took huge mouthfuls with front teeth that formed a monstrous "cookie cutter." Meat is easily digested, so theropods had a relatively short, simple gut as cats do. Leaves and twigs are harder to digest, so the plant-eating dinosaurs needed a long gut that contained leaf-digesting bacteria.

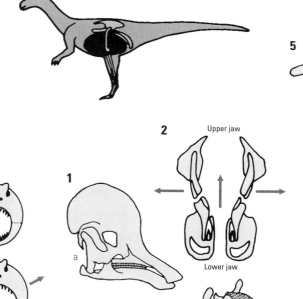

Digestive organs (right)

Digestive organs and hip girdles influenced the body bulk and posture of some groups of dinosaurs.

1 *Primitive dinosaur: a bipedal predator with a small digestive system in front of the pubic bone*

2 *Sauropod: a plant eater whose bulky digestive system in front of the pubic bone helped force it to bear its body weight on all fours. Some of its weight lay in swallowed gizzard stones (**2a**), polished as they ground up food inside the creature's gut.*

3 *Ornithopod: a bipedal plant eater with a bulky digestive system slung beneath a backward-angled pubic bone and so kept below the creature's center of gravity*

4 *Sauropod's hip bones*

5 *Ornithopod's hip bones, with a backward-angled main stem to the pubis*

a *Pubis*

b *Ischium*

c *Ilium*

Predators' jaws

Loose skull construction helped Allosaurus *bite and swallow.*

1 *Jaws in normal position (**a**) and (**b**) pull back the upper jaw to slice flesh gripped by the lower jaw.*

2 *Schematic head-on view shows jaws moving outward to clamp down on a big mouthful of meat.*

Plant eaters' jaws (left)

1 *The duck-billed dinosaur* Corythosaurus

a *Skull*

b *Lower jaw, revealing a pavement of self-sharpening teeth*

2 *Cross section through* Iguanodon's *jaws. Closing the jaws pushed the upper jaws apart, so that the top teeth slid across bottom teeth with a grinding action.*

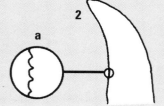
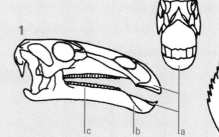
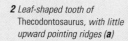

Dinosaur teeth

Like living reptiles, the teeth of most dinosaurs were all one shape. But the plant eaters had very different teeth from the meat eaters, and large dinosaurs tended to have bigger teeth than small dinosaurs. New teeth were always growing and replacing old worn teeth as these dropped out.

Flesh eaters' teeth

*Jaws (**1**) and tooth (**2**) (not to scale) of a large theropod. Such a curved, bladelike tooth with "steakknife" serrations (**a** enlarged), sliced through tough flesh as if it were soft butter.*

Plant eaters' teeth

1 Iguanodon *had an ornithischian's toothless cropping beak (**a**), a gap between beak and teeth (**b**), and cheek teeth (**c**).*

2 *Leaf-shaped tooth of* Thecodontosaurus, *with little upward pointing ridges (**a**)*

3 *Spoon-shaped tooth of* Amygdalodon *("almond tooth"), a sauropod*

© DIAGRAM

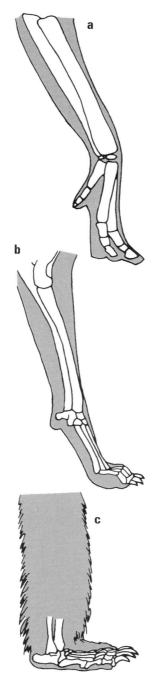

Hips, legs, and feet

Dinosaurs' legs supported their bodies thanks to straight thigh bones, equipped with turned-in tops that fitted into deep sockets into the hip bones. Legs were long in fast-running theropods and ornithopods, and the fastest sprinters seemingly had longer shins than thighs. Pillarlike legs supported the heavy four-legged dinosaurs. All dinosaurs had high ankles with a simple hinge joint and long foot bones. Most walked upon their toes, as dogs do, not flat-footedly like bears. Theropod feet were rather birdlike, usually with three forward-pointing toes armed with large sharp claws and one small claw pointing back. Fleshy "heels" supported sauropods' broad toe pads, which had three or more claws. Ornithischians had three to four toes with hooflike claws.

Hip joints (below)

Two diagrams contrast the hip joints of a semi-improved reptile and dinosaur.

A *Semi-improved hip joint*

B *Dinosaur hip joint*

a *Femur (thigh bone)*

b *Head of femur*

c *Pelvic (hip) bones*

d *Hip socket*

e *supra-acetabular crest*

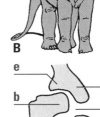

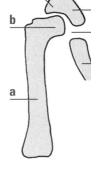

Ankle joints (below)

A *Bent hinge line seen in crocodilians and thecodonts*

B *Straight hinge line as seen in dinosaurs, pterosaurs, and birds. Distinctive ankle joints help to identify fossil dinosaurs. In life*

these simple hinges let dinosaurs move fast on rough ground. Such ankles also let the dinosaurs' descendants, modern-day birds, climb trees.

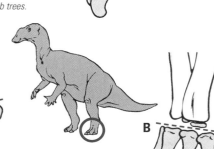

Feet compared (above)

Three diagrams compare the foot bones of a dinosaur with those of two living mammals representing two kinds of foot design.

a *Dinosaur foot: high ankle and weight supported on long toes—the kind of foot known as digitigrade*

b *Dog's foot: also of digitigrade design. Fast-running mammals tend to be long limbed and bear their weight upon their toes.*

c *Bear's foot: rests flat on the ground—the kind of foot called plantigrade*

Stance and gait

Three tetrapods (four-legged animals) with different types of stance appear above simplified cross sections through the limbs and bodies.

1 *Lizard: sprawling stance*

2 *Crocodile: semi-improved gait (hurrying with body held above the ground)*

3 *Horse: fully improved stance and gait, as in the dinosaurs*

a *Body*

b *Thigh*

c *Leg*

d *Foot*

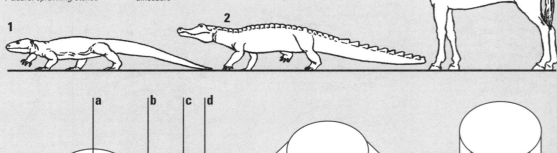

Tails

Dinosaurs' tails were lizardlike with bony cores, but they largely held their tails aloft, not low and dragging along the ground. Long, stiffened tails counterbalanced the necks and heads of running ornithopods and theropods. Long tails also balanced the elongated necks of prosauropods and sauropods. Thick, short, heavy tails sufficed for the short-necked, four-legged horned dinosaurs. Strong tails might have served as props for stegosaurs, prosauropods, and sauropods that reared to graze. Swimming dinosaurs probably waggled their tails, but did so less effectively than crocodiles. Some four-legged dinosaurs fought enemies by using their tails as whips or clubs.

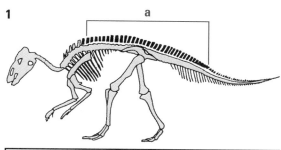

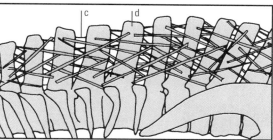

Stiffened tails (left)

Ornithischians had bony tendons that reinforced the backbone and stiffened the tail. This bony corset was best developed among big ornithopods.

1 *Skeleton of a duck-billed dinosaur*

a *Spinal region reinforced by tendons*

b *Enlarged detail of a spine with criss-crossed solid bony tendons (**c**) fixed by ligaments to spines (**d**) rising from the vertebrae*

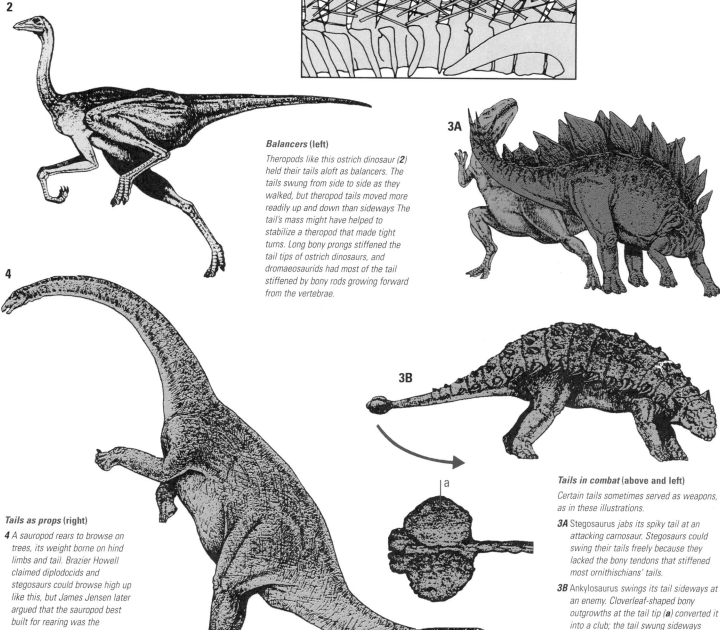

Balancers (left)

*Theropods like this ostrich dinosaur (**2**) held their tails aloft as balancers. The tails swung from side to side as they walked, but theropod tails moved more readily up and down than sideways The tail's mass might have helped to stabilize a theropod that made tight turns. Long bony prongs stiffened the tail tips of ostrich dinosaurs, and dromaeosaurids had most of the tail stiffened by bony rods growing forward from the vertebrae.*

Tails as props (right)

4 *A sauropod rears to browse on trees, its weight borne on hind limbs and tail. Brazier Howell claimed diplodocids and stegosaurs could browse high up like this, but James Jensen later argued that the sauropod best built for rearing was the camarasaurid sauropod Cathetosaurus.*

Tails in combat (above and left)

Certain tails sometimes served as weapons, as in these illustrations.

3A *Stegosaurus jabs its spiky tail at an attacking carnosaur. Stegosaurs could swing their tails freely because they lacked the bony tendons that stiffened most ornithischians' tails.*

3B *Ankylosaurus swings its tail sideways at an enemy. Cloverleaf-shaped bony outgrowths at the tail tip (**a**) converted it into a club; the tail swung sideways when the dinosaur contracted the tail muscles joined to its hips and thighs.*

© DIAGRAM

Skin and scales

Feathered dinosaurs

The small theropod Syntarsus is sometimes shown with a feathered head crest and short feathers covering the body. Some scientists think all small theropods had an insulating covering of down. Were they warm-blooded, these feathers would have helped them keep an even body temperature. Since 1990, several such feathered theropods have emerged in China.

Dinosaurs had thick, tough, scaly skin. Instead of overlapping like a fish's scales, dinosaur scales had round, or many-sided, bumps called tubercles. Large, flat tubercles covered the belly, and in some ceratopsians and hadrosaurs, formed rows or clusters on the back. Big theropods seemingly had big scales on the head, and bipeds had large leg scales like a bird's. Certain theropods and hadrosaurs probably sported frills or wattles, and small theropods might have had a covering of feathers, as did their bird-dinosaur descendant *Archaeopteryx*. Bony plates floated in the armored skin of ankylosaurs and titanosaurid sauropods.

Two kinds of scales (left)

Two lizards illustrate the two types of horny scales found as body covering in living and prehistoric reptiles.

1 *Spiny lizard: a reptile with scales that overlap like the tiles on a roof.*

2 *Gila monster: a reptile with scales consisting of nonoverlapping horny tubercles set in the skin.*

Fossil skin impressions suggest that dinosaurs' scales were designed more like a Gila monster's than a spiny lizard's.

Skin impressions (below)

Some dinosaur skins left their impressions in fine-grained sediments that later hardened into rocks.

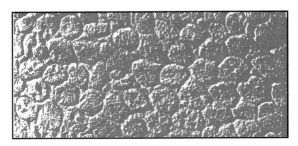

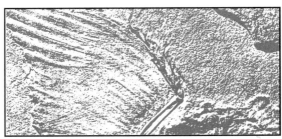

Tyrannosaurid scales (below)

A museum restoration suggests that the scaly head of Tyrannosaurus might have looked like this. The scales are guesswork, though, and might have varied more in size and shape. Carnotaurus's skin impressions, the best from any theropod, reveal that that dinosaur's head scales were mainly small tubercles, but there were also rows of big raised scales forming patterns on the upper snout and around the eyes. Quite possibly Tyrannosaurus also had "display" scales around the eyes and nostrils and in other prominent positions.

Top: *Impression left by a duck-billed dinosaur's leathery skin with horny tubercles that formed a raised pebbled pattern. Hadrosaur skin impressions include clustered larger bumps that might have had distinctive colors. Some hadrosaurs had rows of big bumps on the hips and belly.*

Above: *Feather impressions from the wings of the bird dinosaur Archaeopteryx survive in fine-grained limestone long quarried for making lithographic plates. In the 1980s museum scientists disproved a claim that the feather impressions had been fraudulently added to the fossil bones.*

Keeping warm

To stay active, dinosaurs needed to keep comfortably warm. If they were cold-blooded like lizards, they controlled body temperature by moving in or out of sun and shade. If they were warm-blooded like birds and mammals, their bodies' tissues "burned" food to heat and energize their bodies, and a thermostat in the brain prevented overheating. In this way, small theropods quite likely kept warm day and night, so that they always had the energy for chasing prey or escaping enemies. But sheer size would have kept big dinosaurs warm even had they been cold-blooded. Warmed by sunshine, their huge bodies would have stored heat through the night, and most lived where cold winters were unknown.

Warming and cooling (right)

Three temperature lines show the effects of body size on changes in body temperature among cold-blooded animals during a hot day and a cool night.

A Small alligator

B Medium-sized alligator

C Big dinosaur, if it were a cold-blooded reptile. The dinosaur's is the most constant body temperature because its surface area is smallest compared to volume. Small creatures with a large surface area quickly warm up and cool down throughout their bodies.

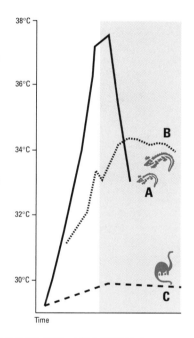

Basking (right)

A This lizard warms up by basking in sunshine.

B To avoid overheating, the warmed lizard moves into the shade. If dinosaurs were cold-blooded animals, they might have moved between Sun and shade to keep their bodies comfortably warm.

Heat exchangers (below)

Sails or flat plates jutting up from their backs probably helped some dinosaurs to warm up and cool down.

C If Spinosaurus stood sideways to the Sun, many rays warmed the blood coursing from its skin sail through its body.

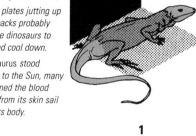

D If Spinosaurus stood with its back to the Sun, few rays warmed its sail, so its blood did not heat up.

Body temperatures (left)

Plotted on this thermometer are the known normal/ideal body temperatures of a bird, mammal, and living reptile and the likely normal/ideal temperatures of two types of dinosaurs.

1 Ostrich 102.6 °F (39.2 °C)

2 Human 98.6 °F (37.0 °C)

3 Crocodile 78.1 °F (25.6 °C)

4 Ostrich dinosaur

5 Sauropod

Items 4–5 assume that birdlike theropods were warm-blooded with a high rate of energy expenditure like birds, while sauropods were cold-blooded creatures like crocodiles.

Blood and bone

Enlarged sections of a piece of bone from three creatures.

1 Living reptile

2 Dinosaur

3 Mammal

2 and 3 feature rings of bony tissue surrounding blood vessels. Such so-called Haversian systems are numerous in living warm-blooded animals. Because the rings also occur in dinosaur bone, some scientists say they, too, must have been warm-blooded. Yet cold-blooded animals also contain several bone types also seen in dinosaurs.

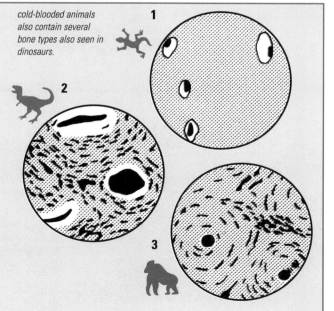

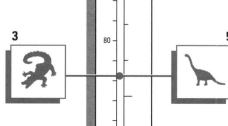

Moving around

1 Sauropod tracks

Washtub-sized depressions left by elephantine feet in mud now hardened into rock show where sauropods once roamed. Finds from Texas and elsewhere hint that sauropods and other herbivores had trudged in herds, some apparently on seasonal migration.

2 Theropod tracks

Predatory dinosaurs large and small left birdlike tracks on the muddy shores of lakes and rivers in the Connecticut valley and elsewhere in the world. Probably some scavenged corpses washed ashore and others ambushed herbivores that came to take a drink.

3 Clues to stance

The left and right feet of horned dinosaurs and others left parallel tracks close together. Matched with fossil skeletons, these tracks confirm the supposition that dinosaurs stood and walked with their limbs held below the body.

4 Tails aloft

Tracks left by ornithopods, some sauropods, and other dinosaurs often do not show any groove left by a dragging tail. Therefore, these creatures held their tails aloft to balance the body and prevent the tail being trodden upon by other members of the herd.

5 Sitting down

Besides footprints, dinosaurs left other marks that give clues to their behavior. Some hint at where a dinosaur sat down to rest or doze, rolled in mud to rid its hide of parasites, or lay in wait for prey.

6 Walking

Tracks with short distances between footprints indicate dinosaurs at slow speeds. By no means did every theropod move leisurely, but all the traces left by sauropods suggest that these creatures always ambled and were never in a hurry.

Feeding

Sauropods and ornithischians browsed high or low according to neck length or the ability to rear, or both. High-feeding sauropods maybe cropped all leaves and twigs within reach, cutting a distinctive graze-line through the trees. Broad-muzzled herbivores were unfussy eaters; narrow-mouthed beasts ate more selectively. All beat paths through forests and created clearings where small dinosaurs could feed. The big herbivores formed food for large theropods. Small theropods ate smaller plant eaters, as well as birds and lizards. Each dinosaur's droppings spread or fertilized plant seeds. Eventually, new plants grew and kept the dinosaurs' food cycle going.

Food chains (right)

Any animal community has food chains of eaters and eaten. Interlinked chains form a food web. This diagram shows who ate whom or what in late Cretaceous western North America. Arrows point to food items. Top predators were the tyrannosaurids, but all dinosaurs also depended on plants.

a Tyrannosaurids
b Dromaeosaurids
c Ornithomimids
d Hadrosaurs
e Ceratopsians
f Ankylosaurs
g Pachycephalosaurs
h Lizards
i Insects
j Plants

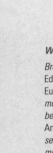

Wide and narrow mouths (left)

Broad-beaked dinosaurs like Edmontosaurus (**1**) and Euoplocephalus (**2**) bit off mixed mouthfuls of plants while narrow-beaked dinosaurs like Anchiceratops (**3**) cropped more selectively. Low-feeding dinosaurs might have helped fast-growing flowering plants to spread at the expense of older forms of vegetation.

Fossil tracks prove conclusively that dinosaurs stood, walked, and ran with limbs held underneath the body. Tracks also reveal where, when, and how sauropods, theropods, hadrosaurs, and others moved and rested on the muddy rims of lakes. Big herbivores, including sauropods, evidently often walked in herds, with tails held aloft. Running dinosaurs left footprints far apart; the faster the dinosaur, the greater the gaps. One such set of tracks suggests that large theropods could run at 25 mph (40 kph). Proof that sauropods and theropods could swim rests on tracks whose incompleteness is really due to erosion and not really swimming. The dinosaurs were probably walking on land.

7 *"Swimming"* (right)

Incomplete footprints once suggested that dinosaurs sometimes swam.

A *The theropod Dilophosaurus left birdlike footprints on land, but claw-tip prints seem to show where this dinosaur touched bottom as it swam across a pool. Such marks are really underprints, and the mud above has worn away.*

B *Forefeet tracks "show" where a swimming sauropod's hind end was buoyed up by water as it made its way across a lake. Again these marks are underprints, and the dinosaur was walking.*

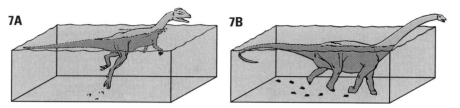

7A 7B

8 Running (below)

Trackways help scientists calculate the sizes and the speeds of running dinosaurs. Small prints usually indicate small animals, and the greater the stride length (a), the faster an animal was moving. Measuring an early Jurassic trackway found in Arizona revealed that an ornithopod or theropod no heavier than a whippet had sprinted as quickly as a horse can gallop. Some paleontologists believe even the tyrannosaurids attained such speeds as they ran to the attack.

8

a

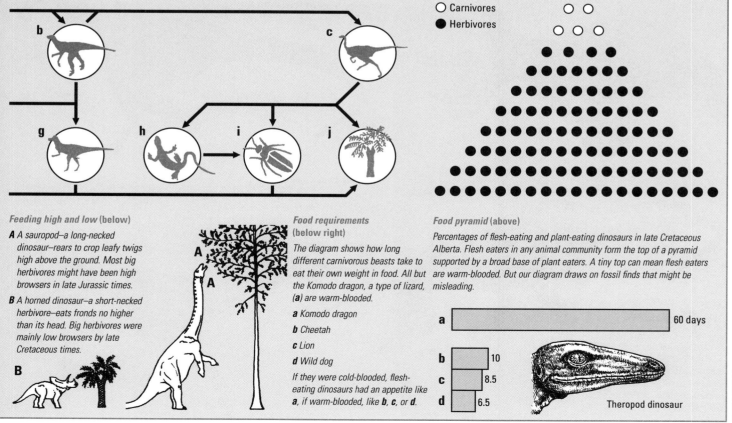

○ Carnivores
● Herbivores

Feeding high and low (below)

A *A sauropod–a long-necked dinosaur–rears to crop leafy twigs high above the ground. Most big herbivores might have been high browsers in late Jurassic times.*

B *A horned dinosaur–a short-necked herbivore–eats fronds no higher than its head. Big herbivores were mainly low browsers by late Cretaceous times.*

Food requirements (below right)

The diagram shows how long different carnivorous beasts take to eat their own weight in food. All but the Komodo dragon, a type of lizard, (a) are warm-blooded.

a *Komodo dragon*
b *Cheetah*
c *Lion*
d *Wild dog*

If they were cold-blooded, flesh-eating dinosaurs had an appetite like a, if warm-blooded, like b, c, or d.

Food pyramid (above)

Percentages of flesh-eating and plant-eating dinosaurs in late Cretaceous Alberta. Flesh eaters in any animal community form the top of a pyramid supported by a broad base of plant eaters. A tiny top can mean flesh eaters are warm-blooded. But our diagram draws on fossil finds that might be misleading.

a | 60 days
b | 10
c | 8.5
d | 6.5

Theropod dinosaur

© DIAGRAM

Attack

Theropods had methods of attack that varied with their size, agility, and victims. Small predators chased lizards, seized them in sharp clawed hands, and swallowed them head first. Hunters from *Deinonychus* up to *Allosaurus* and even *Tyrannosaurus* perhaps roamed in packs, creeping up on big plant eaters then killing with a sudden rush. Theropods struck mainly with their fangs, but sharp toe and finger claws could grip or slash at prey. *Baryonyx* might have seized fish in its crocodilelike jaws, but toothless theropods seem ill-equipped for catching anything but insects or digging up and eating eggs or pecking at plants.

1 High-speed chase

Compsognathus and other lightweight theropods used speed to chase small game. Each agile hunter grabbed prey with its clawed hands, or thrust out its long neck and snapped up lizards, birds, and mammals with its narrow, sharp-toothed jaws.

2 Slashing claws (below)

Members of a Deinonychus pack could have brought down a dinosaur much larger than themselves, just as wild dogs topple zebras. As some grappled with the victim's tail to slow it down, others could have lashed out and ripped its belly with their claws.

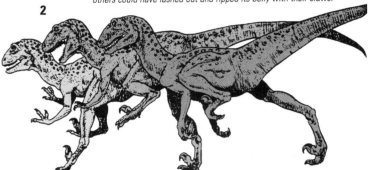

3 Counterattack (below)

A Triceratops at full tilt could have driven off Tyrannosaurus, as today a charging rhino might deter a lion. Counterattack could well have served as a deterrent for other ceratopsians—some as heavy as an elephant, most with two long brow horns, or one long horn jutting from the snout.

4 Crushing bite (below)

Strange, short-headed Oviraptor ("egg thief") lacked teeth for biting prey. Yet two bony prongs pointed down from the roof of its mouth. These might have crushed the shells of other dinosaurs' eggs, as a sharp bone in the neck helps an egg-eating snake crush the birds' eggs that it swallows.

6 Headlong charge (below)

Immense jaws gaping wide, Tyrannosaurus could have run at hadrosaurs head on. Powerful muscles slammed its jaws shut as its fangs took out a massive chunk of flesh from the victims' vulnerable necks. These creatures then quickly weakened and collapsed.

5 Sudden snatch (right)

Baryonyx's crocodilelike head and fish scales found lying where one specimen's stomach would have been suggest that this dinosaur fished like storks or bears. It could have stood in ambush, then seized fish in its sharp-toothed jaws or scooped them up with its claws.

Defense

Each group of dinosaurs had some way of coping with flesh-eating enemies. Sheer bulk and traveling in herds helped protect those big plant eaters, the sauropods and horned and duck-billed dinosaurs. Ostrich dinosaurs and hypsilophodontids relied upon a speedy getaway. Scelidosaurs, stegosaurs, armored dinosaurs, and titanosaurid sauropods relied on tough skins reinforced by tooth snapping studs and plates. Some plant-eaters even counterattacked. *Triceratops* charged like a rhinoceros. *Iguanodon* stabbed with its spiky thumb claws. *Diplodocids* used their tails as whips. Shunosaurus and ankylosaurids wielded heavy tail clubs, and stegosaurs swung tails as spiky as a medieval mace.

1 Body armor (right)

Four-legged ornithischians evolved increasingly effective body armor.

A *Scelidosaurs: rows of bony studs down the back*

B *Stegosaurs: bony spines or plates on back; tail and often shoulder spines*

C *Ankylosaurs: bands of horn-sheathed bony plates. Nodosaurids had long flank spines as in the head-on view of one far right*

D *Ceratopsians: nose and brow horns and bony frill covering the neck*

2 Speed (right)

This skeleton and restoration of an ostrich dinosaur emphasize limb design that allowed a rapid escape from enemies.

A *Relative lengths of hind limb bones suggest the ability to sprint.*

  a *Short femur*

  b *Long shin bones*

  c *Long metatarsal bones*

  d *Long phalanges*

B *An ostrich dinosaur at high speed. Besides running fast, its muscular legs could have delivered deadly kicks.*

3 Toe and thumb claws (right)

Sauropods might have used the large claws on their thumbs and big toes as defensive weapons.

A *Camarasaurus toe bones show a long claw on a big toe. A backward kick with the hind foot might have gored a predator*

B *A rearing Diplodocus brandishes its pointed thumb claws at a threatening Allosaurus. If Diplodocus lunged, it might have stabbed and crushed the predator.*

4 Tails (right)

Areas shown in gray are weapons furnished by types of tails.

A *Bony club: a feature first seen in the sauropod Shunosaurus, but best developed in ankylosaurids, such as the individual pictured here, far right.*

B *Bony tail spikes: seen in stegosaurids*

C *Whiplash: the tapered tail of certain types of sauropods*

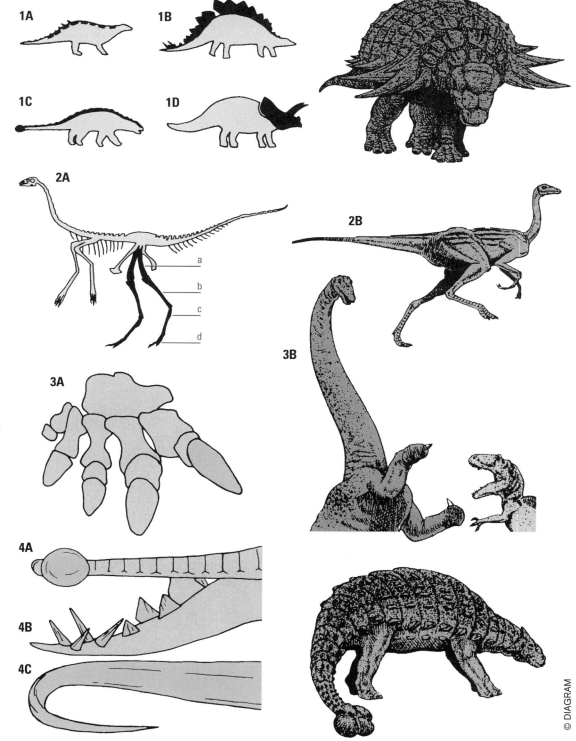

1A 1B 1C 1D 2A 2B 3A 3B 4A 4B 4C

© DIAGRAM

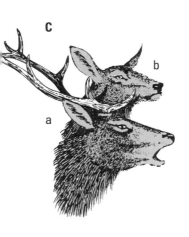

A

b

a

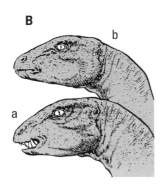

B

b

a

C

b

a

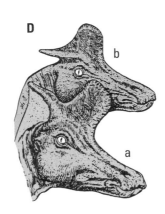

D

b

a

Winning a mate

Tusks and no tusks (left)

Two pairs of heads hint that tusks marked a difference between the sexes in some dinosaurs as well as in some living mammals.

A *Male (**a**) and female (**b**) musk deer. Only the male has long curved tusks.*

B *The tusked dinosaur Heterodontosaurus (**a**) and tuskless Abrictosaurus (**b**) might have been a male and female of the same genus.*

Flamboyant headgear

Two more pairs of heads suggest that showy outgrowths marked a difference between the sexes in certain dinosaurs as well as in some living mammals.

C *Red deer stag (**a**) and (**b**) hind. Only the stag grows antlers.*

D *Lambeosaurus male (**a**) and female (**b**). Both had a crest, but the male's was much more prominent than the female's.*

Male birds, mammals, and even fish and reptiles win mates by attracting females and repelling rival males. So it must have been with dinosaurs. Many males were very likely larger and more showy than females of their kind. The biggest lambeosaurid crests and carnosaur hornlets probably belonged to males. Tuskless *Abrictosaurus* was arguably a female *Heterodontosaurus*, and some say high-domed bone-heads were all males, while low-domed forms were females. The males' horns and crests probably intimidated rivals, but sometimes duels decided which male mated with and ruled a herd of females. Bone-heads butted one another, dromaeosaurids could have sparred with toe claws, and ceratopsians locked horns.

Locking horns

*Similar scenes of combat (**1–2**) hint that some male dinosaurs might have fought like stags to win mastery over females.*

1 *Red deer stags lock antlers, twist heads, and shove against each other. Whichever pushes harder tends to win the fight and dominate the herd.*

2 *Styracosaurus males perhaps clashed the horns projecting from their bony frills, or merely brandished them to scare off would be rivals.*

Banging heads

*Two more combat scenes (**3–4**) suggest a different kind of duel in which male mammals might have had a dinosaur counterpart.*

3 *Male bighorn rams run at one another, rear, and bash their heads together. Reinforced skulls prevent these savage impacts from damaging their brains.*

4 *Maybe male bone-headed dinosaurs also used their heads as battering rams to win a herd of females. Yet, although thick, their skulls appear to have been unsuitable for such shocks.*

Clawing contests

*A third pair of duels (**5–6**) depicts a type of contest fought by male birds probably similar to battles between lightweight theropods.*

5 *Fighting gamecocks leap at one another, stabbing viciously with the long sharp claws called spurs.*

6 *It is very likely that male dromaeosaurids fought like gamecocks (**5**). Swinging their second toe claws, they could strike slashing blows at rivals.*

Eggs

Evidently most dinosaurs hatched from rounded or elongated hard-shelled eggs weighing up to 15 lb, 7 oz (7 kg)–any larger and an egg might break or suffocate the young inside.

Prosauropod, sauropod, ornithopod, and theropod eggs have come from almost every continent. Different species laid on the bare ground, in sandy hollows they then covered with sand, and in nests with raised mud rims. There were nesting colonies of hadrosaurs in Alberta and Montana and of sauropods in Argentina. Mothers very likely guarded eggs until the Sun's heat hatched them.

Laying eggs (left)

Each female Oviraptor *laid 12 or more eggs in a sandy hollow. The eggs formed a spiral, with the narrow ends pointing inward. She evidently sat upon her eggs until they hatched.*

Inside an egg (left)

Like a bird's or turtle's egg, a dinosaur's egg cradled a growing embryo in liquid nourishment protected by a shell.

Safety in numbers (right)

Maiasaura *mothers built their giant nests, each 7 ft (2 m) across, almost in pecking distance of one another. Such guarded colonies were safe from almost any predator.*

Largest egg (below)

A This sauropod egg–length 1 ft (30 cm); diameter 10 in (25 cm); capacity 5.8 pt (3.3 l)–probably belonged to a Hypselosaurus. *No egg much larger could have hatched.*

B Life-size chicken's egg shown for comparison

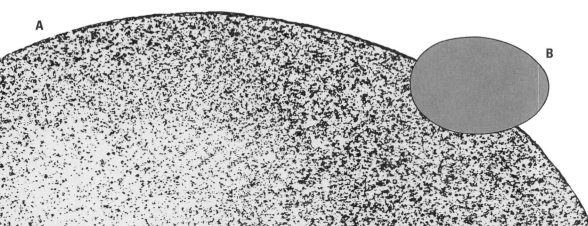

A

B

© DIAGRAM

Young dinosaurs

1 Feeding young (right)

A Maiasaura *mother brings plant food to her young. Scientists think this could have happened because they found the skeletons of young hadrosaurs at a nest. About 3 ft 3 in (1 m) long, these individuals showed signs of tooth wear, yet their limb bones were not strong enough for foraging. Very likely, then, their mother had fed them before they left the nest, as most birds feed their chicks before they begin to fly.*

2 Protecting young (below)

Horned dinosaurs (not shown to the same scale as the adult Maiasaura*) could have formed an outward facing ring to shield their young from marauding theropods, as musk oxen face out to deter wolves.*

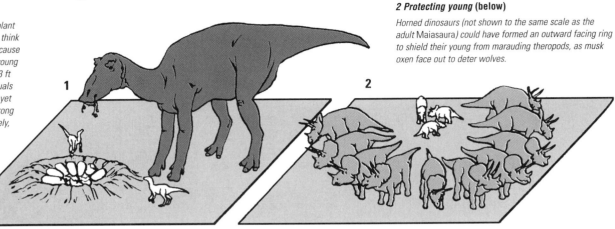

3 On the march (right)

Sauropods evidently marched in herds like elephants. Adults perhaps guarded young; evidence includes the distribution of large and small footprints in a trackway found in Texas. How and when young joined a herd remains in doubt. Baby sauropods came from eggs laid in the ground, but surely these would have hatched after the herd had moved on.

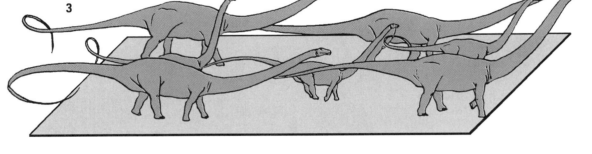

Egg and infant (below)

A prosauropod egg and baby from Argentina reveal that some kinds of dinosaurs began life very small.

A *Egg (shown actual size) found in a nest with the remains of tiny dinosaurs.*

B Mussaurus *skeleton, one of five or six from the same nest as the egg. None was longer than 8 in (20 cm), or no larger than a thrush. Puppylike, outsized, eyes, knees, and feet prove that these creatures had died while still in infancy. Their parents might have been as much as 10 ft (3 m) long.*

Fossil embryos, hatchlings, and adolescents tell us much about how dinosaurs grew up. Hatchlings were quite tiny–as little as one-sixteen thousandth their mothers' size. Hatchling hadrosaurs had legs too weak to forage, and mothers evidently fed them in the nest. *Oviraptor* mothers might have even brought their nestlings other baby dinosaurs to eat. Baby dinosaurs had relatively bigger heads and eyes than adults, although relatively shorter limbs, necks, tails, crests, horns, frills, and plates. At least some parents guarded their young, and it appears that all juveniles grew fast. Despite that, few survived to reach full size.

Changing proportions (right)

Certain bodily proportions changed with age in dinosaurs as others do in humans.

A *Changes in the hind limb of tyrannosaurids*

  a *Young, with a relatively long ankle region*

  b *Adult, with a relatively short ankle region*

B *Changes in tyrannosaurids' skulls*

  a *Young, with relatively big, round eye socket, and slim snout and jaws*

  b *Adult, with relatively smaller eye socket and deep snout and jaws*

C *Changes in proportions of a human head and body*

  a *Newborn baby, with a head one-quarter its total length*

  b *Adult, with a head one-eighth its total length*

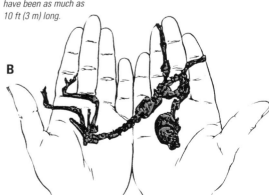

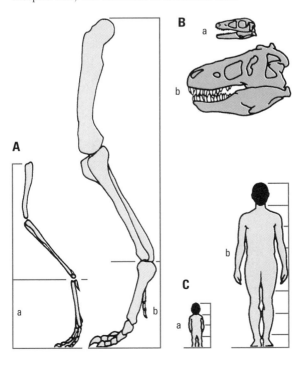

Life expectancy

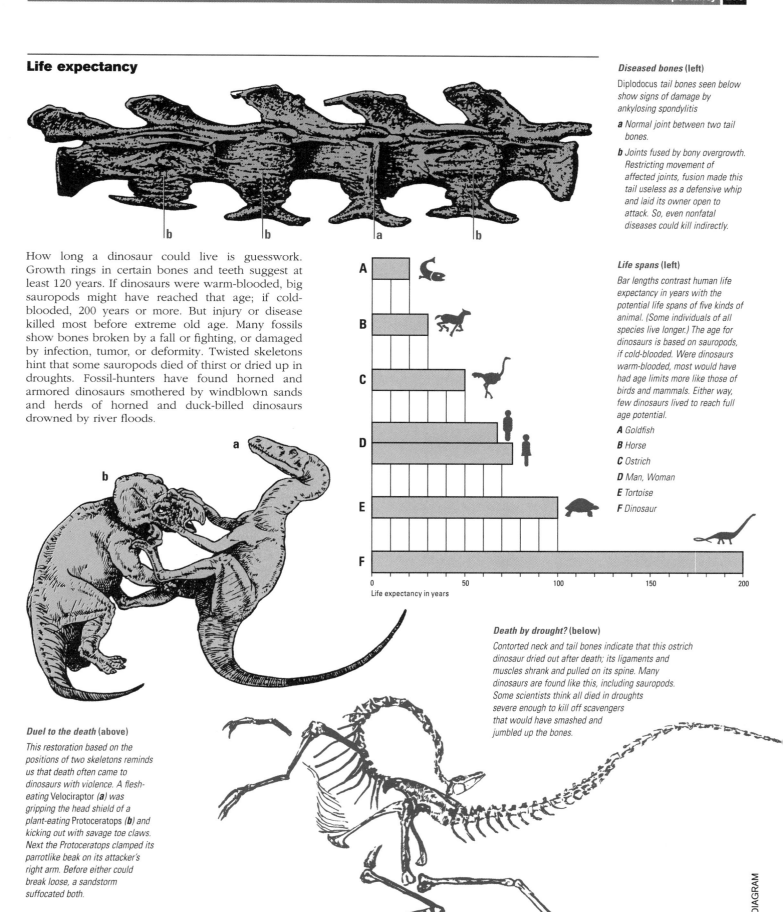

Diseased bones (left)

Diplodocus *tail bones seen below show signs of damage by ankylosing spondylitis*

a *Normal joint between two tail bones.*

b *Joints fused by bony overgrowth. Restricting movement of affected joints, fusion made this tail useless as a defensive whip and laid its owner open to attack. So, even nonfatal diseases could kill indirectly.*

How long a dinosaur could live is guesswork. Growth rings in certain bones and teeth suggest at least 120 years. If dinosaurs were warm-blooded, big sauropods might have reached that age; if cold-blooded, 200 years or more. But injury or disease killed most before extreme old age. Many fossils show bones broken by a fall or fighting, or damaged by infection, tumor, or deformity. Twisted skeletons hint that some sauropods died of thirst or dried up in droughts. Fossil-hunters have found horned and armored dinosaurs smothered by windblown sands and herds of horned and duck-billed dinosaurs drowned by river floods.

Life spans (left)

Bar lengths contrast human life expectancy in years with the potential life spans of five kinds of animal. (Some individuals of all species live longer.) The age for dinosaurs is based on sauropods, if cold-blooded. Were dinosaurs warm-blooded, most would have had age limits more like those of birds and mammals. Either way, few dinosaurs lived to reach full age potential.

A Goldfish

B Horse

C Ostrich

D Man, Woman

E Tortoise

F Dinosaur

Life expectancy in years

Death by drought? (below)

Contorted neck and tail bones indicate that this ostrich dinosaur dried out after death; its ligaments and muscles shrank and pulled on its spine. Many dinosaurs are found like this, including sauropods. Some scientists think all died in droughts severe enough to kill off scavengers that would have smashed and jumbled up the bones.

Duel to the death (above)

This restoration based on the positions of two skeletons reminds us that death often came to dinosaurs with violence. A flesh-eating Velociraptor (a) was gripping the head shield of a plant-eating Protoceratops (b) and kicking out with savage toe claws. Next the Protoceratops clamped its parrotlike beak on its attacker's right arm. Before either could break loose, a sandstorm suffocated both.

SECTION 4

THE FIRST HUMANS

What are humans?

This chapter outlines the combined physical and mental attributes that make our species, Homo sapiens, *unique.*

As evolutionary products, however, our bodies comprise systems inherited from other creatures. Comparisons with various backboned animals—some living, some extinct—reveal the major changes that created human bones, lungs, blood supply, and other features, and show that the biochemicals that build, maintain, and mend our body systems are the same as theirs.

The chapter ends by placing humans in context, as members of the group of mammals known as primates.

Human attributes (below)

Four illustrations show the aspects that collectively distinguish us from other living things.

1 Bipedal walking

Weight is transmitted from the heel through the outer edge of the foot to the ball of the foot and big toe. The leg and foot act as a lever with:

a *Load, transmitted by the tibia*

b *Fulcrum (ball of the foot)*

c *Effort, applied by the Achilles tendon pulling the heel up as the calf muscle contracts*

2 Versatile hands

a *Power grip*

b *Precision grip*

c *Cupping*

3 Binocular vision

Both eyes combine to focus on objects in a wide range of locations:

a *Near*

b *Left*

c *Right*

d *Distant*

4 Big brain

Seen here from above, the big human brain is deeply convoluted. Its wrinkles produce a huge surface area—the part that largely gives the brain intelligence.

a *Normally visible surface*

b *Surface if spread flat: an area of 324 sq in (2,090 sq cm)*

A unique animal

Our species has been defined variously as intelligent, political, tool-using, social, and self-aware. Armed with advanced technology and organized in massive social groups, we now manipulate plants and animals, transforming the Earth's surface to satisfy our needs for food, fuel, living space, and transportation. To defend us from others of our kind we now also have weaponry capable of removing most kinds of life from this planet.

Yet the uniquely powerful being *Homo sapiens* contains just the same chemical ingredients you find in any mammal—elements such as carbon, hydrogen, oxygen, and nitrogen. What makes us special is the way that these are grouped in compounds, cells, tissues, and body systems to create a creature with all-around abilities not shared by any other living thing.

A horse can gallop faster than a human can run. An eagle's eyes are keener than our own. Our teeth and claws are no match for a leopard's. Yet we possess four crucial attributes, combined only in our species: an upright skeleton, manipulative hands, three-dimensional color vision, and a uniquely complex brain. Collectively these four confer advantages that have made us masters of our planet.

Our upright skeleton enables us to travel on two legs with a unique heel-toe action, each step a balancing act demanding split-second coordination of muscles in the back, hips, legs, and feet. Not only can we walk, but we can run, jump, swim, dive, and climb a cliff or tree. Long-distance runners have more endurance than a deer.

With forelimbs not needed for support, we use the flexible and sensitive thumbs and fingers of our hands to explore surfaces by touch and to grip objects strongly or precisely. Swapping tool for tool at will, we control our environment far more effectively than any mammal stuck with forelimbs shod with hooves or armed with claws.

Forward-facing eyes sensitive to color enable us to focus on sharp images, judge distance accurately, and distinguish hue as well as shape and brightness—abilities few other mammals share. Rotating in their sockets, eyes follow movement without the need to move our head. And because we stand high off the ground we see much farther than other ground-based mammals of our size.

Last comes a brain that is large relative to body size and superbly capable of learning, reasoning, speaking and coordinating hand-eye interaction.

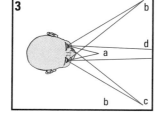

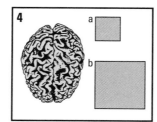

Clues in comparative anatomy

Living and fossil animals with structures that correspond to ours hold clues to common ancestors–the more the similarities, the closer the relationship to us appears. But anatomists carefully distinguish between homologous structures, those which share a common origin (a human's arm and a bird's wing, for example), and analogous structures such as the wings of birds and flies that look somewhat alike yet have an unrelated ancestry.

Primitive living sea creatures much like those of 550 million years ago hint at the great antiquity of our body's basic layout–its inside, outside, front and rear, and right and left sides.

A sea anemone has only two cell layers: an outside that protects and informs it of the world around and a layer lining an inner cavity and handling nourishment and reproduction. Food enters through a single opening to be digested by cells that line this pouch, while the same opening releases eggs and body waste. In worms the pouch has become a tube, with a mouth at one end and an anus at the other–the basic pattern of our own digestive system.

This layout automatically gave its owner a front and rear. Cells specialized and grouped as muscles helped mobile creatures move forward to find food for the mouth. Tentacles or teeth clustered around the mouth for seizing food. Cells specialized for finding food by scent or sight also became concentrated at the front, which gained a head with a brain coordinating signals for an increasingly complex nervous system.

Meanwhile, in humans' early wormlike ancestors, the body had become bilaterally symmetrical: each side a mirror image of the other. This made it easier to travel forward, steer from side to side, and stay the right way up. Our own paired limbs, eyes, ears, and nostrils are legacies of this arrangement.

Front and rear (right)

We probably have lowly, wormlike ancestors to thank for our body's basic layout:

a Central digestive system, with mouth, gut, and anus

b Bilateral symmetry, and with paired limbs and other organs

Homologous structures (right)

A Bat's wing bones

B Human arm and hand bones

Wing and arm may look dissimilar, yet they share structural similarities inherited from a common vertebrate ancestor:

a Humerus

b Radius and ulna

c Five digits

Analogous structures (right)

a Wing of a bat, a vertebrate. This wing comprises skin flaps stiffened from being stretched between arm and finger bones and the legs.

b Wings of a butterfly, an invertebrate. Each wing is a membrane stretched over stiff, tubelike veins and covered by overlapping scales.

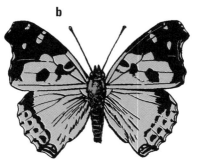

Lowly legacies (left)

This longitudinal section through a worm shows the one-way flow of food made possible by the evolution of three crucial structures:

a Mouth

b Gut

c Anus

Branchiostoma (left)

Branchiostoma, the living lancelet, lacks a head, jaws, or vertebrae, but such beasts might have given rise to all backboned animals from fish to humans. Like a fish, a lancelet has:

a Gills

b Nerve cord

c Notochord (a precursor of the backbone)

d Tail fin

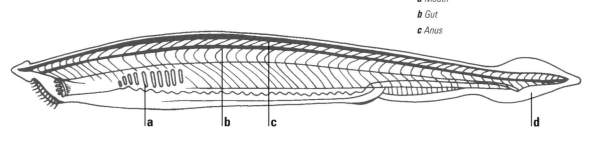

Bones and muscles

Most of the human body is bone and muscle– products of a middle body layer that first appeared between the other two among some early animals without a backbone. Many of these invertebrates evolved an outside shell or skeleton for protection and support, but vertebrates evolved internal bony skeleton–stores of calcium and phosphorus doubling as guards for vital organs and attachment points for muscles, giving leverage for limbs or fins. A crab's shell must be shed from time to time with growth, leaving its owner unprotected until a new shell hardens, but internal skeletons grow at the same rate as the whole body.

In jawless fishes and all later vertebrates, the basic bony structure is a backbone of interlocking vertebrae. These shield the vulnerable spinal cord, while ribs projecting at intervals from each side of the backbone guard soft internal organs and provide attachment points for intervening muscle segments. With these a fish wiggles its body and tail which thrust water back to drive the body forward.

Fishes have an almost straight backbone with relatively weak vertebrae. Vertebrates that walk on land need stronger internal support. The first tetrapods to go ashore had a sturdy backbone curved in a shallow arch–a suspension bridge with the body's trunk slung beneath–and a large rib cage to support the body when lying on the ground. Ribs also probably expanded and contracted to help operate the lungs.

Some land-based vertebrates showed complex spinal changes. As limbs took over locomotion, the tail dwindled to a balancer or fly whisk, and in apes and humans it disappeared, while ribs tended to vanish from the waist and neck. In synapsids ancestral to mammals, neck ribs shrank, allowing freer head movements. Also neck vertebrae curved up to lift the head. In certain mammals, changes to the first two neck vertebrae allowed the head to turn more freely. In humans, a second spinal curve low in the back pushed the chest up and back, bringing chest and head above the hips for good bipedal balance.

Evolving backbones (below)

Six diagrams trace the evolution of the backbone from horizontal rod to cantilevered arch and vertical column.

1 Eusthenopteron's *straight backbone gave its swimming muscles leverage. This fish lived 375 million years ago.*

2 A strong curved backbone supported early tetrapod sprawlers as they crawled on land.

3 Complex changes to the spine and ribs improved land mobility in the mammal-like therapsid Thrinaxodon, *close to the ancestry of mammals.*

4 Flexible backbones of early insect-eating mammals resembling this living tree shrew adapted them for climbing trees.

5 The semi-upright chimpanzee has a straighter backbone than its quadrupedal monkeylike ancestors, whose spine was arched between supporting hips and shoulders.

6 The human spinal column forms a sinuous column combining strength and flexibility. Its curves are shaped to keep the head and body above the center of gravity.

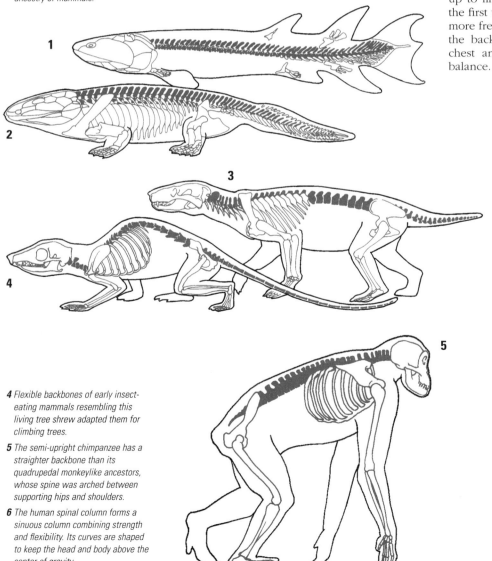

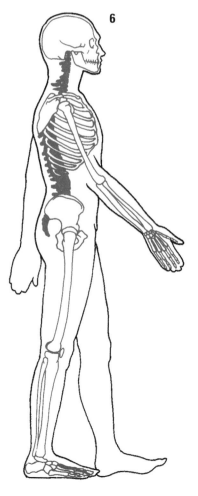

Skull, jaws, and teeth

Our skull, jaws, and teeth have various and complex origins.

Early vertebrates, somewhat resembling those living, jawless fishes the lampreys, had no true skull or jaws, just a box of gristle or bone guarding the brain and internal ear and protecting eyes and nostrils, plus bars of bone or gristle stiffening the gill slits in the sides of the head. Bony plates set in the skin protected the head and neck.

In certain fishes, some gill bars disappeared, but one pair enlarged to form hinged jaws, in time supporting teeth derived from denticles–sharp, enamel-coated points embedded in the skin (as they still are in sharks). Meanwhile, some armor plates migrated from the skin to cover most of the head, fusing with, reinforcing, and largely replacing the braincase and upper jaw, converting all into a single bony skull and adding bones to the lower jaw.

In our own skull, ancient "skin bones" form the top and front and most of the sides and mouth roof. Only the back and base of our brain are still protected by primeval braincase bone.

Almost all our skull bones can be traced back to those in lobe-finned fishes of around 380 million years ago. With redesigning for life on land, bones guarding gills and throat dropped out. Synapsid tetrapods gained differentiated teeth, a skull opening behind the eye to give jaw muscles freer action, and a bony partition above the mouth roof, an aid to breathing while eating. Meanwhile some skull and jaw bones disappeared. Of the early synapsids' seven jaw bones only one–the tooth-bearing dentary–survived in mammals. These gained a new joint where jaw articulates with skull, while tiny bones from the old jaw joint migrated into the skull, becoming two middle ear bones whose vibrations help us hear. Early mammals' braincases also enlarged to fit expanding brains. Further redesigning of the skull accommodated the early primate brain ancestral to our own far larger version.

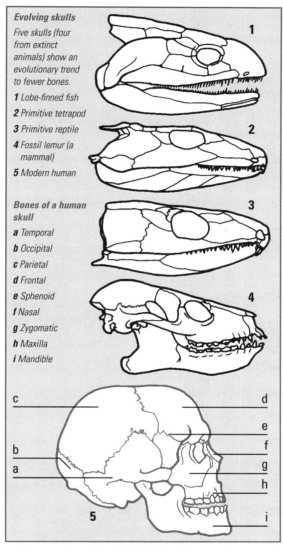

Evolving skulls

Five skulls (four from extinct animals) show an evolutionary trend to fewer bones.

1 Lobe-finned fish

2 Primitive tetrapod

3 Primitive reptile

4 Fossil lemur (a mammal)

5 Modern human

Bones of a human skull

a Temporal

b Occipital

c Parietal

d Frontal

e Sphenoid

f Nasal

g Zygomatic

h Maxilla

i Mandible

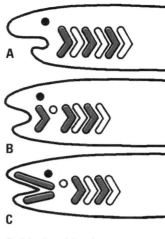

Evolving jaws (above)

Three diagrams trace the evolution of jaws from a fish's gill bars–stiffening gill slits in the sides of the head.

A Jawless fish: bony gill bars (tinted) alternate with gills.

B The first pair of gills shrinks to a spiracle, a tiny hole for drawing in water free from mud.

C The first pair of gill bars expands to form hinged jaws

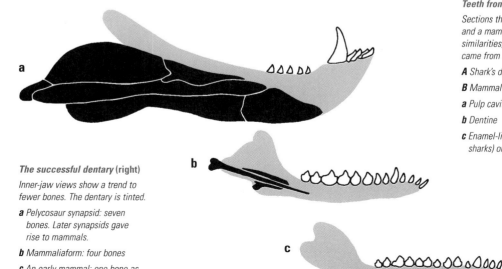

The successful dentary (right)

Inner-jaw views show a trend to fewer bones. The dentary is tinted.

a Pelycosaur synapsid: seven bones. Later synapsids gave rise to mammals.

b Mammaliaform: four bones

c An early mammal: one bone as in modern mammals

Teeth from denticles (right)

Sections through a shark's denticle and a mammal's tooth show similarities, which hint that teeth came from structures set in skin.

A Shark's denticle

B Mammal molar tooth

a Pulp cavity

b Dentine

c Enamel-like vitrodentine (in sharks) or enamel (in mammals).

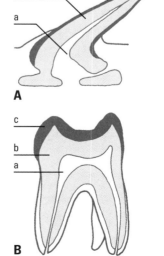

Limbs

Multiplying muscles (below)

a Two muscles are enough to work a fish's pectoral fin.

b Seven muscles operate the shoulder and upper arm of a lizard, a land reptile.

a

b

Legs and arms are outgrowths of the body that we can trace back through the fossil record to the fleshy fins of lobe-finned fishes, one group of which was ancestral to all land vertebrates.

These fins were mainly balancers but were strong enough to haul their air-breathing owners a short way overland. Front fins (the arms' precursors) joined shoulder girdles fixed to the skull. Hind fins (precursors of the thighs and legs) joined pelvic bones inside the body.

In early tetrapods, fins gave rise to jointed limbs. Knees and elbows jutted sideways from the body, but hind limbs joined a pelvic girdle braced by its attachment to the spine, thus aiding forward movement. Meanwhile, the shoulder girdle had been freed from the skull so that head and front limbs now moved separately. Almost every bone inside these ancient prehistoric limbs finds its equivalent in humans. Change has been mainly in the proportion, not the number, of bones.

Advanced synapsids (therapsids) remotely descended from amphibious tetrapods evolved knees and elbows rotated underneath the body, giving a longer stride and faster movement overland. Each limb now ended in five forward-jutting, clawed digits, and the old massive shoulder girdle had grown lighter, making forelimbs much more mobile.

This scheme persisted in the early mammals. Refinements culminating in bipedal walking and manipulative hands figure in the next chapters.

Evolving limbs (left)

Six diagrams trace pelvic and pectoral (hip and shoulder) bone changes that improved limb strength and leverage.

1 Eusthenopteron's *pelvis was unattached to the spine, and this lobe-finned fish's shoulder girdle was joined to an almost rigid skull.*

2 *A pelvic girdle linking hind limb to spine and a shoulder girdle separated from the skull produced stronger limb leverage and freer movement for early tetrapods capable of walking.*

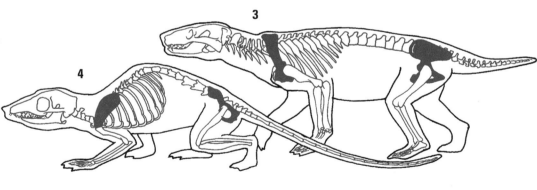

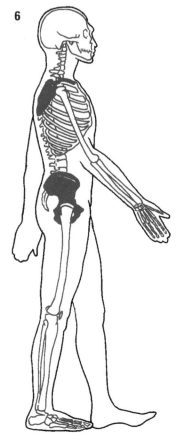

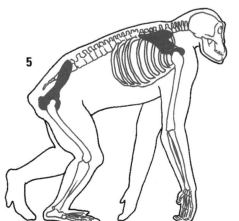

3 Further changes gave therapsids like Thrinaxodon *more limb power and mobility.*

4 A tree shrew's long, narrow pelvis and its flexible shoulder joint, allowing arm raising, are aids to climbing.

5 This ape's pelvis and shoulder girdle show adaptations for walking and climbing on all fours and swinging from branches by the arms.

6 A human's short, wide, pelvis and the broad, flexible shoulder blades on either side of the upper spine allow bipedal walking and free arm rotation.

The skin

Our skin and nervous system both seem to have originated in the outer layer of our ancestral invertebrates' two-layered bodies. As in their descendants, fishes, our own skin protects the body's soft, moist inside from outside dangers, but our only relics of an early fish's bony armor have disappeared or sunk to form our collarbone and large parts of the skull.

Like a pelycosaur synapsid's skin, our own is waterproof, yet our body's only legacy of its horny scales is nails–flattened toe and finger guards derived from claws. Grip-assisting ridges on our toes and fingers are tokens of the tough pads that helped our mammal forebears walk and climb.

Our insulating body hair probably derives from sensitive outgrowths of the skin first seen in the warm-blooded cynodonts, synapsids that led directly to mammals. The origins of skin glands are less obvious, but milk glands probably arose in early mammals from the sebaceous glands, whose oil keeps skin and hair in good condition. Some people, incidentally, have extra nipples, relics of the rows that evidently ran down early mammals' undersides.

Below the facial skin, subcutaneous muscle that evolved with our primate ancestors allows us a series of facial expressions denied to lower vertebrates like fishes, whose faces stay inscrutable, like a mask.

Skin structures

Sections through the skin of a fish, reptile, and human show major features including two shared, basic structures: a thick, deep, fibrous dermis, underlying a thinner superficial epidermis. Both imply a common origin for the skin of all the vertebrates.

1 Fish skin in section

a Epidermis

b Bony scale

c Dermis

2 Reptile skin in section

a Horny scale

b Epidermis

c Dermis

3 Human skin in section

a Epidermis

b Dermis

c Hair

d Duct from sweat gland

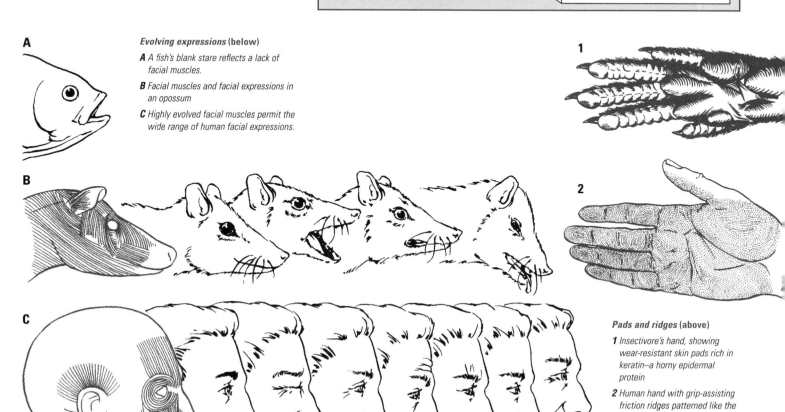

A

Evolving expressions (below)

A A fish's blank stare reflects a lack of facial muscles.

B Facial muscles and facial expressions in an opossum

C Highly evolved facial muscles permit the wide range of human facial expressions.

B

C

Pads and ridges (above)

1 Insectivore's hand, showing wear-resistant skin pads rich in keratin–a horny epidermal protein

2 Human hand with grip-assisting friction ridges patterned like the pads of insectivore ancestors

Nerves and senses

All animals depend on nerve cells for communication and control. Our own complex nervous system originated in the loose nerve net of lowly creatures like the jellyfish. With fishes came a coherent nervous structure, with a spinal cord handling reflex actions; taking signals to a brain from nerve endings specialized for tasting, smelling, seeing, and maintaining balance; and relaying orders from the brain to specific muscle groups.

In us, as in the early vertebrates, key sense organs cluster in the head, the body's old front end. In humans, as in fishes, most work by sensing dissolved substances or vibrations passing through a fluid. Thus taste buds on the human tongue detect substances dissolved in water. And nasal membranes must be moist to pick up scents. Because our nasal membranes are connected to the mouth, flavors are really tastes and smells combined.

As in a fish, fluid flowing in closed tubes of the inner ear provides our sense of balance, but evolutionary changes–first in early amphibious tetrapods, then in early amniotes and early synapsids, and later mammals–remodeled parts of the old fishes' gills, giving ears external openings and making them efficient hearing organs, sensitive to airborne sounds. Internally, our ears convert these to vibrations in liquid that surrounds nerve endings in the cochlea, a coiled tube of the inner ear.

Eyes evolved even earlier than ears, deriving from light-sensitive spots in primitive invertebrates. Even primeval fishes had paired eyes much like our own, designed as cameras. Tear glands, which moisten eyes exposed to air, came with early tetrapods; eyelids later, with early amniotes; while our sharp, binocular color vision originated later still, with diurnal ancestors of apes.

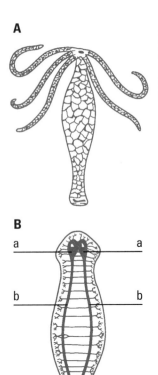

A

B

a   a

b   b

Evolving nervous system (above)

Two invertebrates (shown much enlarged) represent major stages in the evolution of the nervous system.

A Hydra, *a freshwater relative of jellyfish and sea anemones, has a nerve net–a diffused mesh of nerve cells.*

B Planaria, *a flatworm, has bilateral symmetry and a central nervous system with:*

a *Brain in the head end*

b *Nerve cords (foreshadowing our spinal cord)*

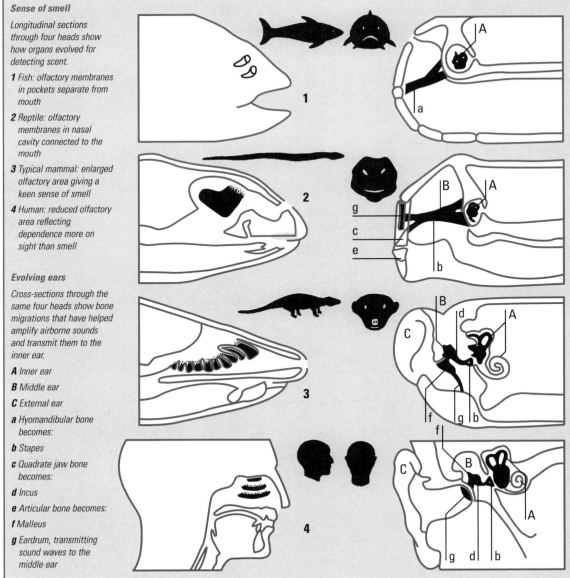

Sense of smell

Longitudinal sections through four heads show how organs evolved for detecting scent.

1 *Fish: olfactory membranes in pockets separate from mouth*

2 *Reptile: olfactory membranes in nasal cavity connected to the mouth*

3 *Typical mammal: enlarged olfactory area giving a keen sense of smell*

4 *Human: reduced olfactory area reflecting dependence more on sight than smell*

Evolving ears

Cross-sections through the same four heads show bone migrations that have helped amplify airborne sounds and transmit them to the inner ear.

A *Inner ear*

B *Middle ear*

C *External ear*

a *Hyomandibular bone becomes:*

b *Stapes*

c *Quadrate jaw bone becomes:*

d *Incus*

e *Articular bone becomes:*

f *Malleus*

g *Eardrum, transmitting sound waves to the middle ear*

The brain

The human brain, which thought up everything from Stone-Age pebble tools to atom bombs, began as a mere swelling of the spinal cord at the head end near the chief sense organs. Brains as coordinating centers of nervous systems occurred in beasts as primitive as the living flatworm, but, like most invertebrates, such creatures acted mainly by instinct; intelligent behavior awaited larger and more complex brains.

Early fishes' brains already showed our own brain's basic three-part structure–hindbrain, midbrain, and forebrain–but a fish's brain is very limited. Its hindbrain handles balance, its midbrain vision, and its forebrain mostly smell.

Reptiles' brains have a relatively larger hindbrain and midbrain, giving improved hearing, vision, and sensory coordination–evolutionary changes geared to life on land.

In early mammals, the brain grew much bigger and more complex than a reptile's brain. The hindbrain gained a large, cabbage-shaped cerebellum, coordinating complex movements. Sense coordination shifted forward to the forebrain, and this acquired a large, many-wrinkled cerebrum to cope with memory and learning. Even in such small-brained mammals as the hedgehog, the forebrain overgrows the midbrain. In more advanced mammals such as monkeys, the evolving forebrain has grown relatively larger still–a process referred to in the next few chapters. In humans, the forebrain's enormously expanded cerebrum, the seat of reason, has overgrown and dwarfed the rest of the brain, remodeling much of the skull.

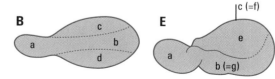

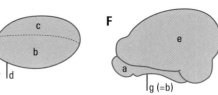
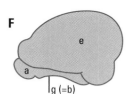

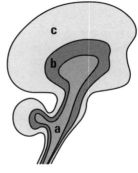

A layered brain (above)

One theory holds that our brain has three layers that betray stages in its evolution:

a "Reptilian" (hindbrain and midbrain): slave to precedent

b Paleomammalian (around the upper brainstem): seat of the emotions

c Neomammalian (cerebral cortex): seat of reason

Cerebral evolution (above)

Schematic side views trace grades in evolution of the brain's left cerebral hemisphere. Most gray matter, rich in nerve cells, migrates to the brain surface to form its cortex or pallium ("cloak")

A Primitive form

B Amphibian

C Primitive reptile

D Advanced reptile

E Primitive mammal

F Advanced mammal

Structures shown are:

a Olfactory bulb

b Paleopallium ("old covering")

c Archipallium ("primitive covering")

d Basal nuclei

e Neopallium (rich in association centers)

f Hippocampus (the old archipallium)

g Olfactory lobe (the old paleopallium, or "smell brain")

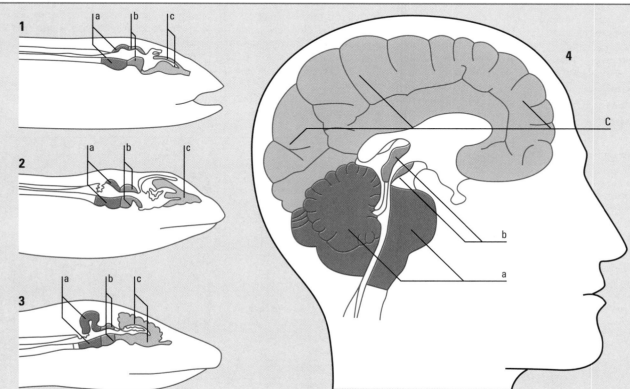

Evolving brains

Longitudinal sections through four heads retrace progressive changes in proportions of the brain's three basic divisions:

1 Fish's brain

2 Reptile's brain

3 Primitive mammal's brain

4 Human brain. For each we show:

a Hindbrain (including its offshoot, the cerebellum)

b Midbrain

c Forebrain

© DIAGRAM

Vanishing tubes (right)

Five diagrams show reduction in the numbers of arterial tubes accompanying changes from gills to lungs.

A *Primitive fish*

B *Lung-bearing fish*

C *Amphibian*

D *Reptile*

E *Mammal*

1–6 *Aortic arches (originally gill-related)*

a *Heart chambers*

b *Lungs*

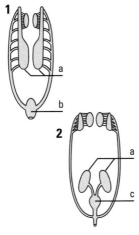

Evolving kidneys (above)

1 *In lower vertebrates kidneys form two long strips that excrete urine through a cloaca along with solid body waste.*

2 *In mammals kidneys form two bean-shaped organs that excrete urine via a bladder.*

a *Kidneys*

b *Cloaca*

c *Bladder*

Three body systems

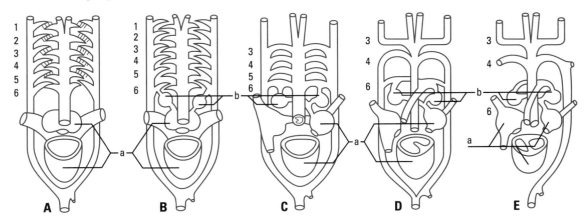

Lungs, blood supply, and kidneys serve vital functions. For instance, lungs provide the body with oxygen for "burning" food to fuel life's processes and expel the combustion waste gas, carbon dioxide. Blood brings cells the nutrients and oxygen they need. Kidneys purify the blood, removing harmful body wastes.

Lungs probably began as moist throat pouches that lobe-finned fishes used for gulping atmospheric air in swampy pools low in oxygen. In amphibians and even reptiles, lung sacs still had and have small oxygen-absorbing surfaces. In mammals, these grew large and complex. Meanwhile an amphibian-type throat-muscle pumping action evolved into the mammals' vacuum pump operated by muscles of the ribs and diaphragm.

In lung-breathing fishes, the nose–at first a smelling organ only–had become also a tube to suck air into lungs while keeping water out. Reptiles gained a bony palate above the mouth partly to separate food from breathed-in air. Mammals added a soft palate, making possible continuous breathing while eating– vital for warm-blooded animals.

Our blood supply is an ancient legacy; indeed, its saltiness hints at our origin from simple cells

designed for life surrounded by the sea. The circulation of the blood, however, has been revolutionized. Since the ancient heart-gill system of ancestral fishes, there has been redesigning of the heart and arteries to take stale blood to lungs and bring fresh blood–enriched with oxygen–from lungs to cells throughout the body. In our cold-blooded forebears, early tetrapods and synapsids, lung evolution outpaced that of circulation. Only birds and mammals have four-chambered "double-barreled" hearts that completely separate fresh blood from stale, providing an efficient circulation system that makes possible the warm bloodedness that keeps us capable of rapid and sustained bodily activity by day or night, even in cold weather.

Kidneys seemingly began among invertebrates as tiny isolated tubes pumping body wastes from cavities between organs. Fishes added filters to these pumps and grouped them into two long strips inside the body. Here, kidneys purified the blood and emptied urine from a common exit. In reptiles, kidneys became two solid masses concentrated far back in the body. In humans and other mammals, each kidney tubule has a loop that rereleases water into the body and prevents it from drying up.

How lungs began (right)

Longitudinal sections show the common origin of land vertebrates' lungs and fishes' swim bladders:

1 *Primitive fish lung, evolved from a throat pouch*

2 *Fish lung modified*

3 *Air-filled swim bladder, controlling buoyancy in bony fishes*

4 *Land vertebrate's lung, with a much-folded inner wall giving more efficiency than the simpler fish lung*

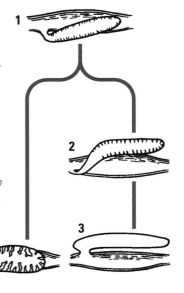

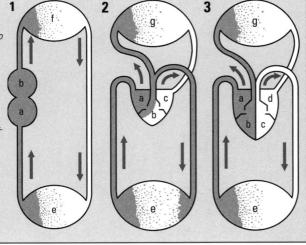

Evolving circulation

1 *Fish circulation: A two-chambered heart pumps stale blood from the body to the gills. Fresh blood flows from the gills to the body.*

2 *One reptilian system: A three-chambered heart pumps mixed blood to the lungs and body.*

3 *Mammal circulation: A four-chambered heart keeps stale and fresh blood separate.*

a–d *Heart chambers*

e *Body*

f *Gill capillaries*

g *Lungs*

Reproduction

How the human egg is fertilized and grows inside the mother's body is very different from the chancy way in which our early ancestors reproduced themselves. Like their living counterparts, these old marine invertebrates most likely shed huge quantities of sperm and eggs haphazardly into the sea. Vertebrates evolved more selective and efficient ways of releasing sex cells and ensuring that egg cells were met by sperm and fertilized.

In primitive vertebrates, sex glands shed sperm and eggs into the body cavity, from where they left through pores near the openings, releasing body wastes. Fishes, however, evolved special tubes to launch their sex glands' products in the outside world.

Like most fishes' eggs, amphibians' lack shells, so they must be laid in water, where they are then fertilized. With amniotes, though, reproduction became geared for life on land. Males injected sperm directly into females' bodies, where moisture kept sperm alive until they fertilized the eggs. Internal fertilization means that a female amniote needs to lay fewer eggs than a frog or toad to ensure that enough will hatch to keep her species going.

Reptiles' eggs are engineered to hatch on land, with a shell, membrane, and fluid-filled sac to guard the growing embryo from injury and drought, a large yolk food supply, a kind of "lung," and a pouch for body wastes.

Humans and other mammals have inherited the plan of this so-called amniotic egg, but while most reptiles lay eggs and leave them for the sun to hatch, placental mammals' eggs develop warm and safe inside the mother's body. There, a temporary organ, the placenta, supplies the unborn young with more food than could be crammed inside an egg surrounded by a shell and removes the fetal body wastes. This reproductive innovation has proved so successful that our species flourishes despite its long pregnancies, most culminating in the birth of just one, single, helpless young.

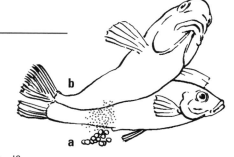

External fertilization (right)

a Female fish releases eggs.

b Male fish sheds a cloud of sperm that fertilize the eggs outside the parents' bodies.

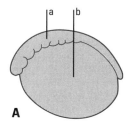
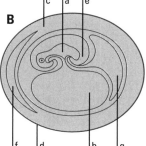
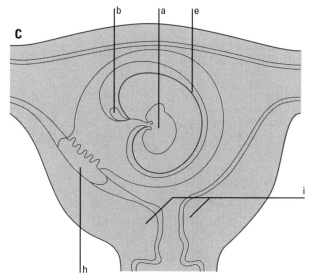

Embryos and evolution (left)

Three sections illustrate changes in protection and nourishment that led to the development of young inside the mother.

A Amphibian embryo

B Reptile embryo

C Human (mammal) embryo

a Embryo

b Yolk (food supply)

c Albumin (food supply)

d Shell (protection)

e Amnion (shock-absorbing liquid-filled sac)

f Chorion (air space letting oxygen in, waste gas out)

g Allantois (area for body wastes)

h Placenta (a temporary organ with chorionic and allantoic structures. Via the mother's blood supply, it provides an embryo with nutrients and oxygen and removes wastes.)

i Uterus (the organ in which an embryo develops inside its mother's body)

Evolving sex organs

Modifications of male and female sex organs aided internal fertilization.

1 Male lower vertebrate: Sperm from testes exit through the cloaca.

2 Female lower vertebrate: Eggs from ovaries exit through the cloaca.

3 Male mammal: Sperm from testes (usually descended) pass via the urethra in the penis (not shown) into the vagina.

4 Female mammal: After a sperm fertilizes an egg, the zygote develops in a uterus. Some mammals have two uteruses.

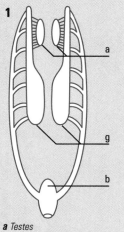
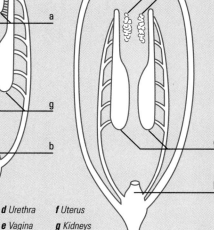
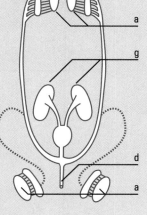
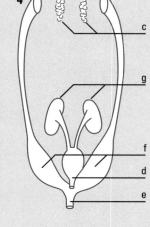

a Testes	*d* Urethra	*f* Uterus
b Cloaca	*e* Vagina	*g* Kidneys
c Ovaries		

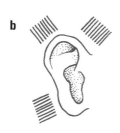

Our hidden history

Parallels between human and other embryos are strong clues to our relationship with different forms of life.

In every animal from worms to humans, the body starts to grow from just two layers of dividing cells–the (outer) ectoderm and (inner) endoderm–that correspond to the double body layer seen in primitive invertebrates like jellyfish. Ectoderm produces skin and nervous tissue. Endoderm produces lining for the digestive tract, related organs like the pancreas and liver, membranes used in gills or lungs, and certain other structures. But in all vertebrates a third, middle, layer–the mesoderm–produces most parts of the body, including bones, muscles, arteries, and veins, most of the genital and urinary systems, and a gristly rod–the notochord–the precursor of the backbone.

Early on in embryonic life, mesodermal cells on each side of the notochord form blocks called somites–bilateral beginnings of a vertebrate's segmented body. At this stage a human embryo resembles an embryonic fish, complete with fishlike brain, "gill pouches" in the neck, limb buds that look like fins, segmented muscles all along the trunk, a tail, a simple fishlike heart and kidneys, and several pairs of big blood vessels like those that link a fish's heart and gills.

Soon, though, our early fishlike structures alter in mammal fashion. Instead of turning into gills, gill bars contribute to a face, jaws, larynx, tongue, ears, and endocrine organs in the neck. Our potential fish's swim bladder develops into lungs. Most paired blood vessels linking heart to "gills" shrink and disappear. Limb arteries get rearranged to service legs and arms. The heart acquires partitions, and mammalian kidneys form. The trunk, by losing muscles, gains a waist. In time, only fused bones at the bottom of the spine remain as a reminder of our embryonic tail.

Between its fourth and sixth week, a human embryo changes from a fishlike organism to one indistinguishable from an embryonic monkey. At two months the fetus is unmistakably a tiny human being.

Vestigial features (above)

Here are three evolutionary products that persist in humans yet serve no valuable purpose:

a Appendix

b Ear muscles

c Coccyx (vestigial tail bone)

Three cell layers (below)

A human embryo a few days old resembles that of any other vertebrate. Each consists of ectoderm, mesoderm, and endoderm—three layers of cells from which all body structures will arise.

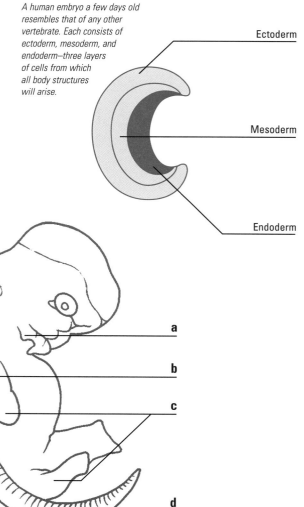

Ectoderm

Mesoderm

Endoderm

Human embryo (right)

Labeled features in this human embryo parallel those seen in other embryonic vertebrates.

a Gill pouches

b Somites

c Limb buds

d Tail

a

b

c

d

Evidence for evolution

Three sets of illustrations trace the development of a fish, pig, and human from egg through embryo to adult form. Each vertebrate passes through similar early stages, suggesting that all three evolved from the same ancient backboned source.

1 Fish   2 Pig   3 Human

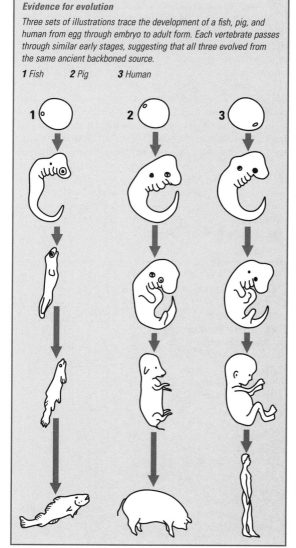

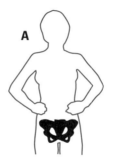

The makeshift mammal

Despite its many advantages, our body's form is flawed. One writer decribed a human being as a "hodgepodge and makeshift creature."

Most major problems stem from upending a skeleton originally constructed as a cantilever bridge. To cope with new needs for twisting and bending, we gained wedge-shaped vertebrae, pivoting on thick front edges, but this weakens the lower spine, so that heavy lifting can dislodge a vertebra or worn intervertebral disc, producing severe back pain. Then, too, the spine's basal curve pushes some vertebrae into the birth canal far enough to give some mothers problems during labor.

Because the body rests on just two limbs, feet sometimes suffer strain and arches of the feet collapse, producing flat footedness, distorted bones, even hammer toes and bunions.

Hernias are another penalty of redesigning for bipedal life. In four-legged animals, the gut is slung from the spine by a broad ligament; in humans this is reduced and less well attached. Intestines may bulge out through our weakened abdominal wall.

Upright posture even hampers blood supply. Blood must overcome about 4 ft (1.2 m) of gravitational pressure to return from the feet to the heart. If faulty leg-vein valves allow blood to fall back, the results are heavy, tired legs and other symptoms of varicose veins. "Milk leg," affecting the left leg in pregnancy, is also due to poor venous drainage, as increased visceral pressure thrusts a vein against a sharp bone where two vertebrae join low in the spine.

A reduced birth canal (a result of bipedalism) and babies' enlarged skulls, which cause childbirth problems, are other penalties we pay for less than perfectly adjusted bodies.

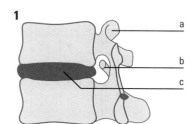

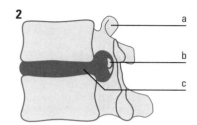

Slipped disk (right)

Prolapse of a cartilaginous disk buffering two spinal vertebrae can produce painful pressure on a spinal nerve and impair mobility.

1 *Normal disk*

2 *Prolapsed disk*

a *Vertebra*

b *Nerve*

c *Disk*

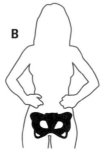

Narrow hips (above)

A *Narrow hips imply a pelvis too narrow to allow normal birth–a common reason for operating to remove a baby.*

B *Broad hips imply a pelvic opening of normal width, unlikely to cause problems in giving birth.*

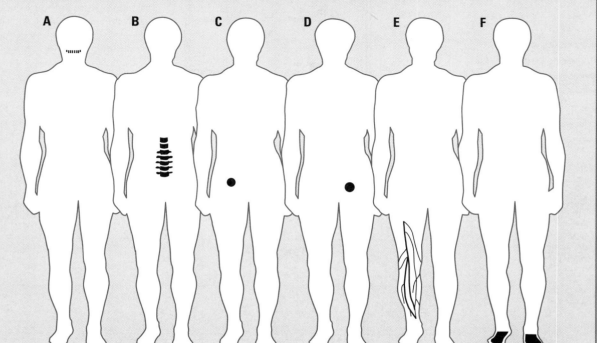

Problem areas

Below and right we indicate a few parts of the skeleton, blood supply, and other systems particularly prone to problems.

A Teeth

Overcrowding is a legacy of jaw shrinkage–a relatively recent product of evolution.

B Slipped disk

Lower back troubles usually reflect degenerative change with age compounded by load transmission via the spine to two limbs, not four as in our early mammal ancestors.

C Appendicitis

This condition involves infection and inflammation of the appendix, a vestigial offshoot of the gut.

D Hernia

Intestine bulges through a weakness in the abdominal wall. Hernias tend to occur in slightly different sites in males and females.

E Varicose veins

Faulty valves allowing blood to pool in veins can affect both the thigh and leg.

F Flat feet

Collapsed arches of the foot are a common condition, related to the fact that two feet support the entire weight of the human body.

Clues in biomolecules

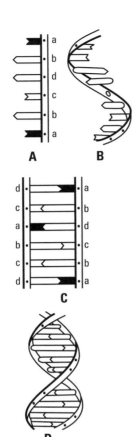

A Bases in part of one strand of nucleotides

B Part of one strand twisted

C

D

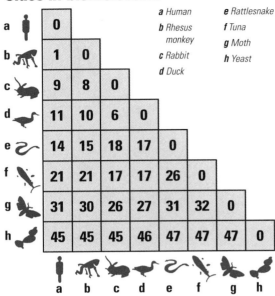

Amino-acid sequences (above)

Organisms differ in the sequence of amino acids in protein cytochrome c, an enzyme used in energy production. The higher the number shown, the greater the difference between any two.

	a	b	c	d	e	f	g	h
a	0							
b	1	0						
c	9	8	0					
d	11	10	6	0				
e	14	15	18	17	0			
f	21	21	17	17	26	0		
g	31	30	26	27	31	32	0	
h	45	45	45	46	47	47	47	0

a Human
b Rhesus monkey
c Rabbit
d Duck
e Rattlesnake
f Tuna
g Moth
h Yeast

Genetic code (above)

The genetic code determining a species lies in the sequence of bases that link two strands of nucleotides to form the double helix that is DNA.

A Bases in part of one strand of nucleotides

B Part of one strand twisted

C Complementary bases joined

D Two strands joined and twisted

a Thymine

b Guanine

c Cytosine

d Adenine

Serological clues (right)

The amount of antigen/antibody reaction produced by a foreign blood serum hints at biological links; the greater the reaction, the closer the supposed relationship.

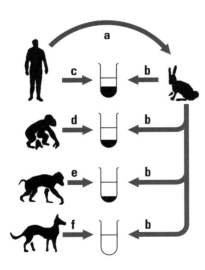

a Human serum into rabbit

b Rabbit serum with antibodies to human serum

c Human serum (100% reaction)

d Chimpanzee serum (97%)

e Baboon serum (50%)

f Dog serum (0%)

Some of the strongest proof of our evolutionary origins come from comparing human biochemicals– the body's building blocks–with those of other living organisms.

Like almost all of these, our body's cells contain the energy-rich compound ATP (adenosine triphosophate,) used in the cells' energy-requiring processes. Animal, plant, and human cells also contain DNA (deoxyribonucleic acid), the inherited material passed on in genes.

Differences between some of our own biomolecules and those of other organisms help to narrow down our relationship to certain groups. For example, phosphocreatine occurs in the muscles of humans and other chordates (creatures with a skeletal rod, the notochord), but not in most invertebrates.

Experts have devised sophisticated batteries of tests to find which living chordates are biochemically our closest counterparts.

Immunological studies revealing how strongly different animals react to foreign blood sera indirectly show how greatly proteins from different species differ from each other.

Other tests include comparing sequences of amino acids that make up a given protein. The more similar the sequences in different animals, the closer their presumed relationship. More difficult to measure is variation in the sequence of nucleotides building long-chain molecules of DNA. As the so-called "ultimate ancestor," DNA enshrines what has been called the "ultimate truth of molecular evolution."

Between them, direct and indirect molecular comparisons confirm the findings of anatomy and physiology: that our closest living relatives are in the group containing apes and monkeys. Thus our origins must lie among its ancestors.

In later pages we shall see just what molecular biology suggests–albeit controversially–about how recently the ape and human lines diverged.

Molecular tree of life

Comparison of hemoglobin molecules in 48 placental mammals from seven groups suggests some evolutionary relationships. The time scale is in millions of years.

a Rodents

b Ungulates (hoofed placentals)

c Insectivores

d Carnivores

e Lagomorphs (rabbits)

f Tree shrews

g Primates (lemurs, lorises, tarsiers, monkeys, apes, and– far right–humans)

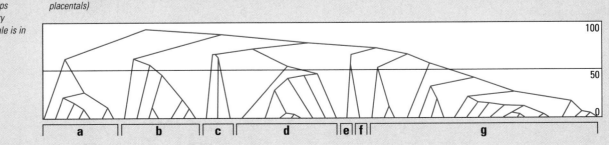

People as primates

While broad aspects of our bodies place us with the mammals, so detailed anatomy collectively identifies us with those agile mammals, primates–the order that includes the lemurs, monkeys, and apes. Most primate features seemingly evolved for life spent mostly up in trees.

First, each primate hand and food has five flexible digits as a rule, with nails, not claws. Thumbs, and usually big toes, are opposable for grasping, and sensitive hands on long, mobile arms serve as tactile organs.

Cheek teeth with relatively low cusps (prominences) and an enlarged lower gut with a fermentation chamber–the cecum or appendix–are geared to break down and digest vegetable food, although many primates are omnivorous.

Treetop communication is easier by sight than scent, so primates tended to evolve shorter noses and a feebler sense of smell than many mammals. Their sense of sight, however, enormously improved.

Big, keen, forward-facing eyes that see in three dimensions–in color in diurnal primates–made it easy to judge leaps from branch to branch.

Enlarged brains show great development of sensory, motor, and coordination areas needed for split-second acrobatic timing.

Reduced muzzle, enlarged eyes, and expanded brain, together with an upright posture ideal for perching on a branch, redesigned the primate skull.

After a long gestation period most females produce a single baby that sucks milk from two glands on the mother's chest. Young stay dependent on their mothers–a survival strategy evolved for life in trees by creatures whose behavior is learned rather than instinctive.

Lastly, most primates benefit from life in groups, where individuals communicate food finds, combine for mutual defense, and pass on learned behavior.

The next few chapters show changing trends in primate groups, whose evolution led to humans.

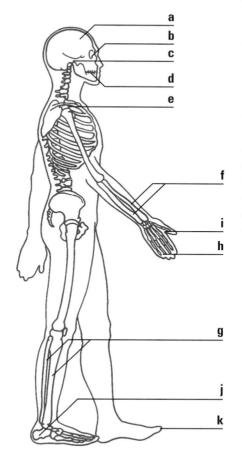

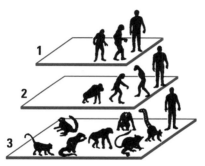

Primate features (left)

*Humans and other primates share these features (**e–h** also occur in various primitive mammals):*

a Enlarged brain, with two unique creases

b Big, forward-facing eyes (with orbits ringed by bone)

c Distinctive middle ear structure

d "Primitive" teeth

e Collarbone

f Separate radius and ulna

g Separate tibia and fibula

h Five flexible digits per limb

i Thumbs usually opposable for grasping

j Distinctive heel bone

k Flat nail on big toe and usually nails (not claws) on other digits

Humans' place in nature (right)

A major 1997 reclassification of mammals ranks humans in 11 progressively higher primate groupings, placing our species in the same subfamily as the great apes.

1 Species: Homo sapiens. Genus: Homo.

2 Subtribe: Hominina. Tribe: Hominini. Subfamily: Homininae. Family: Hominidae

3 Superfamily: Cercopithecoidea. Parvorder: Anthropoidea. Infraorder: Haplorhini. Suborder: Euprimates. Order: Primates

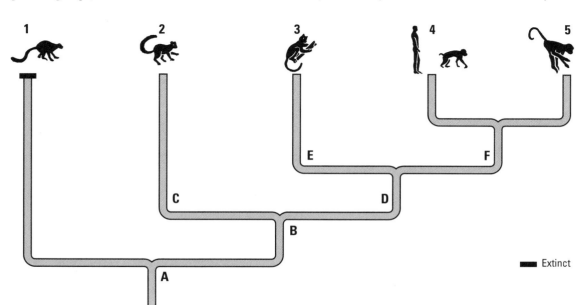

Primates' cladogram (left)

This shows groups living and extinct, stressing those that led to monkeys, apes, and humans.

A Order: Primates

B Suborder: Euprimates ("true primates",)

C Infraorder: Strepsirrhini

D Infraorder: Haplorhini

E Parvorder: Tarsiiformes

F Parvorder: Anthropoidea

1 "Plesiadapiformes"

2 Lemurs and lorises

3 Tarsiers and omomyids

4 Cercopithecoidea or Catarrhini: Old World monkeys, apes, and humans

5 Callitrichoidea or Platyrrhini: New World monkeys

■ Extinct

© DIAGRAM

Primitive primates

Beginning with the controversial origins of primates more than 60 million years ago, we give a brief account of lower primates, often collectively called prosimians. These pages include extinct early forms and their descendants the living lemurs, lorises, and tarsiers. Among their forebears were the ancestors of humans.

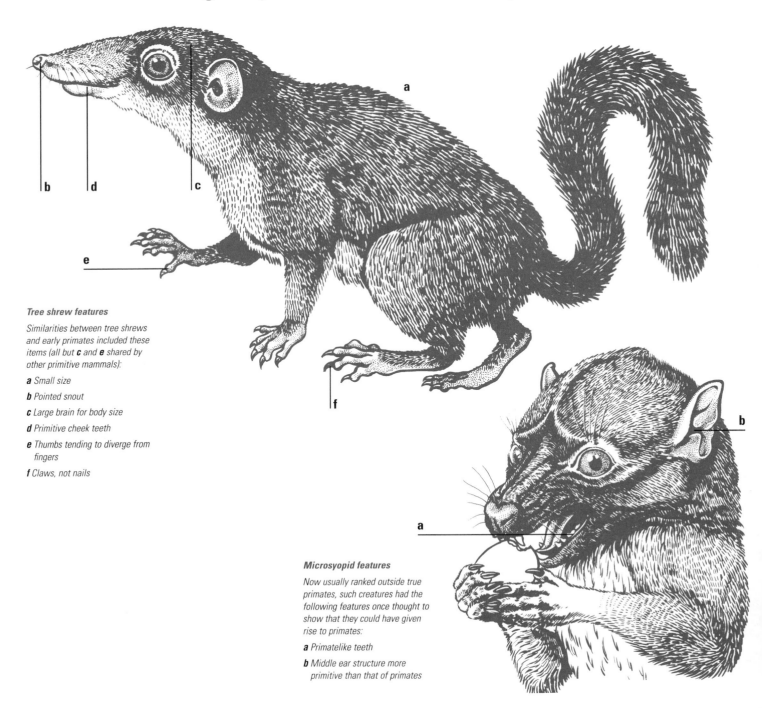

Tree shrew features

*Similarities between tree shrews and early primates included these items (all but **c** and **e** shared by other primitive mammals):*

a Small size

b Pointed snout

c Large brain for body size

d Primitive cheek teeth

e Thumbs tending to diverge from fingers

f Claws, not nails

Microsyopid features

Now usually ranked outside true primates, such creatures had the following features once thought to show that they could have given rise to primates:

a Primatelike teeth

b Middle ear structure more primitive than that of primates

How primates began

Primates are one of the oldest, most primitive placental mammal groups but are of doubtful ancestry. Some experts argue that they stemmed from some line of placental mammals with species still alive today. At one time or another, anatomists have pointed out close similarities between primates and such diverse creatures as colugos, elephant shrews, lagomorphs (rabbits, hares, and pikas), rodents, carnivores, ungulates (hoofed placental mammals), bats, and tree shrews.

Of all these, tree shrews are the primates' closest living relatives. These mammals were once lumped with shrews and hedgehogs as insectivores, for all three have a low braincase, long snout, and unspecialized limbs.

Biomolecular studies show that primates and tree shrews share the same ancestor and are anatomically similar. Small, agile inhabitants of Southeast Asian forests, tree shrews resemble squirrels with long, pointed faces more than apes or monkeys, but like primates, tree shrews have a large brain for their body size, large eyes, primitive cheek teeth, and thumbs that tend to diverge from the fingers. Close study of such features, though, suggests that tree shrews and primates are less alike than people used

to think, although their hemoglobin molecules show striking similarities.

Some experts see the primates' forebears among long-extinct insectivores called microsyopids–known species that lived later than the first known primates yet had a more old-fashioned inner ear design. Perhaps early microsyopids predated and produced the primate pioneers, but most experts are unconvinced by this suggestion, too.

Such inconclusive findings lead some scientists to believe that the primates' ancient order lacks any features that unquestionably link it with another parent group.

Primate teeth (below)

Illustrations compare:

A Teeth of a postulated primate ancestor

B Teeth of a modern catarrhine monkey (Loss of some teeth in evolution has reduced the original 44 to 32.)

a Incisors: cutting

b Canines: piercing or cutting

c Premolars: crushing and/or grinding

d Molars: crushing and/or grinding

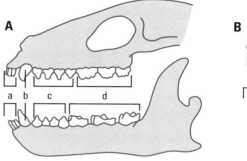

A gallery of candidates

Proposed primate precursors have included ancestors of:

1 Bats

2 Tree shrews

3 Ungulates

4 Carnivores

5 Lagomorphs (rabbits)

6 Rodents

7 Elephant shrews

8 Colugos (dermopterans)

© DIAGRAM

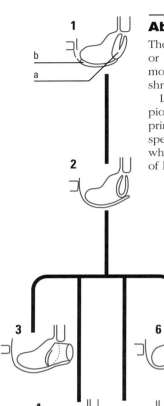

About prosimians

The first primates probably evolved in North America or Europe about 70 million years ago. They were mouse to cat-sized and derived, perhaps, from tree shrewlike insect eaters.

Like their remote descendant, humans, primate pioneers retained five digits on each hand and foot–primitive features that stand us in better stead than the specialized limbs of mammals like whales and horses, who are locked forever in a single habitat or mode of life.

Evolving middle ears (left)

For various prosimians we show possible evolutionary changes to the ectotympanum, a strong ring or tube that supports a primate's eardrum.

a Ectotympanum

b Section along auditory bulla (a bony, hollow prominence enclosing the middle ear)

1 Supposed ancestor of the primates

2 Primitive primate

3 Lemuroid

4 Loroid

5 Plesiadapid

6 Early tarsiiform

Early primates had claws, not nails, and lacked most later primates' large, forward-facing eyes and short faces, but cheek teeth foreshadowed those of monkeys, apes, and humans. Scientists traditionally put them in the Prosimii ("before the monkeys"), a primitive suborder, including the living lemurs, lorises, and tarsiers, now found only in tropical forests in some parts of Africa, Madagascar, and Asia. A later classification split lower primates into the primitive Plesiadapiformes (now known to be a mixed group) and the more advanced Strepsirrhini, with improved grasp-leaping adaptations.

The prosimians' heyday coincided with the Paleocene and Eocene epochs when scores of species were evolving and replacing one another.

Some of the first prosimians might have lived mainly on the ground. From 60 million years ago, however, competition from evolving rodents restricted prosimians to the trees. The sharp insect eaters' teeth of early primates gave way to crushers suitable for pulping leaves and fruits with help from grinding muscles fixed to wide, strong cheekbones. Meanwhile, limb changes made it easier to leap and climb, and eyes moved forward in the head until both focused on one object, making branch-to-branch leaping more accurate and catching insects easier.

By 30 million years ago, however, prosimians were waning–victims of climatic cooling in the northern continents and of competition from their own descendants, monkeys.

Strepsirrhine relationships (right)

*This diagram includes three superfamilies (**E–G**) and eight families (**2–10**) of strepsirrhine "prosimians." **E** and **F** may not form natural groups.*

A Primates

B Euprimates

C Strepsirrhini

D Haplorhini

E Lemuroidea

F Loroidea

G Indroidea

1 Plesiadapiformes

2 Adapidae

3 Lemuridae (lemurs)

4 Daubentoniidae (aye-aye)

5 Archaeolemuridae

6 Palaeopropithecidae

7 Indridae (indris)

8 Cheirogaleidae (dwarf lemurs)

9 Loridae: Galagoninae (galagos or bush babies)

10 Loridae: Lorinae (lorises, and pottos)

11 Tarsiiformes

12 Anthropoidea

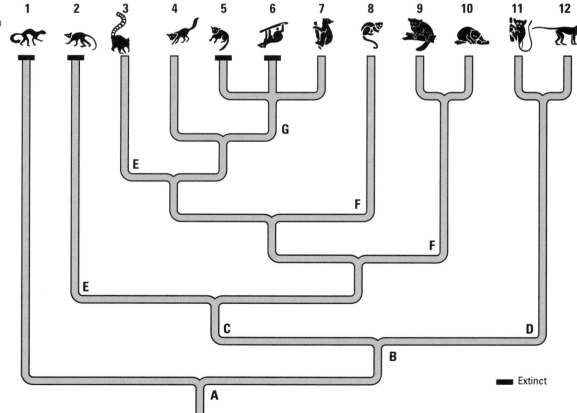

■ Extinct

World background

Early primates inherited a literally changing world. As the Cretaceous period ended 65 million years ago, the two prehistoric supercontinents (northern) Laurasia and (southern) Gondwanaland were breaking up. In the Paleocene and Eocene epochs, landmasses were taking on their present shapes and positions. North America and Europe separated, and South America became an island, with just a narrow strip of ocean between it and Africa at first. Meanwhile, shallow inland seas retreated and advanced in several continents, and the modern Andes, Rockies, and other ranges rose.

Shifting continents affected climates. At first, North America and Europe basked in warmth, but by the Oligocene epoch (34–24 million years ago), climates everywhere were cooling down.

This altered vegetation. Subtropical forest that had been flourishing in much of North America and Europe gave way to hardy trees and grasses.

All this affected the placental mammals, now fast evolving into different forms adapted for the modes of life and habitats left vacant when the dinosaurs died out as the Cretaceous period closed. Early placentals could spread widely through Eurasia and North America, where most early primates flourished. As oceans or mountains split one species into different populations some tended to evolve new forms, but others just became extinct.

By Paleocene times, rat-sized placentals had given rise to larger kinds, notably primitive hoofed herbivores called condylarths and early flesh-eating mammals called creodonts. By Eocene times, both faced increasing competition from early modern ungulates and carnivores, respectively. Meanwhile rodents ousted rodentlike primate pioneers from ground-based habitats. Their agile, tree-climbing successors included the prosimian ancestors of lemurs, lorises, monkeys, apes, and humans.

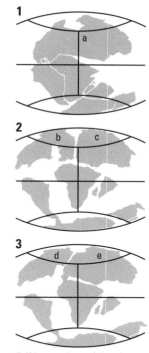

Drifting continents (above)

Three maps show the changes that separated continents, isolating some early primate populations.

1 *200 million years ago*

2 *65–46 million years ago (Paleocene–mid-Eocene)*

3 *46–34 million years ago (later Eocene)*

a *Laurasia*

b *Euramerica*

c *Asiamerica*

d *North America*

e *Eurasia*

Paleocene life

Here are nine prehistoric animals that lived in Paleocene times. They are not shown to scale. Items **c–i** *represent the explosive evolution of the mammals.*

Mammals

c *Pantodont*
d *Dermopteran*
e *Primate*
f *Condylarth*
g *Multituberculate*
h *Perissodactyl*
i *Rodent*

Invertebrates

a *Phoronid*

Amphibians

b *Caecilian*

Eocene life

These 18 prehistoric creatures were among those flourishing in Eocene times. They are not shown to scale.

Invertebrates

a *Coelenterate*
b *Nematode worm*

Mammals

c *Bat*
d *Tillodont*
e *Primate*
f *Creodont*
g *Carnivore*
h *Mesonychid*
i *Dinocerate*
j *Sea cow*
k *Proboscidean*
l *Perissodactyl*
m *Artiodactyls*
n *Edentate (xenarthran)*
0 *Whale*

Birds

p *Gastornithid*
q *Anseriform*

Primate pioneers

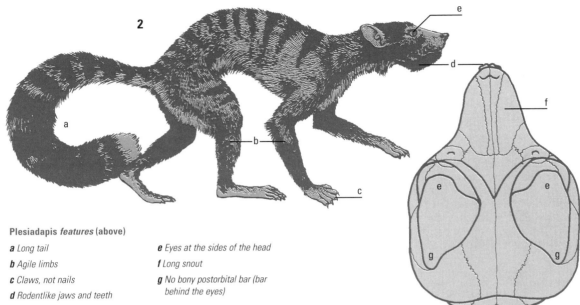

Early primate sites (above)

Early Cenozoic primate sites of western North America:

1 *Gidley Quarry, Montana*

2 *Mason Pocket, Colorado*

3 *Wind River Basin, Wyoming*

4 *Big Horn Basin, Wyoming*

5 *Uinta Basin, Utah*

6 *Bridger Basin, Wyoming*

Plesiadapis *features* (above)

a *Long tail*

b *Agile limbs*

c *Claws, not nails*

d *Rodentlike jaws and teeth*

e *Eyes at the sides of the head*

f *Long snout*

g *No bony postorbital bar (bar behind the eyes)*

Purgatorius *teeth*

*Below are (**a**) side view and (**b**) crown view of a* Purgatorius *molar tooth, both much enlarged. Chewing teeth with an added "heel" helped primates to crush plant foods.*

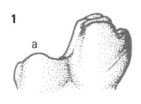

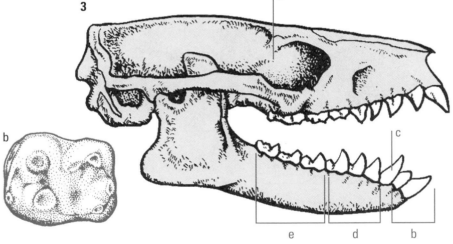

Palaechthon *skull* (left)

*The eye socket narrows at the back (**a**) but lacks a post-orbital bar. Each side of the jaw had two incisors (**b**), one short canine (**c**), three premolars (**d**), and three broad molars (**e**).*

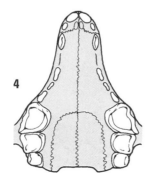

Zanycteris *jaw* (above)

This much-enlarged view of a lower jaw shows simple, low-crowned, batlike molars. Some experts suggest that Zanycteris ate soft fruits, as living fruit bats do.

Primates probably arose among Plesiadapiformes, now known to be a mixed group, including some dermopterans, mammals that glide on webs of skin. Most supposed early primates are identified by internal ear design. Skull, limbs, and long lower incisor teeth also show features not found in later primates. Primates probably evolved from insect eaters, but many species ate tough plant foods. At least seven supposedly nondermopteran early primate families arose, with more than 30 genera ranging in size from mice to cats. Many perhaps resembled rodents. Most are known only from fossil teeth and bits of skull.

Known fossil forms lived about 65–35 million years ago and evidently spread from North America to Europe via Greenland, then a warm, wooded land bridge. Our examples represent four families.

1 Purgatorius, the oldest supposed primate, or near primate, was a ratsized animal with four premolars (more than later primates) and sharp, three-pointed molars, like those of insectivores but with a "heel" to give a bigger chewing surface. Time: late Cretaceous–Paleocene. Place: Montana. Family: Purgatoriidae.

2 Plesiadapis looked like a squirrel with side-facing eyes, long snout, projecting chisel-like incisor teeth, bushy tail, and claws on paws that could not grasp. It ate leaves, leapt well, and maybe lived in troops, often on the ground. Time: late Paleocene–early Eocene. Place: Colorado and France. Family: Plesiadapidae.

3 Palaechthon was a ratsized, omnivorous or maybe insectivorous, creature with blunt-cusped molars in a low skull only 4 cm (2 in) long. Time: early Paleocene. Place: North America.

4 Zanycteris was a tiny mouselike primate with cheek teeth like a bat's. It might have eaten nectar, fruit, or insects. Time: late Paleocene. Place: North America. Family: Picrodontidae.

Adapidae

The lemurlike Adapidae featured strongly in a second burst of primate evolution. At least 34 genera are known, all long extinct. Mostly cat-sized or smaller, many had a longish muzzle, long hind limbs, short forelimbs, and a long tail, though some perhaps resembled the slow-moving, short-tailed lorises. Adapids were agile climbers, and many might have clung and leapt upright in search of fruits, shoots, insects, and birds' eggs.

Unlike plesiadapids, adapids had premolars and vertical front teeth. They were more advanced than early primates in their shorter snout; larger brain; more forward-facing eyes protected by a bony bar behind; nails, not claws; and grasping hands and feet.

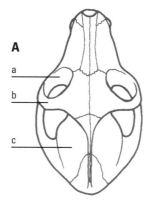

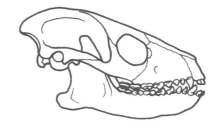

A
a
b
c

d
a
b
c
B

a Forward-facing eyes for stereoscopic vision
b Bony bar protecting eyes
c Relatively large brain
d Reduced snout
e More vertical incisors

e

Adapid *skulls* (right)

*Skulls of (**A**) Notharctus and (**B**) Smilodectes, a short-faced form, show adapid trends not seen in plesiadapids.*

Adapidae

This family flourished mainly in Eocene Europe, North America, Africa, and Asia (about 55–34 million years Ago). They probably gave rise to lemurs, and possibly to higher primates, too. Our examples come from two subfamilies.

1 Notharctus had a rather long muzzle; supple back; long, slender legs; thumbs and big toes separated from the other digits; and a long tail used for balancing in treetop climbing and leaping. Canine teeth were small and tusklike; incisors small and vertical; and the (complete) set of cheek teeth included low-crowned molars capable of grinding leaves to pulp. Length: 33 in (84 cm). Time: early–mid-Eocene. Place: Wyoming. Subfamily: Notharctinae (mostly from North America but also Europe).

2 Adapids, possibly resembled *Notharctus* (or maybe a loris), but its strong, short jaws bit only up and down with no grinding action. Probably it ate tough plant foods. The brain's cerebrum was somewhat primitive, but its temporal lobes were relatively larger than nonprimate mammals'. Length: 16 in (40 cm). Time: mid–late Eocene. Place: western Europe. Subfamily: Adapinae (from Europe, Asia, Africa, and North America).

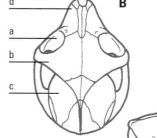

1

2

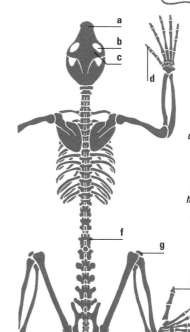

a
b
c
d
f
g
h
e
i

Notharctus *features* (left)

a Long muzzle
b Eye midway along skull
c Bony bar behind eye
d Thumb capable of grasping
e Nails, not claws
f Supple back
g Long, slender, flexible legs
h Big toe capable of grasping
i Very long tail for balancing

Giant lemuroid (above)

Megaladapis *was a recently extinct Madagascan lemuroid as heavy as a woman and as big as a large dog. Probably it browsed on leaves and climbed trees slowly, making cautious jumps.*

A

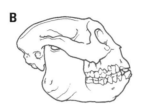

B

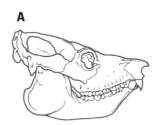

Contrasting skulls (above)

A *Piglike skull of* Megaladapis, *a browsing member of the extinct lemurid subfamily Lepilemurinae.*

B *Deep, short homininelike skull of* Hadropithecus, *a ground-dwelling grazer in the extinct family Archaeolemuridae.*

Lemurs, lorises, and kin

Strepsirrhines, including the Lemuroidea, Loroidea, and Indroidea, are varied groups possibly evolved from the Adapidae. Unlike adapids, all three groups have long, jutting lower front teeth evolved into a comb for grooming fur.

Scientists know of some 28 genera of nonadapid strepsirrhines, 12 of them extinct, half recently. The first probably appeared more than 40 million years ago, in middle Eocene times, but early fossil finds are few.

Six of the eight families appeared in Madagascar, evolving a variety of forms free from major predators until humans arrived a few hundred years ago. Most are sharp-featured, long-limbed, long-tailed climbers that eat fruits, leaves, or insects. The only surviving other family, Loridae, includes the Asian lorises, African pottos, and Africa's galagos, or bushbabies.

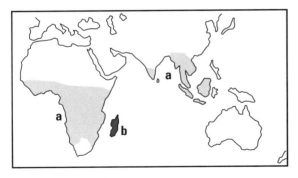

Where they live (above)

This map shows the distribution of living strepsirrhines.

a *Lorids*

b *All other families*

Five strepsirrhines

Our five examples show something of the strepsirrhines' diversity.

1 Lemur catta, the living ring-tailed lemur, has a typical lemuroid's doglike face; 36 teeth; naked nose; big, furry ears; mobile limbs; grasping hands and feet with nails; and a long, bushy tail. Family: Lemuridae.

2 Indri indri, the indri, an indroid strepsirrhine, has long limbs and stumpy tail, and clings and leaps upright. Family: Indridae.

3 Daubentonia madagascariensis, the aye-aye, has a pointed muzzle, huge ears, bushy tail, clawed digits, and only 18 teeth. Its gnawing incisors open coconuts, and it squashes wood-boring insects with its wiry middle finger. Family: Daubentoniidae.

4 Galago crassicaudatus, the fat-tailed galago, has a doglike muzzle; big eyes; mobile ears; long, bushy tail; and broad pads on the fingertips. Length: 25 in (64 cm). Place: Africa. Family: Loridae. (This largest living galago might resemble the early Miocene *Progalago*.)

5 Nycticebus coucang, the slow loris, has a short muzzle, big eyes, thin wrists and ankles, and no tail. Length: 13 in (33 cm). Place: Southeast Asia. Family: Loridae.

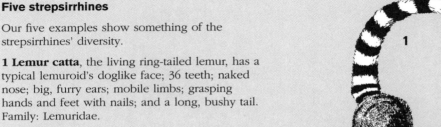

Tarsiiformes

Tarsiiformes comprise more than 40 genera of small, short-faced primates, all but one extinct. Its three huge-eyed, nocturnal species look like goblins from a fairy tale, yet they might be our closest relatives outside the apes and monkeys. Tarsiers, monkeys, apes, and humans all share similarities in nose and eye design, brain structure, fetal membranes, and biochemical ingredients. Indeed, many experts place the parvorder Tarsiiformes with the higher primates in the same infraorder: Haplorhini ("single noses").

The Tarsiiformes evolved in Paleocene times from adapids or from some still undiscovered kind of plesiadapiform. They diversified and spread through northern continents and Africa. Their heyday was the Eocene, but most died out in the Oligocene, probably from failing to compete with the evolving monkeys.

a Long, slim tail
b Long ankle (tarsal) region aids treetop leaping.
c Semi-fused tibia and fibula
d Long, slim toes and fingers
e Backbone articulated with skull from below, not behind (head usually held erect)
f Distinctive middle ear
g Huge eye sockets
h Small nose
i Short jaws

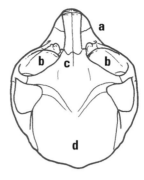

Last refuges (left)

The tarsiers' sole surviving genus, Tarsius, lives in low-lying forests, on only certain Southeast Asian islands. These are the largest:
a Sumatra
b Borneo
c Sulawesi (Celebes)
d Mindanao

Tarsiiform skull (above)

Like other omomyids, extinct Rooneyia differed from modern tarsiids in tooth and middle ear design but shared with them these features:
a Short face
b Big, forward-facing eyes
c Narrow gap between the eyes
d Large braincase

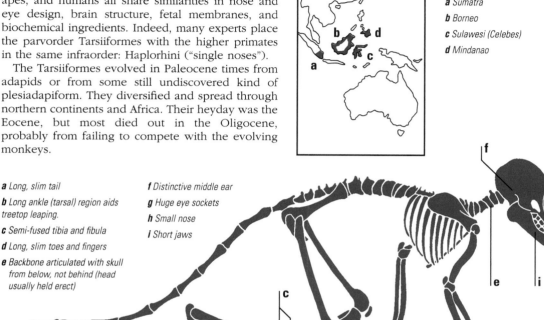

Tarsius *features* (left)

Some features labeled in this skeleton of Tarsius occur in fossil tarsiiforms.

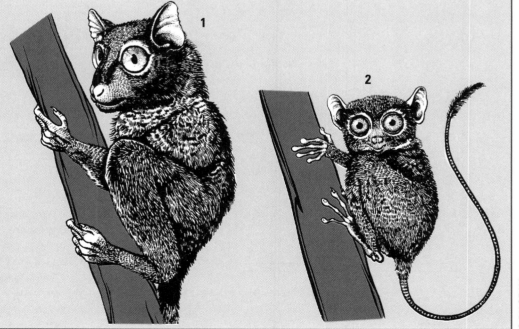

Two tarsiiforms

Our examples come from two of five families.

1 Necrolemur had a short face; big forward-facing eyes; heavy, jutting lower front teeth; and long heel bones. It clung upright to tree trunks and might have leapt from branch to branch erect. Size: as **2**. Time: Eocene. Place: Europe. Family: Microchoeridae.

2 Tarsius, the living tarsier, has a dry, furry nose; 34 teeth; huge eyes; big ears; short arms; long, flexible legs with long ankle bones; disks on finger tips and short nails (but grooming claws on two toes per foot). Length: 4.7 in (12 cm) without the long, slim tail. It eats insects and lizards. Place: Southeast Asia (but extinct *Afrotarsius* lived in Africa). Family: Tarsiidae.

© DIAGRAM

Evolving anthropoids

With this chapter we reach the anthropoids, or higher primates–the group including monkeys, apes, and humans.

Emerging probably in East or Southeast Asia about 45 million years ago, early anthropoids produced the Callitrichoidea or Platyrrhini (New World monkeys and marmosets) and Cercopithecoidea or Catarrhini (Old World monkeys and hominids). These pages feature early anthropoids, some that branched off in different directions, including apes perhaps ancestral to ourselves, and some whose place within the evolutionary scheme remains uncertain.

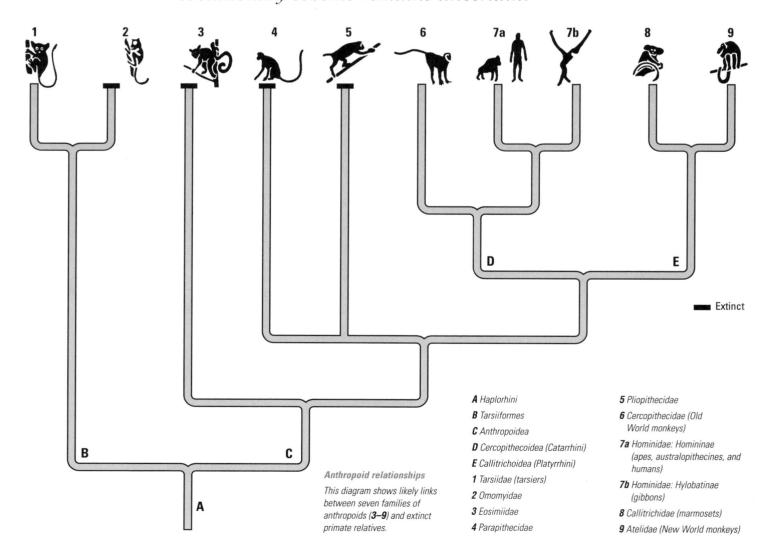

■ Extinct

Anthropoid relationships

This diagram shows likely links between seven families of anthropoids (**3–9**) and extinct primate relatives.

A Haplorhini
B Tarsiiformes
C Anthropoidea
D Cercopithecoidea (Catarrhini)
E Callitrichoidea (Platyrrhini)
1 Tarsiidae (tarsiers)
2 Omomyidae
3 Eosimiidae
4 Parapithecidae

5 Pliopithecidae
6 Cercopithecidae (Old World monkeys)
7a Hominidae: Homininae (apes, australopithecines, and humans)
7b Hominidae: Hylobatinae (gibbons)
8 Callitrichidae (marmosets)
9 Atelidae (New World monkeys)

About anthropoids

Monkeys, apes, and humans–the higher primates–form the Anthropoidea, a parvorder evolved from ancestors of the little living tarsiers or lemurs. The earliest known anthropoid is arguably 45-million-year-old, mouse-sized *Eosimias* from China. Two superfamilies arose: Callitrichoidea or Platyrrhini (New World monkeys) and Cercopithecoidea or Catarrhini (Old World monkeys, apes, and humans).

Living anthropoids range from tiny squirrel-sized tamarins to gorillas three times as heavy as an average man. Some species walk on all fours, some swing from trees using arms, legs, or tails. Only our species regularly walks on hind limbs. Some monkeys have tails longer than their bodies; apes and humans are tailless. One type of monkey moves around at night, other anthropoids by day.

Such variations aside, most anthropoids share certain basic features. Most can sit up, which frees hands for manipulating objects. Hands are helped by a thumb and big toe that can be turned in for grasping. Most species have flat nails on toes and fingers and lack the lemurs' grooming claws.

The head is angled forward from the spine. The snout is generally short, but the eyes are enlarged and forward facing, each set in a protective bony cave, not just guarded by a bony bar as in the more primitive prosimians. The rounded skull shields a brain relatively bigger, more wrinkled, and differently grooved than a prosimian's. It has a shrunken smell sector but enhanced visual and mental areas.

The 30–36 teeth are all vertical. They include enlarged, low-cusped cheek teeth designed for grinding tough food, not just shredding or "juicing," and low premolars that tend to mesh with and hone upper canines, into a point. Such teeth help make many anthropoids efficient omnivores.

Anthropoids have only two breasts, located on the chest. Anthropoid placentas differ from prosimians' and, compared with these primates, anthropoids have longer pregnancies and lives.

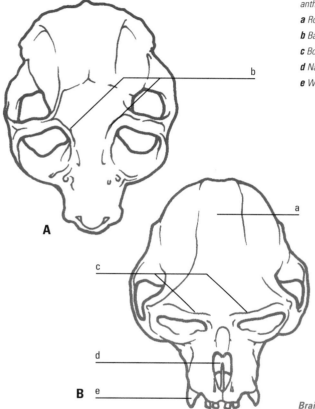

Contrasting skulls
Illustrations contrast two types of primate skull.

A Lemur, a prosimian
B Langur monkey, an anthropoid
a Rounded cranium
b Bars behind eyes
c Bony caves behind eyes
d Narrow nasal cavity
e Well developed canines

Anthropoid features (right)

a Tail long, short, or absent
b Prehensile hands and feet
c Thumbs at least partly opposable to fingers in most
d Big toe turns in for use in grasping in most
e Flat nails on toes and fingers
f Only two nipples, on the chest
g Large, rounded cranium
h Large, forward-facing eyes
i Face protrusion variable
j 30–36 vertical teeth, canines mostly large

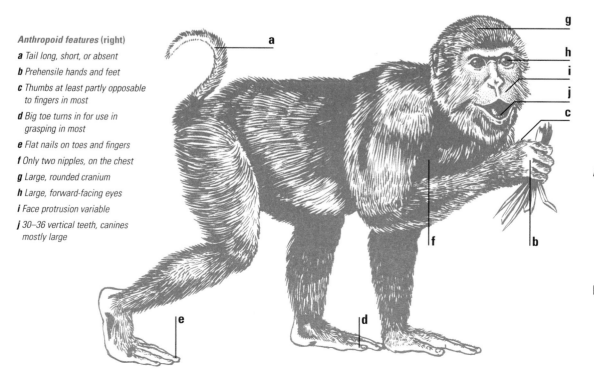

Brains compared (below)

Here are some functional areas and divisions in the brains of (**A**) lemur (a prosimian) and (**B**) macaque (an anthropoid):

a Olfactory bulb (smell)
b Voluntary movement
c Sensations
d Visual area
e Central groove
f Simian groove

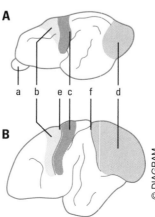

© DIAGRAM

Miocene world background

Miocene world (above)

This world map shows that continents had taken up their present positions by Miocene times. Lines represent the equator, Tropics, and Polar Circles.

Miocene life

Here are 17 prehistoric animals that lived in Miocene times. They are not shown to scale.

Mammals

a *Carnivores*
b *Perissodactyls*
c *Artiodactyls*
d *Proboscidean*
e *Primates*
f *Notoungulate*
g *Monotreme*
h *Litoptern*

Birds

i *Gruiform*
j *Pelecaniform*

Shrinking seas (right)

This shows part of Africa and Eurasia about 16 million years ago. Shrinkage of the Tethys Sea and a new land bridge allowed anthropoids to migrate between Africa, Europe, and Asia.

a *Tethys Sea*
b *Para-Tethys Sea*
c *Arabian land bridge*

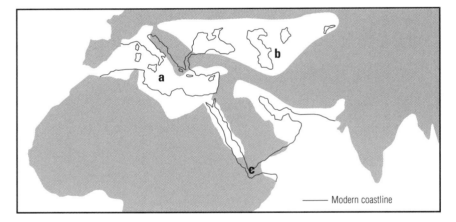

—— Modern coastline

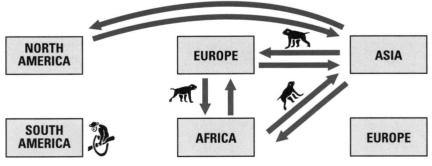

Animal migrations (above)

This diagram gives the pattern of two-way mammal migrations in the Miocene, when land linked northern continents. Yet Old World apes and monkeys never entered North America; perhaps climatic barriers defeated them. New World monkeys evolved in isolation on South America, an island. No primates reached Australia.

By Miocene times (24–5 million years ago) anthropoids were diversifying and colonizing Africa, Eurasia, and the tropical Americas.

The world changed greatly in this time. Ice blanketed Antarctica, India bumped into Asia, the world's great mountain ranges rose. Africa's Rift Valley yawned open to the belching of volcanoes. The vast prehistoric Tethys Sea shrank into big salty pools: the Mediterranean, Black, and Caspian Seas. Animals easily migrated between Eurasia and Africa.

Deciduous and evergreen broad-leafed trees and conifers now covered northern continents. Farther south, some tropical forests shrank under the effects of drying climates. In East Africa, tropical forest still rimmed rivers and low mountain slopes, but great plains became savanna–open, parklike countryside of tall grasses and scattered trees.

The cooler northern climates dating from Oligocene times (34–24 million years ago) probably contributed to the evolution of the anthropoids. Where the year-round leaf and fruit supply dried up, prosimians mostly became extinct or followed the retreating tropical forest south. Primates with flexible food demands and tolerance to cold seemingly gave rise to anthropoids. Influential trends would have included eating less fruit where this grew seasonally scarce but more bark and leaves of evergreens. Another tendency was increased body size, which conserved body heat. This probably went hand in hand with longer pregnancies, smaller litters, a shift from night to day activity, and sight increasingly outranking smell.

New World monkeys

The Callitrichoidea or Platyrrhini ("flat noses") are monkeys of the New World Tropics. They have well-separated, outward-facing nostrils; three premolar teeth in each side of each jaw; a relatively larger and more convoluted brain than the Tarsiiformes; some distinctively interlocking skull bones; long tails (some prehensile); and poorly developed thumb and finger grip. They range from minute tamarins and marmosets to howler monkeys that weigh about 22 lb (10 kg).

New World monkeys probably arose about 35 million years ago, perhaps from North American Tarsiiformes, but colonized only Central and South America. The oldest fossil find is *Branisella* from late Oligocene Colombia, some 25 million years ago. More than one-third of the more than 30 known genera are extinct, but two-thirds of all genera of living anthropoids are platyrrhines.

Where they live (left)

This map of the Americas gives the present distribution of New World monkeys.

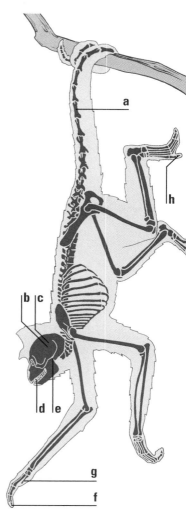

Five platyrrhines

Our living and defunct examples come from both families, largely classified by skull and tooth design.

1 Saimiri comprises squirrel monkeys, with small, expressive faces and tails far longer than bodies. Length: 20 in (50 cm). Time: Miocene–present. Place: South and Central America. Family: Atelidae.

2 Callithrix jacchus, the common marmoset, has ear tufts, 32 teeth with long lower incisors, and not claws but flat nails on the (small) big toes. Family groups eat forest plants and insects. Length: 20 in (50 cm). Time: present. Place: Brazil. Family: Callitrichidae.

3 Stirtonia, a likely ancestor of the howler monkeys, was probably a large, hunched, bearded leaf eater with a prehensile tail and a howling call to threaten rival groups. Length: 3 ft 7 in (1.1 m). Time: mid–late Miocene. Place: Colombia. Family: Atelidae.

4 Cebupithecia had long, narrow, jutting incisor teeth, big canines, and small, crowded premolars. This fruit eater might have resembled today's bearded sakis. Length: 31 in (80 cm). Time: mid–Miocene. Place: Colombia. Family: Atelidae.

5 Tremacebus had huge eyes and maybe resembled the douroucouli, today's sole nocturnal monkey, a fruit and insect eater. Length: 30 in (75 cm).
Time: early Miocene.
Place: Argentina.
Family: Atelidae.

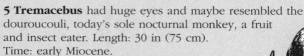

Ateles *features* (above)

Ateles, the living spider monkey, shows these typical platyrrhine features:

a Long, prehensile tail

b Distinct pattern of sutures between skull bones

c Relatively larger, more complex cerebrum than that of the tarsiiforms

d Thirty-six teeth, with three premolars per side per jaw.

Features found in its family, the Atelidae, include:

e Naked, not tufted, ears

f Short, curved, but nail-like claws

g Non-opposable thumb

h Opposable big toe

Old World anthropoids

The Cercopithecoidea or Catarrhini ("down-facing noses") are Old World monkeys, apes, and humans. Some 70 genera are known, more than half extinct.

Catarrhines have nostrils close together and facing down or forward. They tend to have a better thumb-and-finger grip than New World monkeys but none has a prehensile tail. Many later monkeys evolved shortened tails; modern apes have none. Catarrhines share a relatively large brain and similar bony ear passages, and all but primitive species have only two premolar teeth in each side of each jaw. Catarrhines range in size from squirrel-sized *Apidium* to the immense ape *Gigantopithecus*, both long extinct.

Catarrhines seemingly shared ancestors with the "prosimian" Tarsiiformes; they appeared by 45 million years ago in East or Southeast Asia, then diversified and spread across Eurasia and Africa.

Apidium skull (below)

The actual length of this reconstructed face and lower jaw is little more than 1 in (2.5 cm).

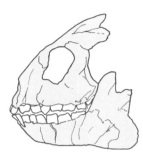

Where they live (right)

This map shows the present distribution of Old World anthropoids.

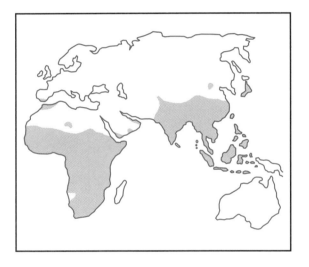

Early fossil finds (below)

A *Northern Egypt, showing the Fayum Depression, site of major finds of early Old World anthropoids.*

B *Section through Fayum deposits with Eocene and Oligocene discoveries.*

a *Lower fossil wood zone quarries: Oligopithecus*

b *Quarry G: Apidium*

c *Upper fossil wood zone: Apidium, Parapithecus, Propliopithecus and Aegyptopithecus*

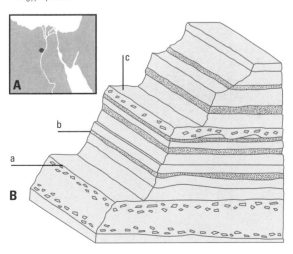

Early anthropoids

Examples given here include some possible precursors of apes and Old World monkeys.

1 Eosimias is the earliest-yet reputed anthropoid, known from jaws, teeth, foot bones, and an ear bone. The mouse-sized creature combined "prosimian" foot bones with a chin and teeth like a monkey's, and it walked on all fours. Time: mid–Eocene. Place: eastern China. Family: Eosimiidae.

2 Oligopithecus has been variously grouped with apes and monkeys but was probably a more primitive anthropoid than either group. Crested cheek teeth hint at leaf and insect eating. Size: that of a small monkey. Time: late Oligocene. Place: Egypt and Oman. Family: Pliopithecidae.

3 Apidium was no bigger than a squirrel monkey, which it possibly resembled. Probably it ran up branches on all fours and munched fruit and insects with its many-cusped cheek teeth. Time: early Oligocene. Place: Egypt. Family: Parapithecidae (monkeylike anthropoids, extinct by the end of the Oligocene).

Tails and nostrils (right)

Illustrations (right) compare key features of New and Old World anthropoids.

A *Old World monkey, with a non-prehensile tail and downfacing nostrils.*

B *New World monkey, with a prehensile tail and well separated nostrils*

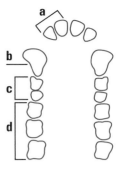

Old World monkeys 1

Old World monkeys of the family Cercopithecidae evolved from the same early anthropoid stock that gave rise to hominids (apes and humans).

Miocene and later fossils give only glimpses of the Old World monkeys' history. Most are small to medium-sized mammals, with a large, well-developed brain; large, rounded braincase; only two premolars on each side of each jaw; small external ears; and a long or short tail that is not prehensile.

There are two subfamilies: Cercopithecinae and Colobinae. Cercopithecines have cheek pouches, tend to be more omnivorous and less tree-bound than colobines, and live in Africa and Asia. They include guenons, baboons, macaques, and geladas.

Here we show three cercopithecines and a strange, extinct anthropoid with some monkeylike features but probably in fact an ape.

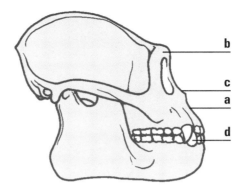

Oreopithecus *skull* (above)

This combined a monkeylike snout (**a**) and brow ridges (**b**) with hominid features such as a short face (**c**) and small canine teeth (**d**).

Tooth formula (above)

Each side of a male baboon's upper jaw shows the typical tooth formula of Old World anthropoids:

a Two incisors

b One canine

c Two premolars

d Three molars

Four cercopithecoids

1 Oreopithecus, a large early anthropoid, had monkeylike and apelike features. It hung from its long arms but sometimes might have walked on two legs. Time: late Miocene. Place: north Italy and Sardinia. Family: Oreopithecidae, perhaps an evolutionary link between the gibbons and great apes.

2 Cercopithecus, the guenons, are small, quadrupedal monkeys with tails longer than bodies. Most live in trees and eat fruit. Time: late Pliocene to modern. Place: Africa.

3 Papio, a baboon genus, features large, quadrupedal ground dwellers (males far bigger than females) with powerful arms and legs of equal length, arched tail, long, doglike face, and massive canines. Baboons live in troops, eating plants and small animals. Time: early Pliocene to modern. Place: Africa, Europe and southwest Arabia.

4 Macaca, the macaques are robust, small to medium monkeys with long, rounded muzzles, and arms and legs of similar length; some lack a tail. Time: late Miocene to modern. Place: northwest Africa to Japan.

© DIAGRAM

Old World monkeys 2

Colobine features

Collectively these features help identify the fossil skeleton of Mesopithecus as a colobine:

a *Globular neurocranium (with, in modern colobines, a brain geared more for limb control than visual ability)*

b *Short, wide but not high, face (but some colobines have long muzzles)*

c *Eyes wide apart*

d *Distinctive teeth with high molar crowns*

e *Long tail*

f *Slim long bones*

g *Long toes and fingers for grasping branches*

h *Reduced thumb*

i *Long body*

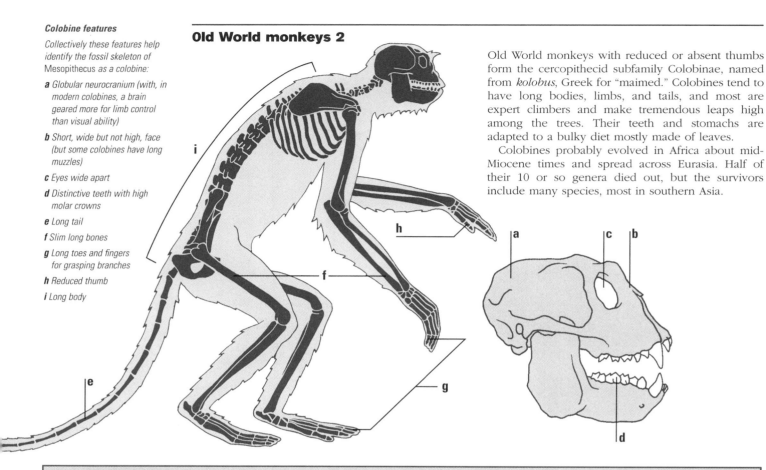

Old World monkeys with reduced or absent thumbs form the cercopithecid subfamily Colobinae, named from *kolobus*, Greek for "maimed." Colobines tend to have long bodies, limbs, and tails, and most are expert climbers and make tremendous leaps high among the trees. Their teeth and stomachs are adapted to a bulky diet mostly made of leaves.

Colobines probably evolved in Africa about mid-Miocene times and spread across Eurasia. Half of their 10 or so genera died out, but the survivors include many species, most in southern Asia.

Four Old World monkeys

Our examples represent different subgroups.

1 Victoriapithecus, one of the earliest known cercopithecids, was possibly ancestral to the colobines, but some fossil finds that bear its name derive from several genera. Size: small. Time: early to mid-Miocene. Place: East Africa.

2 Mesopithecus had long, strong limbs and a longer thumb than any living colobine. It might have given rise to the slim, long-legged, long-tailed langurs of modern Asia. *Mesopithecus* lived in parklike countryside and often walked on all fours on the ground. Size: small to medium. Time: late Miocene to late Pliocene. Place: Europe and Southwest Asia.

3 Colobus is the generic name for long-limbed, agile colobines from Africa, also called guerezas. They lack thumbs and have a short muzzle and slightly overhanging upper lip. Most live high among the trees. Size: 18-24 in (46–60 cm) plus an even longer tail. Time: late Miocene to modern. Place: North, East, and central Africa.

4 Presbytis, the langurs and other Asian leaf eaters, resemble *Colobus* but have short thumbs, and many have a hairy cape or crest. Langurs live in diurnal troops. Length: 16–31 in (40–80 cm) plus even longer tail. Time: late Miocene to modern. Place: Pakistan to Indonesia.

About hominids

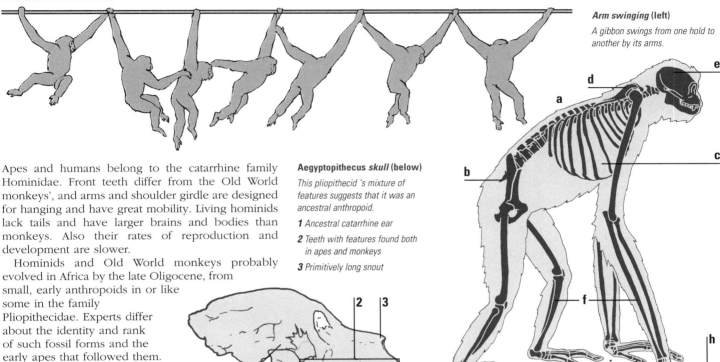

Arm swinging (left)

A gibbon swings from one hold to another by its arms.

Apes and humans belong to the catarrhine family Hominidae. Front teeth differ from the Old World monkeys', and arms and shoulder girdle are designed for hanging and have great mobility. Living hominids lack tails and have larger brains and bodies than monkeys. Also their rates of reproduction and development are slower.

Hominids and Old World monkeys probably evolved in Africa by the late Oligocene, from small, early anthropoids in or like some in the family Pliopithecidae. Experts differ about the identity and rank of such fossil forms and the early apes that followed them. This page looks at pliopithecids, some resembling gibbons, and at these hylobatine hominids, whose ancestry remains uncertain.

Aegyptopithecus *skull* (below)

This pliopithecid 's mixture of features suggests that it was an ancestral anthropoid.

1 *Ancestral catarrhine ear*

2 *Teeth with features found both in apes and monkeys*

3 *Primitively long snout*

Gibbon features (above)

Most of these occur also in other apes and humans:

a *Large size*

b *No tail*

c *Broad chest*

d *Very mobile shoulder joint*

e *Large braincase*

f *Arms longer than legs*

g *Mobile wrist*

h *Long, prehensile hands*

i *Opposable thumb*

Where gibbons live (below)

a *Mainland Southeast Asia*

b *Hainan Island*

c *Sumatra and Java*

d *Borneo*

Here are three pliopithecids and a gibbon.

1 Pliopithecus, once thought ancestral to the gibbons, was gibbon-sized, with a gibbonlike short face, big eyes, and tall, sharp canines, but it lacked the long arms of a gibbon and might have had a tail. It ran, climbed, leapt, and hung from trees. Time: Miocene. Place: Eurasia. Family: Pliopithecidae.

2 Propliopithecus was small to medium, built like a howler monkey, and had a long, low face. It ran on all fours and climbed with grasping hands and feet. Time: late Eocene–early Oligocene. Place: Oman and Egypt. Family: Pliopithecidae.

3 Dendropithecus was no bigger than a gibbon and built slimly like a spider monkey. It climbed, leapt, and hung from trees. Time: early–mid-Miocene. Place: Africa and Asia. Family: Pliopithecidae.

4 Hylobates, the gibbons, are slim, broad-chested, "lesser apes." Family groups eat fruit, call loudly, and swing from tree to tree by arms far longer than the legs. Gibbons briefly walk bipedally. Head–body length: 16–26 in (40–65 cm). Time: Pleistocene to modern. Place: Southeast Asia. Family: Hominidae. Subfamily: Hylobatinae.

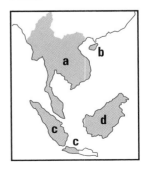

© DIAGRAM

Early African apes

Homininae, the anthropoid subfamily including great apes, "ape men," and humans, evolved a combination of distinctive features. Hominines tend to have arms, shoulder girdles, and wrists evolved to some extent for swinging through trees, plus a broad chest, shortened small of the back, long spinal base (the fused bones of the sacrum), vestigial tailbone (coccyx), and broadened upper hipbones (ilia). Teeth and skull, with its broad and often longish face, are much like those of other Old World anthropoids, but body size and relative brain size have tended to increase.

Hominines (and hylobatines) evidently had their roots in early Miocene Africa, where a great variety of apelike anthropoids and early apes appeared. Most

are known from only scrappy fossils, and experts disagree about relationships and names.

The variously classified early African anthropoids included *Proconsul*, *Afropithecus*, *Dendropithecus*, *Kenyapithecus*, and *Morotopithecus*. About 22 million years old, *Morotopithecus* is the earliest hominine seemingly designed on the same lines as the living great apes.

Mid-Miocene climatic changes that shrank forests in East Africa may explain why fossil finds of hominines are scarcer from that time. Meanwhile, early low-headed African forms had produced deep-headed apes, some spreading through Eurasia.

Female Proconsul *skull* (below)

This skull's small size, short face, and small teeth suggest that female early hominids were smaller and less powerfully built than males. Such sexual dimorphism has featured in most or all later hominids.

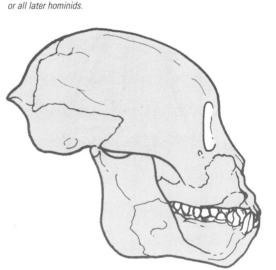

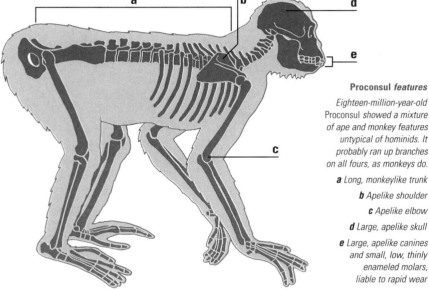

Proconsul *features*

Eighteen-million-year-old Proconsul *showed a mixture of ape and monkey features untypical of hominids. It probably ran up branches on all fours, as monkeys do.*

a *Long, monkeylike trunk*

b *Apelike shoulder*

c *Apelike elbow*

d *Large, apelike skull*

e *Large, apelike canines and small, low, thinly enameled molars, liable to rapid wear*

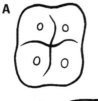

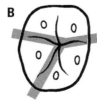

The Y–5 molar pattern (above)

Molar crowns help experts distinguish fossil monkeys from hominids including humans.

A *Monkey molar, with two pairs of cusps (prominences)*

B *Dryopithecine (hominid) molar, with five cusps separated by a Y-shaped fissure pattern. One cusp may be suppressed in modern humans.*

Four early African apes

1 Afropithecus grew as large as a female gorilla, but had a longer, lower head, with massive jaws. Time: early Miocene. Place: Africa and Asia.

2 Proconsul included some large tree climbers, bigger than a monkey and with somewhat jutting, chimpanzeelike faces. Time: early–mid-Miocene. Place: East Africa.

3 Limnopithecus was small and gibbonlike, maybe not a hominine. Time: early–mid-Miocene. Place: East Africa and Asia.

4 Morotopithecus was as big as a chimpanzee and resembled one. It climbed hand over hand and hung from branches. Time: early Miocene. Place: Africa.

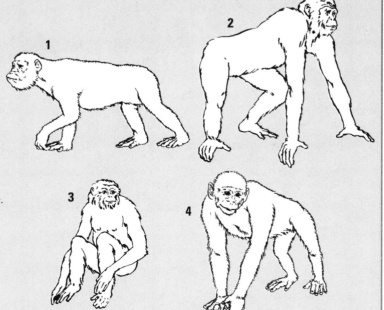

Eurasian apes

Apes probably arose in Africa, but by 10 million years ago, a variety inhabited Eurasia and spread through the belt of broadleaved, summer-drought-adapted woodland that ran from southern Europe to East Asia. One group, called Pongini, included *Sivapithecus*, perhaps the true identity of the similar *Ramapithecus*, and an ancestor of Asia's only living great ape, the orangutan. Close relatives of the pongines included huge *Gigantopithecus*, perhaps the largest-ever ape, bigger even than a male gorilla. Confusion clouds various relationships between Eurasian apes. Some experts think *Sivapithecus* was in fact yet another ape called *Dryopithecus*. Others linked *Dryopithecus* with *Ouranopithecus* and *Ankarapithecus* as apes closer to the tribe Hominini (ape men), Africa's living great apes, and humans.

Fossil finds showing reduced front teeth and big cheek teeth reinforced with thick enamel suggest that many of the late Miocene Eurasian apes could crunch up hard, dry foods such as nuts. They evidently lived where open woodlands replaced rain forest and soft fruits were scarce.

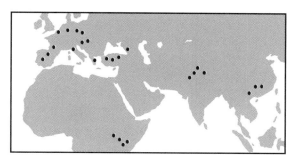

Where they lived (above)

This map of Europe, Africa, and Asia shows fossil finds of pongines and other hominids dating from the Miocene epoch (24–5 million years ago).

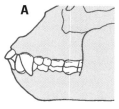

Snouts and teeth (above)

A A gorilla's relatively long snout and large canine teeth

B Ramapithecus's shorter snout and smaller canines

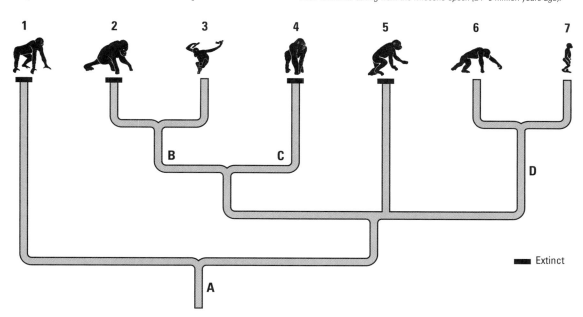

Hominines in perspective (left)

A Homininae
B Pongini
C Gigantopithecini
D Hominini
1 Early African apes
2 Sivapithecus
3 Pongo *(orangutan)*
4 Gigantopithecus
5 Dryopithecus
6 Living African apes
7 "Ape men" and humans

■ Extinct

Three Eurasian apes

1 Sivapithecus had a face similar to an orangutan's, chimpanzeelike foot bones, and wrists it could rotate. Probably it climbed, hung from trees, and walked on all fours. Size: about that of an orangutan. Time: about 15–9 million years ago. Place: Europe and southern Asia.

2 Dryopithecus had a short waist, a broad chest, mobile shoulder joints and long, strong arms. Males possessed large canine teeth. This chimpanzee-sized ape climbed hand over hand and swung from branches, just as living great apes do. There were probably at least two species. Time: about 14–8 million years ago. Place: West and Central Europe.

3 Gigantopithecus, the last and largest prehistoric Eurasian great ape had a deep, short face, powerful jaws, rather small canines used like grinding cheek teeth, and immense molars. Height: up to 9 ft 10 in (3 m). Time: 6–0.5 million years ago. Place: Asia, from Pakistan to southern China.

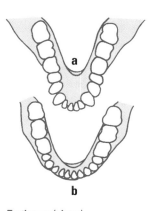

Tooth rows (above)

a Ramapithecus *had a V-shaped tooth row, unlike the U-shaped row of modern apes and the:*

b Human tooth row, a parabola

© DIAGRAM

Apes and humans

By the early twenty-first century paleontologists were coming closer to discovering a common ancestor for modern apes and humans. Meanwhile shared ancestry was obvious in similarities of body build, behavior, and, above all, in biochemical ingredients.

Biomolecular studies point to the great apes of Africa as our closest living relatives. Molecular evidence also suggests that the human-ape evolutionary split occurred a mere five to eight million years ago–far more recently than people had supposed.

Gorilla upper tooth row **(below)**

a *U-shaped tooth row*

b *Large, spoon-shaped incisors*

c *Large conical canines*

d *Gap between incisors and canines*

e *Very large molars*

Orangutan features (right)

a *No tail*

b *Elongated pelvis*

c *Broad, deep chest*

d *Legs shorter than arms*

e *Long hands, with short but opposable thumbs*

f *Skull crest and ridges*

g *Big brain in relation to body size*

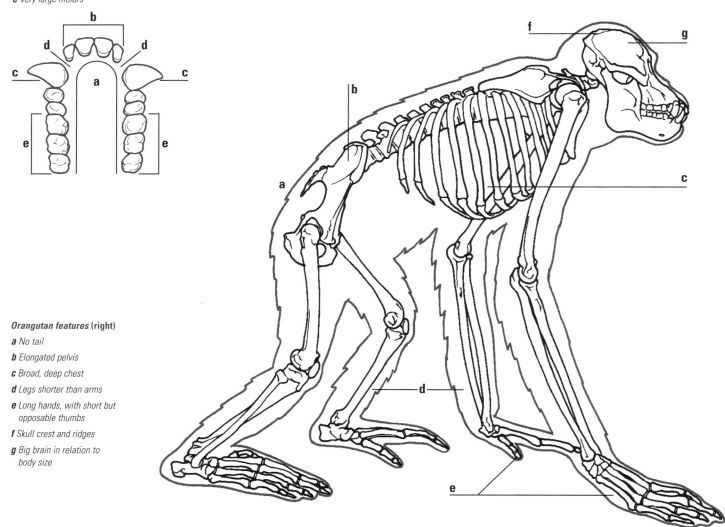

The great apes

The extinct African and Eurasian apes of the previous chapter undoubtedly included ancestors of humans and the great apes–those large, hairy, intelligent inhabitants of tropical forests in Africa and Southeast Asia. The great apes' fossil record is poor, apart from finds connecting the orangutan with the fossil group including *Sivapithecus*, but biological studies have proved that great apes and humans must share a recent ancestor.

Zoologists traditionally set aside one family, Pongidae, to hold all three great apes (orangutan, chimpanzee, and gorilla), placing modern humans with fossil humans and "ape men" in another family, Hominidae. Close study of body build, behavior, and molecular biology now persuades most experts that the Hominidae includes apes as well as humans, however. This chapter reveals similarities so close that zoologists now even tend to rank the orangutan, gorilla, chimpanzee, "ape-humans," and humans in one subfamily: Homininae.

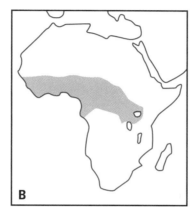

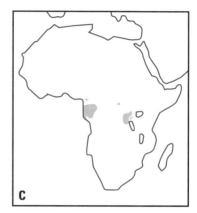

Where they live
A Orangutan
B Chimpanzee
C Gorilla

Great apes

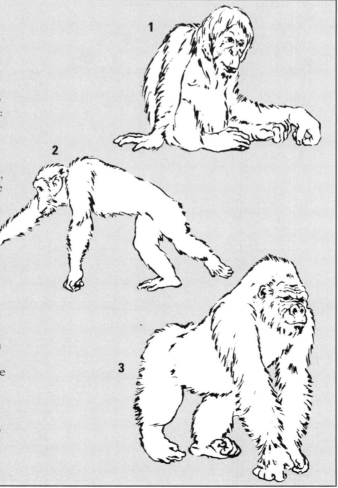

1 Pongo, the orangutan, has a shaggy, reddish coat; long arms; relatively short legs; short thumbs and toes; and big, low-crowned cheek teeth. It eats fruit, swings from trees, and hangs by hands or feet. Size: males up to 55 in (1.4 m) tall and 165 lb (75 kg)–twice as heavy as females. Time: modern. Place: Borneo, Sumatra, and once Southeast China. Subfamily: Homininae. Tribe: Pongini.

2 Pan, the chimpanzee, has a long, shaggy, black coat; longer arms than legs; bare face with big brow ridges; large jutting ears; flat nose; and mobile lips. It eats fruit, leaves, seeds, and small animals; climbs trees with hands and feet; swings from branches; and knuckle-walks on the ground. Size: up to 5 ft (1.5 m) erect and 110 lb (50 kg). Time: modern. Subfamily: Homininae. Tribe: Hominini.

3 Gorilla, the gorilla, is the largest living ape. Males, twice the size of females, reach 6 ft (1.8 m) and 397 lb (180 kg). This strong, stocky ape has thick black hair; bare face and chest; large, flaring nostrils; and relatively small ears. Adult males have a bony skull crest and massive jaws. Gorillas knuckle-walk and eat leaves, shoots, stalks, and roots. Time: modern. Place: equatorial Africa. Subfamily: Homininae. Tribe: Hominini.

Humans, apes, and molecules

What biochemicals reveal

Three sets of diagrams depict the biochemical techniques used to prove that Africa's great apes are our closest kin.

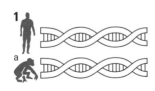

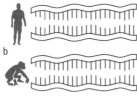

1 DNA annealing (left)

a In humans and chimpanzees, two strands of simple compounds have matching units that zip up to form a DNA double helix.

b Double helices unzipped

c Mixed strands form a hybrid double helix of DNA. Only one unit per 100 is a mismatch.

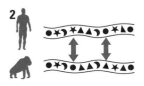

2 Protein sequencing (above)

Humans and gorillas show only two differences in the sequences of amino acids forming the red-blood protein, hemoglobin. (Humans and chimpanzees show no differences. Humans and all other animals show more than two).

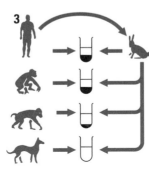

3 Immunological testing (above)

For details, see page 294

Molecular and other studies show astonishingly close relationships between humans and the great apes, especially Africa's gorilla and chimpanzee.

Take DNA annealing, for example. Scientists mix "unzipped" strands from double helices made up of DNA from animals of different species. Mixed strands join to make hybrid double helices, but only matching units in two strands unite. Next, heat tests to separate the strands show each hybrid's thermal stability; the more heat needed, the more matching units there must be, and so the closer the relationship between the animals they came from. This test reveals that chimpanzee and human DNA are almost 99 percent identical.

Comparing the percentage of differences in the amino acids making up a protein gives a similar result. Testing the immunological reactions of primates to antibodies produced by rabbits in response to albumin from human blood just confirms these findings.

All tests show that humans, chimpanzees, and gorillas are related more closely to one another than to the orangutan, their nearest relative. Tests show humans closer to the chimpanzee than to the gorilla.

Traditional wisdom based on scanty fossil finds put the evolutionary human-ape split as much as 20 million years ago. Biochemists reckoned it came much later. They based this notion on the so-called molecular clock whose ticks are random mutations thought to build up at a constant rate as changes to ingredients in proteins. By measuring degrees of difference in molecular structure or immunological response between creatures with an already securely dated common ancestor, the scientists believed they could work out when major primate lines diverged.

According to this theory, great apes and gibbons split 10 million years ago, while humans, chimpanzees, and gorillas shared an ancestor a mere 6 million years back–8 million at the very most.

Objectors argued that the theory was untestable, but supporters claimed that molecular clock dates matched prehistoric dates that could be verified by other means. Fossil finds have since confirmed our recent ancestry among the apes.

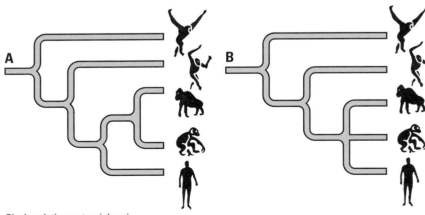

Rival evolutionary tree (above)

A Fossil finds once suggested a long separation between the human line and the ancestor of the chimpanzee and gorilla.

B Molecular studies suggested all three were close enough to share a common ancestor.

A DNA clock (right)

This family tree uses genetic differences based on DNA studies to estimate divergence dates for different anthropoids. Figures represent millions of years ago.

1 Old World monkeys

2 Gibbons

3 Orangutans

4 Humans

5 Chimpanzees

6 Gorillas

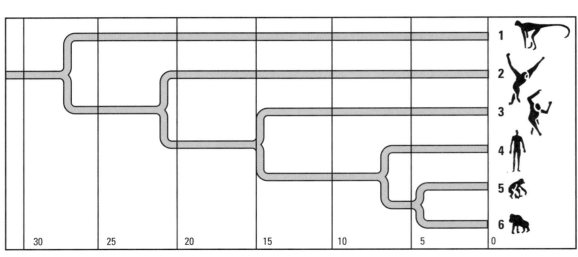

Human-ape anatomy compared

Anatomical comparison strongly suggests that our bodies are apes' bodies redesigned as bipeds. Our arms and shoulders differ little from a chimpanzee's. Unlike apes, however, our legs are longer than our arms, and our hips, spine, thighs, legs, feet, and toes have all been modified for standing and walking in an upright position. (Great apes can only stand on two legs with knees bowed and walk as bipeds with a sideways lurching motion.)

Redesigning of the feet means we can no longer use big toes as extra thumbs. Our thumbs are relatively longer than an ape's, and swing across the palms to meet fingers tip to tip for the precision grip we use in making and exploiting tools.

Bipedal walking, increased intelligence, and an omnivorous diet all contribute to differences between our own and apes' skulls, brains, jaws, and teeth. In relation to body size, our brain and braincase are far larger than an ape's, and the brain is more highly organized, with relatively bigger frontal, parietal, and temporal lobes, collectively concerned with thinking, social behavior, and producing and understanding speech.

Omnivorous modern humans have much shorter, weaker jaws than the chiefly vegetarian apes, with their shock-absorbing brow ridges and bony skull crests to anchor powerful jaw muscles. We lack the thick neck muscles needed to support an adult ape's forward-jutting face. Our parabolic tooth row differs from the U-shaped tooth row of the apes. Their canines are much larger and their molars' cusps much higher than our own, but human molars wear a thicker coating of enamel to resist wear caused by chewing harder foods. Then, too, differences between our tongue and pharynx and a chimpanzee's enable us to make more kinds of sounds, though chimps and people share expressive faces, and human adults show some striking anatomical similarities with young chimpanzees, a likely product of neoteny: survival into adulthood of features found in many species only in their young.

Walking and waddling (right)

A Human lower limbs. Flaring pelvis, inward-angled femur, strong knee joint, and "platform" foot are made for smooth bipedal walking.

B Chimpanzee's lower limbs: Long pelvis, outward-angled femur, knee joint, and grasping toes aid quadrupedal walking but produce a bow-legged, body rocking bipedal waddle.

a Pelvis
b Femur
c Knee joint
d Foot

Pelvic tilting (below)

In humans, contracting gluteus medius and gluteus minimus muscles on one side of the pelvis tilt that side down and lift the other leg, yet help hold the body upright.

a Gluteus medius
b Gluteus minimus

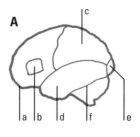

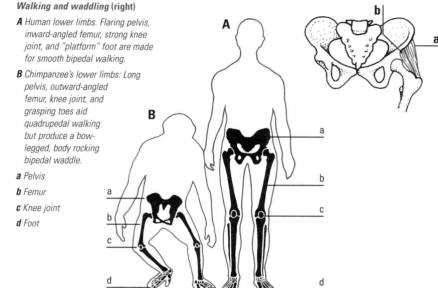

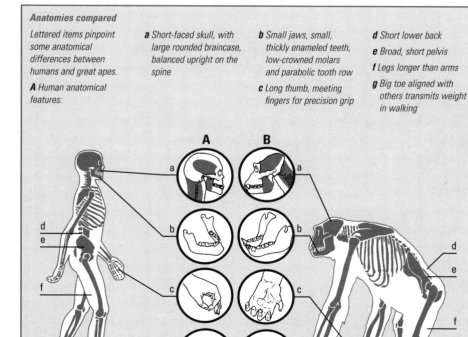

Anatomies compared

Lettered items pinpoint some anatomical differences between humans and great apes.

A Human anatomical features:

a Short-faced skull, with large rounded braincase, balanced upright on the spine

b Small jaws, small, thickly enameled teeth, low-crowned molars and parabolic tooth row

c Long thumb, meeting fingers for precision grip

d Short lower back

e Broad, short pelvis

f Legs longer than arms

g Big toe aligned with others transmits weight in walking

B Gorilla's anatomical features:

a Long-faced skull jutting forward from the spine and ridged to take strong jaw and neck muscles

b Massive jaws with large canine teeth, high-crowned thinly enameled molars, and a U-shaped tooth row

c Long fingers, short thumb

d Lower back relatively shorter than a human's

e Long pelvis

f Legs shorter than arms

g Grasping, divergent big toe

Brains compared (above)

A Human brain
B Chimpanzee brain
a Frontal lobe (various roles)
b Broca's area (a speech center, not prominent in apes)
c Parietal lobe (sensory integration)
d Temporal lobe (memory)
e Occipital lobe (vision)
f Cerebellum (coordination)

© DIAGRAM

A

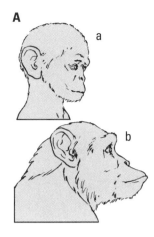

a

b

B

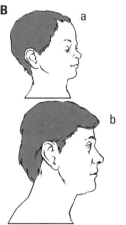

a

b

Young and adult (above)

A *Chimpanzees' heads*

a *Juvenile, held upright and with almost human features*

b *Adult, jutting forward, with ridged brows and projecting muzzle*

B *Human heads*

c *Human child*

d *Human adult, retaining many childhood features*

Humans, the neotenous apes

Impressive circumstantial evidence for humans' shared recent ancestry with great apes comes from neoteny–the survival into adulthood of features found in many species only in their young. Adult humans share numerous features found in baby chimpanzees, but lose these as they grow.

Like humans, baby chimpanzees have a sparse covering of body hair; they have a relatively big brain, shielded by a bulbous cranium; and their skull bones are thin and lack marked brow ridges or crests. Because no muzzle has developed, the face in baby chimpanzees is short, with small jaws and teeth, but a protruding chin. In both, the brain stem joins the brain through a hole beneath the middle of the skull, which thus balances above the spine if its owner walks on two legs. In women and in young female chimpanzees, the vagina faces forward instead of back.

Humans and chimpanzees both share extended childhoods–an advantage for creatures whose behavior will be based on learning more than instinct. Indeed our childhood lasts so long that it prolongs our lives beyond those of any other mammal.

Big brain, small jaws, and upright stance–supposedly the most distinctive traits that separate us from the apes–all therefore seem at least partly the products of neoteny.

The mechanisms transforming apes into humans would have been simply changes to the sets of genes that switch growth on and off, thereby adjusting growth rate and extent for different body systems. These switches tend to act through hormones such as somatotrophin, which stimulates bone growth, and melatonin, which helps to trigger puberty. Natural selection preserved into adulthood those childhood features that favored our ancestors' survival.

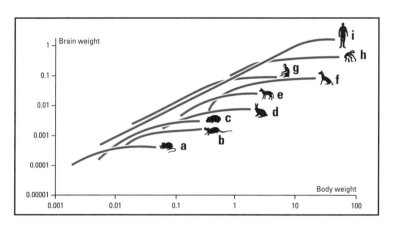

Brain and body growth (left)

This diagram shows how brain and body weights increase (in kilograms) with age among nine animals. Brain growth tapers off at adulthood, so the human brain may owe its relatively large size to an unusually extended human childhood.

a *Mouse*

b *Rat*

c *Guinea pig*

d *Rabbit*

e *Cat*

f *Dog*

g *Old World monkey*

h *Chimpanzee*

i *Human*

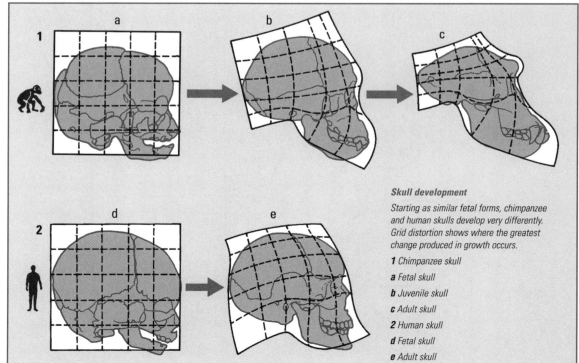

Skull development

Starting as similar fetal forms, chimpanzee and human skulls develop very differently. Grid distortion shows where the greatest change produced in growth occurs.

1 *Chimpanzee skull*

a *Fetal skull*

b *Juvenile skull*

c *Adult skull*

2 *Human skull*

d *Fetal skull*

e *Adult skull*

How apes behave

How nonhuman primates live shows further similarities between the great apes and ourselves. Apes and monkeys live in social groups, obeying rules involving age, sex, and a pecking order, but unlike social groups of animals like birds, these social groups are largely permanent, embrace both sexes, and involve behavior that is largely learned, not just instinctive.

The closest human-ape parallels are seen in chimpanzees–intelligent, strongly social animals living in communities whose cores are bands of males with young females recruited from outside.

Chimpanzees develop both strong and enduring attachments to each other and communicate through many facial expressions, gestures, postures, and sounds. Although they have no exact equivalent of speech, they signal greeting, reassurance, deference, or aggression in almost human ways.

Some chimpanzees make tools, an ability once thought unique to humans. Females in particular eat termites caught on twigs trimmed until they can be poked down holes in termite mounds. Individuals also suck water from sponges made of leaves, use sticks as levers, and brandish natural clubs at enemies.

In some groups males cooperate in hunting monkeys, then share the meat. And although human warfare has no true parallel among these apes, a group of raiding males has killed members of another group, behavior influenced perhaps by overcrowding

due to loss of habitat. Chimpanzees form relatively fluid social groups and live in defended ranges, where members gather food, hunt, breed, and sometimes manufacture simple tools. Add upright walking and tool dependence to these ingredients and you approach the likely lifestyle of prehistoric creatures that had crossed the threshold from ancestral ape to early human.

Play

Like human children, young apes exercise their limbs through play. A common ancestry equips both for swinging by the arms.

Family life (above)

Like humans, chimpanzees develop strong attachments to each other. The mother-child relationship helps each infant through its long learning period. Also, the need to protect their young helps stabilize each troop of chimpanzees.

Tool using (left)

A *Poking a twig into a termite nest to capture termites*

B *Sucking water from a bunch of leaves that have been moistened in a pool*

Facial expressions

Although lacking speech, chimpanzees can communicate emotions by almost human facial expressions. Four are pictured here.

1 *Relaxed*

2 *Greeting*

3 *Smiling: showing only the bottom teeth*

4 *Anger: showing top and bottom teeth*

© DIAGRAM

Human-apes

By maybe 6 million years ago, African apes in the subtribe Hominina were evolving into hominines that walked on two legs only. Bipedalism fostered hand-eye coordination and brain development among those called australopithecines, now popularly known as "ape men." From their later forms emerged the first known species of our genus, Homo *(meaning literally "man"). This chapter explores the forms and lifestyles of these creatures of a million and more years ago.*

Bipedal walking (below)

Pictures illustrate rival ideas about why our ancestors took to walking on their hindlimbs.

A Standing upright to see over tall savanna grasses or to pluck forest fruits.

B Standing upright to wade through shallow water.

A

B

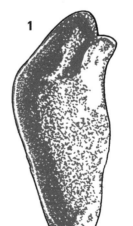

First footprints (right)

1 Fossil footprint from Laetoli, Tanzania. It formed in newly fallen, soft, volcanic ash that soon hardened into solid rock.

2 Contours of fossil footprint.

3 Contours of modern human footprint. (**2**) and (**3**) reveal similarities of shape and weight distribution.

4 Overlapping fossil footprints show where three hominids walked upright more than 3.5 million years ago.

Humankind in the making

By 3.5 million years ago, intensifying Ice Age cold had locked up so much water in the form of ice that worldwide rainfall dwindled, and tropical grasslands spread at the expense of shrinking forests. In Africa, big grazing herbivores and other animals adapted to savanna life now multiplied, while forest creatures suffered loss of habitat.

Incompletely designed for arboreal life, certain creatures derived from African apes seemingly became adjusted to life in open countryside. These "human apes" were the australopiths featured later in this chapter, some evolving toward "true humans." Hominization–the making of humankind–seemingly involved a complex of mutually reinforcing changes, some seen in fossil finds and archaeological discoveries, others just inferred. Fossil footprints 3.8 million years old reveal that by then bipedal walking had freed hands for the making and habitual use of tools, of which the earliest discovered date from 2.5 million years ago. Canines shrank, arguably as tools increasingly performed their tasks. Toolmaking and upright walking stimulated brain development and offered new survival strategies involving foraging for plants and game. In time some hominines lost body hair and gained sweat glands–body changes that helped stop overheating on hot, shadeless plains.

According to one theory, scavenging from carnivores' kills encouraged food-sharing by groups at base camps where communal activities fostered communication that preceded speech. Young learned from elders how to fashion tools, and brain, not brawn or speed, began deciding which hominines survived and which became extinct. This scenario is speculation, however. Most australopithecines were probably no better organized than chimpanzees.

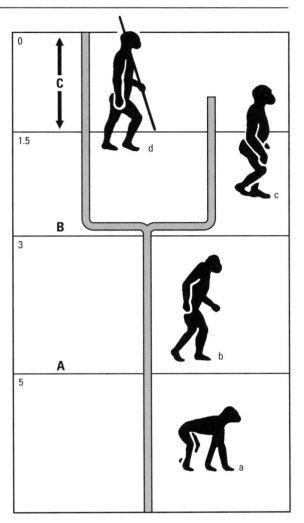

Hominids and climate (left)

Landmarks in human evolution perhaps reflect climatic change caused by Ice Age events, shown in millions of years ago.

a Ancestral ape

b Early australopiths

c Later australopiths

d Homo *species*

A Antarctic ice cap formed

B Arctic ice cap formed

C Glacial-interglacial climatic fluctuations

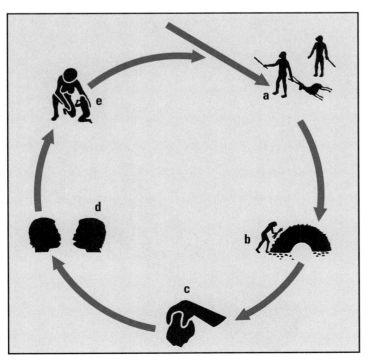

Feedback processes (left)

Environmental change probably promoted hominid evolution by triggering self-reinforcing changes, although perhaps not in the sequence pictured here.

a Group cooperation helped survival on open grasslands.

b A home base where food was shared cemented social ties.

c Toolmaking and tool use promoted hand-eye coordination, food-gathering, hunting, and bipedalism.

d Increasing brain complexity improved communication and the ability to learn to make and use new tools.

e Prolonged infant care and childhood learning aided survival.

Our early relatives

Toward humanity (right)

a Large brain/body weight ratio

b Large cheek teeth with high, square molar crowns

c Canine teeth reduced in height

d Head held erect on spine

e S-shaped spinal curve

f Short, broad pelvis

g Long, inward-angled femur

h Flat-surfaced knee joint

i Long lower limb

j Foot designed as platform

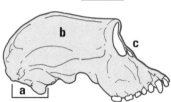

Australopithecus *skull* (above)

Two views show some features not found in our own genus.

a Little of skull behind hole for spinal cord

b Small brain capacity

c Large, dished face

d Wide mid-face

e Distinctive tooth row

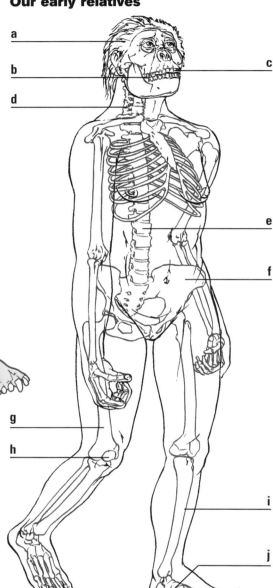

Only hips and legs redesigned for walking upright set apart our early ancestors from apes; differences later reinforced by increased brain size. These "ape men" arguably included at least three genera: *Ardipithecus* ("ground floor ape"), *Australopithecus* ("southern ape"), and *Paranthropus* ("beside ape").

Australopiths–the so-called "ape men"–evolved in Africa 4 million years ago, or even earlier. They evidently came from a chimpanzeelike ancestor yet to be identified. There arose perhaps 10 species (experts disagree). By 2 million years ago, one probably gave rise to the first species of our own genus, *Homo*. Both genera endured side by side for another million years before the last of the australopiths died out, possibly exterminated by its brainier successor.

Australopiths were quite likely hairy creatures, most slightly built and no bigger than a chimpanzee, with males much larger than females. Brain-body ratio was little better than an ape's, and the apelike head had a concave face, flat nose, and chinless muzzle. Jaws and cheek teeth were big and powerful, with a V-shaped or pointed-U-shaped tooth row. But unlike apes' lower limbs, those of australopiths were longer than the arms and designed primarily for walking upright.

Australopiths evidently used hands habitually to carry loads and some made stone cutting tools, although their teeth were suitable for crushing seeds or chewing leaves.

Foraging, scavenging, and sometimes maybe even hunting for their food, small groups ranged the tropical grasslands of eastern and southern Africa. Some might have spread to Asia and Europe.

The next pages give details of the best-known species of these primeval hominines.

A

Ancient finds (above and right)

Illustrations depict two finds perhaps from very early australopiths.

A *Jaw 5.5 million years old from Lothagam in Kenya*

B *Elbow joint 4 million years old from Kanapoi in Kenya*

B

The first bipedal hominid? (right)

This femur with an offset head found in northwest Kenya in AD 2000 might represent a bipedal hominid 6 million years old–far older than the oldest "ape human" named on the next page.

Thigh, jaw, arm, and finger bones and teeth came from individuals evidently eaten by a leopard. Paleontologists Brigitte Senut and Martin Pickford thought Orrorin tugenensis *larger than some australopithecines and built on more human lines. It evidently walked upright but climbed trees and chewed tough-skinned fruits.*

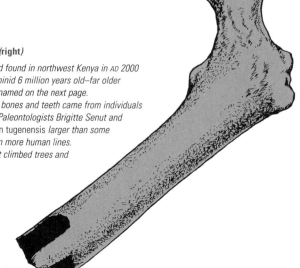

Human evolution: an overview

This shows in millions of years ago when "ape-humans" and humans lived. Some fossils are scanty and relationships uncertain.

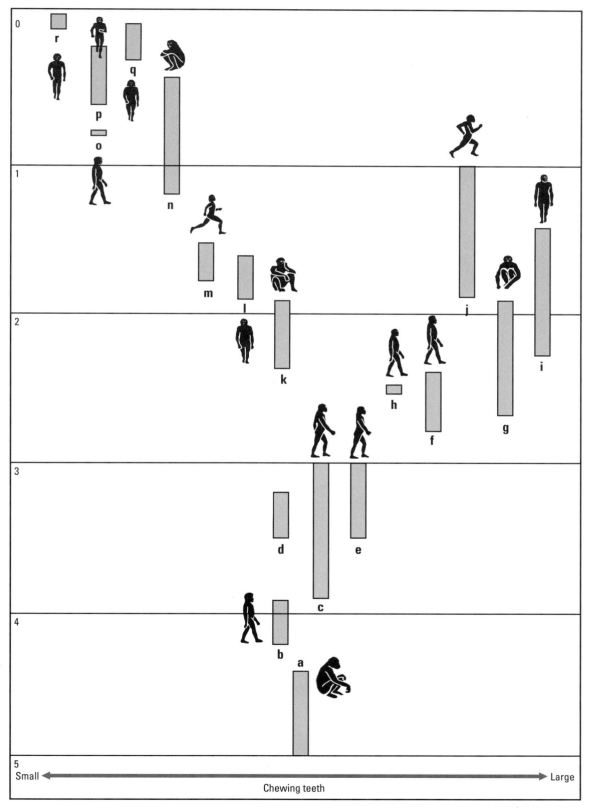

a Ardipithecus ramidus
   Close to chimpanzee

b Australopithecus anamensis
   Oldest known "ape human"

c Australopithecus afarensis
   "Lucy" walked upright

d Kenyanthropus platyops
   A flat-faced hominine

e Australopithecus bahrelghazali
   Resembled afarensis

f Australopithecus africanus
   Maybe evolved from afarensis

g Paranthropus aethiopicus
   Massive jaws

h Australopithecus gahri
   Possibly the maker of the first known stone tools

i Paranthropus boisei
   Broad, concave face

j Paranthropus robustus
   Large chewing teeth

k Australopithecus rudolfensis
   Enlarged braincase

l Australopithecus habilis
   Evolved from rudolfensis

m Homo ergaster
   The first hominid as tall as us, using fire and perhaps making the first stone hand axes.

n Homo erectus
   Derived from ergaster

o Homo antecessor
   First known Homo in western Europe (identity doubtful)

p Homo heidelbergensis
   Very strongly built

q Homo neanderthalensis
   Extremely muscular

r Homo sapiens
   Fully modern humans

© DIAGRAM

Australopithecus afarensis

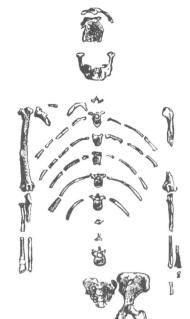

Where afarensis *lived* (above)

1 Hadar
2 Middle Awash
3 Baringo
4 Laetoli

Lucy's skeleton (left)

Nicknamed "Lucy," this partial skeleton of Australopithecus afarensis reveals a bipedal creature with smaller body, relatively smaller brain and longer arms than ours, and slimmer hips than a modern woman's. (Other finds show that afarensis had slightly curved toe and finger bones.) American anthropologists discovered it in north-central Ethiopia in 1974. Lucy's 3-million-year-old skeleton became the oldest known for any hominine.

Australopithecus afarensis ("southern ape of Afar"), the best known "ape human," evolved from an earlier form, perhaps 4 million years ago. Its name comes from find sites in Ethiopia's northern Afar Triangle, but *afarensis* fossils have also been identified at Omo in Ethiopia and Laetoli, Tanzania, site of the oldest known human footprints.

The creature looked like a small yet upright chimpanzee. Some experts interpret larger and smaller individuals as males and females; others think they represent quite separate species. Adults included specimens no bigger than a six-year-old girl, weighing only 65 lb (30 kg). The brain was little bigger than a chimpanzee's and probably could not organize speech. The face was apelike, with a low forehead, brow ridge, flat nose, and no chin, and had jutting jaws with massive back teeth. Front teeth were chipped, perhaps through use as gripping tools.

Afarensis walked slightly bowlegged, and the somewhat chimpanzeelike hips and curved toe and finger bones suggest that it spent much time in trees, perhaps sleeping high among the branches out of reach of predators. Females had much slimmer hips, and therefore narrower birth canals, than modern women, and they must have given birth to young with relatively smaller heads and brains than those of modern newborn human babies.

Family groups would have foraged for plant foods including tough, hard, or fibrous fruits and seeds. Individuals might have made crude tools of wood and stone to scavenge meat from carnivores' kills.

Before dying out by 2.9 million years ago, *afarensis* possibly gave rise directly or indirectly to the other australopithecines and to our genus, *Homo*.

a *Big, apelike incisors*

b *Diastema (gap) between incisors and canines in many specimens of afarensis*

c *Canines larger than in later hominids*

d *Premolars more primitive than later hominids'*

e *Large, thickly enameled molars, worn rather flat*

Two tooth rows (right)

*Two pictures contrast (**A**) afarensis's somewhat apelike tooth row with (**B**) the more smoothly curved tooth row seen in members of the genus Homo.*

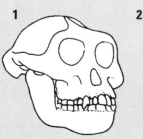

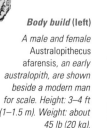

Body build (left)

A male and female Australopithecus afarensis, an early australopith, are shown beside a modern man for scale. Height: 3–4 ft (1–1.5 m). Weight: about 45 lb (20 kg).

Skulls compared

1 *Three-quarter view of A. afarensis skull showing relatively small size, small braincase, low forehead, brow ridge, flat nose, jutting jaws, and no chin. Brain capacity: about 410 cc.*

2 *Three-quarter view of skull of Homo sapiens. Brain capacity: 1,400 cc.*

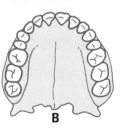

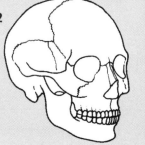

Australopithecus africanus

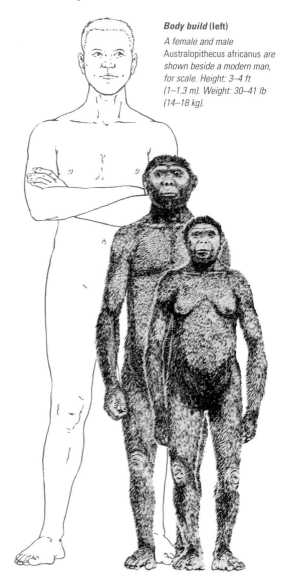

Body build (left)

A female and male Australopithecus africanus are shown beside a modern man, for scale. Height: 3–4 ft (1–1.3 m). Weight: 30–41 lb (14–18 kg).

Australopithecus africanus ("southern ape of Africa") lived perhaps from 3 million to 2.4 million years ago. It possibly evolved from *Australopithecus afarensis*, and some half-jokingly suggest that it gave rise to the chimpanzee.

A small, slight, apelike creature, *africanus* stood as high as, and weighed no more than, a six-year-old American girl. It walked upright, although the leg muscles differed from ours. The arms were relatively long, and the thumb and fingers may have handled objects less skilfully than we can.

The lower face jutted forward, but face and jaws were deeper and shorter than an ape's. Some skulls show traces of a crest that anchored strong neck muscles. The brain was no bigger than a gorilla's, but casts show that brain structure differed somewhat from an ape's. For relative brain-body size, *africanus* ranks midway between modern apes and modern humans.

Experts disagree about its likely mode of life. Tooth and jaw design suggest that this ape-man chewed plant foods but also might have scavenged meat from carnivores' kills. Experts dispute its ability to manufacture tools. Most bone "tools" found near *africanus* fossils have proved to be remains of meals consumed by hyenas or other carnivores.

Some writers have argued that *africanus* fossils are just female robust australopithecines, but robusts seemingly postdated most *africanus* specimens. The earliest alleged *africanus* fossil is a 5.5-million-year-old jaw fragment from Lothagam in Kenya. A suggested end date of 700,000 years ago seems equally unlikely.

Most fossils come from Sterkfontein Cave in South Africa. Others attributed to *africanus* come from Ethiopia, Kenya, and Tanzania.

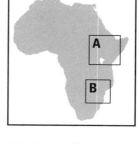

Where africanus *lived*

East African finds might be those of other hominines.

A *East Africa*

1 *Omo River*

2 *Koobi Fora*

3 *Lothagam*

4 *Olduvai Gorge*

B *South Africa*

5 *Makapansgat*

6 *Sterkfontein*

7 *Taung*

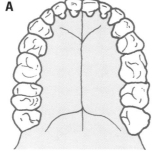

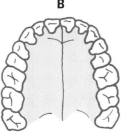

Tooth rows compared (above)

*Illustrations contrast (**A**) africanus's large tooth row and very large back teeth with (**B**) the smaller tooth row and smaller teeth of modern humans.*

Skulls compared

A *Skull of* Australopithecus africanus *in three-quarter view*

B *Three-quarter view skull of* Homo sapiens

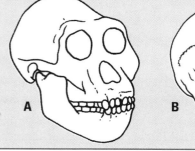

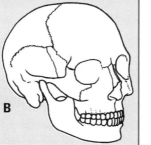

© DIAGRAM

Australopithecus habilis and *rudolfensis*

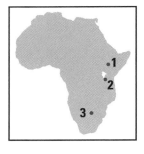

Where habilis **lived** (above)

Where habilis **lived** (above)

1 *Koobi Fora*

2 *Olduvai Gorge*

3 *Swartkrans (possibly)*

There are claims for finds at other sites, mostly in East Africa.

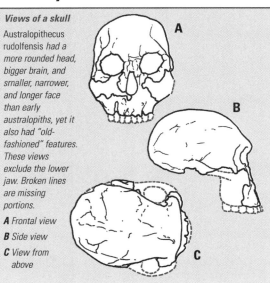

Views of a skull

Australopithecus rudolfensis had a more rounded head, bigger brain, and smaller, narrower, and longer face than early australopiths, yet it also had "old-fashioned" features. These views exclude the lower jaw. Broken lines are missing portions.

A *Frontal view*

B *Side view*

C *View from above*

Widely known as *Homo habilis* ("handy human"), the first known species of our genus was small, with gangly apelike arms, and redescribed in AD 1999 as an australopithecine. Compared with others, however, it had a bigger braincase and smaller, less projecting face, smaller cheek teeth, and larger front teeth. It had an open U-shaped tooth row.

Australopithecus habilis stood 5 ft (1.5 m) tall at most; in fact, one adult measured only 3 ft 3 in (1 m). Its face was still "old-fashioned," with brow ridges, flat nose, and projecting jaws. *Habilis* had a more rounded head than other australopiths, however, and a larger brain (650–800 cc), but it was still only half the size of ours. Inside the thin-walled skull, a bulge shows the brain's speech-producing Broca's area, but the larynx might have been incapable of making as many sounds as ours. Jaws were less massive than a typical australopith's, but arms and hand bones were still designed for climbing and hanging from trees.

Individuals with the largest brains and teeth may have had more modern limb bones. These arguably represent a separate species, *Australopithecus rudolfensis*. Perhaps this led to *Homo*, although its "old-fashioned" face and teeth make that seem doubtful. However, between them, these species lived about 2.4–1.6 million years ago, and so bridged the time gap between *Australopithecus gahri* and *Homo ergaster*, the first undoubted member of our genus.

Artifacts found near *habilis* bones suggest that it made basic stone tools. Probably these helped it gather plant foods, scavenge meat from the carcasses of creatures killed by carnivores, and hunt small game. Supposed evidence that *habilis* built simple shelters now seems questionable, however.

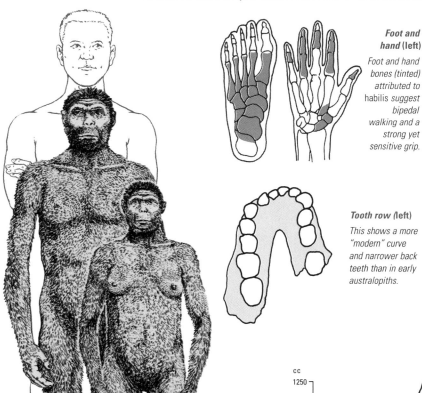

Foot and hand (left)

Foot and hand bones (tinted) attributed to habilis *suggest bipedal walking and a strong yet sensitive grip.*

Tooth row (left)

This shows a more "modern" curve and narrower back teeth than in early australopiths.

Body build (left)

A male and female Australopithecus habilis *are shown beside a modern man, for scale. Height: 3 ft 3 in– 5 ft (1–1.5 m). Weight: about 64–115 lb (29–52 kg).*

Brain size and body weight (below)

The steeper the line, the greater the increase in brain size compared to increase in body weight.

1 *Apes*

a *Chimpanzees*

b *Gorillas*

2 *Australopiths*

c *Australopithecus africanus*

d *Australopithecus robustus*

e *Australopithecus habilis*

3 *Humans*

f *Homo erectus*

g *Homo sapiens*

Paranthropus robustus

Body build

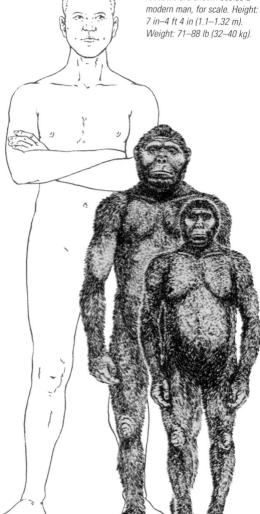

A male and female Paranthropus robustus *are shown beside a modern man, for scale. Height: 3 ft 7 in–4 ft 4 in (1.1–1.32 m). Weight: 71–88 lb (32–40 kg).*

Paranthropus "beside man" *robustus*, also called *Australopithecus robustus*, had more robust jaws and teeth than *africanus* but was even smaller than that species. Some have argued that robust fossils were just males and *africanus* fossils females of a single species, but most experts reject that notion.

About 4 ft 4 in (1.3 m) tall, *robustus* was the height of an 8-year-old boy, but rather heavier at 88 lb (40 kg). Compared with *africanus,* it had a larger, flatter skull, which housed a bigger brain of about 500 cc, and the face was considerably larger and broader in relation to the braincase. A tall central skull crest anchored powerful muscles that worked the massive jaws. Front teeth were no bigger than those of *africanus,* but cheek teeth were large and often worn despite a thick coat of wear-resistant enamel. All this suggests that *robustus* must have eaten hard, tough foods, perhaps including seeds.

Robustus seemingly evolved by 1.8 million years ago, perhaps from a relative of *africanus*. All undisputed *robustus* fossil finds come from South African caves, where the creatures' carcasses were evidently dragged or dropped by carnivores.

The species apparently died out about 1 million years ago. Before then it probably gave rise to *Paranthropus boisei*, although many experts identify that creature with this species. Skull comparisons have even led some scholars to suggest that *robustus* was ancestral to the gorilla.

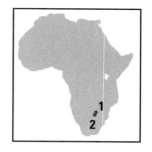

Where robustus *lived* (above)

1 Kromdraai

2 Swartkrans

Many experts would include sites named on the next page.

Tooth row (below)

Massive cheek teeth and small front teeth show that robustus *was a herbivore.*

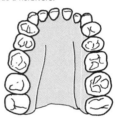

Skulls compared (below)

A Three-quarter view of a P. robustus *skull, showing the skull crest and massive jaws. Brain capacity: 500 cc.*

B Three-quarter view of skull of Homo sapiens. *Brain capacity: 1400 cc.*

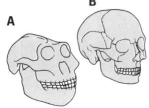

B

A

Tell-tale holes (above)

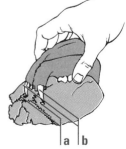

Damaged robustus *bones hint at how their owners died.*

a Holes in a robustus *skull*

b *A leopard's lower canines match the holes.*

Finds in fissures

Robustus *bones found in limestone fissures probably accumulated like this:*

A Old land level

B Present land level

a *Leopard drags* robustus *corpse up a tree, out of reach of hyenas.*

b Robustus *bones fall into limestone fissure.*

c *Layers of sediment bury the bones.*

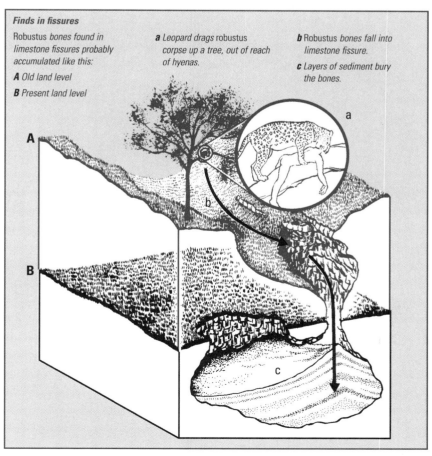

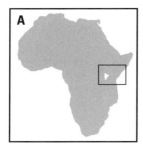

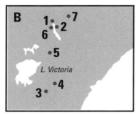

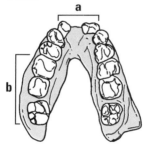

Where Paranthropus boisei lived (above)

A *Africa: A rectangle shows the area involved.*

B *The area enlarged*

1 *Omo*

2 *Koobi Fora*

3 *Olduvai Gorge*

4 *Peninj*

5 *Chesowanja*

6 *Nachukui*

7 *Konso*

Paranthropus boisei

Known also as *Australopithecus boisei* ("Boise southern ape"), this species was named after British businessman Charles Boise who helped fund the fossil hunts that led to its discovery in 1959. A former name, *Zinjanthropus*, means "East Africa man." The animal inhabited that region from about 2.3 to 1.4 million years ago.

This creature supposedly had more massive jaw muscles than *Paranthropus robustus* (from which it probably arose), although many paleoanthropologists consider it just a regional variant of that species. Restorations based on finds of fossil skull and limb bones suggest it had a *robustus*-sized brain, about one-third as big as ours, and grew no taller than a modern 10-year-old girl. Despite muscular jaws, both of these robust australopithecines probably had bodies similar to that of *Australopithecus africanus*.

Like a gorilla's, *boisei*'s skull was large, with brow ridges and a central crest for anchoring immense jaw muscles, but compared with a gorilla, *boisei*'s crest was slighter and located farther forward, its face was flatter, and the canine teeth were smaller.

Immense molars and premolars earned this animal the nickname "Nutcracker Man," but biomechanical studies show that its teeth exerted no more pressure than our own, one-quarter their size. Instead of crunching hard-shelled foods, *boisei* seems to have chewed large quantities of leaves, a low-grade source of nourishment.

Fossil bones found with chipped pebbles about 1.8 million years old suggest that *boisei* might have made or used stone tools, and in AD 2001 came evidence for tool use by its *robustus* relative–sharp bones with wear marks evidently made by digging termites from their earth-mound nests.

Tooth row (left)

This incomplete tooth row (reduced in size) shows features stressed in Paranthropus boisei.

a *Small, biting front teeth*

b *Immense, grinding back teeth*

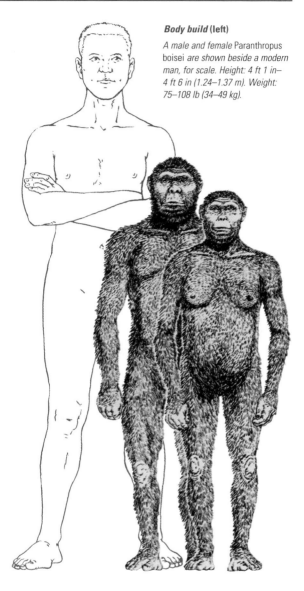

Body build (left)

A male and female Paranthropus boisei are shown beside a modern man, for scale. Height: 4 ft 1 in– 4 ft 6 in (1.24–1.37 m). Weight: 75–108 lb (34–49 kg).

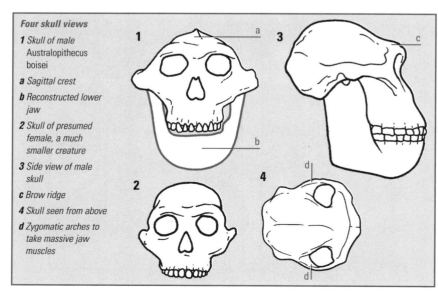

Four skull views

1 *Skull of male Australopithecus boisei*

a *Sagittal crest*

b *Reconstructed lower jaw*

2 *Skull of presumed female, a much smaller creature*

3 *Side view of male skull*

c *Brow ridge*

4 *Skull seen from above*

d *Zygomatic arches to take massive jaw muscles*

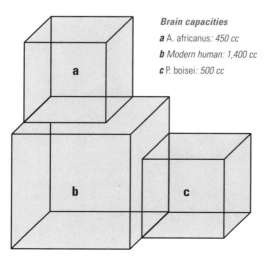

Brain capacities

a *A. africanus: 450 cc*

b *Modern human: 1,400 cc*

c *P. boisei: 500 cc*

Early artifacts

Early humans were slower and weaker than the big carnivores and lacked their built-in weapons of fangs and claws. Yet early hominines learned to make up for these disadvantages. They fashioned lumps of stone, bone, and wood to cut, scrape, or dig. Unlike fangs or claws, such tools could be picked up, put down, or interchanged at will. Tools in time gave humans unprecedented mastery of the environment.

The first tools were probably bone splinters, sharp sticks, and bark trays for collecting food. Such mostly perishable artifacts are lost, but stone proved durable. We know that early hominines in Ethiopia deliberately broke small rocks, perhaps to make hard, sharp edges to cut up meat. From then, 2.5 million years ago, until about five thousand years ago, stone dominated technology.

Of the Stone Age's three subdivisions (Old, Middle, and New), the Paleolithic, or Old Stone Age, period endured wherever humans set foot until about 10,000 years ago. Early Paleolithic toolmakers learned to make sharp tools by bashing stone on stone. They selected only rocks that broke easily when struck and split along fracture lines the fashioners could control. They chose rock hard enough to cut, grind, split, or scrape plant and animal materials.

Flint, chert, quartzite, and rock crystal all proved suitable, but none is available everywhere. In East Africa, most of the oldest tools were made of lava, which yields rougher surfaces than flint.

The best-known early toolkit is the Typical Oldowan from Tanzania's Olduvai Gorge. Here, 1.9 million years ago, *Australopithecus habilis* (or some contemporary australopithecine) chipped basalt and/or quartzite pebbles into shapes identified as crude choppers, scrapers, burins, hammerstones, and (by their shape) discoids, polyhedrons, and subspheroids. Some experts think that the true tools were the "waste" flakes struck off from these artifacts. Certainly, near Kenya's Lake Turkana, hominines used small stone flakes to butcher antelopes 1.5 million years ago.

Tooth marks underlying cut marks made on bones imply that early hominines scavenged most of their meat from carnivores' kills. Yet early man quite likely made hunting weapons, too. Stone balls from Olduvai could have brought down antelopes if tied to thongs and thrown to wind around legs, as cowboys topple cattle with the bolas.

The Oldowan (alias chopper-and-flake or pebble tool) industry, with later variants, spread over much of early Stone Age Africa and Eurasia. In places it flourished until about 200,000 years ago–long after the invention of much more sophisticated Stone Age industries.

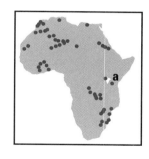

Oldowan Africa (above)

Map symbols show finds of stone tools supposedly like those from Olduvai (**a**).

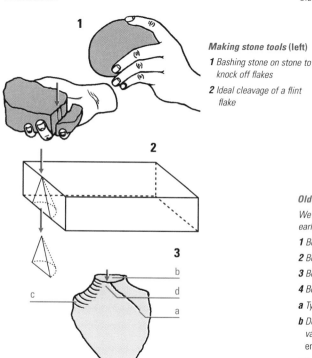

Making stone tools (left)

1 Bashing stone on stone to knock off flakes

2 Ideal cleavage of a flint flake

3 A human-made flint flake:

a bulbar scar

b striking platform

c concentric ripples

d bulb of percussion

Oldowan time scale (below)

We show rock beds, toolkits, and early homines at Olduvai:

1 Bed 1: 2.0–1.7 million years ago

2 Bed 2: 1.7–1.1 million years ago

3 Bed 3: 1.1–0.8 million years ago

4 Bed 4: 0.8–0.6 million years ago

a Typical Oldowan tools

b Developed Oldowan tools–more varied and overlapping Homo erectus

c Australopithecus *species*

d Australopithecus habilis

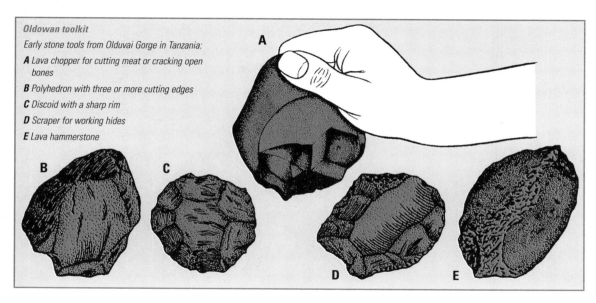

Oldowan toolkit

Early stone tools from Olduvai Gorge in Tanzania:

A Lava chopper for cutting meat or cracking open bones

B Polyhedron with three or more cutting edges

C Discoid with a sharp rim

D Scraper for working hides

E Lava hammerstone

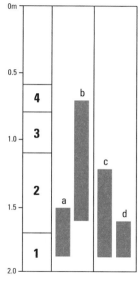

© DIAGRAM

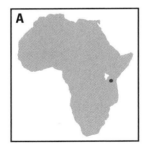

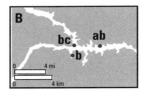

Finds from Olduvai

A *Map of Africa showing the area including Olduvai Gorge*

B *Olduvai Gorge showing a few sites of key early finds*

a "Hut" circle

b Homo habilis

c Paranthropus boisei

C *Section through beds at Olduvai showing finds of hominids featured in this chapter and the next*

1 Australopithecus boisei

2 Australopithecus habilis

3 Homo erectus

The oldest hut?

This 1.8-million-year-old scattering of stones and fossils might represent the oldest-known human habitation. Stones perhaps anchored branches, providing the structure of a lakeside hut at Olduvai.

Early working sites

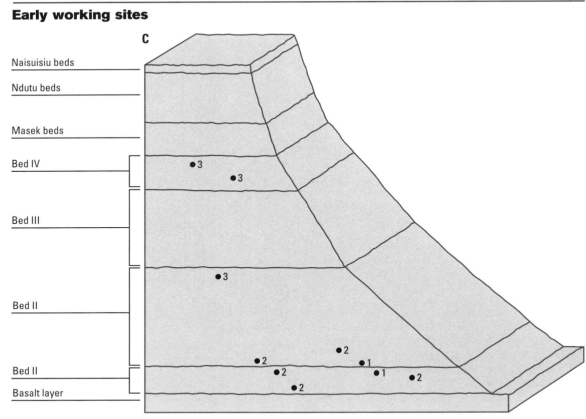

Clusters of stones and bones dug up at Olduvai Gorge in Tanzania suggest that by about 2 million years ago early humans already met in groups at centers where they butchered game, made tools, ate food, and perhaps built the world's first shelters.

Sharpened stones and the cut and broken bones of big grazing mammals reveal, not chance assemblages produced by running water but working floors where families of *Australopithecus habilis* or other hominines shared meat and marrow. They carried in bones scavenged from carnivores' kills and lava lumps from nearby rocks to shape them on the spot. About 1.7 million years ago, they also seemingly used tools brought ready-made from rocks 10 miles (16 km) away, implying maybe even very early trade.

Close study suggests that most of the 20 or so very early sites at Olduvai were carefully located where drinkable freshwater streams flowed into a game-rich alkaline lake. Perhaps the most remarkable discovery is a hint that the ancient hominines began to build. At one site, the scattered pattern of bones and stones suggests that a thorn fence or windbreak protected workers on their windward side. Another site features a stone circle about 13 ft (4 m) across–perhaps support for branches raised to form a hut like those still built in parts of Africa. However, this 1.8-million-year-old feature might just be stones disturbed by roots around a tree.

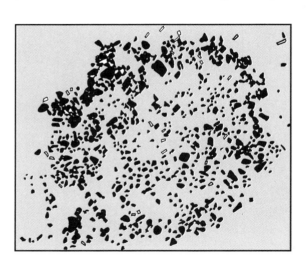

An early home

This reconstruction of an early prehistoric hut is based on finds of old stone circles and building methods still in use by hunter foragers in parts of Africa.
In fact, the roofing might have been a rough-and-ready covering of leafy twigs.

Animals of ancient Africa

Thousands of broken animal bones litter East Africa's early butchery and living floors. Careful studies of sites from Tanzania, Kenya, and Ethiopia show scores of creatures large and small that shared savanna, lake, or forest with hominines 2–1.5 million years ago. Most detailed studies come from the former shoreline sites of a dwindling prehistoric lake in the area now pierced by Tanzania's Olduvai Gorge. Here are examples of these creatures, living and extinct, not shown to scale:

1 Tilapia, a cichlid, is a freshwater fish that tolerates brackish water. Length: up to 12 in (36 cm).

2 Xenopus, the clawed frog, is an aquatic gray frog with a pale belly. Length: up to 6 in (15 cm).

3 Chamaeleo jacksoni, is a slow-moving lizard that catches flies on its long, sticky tongue. Males have three horns. Length: to 12 in (30 cm). Habitat: bush and open woodland.

4 Phoeniconaias, the lesser flamingo, is a long-necked wading bird with a bent beak. Length: 40 in (1 m). Habitat: brackish lakes.

5 Megantereon was a possibly lion-sized saber-toothed cat, stabbing big herbivores with its daggerlike upper canines.

6 Deinotherium was an elephant with downcurved tusks in its lower jaw, perhaps for digging roots. Height 13 ft (4 m).

7 Sivatherium was a short-necked giraffe with antlers. Height 7 ft (2.2 m).

8 Pelorovis was a giant African buffalo with a 6 ft 7 in (2 m) horn span. It belonged to the *Bovidae* (cattle and antelopes), which account for most bones found at Olduvai Gorge.

Life at Olduvai

Shown below are eight creatures with numbers that correspond to their descriptions in the text. These animals are not all to the same scale.

1 Tilapia
2 Xenopus
3 Chamaeleo jacksonii
4 Phoeniconaias
5 Megantereon
6 Deinotherium
7 Sivatherium
8 Pelorovis

© DIAGRAM

Early humans

By 1.9 million years ago, an advanced australopithecine gave rise to the first truly human creature. Homo ergaster *("work man") was as big as and proportioned like ourselves. Superior intelligence and technology helped* ergaster *and its Early Stone Age hunter-gatherer descendants exploit new habitats.* Ergaster *occupied Africa, where it produced the more advanced* Homo heidelbergensis *("Heidelberg man").* Ergaster *also entered Asia, where it evolved into* Homo erectus *(upright man). By 300,000 years ago,* heidelbergensis *had spread across Europe and was evolving into the Neadertals and* Homo sapiens.

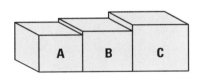

Increase in brain size (above)

A Australopithecus rudolfensis*: 750 cc*

B Homo ergaster*: 905 cc*

C Homo sapiens*: 1,400 cc*

Brains and muscles

Diagrams show skull shapes related to brain size and the size of muscles balancing the head and operating jaws.

A Homo erectus *(small brain, big muscles)*

B Homo sapiens *(big brain, small muscles)*

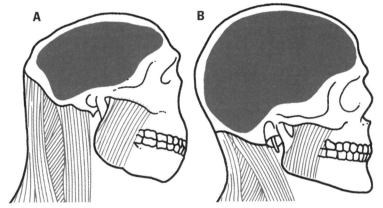

Human family tree

This simplified scheme shows likely trends in human evolution. Figures represent millions of years ago. (When erectus *arose is a matter for debate.)*

1 Australopithecus rudolfensis *or* habilis

2 Homo ergaster

3 Homo erectus

4 Homo heidelbergensis

5 Homo neanderthalensis

6 Homo sapiens

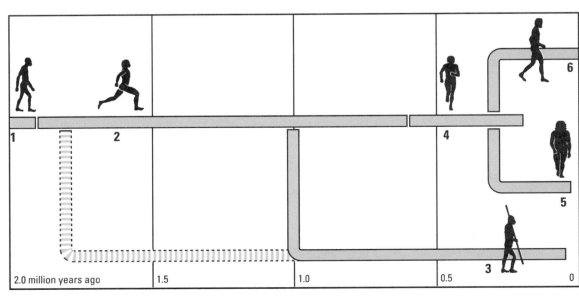

2.0 million years ago   1.5   1.0   0.5   0

Upright man and Work man

Body build

A male and female Homo erectus *are shown beside a modern man, for scale. Height: 5–6 ft (1.5–1.8 m). Weight: 88–160 lb (40–72.7 kg).*

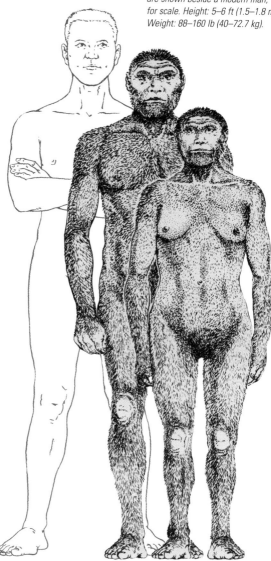

Homo ergaster of Africa and its Asian offshoot *Homo erectus* (also known as "Peking man" or *Sinanthropus*, and as "Southeast Asia man," or *Pithecanthropus*) had a bigger brain and body than their australopithecine ancestors and less difference in size between the sexes. *Homo ergaster's* rather rounded cranium contrasted with erectus's long, low skull, though both possessed a shelving forehead, thick brow ridges, a flatter face than ours, no chin, big projecting jaws, and larger cheek teeth than our own. Early *Homo ergaster* had thinner skull bones than the extremely thick bones of erectus, and, behind its brow ridge, lacked the other's sulcus, or depression. Strong muscles at the back of erectus's neck joined a rear skull bump and stopped the front-heavy head from sagging forward.

Their brains were smaller than our own, with a cubic capacity of about 905 cc for early *ergaster* and 1,000 cc for *erectus*. However, their overall physique resembled ours, although *ergaster* included slender, long-limbed individuals up to 6 ft (1.8 m) tall, while *erectus* tended to be more robust.

Homo ergaster lived in Africa perhaps 1.9–0.6 million years ago, *erectus* in Asia from maybe 1.8 million years ago until as recently as 50,000 BC.

Both possibly owed their large size and ability to spread to the control of fire for cooking nutritious roots and tubers indigestible if eaten raw.

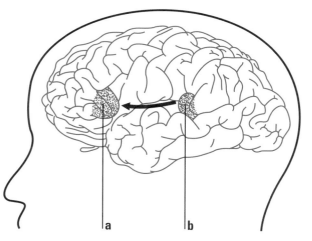

Speech centers

Linked speech centers in the brain's left side produce swellings detectable in early fossil skulls of Homo *(and, confusingly, but less pronounced, in apes).*

a *Broca's area, controlling speech production*

b *Wernicke's area, controlling understanding of speech*

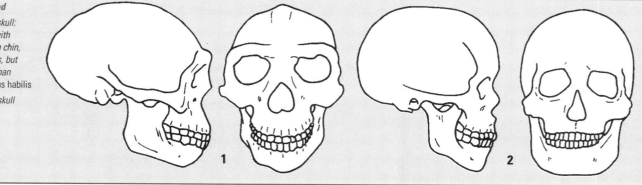

Skulls compared

1 Homo erectus *skull: long and low with brow ridges, no chin, protruding jaws, but smaller teeth than* Australopithecus habilis

2 Homo sapiens *skull*

© DIAGRAM

A changing world

The evolving hominines *Homo ergaster*, *Homo erectus*, and *Homo heidelbergensis* collectively lived through almost all the of Pleistocene–the geological epoch from about 2 million to 10,000 years ago. During these Ice Age times, phases of intense cold, called glacial stages, sent ice sheets and mountain glaciers sprawling over much of northern North America and Northwest Eurasia, only to retreat in intervening warmer spells, called interglacials.

During glacials, even unglaciated Europe and West Africa and East Asia were frost-free for barely a month each year. Accordingly their landscapes ranged from tundra to cool temperate forests of such trees as firs and beeches. Cool conditions favored large mammals, including (in China, for example) hyenas, giant beavers, red deer, and prehistoric species of rhinoceros and elephant.

Meanwhile, depressions forced south by ice sheets brought the subtropics more rain than they get now, but during glacials, the tropics tended to be dry, their luxuriant rain forests shrinking into isolated "islands."

Deprived of the water locked up in vast ice sheets, the oceans shrank. The sea surface sank to at least 328 ft (100 m) below its present level, exposing land bridges that enabled humans to colonize the big Southeast Asian islands.

In interglacials, some northern climates became warmer than they are today. Warmth-loving mammals such as the hippo and Merck's rhinoceros ranged north as far as southern England. At the same time, the sea rose by up to 180 ft (50 m) above the level of today, isolating some offshore islands previously linked to land. Any populations of early humans isolated by climatic change were likely to evolve in slightly different ways, suited to conditions where they lived.

Ice Age world

In glacial stages, the Northern Hemisphere looked like this:

a *Asia*

b *Europe*

c *North America*

(legend)

Extra land exposed in glacial stages

Sea

Glaciated areas

— Summer extent of pack ice

Climatic changes

A graph shows fluctuating July temperatures in degrees Centigrade for Central Europe for about the last 1,200,000 years. (Research now suggests that peaks and valleys occurred more frequently than this.) Homo erectus *perhaps flourished until 50,000 years ago.*

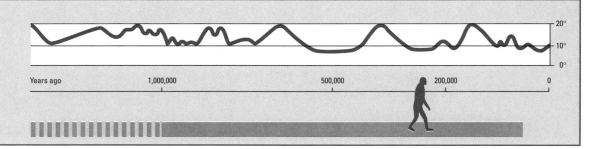

Years ago   1,000,000   500,000   200,000   0

Work man in Africa

Fossil finds point to Africa as the continent where complex feedback processes involving intensified use of hands and tools, together with new food resources, created a genus bigger, more intelligent, and more adaptable than anything before.

Among its scrappy fossil remains, one East African discovery stands out: a *Homo ergaster* skeleton 1.6 million years old, yet more complete than any fossil hominid predating deliberate burials, begun about 70,000 years ago.

Other fossils–mostly bits of skull or jaw–suggest that work man eventually spread from East Africa to the farthest corners of the continent, but because so many fossils are so partial and show no clear progressive evolution and because the dividing line between this species and our own is blurred, African and European *ergaster* (alias *erectus*) specimens more recent than 800,000 years are often assigned to the intermediate species *heidelbergensis*.

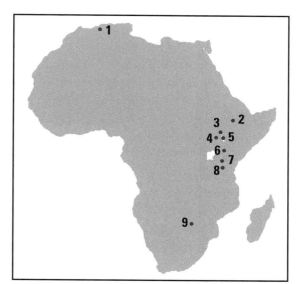

Early **Homo** *in Africa*

Major sites include:

1 *Ternifine*

2 *Melka Kunture*

3 *Omo River*

4 *Nariokotome*

5 *Koobi Fora*

6 *Chesowanja*

7 *Olorgesailie*

8 *Olduvai Gorge*

9 *Swartkrans*

Homo ergaster

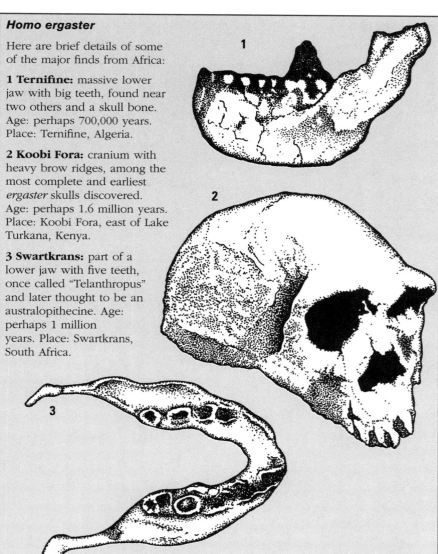

Here are brief details of some of the major finds from Africa:

1 Ternifine: massive lower jaw with big teeth, found near two others and a skull bone. Age: perhaps 700,000 years. Place: Ternifine, Algeria.

2 Koobi Fora: cranium with heavy brow ridges, among the most complete and earliest *ergaster* skulls discovered. Age: perhaps 1.6 million years. Place: Koobi Fora, east of Lake Turkana, Kenya.

3 Swartkrans: part of a lower jaw with five teeth, once called "Telanthropus" and later thought to be an australopithecine. Age: perhaps 1 million years. Place: Swartkrans, South Africa.

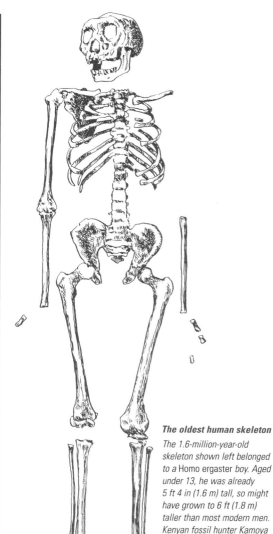

The oldest human skeleton

The 1.6-million-year-old skeleton shown left belonged to a Homo ergaster *boy. Aged under 13, he was already 5 ft 4 in (1.6 m) tall, so might have grown to 6 ft (1.8 m) taller than most modern men. Kenyan fossil hunter Kamoya Kimeu found these ancient bones in 1984, west of Lake Turkana.*

© DIAGRAM

Upright man in Asia

Homo erectus fossils all arguably come from Asia. Almost all were found in Java or China, with a possible *erectus* skull from India.

Very early specimens of *Pithecanthropus* from central Java's so-called Djetis beds could date from more than 1.5 million years ago, while Java's Trinil beds have yielded some possibly 700,000-year-old bones. China's best-known fossil human, *Sinanthropus*, is known as Peking man, from the remains of more than 40 individuals discovered near Peking; all disappeared in World War II, though casts survive. This Chinese form had a larger brain than older Asian forms and thrived in cool conditions about 360,000 years ago.

All these Asian hominids lived near the fringes of the South China Sea, which has been likened to a giant waterhole that filled and emptied as the northern ice sheets melted and advanced. In cold "low water" phases, *erectus* probably colonized the now drowned Sunda Shelf between Indonesia and China and migrated overland between the two.

Back views compared

Below we compare back views of two skulls.

A *Peking man: skull broadest low down, but not as low as for Australopithecus*

B *Modern human: skull broadest high up*

Homo erectus *in Asia*

This map shows important selected sites:

1 *Narmada*

2 *Yuanmou*

3 *Luc Yen*

4 *Lantian*

5 *Yunxi*

6 *Nanzhao*

7 *Beijing (Peking)*

8 *Hexian*

9 *Sangiran*

10 *Perning/Modjokerto*

11 *Trinil*

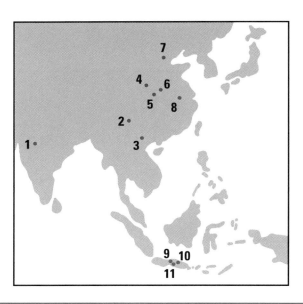

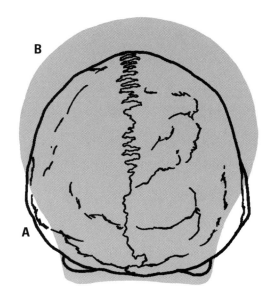

Homo erectus

Here are examples of specimens from Asia.

1 Pithecanthropus 4 includes part of a big, thick skull, also a massive upper jaw with a gap between canine and incisor, as if to accommodate a large lower canine. Age: About 1 million years. Place: Sangiran, Java.

2 Lantian skull: a small, thick skull (cranial capacity 780 cc), with strong, arched brow ridges. A separate chinless lower jaw at Lantian lacked third molars (a congenital condition seen in some people today). Age: about 600,000 years. Place: Lantian, Shaanxi Province, China.

3 Sinanthropus had a low, wide skull (cranial capacity about 1,075 cc) but smaller teeth–without a gap–and a shorter jaw than older Asian forms. Age: 360,000 years. Place: Choukoutien, near Beijing, China.

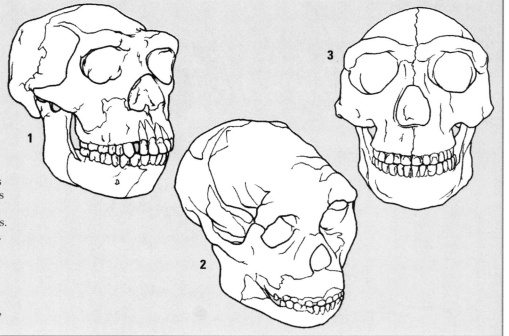

Homo heidelbergensis

Humans reached the edge of Europe 1.7 million years ago, as proved in 1995 with the discovery of a *Homo ergaster* skull in Georgia, a country near Russia. Remains named *Homo antecessor* show humans in north-central Spain 800,000 years ago, but most other early European human fossils date from 500,000–200,000 years ago or less.

Despite "old-fashioned features" (thick walls, brow ridges, big teeth, and massive, chinless jaws), their skulls had larger brains than *ergaster*, and some skull bones were becoming shaped like ours. Accordingly, most finds are now attributed to *Homo heidelbergensis*, the species supposedly ancestral to the Neandertals and *Homo sapiens*. Perhaps this species invaded Europe from Africa in a warm phase of the Ice Age when the northern ice sheets ebbed.

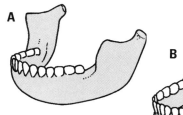
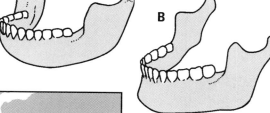

Jaw bones compared (left)

A *Mandible of Heidelberg man. It is big and thick boned, but the structure and evenly proportioned teeth are largely similar to those of modern humans*

B *Mandible of a modern human*

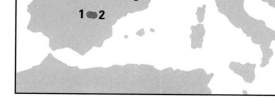

Homo heidelbergensis in Europe (left)

Selected sites show finds of bones or artifacts that have been attributed to Homo heidelbergensis.

1 and **2** *Ambrona and Torralba*

3 *Arago, near Tautavel*

4 *Soleilhac*

5 *Terra Amata, Nice*

6 *Mauer, near Heidelberg*

7 *Bilzingsleben*

8 *Prezletice*

9 *Vértesszöllös*

10 *Petralona, near Thessaloniki*

Homo heidelbergensis

1 Heidelberg man: a massive, chinless lower jaw with teeth, designed to fit a broad, projecting face. Age: about 500,000 years. Place: Mauer, near Heidelberg, Germany.

2 Tautavel skull: a skull with big brows, broad face and nasal opening, flat forehead, and long, narrow braincase. Age: about 400,000 years. Place: Arago Cave, near Tautavel, southwest France.

3 Vértesszöllös skull: part of an occipital bone from the back of the skull–thick, with a ridge for neck muscle attachment. Brain capacity might have been as great as ours. Age: about 400,000 years. Place: Vértesszöllös, west of Budapest, Hungary.

4 Petralona skull: a broad-based, broad-faced skull with beetling brows, sloping forehead, and angulated occipital bone but large cranial capacity: about 1,230 cc. Age: about 300,000 years. Place: Petralona, near Thessaloniki, Greece.

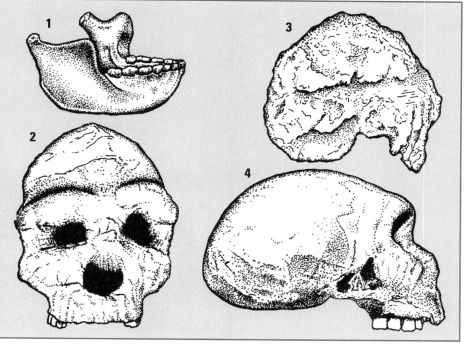

Hand ax grip

The user could have gripped a hand ax by its rounded butt, exerting pressure to cut meat or dig up edible roots.

Acheulian tools (right)

These Angolan examples are half the actual size or less.

1 *Hand ax*

a *Butt*

b *Sharpened edge*

c *Point*

2 *Cleaver*

d *Butt*

e *Side*

f *Cutting edge*

Hand axes and choppers

About 1.6 million years ago, a new, distinctive type of stone tool appeared in East Africa. This so-called hand ax consisted of a fist-sized lump chipped into a shape resembling a hand or flattened pear, with sharpened edges formed by striking flakes from both sides. Experiments suggest that this tool served largely as a butcher's knife to cut up carcasses already skinned by sharp stone flakes, some fashioned into long-edged cleavers.

The earliest hand axes postdate the appearance of *Homo ergaster*, and the foresight needed to produce such standard implements points to this advanced hominid as their probable inventor.

Old Stone Age toolkits featuring hand axes, cleavers, scrapers, and flakes are called Acheulian, from 300,000-year-old finds at St. Acheul in northern France. From Africa, Acheulian toolmaking techniques reached India and Europe, where they persisted until about 100,000 years ago, but only one Chinese site has yielded tools like these.

Meanwhile, cruder chopper-core cultures of the type called Oldowan at Olduvai Gorge in Tanzania spread to Europe and from Asia to the Middle East and Java, the Philippines, and Choukoutien in northern China. Local versions include the Clactonian from Clacton, England (where its biconical stone cores, chopping tools, thick flakes, and notched flakes preceded an Acheulian industry), and the Tayacian from Tayac in the French Dordogne.

In places, Acheulian and chopper-core techniques persisted side by side; elsewhere the tool used probably depended on locally available materials or the job at hand.

Traces of other early *Homo* artifacts include anvils and hammerstones; some of the first known borers, blades, and burins; and early evidence of bone and wooden tools–all from either Ambrona or Torralba, Spain–as well as likely traces of a wooden bowl, from Nice in France.

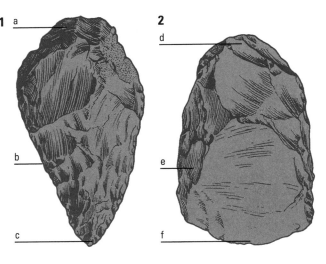

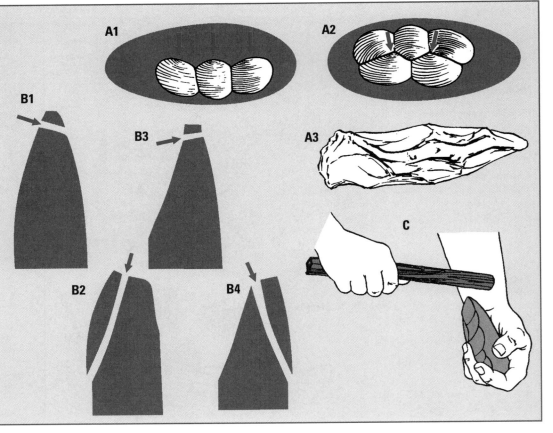

Primitive technique (A 1–3)

1 *Blows with a hammerstone detach flakes from one side of a pebble, leaving deep, short, overlapping scars.*

2 *The pebble is turned over and struck again on ridges created by the scars. This forms another row of scars.*

3 *The result: A hand ax with a strong, blunt, wavy cutting edge produced by deep scars meeting back to back.*

Advanced technique (B 1–4)

1 *A blow removes part of a nodule's edge, leaving a flat striking platform.*

2 *A blow removes a long shallow flake from one side of the nodule.*

3 *A blow prepares a new striking platform.*

4 *A blow removes a long shallow flake from the opposite side. The result will be a slimmer, straighter cutting edge than that produced by the primitive technique.*

Using a baton (C)

*Blows described in **(B)** were probably delivered by a soft springy bone, horn, or wooden baton. These could hit a nodule near its edge without crushing to remove long, thin, shallow flakes. This advanced technique shaped many hand axes already roughed out by a hammerstone.*

Hunting

A number of early *Homo* sites strongly suggest that these enterprising hominids were not just plant gatherers and scavengers but active hunters of big game who combined in groups to plan and execute a chase or ambush. Finds from three continents give clues to hunting methods and the animals attacked. The following three examples all probably date from 500,000–300,000 years ago.

Olorgesailie, Kenya, held one site with the remains of 50 *Simopithecus*. Perhaps early humans had clubbed to death an entire sleeping troop of this large and now extinct baboon, as some Tanzanian tribespeople still kill its modern counterparts.

At Torralba, in north-central Spain, hunters possibly used fire to drive dozens of migrating elephants, wild cattle, horses, deer, and rhinoceroses into a natural trap–a boggy gully in a steep-sided valley. Here died at least 30 elephants of an extinct straight-tusked species larger than the African, alive today. Many beasts may have been butchered at Torralba and nearby Ambrona.

Spectacular Asian evidence is claimed for Zhoukoudian, near Beijing. Supposed cave deposits hint that *Homo erectus* killed and ate many animals, including deer, and practiced cannibalism.

Sceptics argue that none of these sites contains conclusive evidence for early hunting. Carnivores, river action, or other agents could explain the bones found near tools. However, undoubted proof of

hunting are 400,000-year-old wooden throwing spears and horses' bones at Schöningen in Germany.

Sometimes, finishing off a large animal at close range must have been extremely dangerous. This probably explains why some early bones show signs of old, healed fractures.

An ancient feast? (below)

This plan of an excavation at Ambrona, Spain, reveals:

a Bones of fossil elephants and other animals

b Stone tools and waste flakes

c Burnt wood

d Possible hearth stones

Hunters' prey? (below)

a Elephas antiquus, *a now extinct elephant, perhaps trapped in southwest Europe.*

b Simopithecus, *a baboon, perhaps killed in East Africa.*

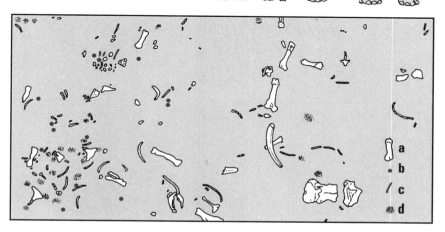

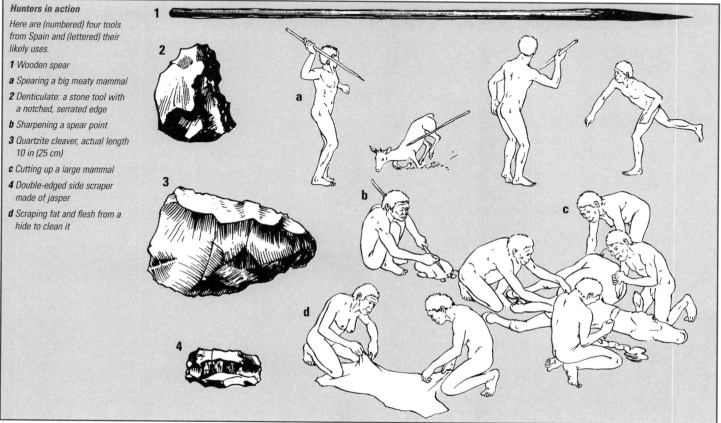

Hunters in action

Here are (numbered) four tools from Spain and (lettered) their likely uses.

1 Wooden spear

a Spearing a big meaty mammal

2 Denticulate: a stone tool with a notched, serrated edge

b Sharpening a spear point

3 Quartzite cleaver, actual length 10 in (25 cm)

c Cutting up a large mammal

4 Double-edged side scraper made of jasper

d Scraping fat and flesh from a hide to clean it

© DIAGRAM

Home-making

A hut at Chichibu

Homo erectus *may have raised brushwood huts like this 500,000 years ago, at Chichibu in Japan.*

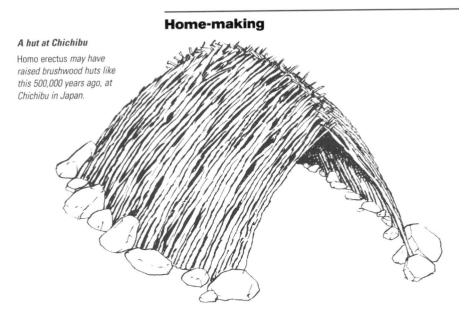

Concentrations of stone tools and bones may mark places where family groups of early *Homo* made their camps. For instance, at Bilzingsleben, Germany, tools, bones, and charcoal covered small patches of ground where people had evidently stayed briefly 350,000 years ago. For a few days they probably planned hunts; butchered and shared out meat and edible plants; drank from a nearby spring, stream, or lake; refurbished their toolkits of wood and stone; and slept and rested.

In the warm Tropics, dry ground often must have sufficed as a temporary home, but in cooler regions, ancient peoples needed some kind of shelter from the weather. North of Tokyo, Japan, 30 stone tools lay near postholes forming two pentagons and have been thought to reveal two huts made 500,000 years ago by *Homo erectus*. Described in AD 2000, these features seem to be the most convincing evidence yet for the earliest human shelters.

In Europe, stone rings at Torralba and Ambrona in Spain recall weights used to hold down hides hung from the central pole of a tepee. At Terra Amata in the French city of Nice, 400,000-year-old living floors supposedly show where groups of *Homo heidelbergensis* raised oval huts of branches braced by stones. Inside, fires may have burned in hearths with stone windshields. Skeptics, however, suspect that most such early "human-made" arrangements of stones were really the natural results of geological processes such as soil creep or stream flow.

Some early peoples used the ready-made shelters of caves. Near Tautavel in the French Pyrenees and at Zhoukoudian near Beijing, people inhabited caves 400,000 years ago. They might have come to the French cave of Arago on a seasonal basis, following migrating game. Prolonged hunters' visits perhaps explain the mass of bones at Zhoukoudian, ranging from small rodents to deer, rhinoceroses, elephants, and *Homo erectus* itself. However, hyenas' bones, toothmarks, and droppings suggest that many bones were the remains of carnivores' meals.

A Riviera home

Oval huts of interlocking branches may have housed hunters on France's Mediterranean shore. Such flimsy shelters vanished long ago, but archeologists can reconstruct them from their stones and postholes.

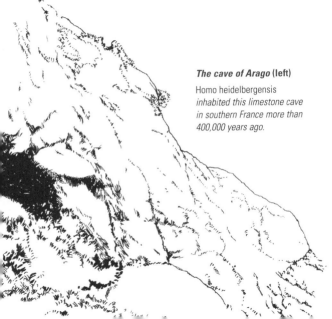

The cave of Arago (left)

Homo heidelbergensis *inhabited this limestone cave in southern France more than 400,000 years ago.*

A base in Spain (below)

An excavated living floor at Torralba in North-central Spain reveals bones of big-game animals, stone tools used to butcher them, and other signs that hunters feasted here perhaps 500,000 years ago.

- ■ Core
- ▬ Cleaver
- ● Flake tool
- ⟁ Bone
- ⬤ Unworked stone

Using fire and crossing the sea

Of all early *Homo*'s technological inventions and discoveries, proved or inferred, probably none mattered more than learning how to use fire. Fire could give warmth, cook roots and tubers, and protect from predators. Perhaps fire-drives helped early humans to hunt big, meaty animals, too. Almost certainly nothing did more than fire to enlarge food supplies and open cool northern lands to early human settlement in warmer phases of the Ice Age.

When humans first mastered fire is uncertain. The main problem here is distinguishing traces of natural fires from fires lit by humans. Campfires and smoldering tree-stumps leave largely similar remains in soil. Brush fires perhaps baked clay at some African sites more than 2 million years old. Forest fires maybe blackened many bones found in Zhoukoudian's caves, and water could have washed the bones into hollows once thought to be hearths.

However, researchers claim there is evidence of high-temperature burning, not found in bushfires, at certain East African sites up to 1.6 million years old. At such places archeologists have also found stone tools where bits had snapped off with so-called potlid fractures–breakages due to intense heat.

Homo ergaster's first experience of fire no doubt came from lightning or volcanic eruptions. In time, though, this species probably learned to keep lit fires started in this way. Techniques for making fire by friction would have come later.

We may never know when *Homo* first learned to control fire and build shelters, but a discovery published in 1998 suggests that early *Homo* was technologically more capable than skeptics believe. That year apparent proof that *Homo erectus* had crossed a 12-mile (19 km) sea gap to the Indonesian island of Flores was found there: stone tools dating from about the same time as the island's dwarf elephants vanished, some 900,000 years ago. Perhaps even those early, small-brained humans knew how to make seaworthy boats.

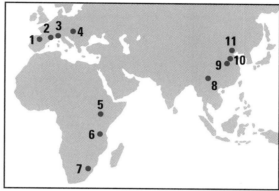

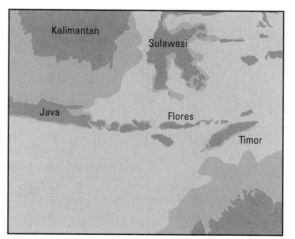

Fire and Early Humans (left)

A map shows sites where humans evidently made fires more than 100,000 years ago. Experts question the evidence for fire at site 11, but sites 5, 6, 8, and 9 may date back a million years old or more.

1 *Torralba*
2 *Escale*
3 *TerraAmata*
4 *Vértesszöllös*
5 *Chesowanja*
6 *Kalambo Falls*
7 *Cave of Hearths*
8 *Yuanmou*
9 *Xihoudu*
10 *Lantian*
11 *Choukoutien*

The first sea crossing? (left)

Homo erectus *must have crossed the sea to reach the Southeast Asian island Flores even if cold phases locked up so much water in ice that the sea level fell, exposing continental shelves (shown tinted).*

Continental shelf

Ancient hearth (right)

Stone windshields helped hunter-gatherers control open fires.

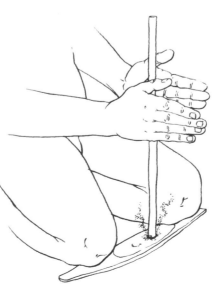

Making fire (left)

Rotating a stick on a wooden "hearth" can produce hot wood dust and a spark to ignite it. Fire-making might have begun in this way.

© DIAGRAM

The Neandertals

By 300,000 years ago, European Homo heidelbergensis *was giving rise to Neandertal (or Neanderthal) man, best known from 70,000 to 40,000-year-old bones and artifacts. Most of us know this last truly prehistoric human from artists' impressions of its projecting chinless face, muscular body, and rather short, stocky limbs.*

Neandertals proved innovative hunter-gatherers of the so-called Middle Old Stone Age, able to endure quite cold climatic phases. Deliberate burials—the oldest known—hint at emergent human sensitivity. Yet Neandertals were undoubtedly a side branch off the evolutionary path to fully modern humans. Although large-brained, they lacked the technology of the fully modern humans who came to share their continent, possibly because they were less dexterous or capable of speech. Outcompeted in one way or another, by 30,000 or so years ago, Neandertals became extinct.

Where they lived (right)

A world map shows approximate locations of six skulls that represent various stages of human evolution 400,0000– 100,000 years ago.

1 *Swanscombe, England (proto-Neandertal)*

2 *Steinheim, Germany (Neandertal and* Homo sapiens *features)*

3 *Kabwe, Zambia (early* Homo sapiens *features)*

4 *Saldanha Bay, South Africa (early* Homo sapiens *features)*

5 *Ngandong, Java (*Homo erectus *features)*

6 *Xujiayao, China (*Homo erectus *and* Homo sapiens *features)*

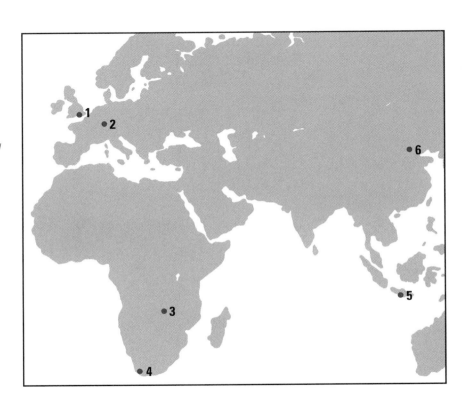

Trends in human evolution

Between 400,000 and 100,000 years ago, humans were evolving in different ways in different regions of the world, influenced by factors including mutations, increasing use of tools for heavy work once done by teeth or muscles, migration, and the isolation of some populations. Even in different parts of the body evolution progressed unevenly, producing skulls with a mosaic of modern and "old-fashioned" features.

Three forms predominated by 100,000 years ago: *Homo erectus*, *Homo sapiens*, and *Homo neanderthalensis*. Skulls with *Homo erectus* features figured in Southeast Asia. Chinese skulls show a mixture of old-fashioned *Homo erectus* and early *Homo sapiens* features. Early *Homo sapiens* features predominate in skulls from Africa. Europe and Southwest Asia were undoubtedly the regions where of the Neandertals were most numerous.

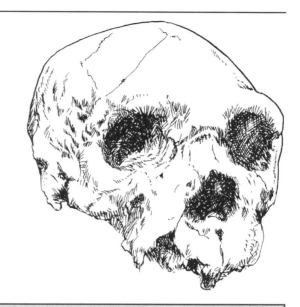

A proto-Neandertal

This 300,000-year old Homo heidelbergensis *skull from Atapuerca, Spain, already shows Neandertal tendencies: a two-arched brow ridge, jutting face, and expanded cheekbones.*

Skulls from three continents

1 Swanscombe skull: parts of a thick female skull with an "advanced" rounded back and large brain capacity (1,300 cc). Age: perhaps 250,000 years. Place: Swanscombe, near London, England.

2 Steinheim skull: low skull with browridges and brain capacity of 1,100 cc but with a rounded back, relatively small, straight face, and small teeth. Age: more than 300,000 years. Place: Steinheim, near Stuttgart, Germany.

3 Kabwe skull (alias Broken Hill skull): skull with sloping forehead, strong browridges, and angulated rear but with steep modern sides and base and brain capacity of 1,300 cc. Age: maybe 200,000 years. Place: Kabwe, Zambia.

4 Saldanha skull: similar to Kabwe skull. Age: at least 400,000 years. Place: Hopefield, Saldanha Bay, South Africa.

5 Solo skull: thick skullcap with sloping forehead, flattened frontal bone, ridged back, and brain capacity of 1,035–1,255 cc; they recall the much earlier Peking man. Age: perhaps more than 100,000 years. Place: Ngandong, Solo River, Java.

6 Xujiayao skull: one of a group of heavy Chinese skulls like *Homo erectus* but rounded at the back. Age: 250,000–100,000 for the group. Place: Datong, Shaanxi Province, China.

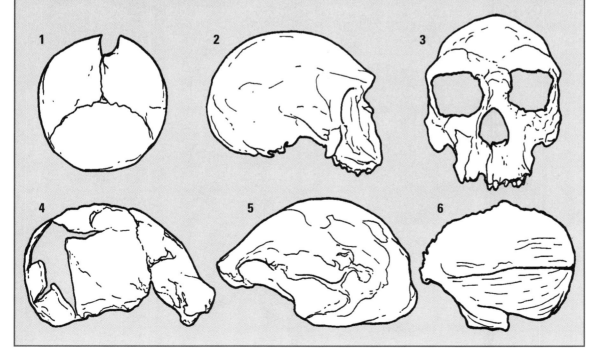

© DIAGRAM

The changing world

Waves of cold with warmer intervening gaps continued dominating northern climates from 200,000 to 40,000 years ago—a time span embracing the Neandertals and their immediate precursors. Geologists traditionally divide this part of the Pleistocene epoch between two glacial stages (in Europe often called the Riss and Würm) separated by an interglacial (the Eemian); in fact, research reveals more glacials and interglacials, each with climatic changes affecting the level of the sea.

At its most intense, the cold drove mammals south in North America and trapped some European species between advancing northern ice sheets and Alpine glaciers. In western and central Europe, temperate woodlands gave way to steppe or tundra. Here only cold-adapted beasts survived, including new species like the woolly mammoth, woolly rhinoceros, and musk ox. When ice sheets shrank, all moved north with the retreating steppe and tundra. Woodland spread in from the south with the hippopotamus, straight-tusked elephant, giant elk, lion, and leopard. As cold returned, migration went into reverse.

Ice sheets and glaciers at their maxium

Permafrost (ground with permanently frozen subsoil)

Old coastline

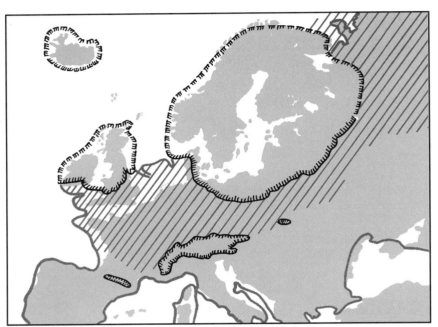

Ice Age Europe (left)

This map shows harsh climatic conditions faced by Europe's Neandertals in the Würm glacial stage. The map includes both old and modern coastlines.

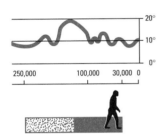

Climatic changes (left)

A graph shows fluctuating July temperatures in degrees Centigrade for central Europe for the last 250,000 years or so. (In fact peaks and troughs were probably more frequent than this.) During this time Homo heidelbergensis *gave rise to classic* Homo neanderthalensis *(the solid bar), who died out by 30,000 years ago.*

Four Ice Age mammals

Here we show four cold-tolerant mammals:

1 Mammuthus primigenius, the woolly mammoth, had long dark hair, woolly underfur, small ears, and huge curved tusks. Height: 9 ft 6 in (2.9 m). Time: mid-late Pleistocene. Place: northern Eurasia and North America.

2 Coelodonta antiquitatis, the woolly rhinoceros, had a shaggy coat and two horns, the front one long. Height: 6 ft 6 in (2 m). Time: mid-late Pleistocene. Place: Eurasia and North Africa.

3 Ursus spelaeus, the cave bear, had a great head with mighty jaws, yet was an omnivore. There were huge and dwarf varieties. Length: up to 9 ft (2.7 m) from nose to tail. Time: mid-late Pleistocene. Place: Eurasia.

4 Ovibos moschatus, the musk ox, has a large, horned head and stocky body with underwool and an outer coat of long, dark, almost ground-length hair. Height: up to 5 ft (1.5 m). Time: mid-Pleistocene to today. Place: northern Eurasia and North America.

About Neandertals

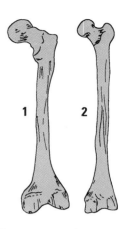

Femurs compared (above)

1 Neandertal femur: thick, strong, and noticeably curved

2 Modern human femur: slimmer, weaker, and straighter than the Neandertals'.

Body Build

A male and female Neandertal are shown beside a modern man, for scale. Height: about 5 ft 7 in (1.7 m). Weight: about 154 lb (70 kg).

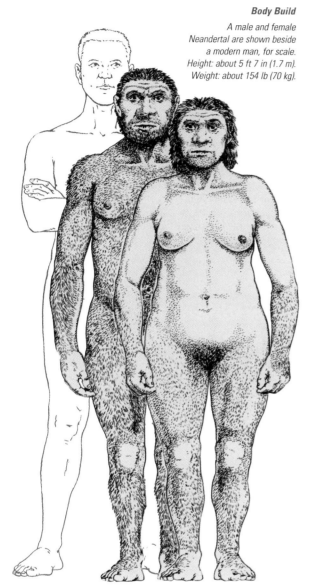

Homo neanderthalensis takes its name from fossils found in the Neander Valley, near Dusseldorf, Germany. The so-called classic Neandertals from Europe had a large, long head, with a bigger brain inside a thicker skull than ours, yet the skull was thinner than that of *Homo erectus*. Somewhat like that species, Neandertals had heavy browridges and a sloping forehead. There was a distinctive bun-shaped swelling at the back of the skull, with a big area below for tethering neck muscles. The broad face projected far forward, its backswept sides creating "streamlined" cheekbones. The large nose might have been either flat or bulbous. The powerful chinless jaw held front teeth larger than ours, and molars tended to contain big pulp cavities.

Classic Neandertals were slightly short, extremely muscular, and stocky, with large joints and hands. Proportions recall the Inuit, whose compact body helps conserve heat in a cold environment. But individuals and populations varied, as the following pages show.

The Neandertal species evolved from European *Homo heidelbergensis* maybe as much as 200,000 years ago. Their physique and improved technology made some of these middle Paleolithic people probably the first hominids able to endure the rigors of winter in a cold climate. Also, supposed Neandertal rituals seem to show a new, high level of sensibility and human self-awareness.

Yet about 30,000 years ago this group apparently died out. Most scientists suppose that the Neandertals were wiped out by fully modern humans who had evolved in Africa. Rival explanations are that Neandertals interbred with or evolved into our own subspecies. Genetic evidence, however, does not support this view.

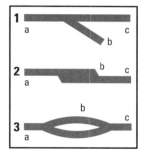

Rival family trees (above)

1 Neandertals as an extinct species

2 Neandertals as an extinct subspecies

3 Neandertals as part of the rootstock of modern humans

a Homo heidelbergensis

b Neandertals

c Homo sapiens

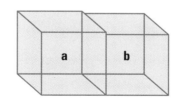

Brain capacities (left)

a Neandertal man: 1,500 cc

b Modern human: 1,400 cc

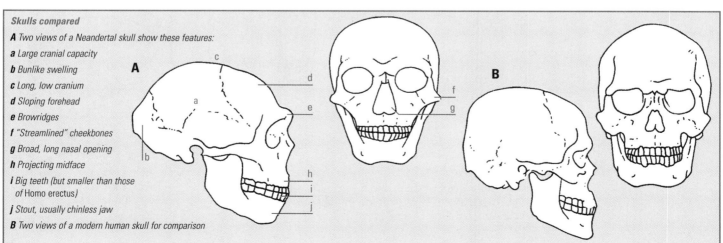

Skulls compared

A Two views of a Neandertal skull show these features:

a Large cranial capacity

b Bunlike swelling

c Long, low cranium

d Sloping forehead

e Browridges

f "Streamlined" cheekbones

g Broad, long nasal opening

h Projecting midface

i Big teeth (but smaller than those of Homo erectus)

j Stout, usually chinless jaw

B Two views of a modern human skull for comparison

© DIAGRAM

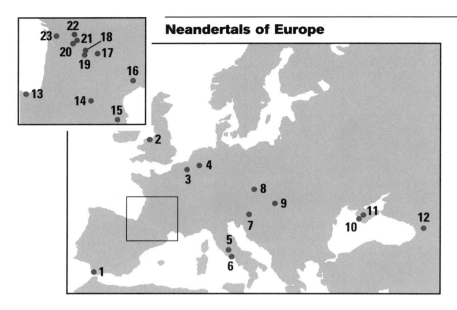

Neandertals of Europe

By the year 2000, scientists in Europe had found remains of more than 200 Neandertal or proto-Neandertal individuals–most in caves. They include the oldest large samples of fossil humans from any continent. Some show that even cohabiting groups varied considerably in skull and jaw design. More than half the individuals came from France, with bits of 116 at about 36 sites. Two sites–Hortus and La Quina–accounted for most French remains. Neandertal features also figure among possibly 24 individuals from Krapina, Croatia; 11 from Italy; 10 from Belgium; eight from Germany; and others from places including Britain, Spain, Gibraltar, Czechoslovakia, Russia, and the Ukraine.

Finds date from maybe 250,000 to 30,000 years old, but most "full-blown" Neandertals come from a time span extending about 127,000 to 40,000 years ago. Our examples represent different finds from different times and places.

Where they lived (above)

Selected European Neandertal and proto-Neandertal sites appear in the map and enlarged area above.

1 Gibraltar
2 Pontnewydd
3 Spy
4 Neander Valley
5 Saccopastore
6 Monte Circeo
7 Krapina
8 Kŏlna
9 Subalyuk
10 Staroselye
11 Kiik-Koba
12 Dzhruchula
13 Urtiaga
14 Mas d'Azil
15 Bañolas
16 Hortus
17 La Chapelle-aux-Saints
18 Le Moustier
19 La Ferrassie
20 La Quina
21 La Chaise
22 Fontéchevade
23 St.-Césaire

European Neandertals

1 Ehringsdorf skull: Remains include a Neandertal-type skull but with a high forehead, and a chinless jaw with small teeth. Age: perhaps 200,000 years. Place: Ehringsdorf, Germany.

2 Pontnewydd: Tooth and jaw remains discovered in the 1980s include features found among Neandertals. Age: about 250,000 years. Place: Pontnewydd Cave, near Rhyl, north Wales, UK.

3 Fontéchevade: This site produced skull fragments with and without browridges. Age: perhaps 150,000 years. Place: Fontéchevade, western France.

4 La Chapelle-aux-Saints: Famous for the arthritic skeleton of an old male classic Neandertal. Age: perhaps 50,000 years. Place: La Chapelle-aux-Saints, south-central France.

5 Gibraltar: This skull's discovery in fact predated that from the Neander Valley. Age: 50,000 years.

6 Circeo is noted for a man's mutilated skull. Age: about 45,000 years. Place: Monte Circeo, near Rome, Italy.

7 Neander Valley: The first-described Neandertal skeleton came from a cave beside this river. Age: maybe 50,000 years. Place: Feldhofer Cave, Neander Tal ("Neander Valley"), Düsseldorf, Germany.

8 Krapina Skulls include broad, short forms with strong browridges, perhaps victims of a cannibal feast. Age: about 100,000 years. Place: Krapina, Croatia.

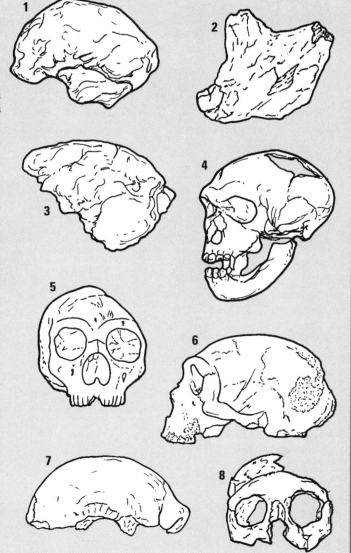

Neandertals outside Europe

Neandertals lived in Southwest Asia and maybe Africa, but some lacked much of the ruggedness of Europe's classic form, probably adapted to intense Ice Age cold. Some had straighter, slimmer limbs, less massive browridges, and a shorter, less sturdy, cranium. Also, browridges and a projecting face could occur in skulls with a high forehead and high, rounded cranium. No typically Neandertal fossils have been found outside Europe and Southwest Asia. By about 40,000 years ago, the last Southwest Asian Neandertals evidently coexisted with people of entirely modern aspect. Some of the following skulls themselves might almost rank as fully modern humans.

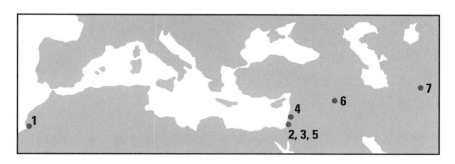

Where they lived

On this map numbered sites correspond to numbered items in the text below.

1 Jebel Irhoud
2 Tabun
3 Skhūl
4 Amud
5 Qafzeh
6 Shanidar
7 Teshik-Tash

Seven skulls

1 Jebel Irhoud skulls were long and low with large browridges but with modern faces and slight "buns." Age: about 70,000 years. Place: Jebel Irhoud, Morocco.

2 Tabūn skull was low with a sloping forehead, browridges, and thick incisors, yet the face and back of the head were modern. The jaw had a chin. Curved limb bones resembled those of European Neandertals. Age: 100,000 years. Place: Tabūn Cave, Mount Carmel, Israel.

3 Skhūl 5 combined a big brain, browridges, fairly high forehead, and modern face and back of head. Age: 90,000 years. Place: Skhūl rock shelter, a burial site on Mount Carmel, Israel.

4 Amud 1 Neandertal-type skull with a brain capacity of 1,740 cc (among the largest known), plus long limb bones. Age: perhaps 45,000 years. Place: Amud Cave, near Lake Tiberias, Israel.

5 Qafzeh also included skulls with modern features. Age: perhaps 90,000 years. Place: Qafzeh Cave, Israel.

6 Shanidar revealed big-brained classic Neandertals, but their browridges were not continuous as in Europeans. Age: perhaps 60,000–40,000 years. Place: Shanidar Cave, north Iraq.

7 Teshik-Tash had a boy with undeveloped browridges and other classic features, yet a more modern face and limbs. Age: perhaps 45,000 years. Place: Teshik-Tash Cave, Uzbekistan.

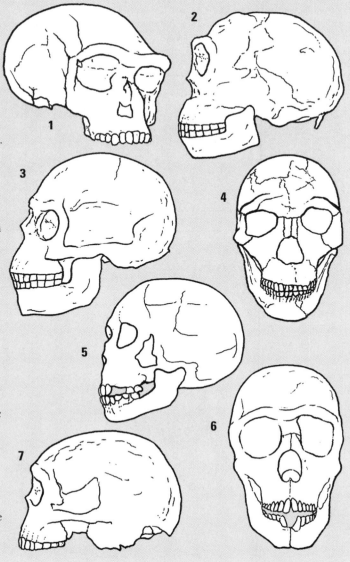

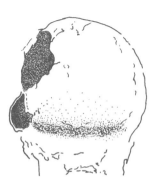

Neandertal skull

A rear view of Shanidar shows a barrel-shaped Neandertal skull, broadest higher up than in skulls of Australopithecus or Homo erectus. Holes betray fatal crushing caused by a rockfall.

© DIAGRAM

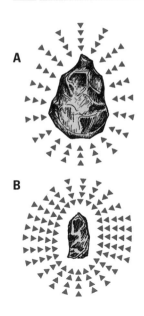

A

B

Advance in technique (above)

A A Homo ergaster *took 65 blows to produce this Acheulian hand ax.*

B A Neandertal took 111 blows to produce this Mousterian knife. Increased numbers of blows and use of prepared cores conserved materials and widened the range of fine, specialized tools.

Working edge produced (right)

A Amount of cutting edge per pound of stone produced by Homo erectus

B Amount of cutting edge per pound produced by the Neandertals

Neandertal toolkits

Neandertal toolkits are termed "Mousterian" from finds made at Le Moustier in France. They marked improvements over earlier chopper-core and hand ax industries.

Key innovations included a variety of specialized, finely retouched stone tools, made from flakes, not cores. Using fine-grained glassy stone like flint and obsidian, Neandertals improved on the already established Levallois technique for striking one or two big flakes of predetermined shape from a prepared core. They made each core yield many small, thin, sharp-edged flakes; then they trimmed the edges to produce side scrapers, points, backed knives, stick sharpeners, tiny saws, and borers. Between them these could have served for killing, cutting up, and skinning prey, and for making wooden tools and clothing.

Europe's several types of Mousterian toolkit might represent different times or cultures, or just different tasks performed.

Mousterian toolkits evolved from the old Acheulian and chopper-core industries and persisted from about 100,000 to 35,000 years ago. They appeared in Europe, North Africa, and Southwest Asia. Related toolkits appeared as far as southern Africa and China.

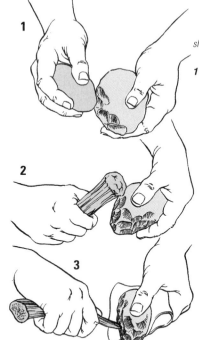

Making a flake tool

Three pictures show stages in making a flint knife.

1 *Roughly shaping a flint flake with a stone hammer*

2 *Refining the shaped flake with blows from a softer hammer of bone or antler*

3 *Trimming the knife edge by pressure flaking*

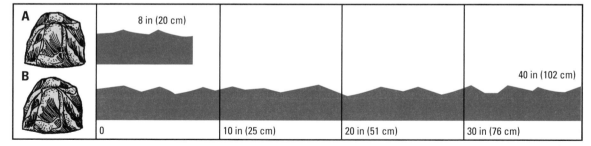

A

B

	8 in (20 cm)			40 in (102 cm)
0	10 in (25 cm)	20 in (51 cm)	30 in (76 cm)	

Mousterian tools

Our examples represent five typical tool types:

1 Point: a flake retouched to make a long, sharp, triangular point, perhaps lashed or wedged into a wooden shaft to form a dart or spear head.

2 Side scraper: a convex scraper retouched to give a thickened working edge, maybe for dressing skins without tearing them.

3 Backed knife: a long, sharp-bladed flake with a blunt back for exerting pressure; used for skinning, cutting meat, or trimming wood.

4 Denticulate saw: a flake with a retouched, saw-edged blade suitable for trimming wood.

5 Notch tool: a notched flake suitable for smoothing sticks perhaps used as spears.

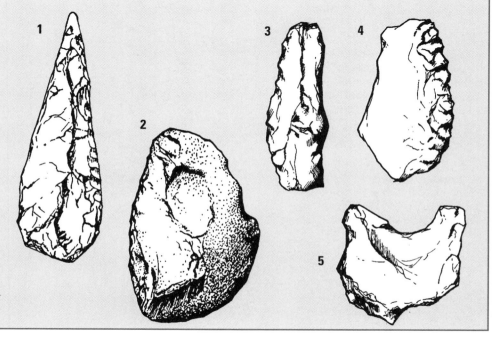

Hunting

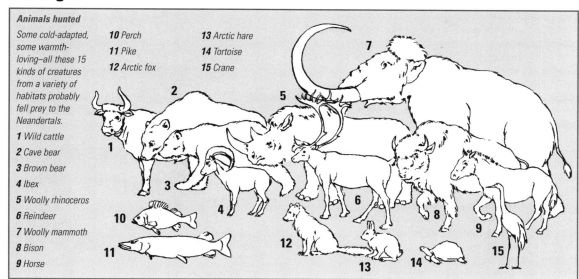

Animals hunted

Some cold-adapted, some warmth-loving–all these 15 kinds of creatures from a variety of habitats probably fell prey to the Neandertals.

1 Wild cattle
2 Cave bear
3 Brown bear
4 Ibex
5 Woolly rhinoceros
6 Reindeer
7 Woolly mammoth
8 Bison
9 Horse
10 Perch
11 Pike
12 Arctic fox
13 Arctic hare
14 Tortoise
15 Crane

Spearing big game

A hunting band jabs stone-tipped spears into a woolly rhinoceros. Neandertals lacked effective long-range weapons.

Neandertals arguably included the most effective hunters that had evolved by their period. They had to be in order to stay alive in harsh, cold Ice Age climates. In summer there were roots and berries to be had, but in winter groups relied on the concentrated nourishment in meat from tundra and cold-forest mammals.

Bones from caves and open camp sites tell us that the chief European prey comprised creatures such as bison, cave bears, horses, reindeer, wild cattle, woolly mammoths, and woolly rhinoceroses. Some hunters specialized, for instance, in bison at Il'skaia in the northern Caucasus and in reindeer at Salzgitter-Lebenstedt, north Germany. Smaller victims included foxes, hares, birds, and fishes. One Hungarian site alone has yielded more than 50,000 bones from 45 species of creatures large and small (although many bear and mammoth bones at certain sites seem to have been scavenged from corpses of beasts that had already perished naturally).

Some animals were doubtless prized for fur, bones, and sinews used respectively in clothes, tents, and snares, as well as for their meat.

We lack much evidence to show how these people killed their prey. Likely methods include hurling spears or bolas, rolling boulders off a cliff, or setting snares and pitfall traps. Hunters would have picked off sick, old, young, or weakened animals, and even hibernating bears. With fire they could have driven whole herds of frightened horses over cliffs or into dead-end canyons for mass slaughter.

Such strategems presuppose keen understanding of the victims' eating, drinking, or migration habits, and would also call for careful planning and cooperation.

In Southwest Asia, outside the coldest zones and times, bands of men doubtless ranged far afield to track down and kill large creatures such as wild cattle, sheep, or goats. Meanwhile, women and children would have scoured the countryside around a home base–their targets: rodents, reptiles, insects, berries, gums, honey, roots, and tubers.

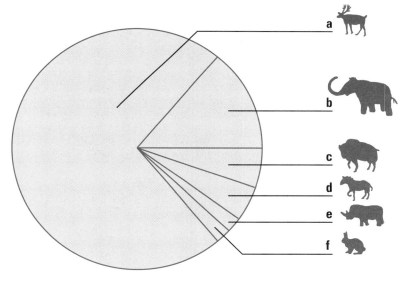

Prey percentages (above)

These are based on bones of beasts killed 55,000 years ago and found at a summer open camp site near Salzgitter-Lebenstedt in north Germany.

a Reindeer 72%
b Woolly mammoth 14%
c Bison 5.4%
d Horse 4.6%
e Woolly rhinoceros 2%
f Other animals 2%

Deadfall trap (right)

In trying to seize meat bait this fox must dislodge a heavy stone that will fall and crush it. Such traps–still used by the Inuit–probably helped Neandertals secure fox pelts for clothing.

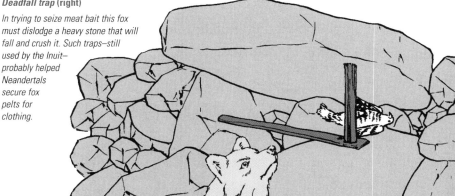

Caves, tents, and clothes

The Neandertals of Europe survived harsh Ice-Age winters in warm microclimates formed by clothes and heated homes.

In some places, caves afforded natural protection. Groups up to 40-strong inhabited many of the scores of limestone caves in the Dordogne of southwest France, and at least two dozen caves in eastern Europe. At Combe Grenal in France. a post hole at a cave mouth hints at a wall of skins that kept out wind, snow, or rain. There was even a stone wall inside the Cueva Morín, in northern Spain.

Where caves were not available, hunting bands built shelters in the open. The most impressive of these bastions against the elements were tents or huts built in Ukrainian river valleys teeming with big game. Here, people might have raised branch frameworks up to 30 ft (9 m) long, 23 ft (7 m) wide, and 10 ft (3 m) high, then covered these with skins weighed down by heavy mammoth bones found lying in the surrounding countryside.

Old hearths show where Neandertals had warmed their tents and caves by burning wood or bones. Discoveries suggest that they knew how to start fires by striking sparks from iron pyrites and using dried bracket fungus as tinder.

Evidence for clothes is mostly indirect. People apparently used stone knives to cut furry skins to shape, bored holes in tailored skins with awls of stone or bone, and then tied the skins with sinews. When skinning foxes, hares, and wolves, they evidently sometimes left the feet intact to serve as ties. The resulting clothes probably included unsophisticated trousers, tunics, cloaks, hoods, and wrappings for the feet.

Tent in a cave? (below)

Excavation of Le Lazaret cave near Nice in France suggests that 150,000 years ago Neandertals made a partitioned skin tent inside a cave to keep out cold.

A *Rear compartment*

B *Front compartment*

a *Shelter wall of stones, perhaps including post supports*

b *Probable entrances*

c *Presumed partition*

d *Litter, perhaps including bedding*

e *Hearths*

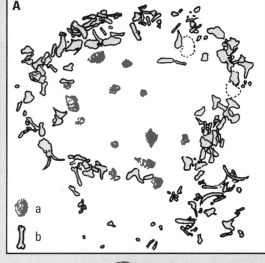

Evidence for huts

A *Excavated ground plan of a hut at Molodova in the Ukraine*

a *Hearths (15 were found)*

b *Mammoth bones*

B *The hut might have looked like this, but long mammoth bones would have served as supports if wood were scarce.*

A

a

b

B

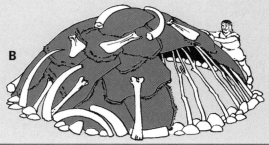

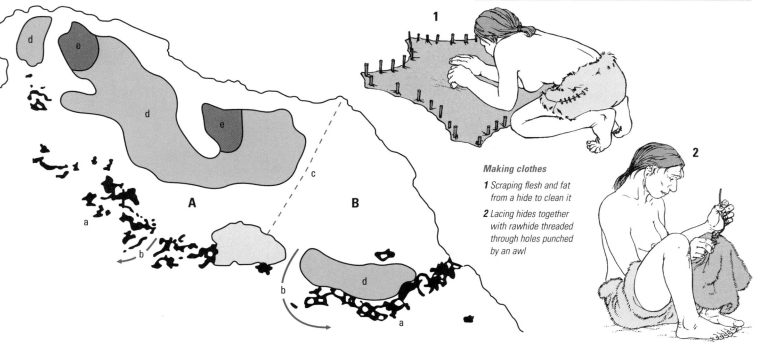

Making clothes

1 *Scraping flesh and fat from a hide to clean it*

2 *Lacing hides together with rawhide threaded through holes punched by an awl*

Burial, ritual, and art

Burial, alleged ritual, and rudimentary art hint that the Neandertals were more self-aware, socially caring, and generally capable of abstract thought than their ancestor *Homo heidelbergensis.*

Neandertals were the first people to bury their dead systematically. By soon after the middle of the 20th century, scientists had excavated 68 burial sites, most in Europe, with more than 150 bodies, almost all in caves.

There is clear proof of deliberate interment. Skeletons lay in holes dug in cave floors. Many had been placed in a sleeping posture, some perhaps (the evidence is inconclusive) with grave goods ranging from cooked meat to a stone pillow, a bed of woody horsetail, and spring flowers, identified by pollen that burrowing rodents may have introduced by chance.

All this suggests that Neandertals attached importance to an individual's life and death and perhaps looked forward to an afterlife. Maybe they showed compassion, too. At Shanidar, Iraq, only caring companions could have kept alive an old man, half-blinded and crippled by arthritis and a withered arm long before he died.

Yet, like their predecessors, these people seemingly ate each other, mutilating skulls and limb bones to extract brains and marrow. Probably the eaters hoped to gain the strength of those they ate.

Cannibalism was evidently one of several rituals. In one cave Neandertals placed mountain goats' horns in a ring; elsewhere they seemingly stacked cave bears' skulls. Perhaps they wanted to please the spirits of the animals they killed.

Ritual perhaps infused art, mainly limited to such items as a bone amulet, scratched pebbles, and lumps of red iron oxide and rubbed manganese–these last evidently used to paint the body. Red maybe symbolized blood and therefore life.

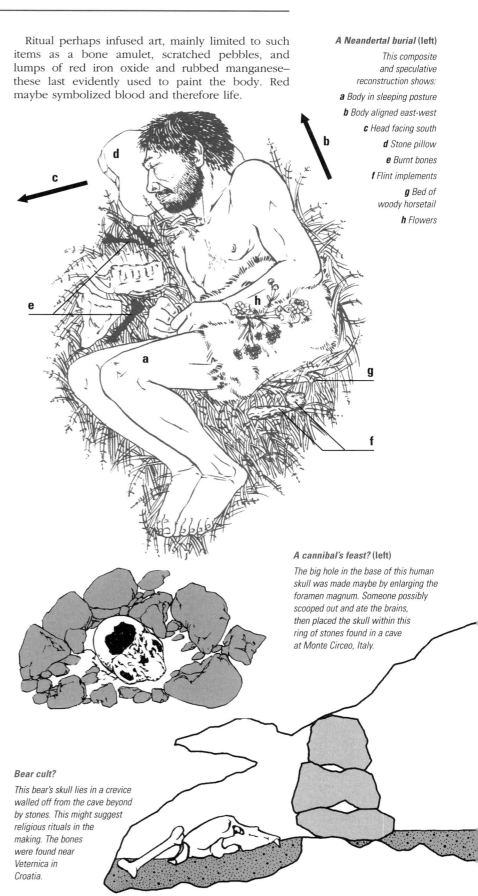

A Neandertal burial (left)

This composite and speculative reconstruction shows:

a Body in sleeping posture

b Body aligned east-west

c Head facing south

d Stone pillow

e Burnt bones

f Flint implements

g Bed of woody horsetail

h Flowers

A cannibal's feast? (left)

The big hole in the base of this human skull was made maybe by enlarging the foramen magnum. Someone possibly scooped out and ate the brains, then placed the skull within this ring of stones found in a cave at Monte Circeo, Italy.

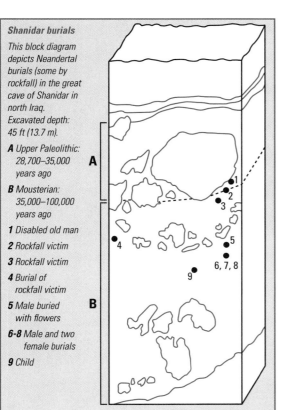

Shanidar burials

This block diagram depicts Neandertal burials (some by rockfall) in the great cave of Shanidar in north Iraq. Excavated depth: 45 ft (13.7 m).

A Upper Paleolithic: 28,700–35,000 years ago

B Mousterian: 35,000–100,000 years ago

1 Disabled old man

2 Rockfall victim

3 Rockfall victim

4 Burial of rockfall victim

5 Male buried with flowers

6-8 Male and two female burials

9 Child

Bear cult?

This bear's skull lies in a crevice walled off from the cave beyond by stones. This might suggest religious rituals in the making. The bones were found near Veternica in Croatia.

Homo sapiens in Europe

Evidence of fully modern humans—the species Homo sapiens—*first emerged with bones discovered at Cro-Magnon in southwest France. Cro-Magnon people left skeletons and artifacts in many parts of Europe. Here, about 40,000 to 10,000 years ago, lived people probably ancestral to Europe's modern so-called whites or Caucasoids. Late Old Stone Age hunters survived the harshest rigors of the Ice Age by making new, sophisticated implements of stone and bone and using them to kill big, meaty animals that ranged across the continent. Then evolved the Mesolithic (Middle Stone Age) hunting-and-gathering cultures that flourished in post-Ice Age Europe 10,000 to 5,000 years ago.*

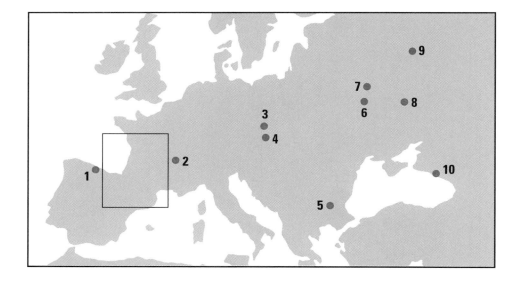

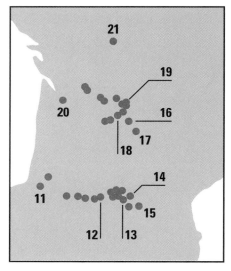

Evolving egg-shaped heads *(right)*

Three heads suggest that the adult human face has tended to become more juvenile.

a Neandertal face: large jaw, large nose, low cranium

b Cro-Magnon face: smaller jaw, smaller nose, higher cranium

c Some humans today: still smaller jaw and nose, still higher cranium

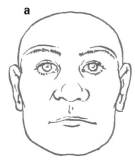

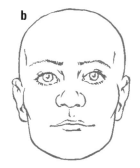

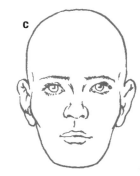

About early *Homo sapiens*

Body build (below)

Cro-Magnon people were probably early Caucasoid ancestors of today's Europeans. Height: 5 ft 6 in– 5 ft 8 in (1.6–1.77 m) Weight: about 150 lb (68 kg)

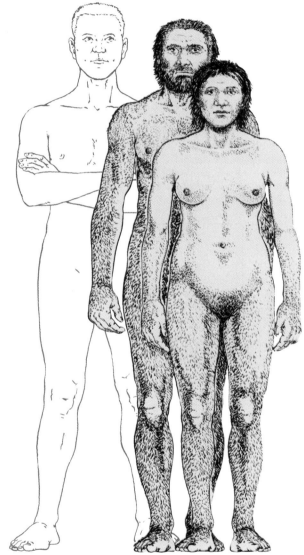

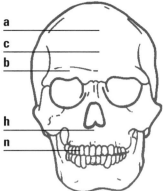

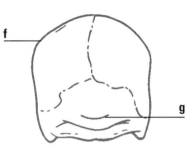

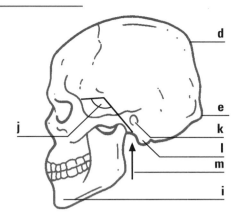

Skull features

Three views of a modern human skull (above and left). Most listed items distinguish it from an older Homo *skull:*

a *Large cranial capacity*

b *No overhanging brows*

c *High, vertical forehead*

d *Convex cranial vault*

e *Low, rounded occiput*

f *Skull widest high up*

g *Small arched torus*

h *Nasomaxillary region not inflated*

i *Projecting chin*

j *Relatively acute sphenoidal angle*

k *Round ear hole*

l *Sizable mastoid process*

m *Central foramen magnum (hole in the skull base)*

n *Pulp cavities of teeth seldom enlarged*

Fully modern humans–the species *Homo sapiens*– crop up widely in the fossil record in 40,000-year-old sites as far apart as Borneo and Europe. Some early skeletons even show similarities to modern whites, blacks, Asians, and aboriginal Australians.

Best known are the bones of early modern Europeans, called collectively Cro-Magnons, from skeletons discovered at Cro-Magnon in southwest France. Cro-Magnons were taller and less rugged than Neandertals, with thinner bones than these or *Homo erectus*. Compared with the Neandertals, the head was relatively tall but short, with a more rounded braincase containing a slightly smaller brain of 1,400 cc average capacity. Other innovations were an upright forehead; a straight, not forward-jutting face; absent or only slight browridges; a smaller nose; smaller jaws; more crowded teeth; and a well-developed chin.

Some paleoanthropologists think that fully modern humans evolved in one continent (probably Africa) and spread to all the rest, replacing local archaic forms of *Homo*. Other experts have argued that local archaic forms evolved into our own subspecies independently of one another. A compromise suggests that modern humans arose in one place but interbred with older, local forms to help produce the races of today.

Fossils fail to show why our own species has proved so successful. Indeed, until about 10,000 years ago, our forebears still lived in largely mobile bands of Old Stone Age hunter-gatherers. Yet they colonized all continents except Antarctica and developed tools, techniques, and new behavior patterns that would transform the human way of life and bring explosive population growth. The next pages trace major trends in later prehistoric Europe.

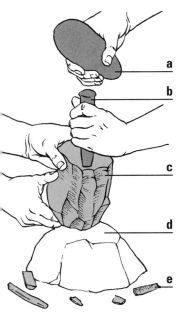

Indirect percussion (above)

This produced long, slim, parallel-sided flint blades

***a** Hammerstone*

***b** Bone or antler punch*

***c** Core*

***d** Anvil stone*

***e** Blades and waste flakes*

Economy with stone (right)

***A** Length of cutting edge per pound of stone produced by the Neandertals' technique*

***B** Length of cutting edge per pound produced by the Cro-Magnons' technique*

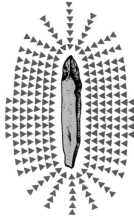

Advance in technique (above)

More than 250 blows (including pressure flaking) went into making a finely crafted Cro-Magnon flint flake knife. Compare this with the fewer blows for implements produced previously by Neandertal peoples and Homo erectus.

New ways with stone and bone

With the first fully modern humans, the Paleolithic, or Old Stone Age, began its late, or upper, phase–its last and finest flowering. In Europe, this ran from 35,000 to 10,000 years ago, coinciding with the frigid last gasp of the Pleistocene.

Like the Neandertals' Mousterian cultures, the Cro-Magnons' Upper Paleolithic cultures used flaked stone tools and weapons geared to hunting. But there were striking innovations, some probably imported from the Near East.

Pressure flaking (right)

Pressing a pointed tool down on a flint flake's outer edge snaps subflakes from its underside.

***a** Pointed stick or bone*

***b** Flint flake artifact*

***c** Bark cushion on stone anvil*

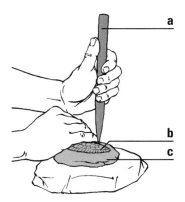

First, Cro-Magnons developed a new and startlingly efficient way of making stone blades. With a stone, bone, wood, or antler hammer a toolmaker struck an antler-tine punch resting on one edge of a cylindrical stone core. This indirect percussion split off a long, flat, narrow, sharp-edged flake. The toolmaker could then delicately trim this flake by pressure flaking–pressing a pointed tool against the blade edge to snap off tiny subflakes. These methods produced more and finer tools from just one stone than any previous technique.

Compared with the Neandertals before them, Cro-Magnons made a far wider and more finely crafted range of knives, scrapers, saws, points, borers, and other stone implements. Half of their tools were bone–tougher and more durable than wood and shaped by chisel-edged stone burins, which also fashioned artifacts of antler, wood, and ivory.

From these materials, Cro-Magnons made such novel implements as eyed needles, handles, fishhooks, harpoons, and spear throwers. Between them, these simple-seeming artifacts enormously increased human control of the environment.

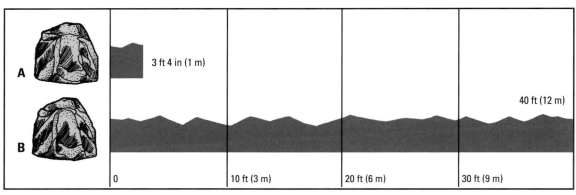

Late Paleolithic tools

Shown right are four tools of flint and one of bone (not all to scale).

(More are shown opposite)

***a** Flint knife, with a back blunted by pressure flaking*

***b** Flint end scraper, rounded at one end by pressure flaking*

***c** Burin chisel, for working antler, bone, or wood*

***d** Microburin drill, for piercing holes in skin, wood, bone, or antler*

***e** Bone needle, with an eye pierced by a microburin drill*

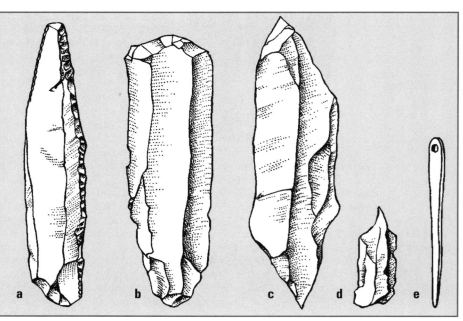

Cro-Magnon cultures

Europe's Cro-Magnon toolkits varied with time and place. Some archaeologists think that this reflects different groups of people. Other experts argue that different toolkits represented only different schools of craftsmanship.

Based on tools and other artifacts, four main upper Paleolithic cultures have been named for western Europe; southwest France is rich in their remains. (Many more cultures come from other regions of the world.)

The Aurignacian, of 40,000–28,000 years ago, included big blades with strongly retouched edges, nosed and other scrapers, burins, and split-based bone points. The Aurignacian evidently spread west through Europe from the Near East. Aurignacian influence probably explains the scrapers, burins and bone artifacts of the Neandertals' Châtelperronian culture in France.

The Gravettian (Perigordian), of about 28,000–21,000 years ago, had many small, slim, backed, pointed blades, burins, and bone tools. It extended from France to Russia and south to Spain and Italy.

The short-lived Solutrean (about 22,000–18,500 years ago) stressed fine workmanship in such articles as slender, leaf-shaped blades tapered at each end and superbly crafted on both sides.

The Magdalenian (about 18,500–11,000 years ago) is noted for hooked rods used as spear throwers and fishing implements from barbed hooks to harpoons.

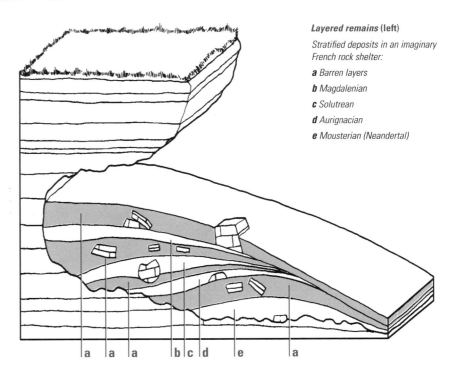

Layered remains (left)

Stratified deposits in an imaginary French rock shelter:

a Barren layers

b Magdalenian

c Solutrean

d Aurignacian

e Mousterian (Neandertal)

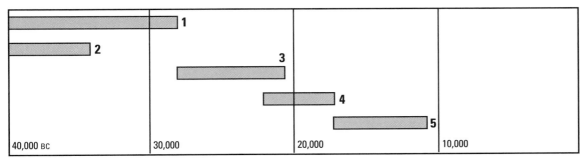

40,000 BC   30,000   20,000   10,000

Cultural complexes (left)

Four lines show time spans of four Late Paleolithic western European technocomplexes.

1 Aurignacian

2 Châtelperronian

3 Gravettian (Perigordian)

4 Solutrean

5 Magdalenian

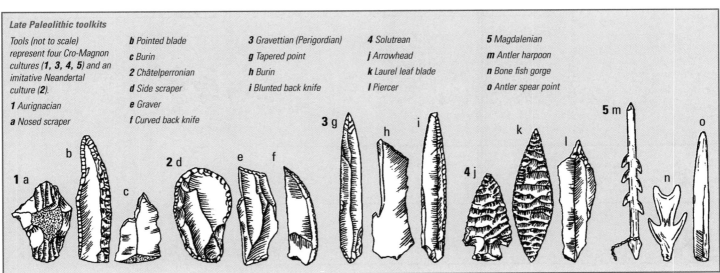

Late Paleolithic toolkits

Tools (not to scale) represent four Cro-Magnon cultures (**1, 3, 4, 5**) and an imitative Neandertal culture (**2**).

1 Aurignacian

a Nosed scraper

b Pointed blade
c Burin
2 Châtelperronian
d Side scraper
e Graver
f Curved back knife

3 Gravettian (Perigordian)
g Tapered point
h Burin
i Blunted back knife

4 Solutrean
j Arrowhead
k Laurel leaf blade
l Piercer

5 Magdalenian
m Antler harpoon
n Bone fish gorge
o Antler spear point

© DIAGRAM

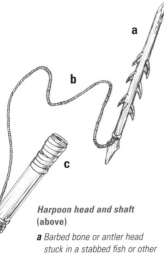

Harpoon head and shaft (above)

a Barbed bone or antler head stuck in a stabbed fish or other prey.

b Cord linking head and shaft

c Shaft socketed to take the head and gripped by the hunter before and after stabbing.

Hunting methods

Archaeological finds suggest that Cro-Magnon hunting weapons and techniques far surpassed those of the Neandertals–with major implications for food supply and population growth. Spear throwers that looked like giant crochet hooks improved the leverage exerted by the human arm, doubling the distance over which a hunter could hurl a spear. Now hunters could kill at long range, before their prey grew scared and ran away. Barbed points led to the invention of harpoons for killing salmon on their spawning run upriver from the sea. Now, for the first time, fish became a major item in the diet, especially in southwest France. Runnels in spearheads increased blood flow from stricken animals, hastening their end. Cro-Magnons snared birds and almost certainly developed deadfall traps for birds, wolves, foxes, and much larger game. Some experts think that pitfall traps had caught the 100 mammoths whose remains were found near Pavlov in the Czech Republic.

Cro-Magnons were arguably the most skilful hunters of big game ever. Seasonal occupation of selected sites implies that they followed reindeer and ibex on seasonal migrations to or from new feeding grounds. Great piles of bones imply that hunters learned the skill of driving herds to easy killing grounds. This might explain the 1,000 bison evidently killed in a ravine in southern Russia. Even more spectacular are the skeletons of 10,000 wild horses found below an inland cliff near Solutré in east-central France. About 17,000 years ago, hunters had seemingly ambushed whole herds on seasonal migration and killed them at the bottom of the cliff.

Using techniques and tools like these, Cro-Magnons won an almost inexhaustible supply of highly nourishing food. This evidently helped them multiply and people even the harsh, cold regions of Siberia.

Wounded bison (right)

Arrows seem to pierce a bison in this late Paleolithic cave painting from Niaux, in southwest France. Despite such images and a few finds of arrowheads, there is little evidence that hunters used bows and arrows before the Ice Age ended.

Migrating herds (right)

Arrows show likely spring migration routes of reindeer from winter quarters to summer coastal and mountain pastures.

a Perigord

b Atlantic coast (now submerged)

c Cantabrian Mountains

d Pyrenees

e Massif Central

f Mediterranean coast (now submerged)

g Alps

Spear thrower in action

1 A Cro-Magnon hunter used a spear thrower like this.

a Spear thrower

b Spear

2 Diagrams below show how this increased the weapon's range.

a Unaided arm power hurls a long spear 70 yd (64 m); actual killing range might be 15 yd (13.7 m)

b A spear thrower helps hurl a spear 150 yd (137 m); killing range increases to 30 yd (27.4 m)

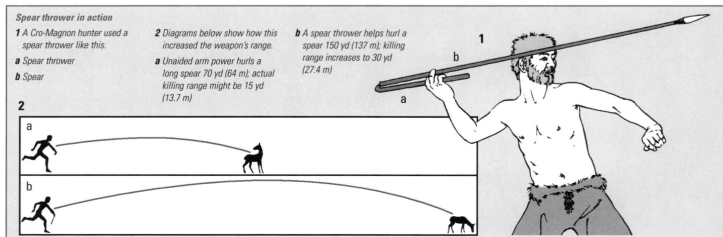

The hunters' prey

Late Old Stone Age Europe teemed with big, wild, meaty and fur-bearing mammals–never again surpassed in numbers or variety. Most species would have been familiar to Neandertals, but Cro-Magnon hunters' abundant, widespread leavings shed new light on which animals lived where.

Wild horses, reindeer, bison, mammoths, saiga antelopes, and woolly rhinoceroses grazed open steppes. Wooded slopes and valleys sheltered red deer, wild boars, cave bears, and cave wolves. Chamois, ibex, and wild goats climbed to high mountain summer pastures. Wild cattle thrived on steppes and in the forest edge.

Local differences suggest that in the early Late Stone Age reindeer and horses predominated in northern Germany, mammoth and rhinoceros in southern Germany, with cattle and horses farther east, around the Black Sea. There was change through time, however. In one Italian site, the chief prey animals–cattle, horse, red deer, and boar–gave way to horse and ass, in turn replaced by boar, red deer, and cattle. Probably climatic changes repeatedly affected vegetation.

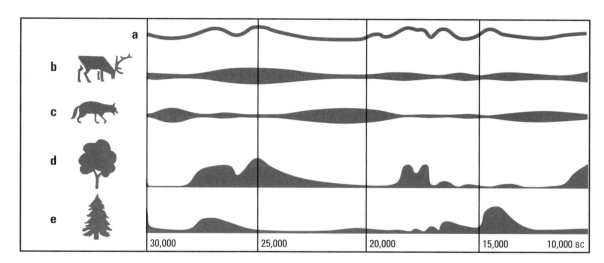

Species wax and wane

Diagram left shows how numbers of various animals and plants waxed and waned in southwest France as temperatures fluctuated in the last part of the Pleistocene.

a Rise and fall in temperature 30,000–10,000 BC.

b Red deer

c Arctic fox

d Deciduous trees

e Conifers

Prey animals

These five species formed the staple items in Cro-Magnon diets:

1 *Rangifer tarandus*, the reindeer. Shoulder height: to 4.6 ft (1.4 m). Time: Pleistocene–modern. Place: circumpolar.

2 *Cervus elephas*, the red deer, is the largest deer in most of Europe. Shoulder height: to 5 ft (1.5 m). Time: Pleistocene–modern. Place: Eurasia and North Africa.

3 *Bos primigenius*, the aurochs was a huge ox. Shoulder height: 6 ft (1.8 m) Time: Pleistocene–AD 1627. Place: Eurasia and North Africa.

4 *Equus caballus*, the horse, was a small, wild subspecies. Shoulder height: to 4.6 ft (1.4m). Time: Pleistocene–modern. Place: northern continents.

5 *Capra pyrenaica*, the Spanish ibex, is a mountain goat. Shoulder height: to 30 in (76 cm). Time: Pleistocene–modern. Place: Spain and once southwest France.

© DIAGRAM

Homes and clothes

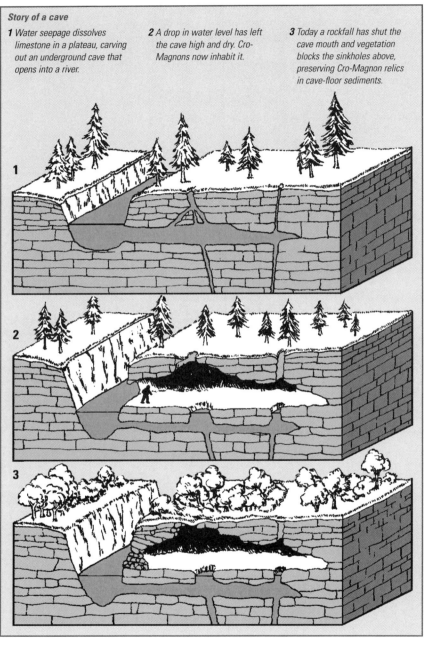

Story of a cave

1 Water seepage dissolves limestone in a plateau, carving out an underground cave that opens into a river.

2 A drop in water level has left the cave high and dry. Cro-Magnons now inhabit it.

3 Today a rockfall has shut the cave mouth and vegetation blocks the sinkholes above, preserving Cro-Magnon relics in cave-floor sediments.

Cro-Magnon homes largely followed old Neandertal traditions, but some homes and probably all clothing incorporated innovations that improved survival prospects in the last cold millennia of the Pleistocene.

Like the Neandertals before them, Europe's cave-dwelling Cro-Magnons made use of the limestone river cliffs of southwest France–especially in the Dordogne River area, but also on the northern slopes of the Pyrenees. Many caves faced south, warmed by sunshine and sheltered from cold northern winds. The caves lay near plentiful supplies of water and commanded views of pastures grazed by big meaty, herbivores. Where food abounded year-round, up to several dozen individuals might have lived permanently in one large cave, but certain caves show signs of only seasonal activity.

Again like the Neandertals, Russia's Gravettians built winter homes in river valleys. Some were paved with stone, some sunk in the ground, and many walled and roofed by tented skins propped up by mammoth thigh bones and weighed down around the rim by other heavy bones and tusks. Maybe the largest structure was an 89 ft (27 m) long longhouse from Kostenki in the Don valley; its central row of hearths suggests that several families wintered here beneath one roof consisting of a row of linked skin tepees with a common entrance.

Other finds and old drawings in French caves reveal that nomadic hunters also put up flimsy summer huts resembling those still built by certain modern people who live in hunter-gatherer societies.

Increased ability to live and work in Ice-Age cold owed as much to novel clothing as to new building methods or the use of fire. Bone needles and carvings of fur-suited people speak to the use of closely-fitting pants, hooded parkas, boots, and mittens–with seams closely sewn to keep in heat.

Dressed for warmth

Carved figurines from Russia show how people kept warm through Ice-Age winters.

a Figure wearing a close-fitting fur costume, with hood and trousers. This mammoth-tusk carving comes from Buret in Siberia.

b Headless female figure wearing a decorative belted costume. This carving comes from Kostenki, south of Moscow.

A Ukrainian longhouse

This is a reconstruction of a communal longhouse sunk slightly in the ground and roofed by tented skins propped up by poles, with mammoth bones and tusks to reinforce the bottom of the walls. Found at Pushkari, northeast of Kiev, the site might really represent three tents ranged close together in a row.

Art and ritual

From 35,000 to 10,000 years ago, Europe passed through its great age of prehistoric art. Works range from engravings of animals and people done on portable bits of stone, bone, ivory, and antler to clay or stone sculptures in the round or half-round and paintings in ocher, manganese, and charcoal dabbed on cave walls with moss or blown through a straw.

Studies of more than 100 caves and rock shelters convinced some experts that art went through four stages of development: Period I (32,000–25,000 years ago) featured animals and other forms mostly poorly drawn on small, portable objects. Period II (25,000–19,000 years ago) produced early cave art, including hand prints and engraved and painted silhouettes of animals with sinuously curved backs. Period III (19,000–15,000 years ago) marked cave art's climax as seen in lively, well-drawn horses and cattle at Lascaux in southwest France, and relief sculpture elsewhere. Period IV (15,000–10,000 years ago) stressed portable art, symbolic marks, and the superbly lifelike creatures in caves such as those of Altamira in northern Spain and Font-de-Gaume in France. This scheme, however, predates the discovery in AD 1994 of 300 fine animal cave paintings made in southern France an astonishing 30,000 years ago.

Most paintings lay deep in caves where artists evidently worked in the light of burning wood or moss-wick lamps. Perhaps their skills had ritual significance. Some illustrations depict part-human, part-animal figures, supposed sorcerers or shamans. Hunting magic or sexual symbolism probably explain the many scenes of meaty creatures of the chase. Fertility symbolism could account for human figurines with exaggerated female features. Geometric patterns suggest notation systems.

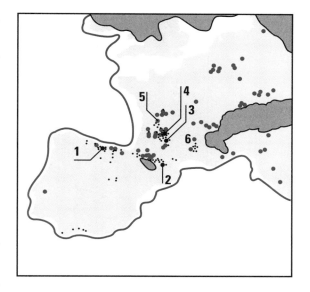

West European art sites

This map of late Paleolithic western Europe includes ice masses and the coastline then and now. Symbols show cave-wall art clustered in northern Spain and southwest France, with engravings, figurines, and other items farther north and east. Selected sources of major art objects include:

1 *Altamira*	**4** *Lascaux*
2 *Niaux*	**5** *Montgaudier*
3 *Pech-Merle*	**6** *Vallon-Pont-d'Arc*

Ice masses

· Cave-wall art

• Engravings and portable art

— Old coastline

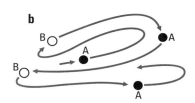

a

b

B○ ─────── ●A
    A●
B○ ───────
       ●
       A

Phases of the Moon?

a Bone plaque from Sergeac, France (somewhat reduced)

b Engraved symbols on the plaque, one per night, may trace phases of the Moon.

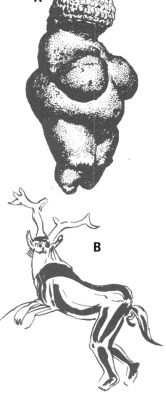

A

B

Two problematic figures (above)

A "Venus" of Willendorf in Austria, a mammoth-ivory figurine with exaggerated female features

B "Sorcerer" from Les Trois Frères cave in France—painting of a figure that seems half stag, half man

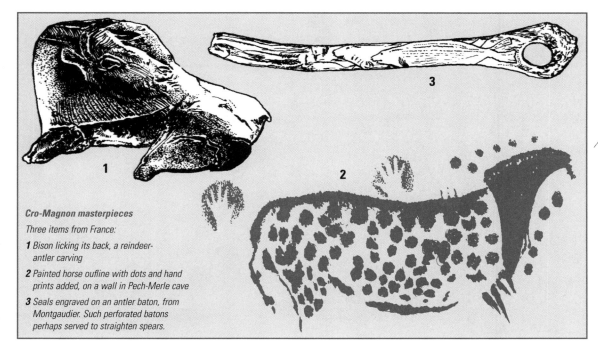

Cro-Magnon masterpieces

Three items from France:

1 Bison licking its back, a reindeer-antler carving

2 Painted horse outline with dots and hand prints added, on a wall in Pech-Merle cave

3 Seals engraved on an antler baton, from Montgaudier. Such perforated batons perhaps served to straighten spears.

© DIAGRAM

Cro-Magnon burials

A princely burial (right)

Two skeletons reveal remains of boys aged 12 to 13 buried head to head 23,000 years ago at Sungir in Russia. The wealth of grave goods buried with them foreshadowed royal burials of much later times.

Ornamented corpse (below)

More than 1,000 beads and other ornaments embellished the fur clothes of an old man whose buried skeleton was excavated at Sungir in 1955. The furs had rotted many centuries ago.

Grimaldi burial (below)

These skeletons were found in a single, shallow burial inside the Grotte des Enfants, a cave in Italy. Distortion after death produced projecting jaws.

A *Youth 5 ft 1½ in (1.56 m) tall.*

B *Old woman 5 ft 3 in (1.6 m) tall.*

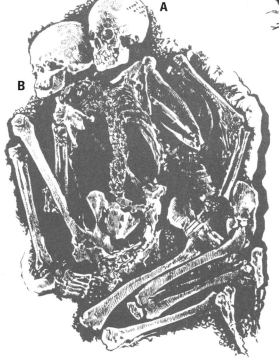

Burials as far apart as France and Russia hold clues to life among Cro-Magnon peoples.

Studied skeletons suggest that two-thirds of Cro-Magnons reached the age of 20 compared to less than half of the Neandertals before them, and one in 10 reached 40 compared with one in 20 Neandertals. Although based on scanty samples, these figures might imply that life expectancy was rising.

More reliably, Cro-Magnon burials speak of symbolic ritual and evolving wealth and status. Many mourners had sprinkled the dead with red ocher, presumably symbolizing blood and life, so hinting at belief in afterlife. Some corpses had gone to their graves richly ornamented–early signs that hunter-gatherer societies had begun producing rich, respected individuals.

Here are just a few burial examples:

The Cro-Magnon rock shelter near Les Eyzies in southwest France contained five adults and an infant colored with red ocher and buried with Aurignacian flint tools and pierced sea shells.

The Grimaldi fossils from the Italian Riviera comprise 16 individuals buried in several caves up to 30,000 years ago. The Grotte du Cavillon contained a man with a stag's teeth crown and a bonnet embroidered with hundreds of whelk shells. The Grotte des Enfants included two children with whelk shell ornaments. The Barma Grande held individuals with necklaces of animal vertebrae.

Prědmost in the Czech Republic revealed 29 deliberately buried skeletons, with clay figurines and tools of horn and bone.

Perhaps the most striking finds of all came from a 23,000-year-old hunters' burial ground at Sungir, east of Moscow. Here lay one old man in elaborately beaded fur clothes. Nearby, two boys wore beaded furs, ivory rings and bracelets; beside them lay long mammoth-tusk spears and two of the strange, scepterlike carved rods called *bâtons de commandement.*

Refined grave goods

Two late Paleolithic necklaces buried with their owners hint at accumulating personal possessions.

1 *A necklace of perforated bone beads and pendants, buried with a child in Siberia*

2 *Part of a three-row necklace with two rows of perforated fish vertebrae, one row of perforated shells, and perforated deer's teeth linking all rows. It was buried with a young man in southeast France.*

The Mesolithic period

By 10,000 years ago, the cold Pleistocene epoch had given way to the Holocene, or Recent, epoch–the mild phase we live in now. As Europe's climate warmed up, expanding forests invaded huge tracts of former tundra and rising sea drowned low shores and river valleys. Climatic change and hunting pressure destroyed the great grazing herds that Cro-Magnons had depended on for food, but land and water now teemed with forest mammals, fish, and waterfowl.

The tools and weapons described on the next page enabled northern Europeans to exploit this food supply. Their distinctive hunter-gatherer societies produced the cultural Mesolithic period, or "Middle Stone Age," so named because it followed the herd-hunting Late Old Stone Age and preceded the entry of New Stone Age farming into northern Europe. Lasting only from about 10,000 to 5,000 years ago, the Mesolithic occupied a mere eye blink of prehistoric time.

Bones found at Mesolithic sites reveal that hunters killed and ate such prey as red and roe deer, wild boar, wild cattle, beaver, fox, ducks, geese, and pike. Huge heaps of shellfish show that these were widely eaten on Atlantic and North Sea coasts. But Mesolithic peoples also gathered roots and fruits including nuts. Groups of people evidently moved from place to place as different foods reached peaks of seasonal abundance.

Archaeologists believe that Mesolithic people lived in groups smaller than their likely ancestors, the Cro-Magnon big-game hunters. Year-round food supply was now more stable, which helps explain why camp sites and evidently population multiplied. It also seems that life expectancy increased. At Vlasac on the River Danube in Serbia, several dozen adult skeletons show that, once past childhood, females at this favored spot attained an average age of 35, males 55. Few known Paleolithic individuals lived as long as this.

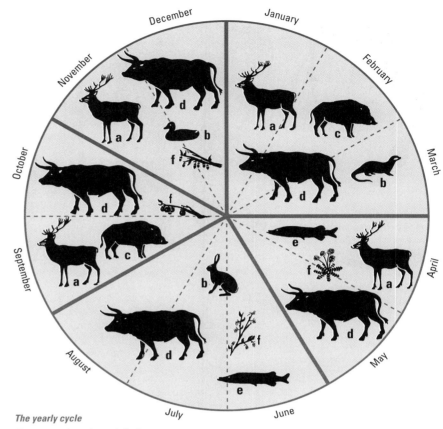

The yearly cycle

Five seasons formed a year's food cycle in northwestern Europe 8,000 years ago. Deer and ox were eaten all year but varied in abundance.

a Red deer **d** Wild ox
b Small game **e** Fish
c Wild boar **f** Plants

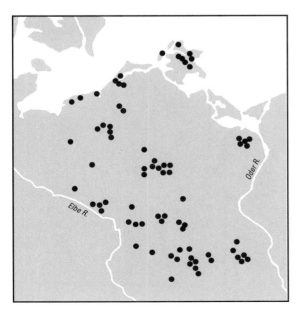

Mesolithic sites in eastern Germany (left)

Dots show contemporary sites, most evidently small. An area of 18,000 sq mi (47,000 sq km) held perhaps only 1,500 people.

The hunters' prey (right)

This shows how many of 165 European sites held each of the most widely hunted mammals.

1 Red deer
2 Wild boar
3 Wild ox
4 Roe deer
5 Fox
6 Badger
7 Wild cat
8 Beaver

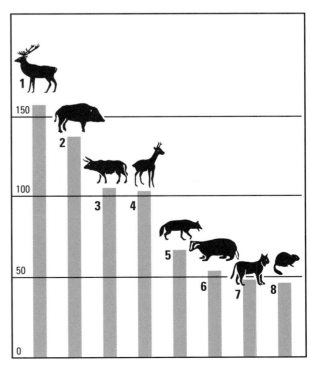

© DIAGRAM

Mesolithic toolkits

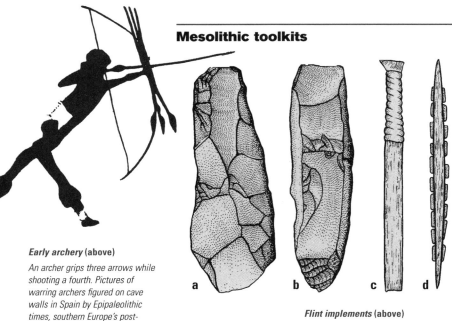

Early archery (above)

An archer grips three arrows while shooting a fourth. Pictures of warring archers figured on cave walls in Spain by Epipaleolithic times, southern Europe's post-glacial equivalent of the Mesolithic period farther north.

Flint implements (above)

These are not to scale:

a Ax

b Adze

c Arrow with microlith head

d Bone fish spear with microlith barbs

Dugout canoe (below)

Flint blades socketed in handles of antler, bone, or wood sculpted a solid tree trunk into this open boat, discovered in the Netherlands.

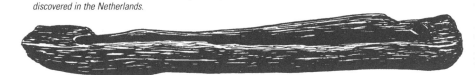

New stone-edged tools and weapons helped Mesolithic peoples exploit the forest and sea that encroached on parts of northwestern Europe after northern ice sheets melted.

Key hunting aids included bows and arrows, probably a late Paleolithic invention. Lighter to carry than a sturdy spear, bows and arrows were also more accurate, afforded greater range, and required less muscle power. A skilled archer could shoot an ibex 35 yards (32 m) away, and if the first arrow missed, there was time to fire another.

Mesolithic arrows were mostly barbed or tipped with small, sharp flints called microliths. Many were no more than 1 cm long, and they were trimmed in standard forms such as crescents, rods, triangles, or trapezes. Resin-cemented into shafts of antler, bone, or wood, microliths could simply be replaced if lost or blunted. Moreover, they were economical to make: a skilled microlith maker could produce 300 feet (91.5 m) of cutting edge from just 2 pounds (987 gm) of flint.

New types of large stone tools helped Mesolithic peoples fell and fashion timber. They chopped down trees with stone-headed axes and shaped trunks and branches with stone-bladed adzes. To sharpen these tools they removed flakes or ground cutting edges on hard stone slabs. Then they hafted the heads in antler sleeves inserted into wooden handles.

Axes and adzes enabled Mesolithic peoples to produce dugout canoes, paddles, skis, and sledges. Between them, these opened up huge water areas for fishing and made it easier to travel over snow and boggy ground.

Making microliths

1 *Flint blade*

2 *Blade notched on opposite sides*

3 *Blade snapped in three*

4 *Central piece retouched as a rhomboidal microlith*

5 *Blade notched on one side*

6 *Blade snapped in three*

7 *Central piece retouched as:*

a Trapeze

b Lunate

c Triangle

Microlith types

These represent four Mesolithic cultures:

1–3 *Azilian, named after the Mas d'Azil cave in the French Pyrenees*

4–6 *Maglemosian (or Forest culture), named after Maglemose in the Dutch province Zeeland*

7–9 *Sauveterrian, named after Sauveterre-la-Lemance in France, but widespread in western Europe*

10–12 *Tardenoisian, named after Fère-en-Tardenois, in northern France*

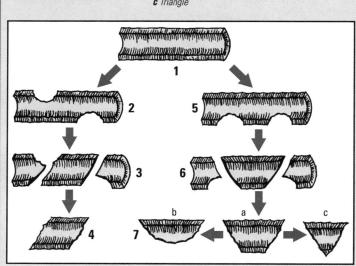

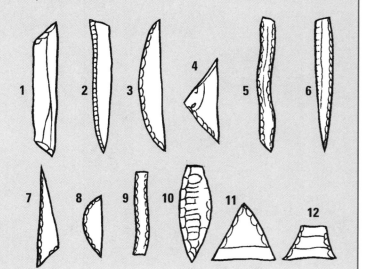

Two famous Mesolithic sites

Two sites far apart in time and place illustrate cultural developments in Mesolithic Europe.

At Star Carr in northeast England, hunter-gatherers set up summer camps beside a lake as long ago as 8,700 BC. Once birchwood and deer herds colonized this region newly freed from ice, these people followed, walking from Scandinavia or Germany before the North Sea rose. Skilled carpenters, using little more than sharp stone tools, they evidently fashioned canoes and paddles. Splitting birch trunks lengthwise, they also laid Europe's first known trackway over boggy lakeside ground. For many summers, for between 250 and 300 years, they managed the lakeside vegetation by burning old, dead reeds. This encouraged young growth, perhaps to draw in grazing deer, wild cattle, and wild boar–creatures that they killed with long, barbed points produced by cutting splinters from the scores of antlers discovered on the site. They also trimmed some antlers, reshaping them as headgear, perhaps used as disguises while hunting deer.

Star Carr supported only summer hunting camps, but at Lepenski Vir in Serbia, Mesolithic people built a permanent village by 6,400 BC. Here, at the Danube River's Iron Gates Gorge, fish, deer, wild cattle, and edible plants provided enough food to last them all the year. About 100 people at a time inhabited a group of fan-shaped wooden hunts laid out across a well-drained sandstone river terrace. Supposedly, the huts' unusual floor plans mimicked the outline of a mountain opposite. An extra large hut, perhaps the village chief's, a central meeting ground, and sandstone "fish god" sculptures by the hearths inside some huts imply levels of cultural development normally expected only in the settled farming communities of later Neolithic times.

Hunter-gatherers occupied Lepenski Vir for about 800 years. Then, about 5,600 BC, farming, spreading up through Europe, added its contribution to the village food supply.

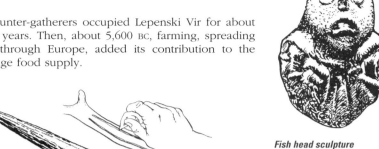

Barbed antler point

To make a harpoon point, a Star Carr hunter cut two parallel grooves close together in an antler and then detached the sliver in between. Careful trimming shaped its barbs.

Hunter's disguise? *(below)*

Tying this stag's skull to his head with string strung through holes bored in its bone might have helped a Star Carr hunter to fool the deer he stalked into thinking he was merely one of them.

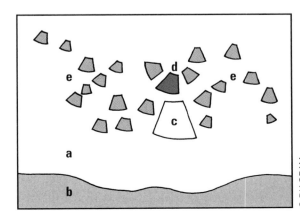

Fish head sculpture

Fish-faced sandstone sculptures found in many huts at Lepenski Vir might represent a fish god. Fish probably provided villagers with a large part of their diet.

Lepenski Vir hut

A typical wooden hut from Lepenski Vir possessed these features:

a Triangular floor plan
b Limestone-plastered floor
c Stone hearth
d Threshold of flat stones
e Wooden framework
f Thatched roof
g Sandstone fish head sculpture
h Stone-filled trench

f
g
h
a
b c d
e

Lepenski Vir

This plan view shows how one of a series of successive village layouts was arranged:

a Sandstone river terrace
b Danube River

c Meeting place
d "Chief's hut"
e Village huts

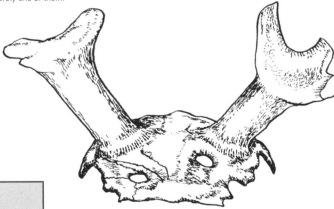

© DIAGRAM

Homo sapiens worldwide

Our own species' emergence in Europe postdated its rapid spread in Africa, Asia, and Australia. Indeed, modern humans probably evolved in Africa 100,000 years or more ago from a local archaic form of Homo sapiens, *perhaps itself derived from an African population of* Homo heidelbergensis.

This chapter briefly surveys early finds of modern people around the world and shows how local differences of climate contributed to racial differences observed today.

Sickle-cell trait

This map shows recent distributions of sickle-shaped red blood cells and malaria in human populations. Sickle cells originated with a mutation in one individual. The gene producing sickle cells confers resistance to malaria but causes anemia if inherited from both parents.

 Sickle-cell distribution

Malaria

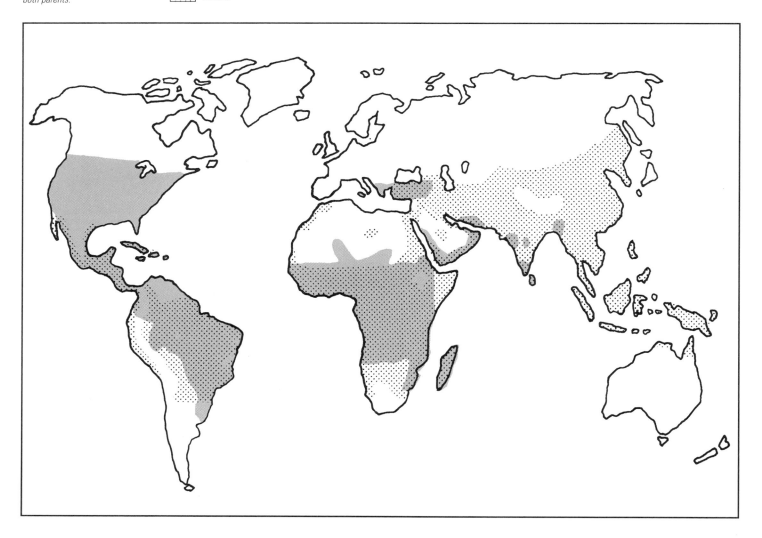

Origins of modern humans

It now seems increasingly unlikely that Neandertals gave rise to Europe's Cro-Magnons, or that these were the world's first fully modern humans. One Portuguese skeleton shows some Neandertal and modern human features, but biochemical evidence says that Neandertals remained a species separate from ourselves. Many scientists believe *Homo sapiens* began evolving from *Homo heidelbergensis* in Africa as early as 500,000 years ago, attaining its fully modern form there perhaps 100,000 years ago.

Fossil skulls that old indeed indicate that Africa is where we came from. Other evidence is in the genes inherited by different racial groups. Scientists once classified these groups by unreliably superficial characters like body form and color. Later, biologists compared more stable features, such as blood groups and their proteins. Because various DNA sequences can produce genes with the same protein products, the surest way to trace long-term inherited relationships is to compare the DNA sequences themselves; now biologists have done that too.

In 1986 British scientists James Wainscoat and Adrian Hill reported using biological agents called enzymes to isolate five DNA fragments from a gene responsible for producing part of the hemoglobin molecule of red blood cells. They recorded the different patterns that these fragments formed in 600 people, including Africans, Britons, Indians, Melanesians, and Thais. It emerged that non-Africans shared a limited number of common patterns, while Africans showed a pattern not found in other groups. The scientists concluded that one small, inbred group of prehistoric Africans had given rise to all the other peoples of the world.

Many subscribers to this theory believe that modern humans evolved in Africa by 100,000 years ago, entered Asia not very much later, and by 30,000 years ago had reached all continents except Antarctica.

US scientists Rebecca Cann and Mark Stoneking reached geographically similar conclusions by studying mitochondrial genes, passed on by females only. These imply that our species began with a woman who lived in Africa 200,000 years ago–much earlier than fossil evidence suggests.

Critics found flaws in these early genetic studies, but later research has tended to confirm them.

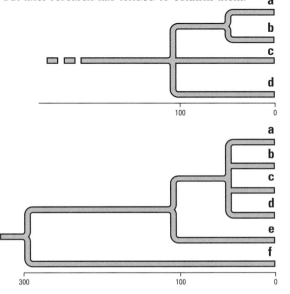

One view of racial origins (left)

Here we show racial origins according to studies of proteins and DNA in chromosomes. Numbers are in thousands of years ago.

a Australian Aborigines
b Asians
c Blacks
d Whites

Racial origins: another view (left)

One study of mitochondrial DNA produced this rival theory of racial origins. Again numbers are in thousands of years ago.

a Most Australian Aborigines
b Most Asians
c Blacks
d Whites
e Some Asians
f Some Australian Aborigines

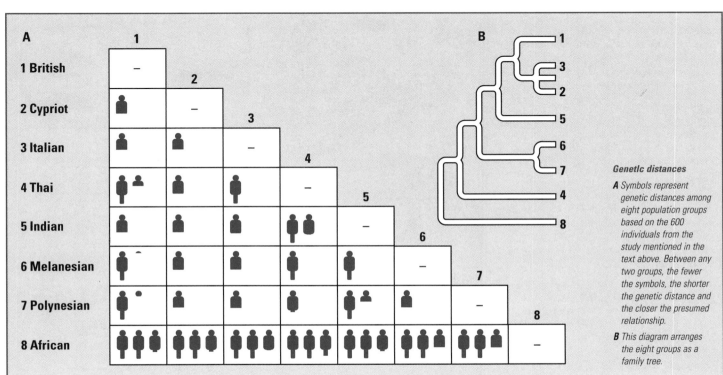

Genetic distances

A Symbols represent genetic distances among eight population groups based on the 600 individuals from the study mentioned in the text above. Between any two groups, the fewer the symbols, the shorter the genetic distance and the closer the presumed relationship.

B This diagram arranges the eight groups as a family tree.

© DIAGRAM

Homo sapiens in Africa

Africa has yielded older fossil finds of fully modern humans than any other continent. Thus from southern Ethiopia comes Omo-Kibish 1, a partial skull, probably more than 60,000 years old, with many modern features. The mouth of South Africa's Klasies River produced 100,000-year-old "modern" fragments, and Border Cave, a "modern" 90,000-year-old lower jaw.

Some other ancient bones foreshadow today's Bantu and Khoisan. Supposed ancestral features of both groups figure in a more than 200,000-year-old skull from Florisbad, South Africa. Distinctive, childlike Khoisan skulls predate the 17,000-year-old first-known fossils resembling Bantu-speaking groups today. The Khoisan group seemingly once occupied all of southern Africa, and bands of Khoisan hunter-gatherers still live an almost Paleolithic lifestyle in Botswana's Kalahari Desert.

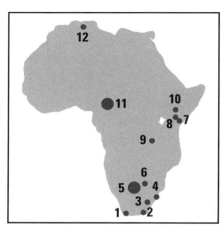

Hunter-gatherers today

Like their Paleolithic forebears, some Khoisan still hunt with bows and arrows and chiefly eat wild plants.

Four African heads

Numbered illustrations depict examples of past and present Africans of modern form:

1 Omo-Kibish 1: a thin-boned skull, with bulging upper sides, rounded back, slight browridges, well-developed chin, and 1,400 cc brain capacity. Age: 127,000–37,000 years. Place: Omo River, Ethiopia.

2 Florisbad skull: a large, low-vaulted skull, with browridges, broad face, protruding mouth, and low, rectangular eye sockets. Age: about 260,000 years. Place: Florisbad, South Africa.

3 Khoisan: a short, slim, yellowish, wiry form of a modern human with high cheekbones and childlike facial features, including a small face; flat, broad nose; and prominent forehead. Time: perhaps dating back 40,000 years. Place: southern Africa.

4 Bantu: member of a dark-skinned group of variable size, with distinctive broad nasal opening, turned out lips, and projecting lower face. Time: perhaps dating back 20,000 years. Place: sub-Saharan Africa (with emigrants worldwide).

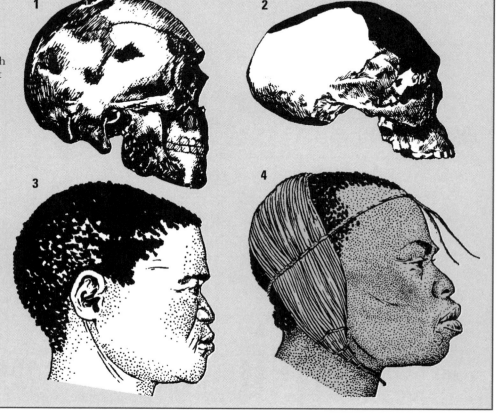

Homo sapiens in Asia

Fossil skulls up to 90,000 years old and attributed to fully modern humans crop up in Asia as far apart as Israel and Java. All have a chin or other crucial "modern" features. Yet there are West Asian and Southeast Asian forms with "old-fashioned" details found in the Neandertals, and some Far Eastern forms recall _Homo erectus_. Experts disagree about what this implies. Multiregionalists would argue that certain similarities between _Homo erectus_ and modern Chinese skulls derive from a shared inheritance. Fossil and biochemical evidence, however, support the "out of Africa" hypothesis.

Certain Chinese skulls suggest that by 20,000 years ago there lived ancestors of today's Asian Mongoloids–short, stocky people, with straight dark hair, sparse body hair, a fold in the upper eyelids, flat faces, wide cheek bones, and narrow noses.

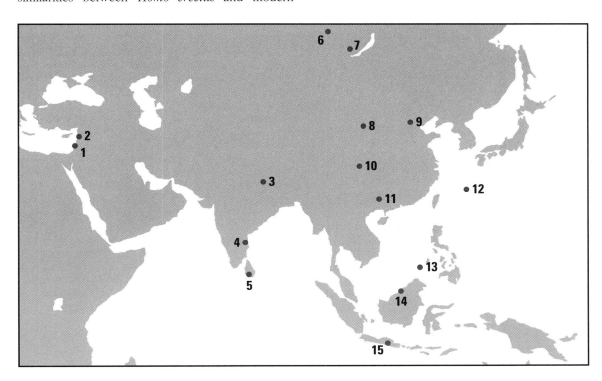

Where they lived

This map shows 15 sites of finds of fully modern people of 100,000–50,000 years ago.

1 Qafzeh
2 Ksar Akil
3 Mahadaha
4 Attirampakkam
5 Batadombalena
6 Novoselovo
7 Mal'ta
8 Ordos (artifacts)
9 Zhoukoudian (Choukoutien)
10 Ziyang
11 Liujiang
12 Minatogaa
13 Tabon Cave
14 Niah Cave
15 Wadjak

Five Asian examples

Numbered illustrations depict past and present Asian examples of fully modern humans:

1 Qafzeh Despite brow ridges recalling the Neandertals, this skull has been identified with fully modern humans. Age: 90,000 years. Place: Qafzeh Cave, Israel.

2 Niah man is known from skull fragments, teeth, and a foot bone from a delicately built youth. Age: 40,000 years. Place: Niah Cave, Borneo.

3 Wadjak skull This was long, with sloping forehead, browridges, jutting mouth, and heavy jaws. Age: uncertain. Place: Wadjak, Java.

4 Liujiang man anatomically represents an early modern human from China. Age: 20,000 years. Place: Liujiang, Kwangsi Province, China.

5 Asian Mongoloid a fully modern skull with a flat face, narrow nose, and angulated cheekbones–features foreshadowed in some fossil Chinese skulls.

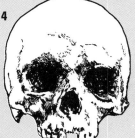

© DIAGRAM

Peopling the Americas

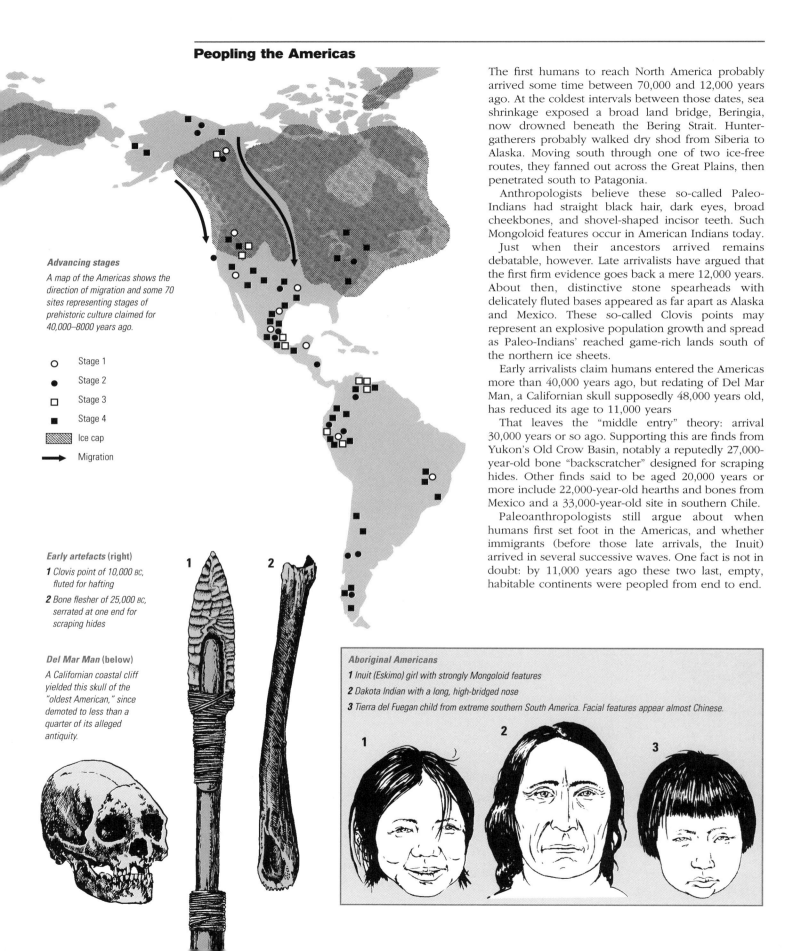

The first humans to reach North America probably arrived some time between 70,000 and 12,000 years ago. At the coldest intervals between those dates, sea shrinkage exposed a broad land bridge, Beringia, now drowned beneath the Bering Strait. Hunter-gatherers probably walked dry shod from Siberia to Alaska. Moving south through one of two ice-free routes, they fanned out across the Great Plains, then penetrated south to Patagonia.

Anthropologists believe these so-called Paleo-Indians had straight black hair, dark eyes, broad cheekbones, and shovel-shaped incisor teeth. Such Mongoloid features occur in American Indians today.

Just when their ancestors arrived remains debatable, however. Late arrivalists have argued that the first firm evidence goes back a mere 12,000 years. About then, distinctive stone spearheads with delicately fluted bases appeared as far apart as Alaska and Mexico. These so-called Clovis points may represent an explosive population growth and spread as Paleo-Indians' reached game-rich lands south of the northern ice sheets.

Early arrivalists claim humans entered the Americas more than 40,000 years ago, but redating of Del Mar Man, a Californian skull supposedly 48,000 years old, has reduced its age to 11,000 years

That leaves the "middle entry" theory: arrival 30,000 years or so ago. Supporting this are finds from Yukon's Old Crow Basin, notably a reputedly 27,000-year-old bone "backscratcher" designed for scraping hides. Other finds said to be aged 20,000 years or more include 22,000-year-old hearths and bones from Mexico and a 33,000-year-old site in southern Chile.

Paleoanthropologists still argue about when humans first set foot in the Americas, and whether immigrants (before those late arrivals, the Inuit) arrived in several successive waves. One fact is not in doubt: by 11,000 years ago these two last, empty, habitable continents were peopled from end to end.

Advancing stages

A map of the Americas shows the direction of migration and some 70 sites representing stages of prehistoric culture claimed for 40,000–8000 years ago.

○   Stage 1
●   Stage 2
□   Stage 3
■   Stage 4
▨   Ice cap
➜   Migration

Early artefacts (right)

1 Clovis point of 10,000 BC, fluted for hafting

2 Bone flesher of 25,000 BC, serrated at one end for scraping hides

Del Mar Man (below)

A Californian coastal cliff yielded this skull of the "oldest American," since demoted to less than a quarter of its alleged antiquity.

Aboriginal Americans

1 Inuit (Eskimo) girl with strongly Mongoloid features

2 Dakota Indian with a long, high-bridged nose

3 Tierra del Fuegan child from extreme southern South America. Facial features appear almost Chinese.

People and animals in the Americas

Between about 12,000 and 5,000 years ago, a great wave of extinctions swept away many of the larger animals of North and South America. Victims included seven prehistoric kinds of elephant (four mammoth species and three types of mastodont), three kinds of camel, the long-horned bison, the horse, certain pronghorns and musk oxen, giant ground sloths, those gigantic "armadillos" the glyptodonts, and sabertooth cats.

Extinctions peaked between about 12,000 and 10,000 years ago, as Paleo-Indians increased their hold upon both continents. Some people see humans as the exterminators. This overkill theory holds that stone-tipped spears launched by spear-throwers accomplished the annihilation. One expert claims that 100 humans advancing south from Canada 10 miles (16 km) a year could have given rise to 300,000 people in 300 years, by which time humans would have reached the Gulf of Mexico and could have killed 100 million big mammals on the way.

Extinctions also coincided with dramatic climatic changes, as northern ice sheets melted. Fluctuating temperature and rainfall drastically affected vegetation, robbing certain herbivores of food and indirectly starving the carnivores that preyed upon them.

A third extinction theory blames humans and climate jointly. This theory holds that climatic change affecting vegetation reduced the feeding areas available for certain animals. Concentrated in these zones and weakened by a lack of food, whole herds would have fallen prey to hunters.

As mammoths disappeared and human numbers multiplied, the successive mammoth-hunting Clovis and Folsom cultures gave way about 10,000 years ago to the Plano culture, combining bison hunting with foraging for wild-plant foods. North America's Paleo-Indian hunting cultural stage was superseded by the more mixed economies of the so-called Archaic stage, which lasted locally until about 2,300 years ago.

Waves of extinction

The map right shows waves of extinction spreading south through the Americas with man. Bands show one theorist's notion of the rate of spread. Numbers represent thousands of years ago.

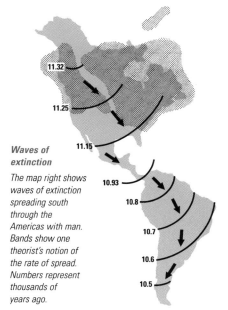

When they went (below)

The large mammals listed below died out in North America. Some experts group their deaths later than the map suggests. Here, numbers show one expert's estimates of how many thousands of years ago each group disappeared.

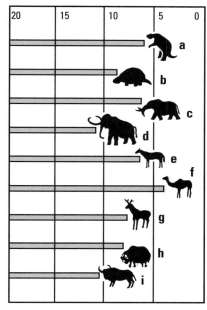

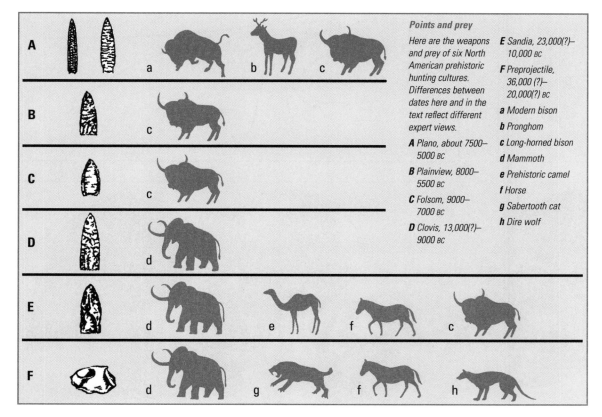

Points and prey

Here are the weapons and prey of six North American prehistoric hunting cultures. Differences between dates here and in the text reflect different expert views.

A Plano, about 7500–5000 BC

B Plainview, 8000–5500 BC

C Folsom, 9000–7000 BC

D Clovis, 13,000(?)–9000 BC

E Sandia, 23,000(?)–10,000 BC

F Preprojectile, 36,000 (?)–20,000(?) BC

a Modern bison
b Pronghorn
c Long-horned bison
d Mammoth
e Prehistoric camel
f Horse
g Sabertooth cat
h Dire wolf

a Ground sloths
b Glyptodonts
c Mastodonts
d Mammoths
e Horses
f Prehistoric camels
g Prehistoric pronghorns
h Prehistoric musk oxen
i Long-horned bison

Hafted spear points (above)

1 Folsom point: fluted
2 Eden point: slender
3 Eva point: barbed

© DIAGRAM

The first Australians

Dated hearths and fossils prove that modern humans lived in Australia at least 60,000 years ago. Some experts think they had moved in by 130,000 years ago, when New South Wales saw a sharp rise in brush fires and the spread of fire-resistant plants of modern kinds, but Australia has not yielded any human skeletons or tools that old.

Most likely, people first arrived in the Ice Age, at a time when the ocean level stood 160 ft (50 m) lower than today and many islands coalesced. Southeast Asian migrants on canoes or rafts had to cross a mere 40 miles (65 km) of sea to get to Meganesia–the landmass that encompassed Australia.

Early Australians were by no means uniform. About 30,000 years ago, Lake Mungo in the southeast was home to people slightly built on modern lines, with some skeletal resemblance to today's Chinese. About 13,000 years ago, Kow Swamp, not far away, had more strongly built individuals with thick skulls, jutting jaws, ridged brows, and sloping foreheads–features found in Solo man–a late form of *Homo erectus* from Java.

Some experts therefore think that Australia received two waves of immigration. Others argue that varied prehistoric forms were just extremes among ancestors of today's Aborigines, whose ridged brows suggest retention of an ancient trait.

Until about two centuries ago, all Aborigines lived a Late Old Stone Age way of life. Small, seminomadic bands of near-naked individuals roamed fixed territories. Men armed with spears or boomerangs hunted game. Women gathered plant and insect foods. Myth and ritual played a major role in life, which featured dancing, painting, and verbally transmitted songs and legends. Such practices survive as insights into prehistoric life worldwide.

Where they lived

Dots mark selected prehistoric sites in Australia.

1 *Cossack*
2 *Devils Lair*
3 *Keilor*
4 *Kow Swamp/Cohuna*
5 *Lake Mungo*
6 *Willandra Lakes*
7 *Talgai*

Peopling Oceania

We show likely migration routes and major regions. Robust and/ or gracile forms produced the Australoids of Australia and Melanesia. Austronesians–a linguistic group–peopled the Pacific from Hawaii to New Zealand.

1 *"Robusts" by 45,000 BC*
2 *"Graciles" by 45,000 BC*

3 *Austronesians (mainly Mongoloids) 5000 BC–AD 1000*
a *Southeast Asia*
b *Australia*
c *Melanesia*
d *Micronesia*
e *Polynesia*

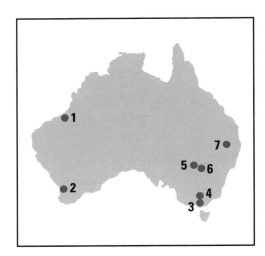

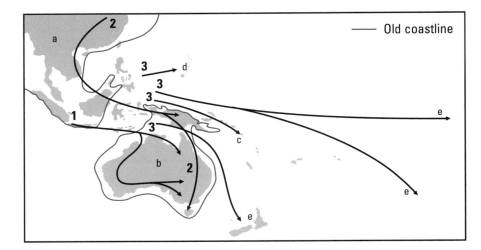

—— Old coastline

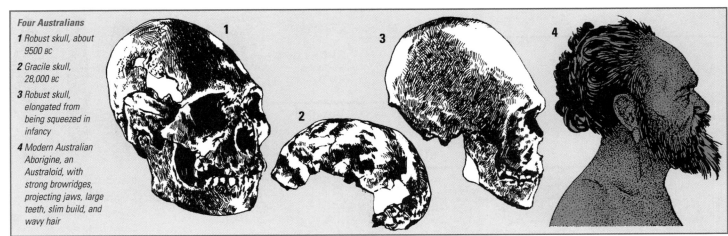

Four Australians

1 *Robust skull, about 9500 BC*
2 *Gracile skull, 28,000 BC*
3 *Robust skull, elongated from being squeezed in infancy*
4 *Modern Australian Aborigine, an Australoid, with strong browridges, projecting jaws, large teeth, slim build, and wavy hair*

Climate, color, and physique

As our species spread around the world, groups of people found themselves in different climatic zones. Natural selection produced physical adaptations to differing conditions. The result: the world's blacks, whites, and mongoloids. Each label by no means indicates a race (a biological breeding group). Africans and Melanesians are blacks as unrelated to each other as they are to whites or mongoloids. And of course all humans still belong to the same species.

With that in mind this page examines briefly how major differences between blacks, whites, and certain mongoloids reflect the way their bodies have evolved to cope with hot or cold climates.

Take skin color first: Among whites, strong tropical sunshine makes pale skins peel and blister, and intense ultraviolet radiation tends to cause skin cancers. Among blacks, skin darkened by the brown pigment melanin is protected from these risks. Yet in cloudy lands outside the Tropics, pale skin is an advantage, for it absorbs enough of the weak ultraviolet radiation to make Vitamin D, a substance promoting healthy bone growth. In cool, cloudy lands, young blacks can suffer rickets.

There are equally good reasons for differences in body shape and size. In relation to body size, a tall, slim, long-limbed Nilotic African has a big surface area, ideal for keeping cool in the Tropics by radiating surplus body heat. In similar conditions a (mongoloid) Inuit's short, squat body with its small surface area would suffer overheating, but this same body form, with its insulating fat beneath the skin, conserves essential body heat in Arctic winters where a lanky body could suffer fatal chilling.

Of course this oversimplifies the world picture; for instance, by no means are mongoloids all built like Inuit. Biological adaptations like those described undoubtedly helped Paleolithic modern humans to populate all habitable continents, however.

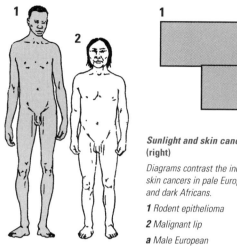

***Physiques compared* (above)**

1 (Equatorial) Nilotic African
2 (Polar) Inuit (Eskimo)

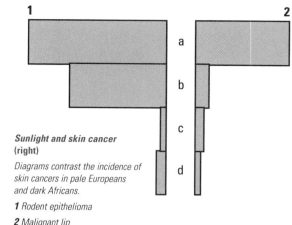

***Sunlight and skin cancer* (right)**

Diagrams contrast the incidence of skin cancers in pale Europeans and dark Africans.

1 Rodent epithelioma
2 Malignant lip
a Male European
b Female European
c Male African
d Female African

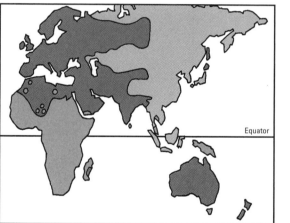

***Hair form* (left)**

Hair form seems related to solar heat. The crinkly hair of some tropical peoples protects their brains against heat radiation from the Sun.

- Crinkly or woolly
- Straight
- Wavy-straight

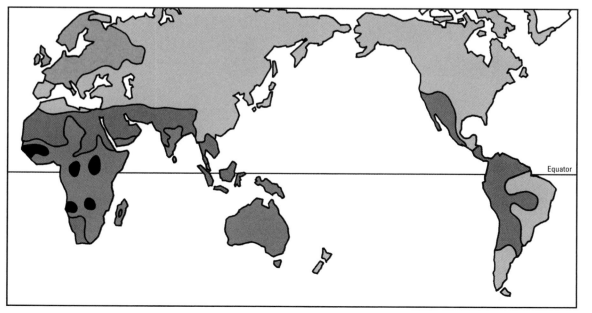

***Skin color* (left)**

Aboriginals' skin tones tally with the strength of sunshine except where recent migration has given natural selection too little time to work.

- Very pale
- Fairly pale
- Medium
- Fairly dark
- Very dark

© DIAGRAM

Since the Ice Age

Humans have altered little physically since the Ice Age ended about 10,000 years ago, but cultural evolution has transformed humankind. This chapter charts major prehistoric innovations, from food production and the growth of metallurgy to the rise of cities and the birth of writing. We see how cultural change has modified physique and vastly multiplied our species' numbers, and we end with a (daunting) glimpse into the future.

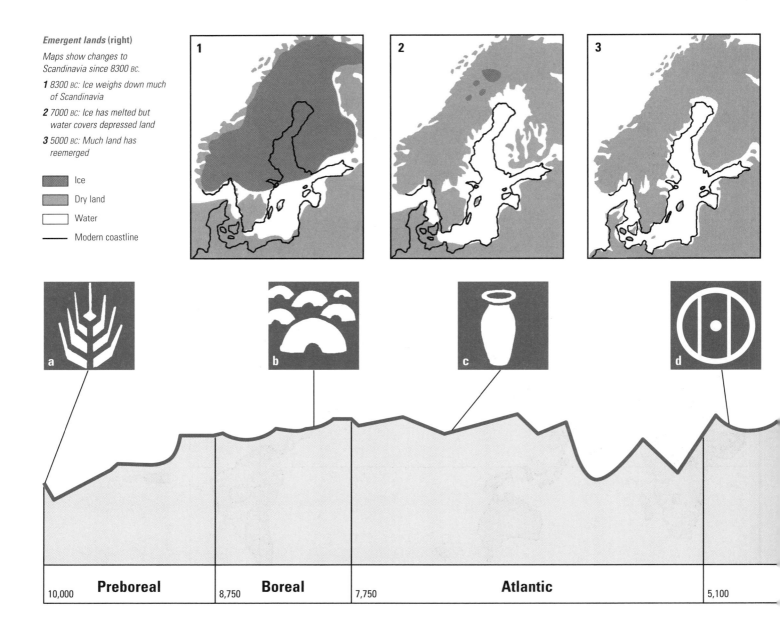

Emergent lands (right)

Maps show changes to Scandinavia since 8300 BC.

1 *8300 BC: Ice weighs down much of Scandinavia*

2 *7000 BC: Ice has melted but water covers depressed land*

3 *5000 BC: Much land has reemerged*

- Ice
- Dry land
- Water
- Modern coastline

| 10,000 | **Preboreal** | 8,750 | **Boreal** | 7,750 | **Atlantic** | 5,100 |

A warmer world

Sweeping cultural advances that would make humans dominant on Earth marked the Holocene, or Recent, geological epoch, which began about 10,000 years ago. This human progress coincided with climatic warming after the last long wave of Ice Age cold that closed the Pleistocene. (In fact, the Holocene is probably a brief, mild interval with further cold to come.)

Global change was under way soon after northern ice sheets began melting 15,000 years ago. Meltwater pouring into oceans slowly raised their level 430 feet (130 m). The seas severed land bridges that had joined Asia and North America, Indonesia and Malaya, the British Isles and Europe. One-twentieth of Earth's land surface drowned. Yet, as ice sheets dripped away, the lands they had pressed down re-emerged. In parts of Canada and Scandinavia, old shorelines now stand 980 feet (300 m) above the present level of the sea.

European studies reveal several climatic stages in the Holocene–each affecting lands and living things. In the Preboreal and Boreal stages (10,000–7,750 years ago) ice sheets, and mountain glaciers shrank, and the midlatitudes and tropics received hugely increased rainfall. As lakes and rivers rose, moist grassland invaded the Sahara and some other arid regions of the world. Wild Eurasian cattle, goats, and sheep moved north, locally replacing elk and reindeer. Early farming villages took root in Southwest Asia.

The Atlantic Stage (7,750–5,100 years ago) was warmer than today in northern lands. Vegetation spread worldwide, except up to the highest mountain tops, and forest ousted much northern tundra. American Indians peopled once glaciated parts of North America, and farming spread across Eurasia.

The Subboreal stage (5,100–2,200 years ago) brought cooler, drier winters to the hearts of midlatitude continents. Steppe and prairie plants and animals multiplied. Farming started in Central America, and city life emerged in several continents. In places, written records of events appeared. Humankind began emerging from its prehistoric past.

About 2,200 years ago the climatically fluctuating Sub-Atlantic stage we live in now began.

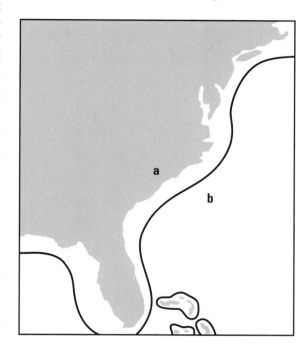

Drowned lands (left)

Southeastern North America shrank when melting ice raised the level of the sea.

a Shoreline now

b Shoreline in glacial times

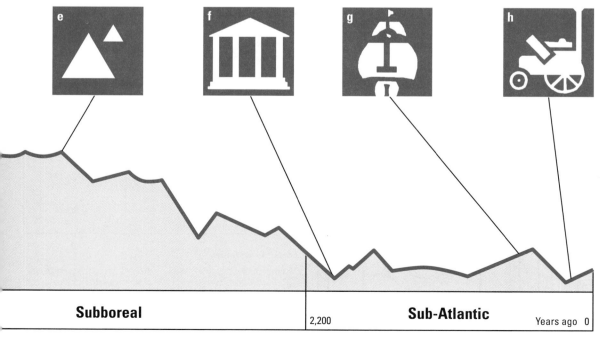

Cultural landmarks (left)

Symbols of cultural innovations appear above a time scale showing temperature fluctuations in the last 10,000 years–since major warming closed the Pleistocene.

a Farming

b Towns

c Turned pottery (also metal smelting and weaving)

d The wheel (also writing and sailing boats

e Nation states

f Classical civilizations

g Age of Discovery

h Industrial Revolution

© DIAGRAM

Wild harvest (below)

In a good season one person could cut 6 lb (almost 3 kg) of wild wheat in an hour, and a family could harvest a year's supply in three weeks.

The rise of farming

An ear of wheat (left)

Four illustrations show structures involved in processes mentioned below:

A *Wheat spike*

B *Spikelet with:*

a *Internode*

b *Glumes (four husks)*

c *Awns*

C *Floret: two inner husks, containing:*

D *Grain, the edible kernel rich in protein and carbohydrates*

By 10,000 years ago, the discovery of farming had begun transforming humankind. A given area of fertile land feeds far more food-producers than hunter-gatherers; thus where farming spread, populations multiplied. Then, too, tending crops encouraged a trend toward a settled, village way of life with craftspeople who produced and bartered such articles as ground stone tools and pottery.

Such Neolithic (New Stone) Age farming and/or stock raising cultures followed Paleolithic or Mesolithic lifestyles but predated the metal-using Bronze Age and Iron Age cultures.

Different Neolithic cultures sprouted, independently it seems, at different times and places. Farming first became widespread around 10,000 years ago in and near the so-called Fertile Crescent that runs from Egypt through Southwest Asia to the Persian Gulf. Here early farmers grew wheat, barley, lentils, and peas. Beginning about 7,000 years ago, the Chinese produced crops such as millet, rice, soybeans, taro, and yams. By 5,000 years ago, Mesoamerica (southern Mexico, Guatemala, and Honduras) was a third great farming nucleus, with maize, beans, squash, and cotton grown.

Experts debate just how and why Stone Age peoples took up sedentary food production. Many hunter-gatherers already had enough to eat and leisure time in plenty. Early farmers worked longer hours for a less varied diet at the risk of famine if their crops should fail.

In places, though, population growth outstripping food supply perhaps forced hunters to seek extra food from plants. Another influence must have been the spread of grasses with big, edible seeds.

By 13,000 years ago, harvesting wild cereals had become a mainstay of at least one group in Israel. Natufians used flint-bladed sickles to cut the ripe seed heads of wild relatives of modern wheat and barley. In time such systematic gatherers began actually sowing seeds, selecting the strains of wheat or barley that proved easiest to harvest. Selective breeding of this kind was to transform small wild seeds, fruits, roots, and leaves into the big domesticated kinds we eat today.

From seed head to flour

Diagrams, below, show how early farmers processed ripe wheat.

1 *Cutting spikes (ears) of wheat with a sickle. Only tough spikes stayed intact and were easily harvested.*

2 *Threshing: beating spikes to break them up into spikelets*

3 *Winnowing: tossing spikelets to let the wind blow away unwanted pieces of straw*

4 *Pounding spikelets to free grains of wheat from protective husks. More winnowing separated grain from husks. The grain could be boiled to make porridge, or ground into flour and baked to make bread.*

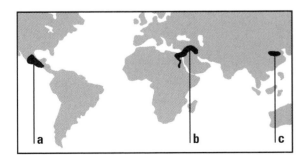

Cradles of cultivation

This world map shows three major regions where early farming emerged.

a *Mesoamerica (maize, beans, squash, peppers)*

b *Fertile Crescent (wheat, barley, peas, lentils)*

c *China (rice, millet, soybeans, tea)*

Living larders

Much as food gathering led to farming, so hunting led to the domestication of animals. Again Southwest Asia formed a major nucleus. By 13,000 years ago, dogs descended from tamed wolves were probably assisting Southwest Asian hunters to drive herds and flocks of wild hoofed mammals into ravines for slaughter. By 8,500 years ago, some hunters had turned pastoralists: keeping sheep, goats, or cattle as "living larders and walking wardrobes." Each group conveniently fed on plants indigestible to humans: goats browsed on trees and shrubs, sheep grazed hillside grasses, and cattle thrived on lush valley pastures. Meanwhile pigs domesticated from wild boar emerged as useful village scavengers.

Selective breeding of all these produced docile creatures with shorter horns or tusks than their wild ancestors and higher yields of meat, milk, or wool. Evidence of this comes indirectly from old barnyard bones.

By 5,000 years ago, tame cattle, camels, donkeys, horses, and (in South America) llamas were shifting loads to transform travel overland.

An ancient harness? (above)

Ropelike features on this carved horse's head from southwest France hint that Paleolithic hunters rode tamed horses 14,000 years ago.

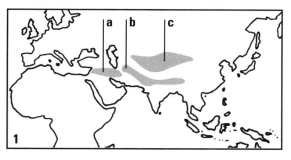

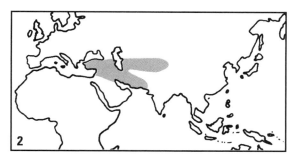

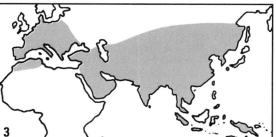

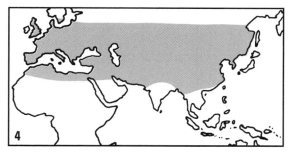

Where they lived

Four maps give distributions of wild mammals ancestral to domesticated species. All but the aurochs still largely occupy these zones today.

1 Ovis, *sheep. Only (**a**) and (**b**) made much contribution to modern breeds.*

a Ovis orientalis, *the West Asian mouflon*

b Ovis vignei, *the urial*

c Ovis ammon, *the argali*

2 Capra aegagrus, *a wild goat known as the bezoar or pasang*

3 Sus scrofa, *the wild boar*

4 Bos primigenius, *the aurochs, an extinct wild ox. The map shows its distribution in the Pleistocene.*

Before the barnyard

Here are brief details of the wild ancestors of four food animals now found worldwide:

1 Ovis orientalis, a wild sheep, has longer horns, hair, and limbs than domesticated sheep. Domestication date: about 11,000 years ago. Place: probably Turkey, Iraq, or Iran.

2 Capra aegagrus, a wild goat, has horns that curve straight back without the spiral twist seen in domesticated goats. Domestication date: about 10,000 years ago. Place: probably Iran.

3 Bos primigenius, the aurochs, was larger, longer, longer-horned, and fiercer than early domesticated cattle. Domestication date: about 8,500 years ago. Place: probably Turkey.

4 Sus scrofa, the wild boar, has a longer snout and denser coat of bristles than domesticated pigs. Domestication date: about 9,000 years ago. Place: perhaps Turkey.

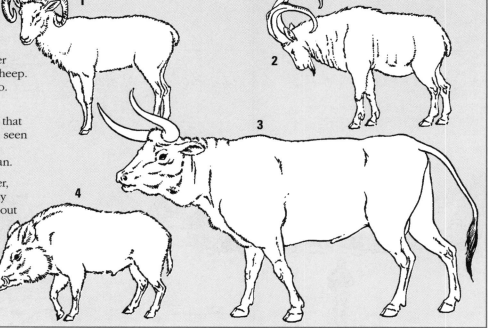

Homes, tombs, and temples

Old World Neolithic cultures never matched the splendid wall art of the Late Old Stone Age, although they did yield figurines and highly decorated pottery. Perhaps their creators' greatest triumphs lay in building in more ways, and more splendidly, than anyone before.

Craftspeople erected villages and towns from locally available materials. Thus Jericho in modern Jordan had mud-brick homes with plaster floors and walls, protected by an outer wall of stones. Mud walled houses served in dry Southeast Europe and Southwest Asia, but timber figured heavily in rainy western Europe. Here, homes had wooden posts and ridge poles supporting sloping roofs that shed rain from eaves jutting over woven wattle walls waterproofed by clay or dung. In Switzerland, wooden stilts protected lakeside dwellings against the risk of flooding. Stone walls roofed with driftwood, skins, and turf formed Skara Brae, a Neolithic village in the windswept Orkney Islands.

The most impressive Neolithic structures served religious functions. More than 8,000 years ago, dozens of shrines stood in the early town of Çatal Hüyük, in what is now Turkey. By 6,000 years ago, rock-cut tombs appeared in Italy and Malta, where Neolithic temple tombs featured huge blocks of stone called megaliths. By 5,000 years ago, megalith builders in the British Isles and Brittany were independently at work on chambered tombs now termed gallery and passage graves.

As the Neolithic merged into the pre-bronze Copper Age, large communities devoted millions of hours of labor to erecting rows and rings of standing stones respectively at sites like Carnac in Brittany and Stonehenge in southern England. Such stone alignments show some knowledge of astronomy.

By 2,700 BC in southern England, communal burial in long barrows (mounds) was giving way to single burials in round barrows. Gold and other rich grave goods hint at the high status of some occupants, perhaps paramount chiefs powerful enough to organize construction of the local monuments. Society was growing stratified.

An early shrine (below)

Bull images and sculptures figure strongly in this shrine discovered during James Mellaart's excavations at the early Turkish town of Çatal Hüyük. Perhaps Neolithic people worshiped bulls as symbols of virility and strength.

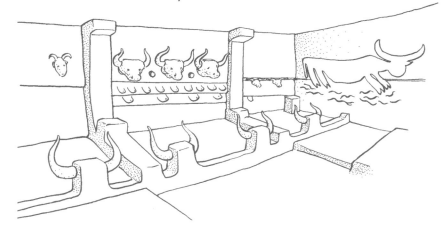

Megalith builders (right)

Bars show when people raised different megalithic building types at various localities in Europe.

1 Temple complexes

2 Passage graves

3 Gallery graves

4 Stone circles

5 Stone alignments

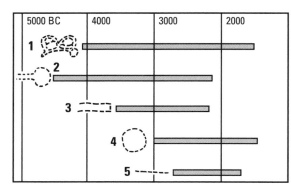

A Neolithic village

Excavated posts and postholes enabled artists to reconstruct this Neolithic lakeside village, found in southwest Germany.

A A plan view shows how huts were grouped and aligned.

B Seen from the lake, the huts appeared like this. Wooden frameworks produced quite sturdy structures.

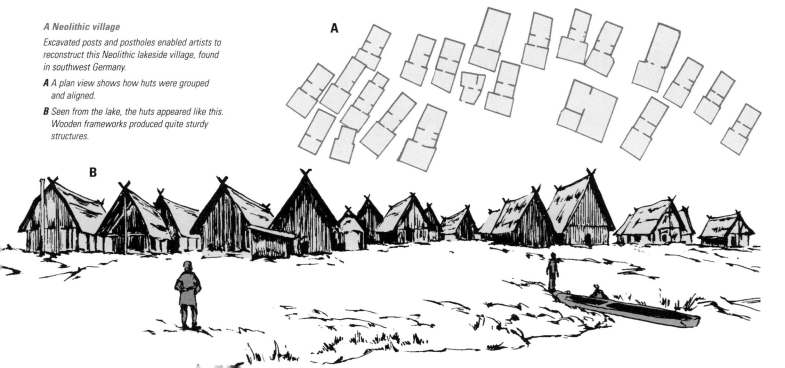

From stone to metal

For more than 2 million years, chipped stone provided the hardest, sharpest tools and weapons, but in the last few thousand years, metal has transformed technology. Like farming, metallurgy evidently arose independently at different times in different parts of Europe, Asia, and the Americas.

About 9,000 years ago, people in southeast Turkey began cold-hammering pure copper into pins, beads, and borers. Copper is tougher and less brittle than stone, and can be more readily reshaped or resharpened, but pure copper is much scarcer than its ore–the metal chemically joined to various impurities. True metallurgy started only about 6,600 years ago when Southeast European and Southwest Asian smiths began extracting copper from its ore by smelting.

Furnaces for smelting probably evolved from potters' kilns heated to 1,470 °F (800 °C)–hot enough for melting copper. Metalsmiths learned to pour molten copper into stone molds. By 5,000 years ago, they were mixing one part tin to nine parts copper to produce the alloy bronze, easier to cast than copper and yielding harder tools and weapons.

By about 1500 BC the Hittites in Turkey had begun producing iron–far more plentiful than copper, but more difficult to smelt. Hittite furnaces did not reach 2,880 °F (1,535 °C)–the melting point of iron. So the product was a "bloom"–a solid mass of iron and slag. Smiths hammered this red hot to separate the slag, added charcoal to the iron to harden it, beat the hot iron into shape as tools or weapons, and made these harder still by quenching them in water.

Forging stayed the only way of shaping iron until high-temperature Chinese furnaces began producing cast-iron objects about 2,500 years ago. By then, Iron Age cultures had succeeded Bronze Age cultures in much of Europe, Asia, and North Africa. In all three, mass-produced iron tools and weapons were promoting farming, war, and trade, and deforesting the land. Elsewhere metals had made less impact. sub-Saharan Africa was passing straight from stone to iron, and Pre-Columbian America never got beyond a Bronze Age level.

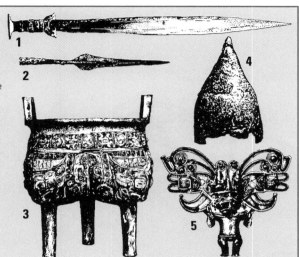

Metal masterpieces

Five products, shown here not to scale, represent the fine craftsmanship of ancient metalworkers.

1 *Two-edged sword from Bronze Age Europe*

2 *Broad-bladed Austrian dagger of the sixth century BC*

3 *Bronze tripod cooking vessel from China's Shang Dynasty (1600–1100 BC)*

4 *Conical Assyrian iron helmet of the eighth century BC*

5 *Tairona cast-gold figure of a god–actual height 5.25 in (13 cm)–from AD 13th century Colombia*

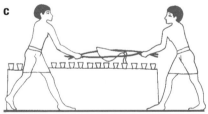

Bronze casting (left)

Scenes from ancient Egypt:

a *Tending a charcoal fire*

b *Lifting a crucible of molten bronze from the fire*

c *Pouring molten bronze into a mold to make a big bronze door*

Realms of gold (below)

Pre-Columbian metallurgy stressed gold ornaments. Here are selected gold-working centers and peoples.

1 Aztec	**4** Veraguas	**7** Chimú
2 Mixtec	**5** Tairona	**8** Mochica
3 Maya	**6** Muisca	**9** Inca

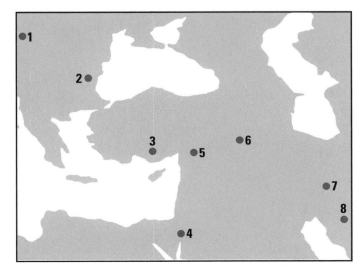

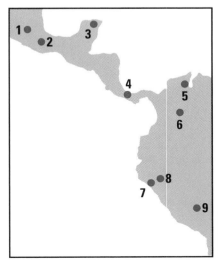

Early metalworking (left)

This map shows selected early sites with evidence of metalworking. Most lay in ore-rich mountain ranges. Despite some very early Southwest Asian dates for hammered copper, southeast Europe perhaps discovered smelting independently.

1 *Tiszapolgar, 4500 BC*

2 *Gulmenitsa, 4400 BC*

3 *Çatal Hüyük, 6000 BC*

4 *Timna, 4000 BC*

5 *Cayönü Tepesi, 7200 BC*

6 *Shanidar, 9500 BC*

7 *Tepe Sialk, 5000 BC*

8 *Tal-I-Iblis, 4000 BC*

© DIAGRAM

The rise of cities

Early empire builder (right)

Sargon of Akkad is probably the subject of this fine bronze head, sculpted more than 4,000 years ago. Under Sargon, Akkadians imposed Semitic-speaking rulers on their Sumerian neighbors to the south.

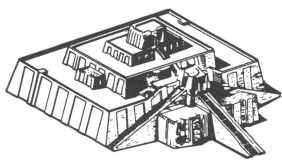

The Ur ziggurat (above)

This stepped temple pyramid dominated the Sumerian city of Ur 4,000 years ago. Organized mass labor must have made and raised millions of bricks to build such human-made "mountains."

City planning (right)

An excavated grid of streets and buildings in Mohenjo-daro suggests that town planners laid out Indus Valley cities more than 4,000 years ago.

By 5,000 years ago, food production and metallurgy had helped some towns expand into the world's first cities. Civilization–our city-oriented way of life–first emerged with the Bronze Age Sumerians of Mesopotamia–the land between the Tigris and Euphrates Rivers in what is now Iraq. Later, early cities sprang up in Egypt's Nile Valley, Pakistan's Indus Valley, by China's Yellow River, and in favored regions of Peru and Mexico.

In all these places, irrigation of rich soils helped farmers produce enough spare food to feed big urban concentrations of full-time non-food-producing specialists. Potters, carpenters, metalworkers, jewelers, scribes, merchants, and others exchanged manufactured goods or services for food produced by local farmers; for raw materials like stone, wood, bitumen; and for metals imported from much greater distances. With such economic change, societies evolved from tribal bands via chiefdoms into states with layered social classes. Kings or priests controlled most wealth and power and ruled through bureaucrats who evidently organized irrigation, taxation, and communal food storage.

New, imposing building types reflect this social structure. Dominating early Mesopotamian cities were ziggurats–huge, stepped, brick pyramids crowned by temples. Temple administrators with knowledge of writing, mathematics, and astronomy seemingly used calendars to tell farmers when to sow, measured fields, and gathered and stored taxes in the form of grain. By 3000 BC, the building of large palaces suggests a shift of power from priests to kings who ruled small city-states. High walls defended their cities' goods from raiding nomads and rival city-states.

In time, wars between rival city-states fused some into the first small nations. By 2279 BC, the ambitious Akkadian ruler Sargon had conquered lands from Turkey to the Persian Gulf to forge what might be called the world's first empire.

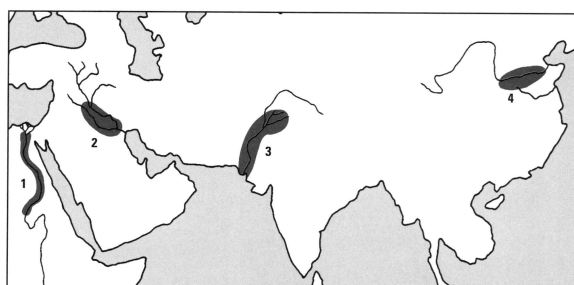

Cradles of civilization

A map shows where city life began in four great Old World river valleys.

1 *Nile Valley*

2 *Mesopotamia*

3 *Indus Valley*

4 *Yellow River valley*

Bronze Age toolkits

The transformation of some Old World Neolithic towns into the world's first Bronze Age cities owed much to several inventions and discoveries.

Bronze itself provided points for spears and arrows but remained too scarce and costly to replace stone farm implements.

The enlarged food surplus that fed Sumerian city populations owed more to oxen, plows, and irrigation. An ox harnessed to a wooden plow tilled far more land each day than a farmer with a hoe. Cattle were plowing fields by 6,000 years ago. Ox power quite likely also helped construct irrigation ditches and canals and raise water to the fields. Warm, fertile, irrigated soil yielded several heavy crops each year.

Another major innovation was the wheel. At Ubaid in Mesopotamia craftspeople were turning pottery on revolving disks 7,000 years ago. By 5,800 years ago, Sumerians evolved a fast-revolving spinning wheel. By 5,500 years ago, wheeled carts began transforming land transportation.

By 5,000 years ago, water travel, too, was being revolutionized. Now, sailing ships were shifting heavy loads up rivers. By putting wind and animals to work, people had begun to tap far greater energy resources than human muscle power.

Meanwhile writing revolutionized communication. By 5,000 years ago, Sumerians used reed pens to draw picture signs called pictograms on soft clay tablets that became durable when dried and hardened. Later, scribes reduced the 2,000 pictograms to fewer phonograms—word/sound symbols based on pictograms. Abbreviation then converted these into a written script that reproduced the spoken language. Scribes used their Sumerian cuneiform (wedge-shaped) script to record law codes, calendars, taxes, and significant events.

Written records meant that new discoveries in science, mathematics, and astronomy could be set down accurately for posterity. Writing thus boosted cultural evolution. And where written records of events began, prehistory ended.

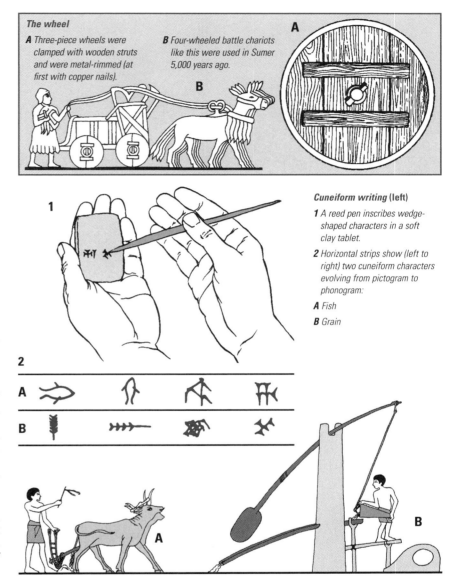

The wheel

A Three-piece wheels were clamped with wooden struts and were metal-rimmed (at first with copper nails).

B Four-wheeled battle chariots like this were used in Sumer 5,000 years ago.

Cuneiform writing (left)

1 A reed pen inscribes wedge-shaped characters in a soft clay tablet.

2 Horizontal strips show (left to right) two cuneiform characters evolving from pictogram to phonogram:

A Fish

B Grain

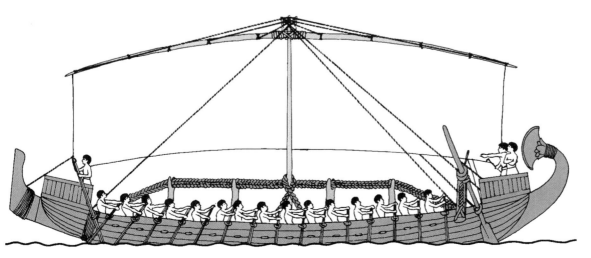

Tending the soil (above)

We show two farming innovations as pictured by artists in Bronze Age Egypt.

A Plowing with a team of oxen

B Irrigating fields with water by shaduf—a device with a vessel dipped in water that is raised by counterbalanced pole, then poured via trough onto the land.

Sea travel (left)

Big wooden merchant ships like this could be propelled by sail, or oars, or both. By 3,500 years ago, such seaworthy Egyptian crafts had sailed south down the Red Sea to the land of Punt (Somalia).

© DIAGRAM

Developments in North America

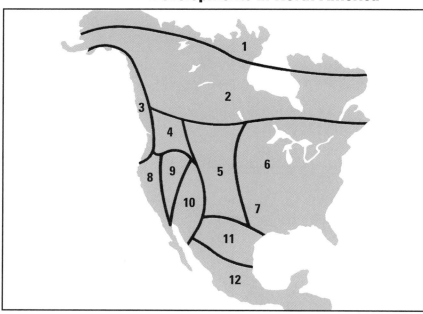

Sea or desert barriers isolated the emergent civilizations of Eurasia from Australia, sub-Saharan Africa, and the Americas. Yet these lands saw cultural advances, too—especially the Americas. The next two pages summarize trends in Pre-Columbian North and South America.

North of Mexico, by 5000 BC, Indians were still big-game hunting on the Great Plains, but sea and river fishing featured strongly in the Northwest. The Eastern Woodlands economy stressed hunting, fishing, and gathering. The Southwest's desert tradition involved seed gathering and small-game trapping. These patterns persisted, but by the early centuries AD, agriculture, pottery, plant-fiber textiles, burial mounds, and ceremonial centers spread north from Mexico to influence the Southwest's Anasazi and Hohokam cultures and the Ohio basin's Adena and Hopewell cultures. After AD 700, the Hopewell gave way to the Mississippi culture, with sizable maize-based communities in the Eastern Woodlands zone.

Where they lived

This map shows cultural areas established in North America by AD 1500.

1 *Arctic: Inuit (Eskimo) hunters*

2 *Sub-Arctic: hunters*

3 *Northwest coast: fishers and hunters*

4 *Interior plateau: fishers and hunter-gatherers*

5 *Great Plains: bison hunters and farmers*

6 *Eastern Woodlands: hunter-fisher-gatherers, and farmers*

7 *Ohio and Mississippi Valleys: farmers*

8 *California: hunters, fishers, and gatherers*

9 *Great Basin: desert gatherers*

10 *Southwest: farmers and gatherers*

11 *Southwest deserts: gatherers*

12 *Mesoamerica: farmers and town and city dwellers*

North American artifacts

These decorative objects represent six local cultural traditions:

1 Storage jar of Arizona's Hohokam culture (about 300 BC–AD 1400), noted for irrigation canals.

2 Textile of the Ohio-centered Hopewell culture (about 200 BC–AD 700), renowned for carved stone pipes, copperwork, and ceremonial earth mounds.

3 Travois: Paired, dog-hauled poles like these moved loads for the tepee-dwelling Great Plains bison hunters.

4 Spoon handle: This stylized Tlingit "beaver" represents the elaborately carved woodwork produced by northwest coast Indians.

5 Birchbark box: Eastern Woodlands Indians used bark for boxes, roofing, and canoes.

6 Ivory head: The Inuit of Arctic North America were carving walrus ivory 2,000 years ago.

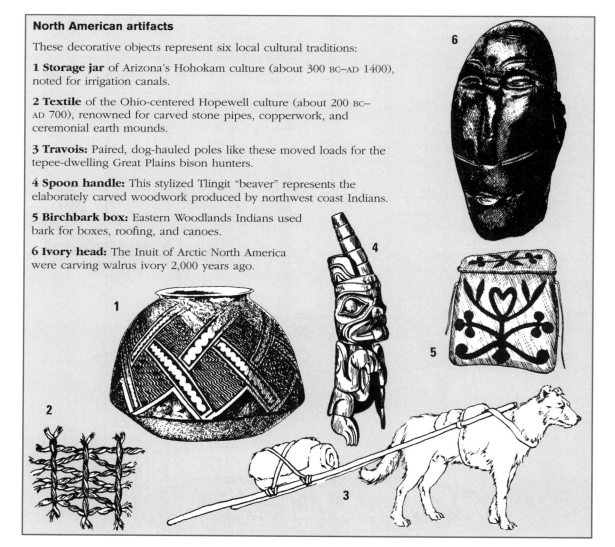

Mesoamerica and South America

North of Mexico, farming villages and towns remained the largest settlements until the Europeans came, but farther south Indians built cities, states, and empires based on agriculture, trade, and conquest. This happened in two regions: Mesoamerica (Mexico through Honduras) and in and near the Central Andes Mountains. Independently of early Old World centers, these areas developed social classes with monarchs, priests, soldiers, artisans, and peasants. Independently, they made fine pottery, sculpture, and painting, discovered bronze technology, and raised pyramids and platform mounds of brick or stone. Mesoamericans even devised pictographic writing. Yet American Indians never mastered iron technology or used the wheel, except for toys.

Centers of civilization

Five major areas of Pre-Columbian civilization figure in this map.

a *Classic and Postclassic Mexican*

b *Olmec*

c *Classic Maya*

d *Postclassic Maya*

e *Inca Empire at its height*

Southern cultures

Numbered illustrations represent major stages of cultural development after 2000 BC:

1 Carved head, a monolith 8 ft (2.4 m) high, produced by the Olmec (1300–400 BC) of the Gulf Coast, Mexico, the likely founders of Mesoamerican culture.

2 Maize god from a Mayan religious book. Mayas built great ceremonial lowland centers in Mesoamerica's Classic epoch (about AD 300–900).

3 Obsidian knife used to kill sacrificial victims by the Aztecs. Their Mexican empire climaxed Mesoamerica's Postclassic epoch (AD 900–1520).

4 Stone puma of the Andes-centered Chavín (900–200 BC), the first highly developed culture in Peru.

5 Portrait vase of the Mochica, a rich, north coast culture of Peru's early intermediate period (200 BC–AD 600).

6 Gold mask made by the Chimú of Peru. Their coastal state (about AD 1300–1465) had fine metalwork, irrigation canals, and a huge capital: Chan Chan.

7 Gold llama made by craftspeople of the Andes-based Inca Empire, which briefly dominated 2,000 miles (3,200 km) of western South America before Spanish conquerors arrived in AD 1532.

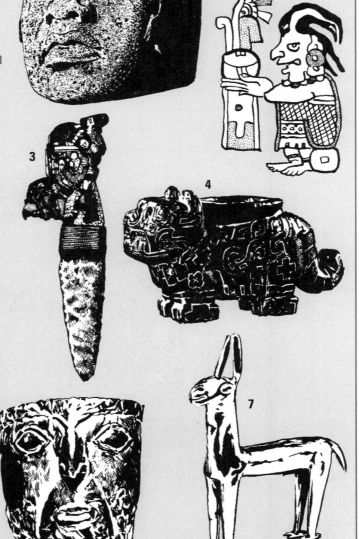

© DIAGRAM

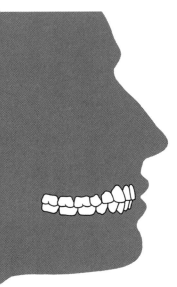

Food and physique

The previous chapter ended by showing how climate helped local racial groups evolve. In and since the Ice Age, food and its preparation have also affected body form and size.

At least some populations with unreliable or inadequate supplies of food are shorter or more slightly built than groups who always get enough to eat. Genetically tiny peoples include the Central African Negrillos and the Negritos found as scattered, mainly island, groups in Southeast Asia and New Guinea. Collectively called pygmies, all were once supposed to be descendants of a single group. Some may be of shared ancestry, while others are hunter-foragers derived from local stocks of normal height but dwarfed by long dependence on uncertain food supplies–tiny people can survive on less food than tall people.

From Egypt east to China, overpopulation has produced huge populations of normal height but very slender build. Arguably long dependence on inadequate subsistence crops has fashioned individuals big enough to produce food for their families but not so big that they must consume more food than they can grow, or so small that they cannot do the necessary work.

Improved diets increase stature in groups where this is not genetically curbed. One 1960s study showed that children of Italian immigrants to the US tended to outgrow their parents.

Cooking and tool use have transformed the human face. Eating soft, cooked foods and using tools for tasks once done by teeth have reduced most facial structures, whose major role is the support of chewing apparatus. Teeth have "shrunk," especially in populations with a long history of using cooking pots. The smallest teeth occur in Europe, the Middle East, and China–the largest among Australian Aborigines. Since Bronze Age times, lower jaws have tended to retreat until top teeth overlap bottom teeth and edge-to-edge bite has given way to overbite.

Since late Paleolithic times, increased use of tools and machines has generally reduced the need for powerful muscles and strong bones. Accordingly, skeletons have tended to become less robust.

Overbite (above)

A view inside a modern human's mouth shows upper teeth overlapping lower teeth. Jaw reduction, responsible for this phenomenon, can cause overcrowding and the failure of some people's wisdom teeth (back molars) to erupt at all.

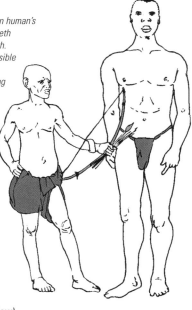

Two Africans

A Negrillo is shown here beside an African of normal stature. Natural selection dwarfed certain groups of hunter-gatherers, probably by weeding out individuals too big to survive food shortages.

Tooth size (below)

A map of four continents shows the distribution of tooth size before European influence affected population characters. The largest teeth occurred among some peoples used to eating tough foods raw.

- Small teeth
- Medium teeth
- Large teeth
- Very large teeth

Where they live (below)

This map shows the distribution of the world's pygmies.

1 *Congo (Zaire) Basin*

2 *Kerala State, India*

3 *Sri Lanka*

4 *Andaman Islands*

5 *Malay Peninsula*

6 *Palawan*

7 *Luzon*

8 *Mindanao*

9 *Sumbawa*

10 *Timor*

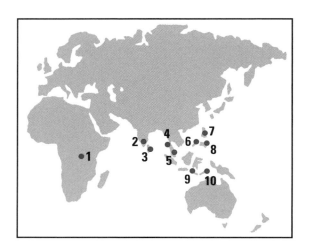

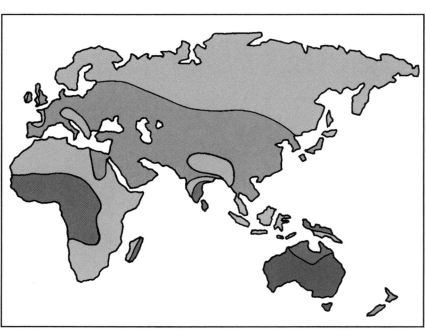

Population growth

Three million years ago the world held probably a few tens of thousands of hominids ancestral to ourselves. By AD 2000, 6 billion people inhabited the Earth. Yet numbers had risen slowly through most of prehistoric time. Growth came in stages as our ancestors evolved, colonized new lands, and stepped up their food supply.

One calculation suggests that 2 million years ago, 1 million herbivorous australopithecines occupied a few habitats in just one continent.

By 500,000 years ago, hunter-gatherers of the genus *Homo* roamed a variety of landscapes in Africa and much of Eurasia, but a given tract of land feeds even fewer hunter-gatherers than herbivores. So some people think the world held only 1.7 million prehistoric humans then.

By 10,000 years ago, *Homo sapiens* had colonized all continents and climates except Antarctica. Yet most people were still nomadic hunter-gatherers unable to control their food supply. The world held 10 million at most.

Population began rocketing only about 7,000 years or so ago, as cultivated crops enlarged the food supply, and people lived who would have starved to death before. New tools and know-how outlined in this chapter further boosted food supply and human numbers. By 500 BC (some say 2500 BC), these passed the 100 million mark. Later, a global interchange of food plants and animals, industrial technology, and scientific medicine sent the population soaring faster still. By AD 2050, 10 billion individuals could be rubbing shoulders on this overcrowded planet.

Food, land, and people

Three squares show amounts of land needed to feed three individuals obtaining food in different ways.

1 Hunter-gatherer: 3.86 sq mi (10 sq km)

2 Dry farmer: 0.19 sq mi (0.5 sq km)

3 Irrigation farmer: 0.04 sq mi (0.1 sq km)

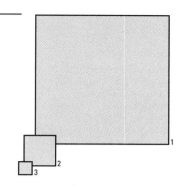

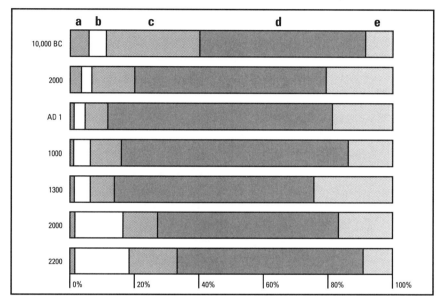

Continental populations (above)

Subdivided bars show estimated continental shares of the world's population at seven dates beginning in 10,000 BC.

a Oceania (including Australia)

b Americas (two continents)

c Africa

d Asia

e Europe

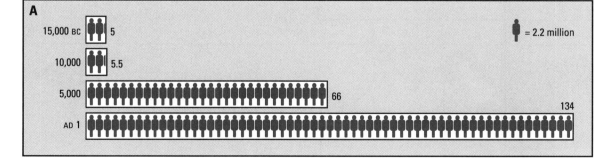

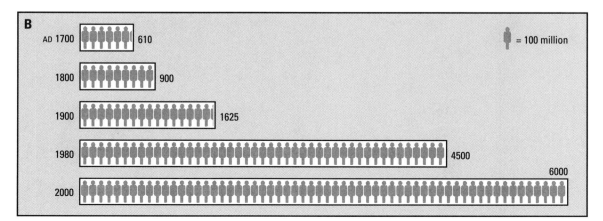

World population (left)

Two bar diagrams show world population growth as estimated for the following periods:

A 15,000 BC to AD 1

B AD 1700 to AD 2000 (Vertical figures relate to time, horizontal population figures are given in millions.)

© DIAGRAM

The future of humankind

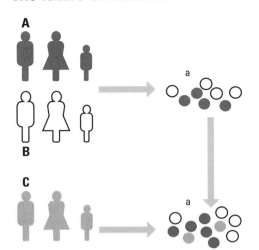

Racial mixing (right)

Interbreeding between racial groups (**A**, **B**, **C**) increases the variety of genes (**a**) in a population. Genes inherited by individuals dictate their characteristics. Thus race crossing can theoretically produce blond blacks or red-haired Chinese.

Migrations (below)

This world map shows major recent migrations from Europe (**A**), Africa (**B**), and Asia (**C**). Migrants interbreeding with each other and with native peoples produce racial mixing.

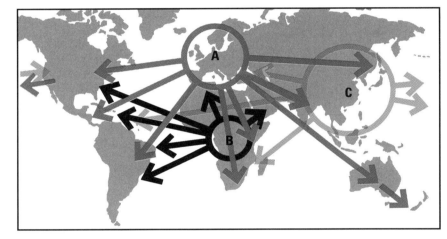

From a vulnerable group of primates, evolution produced our teeming species with its unique ability to multiply, migrate, and mold our planet.

Will humankind continue to evolve? The present answer must be "no." Cultural evolution has buffered us against biological pressures that weeded out the feeble, slow, or stupid. Now, power tools, computers, clothes, spectacles, and modern medicine devalue the old, inherited advantages of powerful physique, intelligence, pigmentation, visual acuity, and resistance to diseases like malaria. Societies hold high percentages of physically weak or ill-proportioned people, and people with poor eyesight or skin color and disease resistance unrelated to the climates where they live. Some individuals who would have died in infancy a century ago survive to breed, handing on genetic faults to future generations.

Migration, too, has helped halt human evolution. No group lives isolated long enough to evolve into a new species as happened in the Pleistocene. And racial differences will decline with increased interbreeding of peoples from Europe, Africa, the Americas, India, and China.

In fact extinction seems likelier than further evolution. Soaring populations depend on rising food and energy production, but both encourage overexploitation of our planet. Overusing soil brings soil erosion, reducing Earth's capacity for yielding food, and fossil-fuel depletion threatens energy supplies. Both problems could worsen with climatic change. Overcrowded, underfed, and underfueled, *Homo sapiens* might fizzle out in famine, war, and pestilence.

Most species last under 3 million years. Our own—the most intelligent—will need all its ingenuity to manage half as long as that.

Vanishing hunters (right)

A world map shows how hunter-gatherer societies have dwindled. Disappearance of their lifestyle marks an end to selective pressures that helped our species evolve. Tinted areas were still occupied by hunter-gatherers 200 years ago. Dots show surviving hunter-gatherers in recent decades:

1 *Warau Indians*

2 *Shiriana Indians*

3 *Bororo Indians*

4 *Negrillos*

5 *Hadza*

6 *Khoisan*

7 *Birhor*

8 *Sakai*

9 *Semang*

10 *Punan*

11 *Tasaday*

12 *Australian Aborigines*

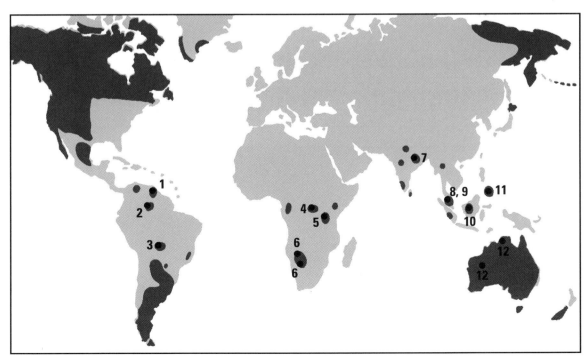

Tomorrow's world

Short- and long-term changes—some brought about by humankind—will drastically affect our planet's atmosphere, continents, and oceans.

By releasing chlorofluorocarbon sprays, we depleted the atmosphere's ozone and let in lethal quantities of ultraviolet radiation. By burning fossil fuels and felling forests, we are warming the atmosphere, shifting climatic zones and spreading deserts. In a few thousand years, variations in the Earth's tilt and distance from the Sun will cool the atmosphere, enlarging ice sheets and lowering the oceans. Later, continental drift will let warm ocean currents into polar regions. Then melting ice sheets may drown lowland but cause a rebound of ice-laden Greenland and Antarctica.

Meanwhile, seafloor spreading and subduction will see oceans grow and shrink. In 30 million years, the Atlantic will be much wider, while the Pacific will have narrowed.

Dramatic changes will affect the land. Already human overuse of soil accelerates erosion and the accumulation of sediments in offshore waters. Longer term, mountains will be worn to stubs, while new ones rise as continents collide.

As Africa heads north, Europe's Alps may grow afresh, and the Rhine fault might split the continent. Iberia could be shoved into the Atlantic. The west Mediterranean may become a landlocked lake while squeezing destroys its east end and plants a mountain range from southeast Italy to Syria. Volcanic islands could appear offshore from Portugal to Norway.

Elsewhere, the Himalayas are still growing. In 15 million years, Australia might override Indonesia. In 25 million years, a north-south sea might split Africa in two. In 50 million years, Los Angeles could be rafted north to join Alaska.

Billions of years will bring many more dramatic changes. A thinned asthenosphere may give the Earth a rigid crust. Because our planet's spin is slowing down, each Earth day could be longer than 50 of today's days. The Moon will move away and hover over the same part of the Earth's surface, producing a fixed high tide. Eventually the Sun will swell up and engulf the Earth. Later still, our solar system may fall into a dense black hole in the middle of our galaxy.

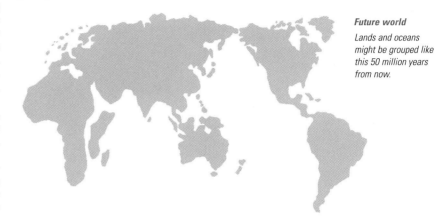

Future world

Lands and oceans might be grouped like this 50 million years from now.

Sun, Earth, and ice

Changes in Earth's tilt and seasonal nearness to the Sun arguably produce ice ages.

A Earth far from the Sun in northern summer with Northern Hemisphere tilted slightly sunward—northern ice sheets will grow.

B Earth close to the Sun in northern summer with Northern Hemisphere tilted far sunward—northern ice sheets will melt.

a Earth in winter

b Earth in summer

c Sun

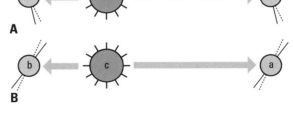

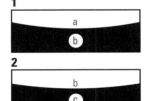

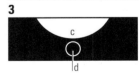

Black hole

Above: Diagrams stress the small size of a black hole.

1 Our Sun (*a*) compared to a white dwarf star (*b*)

2 White dwarf (*b*) compared to a neutron star (*c*)

3 Neutron star (*c*) compared to a black hole (*d*)

Left: A tiny but massive black hole (*a*) may distort the space time fabric (*b*), creating an intense gravitational field that locks in electromagnetic radiation (*c*) and sucks in stars (*d*).

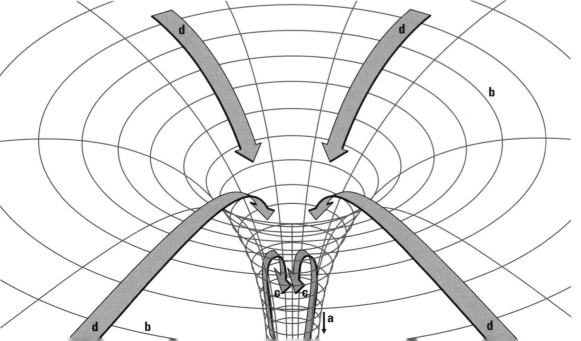

© DIAGRAM

Further reference

The following eight pages supplement this book's four major sections. Included for each section are selected books for further reading; selected websites with links to more on the same topic; an alphabetical list of museums worldwide; and brief biographies of people whose work has made significant contributions to our understanding of prehistory. Please note that many museums listed under one section may include exhibits relevant to one or more of the others.

These items are drawn from vast fields of study, frequently enriched by new insights. Readers wishing to keep abreast of fresh theories and discoveries should consult science magazines such as *Nature*, *New Scientist*, *Science*, and *Scientific American* and the online science news websites posted at naturalSCIENCE:
http://naturalscience.com/ns/nshome.html

SECTION 1: The Evolving Earth

Selected books:

Chesterman, C. W. *National Audubon Society Field Guide to North American Rocks and Minerals*. New York: Random House, 1979.

Lamb, S. and Singington, D. *Earth Story: The Shaping of Our World*. Princeton, N.J.: Princeton University Press, 1998.

Prothero, D. R. and Schwab, F. L. *Sedimentary Geology: An Introduction to Sedimentary Rocks and Stratigraphy*. New York: Freeman, 1998.

Redfern, R. *Origins: The Evolution of Continents, Oceans, and Life*. Norman: University of Oklahoma Press, 2001

Redfern, R. *The Making of a Continent*. New York: Times Books, 1983.

Ritchie, D. and Gates, A. E. *Encyclopedia of Earthquakes and Volcanoes*, New Edition. New York: Facts On File, 2001.

Stanley, S. M. *Earth and Life Through Time*. New York: Freeman, 1986.

Strahler, A. and Strahler, A. N. *Introducing Physical Geography: Updated and Upgraded*. New York: Wiley, 1999.

Vernon, R. H. *Beneath Our Feet: The Rocks of Planet Earth*. Cambridge, Eng.: Cambridge University Press, 2001.

Windley, B. F. *The Evolving Continents*. New York: Wiley, 1995.

Selected websites:

Mineral Museum WebSites: http://www.nhm.org~smmp/sites.htm

University of California–Berkeley, Library Earth Science & Map Library Internet Resources: http://www.minerals.net/mineral/index.htm

Selected worldwide museums

ARGENTINA
Buenos Aires: Museum of Mineralogy and Geology

AUSTRALIA
Ballarat, Victoria: Gold Museum
Coober Pedy, South Australia: Umoona Opal Mine Museum
Kalgoorlie, Western Australia: Hainault Tourist Gold Mine
Melbourne: Melbourne Museum
Sydney: Geological and Mining Museum

AUSTRIA
Hallstatt: Prehistoric Museum
Innsbruck: Zeughaus Tirol Folk Museum
Klagenfurt: Mining Museum
Vienna: Natural History Museum

BELGIUM
Antwerp: Provincial Diamond Museum
Brussels: Museum of Natural Sciences
Liège: Museum of Iron and Coal
Tournai: Museum of Paleontology and Prehistory

BOLIVIA
La Paz: Mineralogical Museum

BRAZIL
Rio de Janeiro: Museum of Geology and Mineralogy

CANADA
Dawson City, Yukon: Dawson City Museum
Edmonton, Alberta: Museum of Geology
Knighton, Ontario: Geological Sciences Museum
Saskatoon, Saskatchewan: Geological Museum
Vancouver: M.Y.Williams Geological Museum

COLOMBIA
Bogotá: Museum of Minerals; National Geological Museum

CZECH REPUBLIC
Prague: National Museum

DENMARK
Copenhagen: Geological Museum

ECUADOR
Quito: Petrographic Museum

EGYPT
Cairo: Geology Museum

FRANCE
Paris: Mineralogy Museum of the Paris School of Mines
Vernet les Bains: Geological Museum

GERMANY
Aalen: Old World Museum of Geology & Paleontology
Berlin: Natural History Museum
Bonn: Mineralogical Museum
Munich: Museum for Paleontology and Geology
Tübingen: Mineralogical Exhibit & Teaching Collection

GHANA
Legon: Museum of the Department of Geology

GREECE
Athens: Museum of Mineralogy and Petrology

GUINEA
Conakry: Conakry Geological Museum

INDIA
Lucknow: Geological Museum

INDONESIA
Bandung: Geological Museum

IRELAND
Dublin: Geological Museum, Trinity College

ITALY
Catania: Geological Museum
Naples: Museum of Mineralogy and Zoology
Rome: Museum of the Institute of Mineralogy

JAPAN
Akita: Mineral Industry Museum
Tokyo: Natural Science Museum
Tsukuba Science City: Geological Museum

MALAYSIA
Ipoh: Geological Survey Museum

MEXICO
Mexico City: Museum of Geology

NETHERLANDS
Amsterdam: Geological Museum of the University of Amsterdam
Leiden: National Museum for Geology and Mineralogy

NEW ZEALAND
Dunedin: Geology Museum of the University of Otago

NORWAY
Oslo: University Mineral-Geological Museum

PERU
Cuzco: Geological Museum

POLAND
Warsaw: Museum of Earth Sciences

PORTUGAL
Lisbon: Mineralogical and Geological Museum

SAUDI ARABIA
Riyadh: Geological Museum

SOUTH AFRICA
Johannesburg: Geological Museum

SPAIN
Madrid: National Geological Museum

SWEDEN
Stockholm: Swedish Museum of Natural History

SWITZERLAND
Zürich: ETH Geology-Mineralogy Collection and Exhibition

THAILAND
Bangkok: Mineralogy Museum

TURKEY
Ankara: Turkish Natural History Museum

UNITED KINGDOM
Birmingham: Lapworth Museum of Geology
Cardiff: National Museum & Gallery
Edinburgh: Cockburn Museum of Geology
London: Natural History Museum (Earth Galleries)
Oxford: Museum of Natural History
Manchester: Manchester Museum

UNITED STATES
Albany, New York: New York State Museum
Albuquerque, New Mexico: Geology Museum
Asheville, North Carolina: Colburn Gem and Mineral Museum
Athens, Georgia: University of Georgia Museum of Natural History
Berkeley, California: University of California Berkeley, Geology Museum
Blacksburg, Virginia: Virginia Polytechnic Institute of Natural History
Boise, Idaho: Museum of Mining and Geology
Bowling Green, Kentucky: Western Kentucky University Geology Department Hallway
Brunswick, Maine: Bowdoin College Geology Department Hallways
Bryn Mawr, Pennsylvania: Vaux Mineral Collection, Bryn Mawr College
Butte, Montana: Montana Tech Mineral Museum
Cambridge, Massachusetts: Harvard Mineralogical Museum
Carbondale, Illinois: Geology Department, Southern Illinois University
Carson City, Nevada: Nevada State Museum
Chicago, Illinois: Field Museum of Natural History
Cincinnati, Ohio: Cincinnati Museum of Natural History
Clemson, South Carolina: Clemson University Geology Museum
Cleveland, Ohio: Cleveland Museum of Natural History
Colorado Springs, Colorado: Western Museum of Mining & Industry
Columbia, South Carolina: McKissick Museum
Columbus, Ohio: Orton Geological Museum
DeLand, Florida: Gillespie Museum of Minerals
Denver, Colorado: Denver Museum of Natural History
Emporia, Kansas: Emporia State University Geology Museum
Fairbanks, Alaska: University of Alaska Museum
Fayetteville, Arkansas: University Museum
Franklin, New Jersey: Franklin Mineral Museum
Golden, Colorado: Geology Museum, Colorado School of Mines
Harrisonburg, Virginia: James Madison University Mineral Museum
Hillsboro, Oregon: Rice Northwest Museum of Rocks & Minerals
Houghton, Michigan: Seaman Mineral Museum
Houston, Texas: Houston Museum of Natural Science
Iowa City, Iowa: University of Iowa Museum of Natural History
Joplin, Missouri: Tri-State Mineral Museum
Knoxville, Tennessee: McClung Museum
Laramie, Wyoming: University of Wyoming Geological Museum
Lincoln, Nebraska: University of Nebraska State Museum
Los Angeles, California: Natural History Museum of Los Angeles County
Madison, Wisconsin: Geology Museum, University of Wisconsin
Marion, Kentucky: The Clement Mineral Museum
Mariposa, California: California State Mining and Mineral Museum
Media, Pennsylvania: Delaware County Institute of Science
Michigan: Cranbrook Institute of Science Mineral Hall
Milwaukee, Wisconsin: Milwaukee Public Museum
Newark, Delaware: University of Delaware Mineralogical Museum
New Brunswick, New Jersey: Rutgers University Geological Museum
New Haven, Connecticut: Peabody Museum of Natural History
New York City, New York: American Museum of Natural History: Rose Center for Earth and Space
Norman, Oklahoma: Oklahoma Museum of Natural History
Philadelphia, Pennsylvania: Academy of Natural Sciences
Phoenix, Arizona: Arizona Mining and Mineral Museum
Pittsburgh, Pennsylvania: Carnegie Museum of Natural History
Pocatello, Idaho: Idaho Museum of Natural History
Providence, Rhode Island: Museum of Natural History
Rapid City, South Dakota: Museum of Geology, South Dakota School of Mines and Technology
Reno, Nevada: W. M. Keck Museum, MacKay School of Mines, University of Nevada
Rock Island, Illinois: Fryxell Geology Museum
St. Johnsbury, Vermont: Fairbanks Museum
St. Paul, Minnesota: Science Museum of Minnesota
Salt Lake City, Utah: Utah Museum of Natural History
San Francisco, California: California Academy of Sciences
Seattle, Washington: Burke Museum of Natural History

Socorro, New Mexico: New Mexico Bureau of Mines Mineral Resources, Mineral Museum
Springfield, Massachusetts: Springfield Science Museum
State College, Pennsylvania: Penn State Earth & Mineral Sciences Museum
Trenton, New Jersey: New Jersey State Museum
Tucson, Arizona: University of Arizona Mineralogical Museum
Tuscaloosa, Alabama: Alabama Museum of Natural History
Washington, D.C.: National Museum of Natural History
White, Georgia: William Weinman Mineral Museum

Selected Earth scientists:
Alberti, Friedrich August von (1795–1878) German geologist who named the Triassic system.

Arduino, Giovanni (1714–95) Father of Italian geology who coined the name *Tertiary* later given to a rock system and geological period.

Beyrich, Heinrich Ernst (1815–96) German paleontologist who introduced the term *Oligocene.*

Brongniart, Alexandre (1770–1847) French geologist who coined the name *Jurassic ground* for rocks later put in the Jurassic system and period.

Conybeare, William Daniel (1787–1857) British geologist who, with William Phillips, in 1822 called certain strata *Carboniferous.*

Dana, James Dwight (1813–95) US scientist who classified minerals chemically and advanced studies of mountain building.

Davis, William Morris (1850–1934) US geographer and geologist; a founder of geomorphology (scientific landform studies).

Desnoyers, Jules French geologist who in 1829 separated Quaternary from Tertiary rocks.

Gilbert, Grove Karl (1843–1918) A US founder of landform studies. He coined the term *orogeny* for mountain building.

Hutton, James (1726–97) Scottish geologist who argued that forces still at work had caused geological change over a vast span of time.

Lapworth, Charles (1842–1920) British geologist who identified the Ordovician system.

Lyell, Sir Charles (1797–1875) British geologist who in the 1830s introduced the terms *Eocene, Miocene, Pliocene, Pleistocene,* and *Holocene* (Recent). Modern geology owes much to his writings.

Mohs, Friedrich (1773–1839) German mineralogist who devised the Mohs hardness scale for minerals.

Murchison, Sir Roderick Impey (1792–1871) British geologist who recognized the Silurian and Permian systems.

Omalius d'Halloy, Jean-Baptiste-Julien (1783–1875) Belgian geologist who produced systematic subdivisions of geological formations and gave Cretaceous rocks that name.

Patterson, Clair C. (Pat) (1922–95) US geochemist who determined the age of the Earth.

Phillips, John (1800–74) British geologist who named the Mesozoic and "Kainozoic" (Cenozoic) eras.

Schimper, Wilhelm Philipp (1808–88) German paleontologist who named the Paleocene epoch.

Sedgwick, Adam (1785–1873) British geologist who named the Paleozoic Era and the Cambrian and (with Murchison) Devonian systems.

Smith, William (1769–1839) So-called Father of English geology. He used fossils to identify sedimentary rock layers and produced the first geological map of England and Wales.

Stensen, Niels (1636–86) Danish geologist, the first to recognize that rock strata and fossils held clues to past changes in the Earth's crust.

Wegener, Alfred Lothar (1880–1930) German meteorologist who in 1912 announced the theory of moving continents later known as continental drift.

Williams, Henry Shaler (1847–1918) US paleontologist who in 1891 introduced the term *Pennsylvanian* for Upper Carboniferous rocks in North America.

Wilson, John Tuzo (1908–93) Canadian geophysicist who in the 1960s coined the term *plates* and contributed to plate tectonics theory.

Winchell, Alexander (1824–91) US geologist who in 1870 introduced the term *Mississippian* for Lower Carboniferous rocks in the Mississippi Valley.

SECTION 2: Evolving Life

Selected general books on paleontology:
Arduini, P. and Teruzzi, G. *Fossils*. Milton Keynes, Eng.: Fireside, 1987.

Benton, M. J. and Sibbick, J. (illustrator). *Vertebrate Palaeontology*. Boston: Blackwell Science, 2000.

Carroll, R. L. *Vertebrate Paleontology and Evolution*. New York: Freeman, 1988.

Fortey, R. *Life: A Natural History of the First Four Billion Years of Life on Earth*. New York: Vintage Books, 1997.

Gee, H. *In Search of Deep Time: Beyond the Fossil Record to a New History of Life*. New York: Free Press, 1999.

Gould, S. J. (general editor). *The Book of Life*. New York: Norton, 2001.

Norman, D. *Prehistoric Life: The Rise of the Vertebrates*. New York: Hungry Minds, 1994.

Palmer, D. (consultant editor). *The Simon and Schuster Encyclopedia of Dinosaurs and Prehistoric Creatures*. New York: Simon & Schuster, 1999.

Thompson, I. and Nehring, C. (illustrator). *National Audubon Society Field Guide to North American Fossils*. New York: Knopf, 1982.

Tudge, C. *The Variety of Life*. New York: Oxford University Press, 2000.

Walker, C. and Ward, D. (scientific editors). *Fossils*. New York: Dorling Kindersley, 1992.

Ward, P. D. *Rivers in Time: The Search for Clues to Earth's Mass Extinctions*. New York: Columbia University Press, 2001.

Selected books on prehistoric plants:
Gensel, P. G. and Edwards, D. (editors). *Plants Invade the Land (Perspectives in Paleobiology and Earth History)*. New York: Columbia University Press, 2001.

Stewart, W. N. and Rothwell, G. W. *Paleobotany and the Evolution of Plants*. Cambridge, Eng.: Cambridge University Press, 1993.

Selected books on prehistoric invertebrates:
Boardman, R. S., Cheetham, A. H., Rowell, A. J. (editor). *Fossil Invertebrates*. Milton Keynes, Eng.: Blackwell Science, 1987.

Briggs, D. E. G., Erwin, D. H., Collier, F. J., and Clark, C. (photographer). *The Fossils of the Burgess Shale*. Washington, D.C.: Smithsonian Institution, 1995.

Fortey, R. *Trilobite: Eyewitness to Evolution*. New York: Knopf, 2000.

Selected book on prehistoric fishes:
Long, J. *The Rise of Fishes: 500 Million Years of Evolution*. Baltimore, Md.: Johns Hopkins University Press, 1995.

Selected book on early tetrapods and amphibians: Zimmer, C. and Buell, C. D. (illustrator). *At the Water's Edge: Fish with Fingers, Whales with Legs, and How Life Came Ashore but Then Went Back to Sea*. New York: Touchstone Books, 1999.

Selected books on prehistoric reptiles:
Benton, M. J. *The Reign of the Reptiles*. Las Vegas, Nev: Crescent Books, 1990.

Callaway, J. M. and Nicholls, E. L., (editors). *Ancient Marine Reptiles*. San Diego, Calif.: Academic Press, 1997.

Wellnhofer, P. *The Illustrated Encyclopedia of Pterosaurs*. Las Vegas, Nev. Crescent Books, 1991.

Selected books on prehistoric birds:
Dingus, L. and Rowe, T. *The Mistaken Extinction: Dinosaur Extinction and the Origin of Birds*. New York: Freeman, 1998.

Feduccia, A. *The Origin and Evolution of Birds*. New Harbour, Conn.: Yale University Press, 1999 [This author controversially rejects a dinosaur origin for birds].

Gauthier, J. A. *New Perspectives on the Origin and Early Evolution of Birds* Peabody Museum, 2001

Selected books on prehistoric mammals and other synapsids:
Benton, M. J. *The Rise of the Mammals*. Las Vegas, Nev. Crescent Books, 1991.

McKenna, M. C. and Bell, S. K. *Classification of Mammals Above the Species Level*. New York: Columbia University Press, 1997 [a technical listing].

Russell, D. E. and Savage, R. J. G. *Mammalian Paleofaunas of the World*. New York: Addison-Wesley, 1983.

Selected websites:
Paleontology and Fossils Resources:

http://dizzy.library.arizona.edu/users/mount/paleont.html

Tree of Life: http://www.phylogeny.arizona.edu/tree/life.phylogeny.html

University of California, Berkeley, Museum of Paleontology: www.ucmp.berkeley.edu

Selected worldwide museums:
ARGENTINA
Buenos Aires: Argentine Natural Sciences Museum
La Plata: Museum of La Plata University

AUSTRALIA
Sydney: Australian Museum

AUSTRIA
Vienna: Natural History Museum

BELGIUM
Brussels*:* Royal Institute of Natural Sciences

CANADA
Toronto: Royal Ontario Museum

CHINA
Beijing: Beijing Natural History Museum

CZECH REPUBLIC
Prague: National Museum

FRANCE
Paris: National Museum of Natural History

GERMANY
Frankfurt am Main: Senckenberg Natural History Museum

GREECE
Athens: Museum of Paleontology and Geology

INDIA
Calcutta: Geology Museum

ITALY
Florence: Natural History Museum

JAPAN
Tokyo: National Science Museum

KENYA
Nairobi: Kenya National Museum

MEXICO
Mexico City: Natural History Museum

MONGOLIA
Ulan-Bator: State Central Museum

MOROCCO
Rabat: Museum of Earth Sciences

NIGER
Niamey: National Museum

POLAND
Warsaw: Museum of Evolution

RUSSIA
Moscow: Paleontological Museum

SOUTH AFRICA
Cape Town: South African Museum

SPAIN
Madrid: Natural Science Museum

SWEDEN
Uppsala: Paleontological Museum, Uppsala University

UNITED KINGDOM
London: Natural History Museum

UNITED STATES
Chicago: Field Museum of Natural History
Cleveland: Natural History Museum
Hays, Kansas: Sternberg Museum of Natural History
Los Angeles: Los Angeles County Museum of Natural History
New York City: American Museum of Natural History
Pittsburgh: Carnegie Museum of Natural History
Washington, D.C.: National Museum of Natural History, Smithsonian Institution

Selected paleontologists:

Agassiz, Jean Louis (1807–73) Swiss-born naturalist who made key studies of fossil fishes and showed that ice caps had covered much of Pleistocene Europe and North America.

Ameghino, Florentino (1854–1911) Argentinian paleontologist who described many South American fossil mammals and dinosaurs, largely from specimens collected by his brother Carlos.

Andrews, Roy Chapman (1884–1960) US leader of American Museum of Natural History expeditions to Mongolia in the 1920s. These made important finds of fossil mammals and dinosaurs.

Anning, Mary (1799–1847) British fossil collector. Near Lyme Regis, Dorset, she found the first British pterosaur and first complete ichthyosaur and plesiosaur.

Barrande, Joachim (1799–1883) French scientist who studied Paleozoic rocks and fossils. His 32-volume work included the first accounts of 4,000 fossil species.

Brongniart, Adolphe (1801–76) French botanist who founded paleobotany. In 1822 he published the first account of all known fossil plants.

Brongniart, Alexandre (1770–1847) French geologist who divided reptiles into four groups (one containing amphibians) and collected Paris Basin fossils.

Bronn, Heinrich Georg (1800–62) German paleontologist and geologist who laid the basis for a chronological study of fossil organisms in Germany.

Broom, Robert (1866–1951) Scottish paleontologist who made major South African discoveries about fossil synapsids and the origin of mammals.

Buffon, Georges, Comte de (1707–88) French naturalist. He helped pioneer the idea that a succession of plants and animals dated back farther than theologians believed.

Clack, Jennifer (1947–) British paleontologist who, with colleagues, has shown that the earliest "amphibians" retained fishlike features, with limbs designed for use in water, not on land.

Collini, Cosimo Alessandro (1727–1806) Italian naturalist who described the first known pterosaur in 1784.

Conybeare, William Daniel (1787–1857) British geologist who first described *Ichthyosaurus.*

Cope, Edward Drinker (1840–97) US zoologist who described many American fossil fishes, reptiles, and mammals, especially from the newly opened West.

Cushman, Joseph (1881–1949) US paleontologist who pioneered the use of foraminiferans as guides to the relative ages of certain rocks.

Cuvier, Georges (1769–1832) French anatomist and paleontologist who pioneered the scientific study of fossil vertebrates. He thought groups of beasts had perished from a series of natural catastrophes.

Darwin, Charles (1809–82) British naturalist who proposed the theory of evolution by natural selection.

Deshayes, Gérard Paul (1797–1875) French conchologist, whose studies of fossil shells laid a basis for subdividing the Tertiary period into epochs.

Edwards, Dianne (1942–) Welsh paleobotanist who has shed new light on the origins of land plants.

Ehrenberg, Christian (1795–1876) German naturalist who pioneered the study of microfossils.

Eldredge, Niles (1943–) US paleontologist who, with Stephen Jay Gould, in 1972 proposed that new species appear in sudden bursts, not through slow, steady evolution.

Fischer von Waldheim, Gotthelf (1771–1853) German scientist who helped pioneer paleontology in Russia.

Gilmore, Charles Whitney (1874–1945) US museum curator and expedition leader. He greatly enlarged the fossil reptile collection of the National Museum of Natural History.

Glaessner, Martin (1906–89) Australian geologist who described Australia's Ediacaran fossils, and helped to establish their Precambrian origin.

Granger, Walter (1872–1941) US paleontologist who specialized in the origins of mammals.

Haeckel, Ernst (1834–1919) German biologist who devised a "family tree" of animals. He named their major groups phyla, and believed that all derived from one-celled organisms.

Hall, James (1811–98) Main founder of the "American school" of paleontology. He wrote on the Paleozoic invertebrates of New York State.

Hennig, Willi (1913–76) German entomologist who developed cladistics, a rigorous way of defining evolutionary relationships between organisms.

Hooke, Robert (1635–1703) English scientist who gave the first descriptions of fossil wood, and foreshadowed the idea of fossils as clues to evolution.

Hyatt, Alpheus (1838–1902) US geologist and paleontologist who helped to classify ammonites.

Lamarck, Jean-Baptiste de (1744–1829) French paleontologist, a pioneer in the scientific study of fossil invertebrates.

Leidy, Joseph (1823–91) US anatomist who pioneered the study of fossil vertebrates in North America.

Linnaeus, Carolus (1707–78) Swedish botanist who established a basis for classifying living things.

Lhuyd, Edward (1660–1709) Welsh natural historian who, in 1699, produced the first book about British fossils.

Margulis, Lynn (1938–) US biologist who has shown that eucaryotic cells originated from symbiotic associations of procaryotes.

Marsh, Othniel Charles (1831–99) US paleontologist whose expeditions in the West and Mid West discovered scores of fossil vertebrates, including many dinosaurs. He described countless fossils.

Meyer, Hermann von (1801–69) Paleontologist who founded German vertebrate paleontology. He named the dinosaur *Plateosaurus* (1837), the pterosaur *Rhamphorhynchus* (1846), and the earliest-known bird *Archaeopteryx* (1861).

Oparin, Alexander (1894–1980) Russian biochemist who theorized that simple chemicals combining into complex compounds gave rise to the first one-celled organisms.

Orbigny, Alcide Charles d' (1802–57) French naturalist whose study of fossil invertebrates revealed regional distributions of species in ancient seas.

Osborn, Henry Fairfield (1857–1937) US paleontologist and expedition leader who wrote over 600 scientific papers and became president of the American Museum of Natural History. He proposed the theory of adaptive radiation: the evolution into different species of ones that spread into a variety of habitats and became adapted to them.

Owen, Sir Richard (1804–92) British anatomist and paleontologist who wrote the first work on general paleontology in English and helped found Britain's Natural History Museum.

Romer, Alfred Sherwood (1894–1973) US vertebrate paleontologist who contributed new ideas about how fishes, amphibians, and reptiles evolved. He wrote major textbooks on fossil and living vertebrates.

Scheuchzer, Johann Jakob (1672–1733) Swiss botanist who wrote one of the first books to picture fossil plants.

Seward, Sir Albert Charles (1863–1941) British paleobotanist who wrote key books on fossil plants.

Sprigg, Reg. C. (1919–94) Australian geologist who, in 1946, discovered the then oldest-known fossils, in South Australia's Ediacara Hills.

Walcott, Charles Doolittle (1850–1927) US paleontologist who discovered a superbly preserved "zoo" of Cambrian fossils in the Canadian Rockies.

Woodward, John (1665–1728) English paleontologist who compiled one of the first classifications of fossils.

Zittel, Karl Alfred von (1830–1904) German scientist who compiled major handbooks of fossils, and a key history of paleontology.

SECTION 3: Dinosaurs

Selected books on dinosaurs:
Carpenter, K. *Eggs, Nests, and Baby Dinosaurs: A Look at Dinosaur Reproduction.* Bloomington: Indiana University Press, 1999.

Currie, P.J. and Padian, K. (editors). *Encyclopedia of Dinosaurs.* San Diego, Calif.: Academic Press, 1997.

Farlow, J. O. and Brett-Surman, M. K. (editors). *The Complete Dinosaur.* Bloomington: Indiana University Press, 1997.

Lambert, D. *The Ultimate Dinosaur Book.* New York: Dorling Kindersley, 1993.

Lockley, M. *Tracking Dinosaurs.* Cambridge, Eng.: Cambridge University Press, 1991.

Norman, D. and Sibbick, J. (illustrator). *The Illustrated Encyclopedia of Dinosaurs.* Las Vegas, Nev.: Crescent Books, 1985.

Paul, G. S. (editor). *The Scientific American Book of Dinosaurs.* New York: St. Martin's Press, 2000.

Weishampel, D. B., Dodson, P., and Osmólska, H. *The Dinosauria.* Berkeley: University of California Press, 1990.

Selected websites:
DinoData: www.dinodata.net/

Dinosaur Mailing List Archives: www.cmnh.org/fun/dinosaur-archive/

University of California Museum of Paleontology dinosaur links: www.ucmp.berkeley.edu/diapsids/dinolinks.html

Selected worldwide museums:
ARGENTINA
Buenos Aires: Argentine Museum of Natural Sciences
La Plata: Museum of La Plata University

AUSTRALIA
Fortitude Valley, Queensland: Queensland Museum
Melbourne: Melbourne Museum
Sydney: Australian Museum

AUSTRIA
Vienna: Natural History Museum

BELGIUM
Brussels: Royal Institute of Natural Sciences

BRAZIL
Rio de Janeiro: National Museum

CANADA
Drumheller, Alberta: Royal Tyrrell Museum of Palaeontology
Edmonton, Alberta: Provincial Museum of Alberta
Ottawa, Ontario: Canadian Museum of Nature
Toronto, Ontario: Royal Ontario Museum

CHINA
Beijing: Beijing Natural History Museum; Museum of the Institute of Vertebrate Paleontology and Paleoanthropology
Beipei, Sichuan: Beipei Museum
Chengdu, Sichuan: Museum of Chengdu College of Geology
Harbin: Heilongjiang Museum
Hohhot, Inner Mongolia: Inner Mongolia Museum
Shanghai: Shanghai Museum
Tianjin: Tianjin Museum of Natural History
Zigong, Sichuan: Zigong Dinosaur Museum

FRANCE
Espéraza, Aude: Museum of Dinosaurs
Paris: National Museum of Natural History

GERMANY
Berlin: Natural History Museum, Humboldt University
Frankfurt am Main: Senckenberg Nature Museum
Munich: Bavarian State Institute for Paleontology and Historical Geology
Münster: Natural History Museum
Stüttgart: State Museum for Natural History
Tübingen: Institute and Museum for Geology and Paleontology, University of Tübingen

INDIA
Calcutta: Geology Museum, Indian Statistical Institute

ITALY
Bologna: G. Capellini Museum

Milan: Civic Museum of Natural History
Venice: Civic Museum of Natural History

JAPAN
Iwaki, Fukushima: Iwaki City Museum of Coal and Fossils
Kitakyushu, Fukuoka: Kitakyushu Museum of Natural History
Kyoto: Kyoto Municipal Science Center for Youth
Osaka: Osaka Museum of Natural History
Tokyo: National Science Museum
Toyohashi, Aichi: Toyohashi Museum of Natural History

MEXICO
Mexico City: Natural History Museum

MONGOLIA
Ultan-Bator: Academy of Sciences

MOROCCO
Rabat: Museum of Earth Sciences

NIGER
Niamey: National Museum of Niger

POLAND
Warsaw: Museum of Evolution

RUSSIA
Moscow: Paleontological Institute
St. Petersburg: Central Geological and Prospecting Museum

SOUTH AFRICA
Cape Town: South African Museum
Johannesburg: Bernard Price Institute of Palaeontology

SPAIN
Madrid: National Museum of Natural Sciences

SWEDEN
Uppsala: Paleontological Museum, Uppsala University

SWITZERLAND
Aathal: Dinosaur Museum

TAIWAN
Taichung: National Museum of Natural Sciences

UNITED KINGDOM
Birmingham: Birmingham Museum
Cambridge: Sedgwick Museum, Cambridge University
Dorchester: Dinosaur Museum
Edinburgh: Royal Museum of Scotland
Glasgow: Hunterian Museum
Leicester: Leicestershire Museum
London: Natural History Museum
Oxford: University Museum
Sandown: Museum of Isle of Wight Geology

UNITED STATES
Amherst, Massachusetts: Pratt Museum (Amherst College)
Ann Arbor, Michigan: University of Michigan Exhibit Museum
Atlanta, Georgia: Fernbank Museum of Natural History
Austin, Texas: Texas Memorial Museum
Berkeley, California: University of California Museum of Paleontology
Boulder, Colorado: University Natural History Museum
Bozeman, Montana: Museum of the Rockies
Buffalo, New York: Buffalo Museum of Science
Cambridge, Massachusetts: Museum of Comparative Zoology, Harvard University
Chicago, Illinois: Field Museum of Natural History
Cleveland, Ohio: Natural History Museum
Denver, Colorado: Denver Museum of Natural History
Dickinson, North Dakota: Dakota Dinosaur Museum
East Lansing, Michigan: The Museum, Michigan State University
Flagstaff, Arizona: Museum of Northern Arizona
Fort Worth, Texas: Fort Worth Museum of Science
Houston, Texas: Houston Museum of Natural Science
Jensen, Utah: Quarry Visitor Center, Dinosaur National Monument
Laramie, Wyoming: Geological Museum
Lincoln, Nebraska: University of Nebraska State Museum
Los Angeles, California: Los Angeles County Museum of Natural History
New Haven, Connecticut: Peabody Museum of Natural History, Yale University
New York City, New York: American Museum of Natural History
Norman, Oklahoma: Stovall Museum, University of Oklahoma
Philadelphia, Pennsylvania: Academy of Natural Sciences
Pittsburgh, Pennsylvania: Carnegie Museum of Natural History
Princeton, New Jersey: Museum of Natural History, Princeton University

Provo, Utah: Earth Science Museum, Brigham Young University
St. Paul, Minnesota: The Science Museum of Minnesota
Salt Lake City, Utah: Utah Museum of Natural History, University of Utah
Vernal, Utah: Utah Natural History State Museum
Washington, D.C.: National Museum of Natural History, Smithsonian
Institution

Selected dinosaurologists:

Alvarez, Luis (1911–1988) and **Walter** (1940–) US scientists who, in 1980, described evidence that dinosaurs had been wiped out by an asteroid striking the Earth.

Ameghino, Florentino (1854–1911) Argentinian paleontologist who, with his brother Carlos (1865–1936), helped to put Argentina's wealth of dinosaurs and prehistoric mammals on the world map.

Andrews, Roy Chapman (1884–1960) US naturalist whose expeditions between 1922 and 1925 pioneered dinosaur discoveries in Mongolia.

Baird, Donald US ichnologist who published articles on fossil footprints in and after the 1950s.

Bakker, Robert (1945–) US paleontologist who claimed in 1968 that dinosaurs had been "fast, agile, energetic and warm blooded." In 1974, with Peter Galton, he argued that birds belonged in the class Dinosauria.

Barsbold, Rinchen Mongolian paleontologist who, in and after the 1970s, named various dinosaurs discovered in Mongolia.

Bonaparté, José F. (1928–) Argentinian paleontologist who named or co-named many of the dinosaurs found in Argentina since the 1960s, adding hugely to our understanding of dinosaurs in South America.

Brown, Barnum (1873–1963) US dinosaur hunter often credited with finding *Tyrannosaurus.* In 1910 he began the "dinosaur rush" along Alberta's Red Deer River. Brown named eight ornithischian dinosaurs.

Buckland, William (1784–1856) British geologist who described *Megalosaurus* (1824), the first dinosaur given a scientific name.

Buffetaut, Eric French paleontologist whose work in Thailand revealed the oldest-known sauropod, *Isanosaurus,* described in 2000.

Carlin, William E. Union Pacific Railroad agent who, with W.H. Reed, in 1877 discovered Wyoming's Como Bluff dinosaur graveyard, among the richest anywhere.

Carpenter, Kenneth (1949–) US paleontologist who had named or co-named eight dinosaurs by 1999.

Charig, Alan J. (1927–97) British paleontologist who, in 1965, worked out that dinosaurs with erect limbs evolved from sprawling reptiles via others with a semi-improved gait.

Chatterjee, Sankar Indian-born paleontologist who named several Triassic dinosaurs and co-named the early Indian sauropod *Barapasaurus.*

Colbert, Edwin (1905–) US paleontologist who named the dinosaurs *Staurikosaurus* and *Scutellosaurus* and, in 1947, discovered a major *Coelophysis* bonebed.

Cope, Edward Drinker (1840–97) US paleontologist, Othniel Marsh's great rival in the race to find and name North American dinosaurs. He named *Camarasaurus, Coelophysis, Monoclonius,* and others.

Currie, Philip J. Canadian paleontologist who named or co-named five dinosaurs by the mid 1990s.

Dodson, Peter Canadian paleontologist who, in 1975, showed that many "species" of crested duck-billed dinosaurs were males, females, and young of just a few.

Dollo, Louis (1857–1931) French-born Belgian paleontologist who provided the first full reconstruction of *Iguanodon.*

Dong Zhiming China's leading dinosaurologist of the later twentieth century, naming 24 dinosaurs by 1998.

Douglass, Earl (1862–1931) US dinosaur hunter who, in 1909, in Utah, found the fossil-rich rocks of what is now Dinosaur National Monument.

Efremov, Ivan A. (1907–72) Russian paleontologist whose expeditions found major bonebeds in Mongolia.

Galton, Peter US-based British paleontologist who has named or co-named more than a dozen dinosaurs, claimed that ornithischians had cheeks, and argued with Robert Bakker that birds are dinosaurs (1974).

Gasparini, Zulma B. Argentinian paleontologist who, with colleagues, in 1988 described the first dinosaur discovered in Antarctica.

Gauthier, Jacques A. US paleontologist who influentially reclassified dinosaurs in the 1980s.

Gilmore, Charles (1874–1945) US dinosaur authority at the American Museum of Natural History (1903–45) who named nine, mostly Asian, dinosaurs.

Hatcher, John B. (1861–1904) US dinosaur hunter and authority on horned dinosaurs. He discovered *Torosaurus,* and probably *Tyrannosaurus.*

Hitchcock, Edward (1793–1864) US teacher who formed the first great collection of dinosaur footprints but thought they had been made by birds.

Horner, John US paleontologist who (with R. Makela and others) in and after 1978 excavated the first dinosaur nests discovered in North America.

Huene, Friedrich von German paleontologist: Europe's leading dinosaurologist of the early 20th century. Between 1922 and 1932 he named 27 dinosaur genera.

Huxley, Thomas (1825–95) British scientist who championed Charles Darwin. He named three dinosaurs and showed similarities between birds and dinosaurs.

Janensch, Werner German Berlin Museum curator whose expeditions (1909–11) to what is now Tanzania found a wealth of late Jurassic dinosaurs.

Jensen, James A. US paleontologist who found giant sauropods, naming *Supersaurus* in 1985.

Kielan-Jaworowska, Zofia Polish paleontologist who led expeditions to Mongolia in the 1960s and 1970s.

Lambe, Lawrence M. Dinosaurologist who hunted fossils in Alberta and (1914–19) named nine dinosaurs.

Leidy, Joseph (1823–91) US anatomist who, in 1856, named *Troodon* and four other dinosaurs, the first named dinosaurs from the Americas.

Lydekker, Richard British paleontologist who named six dinosaurs between 1877 and 1893.

Maleev, E.

A. Russian paleontologist who named *Tarbosaurus* and *Therizinosaurus* in the 1950s.

Mantell, Gideon A. (1790–1852) British physician who largely pioneered dinosaur discovery. He named three dinosaurs including *Iguanodon* (1825).

Marsh, Othniel Charles (1831–99) US paleontologist who described many of the best-known dinosaurs, found by expeditions funded by the Yale Peabody Museum (he was its first director). He named 25 dinosaurs (1877–89), among them *Allosaurus* and *Diplodocus.* Seventeen of his names remain valid.

Maryańska, Teresa Polish paleontologist who, in and after 1974, described various Mongolian dinosaurs.

Meyer, Hermann von German paleontologist who pioneered dinosaur discovery in Germany.

Molnar, Ralph E. US paleontologist who named or co-named several dinosaurs from Australia in the 1980s and identified New Zealand's first dinosaur fossil.

Nopcsa, Franz Baron Hungarian dinosaurologist who named four dinosaurs between 1903 and 1929.

Osborn, Henry F. (1857–1935) US paleontologist who described 11 dinosaurs including *Tyrannosaurus* and *Velociraptor.*

Osmólska, Halszka Polish paleontologist who named or co-named 11 dinosaurs discovered in Mongolia.

Ostrom, John H. US paleontologist, whose discovery of *Deinonychus* (1964) laid the basis for a new view of theropod dinosaurs as agile, warm-blooded animals, and small theropods as the ancestors of birds.

Owen, Richard (1804–92) British anatomist who coined the name *dinosaur* ("Dinosauria") in 1842. He named *Cetiosaurus* and nine other dinosaurs.

Rich, Thomas H. and **Patricia Vickers** US husband-and-wife team working in Australia, and naming five Australian dinosaurs by 1999.

Russell, Dale A. US paleontologist who threw new light on ornithomimids. In 1993 he argued that therizinosaurs resembled chalicotheres.

Seeley, Harry G. (1839–1909) British paleontologist who split dinosaurs into Ornithischia and Saurischia.

Sereno, Paul US paleontologist who reclassified the ornithischians in 1986, and made major dinosaur discoveries in South America and Africa, by 1996 naming or co-naming six dinosaurs.

Sternberg, Charles H. (1850–1943) New York-born dinosaur hunter, working largely in Alberta with sons Charles M. (who later named seven dinosaurs), George, and Levi.

Stromer von Reichenbach, Ernst (1871–1952) German paleontologist who, with Richard Markgraf, discovered *Spinosaurus* and other dinosaurs in Egypt.

Sues, Hans-Dieter German-born paleontologist who has named or co-named various dinosaurs since 1979.

Taquet, Philippe French paleontologist who has named several dinosaurs including *Ouranosaurus*.

Wiffen, Joan An amateur fossil hunter who found New Zealand's first known dinosaur remains.

Yang Zhong-jian (1897–1979) The founder of Chinese vertebrate paleontology. He named 14 dinosaurs.

Zhao Xijin Chinese paleontologist who named 16 dinosaurs in the 1980s and 1990s.

SECTION 4: The First Humans

Selected books on paleoanthropology:
Fleagle, J. G. *Primate Adaptation and Evolution*. San Diego, Calif.: Academic Press, 1998.

Johanson, D. and Edgar, B. *From Lucy to Language*. New York: Simon & Schuster, 1996.

Jordan, P. *Neanderthal*. New York: Sutton Publishing, 2001.

Klein, R.G. *The Human Career*. Chicago: University of Chicago Press, 1999.

McKie, R. *Dawn of Man: The Story of Human Evolution*. New York: DK Publishing, 2000.

Walker, A. and Shipman, P. *The Wisdom of Bones: In Search of Human Origins*. New York: Knopf, 1996.

Selected websites:
Human evolution:
http://anthropology.about.com/cs/humanevolution.index.htm

Prominent hominid fossils:
http://www.talkorigins.org/faqs/homs/specimen.html

University of Michigan Museum of Anthropology:
www.umma.lsa.umich.edu/

Selected worldwide museums:
AUSTRIA
Vienna: Natural History Museum

BELGIUM
Brussels: Royal Museum of Art and History

BULGARIA
Sofia: Museum of Art and History

CHINA
Beijing: Institute of Vertebrate Paleontology and Paleoanthropology; Institute of Archeology, Academia Sinica.

COLOMBIA
Bogotá: National Museum

CYPRUS
Nicosia: Archeological Museum

CZECH REPUBLIC
Prague: National Museum

DENMARK
Copenhagen: National Museum
Silkeborg: Silkeborg Museum

EGYPT
Cairo: Egyptian Antiquities Museum; Egyptian National Museum

ETHIOPIA
Addis Ababa: National Museum of Ethiopia

FRANCE
Bordeaux: Museum of Aquitaine
Les Eyzies, Dordogne: National Museum of Prehistory

Paris: Louvre Museum; Museum of Man
Saint-Germaine-en-Laye, Yvelines: Museum of National Antiquities

GERMANY
Berlin: Berlin State Museum of Near Asia; Egyptian Museum; Museum of Prehistory and Early History
Frankfurt: Museum of Prehistory and Early History
Hamburg: Museum of Ethnology and Prehistory
Stuttgart: Württemberg Museum

GREECE
Athens: Anthropological and Ethnological Museum
Thessaloniki: Paleontological Museum

GUATEMALA
Guatemala City: Archaeological Museum

HONDURAS
Tegucigalpa: Museum of History and Archaeology

HUNGARY
Budapest: Hungarian National Museum

INDIA
Calcutta: Indian Museum

INDONESIA
Gianjar: Museum Gedong Artja

IRAN
Tehran: Archaeological Museum

IRAQ
Baghdad: Iraq Museum

IRELAND
Dublin: National Museum

ISRAEL
Haifa: Museum of Natural History and Prehistory
Jerusalem: Museum of Prehistory

ITALY
Milan: Archaeological Museum
Rome: Collections of the Italian Institute of Human Paleontology; Museum of Anthropology

JAPAN
Tokyo: Tokyo National Museum

JORDAN
Amman: Jordan Archaeological Museum

KENYA
Nairobi: National Museum of Kenya

MEXICO
Mérida: Yucatán Museum of Anthropology
Mexico City: National Anthropological Museum

NETHERLANDS
Amsterdam: Archaeological Museum of the University of Amsterdam
Leiden: National Museum of Antiquities; National Museum of Ethnology

PAKISTAN
Karachi: National Museum

PANAMA
Panama City: Museum of Panama Man

PERU
Lima: Museum of Art

POLAND
Warsaw: National Museum of Archaeology

ROMANIA
Bucharest: National Museum of Antiquities

RUSSIA
Moscow: D.N.Anuchin Anthropology Museum
St. Petersburg: Institute of Archaeology

SOUTH AFRICA
Pretoria: Transvaal Museum

SPAIN
Madrid: National Archeological Museum,

SWEDEN
Stockholm: Historical Museum; Museum of the Mediterranean and near Eastern Antiquities

SWITZERLAND
Zurich: Swiss National Museum

SYRIA
Damascus: Damascus National Museum

TANZANIA
Dar es Salaam: National Museum of Tanzania

TURKEY
Ankara: Museum of Anatolian Civilizations
Istanbul: Archaeological Museum of Istanbul

UNITED KINGDOM
Birmingham: City Museum
Cambridge: Museum of Archaeology and Anthropology
Cardiff: National Museum of Wales
Edinburgh: National Museum of Antiquities of Scotland
Glasgow: Glasgow Art Gallery and Museum; Hunterian Museum
London: British Museum
Manchester: Manchester Museum
Oxford: Ashmolean Museum of Art and Archaeology

UNITED STATES
Austin, Texas: Texas Memorial Museum
Berkeley, California: Phoebe Apperson Hearst Museum of Anthropology
Chicago, Illinois: Field Museum of Natural History
Cincinnati, Ohio: Cincinnati Museum of Natural History
New Haven, Connecticut: Peabody Museum of Natural History
New York City, New York: American Museum of Natural History
Pittsburgh, Pennsylvania: Carnegie Museum of Natural History
Washington, D.C.: National Museum of Natural History

Selected paleoanthropologists and archaeologists:
Alexeev, Valerii Russian anthropologist who named *Homo (=Australopithecus) rudolfensis* in 1986.

Asfaw, Berhane Ethiopian paleoanthropologist who, with Desmond Clark and Tim White, named *Australopithecus garhi* in 1999.

Bass, George Fletcher US archaeologist whose 1960 expedition to a submerged Bronze Age shipwreck off Turkey began scientific underwater archaeology by diving archaeologists.

Bérmudez de Castro, José Spanish paleoanthropologist who, with five colleagues, named *Homo antecessor* in 1997.

Binford, Lewis R. US archaeologist who in the 1960s pioneered the "New Archaeology" by critically reexamining old concepts in the light of worldwide comparative archaeological and ethnographical research.

Black, Davidson (1884–1934) Canadian-born anatomist who in 1927 described a tooth of China's *"Sinanthropus pekinensis" (Homo erectus)*.

Boucher (de Crèvecoeur) de Perthes, Jacques (1788–1868) French archaeologist whose discoveries of stone tools in river gravels showed that human prehistory extended back through geological time.

Braidwood, Robert J. US archaeologist whose early 1950s excavation of Jarmo in Iraq suggested that Middle Eastern agriculture began in the Taurus-Zagros mountain belt, not in the rich river valleys of the Fertile Crescent farther south.

Breasted, James Henry (1865–1935) US archaeologist who coined the term *Fertile Crescent* for the rich belt of land from Egypt to Iraq where Western civilization began.

Broom, Robert (1866–1951) Scottish paleontologist who in 1938 first described *Paranthropus robustus*.

Brunes, Michel French paleoanthropologist who, with others, named *Australopithecus bahrelghazali* in 1996.

Dart, Raymond Arthur (1893–1988) Australian-born South African anthropologist who in 1925 described *Australopithecus africanus*, the first australopithecine to be discovered.

Darwin, Charles Robert (1809–82) British naturalist whose theory of evolution by natural selection (published 1859) laid the scientific basis for a study of human origins, which he believed lay in Africa.

Dubois, (Marie) Eugène (François Thomas) (1858–1940) Dutch anatomist who, in Java, in 1891, made the first known discovery of *Homo erectus*, which he named *"Pithecanthropus erectus."*

Figgins, Jesse D. US paleontologist who in 1927 found proof of human antiquity in the Americas: a stone point between an extinct bison's ribs.

Frere, John (1740–1807) British antiquary who founded prehistoric archaeology. He found flint tools and extinct animals in the same layer of rock.

Groves, Colin Australian anthropologist who named *Homo ergaster* (1975, with Vratislav Mazák).

Johanson, Donald US anthropologist who, in Ethiopia in 1974, discovered the oldest known australopithecine skeleton ("Lucy"), and in 1978 named its species *Australopithecus afarensis*.

Kimeu, Kimoya Kenyan expeditions foreman who in 1984 discovered what proved to be the oldest known nearly complete human skeleton (of *Homo ergaster*).

King, William Irish anatomist who in 1864 coined the scientific name *Homo neanderthalensis*.

Koenigswald, Gustav Heinrich Ralph von German anthropologist who named *Gigantopithecus* in 1935 and discovered *Homo erectus* fossils in Java.

Lartet, Édouard Armand Isidore Hippolyte (1801–71) French geologist, archaeologist, and paleontologist who named *Dryopithecus* and *Pliopithecus*.

Lartet, Louis French archaeologist who discovered Cro-Magnon humans while excavating in the Dordogne.

Leakey, Jonathan (1940–) Louis Leakey's eldest son, who in 1960 discovered *Homo (=Australopithecus) habilis*.

Leakey, Louis Seymour Bazett (1903–72) British anthropologist whose Olduvai Gorge expeditions found evidence that human evolution began in Africa.

Leakey, Mary (1913–96) British-born anthropologist who discovered *Australopithecus (=Paranthropus) boisei* (1959) and led an expedition that found the oldest-known human-like footprints.

Leakey, Meave (1942–) Kenyan paleoanthropologist who, with colleagues, named *Australopithecus anamensis* (1998).

Leakey, Richard (1944–) Kenyan paleoanthropologist who became director of the National Museums of Kenya and in and after the 1960s led expeditions that found *Homo (=Australopithecus) rudolfensis* and the oldest known nearly complete human skeleton (of *Homo ergaster*).

Lewis, G. Edward Scientist who first identified (1932) and named *Ramapithecus*.

Linnaeus, Carolus (1707–78) Swedish botanist who classified living things, and (in 1758) named our species *Homo sapiens*.

Lubbock, Sir John (1834–1913) British archaeologist who coined the terms Paleolithic (Old Stone Age) and Neolithic (New Stone Age).

Morgan, Lewis Henry (1818–81) A US founder of scientific anthropology, tracing cultural evolution "from Savagery through Barbarism to Civilization."

Pitt-Rivers, Augustus Henry (1827–1900) British archaeologist who pioneered modern scientific archeological techniques.

Schoetensack, Otto German professor who in 1908 published details of the Mauer mandible, and named *Homo heidelbergensis*.

Senut, Brigitte French paleoanthropologist, who, with Martin Pickford, named the "oldest ape man" *Orrorin* in 2001.

Stephens, John Lloyd (1805–52) US archaeologist whose explorations of Maya ruins pioneered the archaeology of Central America.

Thomsen, Christian Jurgensen (1788–1865) Danish archaeologist who divided human prehistory into successive Stone, Bronze, and Iron ages.

Weidenreich, Franz (1873–1948) German-born anatomist and anthropologist who in 1940 established the name *Homo erectus*.

White, Tim US paleoanthropologist who, with others, described *Ardipithecus ramidus* (1994–95).

Wilson, Alan C. and **Sarich, Vincent M.** US molecular biologists whose "molecular clock" evidence in 1969 showed human kinship with apes to be more recent than fossil finds had implied.

Woolley, Sir Charles Leonard (1880–1960) British archaeologist whose excavation of Ur (1922–34) gave insights into early Mesopotamian civilization.

Index